SPEAKING OF JESUS

SUPPLEMENTS TO
NOVUM TESTAMENTUM

VOLUME XCII

SPEAKING OF JESUS

*Essays on Biblical Language, Gospel Narrative
and the Historical Jesus*

Willem S. Vorster

EDITED BY

J. EUGENE BOTHA

BRILL
LEIDEN · BOSTON · KÖLN
1999

This book is printed on acid-free paper.

Library of Congress Cataloging-in-Publication Data

Vorster, W.S.
 Speaking of Jesus : essays on biblical language, gospel narrative
and the historical Jesus / Willem S. Vorster ; edited by J. Eugene
Botha.
     p.   cm. — (Supplements to Novum Testamentum, ISSN 0167-9732 ;
v. 92)
 Includes bibliographical references and indexes.
 ISBN 9004107797 (cloth)
 1. Bible.   N.T.   Gospels—Criticism, interpretation, etc.
I. Botha, J. Eugene.   II. Title.   III. Series.
BS2395.V67   1998
226'.066—dc21   98-34823
                                                                  CIP

Die Deutsche Bibliothek - CIP-Einheitsaufnahme

Vorster, Willem S.:
Speaking of Jesus : essays on biblical language, gospel narrative and
the historical Jesus / Willem S. Vorster. Ed. by J. Eugene Botha. -
Leiden ; Boston ; Köln : Brill, 1998
 (Supplements to Novum testamentum ; Vol. 92)
 ISBN 90-04-10779-7

ISSN   0167-9732
ISBN   90 04 10779 7

PRINTED IN THE NETHERLANDS

CONTENTS

SECTION A
BIBLICAL LANGUAGE

SECTION B
NEW TESTAMENT INTERPRETATION

SECTION E
INTERTEXTUALITY

PREFACE

When Willem S. Vorster unexpectedly died of a stroke on the 10th of January 1993 South African New Testament scholarship tragically lost one of its greatest representatives. Few would disagree that Vorster has left an indelible impression on the landscape of New Testament scholarship in South Africa. Le Roux (1994:1) remarks that 'Vorster changed his world: the scholarly world in which we worked since the beginning of the seventies; the way in which people talked about texts, their meaning, history, et cetera. His literary remains are extensive and his contribution many-facetted. . . .' Those acquainted with Willem Vorster's work, can but agree with this statement. Vorster did, despite coming from a tradition which at that stage of his career was more or less fundamentalistic in orientation, challenged South African Biblical scholarship to break out of the fundamentalistic mould, and initiated a process which introduced many South African scholars to new critical concepts. Lategan (1994:121–122) suggests that

> his own interpretation of biblical material was dominated by two strong impulses, directly related to what he considered the two most prominent features of these texts, namely their *historical* and their *literary* nature. . . . Thus he became perhaps the most consistent exponents of a historical critical approach in South African biblical scholarship. On the other hand, recognition of the literary nature of these documents was equally axiomatic in his approach. His linguistic training and proficiency in biblical languages formed the springboard from where he launched his investigation of the gospel genre and numerous studies of biblical narratives, especially of the Gospel of Mark.

His ground-breaking work in these two areas, and the enormous effect his publications and personality had, changed the enterprise of New Testament scholarship in the South African context to this day, and paved the way for the acceptance of some of his later initiatives such as the introduction of Historical Jesus research in the early 1990's (see Van Aarde 1994:235). Not only was Vorster considered a leader by his peers, but a whole generation of younger New Testament scholars was influenced and inspired by him. The logical question to ask is, why? Le Roux (1994:2) ascribes this *inter alia* to his personality:

> In many ways he was *very different*: he formulated things in a different way, he approached the New Testament differently, he looked at life differently, he understood God and the Bible differently, he looked at life differently, and he had the guts to accept whatever happened as a result. Vorster was a *critical scholar*: nothing was just accepted and no view propagated without critical scrutiny ... without fear he vented his critical thoughts and was always ready to explain the 'critical faith' he believed in.

In addition, Vorster also had the ability to constantly stay abreast of new developments, and frequently took the lead to introduce these new developments to his colleagues and students. Lategan (1994:121) remarks that 'Driven by a healthy curiosity (some would say scepticism) and an encyclopaedic grasp of the field, he constantly explored new aspects of this world to which he devoted his academic life. It was almost as if he could not bear not to be abreast with any new development or new approach'. It was inevitable that Vorster would make a lasting impression on South African biblical scholarship.

Willem Vorster was not only a catalyst to bring South African New Testament scholarship up to par with the rest of the scholarly world, but he also impacted international New Testament scholarship significantly. This is evident from his many contributions to international conferences and journals, but particularly by requests to contribute to *Festschriften* for leading international scholars and other collections of essays. He thus experienced unusually wide international recognition as a still relatively young scholar.

Willem Vorster unfortunately never had the opportunity to produce a significant monograph and his dream to start working on a commentary on The Gospel of Mark, was sadly left unfulfilled. However, he has left the scholarly world with an impressive list of articles and essays. The articles presented in this volume were chosen to emphasize the diversity of his scholarship and the development in his thought. Willem Vorster wrote on almost every New Testament topic: linguistics, literary analyses, historical criticism, post modernism, Bible translation, the Historical Jesus, Methodology, and so on. As editor of this volume I hope that I have not only done Willem Vorster justice with the selection of articles, but also that I have provided the reader with a unique selection of examples of Willem Vorster's contribution to New Testament scholarship. The articles were chosen to reflect both the diversity and the integration of knowledge and theological thought of Vorster, and while this principle was the primary concern for the selection of the material, this also posed problems in deciding on which articles to group together. I am aware of the fact that there are many possible ways to categorize this selection, but I am also convinced that no categorization can do justice to the depth, scope and integration of scholarship found in each article. I have thus opted for very broad categories like 'Language of the New Testament', 'New Testament Interpretation', 'Literary Analyses', 'Historical Jesus' and so on. I have done this merely to provide the reader with some broad categories as a point of departure and an organizational principle with which to approach this selection of Willem Vorster's essays.

These articles are not merely carbon copies of the original as they appeared, but they have been edited to present the reader with a more or less homogeneous product which is consistent in terms of abbreviations, references and bibliography. On advice of some of the members of the editorial board of this *Supplements to Novum Testamentum* series, some articles have further been edited and shortened to avoid unnecessary repetition and overlapping between various articles. However, in order to retain the integrity and scope of each individual essay, some duplication between some of the essays is inevitable. In some instances headings were provided or altered for more clarity and consistency in presentation. However, the language of the original articles was left basically unchanged.

I want to express my gratitude to those involved in the preparation of this volume. First of all a word of special gratitude goes to Dr. Kobus Petzer and Mr. Lieb Liebenberg who, spurred by their personal friendship with Willem Vorster initiated this project which I now have the pleasure of completing. I would also like to express my gratitude for the assistance from members of the Institute for Theological Research at the University of South Africa, which was founded by Willem Vorster, especially Jansie Kilian and Nonnie Fouche who provided the *curriculum vitae* of Vorster and assisted with the list of his publications. Invaluable assistance, especially with regard to some bibliographical problems was provided by Natalie Thirion, subject librarian at the University of South Africa.

On a personal note, I also want to note my own appreciation for Willem Vorster and the influence he has exercised on my own scholarly career. He was an inspiration to a whole generation of young New Testament scholars like me, and I was also privileged to have him as supervisor of my own doctoral work. I consider myself

fortunate to have had Willem Vorster both as colleague and friend
at the University of South Africa. This volume is therefore dedicated
to the memory of a great scholar and wonderful human being:
Willem Vorster.

Eugene Botha
Institute for Ecumenical and Cultural Research
St. John's University
Collegeville, Minnesota

Summer 1998

CURRICULUM VITAE: WILLEM S. VORSTER

Willem Stefanus Vorster was born on 1 December 1941 in Roodepoort in South Africa. In 1959 he passed the matriculation examination of the Transvaal Education Department. In 1960 he enrolled for the BA degree at the University of Pretoria. The following degrees were conferred on him by this University:

1963: Baccalaureus Artium (majors Greek & Hebrew)—cum laude
1966: Baccalaureus Divinitatis—cum laude
1966: Baccalaureus Honores (Greek and Semitics)—cum laude
1968: Magister Artium (Greek)—cum laude
1974: Doctor Divinitatis (New Testament).

His DD-thesis which has the title '*Aischunomai and words related to the same root in the New Testament*' dealt with the semantics of the New Testament on the word, sentence and paragraph level. Insights of modern linguistics and particularly modern semantics were applied and interesting results obtained. Prof A.B. du Toit was the promoter and professors J.P. Louw (Classics, University of Pretoria) and J.M.J. de Jonge (New Testament, State University of Leiden, The Netherlands) were co-examiners.

Vorster read Syriac and Aramaic for the B.A. Hons degree and additionally read Coptic (including Sahidic, Bohairic and Achmimic) for 3 years for non-degree purposes at the above university.

In 1965 he was appointed as temporary lecturer in classical Greek at the University of Pretoria. From 1966–1970 he was a full-time lecturer at the same department.

During the period November 1969 to January 1971 he visited Europe where he did research at the University of Groningen under Prof. A.F.J. Klijn. He also spent some time at the University of Manchester. After his return to South Africa he was appointed as senior lecturer in the Department of Old and New Testament Studies at the University of South Africa (Unisa). In 1975 he was appointed as Acting Director of the newly established Institute for Theological Research at Unisa. In 1976 he was appointed as professor and full-time Director of this Institute, a position held until his death. Shortly after this he was also instrumental in establishing the C.B. Powell

Bible Centre as part of the Institute with the specific aim of popu-
larising theological research.

In 1973/4 he visited Europe for a shorter period to renew contact with colleagues in England, the Netherlands and Germany, and
in 1975 spent three months in Bonn doing research on the structure of Mark. He also attended the meetings on New Testament
Scholarship in Leuven, Aberdeen and Bethel (as guest of the Fach-
gruppe Neues Testament). In 1977 he took a group of students to
Lachisch in Israel on an archaeological excavation and also attended
meetings on New Testament scholarship in Leuven and Tübingen.
In 1979 he was awarded an Alexander von Humboldt Stipend and
a senior research grant by the Human Sciences Research Council
(RSA) which enabled him to do research on the Gospel genre at the
University of Göttingen for 8 months. He has attended several inter-
national congresses since then in Leuven, Durham, Rome, Chicago,
San Francisco, New Orleans Göttingen, Copenhagen and Bethel and
has read papers at various national and international meetings of
New Testament scholars.

He has been a leader of a project on methodology and New
Testament Science, including the development of an information
retrieval system on the New Testament and related literature. He
was co-responsible for a History of Religions museum at the University
and for fifteen years from 1977 onwards he had been the organiser
of an annual interdisciplinary seminar on a topical theme of the
Institute for Theological Research at the University of South Africa.
Details of these conferences can be found below on pages xxi–xxii.

Vorster was also co-editor of the influential *South African Theological
Bibliography*. He was also co-organiser of the two international conferences of the Human Science Research Council on '*Paradigms and
Progress in Theology*' and '*Relevance of Theology in the 1990s*' in 1988
and 1990.

He was a full member for the *New Testament Society of South Africa,
The Old Testament Society of South Africa, Judaica and Patristic and Byzantine
Literature Societies of South Africa*, the *Society of Biblical Literature* and the
Studiorum Novi Testamenti Societas (SNTS). He was co-secretary for 10
years and for 5 years general secretary of the *New Testament Society
of South Africa*. He initiated several research programmes under the
auspices of the New Testament Society of South Africa on topics
such as the 'Resurrection of Jesus' and the 'Historical Jesus'.

In 1987 he was appointed as a member of the Discipline-oriented committee for *Theology, Religious Studies, Philosophy and Classical and Near Eastern Studies* of the *Human Sciences Research Council*. Since 1988 he has served as chairperson of this committee. He has served on a variety of University committees both as member and as chairperson.

At his home institution, the University of South Africa he has had the honour to have been nominated a number of times as Merit Professor for outstanding achievement.

Willem Vorster passed away on 10 January 1993.

SELECT BIBLIOGRAPHY OF WILLEM S. VORSTER

This bibliography of Willem Vorster is only a partial indication of his wide scholarly work. In addition to the articles, books and reviews mentioned here, he has also published a large number of other book reviews and some popular essays.

Monographs

1979   *'Aischunomai' en stamverwante woorde in die Nuwe Testament.* Pretoria: Unisa. (Studia 17.)

1981   *Wat is 'n Evangelie? Die plek van die tekssoort evangelie in die literatuur-geskiedenis.* Pretoria: N.G. Kerkboekhandel.

Articles in Journals

1969   2 Korintiërs 3:17. Eksegese en toeligting, in Die Pneuma by Paulus. *Neotestamentica* 3, 37–44.

1971   Matteus 12:38vv en die historisiteit van die gegewens in Jona. *Theologia Evangelica* 4, 223–235.

1971   Moderne linguistiek en Bybelnavorsing. *Theologia Evangelica* 4, 139–148.

1971   The meaning of parrēsia in the Epistle to the Hebrews. *Neotestamentica* 5, 51–59.

1972   A new trend in New Testament scholarship. *Theologia Evangelica* 5, 235–241.

1972   *Phobos kai tromos*: A Greek idiomatic expression with a Semitic background. *Theologia Evangelica* 5, 39–48.

1972   The Gospel of John as language. *Neotestamentica* 6, 19–27.

1974   An information retrieval system for New Testament research. *South-African Libraries* 4, 7–14.

1974   Concerning semantics, grammatical analysis and Bible translation. *Neotestamentica* 8, 21–41.

1974   The messianic interpretation of Genesis 3:15: A methodological problem, in *Studies in Wisdom Literature.* Pretoria: OTSSA Publication, 108–118.

1975   Heterodoxy in 1 John. *Neotestamentica* 9, 87–97.

1975   Hoe konsekwent dink eksegete? *Theologia Evangelica* 8, 126–135.

1976   The Institute for Theological Research: A new era in theological research in South Africa. *Theologia Evangelica* 9, 109–114.

1977   Some remarks on contemporary New Testament scholarship: Methodology and the study of the New Testament. *Theologia Evangelica* 10, 27–40.

1977   The structure of Matthew 13, in The structure of Matthew 1–13: An exploration into discourse analysis. *Neotestamentica* 11, 34–39; 130–138.

1978 The relevance of the New Testament for the interpretation of the Old Testament, in Van Wyk W.C. (ed.) 1978. *Aspects of the Exegetical process*. OTSSA Publication 21 & 22, 190–205.

1980 Die tekssoort evangelie en verwysing. *Theologia Evangelica*. 13(2), 27–48.

1980 Mark: Collector, redactor, author, narrator? *Journal of Theology for Southern Africa* 31, 46–61.

1980 Research at the Institute for Theological Research. *Scriptura* 1, 79–85.

1981 The function of the use of the Old Testament in Mark. *Neotestamentica* 14, 62–72.

1983 Kerygma/history and the gospel genre. *New Testament Studies* 29, 87–95.

1983 I Enoch and the Jewish Literary setting of the New Testament: A study in text types. *Neotestamentica* 17, 1–14.

1984 Der Ort der Gattung Evangelium in der Literaturgeschichte. *Verkündigung und Forschung* 29(1), 2–25.

1984 Historical paradigm: Its possibilities and limitations. *Neotestamentica* 18, 104–123.

1985 Gelykenisse in konteks: Mattheus 13 en die gelykenisse van Jesus. *Hervormde Teologiese Studies* 41(1), 148–163.

1985 The Founding of the C.B. Powell Centre at Unisa. *Theologia Evangelica* 18(1), 3–13.

1986 Die brief aan Rheginos: Oor geloof en rede en die opstanding. *Hervormde Teologiese Studies* 42(2), 211–228.

1986 Readings, readers and the succession narrative: An essay on reception criticism. ZAW 98(3), 351–362.

1986 Readings, readers and the succession narrative: An essay on reception criticism, in Van Wyk, W.C. (ed.). *Old Testament Essays: Studies in the succession narrative*. Pretoria: OTSSA (27[1984] & 28[1985]), 339–353.

1986 The New Testament and narratology. *Journal of literary studies/Tydskrif vir literatuurwetenskap* 2(3), 52–62.

1987 Characterisation of Peter in the Gospel of Mark. *Neotestamentica* 21(1), 57–76.

1987 Literary reflections on Mark 13:5–37: A narrated speech of Jesus. *Neotestamentica* 21(2), 91–112.

1987 Rudolf Bultmann—teoloog en historikus. *Die Hervormer* 78(12), 16.

1987 Rudolf Bultmann as historikus. *Hervormde Teologiese Studies* 43(1 & 2), 138–161.

1987 On early Christian communities and theological perspectives. *Journal of Theology for Southern Africa* 59, 26–34.

1987 Op weg na 'n post-kritiese Nuwe-Testamentiese wetenskap. *Hervormde Teologiese Studies* 43(3), 374–394.

1988 Oor die Nuwe Testament, vertelkunde en prediking. *Hervormde Teologiese Studies* 44(1), 164–177.

1988 'Genre' and the revelation of John: A study in text, context and intertext. *Neotestamentica* 22(2), 103–123.

1988 'Alles is politiek maar politiek is nie alles nie': Het Kuitert gelyk? *Hervormde Teologiese Studies* 44(4), 917–933.

1989 The reader in the text: Narrative material. *Semeia* 48, 21–39.
1989 The Religio-historical context of the resurrection of Jesus and resurrection faith in the New Testament. *Neotestamentica*, 23(2), 159–175.
1989 Die Lukaanse Liedere: Magnificat, Benedictus en Nunc Dimittis. *HTS Supplementum 1*, 17–34.
1989 The in/compatibility of methods and strategies in reading or interpreting the Old Testament. *Old Testament Essays* 2(3), 53–63.
1990 Bilingualism and the Greek of the New Testament: Semitic interference in the Gospel of Mark. *Neotestamentica* 24(2), 215–228.
1991 A reader-response approach to Matthew 24:3–28, *Hervormde Teologiese Studies* 47(4), 1099–1108.
1991 Jesus the Galilean. *Hervormde Teologiese Studies* 47(1), 121–135.
1991 Jesus: Eschatological prophet and/or wisdom teacher? *Hervormde Teologiese Studies* 47(2), 526–542.
1991 In what sense is the Louw/Nida dictionary authoritative? *Hervormde Teologiese Studies* 47(1), 26–38.
1993 The production of the Gospel of Mark: An essay on intertextuality. *Hervormde Teologiese Studies* 49(2), 385–396.

Chapters in Books

1971 The use of the prepositional phrase bmymr' in the Neofiti I version of Genesis, in Eybers, I.H., Fensham, F.C. & Labuschagne, C.J. (eds.), *De Fructu oris sui: Essays in honour of Adrianus van Selms*, 201–214. Leiden: Brill.
1975 Die eksegese van die Sinoptiese Evangelies: Verlede en Toekoms, in Eybers, I.H., König, A. & Borchardt, C.F.A. (reds), *Teologie en vernuwing*, 22–44. Pretoria: Unisa.
1978 Die Nuwe-Testamentiese wetenskap, in Eybers, I.H., König, A. & Stoop, J.A. (reds), *Inleiding in die Teologie*. 2de uitg Pretoria: N.G. Kerkboekhandel. 3de uitg, 1982, 86–107.
1979 'n Loflied van 'n arm vrou: Die Magnificat (Lukas 1:46–55), in Loader, J.A. (red), *'n Nuwe lied vir die Here: Opstelle by die verskyning van die nuwe Afrikaanse Psalm- en Gesangboek*, 13–28. Pretoria: HAUM.
1979 Die Joods-literêre agtergrond van die Nuwe Testament, in Du Toit, A.B. (red), *Handleiding by die Nuwe Testament*. Pretoria: N.G. Kerkboekhandel.
1979 In gesprek met die Landman-kommissie: Oor Skrifgebruik, in Viljoen, A.C. (red), *Ekumene onder die Suiderkruis: 'n Bundel opstelle ter erkenning van die pionierswerk van Ben Marais in die Suider-Afrikaanse konteks, aan hom opgedra in sy sewentigste lewensjaar*, 182–208. Pretoria: Unisa.
1980 Nuwere ontwikkelinge op die gebied van die Markusnavorsing, in *Die Nuwe Testamentiese wetenskap vandag*, 15–31. Pretoria: University of Pretoria (Symposium 2–3 Oct 1980: Departments of New Testament A & B and Department of Greek).
1980 Die Evangelie volgens Markus: Inleiding en teologie, in Du Toit, A.B. (red), *Handleiding by die Nuwe Testament*, vol. IV, 109–147. Pretoria: N.G. Kerkboekhandel.

1980   The Gospel according to Mark: Introduction and Theology, in Du
        Toit, A.B. (ed.), *Guide to the New Testament*, vol. IV, 102–143. Pretoria:
        N.G. Kerkboekhandel.

1981   On the origins of Christianity: A religio-historical perspective, in
        Vorster, W.S. (ed.), *Christianity amongst the religions*, 36–56. Pretoria:
        Unisa. (Miscellanea Congregalia 19.)

1982   Bybelvertaling, in Deist, F.E. (red), *Die Bybel leef*, 265–276. Pretoria:
        Van Schaik.

1982   De structuuranalyse, in Klijn, A.F.J. (red), *Inleiding tot de studie van
        het Nieuwe Testament*, 127–152. Kampen: Kok.

1982   De taal van het Nieuwe Testament, in Klijn, A.F.J. (red), *Inleiding
        tot de Studie van het Nieuwe Testament*, 32–42. Kampen: Kok.

1982   'Formgeschichte' en 'Redaktionsgeschichte', in Klijn, A.F.J. (red),
        Inleiding tot de studie van het Nieuwe Testament, 94–111. Kampen: Kok.

1982   Redaction, contextualization and the sayings of Jesus, in Delobel, J.
        (ed.), *Logia les paroles de Jesus: The sayings of Jesus. Memorial Joseph
        Coppens*, 491–500. Leuven: Peeters. (BEThL 59.)

1983   The Bible and apartheid 1, in De Gruchy, J.W. & Villa-Vicencio, C.
        (eds.), *Apartheid is a heresy*, 94–111. Cape Town: David Philip.

1984   Die Apartheid und das Lesen in der Bibel, in De Gruchy, J. &
        Villa-Vicencio, C. (Hrsg.), *Wenn wir wie Brüder beien ander wohnten . . .
        Von der Apartheid zur Bekennenden Kirche: Stellungnahmer südafrikanischer
        Theologen*, 117–136. Neukirchen: Neukirchner Verlag.

1984   The use of Scripture and the N.G. Kerk: A shift of paradigm or
        of values? in Hofmeyr, J.W. & Vorster, W.S. (eds.), *New Faces of
        Africa: Essays in honour of Ben (Barend Jacobus) Marais*, 204–219. Pretoria:
        Unisa. (Miscellanea 45.)

1985   Markus: Sammler, Redaktor, Autor oder Erzähler? in Hahn, F.C.
        (Hrsg.), *Der Erzähler des Evangeliums: Methodische Neuansätze in der Markus-
        forschung*, 11–36. Stuttgart: Katholisches Bibelwerk.

1985   New Testament sample studies, in Louw, J.P. (ed.), *Lexicography and
        translation, with special reference to Bible translation*, 138–156. Cape Town:
        Bible Society of South Africa.

1985   Meaning and Reference: The parables of Jesus in Mark 4, in Lategan
        B.C. & Vorster W.S. 1985. *Text and reality: Aspects of reference in bib-
        lical texts*, 27–65. Philadelphia: Fortress.

1985   Reader-Response, Redescription, and Reference: 'You Are the Man'
        (2 Sam. 12:7), in Lategan B.C. & Vorster W.S. 1985. *Text and real-
        ity: Aspects of reference in biblical texts*, 95–112. Philadelphia: Fortress.

1986   The annunciation of the birth of Jesus in the Protevangelium of
        James, in Petzer, J.H. & Hartin, P.J. (eds.), *A South African perspective
        on the New Testament*, 33–53. Leiden: Brill.

1986   On miracles and miracle stories: From the earthly Jesus to the writ-
        ten text, in De Villiers, P.G.R. (ed.), *Healing in the name of God*, 48–58.
        Pretoria: C.B. Powell Bible Centre.

1986   Tekste met 'n apokaliptiese perspektief, in Deist, F.E. & Vorster,
        W.S. (reds), *Woorde wat ver kom: Die literatuur van die Ou estament*, deel
        1. Kaapstad: Tafelberg-Uitgewers.

1986   Texts with an apocalyptic perspective, in Deist, F.E. & Vorster, W.S. (eds.), *Words from afar: The literature of the Old Testament*, vol. 1. Cape Town: Tafelberg.

1986   Diskriminasie en die vroeë kerk: Gedagtes oor partydigheid in Jakobus 2:1–13, in Breytenbach, J.C., *Eenheid en Konflik*, 134–149. Pretoria: N.G. Kerkboekhandel.

1988   Oor lees, lesers en Johannes 4, in De Villiers, P.G.R. (red), *Hoe lees 'n mens die Bybel?*, 1–30. Pretoria: Unisa.

1988   The protevangelium of James and intertextuality, in Baarda, T., Hilhorst, A., Luttikhuizen, G. & Van Der Woude, A.S. (eds.), *Text and testimony: Essays on New Testament and apocryphal literature in honour of A.F.J. Klijn*, 262–275. Kampen: Kok.

1988   Towards a post-critical paradigm: Progress in New Testament Scholarship? in Mouton, J., Van Aarde, A.G. & Vorster, W.S. (eds.), *Paradigms and progress in theology*, 31–48. Pretoria: HSRC. (HSRC Studies in Research Methodology 5.)

1989   Intertextuality and Redaktionsgeschichte, in Draisma, S. (ed.), *Intertextuality in Biblical writings: Essays in honour of Bas van Iersel*, 15–26. Kampen, Kok.

1989   On presuppositions and the historical study of the Jewishness of Jesus, in Mouton, J. & Joubert, D. (eds.), *Knowledge and Method in the human sciences*, 195–211. Pretoria: HSRC.

1990   The function of metaphorical and apocalyptic language about the unobservable in the teaching of Jesus, in Jennings, T.W. (ed.), *Text and logos: The humanistic interpretation of the New Testament*, 33–54. Atlanta: Scholars Press.

1990   Hebreërs, Inleiding tot Hebreërs, in Du Toit, A.B. (red), *Handleiding by die Nuwe Testament. Vol. VI*, 73–88. Pretoria: N.G. Kerkboekhandel.

1990   Stoics and early Christians on blessedness, in Balch, D.L., Ferguson, E. & Meeks, W.A. (eds.), *Greeks, Romans and Christians: Essays in honor of Abraham J. Malherbe*, 38–51. Minneapolis: Fortress.

1991   Om te vertel dat Jesus Christus die lydende Seun van God is: Oor Markus en sy teologie, in Roberts, J.H., *et al.*, (reds). *Teologie in Konteks*, 32–61. Halfway House: Orion.

1991   Through the eyes of a historian, in Hartin, P.J. & Petzer, J.H. (eds.). *Text and Interpretation: New Approaches in the Criticism of the New Testament*, 15–46. Leiden: Brill.

1992   Academic Research, in Botha, J.E. & Engelbrecht, J. (eds.). *Succeed at Dissertation: A South African Dissertation Handbook*. Pretoria: Van Schaik.

1992   Promoters and students, in Botha, J.E. & Engelbrecht, J. (eds.). *Succeed at Dissertation: A South African Dissertation Handbook*. Pretoria: Van Schaik.

1992   The Growth and Making of John 21, in Van Segbroeck, F., Tuckett, C.M., Van Belle, G. & Verheyden, J. (eds.). *The four gospels: Festschrift Frans Neirynck*, 3, 2207–2221. Leuven: Peeters.

1992   Oor die gebruik en vertaling van *DUNAMIS* in die Evangelie van Petrus 19, in Barkhuizen, J.H., Stander, H.F. & Swart, G.J. (reds), *Hupomnema: Feesbundel opgedra aan Prof. J.P. Louw*, 330–337. Pretoria: Departement Grieks, Universiteit van Pretoria.

1992   'Gospel Genre', in Freedman, D.N. (ed.). *The Anchor Bible Dictionary*. 6 vols. New York: Doubleday.

1992   'James, Protevangelium of', in Freedman, D.N. (ed.). 6 vols. *The Anchor Bible Dictionary*. New York: Doubleday.

1992   Die Evangelie volgens Markus: 'n Verhaal van glorie of van lyding, in Swanepoel, F.A. (ed.). *Blye boodskap van lyding en bevryding: 'n Oorsig oor die Evangelies en Handelinge*, 11–22. Pretoria: CB Powell-Bybelsentrum.

1992   Nuwe-Testamentiese Literatuur, in T.T. Cloete (red), *Literêre terme en teorieë*, 354–355. Pretoria: HAUM-Literêr.

1992   Readings, readers and the succession narrative: An essay on reception criticism, in House, P. (ed.) 1992. *Beyond Form Criticism: Essays in Old Testament Literary Criticism*, 395–407. Winona Lakes: Eisenbaums.

1994   Lotgenote in God se wêreld, Lukas 10:25–37, in Müller, J. & Vos, C.J.A. (reds) 1994. *God, mens en wêreld*. vol. 4. Halfway House: Orion.

1994   The relevance of of Jesus research for the 'new' South Africa, in Mouton, J. *et al.* 1994. *The Relevance of Theology for the 1990's*. Pretoria: HSRC.

Books Co-Authored

1985.   [With Lategan B.C.] *Text and reality. Aspects of reference in Biblical Text*. Philadelphia: Fortress. (Semeia Supplements.).

Books Edited

1978   *Church and society/Kerk en samelewing*. Pretoria: Unisa. (Miscellanea Congregalia 6.)

1979   *Scripture and the use of Scripture*. Pretoria: Unisa. (Miscellanea Congregalia 9.)

1980   *The Spirit in biblical perspective*. Pretoria: Unisa. (Miscellanea Congregalia 14.)

1980   *Church unity and diversity in the Southern African context*. Pretoria: Unisa. (Miscellanea Congregalia 17.)

1981   *Christianity among the religions*. Pretoria: Unisa. (Miscellanea Congregalia 19.)

1982   *Denominationalism: Its sources and implications*. Pretoria: Unisa. (Miscellanea Congregalia 20.)

1983   *Church and Industry*. Pretoria: Unisa. (Miscellanea Congregalia 22.)

1984   *Sexism and feminism in theological perspective*. Pretoria: Unisa. (Miscellanea Congregalia 24.)

1985   *Views on violence*. Pretoria: Unisa. (Miscellanea Congregalia 26.)

1986   *Reconciliation and construction: Creative options for a rapidly changing South Africa*. Pretoria: Unisa. (Miscellanea Congregalia 27.)

1987   *Are we killing God's Earth?: Ecology and Theology*. Pretoria: Unisa. (Miscellanea Congregalia 30.)

1988   *The right to life: Issues in bioethics*. Pretoria: Unisa. (Miscellanea Congregalia 34.)

1989   *The morality of censorship*. Pretoria: Unisa. (Miscellanea Congregalia 37.)

1990   *Morality of the marketplace.* Pretoria: Unisa. (Miscellanea Congregalia 38.)
1991   *Building a new nation: The quest for a new South Africa.* Pretoria: Unisa. (Miscellanea Congregalia 40.)
1992   *On being unemployed and religious.* Pretoria: Unisa. (Miscellanea Congregalia 43.)

Books Co-Edited

1980   [With C.F.A. Borchardt] *South African theological bibliography/Suid-Afrikaanse teologiese bibliografie* Volume 1. Pretoria: Unisa. (Documenta 22.)
1983   [With C.F.A. Borchardt] *South African theological bibliography/Suid-Afrikaanse teologiese bibliografie.* Volume 2. Pretoria: Unisa. (Documenta 30.)
1984   [With J.W. Hofmeyr] *New Faces of Africa.* Pretoria: Unisa. (Miscellanea 45.)
1986   [With Ferdinand Deist] *Woorde wat ver kom: Die literatuur van die Ou Testament.* Deel 1. Kaapstad: Tafelberg-Uitgewers.
1986   [With Ferdinand Deist] *Words from afar: The literature of the Old Testament,* vol. 1. Cape Town: Tafelberg Publishers.
1988   [With C.F.A. Borchardt] *South African theological bibliography/Suid-Afrikaanse teologiese bibliografie,* vol. 3. Pretoria: Unisa. (Studia Composita 3.)
1988   [With J. Mouton and A.G. van Aarde] *Paradigms and progress in theology.* Pretoria: HSRC. (HSRC Studies in Research Methodology 5.)
1989   [With A.S. Engelbrecht] *Uit genade alleen? Opstelle oor Romeine.* Pretoria: Unisa. (Miscellanea Congregalia 36.)
1989   [With C.F.A. Borchardt] *South African theological bibliography/Suid-Afrikaanse teologiese bibliografie,* vol. 4. Pretoria: Unisa. (Studia Composita 5.)
1990   [With C.F.A. Borchardt & J. Kilian] *South African Theological Bibliography/Suid-Afrikaanse Teologiese Bibliografie,* vol. 5. Pretoria: Unisa. (Studia Composita 10.)
1991   [With C.F.A. Borchardt & J. Kilian] *South African Theological Bibliography/Suid-Afrikaanse Teologiese Bibliografie,* vol. 6. Pretoria: Unisa. (Studia Composita 13.)
1991   [With J.H. Roberts, J.N. Vorster & J.G. van der Watt] *Teologie in Konteks.* Halfway House: Orion.
1992   [With C.F.A. Borchardt & J. Kilian] *South African Theological Bibliography/Suid-Afrikaanse Teologiese Bibliografie,* vol. 7. Pretoria: Unisa.

Selected Book Reviews

1987   Book review of: Louw, J.P., Vosloo, W. & Webb, V.N. 1985. *Die taal van die Bybel en die predikant.* (Universiteit van Pretoria Teologiese Studies nr 1.) *Hervormde Teologiese Studies* 43(3), 590–592.
1989   Book review of Berger, K. & Colpe, C. (Hrsg.) 1987. *Religionsgeschichtliches Textbuch zum Neuen Testament.* Göttingen: Vandenhoeck & Ruprecht. (NTD Textreihe Bd 1.) *Neotestamentica* 23, 359.
1989   Book review of Van Iersel, Bas 1989. *Reading Mark.* Londen: Clark. *Neotestamentica* 23, 360–361.
1990   Book review of Crossan, J.D. 1986. *Sayings Parallels. A workbook*

for the Jesus tradition. Philadelphia: Fortress. Neotestamentica 24(1), 143–144.

1990   Book review of Bilde, P. 1988. *Flavius Josephus between Jerusalem and Rome. His life, his works, and their importance.* Sheffield: JSOT Press. *Journal for the Study of Judaism* 21(1), 98–99.

1990   Book review of Lampe, P. 1987. *Die stadrömischen Christen in den ersten beiden Jahrhunderten. Untersuchungen zur Sozialgeschichte.* Tübingen: Mohr. *Neotestamentica* 24 (1), 144–146.

1990   Book review of Welzen, H. 1986. *Lucas Evangelist van Gemeenschap: Een Onderzoek naar de pragmatische Effecten in Lc. 15,1–17,10.* Dissertation of the Catholic University of Nijmegen. *Neotestamentica* 24(1), 146–147.

1990   Book review of Kodjak, A. 1986. *A structural analysis of the Sermon on the Mount.* Amsterdam: De Gruyter. *Hervormde Teologiese Studies* 46 (1 & 2), 261–262.

1991   Book review of Knibb, M.A. & Van der Horst, P.W. (eds.) 1989. *Studies on the Testament of Job.* Cambridge: Cambridge University Press. *Old Testament Essays* 4(3), 442–443.

1991   Book review of McGovern, AF *1989. Liberation theology and its critics: Toward an assesment.* Maryknoll: Orbis Books. *Missionalia* 19(2), 173.

1991   Book review of Myers, C. 1988. *Binding the strong man: A political reading of Mark's Story of Jesus.* Maryknoll: Orbis Books. *Missionalia* 19 (2), 173–174.

1992   Book review of Roth, W. 1989. *Hebrew Gospel: Cracking the code of Mark.* Oak Park: Meyer & Stone. *Neotestamentica* 26(1), 242–243.

1992   Book review of Schneemelcher, W. 1987. *Neutestamentliche Apokryphen: In deutscher Übersetzung. I. Band, Evangelien.* 5. Aufl. von Edgar Hennecke begründten Sammlung. Tübingen: Mohr. 442 pp. and Schneemelcher, W. (Hrsg.) 1989. *Neutestamentliche Apokryphen: In deutscher Übersetzung. II. Band, Apostolisches Apokalypsen und Verwandtes.* 5. Aufl. von Edgar Hennecke begründeten Sammlung. Tübingen: Mohr. 704 pp. Neotestamentica 26(2), 548–550.

Conferences Organised

As Head of the Institute for Theological Research at the University of South Africa (Unisa), Pretoria, Prof Vorster took the initiative to organise an annual conference on a theological topic of relevance to society in Southern Africa.

1978   Church and society/Kerk en samelewing. Pretoria: Unisa.
1979   Scripture and the use of Scripture. Pretoria: Unisa.
1980   Church unity and diversity in the Southern African context. Pretoria: Unisa.
1981   Christianity among the religions. Pretoria: Unisa.
1982   Denominationalism: Its sources and implications. Pretoria: Unisa.
1983   Church and Industry. Pretoria: Unisa.
1984   Sexism and feminism in theological perspective. Pretoria: Unisa.

1985 Views on violence. Pretoria: Unisa.
1986 Reconciliation and construction: Creative options for a rapidly changing South Africa. Pretoria: Unisa.
1987 Are we killing God's Earth?: Ecology and Theology. Pretoria: Unisa.
1988 The right to life: Issues in bioethics. Pretoria: Unisa.
1989 The morality of censorship. Pretoria: Unisa.
1990 Morality of the marketplace. Pretoria: Unisa.
1991 Building a new nation: The quest for a new South Africa. Pretoria:
   Unisa.
1992 On being unemployed and religious. Pretoria: Unisa.

ACKNOWLEDGEMENTS

Most of the articles included in this volume of essays have appeared elsewhere. The details of their initial publication are as follows:

1977   The structure of Matthew 13. *Neotestamentica* 11, 130–138 (Also: Addendum to Neotestamentica 11, 34–39).

1981   The function of the use of the Old Testament in Mark, in *The relationship between the Old and New Testament*, Neotestamentica 14, 62–72.

1982   Redaction, contextualization and the sayings of Jesus, in Delobel, J. (ed.), *Logia les paroles de Jesus: The sayings of Jesus. Memorial Joseph Coppens*, 491–500. Leuven: Peeters. (BEThL 59.)

1983   Kerygma/history and the gospel genre. *New Testament Studies* 29, 87–95.

1984   I Enoch and the Jewish literary setting of the New Testament: A Study in text types. *Neotestamentica* 17, 1–14.

1985   Meaning and Reference: The parables of Jesus in Mark 4, in Lategan B.C. & Vorster W.S. 1985. *Text and reality: Aspects of reference in biblical texts*, 27–65. Philadelphia: Fortress.

1985   Reader-Response, Redescription, and Reference: 'You Are the Man' (2 Sam. 12:7), in Lategan B.C. & Vorster W.S. 1985. *Text and reality: Aspects of reference in biblical texts*, 95–112. Philadelphia: Fortress.

1986   The New Testament and narratology. *Journal of literary studies/Tydskrif vir literatuurwetenskap* 2(3), 52–62.

1986   The annunciation of the birth of Jesus in the Protevangelium of James, in Petzer, J.H. & Hartin, P.J. (eds.), *A South African perspective on the New Testament*, 33–53. Leiden: Brill.

1987   Characterisation of Peter in the Gospel of Mark. *Neotestamentica* 21(1), 57–76.

1987   Literary reflections on Mark 13:5–37: A narrated speech of Jesus. *Neotestamentica* 21(2), 91–112.

1988   The protevangelium of James and intertextuality, in Baarda, T., Hilhorst, A., Luttikhuizen, G. & Van Der Woude, A.S. (eds.), *Text and testimony: Essays on New Testament and apocryphal literature in honour of A.F.J. Klijn*, 262–275. Kampen: Kok.

1988   'Genre' and the Revelation of John: A study in text, context and intertext. *Neotestamentica* 22(2), 103–123.

1989   The reader in the text: Narrative material. *Semeia* 48, 21–39.

1989   The Religio-historical context of the resurrection of Jesus and resurrection faith in the New Testament. *Neotestamentica*, 23(2), 159–175.

1989   Intertextuality and Redaktionsgeschichte. In Draisma, S. (ed.), *Intertextuality in Biblical writings: Essays in honour of Bas van Iersel*, 15–86. Kampen, Kok.

1989 So many men, so many minds: Reading the New Testament in a postmodern situation. Paper read at the *Studiorum Novi Testamenti Societas* Annual Meeting, Dublin, Ireland, Aug 1989.

1990 Bilingualism and the Greek of the New Testament: Semitic interference in the Gospel of Mark. *Neotestamentica* 24(2), 215–228.

1990 Stoics and early Christians on Blessedness, in Balch, D.L., Ferguson, E. & Meeks, W.A. (eds.), *Greeks, Romans and Christians: Essays in honor of Abraham J. Malherbe*, 38–51. Minneapolis: Fortress.

1990 The function of metaphorical and apocalyptic language about the unobservable in the teaching of Jesus, in Jennings, T.W. (ed.), *Text and logos: The humanistic interpretation of the New Testament*, 33–54. Atlanta: Scholars.

1991 A reader-response approach to Matthew 24:3–28, *Hervormde Teologiese Studies* 47(4), 1099–1108.

1991 Jesus the Galilean. *Hervormde Teologiese Studies* 47(1), 121–135.

1991 Jesus: Eschatological prophet and/or wisdom teacher? *Hervormde Teologiese Studies* 47(2), 526–542.

1991 In what sense is the Louw/Nida dictionary authoritative? *Hervormde Teologiese Studies* 47(1), 26–38.

1991 Through the eyes of a historian, in Hartin, P.J. & Petzer, J.H. (eds.). *Text and Interpretation: New Approaches in the Criticism of the New Testament*, 15–46. Leiden: Brill.

1992 The Growth and Making of John 21, in Van Segbroeck, F., Tuckett, C.M., Van Belle, G. & Verheyden, J. (eds.). *The four gospels: Festschrift Frans Neirynck*, 3, 2207–2221. Leeuven: Peeters.

1993 The production of the Gospel of Mark: An essay on intertextuality. *Hervormde Teologiese Studies* 49(2), 385–396.

1994 The relevance of of Jesus research for the 'new' South Africa, in Mouton, J. *et al.*, 1994. *The Relevance of Theology for the 1990's*. Pretoria: HSRC.

ABBREVIATIONS

The 1988 guidelines of the SBL with regard to abbreviations of commonly used periodicals and reference works (JBL 107/3: 579–596) were followed in compiling this list. An * indicates an item not in the list of the SBL.

ATR	*Anglican Theological Review*
BETL	Bibliotheca ephemeridum theologicarum lovaniensum
BEvT	Beiträge zur evangelischen Theologie
Bib	*Biblica*
BHT	Beiträge zur historische Theologie
BiTr	*The Bible Translator*
BJRL	Bulletin of the John Rylands University Library of Manchester
BTB	Biblical Theology Bulletin
BR	*Biblical Research*
BibRev	*Bible Review*
*BU	Biblische Untersuchungen
BWANT	Beiträge zur Wissenschaft vom Alten und Neuen Testament
BZ	*Biblische Zeitschrift*
BZAW	Beihefte zur ZAW
CBQ	*Catholic Biblical Quarterly*
CRINT	*Compendium rerum iudaicarum ad novum testamentum*
CurTM	*Currents in Theology and Mission*
DBSup	*Dictionaire de la Bible, Supplement*
EKKNT	Evangelisch-katholischer Kommentar zum Neuen Testament
EvT	*Evangelische Theologie*
*GWU	*Geschichte in Wissenschaft und Unterricht*
*HistT	*History and Theology*
HBD	*Harper's Bible Dictionary* (Achtemeier, P.J. *et al.*, eds.)
HTKNT	Herders theologischer Kommentar zum Neuen Testament
HTR	*Harvard Theological Review*
IDB	*Interpreter's Dictionary of the Bible* (Buttrick, G.A. ed.)
Int	*Interpretation*
JAAR	*Journal of the American Academy of Religion*
JBL	*Journal of Biblical Literature*
JR	*Journal of Religion*
JSJ	*Journal for the Study of Judaism in the Persian, Hellenistic and Roman Period*
JSNT	*Journal for the Study of the New Testament*
JSOT	*Journal for the Study of the Old Testament*
JTS	*Journal of Theological Studies*
*JTSA	*Journal of Theology for Southern Africa*
KD	*Kerygma und Dogma*

LB	*Linguistica Biblica*
*NDLitHist	*New Directions in Literary History*
NEB	New English Bible
*NGTT	Nederduits Gereformeerde Teologiese Tydskrif
NIV	New International Version
NLitHist	*New Literary History*
NTD	Das Neue Testament Deutsch
NTS	*New Testament Studies*
NovT	*Novum Testamentum*
OCD	*Oxford Classical Dictionary*
*OTKNT	Ökomenische Taschenbuchkommentar zum Neuen Testament
PT	*Poetics Today*
RAC	*Reallexicon für Antike und Chritentum*
RelS	*Religious Studies*
RevExp	*Review and Expositor*
RV	Revised version
SJT	*Scottish Journal of Theology*
SBT	Studies in Biblical Theology
SBL	Society of Biblical Literature
SBLDS	Society of Biblical Literature Dissertation Series
SBM	Stuttgarter biblische Monographien
SE	*Studia Evangelica*
SNTSMS	Society for New Testament Studies Monograph Series
SR	*Studies in Religion/Sciences Religieuses*
SUNT	Studien zur Umwelt des Neuen Testaments
*TB	Theologische Bücherei
TEV	Today's English Version
ThEv	*Theologia Evangelica*
TLZ	*Theologische Literaturzeitung*
TToday	*Theology Today*
TRev	*Theologisch Revue*
TRu	*Theologische Rundschau*
TRE	*Theologische Realenzyclopädie*
TS	*Theological Studies*
TWAT	*Theologische Wörterbuch zum Alten Testament* (Botterwick G.J. & Ringgren eds.)
TWNT	*Theologische Wörterbuch zum Neuen Testament* (Kittel G. & G. Friedrich eds.)
*TU	Texte und Untersuchungen
UTB	(München: Fink)
VF	*Verkündigung und Forschung*
VT	*Vetus Testamentum*
WTJ	*Westminster Theological Journal*
WUNT	Wissenschaftliche Unterzuchungen zum Neuen Testaments
ZAW	*Zeitschrift für die alttestamentliche Wissenschaft*
ZLL	*Zeitschrift für Literaturwissenschaft und Linguistik*
ZNW	*Zeitschrift für die neutestamentliche Wissenschaft*
ZTK	*Zeitschrift für Theologie und Kirche*

SECTION A

BIBLICAL LANGUAGE

CHAPTER ONE

THE FUNCTION OF METAPHORICAL AND
APOCALYPTIC LANGUAGE ABOUT THE
UNOBSERVABLE IN THE TEACHING OF JESUS

In his book *Theology out of the Ghetto: A New Testament Exegetical Study
concerning Religious Exclusiveness*, Hendrikus Boers has a short section
on 'the ontological grounding of the message of Jesus' in the chapter on 'Jesus and the kingdom of God'. Ever since I first read the
manuscript—still then in unpublished form—this section has been of
interest to me. Reflecting on Robert Funk's distinction between the
'foundational language' of the parables of Jesus and the 'primary
reflective language' of Paul's letters, Boers observes that the fundamental problem is: 'What are the phenomena to which the language
of Jesus pointed? What were the ontological bearings of his language?' (Boers 1971:44). Obviously this has been the million dollar
question since the days of the early church when Christians had to
defend Jesus' talk about the unobservable and their own theological
language. This can be seen, for instance, in Irenaeus' apologetic in
his *Adversus Haereses*, II, 25–28, but also in all subsequent discussions
from the allegorical, fourfold and literal interpretations of the New
Testament, through Strauss' and Bultmann's attempts to deal with
myth and demythologization until the present attempts to deal with
interpretation of theological texts in terms of models and metaphors.
The question is complicated by its epistemological dimensions. How
can humanity know and talk about the unobservable? Why are myth,
metaphor, and revelatory language so often used in religious texts
when the unobservable is spoken about?

Almost two decades after the publication of the book by Boers, I
would like to discuss an aspect of the problem of the status of the
language of the New Testament about things that cannot be observed,
to honour a friend and colleague and to share with others a small
aspect of our common concern about religious talk. I will concentrate on the function of metaphorical and apocalyptic language from
a socio-semiotic point of view in order to show that the problem of
God-talk and talk about the unobservable has a functional side which

complicates the ontological status of theological language in the New Testament, and that this has to be taken into account in any systematic discussion about theological discourse concerning the unobservable. I will develop my argument by first dealing with the problem of the pragmatic function of language with regard to metaphorical and apocalyptic statements in the gospel tradition and then by drawing some conclusions about the cognitive function of these statements in view of a few remarks about epistemological models.

1. *Metaphoric and Apocalyptic Statements and their Function*

1.1   *Language conventions and the unobservable*

The New Testament in general and the gospel tradition in particular abound with imagery and metaphors especially with respect to the unobservable. In addition to terms such as 'kingdom of God' and 'Son of man', shorter statements and units such as sayings of Jesus and parables are phrased in mythic, metaphoric or apocalyptic language. This is typical of the type of discourse which the people of the New Testament world used when they spoke about the unobservable.

Both in the Mediterranean world and the Near East prior to and after the New Testament period people spoke about the unobservable (Hellholm 1983). Myth, metaphor and revelatory language were the conventional vehicles for communication about things which cannot be observed. Oracles made it possible to reveal things which humans cannot see clearly or speak about without special capabilities, and so did visions, dreams and 'flights of the mind' of the philosophers (see Thom 1987). We are told of journeys to otherworldly places, and special functionaries and people with the ability to speak about the unobservable.

Mediators with special insight communicated knowledge about the unobservable to the ordinary person. Generally speaking this is also the situation in the New Testament where Jesus, for instance, is portrayed as somebody who could speak with authority bout the unobservable, and others, like the author of the Revelation of John claim to have had visions which enable them to speak about things which cannot be seen. That this situation continued into the period after the New Testament is clear from the extracanonical literature, especially early Christian apocalypses and gnostic literature, not to mention the vast amount of philosophical thought bout matters of afterlife and so on. What is remarkable is that it is taken for granted that at least some people are able to speak about the unobservable by using certain language conventions such as myth, metaphor or revelatory techniques. When the problem of *how* it is possible to speak about the unobservable is addressed, it becomes quite another matter. A different discourse type is used, namely 'reflective language', if we may use the term of Funk referred to above. Herodotus (*Hist.* 2.33.2) maintains that the unknown should be judged from the plain, that is by way of inference, and although the Empiricists relied on what was seen by one's own eyes, they also allowed for inductive reasoning from the known to the unknown (see Schoedel 1984:37). But, is this type of discourse also applicable to theological matters which cannot be seen by the eye?

By the second century CE, it became apparent that it was not easy to speak about the unobservable in theological terms. In fact, one can even argue that in certain circles people were sceptical about the possibility of talking about the unobservable. It was simply regarded as speculation and also dismissed. In the passage of Irenaeus referred to above, he clearly maintains that men like Valentinus, Ptolemaeus and Basilides who claim that they have knowledge of the whole universe are in the wrong. They first have to explain the things *quae in manibus sunt, et ante pedes, et in oculis, et terrenis . . .*, that is, the things that are in their hands, and at their feet, and before their eyes, and on the earth (*Adv. Haer II.28.9*) see Van Unnik 1979:35–37 for an interesting discussion of the term *ante pedes*. Irenaeus argues that some things known, others not (Van Unnik 1979:43), and that it is better to know that God exists than how things came about (see Schoedel 1984:31). The same anti-speculative tendency is also found in the Mishnah text Hagigah 2.1: 'If anyone speculates about four things, it would have been merciful had he never come into the world—namely, what is above, what is below, what is before, and what is after' (see Schoedel 1984 for a full discussion of the topic). It is obvious that we have two types of discourse here. In the case of mythological, metaphorical and revelatory material it is assumed that the only way to talk about the unobservable, is by using a special kind of discourse. As soon as one starts rationalizing about the unobservable, quite another kind of discourse is needed.

Let us return to the conventional way of speaking about the

unobservable in New Testament texts and the function of statements about the unobservable. First of all we have to explain what is meant by 'function' in this essay because the term is used in many different ways in New Testament scholarship (see Vorster 1988b).

1.2 *Function and the use of language*

Function is used here to indicate the semantic, pragmatic and textual functions of utterances in the New Testament. The intentions of a speaker—that is the functions for which a speaker uses language—are of an *ideational, interpersonal*, and *textual* nature (see Webb 1986:51–52). *Ideational* refers to relating of experiences, providing information (experiential), indicating the relationship between the events described in texts (logical), and the use of language to order thoughts cognitive). *Interpersonal* refers to expression of feelings (expressive), changing of the emotional state of the hearer (emotive), changing the behaviour of the hearer (imperative, persuasive), establishing the speaker's status (egocentric), changing the status of the hearer ('Your sins are forgiven'—performative) and establishing and maintaining contact (phatic). *Textual function* refers to the use of language to give a particular form to the message, for instance, to signal topic. All three types of function are of importance for our topic.

In the past the semantic and textual functions have received most attention from New Testament scholars. In search of the meaning of texts we have realized that certain texts function within certain fields of meaning. (Frow 1980:73–81) makes a useful distinction between field, mode and tenor. He argues that the semantic function of genres should be described by specifying the dominance of field, that is the type of activity in which the text has significant function, tenor, the status and real relationships involved (interpersonal functions) or mode, that is the symbolic mode and rhetorical channels or textual function. The original use of *Sitz im Leben* as a sociological category points in this direction (see Bultmann 1970:4) where cultic, apologetic and other social settings indicated the field within which utterances have meaning. Unfortunately *Sitz im Leben* lost its original purpose, and became a means of speculation about a concrete historical situation or context within which a text could have functioned. Much attention has also been focused upon the textual function or *mode* of New Testament utterances. The study of forms and their functions have been of primary importance in Form

Criticism, for instance. In addition to *Sitz im Leben* the mode of writing of smaller and larger forms has been studied extensively, as can be seen from the literature on sayings of Jesus or that concerning the writing of letters in the world of the New Testament. It is the pragmatic function of the use of language which generally has not received the necessary interest in the past, mainly because of the fact that pragmatics is a relative late-comer to the scene.

It is not possible to overrate the importance of the pragmatic side of language when we talk about the functional of the use of language in any communication. The emphasis on the fact that people do things with words (speech acts) when they communicate, is what I have in mind when I refer to function now. Communication is more than the exchange of words or ideas. Language acts can be informative, expressive, persuasive, aesthetical, social and so on, as we have seen above. That is why it is so important to distinguish between the various functions for which language can be used. One and the same utterance can have totally different functions as is clear from the sentence: The door is open. This utterance can function either as a statement of fact or as an imperative. This also has bearing on the ontological status of sentences or the use of language in the New Testament.

Let us briefly explain pragmatic function with reference to a text from the gospel tradition which is well known. The pragmatic function of the little apocalypse of Mark 13 has to do with the interpersonal level of persuasion. The author of the Gospel of Mark tried to convince the reader that the message of Jesus about future turmoil is authoritative and that the reader/hearer should be confident that his/her following of Jesus will not be in vain. There is no sign that the author wanted to give a concrete or logical description about the future by using the type of language where it is difficult to find out what the sentences are referring to in the real world (cf. verse 14). The function of these sentences is to create a new symbolic universe for the reader in which the return of the Son of man is an important symbol. We will return to this text below.

Social factors also determine the construction of a message and the function of language relates to these factors. Communication between members of subculture or some socio-religious, or socio-political group is determined by the symbols they share. This is reflected in the language they use (see Webb 1986:53–55). In order to be meaningful, a text like a Gospel or the 'Revelation' of John presupposes a group of people who share a common system of meaning, closely knit together in a unit with a strong concern for the beliefs of the group (Malina 1986:13–15). To communicate they use certain language conventions which have certain functions. That is why there has recently been so much interest in the specific nature of theological discourse (see Macquarrie 1967; McFague 1983; Soskice 1985). Function can be a very helpful means to form a conceptual framework of the social context '. . . as the semiotic environment in which people exchange meanings' (Halliday 1978). Function, in other words, is not an empirical category but a theoretical device, and social context is not primarily a particular historical context. This argument has to be developed a little further.

The way in which the material is presented, both with regard to the presentational process (e.g. narrative) and the presented world (e.g. narrative world created by the text), affects the reader and the ontological status of the utterances within a particular text. Ruthrof (1981:138) has made valuable observations in this connection. He argues that in myth, where the narrator functions as an authority (who knows how to speak about the unobservable), the narrative world is presented as a dictate and the implied reader in the text as a minor. In a parable, where the narrator is a preacher, the world is presented as analogue and as teaching, and the implied reader functions as a believer, normally with limited faculties. In prophecy, the narrator is a prophet who presents the world as divine vision and the future truth to rebellious believers as implied readers. This underscores the fact that different kinds of discourse are used for different purposes and for different functions, each with its own ontological status. An illustration will clarify the point.

In his discussion of the oracle of Trophonius with regard to the so-called apocalyptic genre, Hans Dieter Betz deals with the concept of myth. He makes the following remark which is of importance for our discussion of function: 'The genre of *mythos* can do what *logos* cannot do: *mythos* can speak in human words about things that go beyond the human words and language. While *logos* must be understood rationally *mythos* is to be believed' (Betz 1983:587–88). This distinction between *mythos* and *logos* also illustrates the point that on the interpersonal level *mythos* is used to persuade, that is to establish faith. It is hardly possible to think in ontological terms about the things at which myths point in the extra textual real world. Because myths do not refer to extra textual realities, and because they serve the purpose of establishing faith, scholars often distinguish between the meaning and the significance of myths (see Verryn 1987:171–198). It is correct to maintain that: 'David Friedrich Strauss took a great step forward in seeing myth as primarily a construct of the believing community, whereby its faith found expression, . . .' (Macquarrie 1967:170). Perhaps these remarks about the function of myth can also help us get a clearer idea of the function of metaphoric language about the unobservable.

1.3 *The function of metaphoric language in the teaching of Jesus*

A few words about the use of the term 'teaching of Jesus' in this essay will be in order. What I have in mind is simply to take examples and explain the problems we have in dealing with the function of metaphorical and apocalyptic language in the teaching of Jesus. I also have to leave aside any critical discussion about the possibility of reconstructing the *ipsissima vox* of Jesus. For the sake of my argument I simply have to accept some of the domain assumptions of critical scholarship and work with the results.

One of these domain assumptions which I take as certain is the fact that much of the teaching of Jesus has a metaphoric character. Jesus made use of metaphors to say meaningful things about the unobservable. I am referring here to metaphors such as 'kingdom of God', 'father', perhaps 'Son of man', 'heaven', and so on, and also to his parables which I regard as metaphoric teaching (see Harnisch 1979 and Kjaurgaard 1986). He obviously used metaphors in talking about observable things also (all quotations from *Good News Bible*: 'You are like light for the whole world. A city built on a hill cannot be hidden' (Mt. 5:14). I am aware of the difference of opinion concerning the origin of Matthew 5:14a, see Luz 1985:220). Even here the observable, namely light, has a reference beyond the realities which one can see.

Although there still is a great deal of confusion and unclarity about the exact nature of the parables of Jesus as metaphors within New Testament scholarship, as Kjaurgaard (1986:133–197) has convincingly indicated, it is nevertheless clear that there should be little doubt that the parables of Jesus are metaphoric stories, or extended metaphors.

Before we turn to the function of the metaphoric teaching of Jesus about the unobservable, a few remarks have to be made about metaphors in view of current research on the topic. It is generally accepted that metaphors are rather complicated utterances, especially with regard to predication. In his excellent treatment of the subject, Kjaurgaard (1986:133–197) makes use of the findings of interaction theory and argues that the sentence 'Man is a wolf' involves the following: (1) Linguistic-grammatically it is a subject-predicate sentence, while logical-grammatically it contains an explicit primary subject 'man' and an explicit secondary subject 'wolf', and an implicit secondary predicate . . . which is linked to and represented by the secondary 'subject'. 'Man' as primary subject is used literally, whereas the secondary subject 'wolf' is not used literally. (2) The secondary predicate is a complicated system. Logical-grammatically it can be described as a series (e.g. man is a wolf; man is a wolf who is the implicit secondary predicate; man is a wolf who is a, b, c, . . . n). The individual elements of the series '. . . represent concepts, assumptions and ideas that are or can be derived from and are or can be linked to the secondary subject'. (3) The metaphor 'Man is a wolf' is also a performative or speech act. It invites the reader to project the elements of the secondary subject onto the primary subject: 'Man is a wolf who is a, b, c, . . . n'. That is why in the end (4) the metaphor can be formulated as: 'Man is a, b, c, . . . n', since it creates a structural similarity between the primary subject of the metaphor and its secondary subject by modifying the understanding of the sense of the primary subject.

For our purpose it is of vital importance to realize that metaphors are not only semantically complicated. They are speech acts that invite readers to react and to project the elements of the secondary subject onto the primary subject. In the case of the 'kingdom parables', for instance, the reader is invited to understand the meaning of the story about the kingdom and project that meaning onto the 'kingdom of God'. That is why I will argue below that the metaphoric language of the parables of Jesus does not point to some reality outside the text which is unobservable. They invite readers to interpret the sense of the parable with reference to the 'kingdom'.

If we now turn to the parables of Jesus as extended metaphors, it becomes apparent that, as far as function is concerned, we have a very interesting situation. Semantically and textually it is clear that most of these stories function as narratives. They were told by Jesus as short stories within very concrete communication situations. Undoubtedly it is impossible to recover these historical communication situations from the extant canonical and extra-canonical sources. Nevertheless it is obvious that Jesus used these metaphorical stories to do something. On the textual level it seems clear that most of these parabolic utterances are of a narrative character and also reveal the characteristics of narratives (see Vorster 1985a:27–65). In other words they were told as stories, many of them being stories about the unobservable 'kingdom of God'. The question which remains in view of what we have said above about the metaphor, is what is the pragmatic function of metaphoric language in the parables of Jesus.

It is not difficult to apply the insights given above about metaphors to the parables of Jesus and his metaphoric language with regard to pragmatic function. Jesus obviously wanted to do something with words and stories. There may be differences of opinion about the perspective from which Jesus told his stories, that is whether the 'kingdom of God' is a future kingdom, whether the term is used within the ambit of 'wisdom' or 'apocalyptic' theology (see Mack 1987), but there can be little doubt about the fact that Jesus tried to create a new symbolic universe for people who were in despair. By telling metaphoric stories to the 'underdogs' of society in Galilee, Jesus attempted to establish belief in the coming kingdom ruled by God. In such a manner he created new hopes and resocialized people who were at a total loss. He effectively used stories of a metaphorical nature such as the story of the Good Samaritan, the Sower, the Mustard Seed, the Rich Man and Lazarus, the Workers in the Vineyard, the Wicked Husbandman, the Doorkeeper, the Unjust Steward, the Pearl and many others, to change the conduct of people and to make it possible for his followers to get involved in situations which society did not allow. The content of Jesus' message was not all that new. But his message was aimed at having people think in certain ways and do things which fit the rule of God.

The fact that after centuries we New Testament scholars still try to reach a decision on what the 'kingdom of God' refers to in the teaching of Jesus (see also Merklein 1984), is an indication of the metaphoric character of the notion. In short, the function of metaphorical language in the teaching of Jesus has to do with the pragmatic rather than the ontological, when ontological refers to the things at which the stories point in reality. Jesus told these metaphoric stories about the unobservable God, the kingdom and other phenomena to establish faith in the possibilities which the kingdom of God gives. The function is pragmatic!

1.4 *The function of apocalyptic language in the teaching of Jesus*

For almost a century scholars have believed that the teaching of
Jesus, especially regarding the kingdom of God, was embedded in
Jewish apocalyptic. In recent times this has been challenged (Mack
1987) and attempts have been made to argue that the teaching of
Jesus should be related to Jewish Wisdom. For this and other reasons such as the many ways in which the term 'apocalyptic' is used
I shall first make a few general remarks about apocalyptic as a theological perspective before I turn to a discussion of the function of
apocalyptic language in the teaching of Jesus.

Following the research of Hanson (1975) and others, apocalyptic
in my view (Vorster 1986) refers to a phenomenon which arises in
a crisis. Apocalyptic eschatology on the other hand, refers to a meaning system, a theological perspective on God, humanity, and the
world. Apocalyptic usually rises when values and structures of the
particular society lose their meaning for some minority group within
that society and are replaced by new symbolic a meaning system.
It is therefore at the same time a crisis phenomenon and an all-
embracing approach to life in which the future determines the present. Apocalyptic is not concerned with the future only, and adherents
of apocalyptic are not merely interested in the future. The contents of their visions and their revelations also have bearing on the
present and the past. Because life is seen in relation to the future
there is great emphasis on correct conduct and ethics. Eschatology
is of paramount importance. The past, present and future are interpreted in terms of the expectation of a new future or age and a
new world in which supernatural space (heaven) and figures play an
important role.

It is within this frame of reference that I refer to the teaching of
Jesus as apocalyptic. For our present purpose it does not seem necessary to elaborate further on the question whether the teaching of
Jesus was of an apocalyptic or a wisdom nature. More important is
to develop the argument about the function of the apocalyptic teaching on the unobservable. My first example is taken from the macarisms
or beatitudes of Jesus.

> Happy are you poor; the Kingdom of God is yours! Happy are you
> who are hungry now; you will be filled (Lk. 6:20b–21b).

In Matthew's version the sayings read as follows:

> Happy are those who know they are spiritually poor; the Kingdom of heaven belongs to them! Happy are those whose greatest desire is to do what God requires; God will satisfy them fully (Mt. 5:3, 6).

Both sayings probably originated from Jesus although the Lucan and Matthean versions differ considerably. Matthew and Luke both made use of Q in compiling the beatitudes and, as the Greek text indicates, there are close similarities between the two versions of the sayings. Matthew probably edited the Q version considerably by changing the 'poor' to the 'poor of spirit' and 'those who are hungry' to 'those who hunger and thirst for righteousness'. It is probable that in the socio-economic conditions of the followers of Jesus in Galilee, he would have used the terms 'poor' and 'hunger' with reference to economically poor and therefore hungry people. It is possible that originally the sayings were in the third person and not in the second as Luke has them (see Luz 1985:201). Are these sayings apocalyptic sayings about the unobservable? To answer the question we will first have to deal with the different settings within which beatitudes occur in Jewish literature in order to construct possible fields of communication. Beatitudes are used in two totally different *Sitze im Leben* in Jewish literature of the Old Testament and the intertestamental period and therefore reflect two different usages (see Guelich 1982:63–66 for a very useful survey of the problem). In the Wisdom-cultic setting they are used as declarative statements about the well-being of the believers (Prv. 8:34; Ps. 2:11; Wis. 3:13–14; Sir. 14:1–2 and others). The second setting is future-oriented and is primarily found in apocalyptic writings (1 Enoch 103:5, 2 Bar. 10:6–7). Although the last two examples are rather late the roots of this usage probably go back to Isaiah 30:18 and Daniel 12:12. There is quite a remarkable difference between the two usages:

> In the Wisdom-cultic setting, the beatitude is a declarative statement, whose implications border on paraenetic exhortation. The statement of blessing becomes in turn a model to be emulated or a goal to be attained. An ethical tone prevails. In the prophetic-apocalyptic setting, the beatitude is a declarative statement of future vindication and reward. It comes as assurance and encouragement in the face of trouble. The eschatological tone prevails (Guelich 1982:65).

To my mind there is little doubt that these sayings of Jesus are used in the second way, that is in a prophetic-apocalyptic manner. It is interesting to note that both sayings point to the observable as well

as the unobservable. The poor and the hungry refer to real people
in the sayings while the kingdom and 'being satisfied' refer to unobservable realities in the future. What are the functions of these sayings?

Although Jesus did not say what it means that the kingdom belongs
to the poor or that the hungry will be satisfied, he obviously tried
to encourage the poor and the hungry by creating a symbolic universe which includes the future. In other words he encouraged the
poor and hungry to rely on the God who rules and to whose kingdom they belong. The future is not described in concrete terms but
simply referred to. It is the unobservable kingdom and place of relief
which makes life (in the observable conditions of poverty and hunger)
bearable. The sayings have a performative function. They invite the
poor and the hungry to rely on the future kingdom of God. As did
the metaphoric teaching of Jesus the apocalyptic mode enabled him
to encourage people and convince them of the power of a ruler who
cannot be seen. He spoke about this ruler and his kingdom without
a discussion of the exact detail or a description of what the kingdom
is like in observable terms. The apocalyptic sayings of Jesus do not
point to describable or observable realities; they function as speech
acts which invite people to do things or stimulate them to have part
in the kingdom. Let us now turn to Mark 13 from an apocalyptic
perspective.

Obviously the speech related in Mark 13:5b–37 cannot be regarded
as transmitting the exact words of Jesus. The speech has a very complicated history of growth (see Brandenburger 1984:21–46). In addition, scholars also do not agree about the apocalyptic character of
our text. But I believe that there are good grounds to argue that
Mark 13 is an apocalyptic text in the sense discussed above and that
it contains a core of the apocalyptic teaching of Jesus which has
been reworked by Mark to suit his own purpose. For the sake of
our argument this text can be used as a larger unit containing apocalyptic and paraenetic teaching of Jesus.

The eschatological conflict and the return of the Son of man are
two of the master symbols of a new symbolic universe which the
text offers. These aspects make it totally different from the rest of
Mark's Gospel. Mark 13:5–37 presupposes a new context of communication, and presupposes a different implied reader. While the
previous sections of the story of Mark deal with the future mainly
in terms of the death and resurrection of Jesus, Mark 13 focuses
upon the end and the return of the Son of man. In Mark 13 con-

duct is determined by the coming of the end and not by the death
and resurrection of Jesus. The end-time is described in images which
are familiar to those who are acquainted with apocalyptic imagination and theology. How does this text refer and to what does it
point? The history of interpretation of Mark 13 offers an interesting
picture of guesswork in this connection not restricted to the *crux interpretum* in verse 14 (Brandenburger 1984:46, 49–54).

It should be kept in mind that texts written from an apocalyptic
perspective do not refer to extra textual realities in the first place.
That is not their primary function. The image of a future conflict, persecution, tribulation, cosmic changes and the unexpected coming of
the Son of man are used in Mark 13 to persuade the four to whom
the speech is directed (and also the hearers/readers of the text) to
be on the alert and to live with a view to the sudden coming of the
Son of man (Vorster 1987:218). The text obviously bears the marks
of the time and historical context from which it arose, but the individual items which cannot be seen, because they are still to come,
do not refer to extra textual realities.

Mark 13 was written from an apocalyptic perspective, as was the
Revelation of John, not to reveal or describe the unobservable, but
to persuade and instruct readers about their conduct, and to rein-
force their beliefs. The function of apocalyptic texts should therefore
be seen in terms of what they do and not in terms of what they
point to in the metaphysical world.

2. *The Cognitive Function of the Interpretational and Apocalyptic Language of Jesus*

I will be using 'cognitive function' here in restricted sense. Do metaphorical and apocalyptic statements of Jesus also help us to ontologically know the unobservable realities they refer to? Can we claim
cognitive reference for the metaphorical and apocalyptic language of
Jesus? This question will be dealt with briefly in view of current epistemologies, and not in terms of the language reality problem which
I have discussed in another context (see Lategan & Vorster 1985:27–
65, 95–112). The basic problem is obviously: What do metaphorical
and apocalyptic statements refer to, and how do we obtain knowledge bout the unobservable?

The starting point for our discussion of the cognitive function of

the metaphorical and apocalyptic statements about the unobservable
in the teaching of Jesus is the observation that in principle neither
is to be understood literally. In other words there is no direct one-tone
relationship between what is said and what is referred to. The problem is furthermore complicated by the claims of realists that theological language—in some way or other—refers ontologically in spite
of its non-literal character. A few remarks on different epistemological
positions are necessary to explain the different stances on cognitive
function.

There are basically two incompatible epistemological positions
concerning the cognitive function of language which range from
instrumentalism on the one hand to naive realism, positivism and
critical realism on the other. This can also be said in terms of non-
constructivism versus constructivism. Let us start with the first.

> According to non-constructivism, language has no constitutive function
> in the cognition of reality. Language is an arbitrary system of sym-
> bols, and its essential function is to describe the reality objectively exist-
> ing according to experience, having regard to the relations convention
> ally established between language's symbols and reality's objects (Kjaur-
> gaard 1986:106).

This is similar to the position held by instrumentalists as we will see
below. Constructivism on the other hand holds that language has a
constitutive function in the cognition of reality. 'Language contains
terms for a system of categories and concepts and, by virtue of this,
its essential function is a condition of the cognition of reality' (Kjaurgaard 1986:107). The two positions are mutually exclusive. A short
survey of four epistemological positions will clarify the problem.

Instrumentalists hold that theories are products of human creative
imagination. Models are therefore useful fictions with heuristic functions. These models are not true or false. They are mental devices.
That is why '. . . an instrumental (sic!) position would first and foremost imply a definite reluctance to make any ontological claim for
the modes of doctrines of Christian faith' (Van Huyssteen 1987:21),
or, for that matter, utterances about the unobservable, be they in
metaphorical or apocalyptic language. In fact, instrumentalism is the
exact opposite of a realist position as we shall see below.

According to an instrumentalist position models and metaphors in
the Bible will therefore not be depicting reality. They will simply
serve to open the possibility of discovering that which is spoken about

in any given part of the Bible. As such no written text can pretend
to give an exact copy of any event or person, no to mention the
unobservable. Language does not have the ability to copy reality.
The implications of the naive realist position, which is not used here
in a pejorative sense of the word, is given in the following words of
John Updike (1972) in a poem concerning the resurrection of Jesus:

> Let us not mock God with metaphor,
> analogy, sidestepping, transcendence;
> making of the event a parable, a sign painted in the faded credulity
> of earlier ages:
> let us walk through the door.

> The stone is rolled back, not papier-macchea,
> not a stone in a story,
> but the vast rock of materiality that in slow grinding of time will eclipse
> for each of us the wide light of day.

> And if we will have an angel at the tomb,
> make it a real angel,
> weighty with Max Planck's quanta, vivid with hair, opaque in the
> dawn light, robed in real linen
> spun on a definite loom.

The naive realist position simply means that theories, including the
use of language, are accurate descriptions or replicas of that to which
they refer. In the interpretation of the New Testament this position
leads to Fundamentalism. The biblical text is without the mediation
of any theory. That is why we can pretend to walk through the
door. Positivism also poses the same problems since positivists hold
that '. . . it is possible to go directly from observation to theory without the critical use of models . . .' (Van Huyssteen 1987:21). Little
attention is given to the fact that knowledge is theory-mediated and
that in any interpretation theory plays an important role. Biblical
texts are therefore regarded as 'empirical data'. This leads to biblical literalism.

Unlike the instrumentalists, critical realists hold that their theories
are representations of the world as reality, and that the models and
metaphors which are used in the interpretation of the New Testament
refer to reality, even if it is only indirectly by way of redescription
of reality. Critical realists accept that knowledge about reality is mediated through theories, models and metaphors. The point is, however,
that according to this position language has the ability of depicting reality.

The metaphorical language of the Biblical text, as well as the dominant models we have formed from this, represent aspects of the reality of what Christians believe are in no way directly accessible to use. . . . As such they are to be taken seriously but not literally, for although they refer in an ontological or cognitive sense, they are always partial and inadequate (Van Huyssteen 1987:25).

Undoubtedly this is just avoiding the issue. If one accepts the value of models and metaphors in science, one should not forget that the 'is' in every metaphor or model in reality is not equal to an ontological 'is'. It remains 'is' in the sense of 'is like' (see Ricoeur 1975:98). Brown correctly observes with regard to metaphor that '. . . although it should be taken seriously, it should not be taken literally. So e.g. mathematical theories about reality are metaphorical. When the scientist now believes that (sic!) world really is mathematically organized—they have turned the metaphor into a myth' (as quoted in M.E. Botha (1984:55). The problem posed by the different positions which I have briefly introduced, is a problem which has been with us since the days of Plato and Aristotle. It is a mind-boggling problem especially for those who would like to use rational devices to make firm statements about the things which cannot be seen by human eyes. This is not the place to discuss the advantages and disadvantages of the different epistemological positions referred to above. For our purpose it should be clear that no constructivist or realist position can explain how we can get from a text to the reality outside the text other than by making use of 'is like' or 'as if'-arguments. That is one reason among others why an instrumentalist position is preferable to a critical realist position. Instrumentalists are reluctant to make ontological claims in this regard. Basic commitments to realities we cannot observe are faith commitments and therefore not commitments depicting reality in the realist sense of the word.

In the case of the unobservable, both in natural sciences and theology, we have to look for the best theories and hypotheses to explain problems. Not one epistemological position can guarantee that a particular text has cognitive reference. Neither can any epistemological position help the theologian to make claims about the transcendental in ontological terms.

By this time it should be clear that current epistemology cannot help us determine in an ontological sense the 'phenomena to which the language of Jesus pointed' or explain the 'ontological bearings' of the language of Jesus. The cognitive function of the metaphorical and apocalyptic utterances of Jesus is not a means of discovering the 'real persons and the things' that cannot be observed. What we have learnt is that Jesus used metaphoric and apocalyptic language functionally. He did things with words. He tried to resocialize his hearers by offering them a new symbolic universe. In this sense modern theories about language and how it is being used in the Bible help theologians in their attempt to speak meaningfully about the God in whom they believe. That includes the making of new metaphors and the use of metaphorical language about the unobservable.

CHAPTER TWO

BILINGUALISM AND THE GREEK OF THE
NEW TESTAMENT: SEMITIC INTERFERENCE
IN THE GOSPEL OF MARK

1. *Introduction*

It is an accepted fact that most of the writings in the New Testament originated in bilingual or multilingual communities, and that the native language of their authors was Aramaic, and not Greek. In spite of differences of opinion concerning the original version of some of these writings, and the specific nature of 'New Testament Greek', there is good reason to argue that they were written in Koine (κοινή) Greek. There is, furthermore, general agreement that there are signs of Semitic interference in many of these documents. My contention is that the problem of Semitic interference in New Testament Greek should be re-examined, and that special attention should be paid to the phenomenon of bilingualism and the making of New Testament documents.

In spite of the complexities in terminology (see Abudarham 1987b:2ff.), Semitic interference and bilingualism will be used in this essay to refer to the phenomena of deviation from the norms of Greek in the New Testament, and New Testament writers' familiarity with more than one language (see Weinreich 1963:1; also Adler 1977:15ff.). The term Semitic interference refers to the rearrangement of patterns of Greek which resulted from the introduction of Semitic elements into the phonetic, syntactic and semantic systems of Greek because of the contact between Aramaic, Hebrew and Greek-speaking Jews and Christians in the first century CE (see Weinreich 1963:1).

There is good reason to question some of the general presuppositions which prevail in New Testament scholarship, both with regard to the nature of 'New Testament Greek' and with regard to the making of New Testament documents. Since each of these problems can be treated on its own in a separate book, I will have to limit my discussion to aspects which are essential for my argument. In addition to a few observations concerning bilingualism and the use of Greek by Jews and Christians in the first century, I will also address the nature of New Testament Greek from the perspective of Semitic interference and then give a discussion of Semitic interference in the Gospel of Mark. I will argue that Mark's Gospel was written by a bilingual author whose native language was probably Aramaic and his second language Greek. Semitic interference can therefore be ascribed to Mark's use of Greek and not to translation into Greek or the use of Aramaic or other sources.

2. *Semitic Interference, Bilingualism and the Use of*
Greek by Jews and Early Christians

A variety of explanations have been offered for Semitic interference in New Testament Greek over the years. Martin (1987:1) mentions the following: a. the use of Semitic sources; b. translation of entire documents originally written in a Semitic language; c. thinking in Hebrew or Aramaic, either because one of these languages was the vernacular or the author was under the influence of the Greek Old Testament; d. the imitation of the language and style of the Greek translations of the Old Testament. Little attention has, however, been paid to the fact that most of the writings in the New Testament originated from communities which were bilingual or multilingual.

Vergote (1938: cols. 1366–1367), in his oft-quoted article, maintains that most peculiarities in New Testament Greek are Semitisms, resulting from the use of Greek by bilingual authors. The topic of bilingualism and the character of Palestinian Greek has also been dealt with in an article by Silva (1980; see also S. Brown 1989:133–134 and Mussies 1971), but it has not generally been taken seriously by New Testament scholars in general as a possible explanation for Semitic interference in New Testament Greek. There is good reason to do so, however.

Bilingualism is a very complex phenomenon which can be studied from different perspectives. It relates to many aspects of the use of two languages by individuals, as well as to the use of different languages by communities. That is why the phenomenon is studied by linguists, sociologists, psychologists, anthropologists and geographers. From the point of view of New Testament studies, the sociolinguistic and ecological or (geographical) perspectives are perhaps the most important. Let us consider a few aspects of bilingualism with respect to the use of Greek in Palestine in the first century. Since it is possible that Mark's Gospel originated in Galilee, it is necessary to look at bilingualism from the perspective of Greek as a second language in Palestine.

Silva (1980:207) draws attention to the fact that the native language of a bilingual is not affected in the same way as his or her second language. This was also true of Aramaic and Hebrew as the mother tongue of Jews and Christians in the first century CE. Loan words and Greek semantic effects do exist in Aramaic, as Schürer (1979:52ff.) and others have indicated. As far as syntax is concerned, however, there is undoubtedly no comparison between the amount of Semitic influence on Greek as a second language, and that of Greek on Aramaic or Hebrew as native languages in Palestine of the first century.

Bilingualism is furthermore influenced by sociological milieus (Silva 1980:207). The linguistic behaviour of the dominating group is different from that of the dominated group. This is of special importance with regard to the Jews both in Palestine and elsewhere who, under the influence of Hellenism, had to acquire a knowledge of Greek to participate in trade and commerce, and communicate with the inhabitants of Hellenistic towns who did not speak Aramaic, as well as with the rulers and their agents in Palestine and the diaspora. According to Josephus (*Ant.* 20:264) the Jews did not favour polyglots, but this does not mean that they did not learn Greek. He tells us:

> I have also laboured strenuously to partake of the realm of Greek prose and poetry, after having gained a knowledge of Greek grammar, although the habitual use of my native tongue has prevented my attaining precision in pronunciation (Loeb translation by L.H. Feldman).

We also know that Jerusalem was a centre for the learning of Greek. It was even possible that Paul had had his training in Greek during his youth in Jerusalem (see Mussies 1976:1054). It was nevertheless not the native language of the Jews. They were a marginal group in their own country and in the Diaspora with regard to the use of language, and the same also applies to the early Christians. The language of the dominating group had to be learned. How much Greek the Jews (and early Christians) knew, however, is another matter (see Sevenster 1968).

It is difficult to determine the exact level of bilingualism of Jews and Christians in the first century. While Paul might have been thoroughly bilingual, Peter probably would have been able to speak Greek, but not necessarily write it, if we take seriously the remark of Papias that John Mark was the ἑρμενευτὴς of Peter (see Mussies 1976:1056). Depending on language competence and the level of bilingualism, the use of two languages by different individuals is not similar. A person who was thoroughly bilingual might, for instance, have used Aramaic and Greek words as compound signs and not as two signs with the same signifieds (see Weinreich 1963:9). Since θάλασσα acquired the meaning of 'lake' (Sea of Galilee) in Palestine, a Jew such as Josephus might have regarded θάλασσα and ימא as a compound sign with the same signified, and not as two signs. This would not have been the case with somebody who only had a speaking knowledge of the language. Josephus and Paul were probably exceptions in this regard.

Bilingualism plays an important part in the socialisation and assimilation of people. It can be seen in the language behaviour of children (see Adler 1977:3), but also in that of adults who are members of bilingual societies. This aspect of bilingualism was very important with regard to the spread of Christianity.

It is likely that the native language of Jesus and his disciples was Aramaic, and that they also spoke Greek. Jesus probably spoke to the centurion (Mt. 8:5), to the Gerasenes and the people of the Decapolis (Mk. 3:8), the Syro-Phoenician woman (Mk. 7:26), and Pilate in Greek. This would also probably have been the case with Peter and Cornelius (Ac. 10), Paul's relative and the officer (Ac. 23) and others such as the Hellenists who probably were Greek-speaking Jews (see Sevenster 1968:147–148). By speaking to people in their own language it was possible for Jesus and others to communicate their views and associate people who did not speak Aramaic.

Although Greek remained their second language, it is probable that it was much more widespread among Jews and early Christians than 'the mere presence of some Greek schools and synagogues in Jerusalem might suggest' (Mussies 1976:1058). Schürer (1979:74) is probably wrong in asserting that 'it should not be proposed that the Greek language was itself current among the common people of Palestine'. Palestine was far more Hellenised than Schürer seems to think. It was a fragmentised country in the first century, with many Hellenised towns and cities where the Jews did not form the

majority and of necessity had to speak Greek. The 'Hellenistic' area
included:

> ... the entire coastal strip from Raphia to Ptolemais, plus the land of
> the Decapolis, including the towns of Gedara (the 'Assyrian Athens');
> Pella, Scythopolis, Gerasa ... and Philadelphia. Moreover, a number
> of Hellenistic towns were scattered over the remaining territory: Phasael,
> in Judea; Sepphoris and Tiberias, in Galilee; Caesarea-Phillipi and
> Betsaida-Julias, in Batanea; Hesbon and a second Julias in Perea
> (Mussies 1976:1058).

Jesus was raised in Nazareth, which was close to Sepphoris, one of
the major Greek-speaking cities of the period. His ministry was mainly
in this Hellenised area, from which one can gather that he and his
followers often had to communicate with people who did not speak
Aramaic.

No less a scholar than Gustaf Dalman (1965:56–57), the well-known
authority on the language situation in Palestine during the time of
Jesus, maintains that the primitive church in Jerusalem was bilingual
from the very start, and that the gospel sources could have been
written in Greek from the beginning. This presupposes a situation
where the man in the street could read and understand Greek.
Sevenster (1968:190) has convincingly indicated that a knowledge of
Greek was not restricted to the upper classes.

This point of view is corroborated by extant writings, including
inscriptions on stone and graffiti, numismatic inscriptions, papyri,
ostraca and parchments, books written in Hebrew or Aramaic and
then translated into Greek, or works originally written in Greek which
were probably written by bilingual Jews (see Mussies 1976:1042–1050).
This does not deny the fact that the native language of the majority of the Jews in Palestine in the first century was Aramaic (see
Fitzmyer 1970).

Since Christianity was originally a Jewish sect which had started
in Palestine, the use of Semiticised Greek by early Christians is
directly related to the use of Greek as a second language by Jews
in the first century, and to the dispersion of the Jews. It is also
related to the role of the synagogue in the spread of Christianity in
the first century. In most of the larger cities such as Antioch, Corinth,
Ephesus, and Rome (to mention but a few), where the Christian
message was initially spread, it was done among local Jews and
through the synagogues.

Bilingualism is a phenomenon which has to be taken into account

in any discussion of the use of Greek in the New Testament, because
it was written by authors whose mother tongue could have been
Aramaic or Hebrew. In the next section attention will be given to
the nature of New Testament Greek.

3. *The Nature and Characteristics of New Testament Greek*

The term 'New Testament Greek' is used in this essay to refer to
the Greek we find in the writings of the New Testament. The Greek
of the New Testament should not be seen as a dialect, nor as a special kind of Greek. As a matter of fact, the type of Greek that we
find in the New Testament is also the type of Greek that might be
found in other documents of the day. It can therefore be characterised as *Koine*, that is the common language which developed when
Greek became the *lingua franca*. Such a description is obviously too
vague and has to be expanded upon.

One of the main problems in describing the nature and characteristics of 'New Testament Greek' is the fact that it has been compared to the Greek of a variety of Greek texts from different periods
of time. Insights gained since Deissmann discovered agreements
between the Greek in New Testament documents and the Greek
in Egyptian papyri have taught us that it is necessary to compare
the Greek of the New Testament with contemporary, comparable
literature and not with other Greek texts of earlier or later periods (see Rydbeck 1967). If this is not done, unreliable evaluations
are made.

The history of research into the nature of New Testament Greek
is greatly burdened by prejudice, dogmatic beliefs and unattested
assumptions (see the surveys of Friedrich 1974 and Meijer 1976).
For some the New Testament is written in pure classical Greek,
while others believe that there was a Jewish Greek dialect and that
the authors of New Testament documents wrote their works in Jewish
Greek. Others, again, assert that the Greek of the New Testament
has a unique character and even that it was written in 'Holy Ghost'
Greek. The influence of the Septuagint on the Greek of the New
Testament remains an open question, and so does the influence of
Aramaic and Hebrew. Many of the discussions are blurred by the
mixing of theological and linguistic arguments. We already find this
in the remarks of Origen (*Cels.* 1, 62), according to whom some

higher authority behind the words impressed the authors with what they had to say. And Photius (*MPG* 10, 577–592) believed that God gave the authors the correct words, and that this changed fishermen and toll collectors into teachers who could be equated with philosophers. This obviously gave rise to the idea of a God-inspired language.

During the Renaissance and the Reformation there was renewed interest in the language of the New Testament. The 'Purists' believed that the Greek of the New Testament was pure classical Greek—despite the studies of the Humanists, who drew attention to Semitic interference. The Hebraists, on the other hand, believed that the Greek of the New Testament was enriched with Hebrew elements by the Holy Spirit (see Meijer 1976:6). To some extent the 'Purist' and the 'Hebraist' views still dominate scholars' thinking today.

In the eighteenth century J.G. Hamman tried to indicate that the New Testament was written in the Greek of the man in the street (see Friedrich 1974:27). It was, however, the insights of Deissmann that really triggered off an intensive interest in the problems of New Testament Greek in the nineteenth and twentieth centuries. Deissmann was of the opinion that the Greek of the New Testament should be compared to the non-literary sources of Egyptian papyri, ostraca and inscriptions. He furthermore believed that there were signs of Semitic interference in the Greek of the New Testament because the Greek which the Jews spoke was coloured by Semitic influences. He, however, rejected the idea that a special 'Bible Greek' or a 'Jewish Greek' dialect existed, and maintained that the Greek of the New Testament belonged to the Koine (see Deissmann 1965). In this approach he was followed by scholars such as A. Thumb and J.H. Moulton. Although the impact of Deissmann and those who held the same views decreased after their deaths, there are still scholars who defend the position that the Greek of the New Testament should be explained in the light of contemporary Greek texts, and not primarily in terms of the Semitic influence (see e.g. Rydbeck 1967 and Reiser 1984).

On the other hand there are those who maintain that the Greek of the New Testament should first and foremost be described in terms of its Semitic background and characteristics. In the seventeenth century Kasper Wyss in his *Dialectologia Sacra*, and Johann Vorst in his *Hebraismis Novi Testamenti Commentarius*, had drawn attention to Semitic features in the Greek of the New Testament. It is, however, the influence of the works of scholars such as J. Wellhausen, G. Dalman and M. Black which dominates research into Semitic interference in New Testament Greek today. Assumptions concerning the influence of the language of Jesus, the use of Aramaic sources, translations of sources or complete documents, the influence of the Septuagint and the existence of a special Jewish Greek dialect, all influence scholars in this regard.

In spite of differences of opinion, it is generally accepted that there is Semitic interference in the Greek of some of the writings of the New Testament—for example, in the teaching of Jesus.

It is accepted that the native language of Jesus was either Aramaic or Hebrew (see Barr 1970), and that his *logia* had to be translated into Greek for the sake of those who did not speak or understand Aramaic or Hebrew. In this manner Semitic elements, it is argued, were incorporated into the Jesus tradition.

It is, however, a mistake to view the *logia* of Jesus in terms of translation Greek similar to the Greek translations of the writings of the Old Testament. The *logia* of Jesus were translated into Greek and then transmitted orally in Greek. These Greek *logia* were included in writings which were written in Greek, and not in writings which had been translated from Semitic sources (see J. Barr 1969:127).

Another aspect of possible Semitic interference which needs to receive our attention here, is the so-called influence of the Septuagint on the Greek of the New Testament. Jellicoe (1969:199) asserts: 'He who would read the New Testament must know *Koine*; but he who would *understand* the New Testament must know the Septuagint'. When it comes to *influence*, however, one should be very careful not to oversimplify the matter.

In the first instance it is clear that there is no such thing as *the* Septuagint. The term refers to Greek translations of Old Testament writings which are anything but one translation by a single person. The translations of the different documents are quite diverse in character. Different techniques were applied, which resulted in translations that range from literal to free renderings. Interpretative comments are not absent and the quality is not consistent. A good example would be the Greek of Genesis, the Book of Ruth, and Jeremiah 25 and its following chapters.

Semitic interference in the Greek of the LXX is obvious and was caused by the translation of Hebrew and Aramaic into Greek. In other words, Semitic thoughts were translated into Greek. That explains the interference with regard to the semantics of words. The meaning of Greek words was in some cases extended, because they were used to convey Hebrew and Aramaic meanings (see Silva 1983:53–73). But also with respect to syntax there are clear indications of Semitic interference (see Tabachovitz 1956).

It is also important to remember that these translations were read in Greek and not against the Hebrew texts. They were Greek texts, to be understood in Greek and not in comparison with the originals (see also J. Barr 1968). Greek words with Hebrew meanings became part of the Greek lexicon of the users of the Septuagint and this also happened with regard to Semitic interference in Greek syntax.

The influence of the Septuagint on the New Testament should be seen in terms of *convention*, and not in terms of direct influence or in terms of imitation. Because the Greek translations were used frequently, features of expression also became part of Greek use by those who heard and read these translations. Greek with a Semitic influence became part of the language of these people. Unless there are direct signs of imitation, New Testament scholars should therefore think of the influence of the Septuagint on the New Testament in terms of convention.

There is no reason to doubt the importance of the Septuagint in Jewish or Christian religious circles. Quotations and allusions to the Septuagint in the New Testament witness to the fact that the authors of New Testament writings were acquainted with the Septuagint. And so do the similarities in semantics and syntax.

It should be underscored that the New Testament, including the Gospels, was written in Greek. Their authors produced Greek texts. They did not make translations. This clearly indicates the importance of the study of language use, and not of the history of the development of the language of a particular document. It also stresses the importance of convention in language use, and in particular the importance of bilingualism with regard to the Greek of the New Testament.

I do not accept the existence of a separtate Jewish Greek dialect (see Hill 1967 and especially Büchsel 1944). The *lingua franca* of the Persian Empire was Aramaic. When it became Greek through the victories of Alexander the Great, Jews and non-Jews had to use a new language. The remains of Aramaic elements in Greek are due to bilingualism and not to the existence of a separate dialect.

The New Testament documents were written in Koine which reflects Semitic interference due to bilingualism, the influence of the Septuagint on the ground of convention, and the influence of the transmission of the translated Jesus tradition. Let us now turn to Semitic interference in the Greek of the Gospel of Mark.

4. *Semitic Interference in the Gospel of Mark*

Until recently (see Reiser 1984:163) the use of Greek by the author of the Gospel of Mark was commonly described in negative terms such as 'volkstümlich, originell und ungekünsteld, drastisch und derb, stark aramaiserend' (Wellhausen as quoted by Reiser 1984:3), and regarded as translation Greek (Wellhausen and Lagrange, see Reiser 1984:3). C.H. Turner even asserted that: 'His grammar, if (as I conjecture with other scholars) he was the son of the οἰκοδεσπότης of Mark XIV 14, may reflect the rough but effective Greek of the inn and the stableyard . . .' (as quoted by Reiser 1984:163). More recently it has been said: 'On the one hand, it was felt that Mark's style is unpretentious, verging on the vernacular; on the other, that it is rich in Aramaisms' (Turner 1976:11).

This kind of evaluation is partly the result of the influence of well-known scholars on the history of research into the problem of style in the Gospel of Mark, and the role of presuppositions in Marcan research. This is not the place to give a complete survey of opinions on Semitic interference (see Maloney 1981:7–25), but rather the place to draw attention to presuppositions which play a role in this regard.

The history of research into the use of Greek by the author of the Gospel of Mark has been dominated by the two schools of thought mentioned above. Scholars such as Deissmann, Moulton and Thumb have argued that most of the New Testament was written in vernacular Greek. They have argued that New Testament Greek belonged to the Koine language of the period, and that wherever there was a sign of Semitic interference, it was due to the influence of the Septuagint and direct translation of Semitic sources (for a discussion of these views see Maloney 1981:7–11).

In these circles it was contended that Mark wrote his Gospel in Greek. The form and level of Greek in which he wrote, however, had to be explained. Different attempts were made to explain the language use ink of the first century. The argument was that the Greek evidence should first be examined before attempts were made to explain the Greek of Mark in the light of Aramaic (see Maloney 1981:13–23 and Reiser 1984:1–12).

Exponents of the 'Aramaic school', on the other hand, maintained that because of the alleged underlying Semitic syntax, Mark was based on Aramaic sources which were either written or oral, or that Mark initially wrote his Gospel in Aramaic and then translated it into Greek (see Reiser 1984:4 and Maloney 1981:13–25). It was to a certain extent the latter point of view which dominated research into the use of Greek by Mark.

The presuppositions which play a role in the history of research with regard to Semitic interference in Mark are clear. It is generally agreed that there are very few so-called Septuagintisms in Mark. Semitic interference in Mark can therefore only be explained in terms of the use of Aramaic sources or the translation of the whole Gospel, or parts of it, from Aramaic into Greek, on the ground of the author's Semitising Greek, or because he used Aramaic syntax and Greek vocabulary (see Turner 1963:4 for the latter). We will return to these. To develop our thesis it is necessary to give a short survey of what can be regarded as Semitic interference in the Gospel.

What are we talking about when we use the phrase 'Semitic interference' with reference to Mark? It will not be possible or necessary to give a complete list of possible Semitisms in the Gospel, or even to discuss them. To develop our argument we will, however, have to pay attention to a number of items that are relevant for our argument in this section.

I have said that Semitic interference is related to the phonetic, semantic and syntactic structure of the language used in the Gospel. For our purpose, focus will be on the semantic and syntactic systems of the Gospel of Mark.

As to the semantic system I will first give a few examples of loan words from Aramaic and then a few examples of words which point to semantic change in the Greek lexicon. Mark, in other words, used these words with Semitic meanings as part of his lexicon.

The following Aramaic names occur in Mark's Gospel (see Rüger 1984):

Βαραββᾶς (Mk. 15:7, 11, 15); Βαρθολομαῖος (Mk. 3:18); Βαρτιμαῖος (Mk. 10:46); Βεελζεβοὺλ (Mk. 3:22); Βηθσαϊδά (Mk. 6:45; 8:22); Βοανηργές (Mk. 3:17); Γεννησαρὲτ (Mk. 6:53); Γολγοθᾶ (Mk. 15:22); Θωμᾶς (Mk. 3:18); Καναναῖος (Mk. 3:18); Λαφαρναοὺμ (Mk. 1:21; 2:1; 9:33). In addition he also uses the following loan words from Aramaic: ἀββά (Mk. 14:36); γέεννα (Mk. 9:43); Ελωι ελωι λεμα σαβαχθανι (Mk. 15:34); Εφφθα (Mk. 7:34); Κορβᾶν (Mk. 7:11); πάσχα (Mk. 14:1, 12, 14, 16); ῥαββουνι (Mk. 10:51); σάββατα (Mk. 1:21; 2:2, 23, 24; 3:2, 4; 16:2) and ταλιθα κουμ(ι) (Mk. 5:41). What is remarkable is that our author translated into Greek most of the loan words and expressions, for the sake of his readers. The implication is that he knew the Aramaic words and their translated equivalents in Greek.

He also used Greek words with Aramaic or Hebrew meanings or, to put it more correctly, words in which semantic changes had taken place. The following examples will illustrate the point:

In Mark 3:20 ἄρτος is used for the meaning *food*, a meaning which is directly related to the Aramaic לחמא or לחם (same root in Hebrew). Wensinck maintains that ποιεῖ in the phrase ποιεῖ κλάδους μεγάλους in Mark 4:32 should be translated as 'produce' on the ground of Targum Onkelos Genesis 49:15 (see Black 1967:302). Black (1967:133) furthermore suggests that the meaning of ὄρος might correspond to that of טורא ('country') in Aramaic, and πλήρωμα ('patch') with a meaning of a Syriac word. Lastly, words such as ἄγγελος (see מלאך), γραμματεύς (see ספרא), δόξα (כבור), εὐαγγελιον (בשרא) and θάλασσα (ימא) are used in Mark with meanings which overlap with meanings for which Aramaic and Hebrew words are used. These examples illustrate Semitic interference with regard to semantics on the word level. Let us now turn to Semitic interference with regard to syntax.

It has often been argued that Mark's syntax is affected by Semitic interference, and the following aspects have been mentioned in this respect (see Turner 1976:11–25): word order, including the position of the genitive, co-ordinating particles, and the position of the verb in nominal as well as verbal sentences; parataxis; redundancy; pleonastic auxiliary; the abundance of the historic present; periphrastic tenses; the use of the article; pronouns; prepositions; the use of positive degree for the comparative and superlative and the use of the cardinal for the ordinal. It is remarkable that Semitic interference is not restricted to certain parts or particular kinds of material in Mark. It occurs in the narrative framework and elsewhere, which already suggests that it formed part of the language of the author.

One of the major problems is the difference of opinion between scholars concerning what should be regarded as Semitic interference and what not, and the presuppositions that play a role in this regard. Let us take a simple example.

Black (1967:55) argues that: 'Asyndeton is, on the whole, contrary

to the spirit of Greek language'. He ascribes the many sentences or
parts of sentences in Mark which are connected without conjunctions or other linking words to Semitic interference. Either Mark
wrote 'Jewish Greek' or 'he is translating Aramaic sources or employ-
ing such translations' (see Black 1967:60). According to him, the four
instances in Mark 13:6–9 are examples of translation Greek. The
text reads as follows:

13.6 πολλοὶ ἐλεύσονται ἐπὶ τῷ ὀνόματί μου λέγοντες ὅτι Ἐγώ εἰμι, καὶ
πολλοὺς πλανήσουσιν. 13.7 ὅταν δὲ ἀκούσητε πολέμους καὶ ἀκοὰς
πολέμων, μὴ θροεῖσθε· δεῖ γενέσθαι, ἀλλ᾽ οὔπω τὸ τέλος. 13.8 ἐγερθήσεται
γὰρ ἔθνος ἐπ᾽ ἔθνος καὶ βασιλεία ἐπὶ βασιλείαν, ἔσονται σεισμοὶ κατὰ
τόπους, ἔσονται λιμοί· ἀρχὴ ὠδίνων ταῦτα. 13.9 βλέπετε δὲ ὑμεῖς
ἑαυτούς· παραδώσουσιν ὑμᾶς εἰς συνέδρια καὶ εἰς συναγωγὰς δαρήσεσθε
καὶ ἐπὶ ἡγεμόνων καὶ βασιλέων σταθήσεσθε ἕνεκεν ἐμοῦ εἰς μαρτύριον
αὐτοῖς.

There is no doubt that there are many sentences and parts of sentences in Mark's Greek which are not linked by conjunctions (examples are listed in Maloney 1981:77), and Mark 13:6–9 is a good
example. Are the asyndeta in these sentences caused by Semitic interference? And can one really in the case of Mark 13:6–9 assert that
it is due to translation Greek? With regard to the particular instance,
and Black's remarks about it, Reiser (1984:165) refers his readers to
Herodotus Book 3:53, 3, the Grammar of Kühner-Gert, Menander,
and Greek novelists of the first century. He (see Reiser 1984:165–166)
concludes:

Die Verwendung des Asyndetons in der Erzählung beweist geradezu,
dass es sich beim Stil des Markusevangeliums um einen *literarischen* Stil
handelt, der sich von der lebendigen, gesprochenen Sprache durchaus
abhebt. . . .

The views of Black and Reiser are not only in opposition, but contradictory. One will obviously have to take more into account than
the fact that asyndeton occurs in both Semitic and Greek texts of
the period to argue a case for or against Semitic interference in
Mark 13. While Reiser argues his case on the fact that asyndeton
is not unusual in Greek, and that therefore there is no reason to
think of Semitic interference in Mark 13, Black assumes both the
use of sources and the possibility of translation Greek. The many
hypotheses about the origin and growth of Mark 13 are well known,
and Black might appeal to such arguments. He moreover presupposes the existence of 'Jewish Greek', something which is very doubtful.

He also disregards the fact that Mark *produced* a Greek text. If one accepts Semitic interference in this regard, one will have to look for the cause in the use of language by Mark. Unless Mark had a copy of a text in which the sentences mentioned were joined asyndetically and he slavishly followed his *Vorlage*, there is no ground for Black's assertions.

Maloney's study is a thorough investigation of the syntax of Mark from the perspective of possible Semitic interference. He has convincingly argued that there are different aspects of Mark's use of Greek which seems to reflect Semitic interference. He gives a very useful summary of his results at the end of his book, in the form of a list of the syntactical devices he investigated and his conclusions (see Maloney 1981:246–252). He explains his conclusions in terms of the causes of Semitic interference. In each case he says whether a syntactical feature is a Grecism or whether frequency is due to some sort of Semitic interference such as the Greek Old Testament, Hebraism, Aramaism or Semitism. How the interferences came about is not explained in Maloney's book, and this is exactly the problem to be explained. How was Mark influenced in his use of Greek?

Reiser, on the other hand, attempted to show that, of the examples given by scholars who explain the history of Mark's language from the standpoint of Semitic interference, most can also be explained in terms of the use of these features in Greek sources of the period. He made a thorough investigation of the position of the subject and predicate, parataxis with καί, and asyndeta in Mark, and has convincingly shown that for each of these features there are parallels in contemporary Greek literature. He does not deny Semitic interference in the Gospel of Mark (see Reiser 1984:11), but maintains:

> Der Eindruck des Semitischen an Syntax und Stil jedoch scheint vor allem bei jenen Forschern zu überwiegen, die sich mehr mit semitischen als mit griechischen Texten befasst haben und denen darum vieles semitisch vorkommt, was nicht semitisch zu sein braucht, und so manches als ungebräuchliches Griechisch, was dort zu allen Zeiten geläufig war.

There is general agreement concerning Semitic interference in the Greek of Mark, but it is important to note that there are great differences of opinion as to the extent and the cause of this interference.

I am of the opinion that there will not be any progress in the debate about possible Semitic interference in Mark's language if we continue the discussion in terms of either the Semitic or the Greek background of such features in semantics and syntax. What should be taken seriously is the fact that scholars agree that there are features of Mark's Greek which reflect Semitic interference. In addition, we should start thinking in terms of the making of Mark's Gospel and not in terms of the growth of the material. Whoever the producer of the text might have been, he did not simply collect his material. He was neither a passive transmitter of tradition nor a conservative redactor of transmitted material (see Vorster 1980b). These concepts reveal the history of a century of scholarship based on a variety of presuppositions regarding the growth of material. They do not reflect any of the aspects involved in the making of a text or the positive use of language.

Our author produced a text whose language reflects Semitic interference, and which we have to take seriously as something to be explained historically. In other words, both the making of the text and the author's use of language (as historical phenomena) have to be explained historically.

Two recent attempts at explaining the making of Mark are worth mentioning, although I do not necessarily subscribe to either. According to Mack (1988:322–323), Mark's Gospel was:

> . . . not a pious transmission of revered tradition. It was composed at a desk in a scholar's study lined with texts and open to discourse with other intellectuals. In Mark's study were chains of miracle stories, collections of pronouncement stories. . . .

Obviously, not many scholars trained in traditional historical criticism would agree to this. The point is, however, that Mack has taken the realities of text production in the first century seriously. Whether one agrees with the outcome of his reflection is not the point. The point is that Mack forces one to reflect on how the Gospel of Mark was *made*, not how it *evolved* from tradition.

Botha, on the other hand, proposes that Mark was a producer of oral texts and that his Gospel reflects the end process of oral production. Mark dictated his text to somebody who wrote down his words (see P.J.J. Botha 1989:76–77). Again, Mark is taken seriously as the producer of a text and not as a conduit through which the stream of tradition flowed, or the (passive) exponent of a community out of which his text arose (see also Vorster 1980b).

Both these proposals take seriously tradition and transmission of tradition. One need not accept the precise way in which these two authors worked out their positions. However, one has to take seriously the fact that Mark made a text. My own position is that Mark made use of existing material which he not only arranged in the form of a story about Jesus, but also wrote down in his own words and in his own Greek.

Whether the Gospel of Mark was written in Rome (see Hengel 1984) or in Galilee (see Marxsen 1964:128), there is reason to assume that our author was *bilingual*. Jews in both places (see our discussion above and Lampe 1987) were bilingual (and in both places their Greek was probably influenced by their Semitic background) and so were the early Jewish Christians. We cannot say with certainty who our author was, but the fact that he was able to explain Aramaic expressions and words, and that there are signs of Semitic interference in his use of Greek, make it probable that he was a bilingual Jew who wrote to Greek-speaking readers.

Semitic interference in the Gospel of Mark was not caused by translation of original Aramaic documents (whether his Gospel or assumed sources which our author might have used), by translation Greek or the influence of the Septuagint, or the fact that he used 'Jewish Greek'. It was caused by the fact that our author was bilingual, and by the fact that his second language was Greek. Both the fact that Greek was the second language of many early Christians, including our author, and the nature of 'New Testament Greek' make it necessary that we study the Greek of a document such as the Gospel of Mark from the perspective of bilingualism.

CHAPTER THREE

IN WHAT SENSE IS THE LOUW/NIDA
DICTIONARY AUTHORITATIVE?

1. *Introduction*

The *Greek-English lexicon of the New Testament based on semantic domains*,
edited by J.P. Louw & E.A. Nida, and hereafter referred to as *L&N*,
has received a remarkably positive reception by the scholarly world
until now. According to Reese (1988:150): '[T]he publication of this
attractively presented lexicon will force the scholarly guild to pay
attention to the linguistic methodology underlying this revolutionary
achievement'. In a similarly positive review, Silva (1989:165) maintains: '[T]his work has to be regarded as a prodigious step forward
in the field of lexicography generally, and in the study of NT vocabulary specifically' (see also Boers 1989; J. Botha 1989; Elliott 1988;
Lategan 1988; Snyman 1988). I am also of the opinion that it is a
major achievement in lexicographical studies of the vocabulary of
the Greek New Testament. The dictionary offers a new approach
to lexical semantics in this field, and it is in many ways totally
different from existing dictionaries on the New Testament. This gives
rise to the question of how authoritative this lexicon is. I the introduction to *L&N* the compilers assert that:

> The principal reason for a new type of Greek New Testament lexi-
> con is the inadequacy of most existing dictionaries, which for the most
> part are limited in indicating meanings, since they depend principally
> on a series of glosses (Louw & Nida 1988:viii).

Rather than asking whether these inadequacies have been overcome in this new dictionary, I decided to address the problem of
the authority of *L&N* (see C.L. Barnhart 1980). By this I mean
whether the scholarly world can rely on this dictionary as an 'authority' for the lexical meanings of the words used in the Greek New
Testament. 'Authority' is used here in the sense of 'the power or
right to control, judge or prohibit the actions of others' (Collins 1986
s.v.). It is apparent that there are aspects on which this dictionary

cannot be regarded as authoritative since, it was not designed to give information on such aspects. It is, for example, not authoritative on etymology, morphology, pronunciation, syntax, the lexical meaning of each occurrence of a particular word in the New Testament, and the meaning of the words discussed in their usage outside the New Testament, to mention but a few things. *L&N* is a semantic dictionary dealing with the lexical meanings of the Greek words in the New Testament. It can therefore only be authoritative with regard to the meaning of words in the New Testament. The question of authority will therefore be addressed in this respect.

It should be kept in mind that *L&N* was developed primarily for use by translators. This explains the many annotations relating to translation included in the dictionary. This does not, however, imply that the dictionary cannot be an authority or a help for other users such as students, exegetes, theologians and all other persons interested in the meaning of New Testament words. On the contrary. The dictionary gives a comprehensive treatment of approximately 25,000 meanings of some 5,000 words which are used in the New Testament. I shall limit my discussion of the question of the authority of *L&N* to lexical semantics only.

According to Louw (1979:109): 'The purpose of the Wordbook is to provide accurate and practical guidance in determining satisfactory equivalences for the Greek NT vocabulary'. This means that translators and exegetes are provided with 'clear descriptions of areas of meaning of single words, set phrases and idioms', and that indications are given of 'how equivalences of meaning may be satisfactorily expressed in other languages' (Louw 1979:109). How successful is *L&N* in this regard? This question will be approached from different perspectives. Let us first deal with the arrangement of meaning in the dictionary.

2. *Arrangement of Meaning*

The main difference between *L&N* and other bilingual dictionaries on the New Testament is that in *L&N* the focus is on the related meanings of different words, and not on the different meanings for which a particular word is used in the New Testament. That is why the many meanings for which Greek words are used in the New Testament are organised into ninety-three semantic areas or domains.

This is perhaps the most innovative aspect of the dictionary since it is the first time in history that an attempt has been made to arrange the different meanings of the complete New Testament vocabulary into semantic domains.

The idea of the arrangement of meaning into semantic domains is nothing novel (see Geeraerts 1986:67–148). What is new is the arrangement of the different meanings of Greek New Testament terms into semantic fields. The question we have to ask is what this arrangement is based on, and what makes the arrangement of *L&N* authoritative.

The compilers of the dictionary assert that the semantic domains of *L&N* reflect the classification of words into semantic areas on the ground of three basic kinds of semantic components, namely shared or common components, distinctive or diagnostic components, and supplementary components (see Louw 1979:109). According to their view (see Louw 1979:108f.; also Louw & Nida 1988:ix) these domains do not follow a system of classification based on, for example, logico-philosophical categories as in the case of Roget or the classification proposed by Friedrich (1973). The assumption is that *L&N's* classification reflects the semantic structure of the Greek of the New Testament. Louw (1979:109) even claims that their classification is based on an 'emic' approach, 'that is to say, an assignment of meanings as they would have been classified by native speakers of Koine Greek'. In accordance with the view of the ancients who regarded 'fire' as one of the four basic elements, πῦρ, for example, is classified as a substance and not as a process, it is argued (see also Louw & Nida 1988:xiv).

There are a few basic insights, and perhaps even problems, which have to be dealt with before we continue our discussion of the authority of the dictionary in this regard. First of all it is necessary to decide what the compilers of the dictionary did when the classification of the different meanings of the Greek New Testament vocabulary was made. Did they discover, analyse or find the semantic domains inherent in the vocabulary, or did they create them?

It is well known that the terms 'emic' and 'etic' were first used by anthropologists in the description of behaviour (see Pike 1966). These terms represent two standpoints 'which lead to results which shade into one another' (Pike 1966:152). While the etic (coined from phonetic) standpoint studies behaviour and language from outside a system, the emic (from phonemic) standpoint studies the system from inside. There is a vast difference between the two approaches, especially with regard to the Greek of the New Testament, although there also is no reason for a dichotomy between the two approaches. The one is dependent upon the other.

Pike (1966:1530) gives a very useful survey of the most important characteristics of the two standpoints. It becomes clear that, if we apply these characteristics to the study of the language of the New Testament, one can hardly speak of studying the Greek vocabulary solely from an emic point of view. While the emic structure of a system, for example, has to be discovered, the etic structure is created, Pike (1966:153) argues. With regard to New Testament Greek one will have to assume two things, if one holds the view that it is analysed emically. The first assumption is that there is an inherent system in the language, and the second is that it is possible to discover it. Both these views are problematic. Let us deal with the latter first.

We study the Greek of the New Testament, which is part of Hellenistic Greek of that era, mainly from an etic point of view. Due to the lack of native speakers and the lack of exact information on the spoken language of the writers of the New Testament documents, there is no reason for any scholar to claim that the language of these documents is studied or described from inside, that is from the standpoint of a native speaker of that language (see also Ossege 1975:79). The problem is that we know so little about the 'language of the New Testament'. It is only for the sake of convenience that we speak of 'New Testament Greek'. The documents were written by different authors, in different parts of the Near East and Asia, at different times and in different circumstances. Some of the documents were written by bilingual authors whose second language was Greek, others by authors who had a good command of the language. In what sense can one then speak of the semantic structure of *the* Greek of the New Testament? These factors contribute to the difficulties involved in having an emic view of the 'language' of the New Testament. It is more than difficult to discover the cultural key—that is, the knowledge of the emic system—of the Greek of the New Testament. What we actually do is to construe the cultural key by studying the language from outside. This, in my opinion, also applies both to the classification of the semantic structure of the New Testament vocabulary into semantic domains by Louw and Nida, and their definition of lexical meanings of this vocabulary. The semantic domains were created rather than discovered, and so was the definition of meanings with the help of componential analysis. Let us elaborate.

The compilers of *L&N* correctly reject the structure proposed by Friedrich and have convincingly drawn attention to problems involved in the structuring of the lexical meanings of the New Testament vocabulary in existing dictionaries (see Louw 1985b:53ff.). But what about their own structure? Are their domains built on that inherent in the semantic structure of the New Testament vocabulary, as they presume?

The domains of *L&N* obviously reflect the theory on which the dictionary is based. In the first place they reflect the idea that words can be divided into four main categories namely—*events, objects, abstracts and discourse referentials*. Furthermore, they reflect the idea that the meaning of words can be determined by an analysis of their components, and that this excludes the use of encyclopaedic knowledge, to mention only two further aspects. There are more. This has resulted in a very impressive classification of the different meanings of related words into ninety-three main domains of meaning. One should, however, not forget that the three mentioned principles of classification form the basis of this classification. In fact, they explain what the compilers discovered and how they succeeded in creating their classification. Whether these principles comply with the way in which first-century Greek-speaking Christians used lexical meanings is another matter.

Some of the domains may certainly overlap with the way native speakers may have understood the relation between related meanings. This is particularly true with regard to semantic domains which are easy to recognise—such as plants, animals, foods, body and parts of the body and kinship terms. There are, however, numerous fields which are not so clear. A good example is domain 25, 'Attitudes and Emotions', where we find ἀγαπάω and ἀγάπη grouped together with words such as φιλέω, φιλία, φιλαδελφία, φιλάδελφος, ἄστοργος, ζηλόω, στενοχωρέομαι ἐν τοῖς σπλάγχνοις, συμπαθέω, κτλ. What is remarkable, is that we do not find μισέω here. We find μισέω under the subdomain 'Hate, Hateful' with words such as κακίας, πικρία[b], πικραίνομαι, ἀστυργέω, θεοστυγής, κτλ. Subdomain 88, of which these words form part, concerns 'Moral and Ethical Qualities and Related Behavior'. This is a matter of interpretation. If 'hate' belongs to this domain, does 'love' not also belong here, and why are πλούσιος and related words not included under domain 88 (see Malina 1987)? How would native speakers have understood these terms? Another example might help us a little further.

Μμακάριος is also listed under domain 25 with words such as ἱλαρότης, εὐφροσύνη, χαρά^a, συγχαίρω, συνήδομαι, κτλ in subdomain 25.K: 'Happy, Glad, Joyful'. There are, however, interpreters who argue that the 'beatitudes' should be read as apocalyptic blessings (see Guelich 1976). These might argue that the meaning of μακάριος would not be 'pertaining to being happy, with the implication of enjoying favorable circumstances', but that the word should be placed under domain 53, 'Religious Activities'—that is, 'pertaining to being blessed by God'. Such examples can be multiplied. One soon realises that semantic domains can easily be structured in different ways depending on what one sees as the distinguishing component of meaning (see also Geeraerts 1986:1 12ff.). A good example would be ἐσθίω. According to *L&N* the word means 'to consume food, usually solids, but also liquids'. The last part of the definition is included to accommodate the use of τίς ποιμαίνει πίμην καὶ ἐκ τοῦ γάλακτος τῆς ποίμης οὐκ ἐσθίει; in I Corinthians 9:7. To my mind the use of the preposition ἐκ with the verb has to be taken seriously. I think that ἐσθίω means 'to consume food' and that it is used in the New Testament for that meaning only, also in 1 Corinthians 9:7. It is furthermore used as a close synonym of τρώγω and is not used in the sense of 'eating liquids'. If I had to structure the subdomain, I would have placed ἐσθίω first and then τρώγω and so on, in this order. This is just to show that the structuring of the domains is determined by one's interpretation of the lexical meaning of words. Both the structure and the definition of meanings are ascribed, obviously normally on good grounds, not discovered. Let us go a little further.

[W]ords are rooted in social systems; they realize meanings from social systems (Malina 1987:358). To classify the meaning of Greek New Testament words into semantic domains presupposes the ability to reconstruct original contexts of communication in the first-century Mediterranean world. This is an almost impossible task. The most we can do is to construct possible cross-cultural contexts of understanding.

The idea that there is an inherent semantic structure in language, which has to be discovered and described, is equally problematic. It is based on structural semantics, which was in vogue from 1930–1975.

One of the main problems is that too little distinction is made between knowledge of language and knowledge of the world. Structural semantics presupposes that language has its own semantic structure—which has nothing to do with encyclopaedic knowledge. In the words of Louw (1985a:80): 'It is ... important that we should add strictly semantic dictionaries to our list of different types of dictionaries'. This view has been rejected as illusionary since it is argued that the difference between encyclopaedic and 'pure' semantic knowledge does not exist (see Geeracrts 1986:187).

From the perspective of cognitive semantics, 'universals', such as *objects, events, and abstracts*, are not regarded as common structures or elements of language. They are regarded as common strategies to classify experience. Language is furthermore seen as part and parcel of cultural contexts (see Geeraerts 1986:1980. 'Semantic structures are taken to be nothing other than conceptualizations shaped for symbolic purposes according to the dictates of linguistic convention' (Langacker as quoted by Geeraerts 1986:211).

The point I wish to make is that the compilers of *L&N* are responsible, on both emic and etic considerations, for their classification of related meanings into domains and subdomains. They did not discover these categories in the semantic structure of the Greek New Testament vocabulary. They created these domains in the light of their analysis of the related meanings of words. Once one realises this, the dictionary can be used in an interactive fashion. If one knows that the domains of *LAN* are possible ways of dealing with related meanings in the New Testament, the user can start using the material critically. This is exactly what makes *L&N* authoritative. It is not because the last word has been said about the relation between related meanings of different words in the New Testament that this lexicon is an authority that has to be followed. It is because the dictionary enables the user to see a particular word within the context of other words which are possibly related that it is to be regarded as an authority. In the words of Louw and Nida (1988:x):

> The primary value of a lexicon based upon semantic domains is that it forces the reader to recognize some of the subtle distinctions which exist between lexical items whose meanings are closely related and which in certain contexts overlap.

3. *Definition of Meaning*

A second factor which makes *L&N* authoritative is the definition of the meaning of individual words. In this respect, the dictionary is totally different from all existing bilingual dictionaries on the vocabulary of the New Testament.

The description of meaning by way of definition instead of in glosses and translational equivalents makes this dictionary unique. The definitions are the result of the analysis of the components of the lexical meaning of each individual word. In most cases the definitions reflect the diagnostic components of the particular meaning. In this manner the different meanings are identified and made more precise. The advantage of definitions of meaning over translational equivalents is obvious. While translational equivalents are approximate presentations of the lexical meaning of a word in the source language, definitions are supposed to be more precise.

Componential analysis is not an unknown method of analysing the lexical meanings of words. The advantage of defining meaning in this way is that the focus is on those components that distinguish the meaning of particular words from one another. It also helps to see which components are shared by words with related meanings and which are supplementary. Ideally, this is one of the best ways of dealing with meaning. There are, however, also disadvantages in this approach to the analysis of meaning.

As we have seen above, with regard to domains, it appears an illusion that semantic fields can be clearly marked in accordance with an inherent semantic structure. Since semantic domains are fuzzy, and since the boundaries of lexical meanings are also fuzzy, one can never say with certainty that a particular feature is *the* diagnostic component of the lexical meaning of a particular word (see also Geeraerts 1986:1 12ff.). Meanings overlap and are dependent on subtle distinctions and on connotative and associative elements, and can therefore never be analysed in a mechanical or machine-like manner. That, perhaps more than anything else, explains why some of the definitions of *L&N* are better than others, and why some are totally inadequate. A few examples may illustrate the point.

I would regard the definition of the meaning of θυμιάω as 'to burn aromatic substances as an offering to God' (53.25), for example, of τύφομαι as 'the process of burning slowly, with accompanying smoke and relatively little glow' (14.64), of as 'a sudden and severe movement of the earth' (14.87), and all the meanings defined in 15 as adequate and good definitions of the lexical meaning of the particular words. Others, however, are unconvincing and inadequate for different reasons. The definition of βαπτιστής (53.42) as 'one who baptizes' does not explain the meaning of the word. What is the difference between the lexical meaning of the idioms στρατιὰ οὐράνιος (12:30) and στρατιὰ τοῦ ὑρανοῦ (12:45)? I find the definitions 'a large group or throng of angels' (12:30) and 'the stars of heaven as symbols of various supernatural powers' (12:45) unconvincing. What does it mean to be 'free' as in the case of ἐλευθερία ('the state of being free') and ἐλεύθερος ('pertaining to being free')? The vagueness of these definitions becomes a problem when one compares them with ἐλευθερία (87.84), 'pertaining to a person who is not a slave, either one who has never been a slave or one who was a slave formerly but is no longer'.

The fact that definitions of meaning are omitted in some cases also causes problems. The meaning of ἐκκεντέω (19:14) is defined as 'to pierce with a pointed instrument', while the meaning of νύσσω is not defined. Both are then translated by 'to pierce'. In the case of the latter there is an annotation—reading: 'normally not as serious a wound as is implied by ἐκκεντέω'. This example also illustrates the problem of defining the meaning of words from the outside. Although the compilers hold the view that there is no such thing as words having completely the same meaning (Louw & Nida 1988:xv), they are unable to distinguish the subtle differences between these words that are used by the same author in close connection (see, however, 19.18 and 19.19). The entries under 53.4–7 also illustrate that it is almost impossible to define close synonyms in the New Testament with the help of componential analysis. We just do not have the competence to distinguish the subtle differences in the meanings of these words.

The compilers are moreover, not always consistent in their definitions of lexical meaning. A good example is the definition of words referring to specific festivals (see 5 1.5–12). In some cases even the date of the festival is given, while in others it is not. The same applies to words for coins in 6.76–82. In most cases it is said whether the coins were Roman or Greek. Only in the case of λεπτόν, and στατήρ is this not done. Are these features not diagnostic for outsiders as well in these two cases?

Some definitions display the convictions and beliefs of the compilers

more than others. One such case is the entry on θεός (12.1) which
certainly contains much more than semantic information, especially
when it comes to matters such as the patropassion heresy! Is the
definition 'a title with Messianic implications used by Jesus concerning
himself', a definition of the diagnostic components of the words υἱὸς
τοῦ ἀνθρώπου? Why is it regarded as a title? New Testament scholars do not agree about this. Why Messianic? The same applies to
the annotation(?) in brackets after πνεῦμα[a] (12.18), which reads: 'a
title for the third person of the Trinity. . . .' Does this annotation
define the meaning of the word? And if so, is it from an emic point
of view?

The definitions of the meanings of ἀληθής, 'pertaining to being
in accordance with historical fact', and of ἀλήθεια, 'the content of
that which is true and thus in accordance with what actually happened', reflect a positivist perception of truth. It is doubtful whether
these definitions reflect the lexical meanings of the words in the New
Testament.

There are other definitions which are also debatable, but the above
examples will suffice. In spite of the problems I have discussed with
regard to the definition of meaning in some entries, one should not
get the impression that *L&N* is not generally speaking authoritative
in this respect. I would like to underscore the fact that the description of meaning by way of definitions is far more appropriate than
the giving of translational equivalents. A clear distinction is furthermore made between *meaning* and *reference* by the compilers of *L&N*
(Louw and Nida 1988:xvii). In this respect, too, the lexicon is authoritative. There is a tremendous difference between what a word means
and what it refers to, something of which scholars are not always
aware. *L&N* is very helpful in this regard. In some cases, however,
it is not clear whether certain definitions in *L&N* are given in terms
of meaning or reference (see 11.59–64, also 11.66 and 53.52). Let
us consider a few examples.

It is possible that ὁ ὄφις ὁ ἀρχαῖος in Revelation 12:9 and 20:2
has the meaning 'devil'. The term clearly refers to the 'devil', and
it is probable that ὄφις could have acquired this meaning in Jewish
Christian circles. Just as ὄφις[b], 'evil person' is a figurative extension,
the meaning 'devil' would also be a figurative extension. References
become meanings of words through convention. Another, perhaps
even clearer, case would be ὀφθαλμὸς πονηρός[a,b]. Both meanings are
regarded as idioms in *L&N*. They have been defined as 'a feeling

of jealousy and resentment because of what someone else has or does' (88.165), and 'to be stingy'. Nowhere does one, however, find a reference to the belief in an Evil Eye which was common at the time of the New Testament in the Mediterranean world, as J.H. Elliott (1988) has convincingly shown.

The inclusion of οὐρανός^c (12.16) under 'Supernatural Beings' is furthermore understandable, but nevertheless problematic. Instead of giving a definition of the meaning of the word, an annotation explains the term. It reads 'a reference to God based on the Jewish tendency to avoid using the name or direct term for God'. If οὐρανός is used, like שמים, as a replacement for the name of God, one would first of all expect the term under 'Names of Persons and Places' (93).

Since there are many annotations included in *L&N* for the sake of the translator, it would have been of help had there been more remarks about reference in cases where it is possible to determine what words refer to.

4. *The Layout*

A final factor which makes this dictionary authoritative is its layout, since it compels the user to consider thoroughly whether a particular meaning is applicable. It therefore has an educational function.

Users of lexica often tend to think that the purpose of bilingual lexica is to provide the user with the meaning of a word in a particular context. It is often not realised that a lexicon is only an aid for the *user* to determine the meaning of a particular word in a particular context. It is the user, not the lexicon, or the compilers of the lexicon, who has to determine the meaning of a word in use. The way in which *L&N* presents information on the lexical meaning of New Testament words forces the user to make use of the information in a creative way.

Although *L&N* gives a complete survey of all the meanings for which the different words in the New Testament are used, it is not complete with regard to each case where a particular meaning is applicable. This simply means that the user has to make full use of the information provided in the dictionary. If a particular case is not mentioned in the reference index, the user has to consult the other indices. Having decided that a particular word mentioned under a Greek entry might be applicable, both the definition of that

meaning and the definition of other related meanings in its immediate area have to be consulted. This is the only way to be relatively sure that a chosen meaning is applicable in a particular context.

Instead of going through the list of different meanings of a particular Greek word, as they normally occur in an alphabetically
arranged dictionary, the user is introduced the semantic area of
related meanings of different words. This has the advantage that, in
addition to the different meanings of the same word, the user also
sees the related meanings of different terms in the same semantic
domain. Since meaning is also mostly defined and not presented in
the form of glosses or translational equivalents, the user has to divide
actively, with the help of semantic information provided by the dictionary, whether a particular choice is applicable.

5. *Conclusion*

I have discussed four factors which make *L&N* an authority on lexical meanings of the New Testament vocabulary. There are others.
I am thinking of the importance of figurative extensions of meaning, the treatment of meanings of word groups and especially of
idioms. The fact that idioms are listed and treated makes *L&N*
unique. Space does not allow me to go into these factors further.
Enough has been said to indicate that there are good reasons for
this dictionary to be regarded as authoritative in different aspects
and on different grounds. The publication is a milestone in the history of New Testament lexicography.

SECTION B

NEW TESTAMENT INTERPRETATION

Section B.1

Historical Perspectives

CHAPTER FOUR

SO MANY MEN, SO MANY MINDS:
READING THE NEW TESTAMENT IN A
POSTMODERN SITUATION

My reaction to the activities and results of the seminar of the *Societas Novi Testamenti Studiorum (SNTS)* on *The Role of the Reader in the Interpretation of the New Testament* will be given from two perspectives. I shall first pay attention to the frame of reference from which the seminar was conceptualised, and secondly I shall deal with the challenges of post-structural and postmodern views on literature for the reading of the New Testament. My reaction should be read as a reaction from inside and not outside the group. I feel myself responsible for the planning, flow, activities and the results of the group. I have learnt a lot from our discussions and also have a great appreciation for the input of the organisers and the contribution of each member.

1. *The Fetters of the Text*

In one of the early communications about the seminar, it was said that the purpose of the seminar was 'to investigate and explicate the role which is played by the real reader in the reading and interpretation of New Testament texts'. Although the emphasis was put on the reader of New Testament texts, and on reception theory, it was clear from the very start that the investigation would be done within the limits of the then current text theory of New Testament scholars. There was a clear shift in interest, as we have often said, and reminded ourselves, in literary criticism and therefore also in New Testament criticism from the author to the text, and then to the reader and the act of reading. What remained unchanged wittingly or unwittingly, was the concept 'text'. This was based on the idea that texts, and in particular New Testament texts, have meaning which has to be decoded by readers. We planned our programme in view of structural aspects, and textual, historical and sociological constraints, and studied the reader from the perspective of conditions inside and outside texts of the New Testament which shape the reader and the reading process. The meeting of 1988 offered the opportunity to take cognisance of the fact that the history and practice of the interpretation of New Testament texts such as Romans 13 teach us that readers ascribe meaning to texts irrespective of any constraints inside or outside the text. It also opened the possibility of facing the challenges of the implications of a text theory which is not based on structural insights only. Because of the parameters which were set by our planning, however, it was impossible to move beyond the limits of a structural, historical approach to the problem under investigation.

In her reaction to the forthcoming volume of *Semeia* in which a number of essays resulting from the *SNTS* seminar on the role of the reader will be published, Temma Berg correctly observes that most of the essays are written from a structuralist perspective. Her observation is to the point and discloses one of the fundamental problems of the seminar. While we are facing the challenges of postmodern thought, most New Testament scholars have difficulty, and are frequently unwilling to move beyond the 'certainties' and 'stability' which historical criticism and structural approaches pretend to offer. It is necessary to elaborate on this.

There is no doubt that the group took cognisance of developments in *Reception Theory* and the implications thereof for the interpretation of New Testament texts. Through the study of literature concerning the act of reading and 'the' reader, including thorough studies by members of the group on the many different instances who/which are included under the term 'reader' (see Fowler 1985), a common understanding of many of the aspects which were involved was developed. On the other hand, there were also matters concerning reading and readers where no agreement was reached. One of these was the many different ways in which a term such as 'implied reader' was used, and the almost consistent refusal to accept the fact that the term is a literary device. There was also no agreement concerning the possibility and implications of 'reconstructing' the original contexts of communication. Probably this was mainly due to underlying views on text theory and interpretation, as well as historical construction. It must be stressed that our whole undertaking was done within the framework of historical (that is historico-critical) and structural approaches.

Keeping in mind the danger of generalising too much, I think it would be fair to say that most of the participants of the group see their task as interpreting ancient religious texts for modern users of these texts. It is assumed that New Testament texts have meaning and that the interpreters (readers) have to discover and decode the meaning and sense thereof. Although opinions might differ in detail, I sensed the feeling that there was general agreement about the 'object' which is to be interpreted. This can be put in the words of one of the chairpersons of the group in a recent discussion about the nature of the biblical text in another context. Lategan (1988:69) maintains: 'The three basic features of the text are its historical, structural and theological or contextual aspects'. According to him the biblical text is historical because it is a historical phenomenon and also part of human history. Structurally the text consists of a network of relations on the linguistic, literary and theological level. It furthermore speaks about God and his relationship with humans, and is used, according to Lategan, for explicit theological purposes, and is read in a particular interpretative community, that is a community of believers. These remarks which are representative of the views presented in the seminar group, are based on a particular perception of *what a text is*, and implies a very limited perspective of the act of reading and readers in general. Let us first turn to the phenomenon 'text'.

Before the advent of deconstruction and different post-structural modes of reading, texts came to be regarded as structures with centres and edges, signs in the process of communication. Meaning was regarded as *present* in the text, and texts were regarded as presentations of reality, or as windows or mirrors of reality. The very nature of texts, their ability to present aspects of reality, their structure as networks of linguistic, literary and other codes, implied that they had to be read with the view of discovering the message they convey, their meaning and sense. The relationship between the signifiers, the signifieds and the reading subject was one of discovering and assigning meaning to words and images, relating parts to wholes in order to make the text comprehensible. The task of the reader (interpreter) was to integrate the elements of the text into a whole. This was also the view of text which has dominated the *SNTS* seminar group on the role of the reader during the past few years. Views about the 'object' of interpretation determined the outcome of the discussions.

With such a view of 'text' in mind, the role of the reader and the act of reading are in many ways limited to discovering the meaning and sense of texts by assigning meaning within the constraints of the texts. It is assumed that by the use of different codes, the reader and the meaning of the text are written into the text, and that the sensitive and trained reader is able to decode the text, because meaning is present in the text. Even in the application of the insights of reception theory, such as 'gaps' and 'indeterminacies', the 'object' of interpretation of the seminar group, was regarded as an object in search of (a) valid interpretation.

Although there is a general awareness among New Testament scholars that very little is known about the authors and addressees of New Testament documents, or of the historical context of communication, it is nevertheless assumed that information about these matters is important for the act of reading and that it is possible to 'reconstruct' them. At the Göttingen meeting during 1987 several attempts were made from various angles and vantage points, with the help of various methods, to get to grips with the problem, to my mind without success. This is basically due to the fact that it is often assumed that by inference it is possible to reconstruct historical reality. There are two basic problems to this assumption. The first regards the view of what New Testament texts are, namely representations of reality, even if they present remade reality. The other concerns the view of historical interpretation as reconstruction.

As far as the first assumption is concerned, there is a problem in terms of language as representation. The relationship between signifier and signified is a problem which has been with us since the days of Plato and other ancient thinkers. And it is known that the Saussurean views have lately been reviewed (see Derrida 1976). To make inferences about realities outside texts as we do in constructing the communication situation, or the addressees, for example, of New Testament texts, is a risky business. And we still sometimes pretend that we *re*construct these matters. Secondly, it is clear that the past can never be *reconstructed*. It can only be constructed. These constructions are interpretations based on historical argumentation, they are not attempts to capture the past in words, but to explain it. That is why it is possible to construct different possible historical situations within which the same New Testament document could originally have functioned. It has therefore become necessary to read New Testament writings in different contexts and to assign meaning to them in view of these different possible constructed situations. This became abundantly clear at the said meeting. As one of the participants of that meeting correctly observed about New Testament texts: 'The problem is epistemological: what I see are black spots on a page'. The implication is that these black spots have to be filled with meaning by the reader, and that depends on competence. But more than that, it depends on the theories we hold and the perspectives from which these texts are being read. All the beliefs we hold on what texts are and how they function are theory-mediated. I think it was a mistake to have spent so much time on historical and sociological *re*construction.

Another assumption which played a dominant role in the discussions of the role of the reader in the interpretation of the New Testament in the *SNTS* group, was the fact that the interpretative community was fairly homogeneous. The group consisted of traditionally-trained New Testament scholars with an interest in reception theory and the implications thereof for the interpretation of the New Testament. There were no feminist, liberationist, Marxist or other readers in the group. The implications of the inclusion of such readers were to a certain extent taken seriously in 1988 when different readings of Romans 13 were studied. Unfortunately for me, I was not present, but I could not gather from the minutes that it led to a radical questioning of the basic assumptions of the nature of the text, or to a reformulation of the role of the reader and the act of reading. Except for Brown's paper on the 'resistant reader' and the response of Fowler, which seemingly were not accepted, it appears as if the role of the reader in the interpretation of the New Testament was still conceived in terms of the above text theory and convictions about the role of the historical context in reading a text.

In summary it could be said in general that the role of the reader and the act of reading as perceived by the *SNTS* group were determined by a structural-historical approach. This led to findings which are in accordance with structuralist and historical views held by New Testament scholars on the nature of texts in general and New Testament texts in particular. It is not so much the reader that assigns meaning to these texts according to these views. Rather than assigning meaning, the reader decodes the meaning inscribed in the textual codes and context. In spite of the fact that it was said on occasion that the reader creates a new text by reading or misreading the text, it was believed that the meaning of texts are present in texts. It is remarkable that not even the idea of the fusion of horizons, or the filling in of gaps, or the ignorance concerning authors

and readers and historical contexts of communication, or the fact
that there are so many different interpretations of the same passages
and texts from the New Testament, could lead the group to a radical questioning of vantage points concerning texts and readers of
texts. Many reasons could account for this state of affairs which we
need not consider now. The question which has to be addressed
though, is whether or not we New Testament scholars are willing
to move beyond structuralism. The second part of my reaction bears
on this.

2. *Moving beyond Structuralism*

From the perspective of theory of literature, a major disadvantage
of the *SNTS* seminar on the role of the reader was that it was conceptualised from a structuralist perspective without taking into account
the implications of post-structural developments. It meant that knowledge of post-structural developments had to be bracketed out for the
sake of discussing the role of the reader and the act of reading from
a structuralist perspective. Because of the differences between structural and post-structural approaches to literature, this approach had
far-reaching consequences for the discussions and for the preparation of seminar papers. It has been said: 'that to adhere to phenomenological or structural models of thought or of texts is as untenable in
our times as to cling to Newton's Laws' (Brink 1985:13).

From 1960 onwards, great changes have taken place in the field
of literary theory and philosophy. These changes are often related
to deconstruction as a philosophical attitude and literary strategy.
But there is much more involved in the changes which have occurred
in the move from structuralism to post-structuralism and postmodernism. Both terms are difficult to define and should rather be seen
in relation to structuralism and modernism respectively. Not only
was the possibility of objective description radically questioned, the
very status of science came into question (see De Beer 1985:1–9;
Hassan 1987). This is not the place to discuss post-structuralism and
postmodernism in detail. What is necessary is to consider the views
about texts and readers described above from this perspective.

Post-structuralist literary theories include *Reception Theory, Deconstruction,
Psychoanalysis, Materialist literary criticism,* and *Feminism.* The common
denominators of these theories are a redefinition of the role of the

subject who reads (in some cases, interprets) and the relation between signifiers and signifieds. Much more emphasis came to be placed on the reader as a *semiotic topic* and his/her role as the person who assigns meaning, and the Saussurean language model was radically reformulated. The real break with the past, however, emerged with the advent of deconstruction.

Perhaps most important for our understanding of post-structuralist approaches to literature is Jacques Derrida's attack on the traditional logocentric view of textuality (see Derrida 1976). Logocentrism refers to the priority which has traditionally been accorded to speech over writing by linguists. It also refers to the fact that readers have traditionally searched to locate the centre of a text, thus closing the text 'on a determined meaning allegedly *present* at that centre' (Harty 1985:5). Derrida radically reformulated these views. Taking his cue from Saussure's view that *difference* is a characteristic of relations essential for the constitution of meaning, he maintains that, unlike the spoken word, the meaning of the written word can never have a 'presence', it is deferred indefinitely (cf. his term diffearance). Meaning is never absolutely present or absent in a text. There are only differences and traces of traces. In the words of Leitch (1983:44):

> When we use signs, the being-present of the referent and the signified, incarnated in the self-present signifier, appears to us immediately, but it is delusion, misperception, dream. There is neither substance nor presence in the sign, but only the play on differences. Difference invades the sign, allowing its operation as trace—not self-present sign.

In view of this, texts can no longer be regarded as closed systems or objects. The epistemological presupposition of the autonomy and determinacy of the text gave rise to serious thought. It is no longer held that texts are objects that can be known since they contain meaning. The idea that authors create meaning in their texts which have to be sought for within the boundaries of the text have also been rejected (see Ryan 1985:16ff.). Texts are networks of traces of other texts without centres or margins, continually referring to other texts. Meaning never seems to be present in a text. Texts do not have meaning because of their structure, but because of their relationship with other texts in a network of intertextuality (see Derrida 1979:84; Ryan 1985:16). These views imply a totally different *epistemological* status of the phenomenon 'text' and a totally different reading strategy. Reading, and for that matter interpretation, creates a radically new text. (Deconstruction rejects the idea of 'interpretation'.)

Looking from this perspective back to the implications of reception theory and the interpretation of the New Testament, the act of reading is more than decoding the message of a text. Even the adoption of Iser's view of the reader actively filling in gaps and actualising what the text leaves indeterminate, entails much more than decoding encoded codes in a system of signs. It implies the creating of a radically new text. Reading is an active process of attributing meaning. This explains why, in spite of different critical theories of interpretation and objective attempts at interpretation, there is no critical consensus on the meaning of, for example, different parts of the New Testament. This means that the phenomenon 'text' has become unstable, causing a lot of frustration and fear in those circles where the Bible is regarded as a book which has a message waiting to be discovered. Whether we like it or not, once we move into the area of reception theory, we move beyond structuralism. Reception theory is a post-structuralist theory, undoubtedly not as radical as deconstruction, but nevertheless a post-structuralist theory. It assigns a totally different epistemological status to the phenomenon 'text'.

The emphasis of the interaction between the text and the reader furthermore led to the rewriting of the position held by the *subject*, in that the subject became a semiotic topic. This is seen in feminist, neomarxist and psychoanalytical approaches to literature. The study of the subject in post-structuralist approaches focuses on gender difference, for example, as an organising principle in the attribution of meaning, or on socio-economic conditions which determine the production of meaning in texts. Feminist interpreters contend that authoritarian language and pronouncements result from a male orientation. In this manner, the subject is part of the effect of the discourse. It furthermore implies that the reading subject should be seen in the person's capacity as a member of society.

Again the view of the reader as a semiotic topic has implications for the study of the role of the reader in the interpretation of the New Testament. Any science operates within a scientific circle which has a social dimension. Feminist theologians have succeeded in opening our eyes to male dominant interpretations of the New Testament in the past (see Schüssler Fiorenza 1986). In a similar manner, the application of materialist strategies has opened our eyes for the way in which our own scientific work is dominated by our own social contexts (see Clevenot 1985). Reading the New Testament means reading it from a certain perspective for a certain purpose which determines the outcome of the act of reading. In view of this there seems to be no neutral or objective reading of any text possible. It also means that the New Testament can be read critically, that is with the possibility of rejecting that which is read. It is here that the postmodern perspective comes to the fore, because the 'post-modernist thinker wished to dig towards the place where questions are unconstrained', says Ryan (1988:250), and because it is driven 'by idealism or the will to expose and explain that which chooses not to be exposed or explained' (Ryan 1988:251).

A post-structuralist approach to the role of the reader and the act of reading emphasises the importance of the question: Who reads what? This does not simply mean a listing of different readers, but a radical questioning of what is meant by reading, the reader, and text. The differences between a structuralist-historical and a post-structuralist approach to reading the New Testament are apparent. If we evaluate the *SNTS* seminar from the perspective of post-structuralism and postmodernism, it seems that there is a need for radical thought on what the New Testament text is, what the role of the reader is, and also what the act of reading really entails. A post-structuralist view of the reader simply forces one to question the presuppositions of New Testament research radically.

If one wishes to apply insights from literature theory to the interpretation of New Testament texts, there seems to be no reason why certain texts should have a privileged position above others. The fact that New Testament texts are religious texts does not mean that they cannot be subjected to the same scrutiny as other texts. If one subjects these texts to literary investigation, they have to be treated as texts. Perhaps the current interest in rhetorical criticism could help us realise how the authors of the New Testament created texts to do things with words, that is to manipulate, persuade, legitimate and inform.

Post-structuralist approaches to literature challenge New Testament critics to question their beliefs about these texts, to reflect on the epistemological status of these texts and to get to grips with the reality of multiple readings and interpretations of the same text.

The concept of intertextuality carries a lot of promise for the study of the New Testament. For a long time, New Testament texts have been studied in terms of their growth and not in terms of their making. If one accepts the notion that a text is a fabric of traces of other texts, it can be interesting to read the traces from other texts in New Testament texts within this framework, and not in terms of their origin.

The overall impression of so many men, so many minds, should not scare us away from the challenges of post-structuralism and postmodernism. It is simply no longer possible to defend our views about texts and readers on the ground of foundationalist and/or positivistic grounds, let alone fundamentalistic beliefs about the New Testament.

CHAPTER FIVE

THROUGH THE EYES OF A HISTORIAN

1. *Introduction*

There are many reasons why the New Testament and aspects thereof should be interpreted and explained historically. In fact, historical interpretation of the New Testament is necessitated by the very nature of these writings.

The New Testament is a collection of ancient books, each of them written at a different time during the first and beginning of the second centuries CE. Different purposes, different sociological contexts, different authors, and different recipients were responsible for the form in which we now have these writings. We do not possess a single original copy of any of these books, and in many cases we do not know who wrote them, for whom, or under what circumstances. It was long after they had been written that they were collected and canonized as the New Testament, or the second half of the Bible.

The origin, contents, transmission, reception and canonization of the New Testament writings are only some of the factors that make the New Testament an object of historical interest. In addition there is also a past standing behind and a future standing in front of the individual texts. Some of them apparently represent the end phase of a process of oral transmission of tradition. The 'growth' of the inscripturated tradition is thus another aspect of historical interest, and so is the transmission of the written text through the ages. The writings of the New Testament are furthermore the products of human beings, reflecting the thoughts of people in whom we are interested. But they also reflect the processes of text production in early Christianity, which are obviously of great interest to us. They moreover serve as sources for the discovery of the past, including the recovery of persons, events and thought processes. And, last but not least, there is the interpreter who is also a historical figure, limited by his/her own time and context and knowledge all of which are historically conditioned. Taken together, all these factors make historical explanation, interpretation and construction with regard to the New Testament evident, and necessary.

Historical criticism of the New Testament concerns two fields of interest: (1) Historical interpretation and explanation of the individual writings or aspects of these writings. (2) The history of the people about whom the New Testament writings speak, that is Jesus and the early Christians. In this essay we shall concern ourselves with both aspects, although more attention will be paid to the first. Much of the material is based on an essay, that I have published elsewhere (cf. Vorster 1984). I have, however, reworked the material extensively.

2. *What is Historical Criticism of the New Testament?*

The term *historical criticism* often carries a negative connotation, especially with opponents to this approach. There is, however, reason to argue the opposite. In this essay the term will be used in the sense of discerning appreciation of historical phenomena in and concerning the New Testament. In this manner the term is used positively. That is not to deny the history of historical criticism from the early days of Reimarus (1694–1768) through the nineteenth and twentieth centuries and all the negative results that have been reached by New Testament scholars during this period. However, as I have indicated, the very nature of the New Testament calls for historical interpretation.

Historical criticism is more than a method, or a set of methods applied to historical phenomena. It is a way of thinking, an attitude and an approach to the past and past phenomena. In his well-known essay on historical and dogmatic method in theology, Troeltsch (1913:730) remarks that once the historical method is applied to biblical scholarship and church history, it operates like yeast. Everything changes and in the end the complete character of the theological method is changed. He insisted on the principles of *probability* (methodological doubt, or criticism), *analogy* and *correlation* in the historical study of the Bible; principles that still follow us like a shadow (cf. Harvey 1967:3ff.; Stuhlmacher 1979:22ff.). Our knowledge of the past is mediated by our historical judgements based on probability, analogies and the correlation between what we know and what might have been in the past.

Although the interest in historical investigation (historical criticism) of the Bible since the Reformation resulted in important studies, such as text editions, grammars, the nineteenth century's quest for the historical Jesus, and the sources behind the Gospels, to mention a few aspects, the beginning of the twentieth century marked a noticeable change in our understanding of the making of the Bible, the origins and the history of the primitive church, and so on. Like Troeltsch, others after him accepted the challenge of the discovery of the historical consciousness of man during the nineteenth century. By the middle of this century, historical criticism became widely accepted by New Testament scholars, and in many circles it was taken for granted that the methods applied in biblical research are those used by contemporary historians (Krentz 1975:33).

One should, however, not forget that historical thought is a way of thinking and that there are other ways of thinking too. Although historical thought is common to biologists, physicists, theologians and semanticists, who might think about their own subject in historical terms, each of these scientists also has his/her own particular way of thinking. Biologists think about reality as biologists. The same is done by physicists, theologians and semanticists.

> To think historically, means to take seriously the difference and distance between one's own world and that of another who lived at an earlier stage, and to develop a willingness to enter into conversation with the (dead partners of the) past about something, somebody or some event (cf. Demandt 1979:463–78).

Historical thought is obviously based on theories and hypotheses that are human-made attempts to manipulate data for the purpose of explaining, be it the present or the past. The history of historical criticism reminds us that there are constant shifts in theories. These shifts include shifts in the theory of history, historical interpretation and historiography (cf. Stern 1970), something that is not always realised in New Testament scholarship. It is therefore unsatisfying to speak of historical criticism of the New Testament as if it were one model, namely *the* historico-critical method (cf. Hengel 1973:85). This is illustrated by the many shifts from Von Ranke to the present (cf. Koselleck & Stempel 1973; Gilliam 1976; White 1975). Theories are devised to explain; they are systems of explanation that develop and are improved. Let us illustrate the point.

Historical criticism is always historical criticism current in the period of application or used by the interpreter in that period. Under influence of positivism, for instance, much attention was, and sometimes still is paid to *causality, genesis* or *origin* in New Testament scholarship. The reason being, so it is argued, that no written text can be explained without a proper knowledge of the author, his/her life and life setting, and the things that caused certain events and actions. Tremendous efforts have been invested in New Testament scholarship in constructing the original authors of New Testament writings, their lives, the *Zeitgeist* and their thoughts in order to explain these writings. This theory is based on the assumption that literature can only be understood through biography of the author (cf. Maren-Griesbach 1977:10ff.; Wellek & Warren 1963:73). This is a theory of literature that has come under sharp attack and is rejected nowadays, although it is still maintained by many in New Testament circles.

Historical criticism is used in this essay in a broad sense. The term covers historiography, historical explanation and historical interpretation. One should, however, be clear about terminology because of the theories on which they are based. It is to my mind necessary to distinguish between historical interpretation, historical understanding (*Verstehen*), historical explanation (*Erklärung*) and historiography. In positivism there used to be no difference between the humanities and natural sciences. Everything was explained in terms of causality and genesis. Dilthey, on the other hand, propagated the idea that there is a great difference between the humanities and the natural sciences. In the first, phenomena are understood, while in the latter they are explained. However, let us remind ourselves that phenomena such as texts and the conduct of people are nowadays also explained and interpreted in the light of theories, for example, literary theories or sociological theories, and not only understood as Dilthey and his followers wished. Scientific investigation is based on theories, and theories form the framework within which phenomena are explained.

In view of the aforesaid, two things must be kept in mind. The first is that, given the fact that historical criticism is commonly accepted by New Testament scholars, it is necessary to be aware of shifts in the theory and practice of historical interpretation. Many of the methods and assumptions, as we shall see later, are based on theories of historical criticism that are no longer accepted. Secondly, it is a grave misunderstanding to assume that historico-critical methods used by New Testament scholars are necessarily the same as those used by contemporary historians. For this purpose, it will be necessary to relate aspects of historico-critical research to underlying theories and simultaneously to mention current views on relevant aspects of historical research with regard to literature. In the rest of the essay an attempt will be made at describing the different methods that are used in historical interpretation of the New Testament, and also to deal with aspects of New Testament historiography.

2.1 *Historical interpretation of New Testament texts*

2.1.1 *On the assignment of meaning*

Texts do not have meaning. Meaning is attributed to texts by an active interplay between text and interpreter. That explains why it is possible to interpret the same text in various ways depending on the method of interpretation. By consciously choosing a specific approach to literature, for example, a feminist or Marxist interpretation may be given of a particular text. On the other hand, one might approach a text with a specific problem in mind and interpret the same text psychologically or sociologically, or sociolinguistically. In each of these cases meaning is attributed to the text on the ground of a particular theory (cf. Van Luxemburg, Bal & Weststeijn 1982:75ff.).

Historical interpretation is also interested in the meaning of texts and is obviously also based on a theory or theories of literature. Within this framework meaning is constituted by authorial intention, genetic contexts, extratextual reality and by the original readers. The different aspects may be schematized as follows:

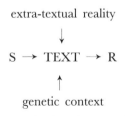

extra-textual reality

$\downarrow$

S → TEXT → R

$\uparrow$

genetic context

→ elements constituting the meaning of a text

The first thing that comes to mind when we think of the New Testament within the framework of this model is the fact that the interpreter is expected to do a lot of constructive interpretation. We have already said that we do not possess a single original copy of any text in the New Testament. So obviously the interpreter is expected to establish an authentic text. The method by which this is done is called Textual Criticism (cf. chapter 2 below). Since we nowadays have a number of critical editions of the New Testament, the task has become much easier for the historico-critical interpreter in this respect.

What we have are *contextless texts* that have to be interpreted historically. In each particular interpretation one has to establish who wrote the text, to whom, under what circumstances and about what. This is in short what is expected from the interpreter who wants to interpret a text historically. Many of these problems are dealt with in so-called *Introductions to the New Testament* where attention is paid to authors, receivers, places and purposes of writing of the individual books, and also in books about the history of the first century CE (*Zeitgeschichte*). In each particular case, however, the interpreter is expected to take into account all the (re)constructed detail in order to make sense of text.

Generally speaking the New Testament consists of narrative and argumentative texts. The Gospels, Acts and the Revelation of John are narratives, while the letters are argumentative texts. Both sets of texts offer different historical problems, and various methods are used to reconstruct information related to these matters.

Let us now turn to an example from an argumentative text in order to illustrate historical interpretation of a fragment of an argumentative text. Romans 13:1–7 forms part of the letter of Paul to the Romans. What Paul had in mind is dependent upon a number of things that the interpreter has to construct. There is no doubt that Paul wrote this letter after his conversion, and according to Romans 16:1 it is probable that he wrote the letter when he was in Corinth. In order to establish when this happened one has to take into account the chronology of Paul.

The only fixed point in Paul's life is derived from the Gallio inscription (cf. Kümmel 1965:177f.). This inscription was found in Delphi during 1897, and is dated in the twenty-sixth acclamation of the Emperor Claudius. The probable date of Gallio's term as proconsul is spring 51 to spring 52. If the data in Acts 18:11f. are correlated with the term of Gallio, it is possible to infer the probable date of the ministry of Paul in Corinth. Taking this as a vantage point, the different dates in Paul's ministry can be established. Paul's letter to the Romans is thus normally dated in 56/7.

The addressees are known from the letter. They are referred to as gentiles (cf. 1:5, 13; 11:13), that is gentile Christians, in their relationship with Jewish Christians (cf. 4:1; 7:4–6; 9–11; 14:4–6, 13–23). The church of Rome therefore most probably consisted of gentile and Jewish Christians. Did Paul have Jewish Christians in mind when he wrote Romans 13:1–7? This is possible if we take into account the remark of Suetonius (cf. *Claudius* 25) in connection with the expulsion of the Jews (= Jewish Christians) from Rome. This took place in the year 49. But who were these people and what did they think? Were they Jewish Christians who lost their property when they had to leave Rome, returned to Rome after the death of Claudius in 54, and then had to be kept under the thumb? Were they anti-Roman charismatic Christians filled with the Spirit, regarding themselves as members of another world, indifferent to the Roman Empire? Were they perhaps revolutionaries who wished to overthrow Roman rule?

Romans 13:1–7 reflects the language usage and characteristics of a Hellenistic Roman (constitutional) legal situation of the first century CE (cf. Friedrich, Pohlmann & Stuhlmacher 1976:135ff.). In an attempt to construct the authorial intention, one also has to construct Paul's frame of mind. Did Paul write from an apocalyptic point of view with the expectation of the imminent return of the Lord coming to establish the kingdom of God? Or did he lay down principles for the ethical conduct of future generations?

From these various possibilities, of which I have mentioned only a few for the purpose of illustration, one has to recover a probable historical setting for a historical reading of the text. Because of the lack of external information from contemporary writings and other historical sources, it is very difficult if not impossible to reconstruct a historical setting for Romans 13:1–7 as Strecker (1972:27) and others have correctly pointed out. The same holds for the reconstruction of the authorial intention, the original recipients and what they thought about the matters referred to in the text.

Romans 13:1–7 is no exception to the problems involved in historical interpretation of the meaning of New Testament texts. The historical setting and the date of writing make quite a difference to the meaning that is ascribed to aspects of the Gospel of Mark, for example. Quite different situations are assumed by placing the Gospel in Rome, Syria or Galilee, and the same goes for dating the Gospel before or after the fall of Jerusalem. Similar problems occur when James, the brother of Jesus or another James is taken as the author of the letter of James, to mention a few examples.

The theory behind this approach is that it is possible to infer from a text the authorial intention, the historical situation referred to in that text, information about the subject matter and about the intended original recipients. Texts are regarded as windows through which the interpreter can see the reality to which they refer. This approach to literature has, however, been rejected by literary critics (cf. Wellek & Warren 1963). There is no direct route via the text to the mind of the author, the actual readers or the events referred to in the extra-textual world of the text. That is why a historical interpretation of a text can never be called a *reconstruction* of the mentioned aspects. It always remains a construction of the interpreter based on probabilities, as we have illustrated above. The interpreter constructs the necessary information in order to make a historical interpretation and gives an interpretation within that framework. This is sound historical thinking and the most we can do with re-enacting the past.

Although the different historico-critical methods, or at least some of them, are also applied to argumentative material, they are normally used to analyse narrative material. That is because of the concept of the text which underlies the approach.

2.1.2   *On texts and methods*

2.1.2.1   *What is a text?*—There is reason to believe that most of the written narratives we find in the New Testament are based on sources, be they written or oral. According to Luke (1:1–4) the author of the Gospel made a thorough investigation into the things that had been handed down and written about Jesus before he wrote his story of Jesus. And Paul also tells us about the *tradition* that he had received concerning the death and resurrection of Jesus (cf. 1 Cor. 15:3f.). In addition, the Old Testament writings and other extracanonical writings are often quoted or alluded to (cf. the list of *Loci citati vel allegati* in the Nestle-Aland edition), which makes it all the more necessary to pay attention to the 'sources' on which the narratives are based and how they were used in compiling the final texts. If one furthermore takes into account the agreements among the synoptic gospels (see below), there seems to be enough reason to take seriously the view that these writings are based on sources, it is argued.

Historico-critical methodology started developing during the nineteenth century, and one should expect the underlying text theory to be from that period. The idea of *origin* and growth is basic to what a text is according to traditional historico-critical thought. New Testament narratives are the products of sources, which have not only been used by the compilers of these texts, but might have undergone changes and developments in the process of transmission and eventual inscripturation. In fact, the narratives originated from the sources, it is argued.

The first step in the development of historico-critical methodology was to devise a method by which the sources underlying a particular text could be discerned. Nineteenth century analysis of the New Testament bears witness to this stage. It was, however, realised that these sources underwent changes and that since they were transmitted orally, it was necessary to investigate the oral stage of tradition, the history of traditions, the transmitters of tradition, and the role of the setting which gave rise to particular forms in which the tradition was transmitted. After the Second World War, attention came to be paid to the purposes for which the final compilers of narrative texts, such as the gospels, used the material that they received. It is clear that the application and development of methodology had an influence on the concept of text of historico-critical methodology and that one should be aware of this. There is a clear difference between current views depending on insights from redaction criticism and, for instance, those of early practitioners of source criticism. The main idea, nevertheless remains. New Testament narratives are the products of communities and bear traces of processes of growth and development. With this in mind, let us now turn to the individual methods, which were mainly developed by German scholars for the interpretation of narrative material, but are nowadays commonly accepted by scholars who are involved in historico-critical study of the New Testament.

2.1.2.2 *Source criticism*—Source criticism is the more acceptable English equivalent for the German *Literarkritik*, which is sometimes translated by literary criticism. Since the purpose of *Literarkritik* is to determine the sources that have been used in a given text, it is inappropriate to use the term literary criticism, which is the name of a totally different discipline.

The main concern of source criticism is to determine the source/s that presumably lie/s behind a particular text. One of the major

problems in this connection in the New Testament is the relationship between the so-called Synoptic Gospels, that is the Gospels of
Matthew, Mark and Luke. They are called synoptic (seeing together)
because they sometimes relate the same material in the same wording and in the same order.

Different solutions have been offered for the phenomenon of the
striking agreements but also remarkable differences in *wording, order
of material, style* and *contents* among the first three Gospels, since
G.E. Lessing (1729–1781) first suggested that they are based on a
common gospel (*Urevangelium*) that is no longer extant. J.G. Herder
(1744–1803) proposed that the synoptic gospels were based on a
series of oral traditions that the individual compilers of the gospels
reworked for their own purposes. And in the same vein F.D.E.
Schleiermacher (1768–1834) thought that the problem could be solved
by assuming written and not oral sources behind the gospels.

These solutions assume a source or sources behind the synoptic
gospels. Quite another model was proposed when it was suggested
that there are signs of *literary dependence* among the synoptic gospels.
I will mention two important hypotheses in this regard. Some scholars, following Griesbach, argue that Matthew is the oldest extant
gospel. The Gospel of Mark is a shortened version of Matthew and
its author also used Luke to compile his Gospel (cf. Farmer 1964).
Contrary to this, the hypothesis that is commonly accepted is the
so-called two-source hypothesis. Priority is given to Mark and it is
argued that Matthew and Luke made use of Mark and an assumed
sayings-source called Q. Q stands for *Quelle*, that is 'source'. It
is maintained by many that by accepting the priority of Mark and
existence of Q, one can best explain the differences and agreements
among the synoptic gospels.

It makes quite a difference which hypothesis one prefers. To mention one problem in this regard: our construction of the development of ideas in early Christian thought is totally dependent on the
solution of the synoptic problem. Since the Gospels of Matthew and
Mark characterise Jesus differently, it is obvious that these differences
would influence one's presentation of the development of Christology.

This is not the place to elaborate on the detail concerning these
hypotheses. Suffice it to say that the synoptic problem is one of the
most intriguing problems of New Testament scholarship and that it
has certainly not been resolved. The most important synoptic relationships have conveniently been summarised by Sanders and Davies
(1989:53f.). They are the following:

* The triple tradition, that is, passages that occur in all three synoptic gospels.
* The placement of the material often agrees in the case of the triple tradition.
* More than ninety percent of the material of Mark is found in Matthew and more than fifty percent in Luke.
* In addition to *verbatim* agreements in the triple tradition, there also are substantial agreements between Matthew and Mark against Luke, but fewer between Matthew and Luke against Mark.
* The agreement between Matthew and Luke begins where Mark starts and ends where Mark ends. This also occurs in individual pericopes.

These observations emphasize the fact that Mark is closer to Matthew and Luke than Matthew is to Luke and *vice versa*.

In addition, it is remarkable that Matthew and Luke have a lot of material in common that is not found in Mark, most of which are sayings of Jesus. It is also remarkable that this material is not arranged in the same way in Matthew and Luke.

Source criticism is an attempt to explain, amongst other things, the agreements and disagreements of the synoptic gospels in wording, order, contents (e.g. omissions, doublets and misunderstandings), style, ideas and theology.

To enable scholars to study the relationships between the gospels, J.J. Griesbach already in 1774 published a critical synopsis in which the gospel material was arranged in parallel columns. We now have a large number of synopses of the synoptic gospels (cf. Sanders and Davies 1989:51f.), each based on different assumptions. They allow us to investigate the different Gospels simultaneously.

Source criticism does, however, not only concern the synoptic problem in the New Testament. Literary relationships in New Testament texts are usually explained by the assumption of sources underlying texts. These relationships are of two kinds. First there are texts that seem to show a literary dependence upon other known texts. This is the case with the synoptic gospels, Colossians and Ephesians, 2 Peter and Jude, for example. In such cases the direction in which dependence lies has to be explained. There are, furthermore, single texts that are presumably based on unknown sources. In John 4:1, for example, it seems as if the author had used a source according to which Jesus and his disciples baptised people. In verse 2 he apparently corrects this view by asserting that Jesus himself did not baptise. Furthermore, because of the difference in vocabulary and the fact that John 20:30 seems to be a natural ending for the Gospel, it is often assumed that John 21 is based on another source not written by the same author who originally compiled the Gospel. Paul inserted hymns into his letters (cf. Phlp. 2:5–11 and Col. 1:15–20) and made use of pre-Pauline material in writing his letters (cf. 1 Cor. 15, etc.). How does one determine whether an author made use of a source if he does not mention it, as is frequently the case of quotations of the Old Testament and so on (cf. 1 Cor. 11:23ff.)?

Sources are normally assumed when there are inconsistencies in a text (see the detailed discussion of Wenham 1985:144f.). These include inconsistencies in the sequence of a text (e.g. breaks/seams and dislocations; cf. the relationship between Jn. 14:31; 18:1 and Jn. 15–17); stylistic inconsistencies (see the hymns in the infancy narrative of Luke); theological inconsistencies (cf. Rm. 3:25–26 with Rm. 1–2) and historical inconsistencies (e.g. doublets in the same document).

Originally source criticism was used to get as close as possible to the events being described in the New Testament, and in particular to the events in the life of Jesus. Especially in the nineteenth century it was maintained that the original sources behind the texts were closer to how things really happened, that is, to the historical events that are fundamental to Christian faith, and that special efforts should be made to determine and reconstruct these sources. This was part of the philosophy of history of that time and also of the concept of truth. The only truth is historical truth, that is truth which is based on facts (cf. Lührmann 1984:42). There are few scholars today who would still defend this view. The purpose of source criticism has shifted from the search for sources and 'reliable facts' to the explanation of the production of early Christian literature. It is therefore used nowadays in form critical and redaction critical studies to determine the tradition/s behind a written text.

2.1.2.3 *Form criticism*—In answer to the question where the authors of New Testament writings obtained their material, we have already noticed in our discussion of source criticism that much attention is paid to the use of sources in traditional historical criticism of the New Testament. Form criticism did not replace source criticism and still does not do so. It also concerns the origin of New Testament material, obviously from quite a different perspective, as we shall soon see.

Form criticism is a translation for *Formgeschichte*. The German term refers to the fact that form critics are interested both in the *forms* of material, which are found in the New Testament, and in their *pre-*

literary history, that is, their oral growth and origin. Form criticism is therefore not only interested in the study of forms as the (English) term suggests. Forms *and* their history are the focal point in form-critical studies. Although scholars sometimes distinguish between the study of forms (form criticism) and the history of the traditions that constitute part of the content of a form (tradition history), it is difficult to do form criticism in the traditional sense of the word without studying the history of the traditions involved. This is clear from the standard works of R. Bultmann and M. Dibelius on form criticism. They should be regarded as the pioneers in this approach, although they built on the insights of their predecessors and contemporaries.

The publication of W. Wrede's book *Das Messiasgeheimnis in den Evangelien: Zugleich ein Beitrag zum Verständnis des Markusevangeliums* in 1906 brought to an end the idea that the oldest Gospel, that is the Gospel of Mark, was a chronicle of the life and works of Jesus. He illustrated how Mark portrayed Jesus to his readers by his theological construction of the secrecy and revelation of Jesus in the Gospel. That ruled out the idea that Mark's Gospel can be used as a basic history of the life of Jesus as had been believed in the nineteenth century. On page 41 of his book, *Kyrios Christos: Geschichte des Christusglaubens von den Anfängen des Christentums bis Irenäus*, which was published in 1913, W. Bousset furthermore drew attention to the need of investigating the 'laws' that regulate oral tradition and transmission. In 1919 three books were published that became classics in New Testament scholarship, one on source and the other on form criticism. In his book, *Der Rahmen der Geschichte Jesu: Literarkritische Untersuchungen zur ältesten Jesusüberlieferung*, K.L. Schmidt argued that the Gospel of Mark consists of small episodes that Mark edited and then put into a seemingly chronological and geographical framework. In *Die Formgeschichte des Evangeliums* M. Dibelius was the first to use the term *Formgeschichte* with regard to the study of the pre-literary oral forms of the gospel tradition. He went about constructively by assuming the missionary context and preaching as the life setting of most of the material in the gospel tradition. R. Bultmann worked analytically and in his book, *Die Geschichte der synoptischen Tradition*, concentrated on the history and characteristics of the forms of the Jesus tradition. Both regarded form criticism as a sociological approach in the first instance that helped the New Testament scholar to trace the history of the traditions we find in the New Testament.

When one pages through a synopsis and compares the introductions

and endings of smaller units, such as parables, miracles or other narratives, one soon realizes that the frameworks of the same stories
are not always similar in all the Gospels. Matthew 18:10–14, for
example, has it that Jesus told the parable of the Lost Sheep to the
disciples. But according to Luke 15:4–7, it was directed against the
Pharisees. There also seems to be a limited amount of forms in
which the gospel tradition was transmitted. These and many other
details indicate that the individual units had their own life of transmission and that they were used in many different contexts by the
primitive church depending on the needs of the church.

Taking their cue from the Old Testament scholar, Herman Gunkel,
New Testament that the content of the Jesus tradition, for example,
was transmitted in certain forms and that there seemed to be a relationship between form, content and the situation in which a particular form originated. A major component of the teaching of Jesus
appears in the form of parables, and his conflicts with opponents
are normally narrated in the form of controversy stories, to mention
two examples. It was argued that a particular setting in life (*Sitz im
Leben*) is the occasion of a certain form. There seems to be a correlation between the form of the material and the occasion or setting
out of which the material originated and was transmitted. Funeral
notices, for instance, are normally occasioned by the death of somebody in a society. Similarly other sociological settings are responsible for other forms. Controversy stories or debates, for instance, can
be traced back to internal strife in the primitive church or debates
with opponents of the Christian sect at an early stage. In order to
find a possible *Sitz im Leben* for a particular form it is helpful to
relate the form to a particular activity of the primitive church, for
instance, the cult, teaching, preaching or mission.

The purpose of form criticism is twofold. First it describes the
genres, forms and formulas that occur in the New Testament. Secondly
it focusses on the pre-literary history and growth of traditions and
smaller literary forms, such as parables, miracle stories, birth stories
and so on.

New Testament writings can be divided into four larger forms
(*Gattungen*) or *genres*, namely gospels, a historical monograph (Acts of
the Apostles), letters and an apocalypse. Each of these has its own
characteristics that are important for the study of the particular writing. Incorporated into these larger forms are smaller ones (*Formen*)
such as hymns, parables, miracle stories and so on. Then there are

also formulas (*Formeln*) incorporated into the material that the authors of the New Testament writings used, such as credal formulas (cf. Rm. 5:8; 10:9; 1 Cor. 15:3). These could have formed part of early Christian catachesis. We also find confession formulas (Phlp. 2:11) that could have been used at baptism ceremonies. There are furthermore liturgical formulas and texts such as acclamation (1 Cor. 8:6) and praise formulas (Rm. 16:25–27), prayers (Ac. 4:24–26) and so on. These forms and formulas also indicate that the writings of the New Testament constitute part of the tradition of the church at an early stage of its development. Form criticism is interested in both the form and the prehistory of these larger and smaller forms. For reasons that are clear, the emphasis is on the Gospel tradition, although, as we have just seen, it is not restricted to that.

A number of *presuppositions* play a role in form criticism, of which the most important is the assumption that our written Gospels originated from oral tradition. During the time between the ministry of Jesus and the writing of the first Gospel, the sayings of Jesus and the stories concerning his words and works were circulated *orally*. It is also maintained that even the written sources that the authors of the Gospels might have used to compile their narratives originally circulated in oral form. They are folk or popular literature, and do not have the characteristics of literary texts in the classical sense of the term. The 'authors' of the Gospels can therefore not be regarded as real authors. The Gospels are the products of a process of evolution with the community as a collective institution, the generating force behind the process of transmission. Not individuals, but the community is the creative force behind the gospel traditions. They transmitted and even created the Jesus tradition that we now find in the written Gospels. The authors of the Gospels are regarded as compilers, collectors of traditions, tradents and exponents of their respective communities.

A further assumption is that it is possible to study the pre-literary form of tradition, be it in written or oral form. It is assumed that the written Gospels reveal traces of oral transmission and that the New Testament scholar has the task of constructing the history of the transmission of traditions. This is done, amongst other things, by investigating how close a particular unit or pericope is to the 'pure form' of that particular form. Since miracles and other forms that we find in the Jesus tradition also occur in other writings of the same period, a particular form is compared to that in extra-

canonical literature in order to determine the characteristics of the
so-called pure forms. A typical form critical argument would be that
the miracle story of the Healing of the Paralytic in Mark 2:1–12
originally did not contain the saying concerning forgiveness. It may
have been added by inserting the controversy about Jesus and the
forgiveness of sins into the story. This resulted in a mixed form, that
is, a miracle story mixed with a controversy story. It is argued that
by comparing parallel accounts of the same unit of tradition, their
wording, placement and context, it is often possible to trace the history of a particular unit to its possible original form. The parables
of Jesus offer an excellent opportunity to apply this approach, since
many of them occur in all three synoptic gospels as well as in the
Gospel of Thomas.

Since it is furthermore believed that the original forms were initially circulated without their current narrative frameworks, and also
transmitted in other frameworks, it is theoretically possible to distinguish redaction from tradition in order to get closer to the original form. Let us now turn to *pre-literary forms* in the Jesus tradition.

It is obvious from the way in which Dibelius and Bultmann divided
and treated the Jesus tradition that there is no such thing as a pure
form and that it is possible to name the forms differently. This is
not the place to enter into detail. A few remarks are nevertheless
necessary.

Dibelius divided the material into paradigms, novellets, legends,
myths and paranesis. Bultmann, however, divided the Jesus tradition
into sayings (*logia*) and narrative material. This is also the division
that to this day is followed to a greater or lesser extent by scholars.
We shall give a short discussion of the different forms by which the
tradition was transmitted. The *sayings tradition* will be dealt with first.

The term *apophthegm* was used by Bultmann for controversy stories, school debates and so-called biographic apophthegms. These
small units normally refer to a short narrative containing a short
and pointed independent saying as the hub of the particular story.
Dibelius called them paradigms because of their exemplary function,
while others preferred the term 'pronouncement story'. These stories
are best explained in the light of similar short narratives containing
a saying, called *chreiai* which abound in Greek literature (cf. Robbins
1988 and Sanders & Davies 1989:146ff.). A few examples of *chreiai*
in the Gospels are the Healing of the Paralytic in Mark 2:1–12; the
Call of Levi (Mk. 2:14); the Question about Fasting (Mk. 2:18–22);

and others which indicate the importance of the pointed saying within the short narratives.

Another important group concerns the *figurative speech* of Jesus, which refers to his proverbs, overstatements (Mt. 5:29–30), images (Mk. 2:17), metaphors of all sorts, including similitudes (e.g. Lk. 14:28–32), parables (Mt. 20:1–16) and exemplary stories (Lk. 10:30–37). The figurative speech of Jesus has been scrutinized intensively by form critics since the critical study of A. Jülicher, which put an end to the allegorical interpretation of this material by the church for a long period. Scholars such as T.A. Cadoux, C.H. Dodd and J. Jeremias did pioneering work in this connection and are worthwhile consulting. Especially with regard to the teaching of Jesus on the kingdom of God, and therefore with regard to the question of what Jesus taught, it is important to be aware of the problems involved in interpreting this material from a form critical perspective (cf. Jeremias 1970).

The *sayings of Jesus* also occur in different other contexts, such as dialogues (cf. Mk. 13) and other narrative material. With regard to content and form these sayings are clearly recognizable. I am referring to wisdom sayings (Mk. 9:49), prophetic and apocalyptic sayings that can be comforting (Lk. 6:20–23), threatening (Lk. 6:24–26), or admonishing (Mk. 1:15). These sayings are uttered for the benefit of the church. There are also law sayings which are either apodeictic (Mt. 7:6): 'Do . . .' 'Do not . . .', or casuistic (Mk. 8:38): 'If . . . then . . .', in form. These sayings originated, according to the form critics, in catechetical contexts or they were used in polemics. The I-sayings constitute a special group (Lk. 14:26). By these sayings Jesus revealed something about his person or his coming (Mk. 2:17). Many of these were built on the model of the original I-sayings of Jesus and are therefore not authentic, as Bultmann and others have convincingly indicated. This obviously applies to the Jesus tradition in general and not only to the I-sayings. The primitive church used and reused the same sayings of Jesus and events in his life in many different situations for different purposes. That explains the diversity in the transmission of tradition.

The *narrative material* in the Jesus tradition is also the object of form critical studies. Bultmann divided this material in accordance with content.

Similar to other contemporary miracle workers, Jesus also performed miracles, and therefore the Jesus tradition has different *miracle stories.* These stories range from stories concerning exorcisms, healing miracles to nature miracles. Although the amount of detail differs, most of the stories have a common structure: there is a need and the need is eventually overcome. They are used to illustrate the authority of Jesus, and for apologetic and missionary purposes. Miracles stories performed by the followers of Jesus are also told in the Acts of the Apostles (cf. Ac. 5).

In addition to miracle stories, the Jesus tradition also includes *historical narratives* and *legends.* These stories concern the infant narratives, baptism of Jesus, his entry into Jerusalem, the passion narrative, and the empty tomb narrative. It is very difficult to distinguish between what is historical and what is legendary in this material. Dibelius used the term legendary with regard to narratives that go back to inquisitiveness to know more about a person or an aspect of a person's life (cf. Lk. 2:41–49). Myth, according to Dibelius, refers to supernatural events. The baptism of Jesus, his temptation and transfiguration are classified as legends by Dibelius.

Since form critics are also interested in theological reasons why traditions were transmitted in particular ways, the application of the method sheds light on theological trajectories in the primitive church.

Form criticism has been subjected to fundamental criticism. This is not the place to discuss the criticism. Let me conclude this section with a remark and references. The production of texts, the conception of what texts are, how authors use other and previous texts to make new ones, the role of oral tradition in the writing of New Testament texts and many other aspects of importance to form criticism have become a bone of contention (cf. Güttgemanns 1970; Sanders & Davies 1989:128ff. and Vorster 1982b:103f.).

2.1.2.4   *Redaction criticism*—In the period between the two world wars scholars focussed on the smaller units and their prehistory even though persons like Bultmann already in his book on the history of the synoptic tradition drew attention to the Gospel writers as editors. After the Second World War there was a change of interest and a new method was applied to determine the theological purpose of the individual Gospel writers in their redaction of the Jesus tradition. The emphasis came to be placed on the Gospels as complete texts and not so much on fragments that the writers of the Gospels used in their compilation of their texts.

I have already referred to the works of Wrede and Schmidt, which in a certain way opened the possibility of investigating the role of the Gospel writers as editors and their individual theological intentions. Wrede emphasised Mark's theological scheme of the Messianic secret and Schmidt showed that the frameworks of the narratives about Jesus are not original. In addition, scholars such as R.H. Lightfoot, who, after his return to England from Germany where he studied under Dibelius, wrote a book on the function of the prologue of Mark, and E. Lohmeyer, who contended that the Gospel of Mark was built around geographical and theological themes. However, they were not taken seriously until the end of the Second World War as far as the Gospels as a whole were concerned.

In 1948 G. Bornkamm published an essay on the Calming of a Storm (Mt. 8:23–27) in which he compared the pericope with its parallel in Mark 4:35–41. He argued that by placing the pericope after the Sermon on the Mount where Jesus was portrayed as the Messiah of the word, in this pericope he is shown as the Messiah of the deed. He also showed that imitation is an important theme in the previous as well as the following pericopes. These and other details, he maintained, indicated the importance of the redaction of the material by Matthew.

H. Conzelmann made a major contribution to the study of Luke with his book entitled, *Die Mitte der Zeit: Studien zur Theologie des Lukas*. He argued that Luke was not a reliable historian. On the contrary he was more of a historian who tried to portray the salvation history of the world in three periods: the time of Israel until John the Baptist; the time of Jesus, which is central, and the time of the church. According to him Luke was much more interested in showing the importance of Jerusalem in the history of salvation than in writing an accurate history.

Both these studies were based on the priority of Mark and therefore it was relatively 'easy' to determine the way in which Matthew and Luke used their sources and to point out the theological interests of the evangelists. In the case of Mark (and John for that matter) it is different if the two source hypothesis is accepted. Attempts to determine Mark's theological intentions and purpose were soon investigated.

W. Marxsen, who was the first New Testament scholar to use the term *Redaktionsgeschichte* as a name for the new method, maintained that redaction criticism is independent from form criticism. He was more interested in the methodological aspects of redaction criticism and wrote a book on *Der Evangelist Markus: Studien zur Redaktionsgeschichte des Evangeliums.* His book is an attempt to show in four separate studies on John the Baptist, Galilee, the term 'gospel' and Mark 13, that Mark independently reworked tradition for his own purpose and theological intentions.

These studies were the beginning of a renewed interest in the activities of the persons who were responsible for the final Gospels in their written form. Detailed comparisons were made of how the evangelists altered their traditions, changed the order of material, added, omitted material, inserted the material in their own frameworks and so on, in order to put their own emphasis on the material. By assuming that Luke used Mark, it can be argued that he changed the saying of Jesus in Mark 8:34 from:

> If any man would come after me, let him deny himself and take up his cross and follow me

to

> If any man would come after me, let him deny himself and take up his cross *daily* (my italics) and follow me

The insertion of 'daily' makes quite a difference to the meaning of the saying. This is but a small example of what is implied by the assumption that the evangelists used sources which they edited for their own purposes in order to portray Jesus in their own chosen way. Obviously the contributions of the evangelists cannot be restricted to minor changes in wording. It also concerns major changes in arrangement of material, such as the Sermon on the Mount in the Gospel of Matthew or the programmatic summary of the preaching of Jesus in Luke 4.

It is clear that traditional redaction criticism is based on detailed comparisons between different texts that presumably are dependent on detailed investigations of what could possibly be regarded as redaction where the sources are unknown. Whenever traditional material is isolated, however, it is possible to ask how a particular author interpreted the tradition by editing it.

The important question in redaction criticism is how did an author make use of a precursor text, be it a tradition, a complete text, or a quotation. Are there signs of editing of the precursor text or tradition? What are the characteristics of a particular writing in wording, style and thought? Is there any indication that these characteristics form part of the redaction of material? These questions are not only applicable in the case of Matthew and Luke, where it is assumed that they used Mark and Q, but also in all texts of the New Testament where it is presumed that an author used and interpreted tradition or other texts for his own purpose.

There have been major shifts in the theory and practice of redaction criticism during the past three decades. Although from the beginning there has been an emphasis on a holistic approach to texts in redaction criticism, the fact that the Gospels, for example, were still regarded as the products of a process of evolution, prevented scholars from taking the evangelists seriously as authors. In spite of their activities as editors, they kept on being tradents and exponents of the communities they represent. Mark is, for example, regarded as a conservative redactor who changed only slightly the traditions he received (cf. Vorster 1980b for a discussion of the problem). Only lately with the introduction of narratology have scholars started focussing on the internal structure and meaning of texts as wholes, and redaction critics have come to realize that they should pay more attention to the texts themselves than to their history of growth.

The result of redaction criticism is that scholars nowadays commonly speak of the theology of the different authors of New Testament texts, such as the theology of Mark, and so on.

At this point it seems necessary to make a critical remark about the methods we have now discussed. Traditional historical criticism of the gospel tradition has reached its limits. There is little that can be added to current hypothesis on the synoptic problem, or, for example, the relationship between the synoptics and the Gospel of John in view of traditional historical criticism. This is mainly due to the present state of evidence. Our sources are very limited. It is important to realize that there is such a problem as the synoptic problem, and it is imperative to make readers of the New Testament aware of it. When it comes to the methods we have treated, it becomes difficult to continue the process of 'disintegrating criticism'. The assumption that there is a direct continuity between the oral and literary phases of the gospel tradition, on the grounds of which the pre-literary oral stages can be reconstructed in more than a speculative way, is no longer tenable (cf. Kelber 1983:1ff.). Recovery of the pre-literary forms and their meanings is well-nigh impossible— in view of our limited knowledge of the pre-literary stages of the gospel tradition. Once oral tradition is inscripturated, it becomes completely changed. In a certain sense it is stripped of its past because all that remains in the written texts are traces of tradition without their pre-literary contexts.

2.1.2.5 *Historico-religio approach*—We have noticed how important it is to understand a particular text within its own time and circumstances. In addition to socio-historical information, knowledge of religious ideas which were current in the area and period when a text was written is also of significance. Although Christianity has its origin in Judaism and started in Palestine, hellenistic religions and religious ideas are of great significance for the study of the religious world of the New Testament, because of the influence of Hellenism on the people living in Palestine and Asia Minor in the first century CE.

At the turn of this century the religio-historical study of the New Testament was stimulated by a series of studies by members of the so-called *Religionsgeschichtliche Schule* of Göttingen (cf. Lüdemann & Schröder 1987). Gunkel (1910), one of the pioneers in this field, proposed the hypothesis that the 'religion of the New Testament' was influenced in its origin and development by foreign religions, and that these influences were transmitted into early Christian religion through Judaism. With regard to resurrection, for example, he asserts (1910:78) that Jewish ideas about resurrection (cf. 4 Ezr. 7:29), with which the disciples were acquainted, should be understood against the background of dying and rising gods in non-Jewish religions and their influence upon Judaism. However this may be (cf. Vorster 1989c), what is noteworthy is the fact that Gunkel and others assumed that the Christian religion was influenced in its beginnings by more religions than Judaism. 'Influence', 'background', 'motifs' and parallel thoughts and statements were basic to this approach in the early days of its application to the New Testament. It was maintained that to explain any religious idea, such as resurrection, one has to study the genesis of such beliefs by comparing parallel statements and motifs in different religions.

The purpose of religio-historical investigation has, however, been redefined (cf. also Berger & Colpe 1987). It is better to define it in terms of historical understanding and explanation of what people thought and believed when they spoke about religious phenomena. The main emphasis, in other words, is not on the searching for influence and genesis. It is an attempt to study patterns of thought with a view of understanding the thought world of the New Testament; that is, the religio-historical context of New Testament thinking about religious phenomena. Not what we think about baptism or life after death, but what people in the religio-historical context of the New Testament thought about these phenomena is important. This context is very large and includes Judaism, Hellenistic religions, such as the traditional Greek and Roman religions, mystery religions and gnosticism.

Each pattern of thought, each parallel statement or tradition should be studied in its original context, its reinterpretation(s) and in its use in the New Testament in order to establish what New Testament authors tried to communicate. It is of no use, for example, simply to establish that Jews and Christians believed in life after death or that immersions occur in the Qumran community and early Christianity. What is important is what they believed. In order to determine that one needs to investigate common thought patterns very carefully. What is more, one has to take into account that ideas often develop and are reinterpreted. Although the Pharisees, for instance, were Jews, their thoughts on a particular aspect of Jewish belief need not necessarily be the same as, say, the Maccabees, who were also Jews. That is why it is so important to establish what people thought at a particular time. Even when the Old Testament is quoted or alluded to in the New Testament, it is important to determine which version was used, a Hebrew or a Greek version, since the translation of the Hebrew text into Greek was also a transformation of Hebrew thought into Greek thought.

Religio-historical criticism helps the reader of the New Testament to understand and explain New Testament religious ideas historically, that is within the context of first century religiosity.

2.2   *The New Testament and historiography*

Historical criticism also concerns the history of the life and works of Jesus and the birth and growth of the primitive church, that is, the history of the persons and events concerned. In view of the lack of other sources, the New Testament and its writings are important for the construction of the history of the period concerned. Since I have dealt with the problem elsewhere I shall largely make use of the material and arguments I have advanced in that respect (cf. Vorster 1984a). The first question we have to deal with is whether we can in any respect regard the New Testament or parts of it as history.

2.2.1 *The New Testament as history*

Very few scholars, if any, would nowadays claim that the New Testament or parts of it, which include the writings of Luke, are history books in the modern sense of the word. In spite of the fact that Luke is often regarded as a historian, albeit a Hellenistic historian (cf. Plumacher 1972), that does not mean that we can regard Luke's writings as history books of Jesus and the early beginnings of the church from Jerusalem to Rome. The following questions therefore immediately arise: What is history? And, how could Luke be regarded as a historian and his works not be history? It is often argued that there is a great difference between ancient (uncritical) historiography and 'modern' critical historiography, and that Luke as historian must be judged in terms of what can be expected of a historian of his age and not of a historian of the post-Enlightenment period (cf. Den Boer 1986; Van Unnik 1978). This is acceptable only if it does not lead to an uncritical acceptance of Luke's writings as 'factive' (historically true in the uncritical sense) and other non-canonical writings of the same kind as 'fictive'. Even in the first century historians were expected 'to say (exactly) what happened', 'to sacrifice to truth only' and to be 'fearless, incorruptible, free, a lover of free speech and the truth, as the comic poet says, calling figs figs and a boat a boat' (cf. *Lucian*, Πῶς δεῖ ἱστορίαν συγγράφειν 39, 41). Even so, there is much more to the problem than simply to accept that Luke was a Hellenistic historian who kept to the rules of Hellenistic historiography, important as the comparison between Luke and his contemporary historians may be (cf. Güttgemanns 1983).

The crux of the matter lies in the relationship between history and language, irrespective of whether we are referring to the first or the twentieth century. I am referring to the problems of language and reference, text and reality, history and truth, objectivity in history and similar matters. These are the concerns of historians of life and works of Jesus and the beginnings of Christianity.

There is no possibility of regarding the writings of the New Testament or parts of them as 'history' in the modern sense of the word. That does of course not imply that there are not historical references, historical material, artefacts, so to speak, that can be used for historical construction in the New Testament. On the contrary, the writings of the New Testament are invaluable sources for the writing of the history of Jesus and the primitive church, as we shall see below.

2.2.2   *The New Testament as a source for history*
None of the writings of the New Testament were written specifically
with a view to giving a historical survey of the words and deeds of
Jesus or the birth and growth of the church and the birth of
Christianity. And none of these present reality as it really happened.
Even Luke-Acts, which comes closest to what may be called a history of Jesus and the primitive church in the ancient sense of the
word 'history', is anything but historical in the post-Enlightenment
sense of the word. And there is no other book of the New Testament
that gives a historical survey of any person or event.

This does not imply that the writings of the New Testament cannot be used as sources for historical construction. On the contrary.
Except for a few extra-canonical writings these are the only written
sources we have to construct a history of the life and works of Jesus
and early Christian beginnings. We are limited in more than one
way. First of all there is a lack of sources and secondly our sources
are totally insufficient as far as events and persons are concerned.
What do we really know about 'the Twelve', Simon Peter, James
the brother of Jesus, James and John the sons of Zebedee, Thomas,
Joseph, Barnabas, Apollos, Paul and his helpers and the evangelists
Matthew, John, Mark and Luke? There is, however, no reason for
despair. Historical construction is in any case a painstaking undertaking in which 'fact' and 'fiction' struggle against each other in
terms of *probability*. The nature of our sources and the nature of historiography explain the diversity in approaches and findings about
Jesus and the origins of Christianity, including the history of the
early period of the church.

The reasons why people are interested in historical construction
and the purpose for which it is done are not always the same. This
can be illustrated by the interest in the historical Jesus with regard
to the so-called Old and New Quests. In the Old Quest people were
interested in reconstructing the life of 'Jesus of Nazareth as he actually was' by means of the 'objective historical method' of the nineteenth century. 'Jesus of Nazareth' thus became the synonym for
'the historical Jesus' because the two terms coincided. As Robinson
(1983:28) observes, 'For the twentieth century this is no longer obvious', because of a new view on the nature of history and the possibilities of reconstruction. In view of this, the term 'historical Jesus'
came to refer to 'what can be known of Jesus of Nazareth by means
of scientific methods of the historian' (Robinson 1983:29), that is,

'the historian's Jesus'. The 'historical Jesus' of the New Quest is therefore no longer 'Jesus of Nazareth as he actually was', since the hope to reconstruct such a Jesus is fiction. The history of Jesus survived only a *kerygma*. For this reason and also because of the historian's own historicity,

> ... it is easy to see that all that Jesus actually was is not likely to be fully grasped, objectively demonstrated and definitely stated by historical research in any given period (Robinson 1983:30).

The New Quest was, in view of the aforesaid, never intended as a renewed attempt to restore Jesus of Nazareth as he actually was. The purpose of the New Quest was: '... to test the validity of the *kerygma's* identification of *its* understanding of existence with Jesus' existence' (Robinson 1983:94). Or to put it differently, to test the continuity between the historical Jesus and the *kerygma* that we find in the New Testament (cf. Bultmann 1965:6ff.). In order to avoid docetism, a New Quest was necessitated, it was argued, because the *kerygma* was concerned about the historicity of Jesus—the relation between the message of Jesus of Nazareth and the *kerygma* of the church.

It is clear from both these quests that historical inquiry was not and cannot be the foundation of Christian faith. It is not on the ground of the historicity of any matter mentioned in the New Testament that Christians believe. If the purpose of historical interpretation is regarded as the search for reasons to believe, historical investigation becomes disastrous. It is the *kerygma* of the church which forms the basis of faith, not historicity. On the other hand, one should keep in mind that 'historical events' seem to be very important to many post-Enlightenment Christians. Not everybody will be willing to accept Lessing's statement that *accidental truths of history can never become proof of necessary truths of reason* (cf. Peters 1977:229–34; Hartlich 1978:467–84). For many historical investigation provides confidence.

The difficulties of historiography concerning Jesus and the birth of the church, can further be illustrated by current investigations about Jesus. One of the problems with the gospel tradition, as we have seen, is the different contexts, forms and wording in which the Jesus tradition was transmitted. This is specifically true of the sayings of Jesus. One of the pioneers in the field of establishing the exact wording (*ipsissima verba*) of the sayings of Jesus was J. Jeremias, a New Testament scholar of Göttingen. He and others developed so-called criteria for the authenticity of the sayings of Jesus. In spite of these criteria and recent attempts to refine and improve these criteria (cf. Boring 1988), there is little consensus about what Jesus really said and how many of the sayings that bear his name in the Gospels are original. The problem is further complicated by the fact that it is clear that it will never be possible to construct the actual contexts of communication of the sayings of Jesus completely. Since the sayings are often transmitted in different contexts of communication by the evangelists, it is probable that the original contexts are lost for ever. On the other hand, since historiography is about probabilities and interpretation, possible frameworks for the teaching can be constructed, and has been done successfully. This is illustrated by the conviction that eschatology is an important formative factor in the teaching of Jesus, and especially with regard to his teaching about the kingdom of God.

Because of the difficulties mentioned, E.P. Sanders (1985), approached the problem of the life and works of Jesus from another perspective by focusing on the indisputable facts in the life of Jesus. These are:

1 Jesus was baptized by John the Baptist.
2 Jesus was a Galilean who preached and healed.
3 Jesus called disciples and spoke of their being twelve.
4 Jesus confined his activity to Israel.
5 Jesus engaged in a controversy about the temple.
6 Jesus was crucified outside Jerusalem by the Roman authorities.
7 After his death Jesus' followers continued as an identifiable movement.
8 At least some Jews persecuted at least parts of the new movement.

(Sanders 1985:11)

This is an improvement on the emphasis normally put on the sayings material, since the evidence is at least more secure for these so-called facts, and because it opens the field of inquiry. The problem, however, is that these facts are not self-explanatory and self-interpreting. They still have to be interpreted and put into a framework of understanding. That explains why D.J. Harrington (1987:36) has recently drawn attention to

seven different images of Jesus that have been proposed by scholars
in recent years, the differences relating to the different Jewish backgrounds against which they have chosen to locate their image of the
historical Jesus.

These images include Jesus the Jew being any of the following: an
eschatological prophet, a political revolutionary, a magician, a Hillelite
or proto-Pharisee, an Essene, a Galilean charismatic or a Galilean
rabbi. These images are the result of historical investigation and underscore the difficulties of constructing an image of Jesus of Nazareth.

Similar problems exist with regard to other aspects of the history
of the birth and growth of the church. Our sources are scanty and
insufficient. What are the roots of the church in Egypt, for example?
Who were the first Christians in Rome and other centres in Asia
Minor? Who were the so-called opponents of Paul? These and many
other questions of importance for historians can be answered only
partly. Suffice it to indicate that historical criticism is a challenging
and an important endeavour of New Testament scholars to understand the sources and the beginnings of Christianity.

Historical construction is, however, not limited to historical fac-
ticity, as many would have it. The purpose of historical construction is to provide a background against which the writings of the
New Testament can be read—and is read knowingly or unknow-
ingly. Those who think that Christianity formed a monolithic unity
from the beginning are sometimes stunned by the discovery that the
New Testament contains diverse ideas about such important things
as Christology. We have already noticed above how important the
priority of one or other Gospel is for the development of ideas in
early Christianity. Part of the history of the primitive church is the
sequence and order of events from Jesus to the evangelists and from
the early apostles to Paul and eventually to his followers. That is
why it is necessary to construct the history of the church and what
the early Christians thought.

Although we do not have an exact picture of the early history of
Christianity, it is usually held that primitive Christianity first became
a Jewish sect. Afterwards it became largely Gentile under the influence
of Hellenism. This vague outline has to be filled out by constructions of the birth process and growth of a religious movement, but
also of a thought process, namely the doctrine and beliefs of that
movement. It is traditionally being done in terms of Judaism versus
Hellenism. This is obviously an oversimplification, as recent studies

on the spread and influence of Hellenism have shown (cf. Vorster 1981b:48–52). Despite the limited sources, our insights develop by testing the validity of hypotheses, revisiting old problems and applying new methods.

During the last two decades historians of the New Testament era have approached a number of problems of historical nature afresh by using insights of other disciplines such as sociology and anthropology. Although this has advanced research, the main problem that confronts us is the lack of sources. Many of these studies have broadened our vision and have stimulated scholars to rethink old axioms (cf. Theissen 1977). Even the study of the social history of New Testament times has profited from these new impulses (cf. Meeks 1983). In addition, much has been done to unlock the world of the New Testament in terms of archaeology of the ancient world. There seems to be a growing interest in archaeological evidence from Palestine and elsewhere and slowly, but surely a new picture of the social history of early Christianity is formed (cf. e.g. Lampe 1987).

3. *Conclusion*

In conclusion, it is important to address a few important aspects of historiography—ideas about which have changed through the ages. I am referring to matters such as history and language, history and truth, and history and objectivity. We have already noticed with regard to the Old and New Quests that the purpose of historiography is different in the two approaches. Insights into the nature of historiography, and therefore also historical criticism, develop and change, and it is important for New Testament scholars to take note of these changes. The first question we have to address is what happens when 'facts' are described? Do we have a verbal representation or imitation of reality?

A history book does not offer a one-to-one correspondence between object and description, because language does not work in that way. What does it then offer? Historians normally select and arrange their material with respect to change in space and time. Historical description, in other words, is nothing else than narrative, human construction of past events and persons. Lévi Strauss's idea that history is never only *history of*, but always *history for* in the sense of being written with some ideological view in mind, is very attractive. He

argues that to historise any structure, to write history, is to mythol-
ogise it (cf. White 1975:51). If history is a kind of narrative and narrative is the remaking of reality, matters such as text and reality,
historical truth and objectivity become very interesting. Remaking of
reality is not reality *an sich*.

What is historical truth? Truth is very often regarded as *correspondence*
between an idea and an object,

> . . . a statement is true if it corresponds to the facts, that is, if the state-
> ment expresses a relation which holds between the real object sym-
> bolized by those terms (cf. Gilliam 1976:244).

On the other hand truth can also be explained in terms of *coherence*,
'. . . the locus of truth is internal to the world of historical idea, and
its criterion is coherence'. Consider the following examples. The resurrection of Jesus is a historical truth only if he really had been
raised from the dead (correspondence theory). Likewise the miracle
stories can only be true if they really happened. We soon run into
trouble with such a view of truth. What about the speeches in Acts
and elsewhere in the New Testament (cf. the Sermon on the Mount!)?
Are they true in the sense of a correspondence theory? Certainly
not. But Lucian (πῶς δεῖ ἱστορίαν συγγράφειν, 58) already reminds
us that,

> If a person has to be introduced to make a speech, it is especially
> important that his language suits his person and the subject, and that
> he speaks as clearly as possible.

'Factive' and 'fictive' are very misleading terms when it comes to
historical truth and history as the remaking of reality. This has been
realised long ago by ancient authors like Quintilian and Cicero (cf.
Güttgemanns 1983:16ff.).

Objectivity in historiography is related to the problem of historical truth because it also depends on one's views about historiography and philosophy of history. Because history is narrative, and
narrative is told from a certain perspective for a specific purpose,
one can hardly speak of objectivity in the sense of a correspondence
theory. On the other hand, however, the historian is a member of
a 'scientific community' and his findings and his narrative have to
comply with the rules of the game. His results are subjected to control and scrutiny, and in that sense a 'set of rules' confirms its objectivity (cf. Nipperdey 1979:329–42; Junker & Reisinger 1974:1–46;
Rüsen 1980:188–98).

These few introductory remarks illustrate the difficulties and the importance of historical criticism in the process of understanding and interpreting the writings of the New Testament. Historical criticism has come to stay. What changes are our insights into the nature of literature, history and historiography. That is why each reader of the New Testament, but especially New Testament scholars have to face the challenges of discovering the past of which Jesus of Nazareth, the birth of Christianity, and the history of early Christian writings form an important part, in order to discover the truth of their own existence.

CHAPTER SIX

THE RELIGIO-HISTORICAL CONTEXT OF THE RESURRECTION OF JESUS AND RESURRECTION FAITH IN THE NEW TESTAMENT

1. *Resurrection and History of Religion: Early Beginnings and Current Aims*

At the turn of the century, religio-historical study of the New Testament was stimulated by a series of studies by members of the so-called *Religionsgeschichtliche Schule of Göttingen* (see Lüdemann & Schröder 1987). In his seminal publication *Zum religionsgeschichtlichen Verständnis des Neuen Testaments* Herman Gunkel (1910:77) argues that the resurrection and ascension of Jesus, which belong together, are the opposite of the descent into hell, and that both conceptions are mythological. Jesus Christ, he maintains, was not the first and only being of divine character who was believed to have risen from the dead. On the contrary, faith in the dying and rising of gods was common in the Near East. This phenomenon was known in Egypt in the first instance, where it was a common belief, as well as in Babylonia, Syria, and Phoenicia. In Crete the grave of Zeus of Crete can be visited to this day; obviously the grave is empty (Gunkel 1910:77).

Gunkel (1910:77ff.) maintains that the disciples' belief in the resurrection of Jesus was influenced by conceptions, from religions other than mainstream official Judaism, about the rising of gods after death. It is of importance for the purpose of our study to give a short summary of Gunkel's argument, both from the perspective of methodology and with regard to the relevance of religio-historical material for the understanding of resurrection and resurrection faith.

The hypothesis that the 'religion of the New Testament' was influenced in its origin and development by foreign religions and that these influences were transmitted into early Christian religion through Judaism is of paramount importance for the understanding of Gunkel's views (1910:1). With regard to resurrection, he asserts (1910:78) that the Jewish ideas about resurrection (see 4 Ezr. 7:29) with which the disciples were acquainted should be understood against

the background of dying and rising gods in non-Jewish religions and
their influence upon Judaism. With this in mind he investigates the
background of resurrection motifs in the New Testament.

First there is the date of the discovery and announcement of the
resurrection of Jesus. According to our sources, it happened on *Easter
Sunday at the rising of the sun* (see Mk. 16:8parr). The fact that this
date coincides with the important Sunday on which the sun rises
after winter, which was most probably regarded as the day of the
rising of the gods, is probably an indication that early Christians
borrowed the date of the 'day of the resurrection' from ancient Near
Eastern beliefs (Gunkel 1910:79).

Even more important is the motif of 'after three days' or its variant 'on the third day'. The value attached to this motif is seen in
its repetition in early Christian sources and its inclusion in the
Apostolic Creed. Gunkel (1910:79ff.) regards it as one of the first
dogmas which the early Christians derived from other religions. He
traces it back through the story of Jonah in the fish, the motif of
three and a half periods in Daniel, to similar and parallel motifs and
ideas in the history of other religions (see also Leipoldt 1988:289ff.).
This material gives an explanation for the importance given to the
three day motif in the resurrection of Jesus by early Christians. They
borrowed the idea from other religions through their Jewish heritage. Gunkel (1910:82) concludes that the material not only explains
the importance of the motif with regard to the resurrection of Jesus,
but also that there was a belief in the death and resurrection of the
messiah in Jewish syncretistic circles before Jesus. After the death of
Jesus, his disciples made use of extant conceptions about death and
resurrection to interpret his death.

Paul's teaching on baptism (Rm. 6) is also clearly based on the
idea of dying and rising: from death to resurrection. Baptism is a
symbol of the Christian's dying and rising with Christ. Gunkel
(1910:84) compares this to the myth of the Egyptian god Osiris who
was killed and rose from death and he considers that this gave rise
to resurrection hope. By being united with his/her god, the believer
can be assured that it is possible to obtain eternal life through death.
Gunkel (1910:82f.) maintains:

> Die historische frage is demnach nicht, wie der Glaue und die Aufer-
> stehung überhaupt entstanden ist, . . . sondern das eigentliche Problem
> ist das engere: wie es möglich gewesen ist, den Glauben an die Aufer-
> stehung auf die Person Jesus, des schimpflich am Kreuz hingerichteten
> Jesus zu übertragen.

These few remarks sufficiently illustrate the assumptions, presuppositions and approach of Gunkel in studying the resurrection of Jesus from a religio-historical perspective. 'Influence', 'background', 'motifs' and parallel thoughts and statements, are basic to Gunkel's approach. To explain resurrection and resurrection faith in the New Testament from a religio-historical perspective is to study the genesis of such beliefs by comparing parallel statements and motifs in different religions. Gunkel did not, however, speak the last word on this subject.

In an equally important study entitled *Sterbende und auferstehende Götter*, Leipoldt (1923; see also 1988) takes the issue of the myths of dying and rising gods a little further by drawing attention to both similarities and differences between these myths and the narratives about Jesus. Despite the similarities there are important differences, according to Leipoldt. Most important is the fact that Jesus is never understood in the New Testament in terms of the nature gods who die and rise like the plants of nature; secondly, he did not have a divine female partner; and thirdly, unlike the dying and rising gods, he was not raised by a miracle worker. This does not detract from the fact that Christian narratives about the empty tomb and the christophany narratives of Jesus contain motifs which also occur in narratives about dying and rising gods and resurrection stories of the Hellenistic and Roman periods. Like Gunkel, Leipoldt (1988:290ff.) draws attention to the three day motif, but adds a number of significant motifs in the New Testament narratives about Jesus which can be explained religio-historically.

Leipoldt proceeds from the assumption that the resurrection of Jesus as experienced by his disciples is totally foreign to Jewish thought and can only be explained from a non-Jewish religio-historical background. Since the days of Gunkel and Leipoldt and the many other studies on the possible influence of the mystery religions upon the development of New Testament thought (see Wedderburn 1987: 90–163), the religio-historical investigation of the resurrection of Jesus has become much more complicated. While Gunkel argues that the influence of other religions on Christianity can be traced through Judaism, Leipoldt prefers to explain the differences and similarities without the mediation of Judaism, because in his view the resurrection of Jesus was totally incomprehensible for a Jew.

We have to remember that the days of Gunkel and Leipoldt were the childhood days of the religio-historical approach to the New Testament. This explains why after almost a century of scholarship most of Gunkel's explanations and intuitions concerning the dying

and rising motif as the context within which resurrection and resurrection faith in the New Testament are to be understood, have
become problematic (see e.g. Wedderburn 1987). His assumptions
on how phenomena such as resurrection should be studied from a
religio-historical point of view have also been challenged (see Paulsen
1978; K. Müller 1985). On the other hand, it has become clear that
Gunkel was correct in arguing that belief in resurrection is not a
unique Christian phenomenon. Long before this phenomenon was
related to Jesus, there were people who believed that death was not
the end and that the body would be revived after death. To understand resurrection and resurrection faith in the New Testament historically, one needs first to understand the religio-historical context
in which these conceptions functioned. This implies more than noting correspondence between motifs in different religions and searching for the roots of the New Testament idea of resurrection, however
important these might be. It also implies understanding the religio-
historical context of phenomena and their explanation within such
a possible context.

The question of whether the resurrection of Jesus and resurrection faith can be explained against the background of the dying and
rising of gods will be dealt with below. A few words about the purpose of this study and the position taken will now be in order.

The purpose of a religio-historical investigation of phenomena such
as the resurrection of Jesus and resurrection faith in the New Testament
is to try to understand and explain historically what people thought
and believed when they spoke about these phenomena. This essay
is not concerned with the genesis of Easter faith in the first instance.
It is also not a study in parallel statements and 'events' in other religions just for the sake of parallels. Patterns of thought will be studied with a view to understanding the thought world of the New
Testament; that is, the religio-historical context of New Testament
thinking about the resurrection. Furthermore, it is not concerned
with the influence of other religions on the formation of resurrection and resurrection faith in early Christianity as such. It is a study
about the beliefs of people who lived in the times of the genesis of
New Testament writings and about the distinctive elements, if any,
in their thoughts on resurrection. To get a clearer picture of the
religio-historical context of resurrection and resurrection faith in the
New Testament, special attention will be paid to resurrection beliefs
in the first century as well as before the New Testament. Since this

material has been studied repeatedly in the past, I will limit my discussion to the possible religio-historical context of interpretation without detailed discussions of all the problems involved. Space does not allow this.

Since the ancients, like ourselves, had many views about life after death, it is necessary to say at the outset what is meant by 'resurrection' in this essay. 'Resurrection' refers to the revival of the body of a human being, that is, man as a whole, into a new existence after a period of death. It is not concerned with any other ideas about life after death, such as immortality or reincarnation. It is only in Zoroastrianism, Judaism, Christianity and Islam that this phenomenon is found; although some would argue that there are analogies to resurrection in Chinese Taoism and also in ancient Indian and Egyptian religions (see Ringgren 1987:344).

2. Jewish Beliefs about Resurrection Before the New Testament

Given the limits of this essay, it is impossible to do much more in this section than to give a survey of beliefs in resurrection in a few relevant texts from the period and to explain where they come from and how they function.

2.1   Origins of resurrection faith in Israel

Although it is sometimes argued that there are indications of resurrection faith in Israel in documents as old as the ninth century BCE (see Greenspoon 1981), it is generally maintained that resurrection was a newcomer on the scene of Israelite religion (see Nickelsburg 1972). It would take too long to go into detailed arguments about the possible origins of the Israelite belief in resurrection. A few words about the matter, will, nevertheless, be in order.

Greenspoon (1981) maintains that despite the absence of direct textual evidence, the origin of resurrection faith lies in the idea of YHWH as the Divine Warrior who rules over nature, chaos and death, and in the belief that his followers are incorporated into his kingship of victory over death. The three resurrection or resuscitation stories in the Elijah and Elisha cycles (ninth to eighth centuries), namely the stories of the son of the widow of Zarephtath (1 Ki. 17:17–24), the son of the wealthy woman in Shunem near Megiddo

(2 Ki. 4:18–21; 33–37) and the story of the man who came into
contact with the bones of Elisha (2 Ki. 4:18–21, 32–37), are stories
about resurrection set in this world. These resurrections resulted in
the revival of the bodies of three persons after death and their rein-
troduction into the same human society. According to Greenspoon
(1981:319), these stories are associated with YHWH as the Divine
Warrior and there are early indications of resurrection faith in the
Northern Kingdom.

Greenspoon furthermore develops his argument about the association of the theme of YHWH as Divine Warrior and resurrection
faith in Israel through the vision of Ezekiel 37 concerning the national
resurrection of Israel, the apocalypse of Isaiah and material from
Trito-Isaiah through Daniel. In Daniel, however, the scope of the
process of resurrection is limited to the righteous who will awaken
to be vindicated and rewarded.

Quite a different approach is taken by those scholars who find
the origins of Judaic resurrection faith in Iranian Zoroastrianism (see
Barr 1985). Zoroastrianism has a fully developed doctrine of the resurrection of all mankind (see *Bundahishn* 34). Resurrection is associated with judgement of the good and the evil deeds of man which
will be revealed when all mankind is resurrected and gathered for
judgement. The righteous will be rewarded with the bliss of entering paradise, while sinners will be punished (see Ringgren 1987:345).
This is not the place to go into detail about the scholarly discussions of the Iranian influence on Judaism, and for that matter on
Christianity, concerning resurrection faith. Suffice it to say that the
development of conceptions such as angels, dualism, eschatology, and
resurrection is surprising, at least in theory; for the Jews lived about
two centuries under the *pax Persica*, and some of their most important books were written in that time' (J. Barr 1985:201).

A variety of other texts, the dating and origin of which are obscure,
are often taken into account in discussions about the origin and
development of resurrection faith in the Old Testament. I am referring here to texts such as Psalms 16, 49 and 73, as well to the apocalypse of Isaiah 25–26, which is probably a post-exilic text and
appears to be one of the earliest texts of Israel to express the hope
of the resurrection of the righteous. They will arise, while the oppressors will remain dead (Is. 26:14–19. See Greenspoon 1981:284). The
locus classicus is, however, a text from Daniel. Let us now turn to
Daniel 12.

2.2   *Daniel 12:3*

> Many of those who sleep in the dust of the earth will wake, some to
> everlasting life and some to the reproach of eternal abhorrence (*NEB*).

The wording of Daniel 12:2 closely parallels Isaiah 26:19 as Nickelsburg (1972:17) has clearly indicated. Chapters 26–27 of Isaiah deal
with the restoration of Israel, and the reference to dead bodies which
will rise should be taken figuratively. Daniel goes beyond this, however. Nickelsburg (1972:19) correctly observes:

> For Isaiah the resurrection of the righteous is in itself vindication for
> the righteous. For Daniel resurrection is a means by which both the
> righteous and the wicked dead are enabled to receive their respective
> vindication or condemnation.

The author of Daniel envisages a bodily resurrection of some of
those who were dead. He is not thinking of a universal resurrection
for judgement; many, not everybody, will rise. Interestingly the LXX
translates the Hebrew word for 'awake' by ἀναστήσονται (see Theo-
dotion ἐξεγερθήσονται, a term which is also used in the New Testament
for resurrection.

The Book of Daniel was written between 167 and 165 BCE, during the persecution of pious Jews and the destruction of the cult in
Jerusalem by Antiochus Epiphanes (see W.H. Schmidt 1982:287).
Daniel 12:3 forms part of the apocalypse in chapters 10–12. The
apocalypse describes the events in the history of Israel to the persecution by Antiochus and his end (10–11:45). It reaches its climax
in a short description of the judgement in 12:1–3.

Daniel 12:1–3 is a response to the course of the events of the
Maccabean revolt when the righteous suffered because they adhered
to the law, while the unrighteous prospered, even at the cost of the
righteous. It was a consolation for people who had suffered terribly.
It is also the only clear reference to resurrection hope in the Hebrew
canon, although there are other passages from this canon which have
been interpreted in the course of history from the perspective of resurrection (*BerR* 14 and *WayyR* 14. See also Lapide 1983:44ff.).

2.3   *2 Maccabees 7*

The second Maccabean history was most probably written during
the period from 125–63 BCE (see Attridge 1984:177). This book

concerns the caring love of God for his people by rewarding the pious and punishing the impious. Antiochus Epiphanes and Nicanor are portrayed as the opponents of God and his people by their disregard for God and his law. The pious suffer at the hands of the adversaries of God. They are, however, encouraged by their belief in future resurrection.

In chapter 7, an interesting legend about the martyrdom of seven courageous young men and their mother is related. The young men and their mother are commanded by Antiochus to eat pork and thus to disobey the law of their God. On their refusal they are tortured in the most brutal way. In vivid language the torture and suffering of the boys are described. Courageously they speak their minds and confess their hope of resurrection. The destruction of their bodies will simply lead to their resurrection by '. . . the King of the universe who will raise us up to a life everlastingly made new' (2 Mac. 7:9). One after the other they are tortured. In answer to his own suffering, one of the boys' response is that there will be no resurrection to life for the torturer (verse 14). Instead there will be torment for the torturer and also for his descendants (verse 17). In the end, after all seven are killed, the mother says:

> You appeared in my womb, I know not how; it was not I who gave you life and breath and set in order your bodily frames. It is the Creator of the universe who moulds man at his birth and plans the origin of all things. Therefore, he, in his mercy, will give you back life again, since now you put his laws above all thought of self (*NEB*).

The most striking thing about this legend is the fact that the youths are the suffering servants of the Lord, whose deeds will be vindicated. The theme of retaliation is characteristic of the thought structure of the book (Stemberger 1972:17). The legend is a clear example of resurrection hope in Israel during the second century. The function of resurrection is to compensate for the lack of divine judgement in this world. It is also a reward for the deeds of the young martyrs in the legend who suffer for the sake of God!

2.4   *Psalms of Solomon*

Eschatological hope for the individual is also a theme in the Psalms of Solomon. These psalms are the product of a Jewish community of the first century (BCE) 'bound together by persecution and hope for the future' (R.B. Wright 1985:641). Eternal destruction is the fate of the sinner, whereas the righteous can hope for eternal life because God looks after the righteous in spite of their sufferings.

> The destruction of the sinner is forever,
> and he will not be remembered when (God) looks after the righteous.
> This is the share of sinners forever,
> but those who fear the Lord shall rise up to eternal life,
> and their life shall be in the Lord's light, and it shall never end
> (PssSol 4:10; see 13:11; 14:10, Wright's translation).

In the Psalms of Solomon, resurrection functions as a recompense for the suffering of the righteous. They will be rewarded by eternal life after the 'day of mercy', while sinners will be punished. Similar ideas about resurrection and judgement are also found in the Testaments of the twelve patriarchs (see TBenj. 10:5–11) and in 1 Enoch (see 1 En. 22–27; 92–105). It should however, be noted that in the Psalms of Solomon, unlike in Daniel, resurrection is only for the righteous. It is not a general resurrection for judgement (see Dn. 12:2; 2 Mac. 7:9; 2 Bar. 30:1–5; 4 Ezr. 7:32 etc.).

Nickelsburg (1972:124) correctly observes that faith in resurrection has different functions in Jewish texts written before the Christian Era. In Daniel and in 2 Maccabees, God will raise the righteous because they suffer unjustly for his sake. This is not the case in 1 Enoch where God raises the dead simply because they suffer unjustly, not because they suffer for he sake of God. Resurrection is also not the answer to unjust death. 'It speaks to the problem of *suffering* and *oppression*, even when it has not resulted in death' (Nikelsburg 1972:124). In the Testament of Benjamin 10:5–11, resurrection encompasses *all*, not only the persecuted righteous.

It is difficult to determine whether the Qumran community had specific views about resurrection. Scholars differ about the interpretation of the relevant texts. The fact that members of the community were buried in a north-south direction points to the belief that paradise is in the north and that the community believed in the resurrection of the dead (see Stemberger 1979:445).

Strikingly different from belief in resurrection of the body of the righteous martyrs is the development of the idea of the immortality of the soul in 4 Maccabees and in the Wisdom of Solomon. Both these books most probably come from the first century of the Christian Era (see H. Anderson 1985:533ff.; Gilbert 1984:312). In 4 Maccabees, resurrection of the body is replaced by immortality and eternal life, beginning at the moment of death (see 7:3; 9:22; 13:17; 14:5–6; 15:3 etc.). The Wisdom of Solomon also deals with immortality. It is God's gift to the righteous, already during their earthly life (see SapSol 1:12–16).

Although textual evidence for the belief in resurrection in Judaism before the birth of Christianity might seem scanty and perhaps even minimal, one should not disregard the entire context of religious thought about afterlife. It is during this period that there was an important development in messianism in Israel. Although there had been an expectation of a better future for Israel in the older prophets, messianic hope and hope about the future of the world, not only for Israel, underwent radical changes (see Schürer 1979:429ff.). The socio-political and religious contexts of the period before the birth of Christianity gave rise to a totally new eschatology in which the individual and his/her life after death played an important role.

3. First Century Beliefs in Resurrection

3.1 Resurrection faith in first century Palestine

Both Jewish and other documents display a diversity in beliefs about life after death in first century Palestine, in spite of the similarities with the beliefs we discussed in Section 2 of this essay. This is apparent from what the New Testament and Josephus say about the beliefs of the Sadducees and the Pharisees, for example, concerning resurrection.

3.1.1 Pharisees and Sadducees on resurrection
The short controversy story in Mark 12:18–27, which in its present form is probably not original (e.g. verse 26. See Bultmann 1970:25; 1974:24; Gnilka 1979:156ff.), tells of the conflict between Jesus and the Sadducees about resurrection. According to the narrative commentary of Mark in verse 18, the Sadducees are 'those who argue that there is no resurrection'. Mark uses the word ἀνάστασιν for 'resurrection'. This view of the Sadducees is supported by Luke. He also maintains that the Sadducees did not believe in the resurrection (Ac. 4:1f.; 23:6–8). According to Luke, Paul defended his position as a Pharisee in his defence before the council in Jerusalem.

Luke's description of the beliefs of the Sadducees corresponds with that of Mark. He uses exactly the same words as Mark quoted above (Ac. 23:8), but adds that they also say that there '. . . are no angels, or spirits, but the Pharisees believe in all three' (*TEV*). This addition of Luke is significant since in Mark 12:25 it is narrated that Jesus said: 'For when the dead are raised, men and women will not marry, but they will be like angels in heaven'. Apparently it was believed in some Jewish circles by the end of the first century that the resurrected become angels or angel like. This view is also found in 2 Baruch 51:10:

> For they will live in the heights of that world and they will be like angels and be equal to the stars (Klijn 1983:638).

Josephus' description of the beliefs of the Sadducees and the Pharisees is different in some respects from that of the New Testament (*BJ* 2.162–66; *Ant.* 18.13–17). According to him the Pharisees maintained that the soul is imperishable, and that only the souls of the good pass into another body, that is, to a new life. The souls of the wicked suffer eternal punishment. Reward or punishment await those who have led lives of virtue or of vice 'under the earth' (*Ant.* 18.14). The Sadducees on the other hand believed that the soul perishes with the body. Josephus (*Ant.* 18.8) also asserts that the Essenes believed in the immortality of the soul. Unlike the New Testament, he does not mention resurrection directly. He discusses the beliefs of the different groups about life after death from the perspective of body/soul. Both the New Testament and Josephus agree that the Sadducees did not believe in life after death.

What the Pharisees actually believed in the time of Jesus is difficult to say because of the nature of our sources. Later sources claim that the chief Pharisaic schools of Hillel and Shammai believed in bodily resurrection at the beginning of the first century (see Strack & Billerbeck 1969:1172). It is clear from the Rabbinic literature that Rabbinic Judaism developed a complete doctrine of resurrection (see Stemberger 1979:446ff.). In the end, the views of the Sadducees about life after death were totally rejected and replaced by the development of Pharisaic beliefs.

3.1.2   *2 Baruch and 4 Ezra*

By the end of the first century (CE) and the beginning of the second, different aspects of eschatological speculation had developed both in Judaism and in Christianity (see the Revelation of John). This is clearly illustrated in 2 Baruch and 4 Ezra. Although both books were probably written early in the second century (see Klijn 1983:616f.; Metzger 1983:520) as responses to the fall of Jerusalem, I include them under the heading of first century beliefs because they illustrate the development in eschatological speculation during the first and second centuries.

The fall of Jerusalem played an important role in the development of eschatology in Judaism. The hope of a new world and a new heaven, based on Isaiah 65:17 and 66:22, is one of these beliefs (see Schürer 1979:537ff.). Two views concerning the start of the new world were propagated. According to some it would begin at the start of the messianic age (see 1 En. 45:5), while others maintained that it would start at the end of the messianic age (see 4 Ezr.). In 2 Baruch the messianic age is placed between this world and the world to come (2 Bar. 74:2–3; see Schürer 1979:537f. for detail). Speculation about the new world obviously also included speculation about what would happen in this new world. It is in this connection that resurrection plays a role.

According to 2 Baruch, the present corrupt age will be followed by the judgement of God after which there will be an everlasting incorruptible age. The last judgement will be preceded by a general resurrection of the dead (see 2 Bar. 30:1–5; 50:1). The souls of the dead are kept in 'treasuries' in the realm of death (Sheol. See 2 Bar. 21:23; 30:2–5). The dead will be raised in their original form so that those who knew them previously can recognise them (2 Bar. 50:2–4). Then the judgement of the Lord will take place. The wicked will first see how the righteous are freed from the limitations of the corrupt age and receive the splendour of the incorruptible age before they themselves go away to be tormented (2 Bar. 51:6). The righteous will enjoy the glory of paradise.

The views of the author of 4 Ezra on resurrection are closely related to those of the author of 2 Baruch. During the interval between death and resurrection the souls are kept in 'chambers' or 'dwellings' (4 Ezr. 4:35) where the righteous experience a preliminary state of peace and blessedness, while the souls of the wicked are tormented in a place apart from those of the righteous (see 4 Ezr. 7:75–107. Here 'spirit' is used). There they will remain until the ressurection for the final judgement. The function of resurrection is also to reward or punish one's deeds. The righteous will enter the glory of paradise, while 'Hell' is the place of torture for the wicked. In both books the purpose of resurrection is not participation in the messianic kingdom, but judgement, reward and punishment.

3.1.3 *Summary*

There was no uniform doctrine of afterlife in Palestinian Judaism during the first century. But resurrection was undoubtedly one of the important views among Jews. The dominant conception of resurrection in first century Judaism in Palestine was most probably a realistic one: a restitution of the body. After judgement there will be a general resurrection for judgement. The righteous will be rewarded for their deeds and the wicked will be punished. These ideas are on the one hand a continuation of those found in Daniel; but on the other hand they are also the development of speculation about the nature of resurrection which found its climax in the second century in both Judaism and Christianity. Spiritual or symbolic resurrection played no role (see Wedderburn 1987:173ff.). The Sadducees rejected the idea of resurrection and so did the Samaritans (see Ferguson 1987:439), while Hellenistic Jews and those under their influence believed in the immortality of the soul (see *4 Mac; Jub; SapSol; Philo*).

3.2 *Resurrection faith in the Graeco-Roman world?*

It is often said that the Graeco-Roman world was familiar with the phenomenon of resurrection from the 'dying and rising gods', and that Christian resurrection faith was influenced by its environment (see Braun 1969:27, 154). Lack of space makes it impossible to go into detail, but a few remarks are nevertheless necessary.

Belief in the dying and rising of gods was probably widespread in the Mediterranean world of the first century. One has, however, to be very clear about definitions, and about the understanding of the resurrection of Jesus by people from the Graeco-Roman world. As to the definition of resurrection in terms of the dying and rising of gods, it seems that Jewish and Christian understanding of the revival of a body after death is not precisely the same as the revivification of Osiris to become the ruler of the dead or as the resuscitation of Adonis (see Wedderburn 1987:190ff.). On the other hand, would people from the Graeco-Roman world not have understood the resurrection of Jesus in exactly the same way as the myths mentioned? This is most probable. It is good to remind ourselves that the church

Fathers understood the fate of Tammuz and Adonis, for example, as death and resurrection (see Wedderburn 1987:200ff. for detail).

Belief in the possibility of the revival of a dead person is illustrated by different narratives from the Graeco-Roman world about people who were resuscitated (see Leipoldt 1988:290ff.). In this sense one can speak of resurrection faith. The function of these stories is to illustrate the miraculous. In the discussion of the New Testament below I will go into more detail.

The Graeco-Roman world had definite ideas about afterlife (see Ferguson 1987:195ff.). At the death of a person, the soul let the body and departed to a cavity under the earth. It was believed that the soul was immortal, and this belief was later combined with resurrection faith in the Christian tradition. Immortality of the soul and resurrection are, however, not the same.

These few remarks are sufficient to indicate that I am not of the opinion that resurrection and resurrection faith in the New Testament can be understood or explained against the background of Graeco-Roman beliefs. This does not mean that beliefs from that world did not mediate the message of early Christians about the resurrection to non-Jews. That is, however, another matter.

4. *Conclusion*

It is now left to consider how resurrection and resurrection faith in the New Testament fit into the material discussed in the previous sections.

The whole of the New Testament was written from a post-resurrection perspective. In almost every writing there is an indiction of the importance attached to the resurrection of Jesus and to resurrection faith, in spite of the fact that the New Testament clearly says that NOBODY witnessed the resurrection of Jesus. The New Testament offers us a picture of resurrection faith and not of the event of the resurrection of Jesus (see however the story of Lazarus in Jn. 11 and the raising miracles in Mk. 5 and Lk. 7). It was believed that Jesus was raised from the dead, and as a consequence that those who believe in him will also be raised after death to live a new life. The different versions of the empty tomb narrative; the christophanies; the belief in the fact that God can raise a body from death, that he raised Jesus from the dead, and that because of the resurrection of Jesus those who believe in Christ will also be raised, all form the backbone of what the New Testament has to say about resurrection and what early Christians believed. The major emphasis is on the conviction that in the resurrection of Jesus, God started the eschatological process. His resurrection is the guarantee that those who have died will also be raised.

The New Testament furthermore displays the same diversity in conceptions concerning resurrection and resurrection faith as Judaism (see 1 Th. 4:16ff.; Rv. 20:5, 6). The same expectation of the renewal of the world which we found in Judaism is also present in early Christianity (see Mt. 19:28; 2 Pt. 3:13; Rv. 21:1). There seems to be an expectation of the immediate transfer of the just to haven (see Lk. 23:43; 2 Cor. 5:8; Phlp. 1:23; Ac. 7:59; Rv. 6:9ff.; 7:9ff.). The New Testament also teaches the judgement of God, and in this respect these ideas can also be linked to those of Judaism (see Jn. 5:29; Rm. 2:16). The main emphasis in the New Testament is on the christological interpretation of resurrection. The death and resurrection of Jesus inaugurated the eschatological process (Ac. 26:23; 1 Cor. 15:20, 21; Col. 1:18). This is God's vindication of the persecution of Jesus (see Rm. 4:24; 8:11). Except for the link between baptism and resurrection (see Rm. 6; Eph.; Col.), the idea of a 'present resurrection' of the kind developed by the gnostics (see Wedderburn 1987:210ff. for detail) is rejected (see 2 Tm. 2:18). In short, the New Testament reveals the process of development of ideas about resurrection and is only the start of the resurrection speculation which reached its climax in the second century (see Tert *ResCarn* 3; *Or. Cels*; Just *Apol*; Athen *Res*).

The christological interpretation of resurrection in the New Testament did not originate from the preaching of Jesus. Although he most probably shared the current Jewish views about resurrection held by his contemporaries (see Mk. 12:18ff.), Jesus did not interpret his life in terms of the inauguration of the eschatological process of resurrection. The passion and resurrection predictions in the gospel tradition (see Mk. 8:31; 9:31; 10:32–34parr) are redactional and come from primitive Christianity (see Bultmann 1970:163; Strecker 1979: 52–75).

Belief in resurrection and resurrection stories was made possible by the world in which Christian religion originated. The fact that the body of a person could disappear after death and not be found because it had been taken into heaven, or that a body could disappear from its grave and appear and speak to those who knew the person in life, is not totally unknown to the world of the New Testament. The Testament of Job, a Jewish-Hellenistic writing from the first century prior to or after the coming of Christ, relates the story of the destruction of the house of Job by Satan and the disappearance of his children's bodies after death because they were taken to heaven by their creator (TJob 39:8–40:4. See also the empty tomb story of Callirrhoe, the wife of Chariton. See Liepoldt 1988:290f.). Furthermore the story which Plutarch (45–125 CE) relates about the appearance of Romulus after his death in his *Parallel Lives* 28, bears a close resemblance to the christophany narratives (see Berger & Colpe 1987:91; Mk. 16:1–8 parr; Lk. 24:51ff.; Jn. 20:17; GPt. 10: 38–40; Plut *VitPar.* 28). This simply goes to show that some people in the period of the genesis of the New Testament, in both the Jewish and the Hellenistic worlds, would not have had any problem with the telling or believing of stories about the afterlife of the dead. The story of the appearance of Romulus after his death would have been as credible as that of the empty tomb of Jesus among the 'believers' in the circle from which these stories grew. Even Tertullian (*Apol.* 21:23) found some similarity between the ascension of Jesus and that of Romulus. This gives us some indication of the reception of these stories the ancient world.

To my mind, it is doubtful whether the resurrection of Jesus can be explained against the background of the dying and rising of gods. Although the myth of dying and rising gods was widespread in the Near East (see Frazer 1963; S. Wissmann 1979:443), it does not seem to have been the dominant belief in first century Palestine where Jesus was crucified and then believed to have been resurrected (see also Leipoldt 1937). The religio-historical context of resurrection and resurrection faith in the New Testament appears to be predominantly Jewish. 'To define hope in terms of a return to "bodily" existence was not what the educated pagan would have wanted' (Ferguson 1987:487). This probably also holds for the non-Jewish man in the street in first century Palestine. Paul used the natural cycle to illustrate the nature of resurrection in 1 Corinthians 15:36–37. Whether in fact he had in mind the idea of dying and rising gods, is a totally different matter.

CHAPTER SEVEN

STOICS AND EARLY
CHRISTIANS ON BLESSEDNESS

The interest of scholars in Cynicism and Stoicism in their study of early Christianity during the last century and the early twentieth century was to a great extent replaced in the mid-twentieth century by studies of Judaism as the context of the interpretation of Christianity, and Cynicism and Stoicism were therefore also often neglected. There is currently a renewed interest in the Greco-Roman context within which Christianity originated.

In spite of the conviction about the apocalyptic nature of the preaching of Jesus, for example, which had dominated scholarship since the late nineteenth century, it was recently asserted that 'a Cynic Jesus does appear to fit the Hellenistic cast to Galilean culture much better than the apocalyptic Jesus.' (Mack 1988:608). This is only one of many recent attempts to place Jesus, Q, and aspects of early Christianity in a Greco-Roman context (see Downing 1984, 1988 and the work being done in the *Corpus Hellenisticum* project).

In this respect the Cynics and Stoics are of special interest, both because of their ways of life and also because of their views. It is nevertheless widely agreed that both Jewish and Greco-Roman contexts are necessary for the interpretation of the spread and beliefs of early Christian thought patterns. This is substantiated by the wide-ranging interests of New Testament scholars in matters such as Judaism, Gnosticism, mystery religions, healing cults, and Hellenistic philosophical thought. One should, therefore, welcome the renewed interest in Cynicism and also take cognizance of the ongoing interest in Stoic philosophy and the New Testament. But, in contrast, there also seems to be reason not to jump to conclusions too quickly about the Cynic character of the teaching of Jesus, and so-called parallels between Christian and Greek philosophical thought.

The purpose of this chapter is to explore the way in which Stoics and early Christians conceived blessedness, that is, happiness. *Blessedness* and *happiness* are translation equivalents for exactly the same terms and concepts in Greek and will be used as synonyms in this chapter. Even in the New Testament there is no reason to attach some special 'religious' connotation to words such as *makarios*. The so-called difference between *happiness* and *blessedness*, or *happy* and *blessed*, as translation equivalents for Greek and Hebrew words in the Bible, derives from the erroneous idea that the אשרי formulas originated in the cult as blessing formulas. (See also Cazelles 1970:481–485). I am interested in how Stoics and early Christians constructed their views on happiness and how these views fitted into their views on reality. This is not an attempt to investigate influences or parallel thought patterns in the first instance. Although there might be similarities between the two systems of thought, I am convinced that most of the statements about happiness in the New Testament have their background in Jewish wisdom and eschatological, including apocalyptic, thought (e.g. Maahs 1965, Kähler 1974).

The essay has three parts. The first deals with Stoic views on happiness. Although reference will be made to different members of the Stoic tradition, I will use Epictetus as my main representative. In the second section, early Christian views on happiness will be dealt with. Again, I will restrict my discussion to the treatment of a limited amount of material in the New Testament. In the last section, I will focus on a few parallel statements concerning happiness in Stoicism and the New Testament.

The Stoics believed that the ultimate end of life, τὸ τέλος, was happiness. According to Cicero (*Fin.* 3.26), the *sapiens* (wise person) is always happy, because the final aim in life is to live in accordance with nature. It naturally follows, he asserts, that all wise persons at all times enjoy a happy, perfect, and fortunate life, free from hindrance, if they live in agreement and harmony with nature. This, in short, is a summary of the Stoic view of blessedness. According to Luke 6:20–22, in contrast, Jesus taught that those who are poor and hungry, those who weep, and those who are hated, rejected, insulted, and accused of being evil because of the Son of Man are happy. They are regarded as happy because God will take care of their needs. How do these two views compare? Are they totally different, contradictory, or perhaps related?

1. *Stoics on Blessedness*

Different terms are used in Greek literature for happiness. In Homer, the gods are called οἱ μάκαρες (Blessed Ones). They live a life of happiness beyond care (Od. 5.7). The term μάκαρ is later used to denote the godlike blessedness of humankind hereafter in the isles of the blessed (Hes. *Op.* 141). Its cognate μακάριος similarly first describes the blessed state of the gods and is then used of the dead who have obtained this blessed state. From the time of Aristotle onward it becomes a much weaker term and is used as an everyday word for happiness. Aristotle still ascribes full blessedness (μακάριος) to the gods only and uses the term εὐδαιμονία for the happiness of humans. Hauck (1942:365–367) gives a detailed discussion and references of this concept. In the second century CE Lucian maintains in his *Bis accusatus sive tribunalia* 'Plague take all philosophers who say that bliss is to be found only among the gods!' (see also his *De sacrificiis 2*). It is the latter term that became the leading word for inner happiness in Greek philosophy.

Happiness is defined in Stoic terms as εὐδαιμονία, being the goal of life. From Zeno, the founder of the Stoic school of philosophy, through the middle and later Stoa, the theme of εὐδαιμονία runs like a golden thread. In order to understand the term properly, one has to see it within the frame of reference and thought within which it was used. Happiness in the Stoic sense of the word is directly linked to the moral purpose of humankind (προαίρεσις), a deliberate choice that must be in harmony with nature (κατὰ φύσιν). It is furthermore related to what is good and to virtue (ἀρετή). In short, happiness is governed by reason (λόγος). All these different concepts are integrated into a view of reality that will now receive our attention, mainly in the writings of Epictetus, a contemporary of early Christian authors.

Epictetus (55 to 135 CE) was born at Hierapolis in Phrygia. The son of a slave woman, he was a slave himself, and from the Phrygians he inherited an intense interest in their deities and a passion for his personal god. He was taken to Rome and was brought up in the house of Epaphroditus, a powerful freedman of Nero. Because of his interest in philosophy, he was allowed to take lessons from Musonius Rufus, a very important Stoic philosopher of the time. He was granted his freedom and was later banished from Rome with other philosophers in 89. He went to Nicopolis in Greece and started his own school. Epictetus suffered from bad health and was lame (Ferguson 1987:291–293).

He wrote nothing himself, but fortunately his pupil Flavius Arrian reorded and published his notes as discourses (diatribes), of which four complete books are extant. Arrian also sumarized the basic ideas of Epictetus in the ΕΓΧΕΙΡΙΔΙΟΝ, or *Manual*. A number of other fragments also exist.

Epictetus was a representative of Stoic philosophy and agreed with most of the main teachings of the school. He also regarded himself as a Cynic, a messenger from Zeus whose purpose it was to teach people how to live and to make decisions between good and evil (*Diss.* 3.22). As a philosopher, he reflected on physics, logic, and especially on ethics. His views of reality are dominated by his theology.

According to Epictetus, the universe is the work of God and the product of divine providence. This explains the order and unity in the universe. God has not only taken care of everything that happens; he has also given humankind the faculties to understand it (*Diss.* 1.6) and to live a life in harmony with nature (1.4.18), that is, orderly and self-sufficient (3.7–8): 'Assuredly from the very structure of all made objects we are accustomed to prove that the work is certainly the product of some artifice, and has not been constructed at random' (*Diss.* 6.8). There is a very close relationship between nature and reason in Stoicism. Seneca puts it as follows:

> Man is a reasoning animal. Therefore, man's highest good is attained, if he has fulfilled the good for which nature designed him at birth. And what is it which this reason demands of him? The easiest thing in the world—to live in accordance to his own nature (*Ep.* 41.8–9 in Loeb translation).

People fit into this orderly universe as beings with all sorts of faculties, which allow them to make judgments and choices, right or wrong. That is why people should be educated in order to reach their goal in life, which is happiness (Epictetus *Diss.* 2.9.29). Certain things are good, whereas others are evil. And in addition, there are virtue and vices, as well as things that are indifferent. To be free is to be master of oneself (Epictetus frg. 35). Some things are under our control, whereas others not, and one has to know how to deal with the things that are under one's control while accepting those that are not (Epictetus *Diss.* 1.1; also Epictetus *Each.* 1). Epictetus asserts:

> Remember that you are an actor in a play, the character of which is determined by the Playwright: if He wishes the play to be short, it is short; if long, it is long; if He wishes you to play the part of a beggar, remember to act even this role adroitly; and so if your role be that of a cripple, an official, or a layman. For this is your business, to play admirably the role assigned to you; but the selection of that role is Another's (*Ench.* 17).

Within this framework, Epictetus maintains that some things are under the control of humans, whereas others are not: 'Under our control are conception, choice, desire, aversion, and, in a word, everything that is our own doing; not under our control are our body, our property, reputation, office, and in a word, everything that is not our own doing. Furthermore, the things under our control are by nature free, unhindered, and unimpeded; while the things not under our control are weak, servile, subject to hindrance, and not our own' (*Ench.* 1.1; see also *Diss.*).

In accordance with ancient Stoic views, Epictetus maintains that false judgments give rise to unhappiness. The most important faculty that the gods have given humankind is the faculty to make correct judgments concerning external impressions. The first task of the philosopher is to test the impressions and discriminate between good and evil, as well as to apply nothing that has not been tested (*Diss.* 1.6.7, see also Colish 1985:42). Seneca (*Ep.* 95.57) also remarks: 'Peace of mind is enjoyed only by those who have attained a fixed and unchanging standard of judgment; the rest of mankind continually ebb and flow in their decisions.' Since wealth, health, fame, and so on are not under the control of humans, it is important to realize the significance of being able to use external impressions correctly. Happiness depends on correct judgments about external impressions (2.19.32). People are to contemplate making right judgments.

The Stoics also taught that all events in nature are good. Evil does not stem from nature but from the acts of humans (Colish 1985:42–50). 'The nature of the good as well as of the evil lies in a use of the impressions of the senses' (Epictetus *Diss.* 2.1.4). Prudence, courage, temperance, and justice are the four virtues of Stoicism. For our purpose it is important to note that prudence is a synthesis of speculative and practical wisdom (Colish 1985:43). People have to strive for wisdom and to avoid vice. That is done by moral choice (προαίρεσις).

Προαίρεσις has an intellectual basis in Epictetus; it is not merely a matter of will (*Diss.* 1.29). It is preceded by διαίρεσις, the distinction between what is under one's control and what is not (2.6.24). Moral purpose concerns the making of good judgments (3.9) in harmony with nature (1.4.18).

By constructing reality as a self-sufficient, orderly universe under the providence of the Divine, in which people control certain things in accordance with moral purpose, the Stoic becomes a person whose ultimate goal in life is happiness. Despite his bodily problems and the fact that he grew up as a slave, Epictetus had an extraordinarily optimistic view of reality. As a Stoic he believed in the possibility of being happy irrespective of one's position in life: 'Show me a man who though sick is happy (εὐτυχοῦνται), though in danger is happy, though dying is happy, though condemned to exile is happy, though in disrepute is happy. Show him! By the Gods, I would fain see a Stoic!' (*Diss.* 2.19.24).

It is within this frame of reference that Epictetus understands happiness as the goal of life. The terms he employs for happiness include γαλήνη, words related to the stem εὐδαιμον-, εὐδία, εὔροια κτλ., εὐσταθ-, εὐτυχ-, and words related to the stem μακαρ-. These words give an idea of the semantic field within which happiness functions in Epictetus. The words related to the stem εὐδαιμον- dominate the statements of Epictetus on happiness, whereas terms such as μακάριος κτλ are used as close synonyms. He maintains: ὁ γὰρ θεὸς πάντας ἀνθρώπους ἐπὶ τὸ εὐδαιμονεῖν, ἐπὶ τὸ εὐσταθεῖν ἐποίησεν (For God made all mankind to be happy, to be serene; *Diss.* 3.24.4).

God has made humankind to be happy and not to be unhappy, and for that reason God has put some things under the control of people and others not. Because they are begotten by God, humans have reason (λόγος) and intelligence (γνώμη) in common with the gods, which is a divine (θεία) and blessed (μακαρία) relationship. Only some are inclined to this relationship. Others are inclined to the body, which humans have in common with all living creatures. They cannot be happy. One should concentrate on the things that are under human control and act accordingly (Epictetus *Diss.* 1.3.3). Moral purpose is the highest of all things. When it is attended to—that is, when one makes right decisions—a person becomes good and is fortunate and happy. When moral purpose is ignored, evil arises.

Virtue can produce happiness, calm, and serenity. This explains the necessity to make progress toward virtue: 'For it is always true that whatsoever the goal toward which perfection in anything definitely leads, progress is an approach thereto' (Epictetus *Diss.* 1.4.4). Progress occurs where people turn their attention to their moral purpose, cultivating and perfecting it in harmony with nature, free and unhindered. Therefore, people must strive to avoid things that are not under their control, because those (1.4.18–19). Possessions, children, marriage, slaves, and friendship are of no use is a person does not attend to the things that can produce happiness. Humans should know what God is, what humanity is, and also what is good and what is evil. Ignorance of these things produces unhappiness: 'Some persons, like cattle, are interested in nothing but fodder; for to all of you that concern yourselves with property and lands and slaves and one office or another, all this is nothing but fodder' (2.14.24–25).

Happiness does not reside in the body, in possessions, in an office, in external appearance, or in royalty. According to Dio Chrysostom (*Or.* 3.1), 'Man's happiness is not determined by any external possessions, such as gold plate, cities or lands, for example, or other human beings, but in each case by his own self and his own character'. Happiness is found in freedom from the things that enslave humans (Epictetus *Diss.* 3.22.26–40). Suffering, death, bad health, a crippled body, exile, and so on cannot be reasons for humans to be unhappy. These things are not under human control. Happiness can only be reached by attending to that which is under one's control. This does not mean that Epictetus accepted life passively. On the contrary, because of his views on reality, he believed in the active participation of humans in their perfection and happiness.

Because of his belief in divine providence, the intellectual ability of humans, and the importance of moral purpose, Epictetus could accept life as a gift from God that has to be lived in accordance with nature. Happiness is the ultimate goal of life. It is not a disposition in the first instance. According to Epictetus, as a state of mind, happiness is something that has to be achieved. It is an activity. This is in line with the Stoic concept of εὐδαιμονία as the ultimate goal of life: '*Eudaimonia* is in Stoic ethics, according to our analysis, primarily to act virtuously so that one's life accordance with the universal nature (ὁμολογία), and secondarily it is possibly a state of exhilaration (χαρά, εὐφροσύνη, etc.) which comes into being as an γέννημα "subsequent manifestation"] of virtuous activity.' (Tsekourakis 1974:97).

Happiness, according to Epictetus, is practical wisdom. This is a common theme in Stoicism. (see Cicero *Fin.* 3.26). In accordance with his view of reality, he taught people how to live and how to make judgments that could help them in achieving the ultimate goal in life, that is, happiness.

2. *Early Christians on Blessedness*

Unlike in Stoicism, in the New Testament εὐδαιμονία is not used to express happiness. Μακάριος and χαίρω dominate the semantic field of happiness in these writings. Other terms functioning in the same semantic field in New Testament writings are ἀγαλλίασις, ἀγαλλιάω, ἀσμένως, ἀσπάζομαι, εὐφραίνομαι, εὐφραίνω, εὐφροσύνη, ἡδέως, ἱλαρός, ἱλαρότης, μακαρίζω, μακαρισμός, σκιπτάω, συγχαίρω, συνήδομαι, and χαρά (see Louw & Nida 1988:302–304). Because of the lack of space, I will have to limit my discussion of happiness in early Christian perspective to a few important aspects.

As in Stoicism, New Testament beliefs about happiness are motivated by conceptions of reality and symbolic universes. Because New Testament writings are in the first place religious texts, it is not amazing that happiness is related to God as the giver of happiness.

According to the New Testament, early Christians regarded themselves as a community of joy and happiness. The coming of Jesus inaugurated a new era, that is, an era of happiness. He made the blind see again and the lame walk; he cured those who suffered from illnesses, made the dead come alive, and made the good news known to the poor (Matt. 11:5). The days of fasting were something of the past, because the bridegroom had arrived, it was said (see Mark 2:18). The teaching and the deeds of Jesus created a new world view for a group of people who most probably despaired because of their socioeconomic and political situation. In their interpretation of the life and the works of Jesus, and of his message concerning the kingdom of God, followers of Jesus saw the basis for a new conception of happiness. Although it had a present aspect in that his coming gave reason for happiness, his teaching about the kingdom of God most probably also included a future aspect—that real happiness would come in the end (see Matt. 8:12; Mark 14:25).

After the death of Jesus, happiness was motivated christologically. His complete life was seen as the sole basis of happiness. Especially in the case of Luke, we notice how the life of Jesus from his birth to his resurrection is described from the perspective of joy and happiness. Luke is even called the evangelist of joy, and some scholars speak of the Lucan theology of joy (cf. Du Toit 1983:585–586; Conzelmann 1979:350–362). The infancy narrative was written from the perspective of joy (see Luke 1:14, 41, 44, 46–55, 68–79; 2:10), and so was the rest of Luke's story of Jesus. Jesus started his mission, according to Luke, with a sermon in the synagogue of Nazareth concerning the good news of the liberation of the oppressed that he brings about (Luke 4:18–19, 21). The Gospel ends on a happy note when the followers of Jesus are seized by the happiness of Easter (see χαρά in Luke 24:41, 52). Lucan Christians are happy because Jesus is born, because he brings a message of happiness and makes people happy, and because Jesus is raised from the dead. Happiness in Luke has both a present and a future character.

In Paul, happiness becomes happiness 'in Christ' or 'in the Lord' (see especially Phil. 3:1; 4:4, 10). Because of the death and resurrection of Jesus, believers share in Christ, that is, in his suffering and in his triumph (see Romans 8), and that is why Christians become a community of happiness (see 1 Cor. 12:26; 2 Cor. 2:3) even when they suffer (see 2 Corinthians 10). Happiness is, however, also something to be hoped for (Rom. 12:12). Happiness in spite of suffering and happiness in suffering is quite a common theme in early Christian thought (see Matt. 5:11; Luke 6:22; Jas. 1:2–4, 12; 1 Pet. 1:6–8; 4:12–14).

In the Johannine writings, special emphasis is laid on happiness as something that is fulfilled in the present. It is not something for which Christians have to wait. It is given in Christ (see John 16:24; 17:13; 1 John 1:4). This is quite a different perspective from that which we find in Revelation, where real happiness will come on the 'new earth' and in the 'new heaven' when all unhappiness will be removed forever.

In short, happiness is to be found in Christ. He is the inaugurator of happiness. In sorrow or pain, poverty or sadness, he is the reason why Christians can be happy. In Christ, God gives happiness. Happiness is both present and eschatological. In this sense, happiness appears to be a state of mind.

There is a certain tension between a world view that emphasizes present happiness and one that projects happiness into the future, especially if the future is seen in apocalyptic terms. Both strands of tradition are present in early Christian documents, and in some cases the interpretation of statements about happiness becomes a moot point. It is not always clear whether present happiness is an imitation of future happiness or whether the present is seen in relation to the future when full happiness will be reached. Two symbolic universes may be involved. This needs to be discussed now with respect to some of the so-called macarisms, or beatitude formulas, in the New Testament. I shall concentrate mainly on the macarisms that Jesus expressed according to Matthew (5:3–12) and Luke (6:20–25) and discuss happiness in terms of wisdom theology and apocalyptic theology.

There are several problems involved in the interpretation of these macarisms, and opinions differ greatly (see Luz 1985:198–218). This is not the place to discuss all the issues, because I am only interested in showing how different views of reality influence our understanding of early Christian views concerning happiness. Should the macarisms of Jesus be seen from the perspective of wisdom theology or from the perspectarisms in Matthew 5 and Luke 6 'entrance requirements,' or are they 'eschatological blessings'? (see also Guelich 1976:415–34).

The macarism was known to both the Greek and Semitic worlds. In Classical Greek, the formula was introduced by ὄλβιος or by μάκαρ followed by a relative clause and a finite verb, mostly in the third person. In Hebrew, the formula was introduced by אַשְׁרֵי followed by a participle, a noun, or a pronoun. Unlike the בָּרוּךְ formula, the אַשְׁרֵי formula *is not* a blessing formula, in spite of the fact that it has often been viewed in this manner (e.g. Cazelles 1970:481–85; Guelich, 1982:64). Because it was related to the cult, אַשְׁרֵי was translated as 'blessed' in the sense of somebody who receives a blessing. This was also transferred to the Greek μακάριος, by which the Hebrew word is normally translated. The 'congratulation' of happiness never refers to God. It always refers to the 'life-enhancing' behavior of the believer; that is, coming to Zion (Ps. 65:5), fearing God (Ps. 94:12), studying and obeying the Torah (Prov. 29:18), caring for the poor (Ps. 41:2), finding wisdom (Prov. 3:13), listening to wisdom (Prov. 8:33), and so on (Perdue 1986:17). These formulas appear almost exclusively in the Psalms and Wisdom literature of the Old Testament. In these contexts, the formulas normally have a parenetic function of religious and moral exhortation. Persons who abide by the rules of moral conduct are happy. Happiness corresponds with Israel's understanding of 'well-being.' It concerns everything that makes people happy: life, security, deliverance, posterity, military success, prosperity, and so on. Guelich (1982:63 observes:) 'Any hint of an eschatological hope is rare' (for example, Isa. 30:18; 32:20; Dan. 12:12). This is in accordance with the use of macarism formulas in practical wisdom in Egypt (see Cazelles 1970:484).

In the intertestamental literature, beatitude formulas are used in two different ways. In continuity with Old Testament usage, macarisms appear in Wisdom literature, where they have a parenetic function. They are also used in apocalyptic writings, where they are future oriented, and their function is to encourage. Guelich correctly observes that the context of these beatitudes is different from that of those used in Wisdom literature (see Guelich 1982:65). The persons who are called lucky in apocalyptic writings are those who are in distress and under pressure. The promise of happiness concerns otherworldly happiness. There is no hope in this world, but in the world to come, the roles will be changed, and the 'underdogs' who are righteous will be happy.

The difference between the two usages is important, since wisdom theology and apocalyptic theology are based on two different world views. Reality is constructed in two totally different ways, even though one often finds wisdom traits in apocalyptic theology (for example 1 *Enoch*). Wisdom theology underscores the order and unity in God's creation. The sages believed that deeds have effects both for people and for their environment. That is why one should live as a *sapiens* (wise person) by pursuing wisdom. Deeds, good or bad, have their consequences. Apocalyptic theology, in contrast, puts its hope in the world to come, and actions are motivated by hope of a better future.

Let us now turn to the beatitudes in Matthew 5 and Luke 6. It is not clear how many of these statements originated with Jesus and what their original wording was. However, what is clear is that Matthew and Luke interpreted the macarisms differently and wanted their hearers/readers to understand them in particular ways. Whereas Luke places the emphasis on the socioeconomic pressures of poverty, unhappiness, hate, insult, and rejection because of the Son of Man, Matthew seems either to have retained the original parenetic character of the macarisms or to have ethicized them. He refers to the 'spiritually poor,' the 'humble,' and those who seek 'righteousness' and 'show mercy,' and in this manner seems to have the emphasis fall on 'life-enhancing behavior.' (See Strecker 1984:29–30.) This explains why the macarisms have often been understood as 'entrance requirements' for the Kingdom in the mouth of Jesus.

The apodoses of the macarisms are normally interpreted eschatologically because of the use of the future tense, the *passiva divina* (passive as circumlocution for naming God), and the reward in heaven. It is nevertheless remarkable that in both Matthew and Luke, it is said that the kingdom *belongs* (present tense) to the μακάριοι (Matt. 5:3, 10; Luke 6:20). It is possible to argue that in Matthew the connection between moral conduct and heavenly recompense is emphasized, whereas Luke stresses the promise of eschatological blessings to the 'underdogs.' This does not imply that both Matthew and Luke interpreted the macarisms in line with the intertestamental apocalyptic use of the beatitudes. On the contrary, one can make out a strong case that these macarisms should be read as wisdom sayings in both Matthew and Luke, even though it is clearly possible to interpret them apocalyptically.

When the focus is placed on the parenetic function of the macarisms, blessedness or happiness is not simply a state; it implies conduct, a goal that is to be achieved. In terms of Matthew, the goal is to become τέλειοι (5:48). This is in line with other μακάριος statements in the teaching of Jesus, which also reflect the wisdom perspective: 'Happy is the person who takes no offense at me' (Matt. 11:6 ‖ Luke 7:23); 'Happy are the eyes that see what you see and the ears that hear what you hear' (Matt. 13:16 ‖ Luke 10:23); 'Happy is the person who comes in the name of the Lord' (Matt. 23:39 ‖ Luke 13:35); 'Happy are those who hear the word of God and keep it' (Luke 11:28); 'Happy are those servants whom the master finds awake when he comes' (Luke 12:37); and 'Happy is the servant whom the master will find so doing when he comes' (Luke 12:43).

These sayings can be regarded as wisdom sayings declaring wellbeing to those who engage in proper conduct. 'The state of blessing already exists, though the tangible rewards may still lay [lie] in the future.' (Perdue 1986:17). Happiness is not something that the followers of Jesus will receive in the afterlife; it is a state that they already experience. Being poor, hungry, marginalized, and so on does not imply unhappiness. On the contrary, because they are members of the kingdom of God, they are happy. This is true of both Matthew's and Luke's versions of the macarisms in spite of their differences with regard to who the blessed are.

It is furthermore remarkable that Matthew presents the Sermon on the Mount as a speech of Jesus the teacher (Matt. 5:2), under-scoring the fact that he was a teacher of wisdom. Taking into account how much of the teaching of Jesus can be regarded as wisdom the-ology simply strengthens the possibility of interpreting the macarisms of Matthew 5 within this framework. Perdue (1986:3–35), gives a very useful survey of the wisdom teaching of Jesus in this regard. The macarisms that were included in Q would most probably have been understood as wisdom sayings of Jesus the teacher of wisdom, because Q was most probably a wisdom document. See for example Kloppenborg 1984 and 1986:35–56). In this framework, Christians are expected to live as sages irrespective of their socioeconomic or political situation. Under all circumstances they can be happy. Well-being is connected to conduct. Deeds have effects.

If, however, we interpret these sayings within an apocalyptic frame-work, happiness has a totally different connotation. Happiness is then related to the hope of an afterlife. Some day the followers of Jesus will be happy. They must bear with their poverty, hunger, and so on, because in the afterlife things will change, and they will receive full happiness.

This is not the place to determine whether early Christians under-stood their happiness only from the perspective of wisdom theology or whether they understood it apocalyptically. I am convinced that both trends were present in early Christianity. It is clear from the New Testament that there were wisdom, as well as apocalyptic, tra-jectories in early Christianity. The point I wish to underline is that happiness can be conceived differently within early Christian per-spectives because of the different world views that were involved.

Although early Christians did not have a particular doctrine about happiness, they undoubtedly formed part of a tradition where happi-ness was related to God as the giver of happiness. In the New Testa-ment, happiness is related to the coming of Jesus and to his teaching.

3. *Parallel Statements on Blessedness*

A few examples of parallel statements about happiness in Stoic and early Christian writings will help give an idea of corresponding views. These will then be viewed against the background of the foregoing discussion of happiness in Stoic and early Christian perspective.

In a recent article on Cynics and Christians, F. Gerald Downing

(1984:587) claims that Cynics and early Christians had similar ideas about true blessedness. Epictetus, for one, he argues, was sure that true happiness 'lay in the right relation with deity.' Cynics and Stoics are one and the same in Downing's article, as can be seen from the sources he uses. Downing furthermore draws attention to the fact that Cynics, like Christians, were ready to invite trouble. Epictetus, for example, said,

> Think the matter over more carefully, know yourself, ask the Deity, do not attempt the task without God. For if God so advises you, be assured that He wishes you either to become great, or to receive many stripes. For this too is a very pleasant strand woven into the Cynic's pattern of life; he must needs be flogged like an ass, and while he is being flogged he must love the men who flog him, as though he were the father or brother of them all (*Diss.* 3.22.53 54).

The acceptance of one's role in life and of brotherly love enabled Cynics (and Stoics) to live happily. Especially with regard to Q and 'special Matthean' material', there seems to be a close relationship between Cynic and Christian views about happiness, according to Downing. Neither of the two groups was interested in wealth and property as grounds for happiness, and both relied on their gods to take care of their needs and problems:

> Consider the beasts yonder and the birds, how much freer from trouble they live than men, and how much more happily also, how much healthier and stronger they are, and how each of them lives the longest life possible, although they have neither hands nor human intelligence. And yet, to counterbalance these and their other limitations, they have one very great blessing—they own no property (Dio Chrys. *Or.* 10.16).

This reminds one of the teaching of Jesus about trust in God for daily needs in Luke 12:22–31. Cynics and early Christians may also be compared with regard to their practical life-styles as the pursuit of wisdom (see Downing 1984:588).

Let us now turn to a few μακάριοι statements in the New Testament that can be compared with similar statements in Dio Chrysostom. In my search for parallel statements (on happiness I found the works of scholars involved in the *Corpus Hellenisticum* project most helpful (e.g. Mussies, 1972; Van der Horst 1974:306–315; 1975; 1981:165–72). The statements I wish to examine are:

Happy are the poor in spirit (Matt. 5:3).

Happy are you [scil. the good king] in your gracious and excellent nature, and happy are we who share its blessings with you (Dio Chrys. *Or.* 1.36).

Happy are you poor, for yours is the kingdom of God (Luke 6:20).

I desired to show in some way or other that poverty is no hopeless impediment to a life and existence befitting free men who are willing to work with their hands, but leads them on to deeds and actions that are far better and more useful and more in accordance with nature than those to which riches are wont to attract most men (Dio Chrys. *Or.* 7.103).

It is more blessed to give than to receive (Acts 20:35).

Therefore he finds greater pleasure in conferring benefits than those benefited do in receiving them (Dio Chrys. *Or.* 1.23).

Happy is the person who does not feel guilty about what he approves (Rom. 14:22).

Whose life is safer than his whom all alike protect, whose is happier than his who esteems no man an enemy, and whose is freer from vexation than his who has no cause to blame himself (Dio Chrys. *Or.* 1.35).

In spite of similarities, it is obvious that statements concerning happiness in Stoicism and early Christianity differ because of the broader framework in which they were conceptualized, as well as the way in which both groups constructed reality. Stoics and Christians had similar views on certain conditions for well-being, but they nevertheless did not share the same world view.

From the above treatment of happiness in Stoic and early Christian thought, it has become clear that both Stoics and Christians held happiness in high esteem. To be happy is the goal of life for Stoics, and for Christians, happiness is something that believers receive from God. Happiness is not something that God alone has. In Philo, for example, happiness (μακαριότης) belongs to God alone. It is only when the divine nature becomes part of earthly life that earthly beings like humans have part in divine blessedness. In Philo. *Abr.* 202 it is stated: 'But the nature of God is without grief or fear and wholly exempt from passion of any kind, and alone partakes of perfect happiness and bliss'. (See also Philo *Vit. Mos.* 2.184. It is part and parcel of a life in Christ. Inner happiness is not only a disposition in Stoicism; it is something that humans have to attain by living in accordance with nature, that is, by virtue and moral purpose.

Because happiness is a gift from God and is found in the believers'
relationship with God, it seems that happiness, according to early
Christianity, is an inner state of the mind, a condition. There is,
however, also another side to the picture. Early Christians were also
happy because of their conduct. Deeds have consequences, and proper
conduct leads to happiness. Except for those who saw life in an
apocalyptic perspective, both early Christians and Stoics had an optimistic view of life. They both accepted life as it was and tried to
live happily. To be happy is to become wise in the eyes of both
Stoics and early Christians.

Christianity originated in a society that was dominated by Judaism.
This explains the many Jewish traits in the understanding of a happy
life by early Christians. One should, nonetheless not disregard the
Greco-Roman influence in Galilee, where the ministry of Jesus took
place. His preaching about the kingdom of God created a new understanding of life for the underdogs of lower Galilee, who were his
first followers. These people were probably acquainted with ideas
about happiness in the Greco-Roman perspective, and they probably shared some of these with their non-Jewish contemporaries.

Professor Abraham J. Malherbe has contributed greatly to the fact
that the study of Greco-Roman documents of the period of the development of early Christianity has become *a sine qua non* for students
of the New Testament and early Christian writings. With his motto
ad fontes, he has opened the Greco-Roman world to many. I am
grateful that I can share many of his views and, therefore, present
this essay with admiration to him.

Section B.2

Gospels

CHAPTER EIGHT

KERYGMA/HISTORY AND THE GOSPEL GENRE

The thesis I wish to propound in this article is that neither kerygma nor history is a distinctive characteristic of the genre of the gospels. For the literary critic this remark may seem superfluous while a New Testament scholar may find it ridiculous. In view of the history of the interpretation of the genre, however, and also in view of current discussion on the problem in New Testament scholarship the thesis is understandable. The article falls into two parts. In the first a short survey is given of the problem and its development. In the second kerygma and history are discussed with reference to the gospels as narratives.

1. *The Problem and its Development*

The Enlightenment, and as a result of that, the rise of historical awareness created grave problems in the interpretation of the gospels. There was no room in the post-Enlightenment world for the miracles, angels, and demons, for example, referred to in the gospel narratives. Various attempts have been made to 'solve' this problem, ranging from the suggestion that the gospel narratives are factually true to the opinion that factual history has to be reconstructed from the narratives by separating fact from fiction, legend or myth. It is regrettable that research on the genre of the gospels has been dominated for more than half a century by the controversy about the gospels and history. The end of this controversy is still not in sight. Perhaps this is best illustrated by the following characterizations of the genre of Mark's Gospel, which is commonly accepted as the first example of the gospel *Gattung* (see Gnilka 1979:22–24): '*Geschichtsdarstellung*' (J. Roloff), '*Geschichtserzählung*' (S. Schulz), '*Kerygma einer bestimmten Lage und Aufgabe*' (E. Stegemann following J. Schniewind and R. Bultmann, see also Bultmann 1970:362), '*Verkündigung als Bericht*' (G. Strecker, see Strecker 1979a:51, where he uses the term 'Botschaft als Bericht'), '*indirekt Predigt, direkt Geschichtserzählung*' (R. Pesch), '*Bericht als Verkündigung oder im Dienst der Verkündigung*' (J. Gnilka). These descriptions, inadequate as they are in their characterization of the distinctive features of the genre, clearly indicate the importance of kerygma and history for New Testament scholars and also the relevance of the topic under discussion. The reasons for this are not unknown but I nevertheless find it necessary to give a short survey of the development of the problem.

There are at present, roughly speaking, two ways in which the genre of the gospels is defined. In the first an evolutionistic model is used while in the second the genre is explained with an analogy model by comparing it to other literary forms (Vorster 1991:9ff.).

Basic to the first model is the idea of a nucleus, the *kerygma* which generated the gospel *Gattung* (Koester 1971:150). Before the rise of *Formgeschichte*, mainly as a result of and in opposition to the mythical interpretation of the gospels by D.F. Strauss, the Gospel of Mark used to be regarded as a history of the ministry of Jesus. The form was compared to ancient memoirs, lives and biographies, and Mark's Gospel used for the reconstruction of the life of Jesus. This interpretation was challenged by Wrede (1969) and especially by the founders of the form critical interpretation of the gospels, namely K.L. Schmidt (1964), R. Bultmann (1970) and M. Dibelius (1966). In his epoch-making essay on the place of the gospel *Gattung* in the history of literature Schmidt (1923) argued that the separate units in the gospel tradition were transmitted orally by illiterate unknown persons who could not be regarded as authors. The evangelists collected these units and compiled their gospels which he maintained should be viewed as popular cult legends, not biographies, 'Kleinliteratur' and not 'Hochliteratur': 'Das Evangelium ist von Haus aus nicht Hochliteratur, sondern Kleinliteratur, nicht individuelle Schriftstellersleistung, sondern Volksbuch, nicht Biographie, sondern Kultlegende', Schmidt (1923:76) wrote. Schmidt's views were supported and amplified by those of Dibelius and Bultmann on the history and growth of the traditions in the gospels and their life settings. It soon became commonly accepted that the gospel genre was generated by an impersonal, collective sociological force namely the cult of Christ, the kerygma or the primitive community. It was now thought that only as a result of the existence of a kerygma which proclaimed as Lord a man who lived on earth, is it possible to explain the origin and form of the gospels (Schniewind 1930:163). The gospel *Gattung* which came about by way of a process of evolution and development was a unicum, *sui generis*. (Norden already promoted the idea that Mark had created a new literary form, see Norden 1958:480–481).

Most probably no other construction has had a greater influence on New Testament scholarship than the kerygma-hypothesis of M. Dibelius (see Dibelius 1966 and Gütgemanns 1970:190ff. for a comprehensive discussion of the theory). He argued that the sermon or proclamation, taken as missionary, cultic and catechetical preaching, was the origin of early Christian literary creativity. Proclamation played a decisive role in the formation, development and transmission of the Jesus tradition and for that matter in the formation of the gospel genre. This was the start of a chain reaction which is still in sway today. The New Testament and especially the gospels were and still are regarded first of all as proclamation—kerygma.

According to this theory the gospel genre is something very unique. As a result of an immanent process of growth, evolution and development the cultic myth or credo (Gütgemanns 1970:208) of the death and resurrection of Jesus became a gospel. It has no literary parallels prior to its origin and outside the canon. Following the ideas of Dibelius in connection with the kerygmatic aspect of the gospel, C.H. Dodd (1944:7–35; 1953:1–11) gave the theory a historical basis. He argued that Mark's Gospel was a commentary on the kerygma which consisted of a basic (historical) framework or outline to be found in 1 Corinthians 15:3–7, 11:23–25, Acts 10:37–41 and 13:23–31 for example (Dodd 1953:9f.). This outline became the substance for the kerygma out of which the gospel genre grew. In view of this the gospel genre is not a product of the literary activity of Mark but that of the apostolic preaching of Jesus from which it developed. The possibility of creative authorship was effectively ruled out by an evolutionistic view of tradition. Pre-literary traditions and units of tradition developed into literary products like the Gospel of Mark, generated by the kerygma. The evangelists did the collecting but '. . . they were believed to have responded to forces of form and content that were inherent in the traditions and recognized by the religious communities' (Petersen 1978:12).

The importance of the historical dimension for the kerygma was highlighted in the period after the Second World War. (Both the New Quest and the rise of *Redaktionsgeschichte* contributed to the renewed interest in the historical dimension of the kerygma. Useful

surveys of the discussion are given in Baarlink (1977:13–26) and
Roloff (1973:9–50). The following remark by Strecker (1979b:92) is
illustrative in this connection:

> Während aber die Formgeschichte die kerygmatische Akzentuierung
> der Überlieferungseinheiten betonte und teilweise die 'Predigt' als Basis
> der Traditionswerdung ansah, scheint in der Redaktions-forschung die
> Tendenz impliziert zu sein, den Evangelienverfassern nicht eine direkt-
> kerygmatische, sondern eine historische Intention zuzuerkennen und
> darin—wenn auch in einer ausserordentlich modifizierten, nicht auf
> das authentische Leben Jesu ausgerichteten Weise—die historisch akzen-
> tuierte Betrachtung der Evangelien durch die liberale Leben-Jesu-
> Forschung wiederaufzunehmen.

Bultmann's attempt to demythologize the gospel narratives aroused
reactions comparable to those on Strauss' mythical interpretation in
the previous century. The essay by Käsemann (1954; also 1964:31–68)
on the historical Jesus and the subsequent discussion clearly indicated the importance of the historical dimension for the kerygma.
Bultmann's answer to the reproach that he ignored the continuity
between the historical Jesus and the kerygmatic Christ is to the point
(Bultmann 1965:8):

> Ich sage ausdrücklich: zwischen dem historischen Jesus und der ur-
> christlichen Verkundigung; nicht: zwischen dem historischen Jesus und
> Christus. Denn der Christus des Kerygmas ist keine historische Gestalt,
> die mit dem historischen Jesus in Kontinuität stehen könnte. Wohl
> aber ist das Kerygma, das ihn verkundigt, ein historisches Phänomen;
> und nur um die Kontinuität zwischen diesem und dem historischen
> Jesus kann es sich handeln!

Form critical studies proved that the gospels did not present factual
history in the sense of describing how it really happened but it was
also unacceptable to ignore the problem of 'Historie', the historical,
in the gospels. The 'dass' of Bultmann seemed to be too little and
it started the controversy about the continuity between the historical Jesus and the kerygmatic Christ anew (see Cystamine 1954 and
Bultmann 1965). This also had an influence on genre studies. The
pendulum swayed from kerygma to history and from history to
kerygma and today we have reached the stage referred to above
where even the genre of the gospel is described in terms of history
and/or kerygma.

   The relevance of the historical dimension for the kerygma became
more problematic with the rise of *Redaktionsgeschichte* (see Roloff 1973:

40–47 and also the remark by Strecker 1979b:92 in footnote 1 above). It became clear that the evangelists were more than compilers and their gospels more than collections of traditions. They were now regarded as theologians in their own right who organized their material according to preconceived plans of composition (Vorster 1980). Although they were based upon events and persons in history the gospels proved to be made-up stories. Especially as far as the oldest gospel was concerned it was argued that it did not only present kerygma; it was kerygma (Marxsen 1956:345–8). In view of the concept of redaction and the gospels as edited tradition more emphasis was laid on the theology of the separate gospels. In recent studies, however, it was argued that the redactional activity of Mark for example had been overestimated by Redaktionsgeschichte and that Mark was in fact a conservative redactor (Pesch 1976:2, 22). As a result the historical dimension and its relevance for the redaction of the gospel of Mark was again emphasized (Roloff 1973). This is why the gospel genre is characterized in terms of history and kerygma.

Redaktionsgeschichte with its greater emphasis on the literary activity of the redactors of the gospel tradition opened the possibility of investigating anew the similarities and differences between the gospels and other text types (Vorster 1981). In search of an ancient genre which could have served as a model for the first author of a gospel this text type has been compared with Semitic ones such as an apocalypse, the legend of Achikar, Exodus, the book of Jonah, a Passover Haggadah, Midrashim and the Mishnah. In the case of Hellenistic texts the biographies and memoir literature, aretalogy, tragedy and tragicomedy were taken into account (Vorster 1981c:13ff.). What is remarkable in most of these studies is that the authors take their cue from the proponents of the form critical explanation of the gospel genre. Or to put it in another way, the problem of kerygma and history also plays a role in the analogical approach to the gospel genre, not because of the relevance of these categories as characteristics of genre but because of the importance of a historical basis for the gospel material. The following remark of Via (1975:93) is striking: 'Mark came to be written because the/a kerygma proclaiming, and the faith in, the death and resurrection of Jesus reverberated in the mind of Mark and activated the comic genre whose nucleus is also death and resurrection. (Jesus, kerygma, and believing community are historical phenomena.) The story took the shape it did because the comic genre—a deep, generative structure of the human mind—generated the Gospel of Mark as a performance text, a transformation of itself'. In this remark Via attempted to accommodate both a structuralist approach to the problem of genre and results of the historico-critical approach to the problem which explains the strange combination of ideas. Talbert's study, to mention yet another recent study on the genre, is in a certain sense nothing more than a commentary on Bultmann's reasons why it is incorrect to compare the gospel genre to ancient graeco-roman biographies. In his study he convincingly refutes Bultmann's point of view on ancient biographies and as a result of his own investigations defines ancient biography as '... *prose narration* (my italics) about a person's life presenting supposedly historical facts which are selected to reveal the character or essence of the individual often with the purpose of affecting the behaviour of the reader' (Talbert 1977:17). It is a pity that Talbert did not analyse the gospel genre in view of this definition. He was influenced instead by recent views on the gospels as aretalogy and as attempts to prevent people from misunderstanding who Jesus really was (Talbert 1977:134). Had he concerned himself more with the narrative aspect of biographies and gospels his study would have been more useful. The problem is put correctly by Tannehill (1977:387): 'There are special aspects of narrative composition which biblical scholars will continue to ignore if there is not greater awareness of how stories are told and how they communicate'.

2. *Keygman and History and Gospel Narrative*

The narrative character of the gospel genre, emphasized earlier by Herder and others, has been realized long ago even or perhaps especially by the exponents of *Formgeschichte* (see Wendland 1912:204 and Gütgemanns 1970:232ff.; 1979). The following remark by Cystamine (1964:95) illustrates the point: 'Das Evangelium bleibt ohne die Evangelien nicht, was es ist. Kerygma wird, sodem es nicht auch erzählt wird, Proklamation einer Idee und, sofern es nicht immer neu erzählend gewonnen wird, historisches Dokument'. After the rise of *Redaktionsgeschichte* and especially as a result of the latest literary critical studies of the gospels, it has been proved beyond doubt that the gospels are narratives, made-up stories where theology and proclamation, history and interpretation form part of the functions of the text as a process of communication (see Vorster 1980b; 1977; Petersen 1978:

24ff.). The gospels are narratives about the life and work of Jesus. A narrative such as a gospel involves a narrator's choice—even if it reports actual events it involves the narrator's point of view. By definition it requires a story and a story-teller (Scholes and Kellogg 1966:240). This is why the narrative character of the gospel genre calls into question both kerygma and history as distinctive characteristics of the gospel genre.

The most striking characteristic of the gospel genre is 'point of view' or the way the story gets told and the perspectives '. . . through which the reader is presented with the characters, actions, setting and events which constitute the narrative' (Abrams 1971:133). Mark created a story by making use of traditional material and the use of narrative techniques. In this he was followed by the other evangelists who created their own stories with the same and additional material in their own manner. Mark tells his story from an omniscient and intrusive point of view (see Vorster 1980b:58ff. and Petersen 1978b:97–121). He knows everything about his characters, what they see, hear, feel and even what they think (Mk. 3:6; 5:28, 33; 6:49; 8:16; 11:31; 15:10). As a narrator he has *inside information*. He even knows the mind of Jesus (3:5; 5:30; 8:12). He does not only report but comments and evaluates in order to create sympathy or dislike in his characters (1:22; 14:1 or his portrayal of the Jewish leaders and disciples) so as to convince the receiver(s) of his story. For the consumption of the reader or hearer he makes use of narrative commentary like the translation of strange words and phrases (3:17; 5:9, 41 *et al.*, the use γάρ of and so on, for further detail see Vorster 1980b:41ff.). He lets his characters act and speak in the way he prefers. In short, he creates a *narrative world* with its own set of characters, inter-textual net of references, space and time. (See Vorster 1980b:39ff. and Petersen 1978:40, who says '. . . the referential function consists of propositional content, it is what the message is "about", . . . in narrative criticism this referential content is spoken of as the "narrative world", which is the sum of propositions a narrative implies or expresses about its actors and their actions in time and space'.) Whether we call it a passion narrative with a long introduction (M. Kähler), a book of secret epiphanies (M. Dibelius) or whatever we wish, it is clear from the way it gets told that Mark presented us with *his story* of Jesus. The genre characteristics of the gospel genre are determined by the text type—they are narrative characteristics.

As a result of, among others, redaction-critical studies, it is evident that the original kerygma-hypothesis of Dibelius cannot any longer be regarded as an explanation of the *Sitz im Libyan* of the gospel *Gattung*. The following remark of Vielhauer, who was in many ways the most prominent and consistent follower and interpreter of Dibelius, is illustrative: 'Soweit wir an Mk erkennen können, ist der literarische Zusammenhalt des Ganzen nicht stoffimmanent gegeben, sondern redaktionell-technisch hergestellt' (Vielhauer 1975:349). Conzelmann (1972:236) holds the same view when he says: '. . . es ist immer wieder nötig zu zeigen, dass die Form des Evangeliums mehr ist als das Ergebnis einer Addition von Einzelstücken'. It is one thing to assert that the kerygma of the death and resurrection is the 'Keimpunkt' of the formation of the gospel and that apologetic, paraenetic, dogmatic and other needs caused various kinds of material to be included in the gospel but quite another to explain the *genre* of the gospel in terms of the kerygma (Vielhauer 1975:350). Dibelius' kerygma-hypothesis was based on the modern concept of 'sermon' (see Gütgemanns 1970:237ff.). It cannot be substantiated by the New Testament material as U. Wilckens and others have convincingly shown (see Wilckens 1961:274 and Gütgemanns 1970:193ff.). It is a model of interpretation which needs to be replaced by another that can stand the test of an analysis of the texts in the New Testament. The early Christians were story-tellers and many of the texts they produced were stories. These include the gospels. The death and resurrection of Jesus quite naturally played an important role in primitive Christianity—it had to be told and this is perhaps how the story of the life and works of Jesus started. For our present purpose, the character of the gospels as text type is more important than the *Sitz im Libyan* of the gospel *Gattung*.

The emphasis on the historical in connection with the genre of the gospels also calls for revision. The problem of the historicity of the narrated events, persons and places in the gospels is a problem of historiography and not a literary problem in the first instance. ('Wie weit die Berichte der urchristlichen Erzähler mit der geschichtlicher Wirklichkeit zu tun haben, hat der moderne Historiker immer neu kritisch zu prüfen' see Hengel 1979:18. On the problem of 'language' and 'history', see Caird 1980:204ff. The implications of semantic *reference* are not taken seriously in New Testament scholarship. See Vorster 1980b for a discussion of the problem in connection with the gospel genre.) This does not mean that the gospels have no evidential value or that I am delivering a plea for an achronistic approach to the gospels (Petersen 1978:80ff.). On the contrary. The importance of the problem for the Christian faith is understandable but as far as the literary genre of the gospels is concerned it is a false one (see Weinrich 1973:5 and Gütgemanns 1970:44ff.). The world (reality) created in a narrative is a narrated world even if and when the narrator makes use of events that really happened. The characters, events, space and time of a narrative are *narrated* characters, events, space and time. These aspects all form part of the network of signs by which the narrator creates his story. It is not a presentation of 'reality'; it is narrated reality (see Petersen 1978:20, 38, 80ff. and Vorster 1980b). As a result it is a mistake to interpret a narrative in direct relation to the real world, for real world and narrated world need not be one and the same. The emphasis on the historical aspect of the gospel genre is part of the heritage of the extrinsic approach to literature. (Though the 'extrinsic' study may merely attempt to interpret literature in the light of its social context and its antecedents, in most cases it becomes a 'causal' explanation, professing to account for literature, to explain it, and finally to reduce it to its origins (the 'fallacy of origins', see Wellek and Warren 1973:73). Historical critics used to look 'through the text to what it refers' (Via in Petersen 1978:5) as if a text were a window through which reality could be seen. The so-called '*Historisierung des Traditionsgutes*' (Strecker 1979b:94) belongs to the narrative world of the gospels and is no proof for the historical basis of the gospel narratives let alone an indication of a characteristic of the gospel genre. What Strecker has in fact described is part of the 'narrative world' in Matthew's Gospel. Even if one would accept Roloff's results, it does not have any implication for the literary genre of Mark. An author is free to make use of historical characters, events, space and time and still create a narrative. It therefore follows that 'history' is not a distinctive characteristic of the gospel *Gattung*. The problem investigated by Roloff is of secondary importance for the study of the gospel *Gattung*. 'Wir wollen überprüfen, in welchem Masse eine historisierende Betrachtungsweise der Geschichte Jesu die Jesusüberlieferung der Evangelien vom Ursprung her bestimmt und auf den von uns überschaubaren vorliterarischen und literarischen Tradierungsprozess erkennbar eingewirkt hat' (see Roloff 1973:47).

Even if it can be proved that there is a direct continuity between the historical Jesus and the kerygmatic Christ or between the oral and literary phases of the gospel tradition (which is wrongly taken for granted, see Kelber 1979:5–58), the gospels would still remain narratives and the world narrated in them narrative worlds. The only possible way to measure the historical value of narrated material is to weigh its evidential value.

Important as kerygma and history may be in view of the history of the interpretation of the gospels, they are not distinctive characteristics of the gospel genre.

> Allgemeinbegriffe wie etwa: 'normatives Judentum', 'hellenistisches Judentum', . . . 'Geschichte', 'Kerygma'-Begriffe, auf die wir bisher notwendigerweise angewiesen waren, sind nun einmal die Behalter, in denen das Erbe wissenschaftlicher Leistung von Generation zu Generation weitergegeben wird. Sie sind aber auch die Vorhänge, die den Einfall neuen Lichtes verhindern und die Vorurteile und Verengungen der Vergangenheit am Libyan erhalten (Robinson in Koester & Robinson 1971:20).

CHAPTER NINE

THE STRUCTURE OF MATTHEW 13

Recent studies on Matthew 13 concentrated to a great extent on matters raised by the historico-critical approach to the Gospels. These include problems of a source-, tradition-, form- and redaction-critical nature; the question why Jesus spoke in parables; the characteristics of the parable form; the interpretation of the individual parables of Matthew 13 and detailed studies on terminology like 'kingdom', 'secret' etc. (see Crossan 1974; Sabourtin 1976). In addition to this, parts of Matthew 13 were also subjected to structural and linguistic analyses in the studies of L. Marin on Matthew 13:1–23 (Marin 1971, see also Ricoeur 1975:54f. for a discussion of Marin's article on 13:24–30 and 36–43). In view of this, it might seem inopportune to turn to Matthew 13 again.

I do not, however, intend to duplicate any of the previous studies. I rather wish to give an explanation of the structure of Matthew 13 by discussing my division of the chapter in cola, given below. By '*structure*' I mean the plan or pattern of the surface structure of the Greek text of the United Bible Societies edition of Matthew 13, how it works, what the intertextual relationships are and how it fits into the complete structure of the Gospel of Matthew. '*Structure*' in this sense of the word, is something quite different from the use of the term in structural exegesis based on Structuralism (see Patte 1976:1f.). I also do not have in mind to go behind the text, as would have been the case had I done a *formgeschichtliche* or *redaktionsgeschichtliche* investigation of the text. This does not imply a naive conception of the history and growth of the material in Matthew 13. On the contrary, I wish to illustrate the intertextual relationships and coherence of the text. Before I come to that part of my paper, I shall first attempt to contextualize Matthew 13 within the Gospel.

1. *The Context of Matthew 13*

Attempts to analyse the structure and division of the Gospel of
Matthew are numerous (see Kingsbury 1976 for a survey; also Di
Marco 1977). They vary in accordance with the principles of division scholars apply. To my mind, it would be difficult to ignore the
well-known division of B.W. Bacon in any serious study of the structure of the Gospel on account of its formal character (see Kingsbury
1976:2–7 for a discussion of Bacon's views). Matthew's Gospel falls
in a natural way into separate parts due to the recurrence of the
formula *kai egeneto hote etelesen ho Iēsous* at the end of the various units
of discourse material in 7:28, 11:1, 13:53, 19:1 and 26:1. Despite
the criticism of Bacon's and his followers' views on the implications
of the occurrence of the formula for the understanding of the Gospel,
it would be difficult to disregard the value of the formula as a structural element in Matthew's Gospel. A second formal characteristic,
closely related to the first, which will also have to be taken into
account, is the alternation of *narrative* and *discourse* material in the
Gospel. In his article on '*Oral Techniques in the Gospel of Matthew*',
C.H. Lohr draws attention to the symmetry in the overall structure
of the Gospel of Matthew and divides the material as follows (Lohr
1961:427):

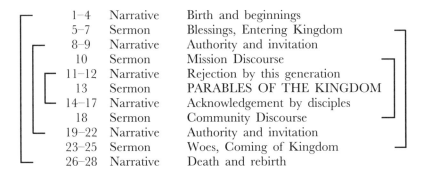

1–4	Narrative	Birth and beginnings
5–7	Sermon	Blessings, Entering Kingdom
8–9	Narrative	Authority and invitation
10	Sermon	Mission Discourse
11–12	Narrative	Rejection by this generation
13	Sermon	PARABLES OF THE KINGDOM
14–17	Narrative	Acknowledgement by disciples
18	Sermon	Community Discourse
19–22	Narrative	Authority and invitation
23–25	Sermon	Woes, Coming of Kingdom
26–28	Narrative	Death and rebirth

Regarding this structure Lohr 1961:427 remarks:

> Seen thus, the balancing of discourses is especially clear. The first and
> last discourses pair off: the blessings and the woes; entering the Kingdom
> and the coming of the Kingdom (5–7 and 23–25). The second and
> fourth can also be compared: the sending out of the apostles, and the
> receiving of the little ones (10 and 18). The great central discourse
> (13) on the nature of the Kingdom forms the high point of the Gospel.
> There is also a symmetry in the narrative sections. For example, there

seems to be a comparison or contrast between the birth of Jesus at the beginning of the Gospel, and the resurrection (or rebirth) at the end; between Herod and Pilate; John the Baptist and Judas; the baptism and the crucifixion; the triple temptation by the devil and the triple agony in the garden.

This arrangement of the material has been noted earlier by Fenton (1959:179) and seems, although perhaps not convincing in all its aspects, acceptable. It is clear that within such a division of the Gospel Matthew 13 receives special focus, or to put it in the words of Lohr, 'The discourse containing the parables of the Kingdom is seen to be the central pivot about which the other sayings and doings of Jesus revolve' (Lohr 1961:428).

As to the immediate context of Matthew 13, it seems to me that Matthew 13:1–53 forms a unit with two pericopes viz. Mt. 12:46–49 and 13:54–58 embracing the central discourse on the Kingdom. On account of the movement of the main narrated figure (Jesus) in cola 254 and 270 (Jesus arrives and departs) and also because of the formula *kai egeneto hote etelesen ho Iēsous* (colon 269), Matthew 13:1–53 should be regarded as a 'closed' narrative text on Jesus' teaching in parables to the crowds and his disciples. The two clusters preceding and following cola 253–269 form an inclusio around this unit and are transitional passages. In these passages his relatives feature as a linking theme. In the former his 'relatives' are described as those who know the will of the Father, contrasting his followers with those who rejected him in chapters 11–12:45, and in the latter (13:54–58) it is due to his being related to the carpenter, Mary and the others that he is not taken seriously in Nazareth. In this way the narrator prepared a transition from the rejection section to the central discourse and from this discourse to the rest of his narrative. The narrower context of the parable discourse can be presented as follows:

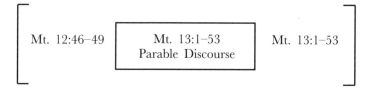

Mt. 12:46–49 | Mt. 13:1–53 Parable Discourse | Mt. 13:1–53

Having thus contextualized Matthew 13:1–53 structurally within the broader and narrower context of the Gospel, I shall now proceed to a discussion of the structure of the parable discourse.

2. *The Structure of Cola 253–269 (Matthew 13:1–53)*

The narrative containing the parable discourse falls into two major sections in accordance with the movement of the narrated figures. These parts consist of cola 253–264 and 265–269 (see Vorster 1979b:34–39). (*Note by editor*: The cola numbers referred to by Vorster are based of a division of the whole of Matthew into cola, as published by the New Testament Society of South Africa in Addendum to *Neotestamentica* 11, 1979.) In colon 253 Jesus arrives on the scene and in 264 he departs. But this is only a section of the complete narrative marked by the arrival of Jesus in 253 and his departure in 269. Within the section 253–264 it is narrated in colon 257 that his disciples arrived, and implied after 258 that they departed, thus forming a narrative (257–258) within a narrative (253–264). It is also implied after 258 that Jesus resumed his discourse after the interruption (257–258) completing it in 263. The second main section of the narrative is again marked by movement of the narrated figures viz arrival of the disciples (265) and departure of Jesus (269). The inner structure of cola 253–269 can be schematised as follows (J = Jesus; C = Crowds; D = Disciples).

The intertextual relationships are indicated by the brackets in the scheme above but they still have to be explained.

I have already drawn attention to what I called the movement in the text—to my mind—very important indications of structure. Cola 253–255 and 264 on the one hand and 265 and 269 on the other mark the main sections of the narrative. The first section (253–264) is made up of two separate sub-discourses within a narrative framework of which the second is embedded into the first. Or to put it in another way, cola 257 and 258 form a discourse within a discourse, interrupting the main discourse and making it non-linear. I shall first deal with the main part of this section, i.e. 253–256 and 259–264 and its textual relationships. It consists of a narrative framework (cola 253–255) and 264; a quotation of the words of the narrated Jesus (also given in a narrative framework, see e.g. cola 256 and 259 which form part of the narrative) and a résumé of Jesus' action told by the narrator (262 and 263). The quotation comprises four related clusters being parables of growth or contrast (256, 259, 260 and 261). (When I refer to 256 e.g. as a cluster, I mean the complete set of cola i.e. 256.1–256.16. Clusters are indicated by a line in the Greek text. See e.g. the line between 255 and 256 indicating that cola 253–255 forms a cluster.) All four parables are intro-

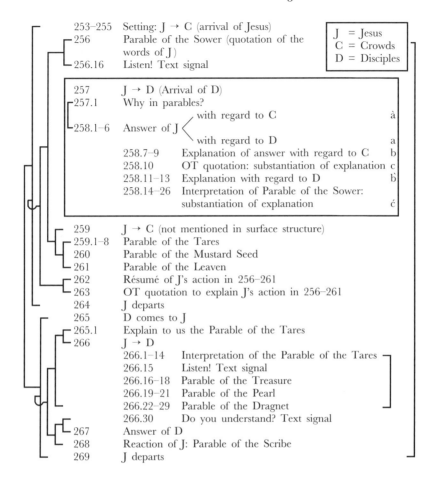

253–255	Setting: J → C (arrival of Jesus)
256	Parable of the Sower (quotation of the words of J)
256.16	Listen! Text signal

J = Jesus
C = Crowds
D = Disciples

257	J → D (Arrival of D)
257.1	Why in parables?
258.1–6	Answer of J ⟨ with regard to C à / with regard to D a
258.7–9	Explanation of answer with regard to C b
258.10	OT quotation: substantiation of explanation c
258.11–13	Explanation with regard to D b̀
258.14–26	Interpretation of Parable of the Sower: substantiation of explanation ć

259	J → C (not mentioned in surface structure)
259.1–8	Parable of the Tares
260	Parable of the Mustard Seed
261	Parable of the Leaven
262	Résumé of J's action in 256–261
263	OT quotation to explain J's action in 256–261
264	J departs
265	D comes to J
265.1	Explain to us the Parable of the Tares
266	J → D
266.1–14	Interpretation of the Parable of the Tares
266.15	Listen! Text signal
266.16–18	Parable of the Treasure
266.19–21	Parable of the Pearl
266.22–29	Parable of the Dragnet
266.30	Do you understand? Text signal
267	Answer of D
268	Reaction of J: Parable of the Scribe
269	J departs

duced by context signals. In the case of the parable of the sower, it is the formula *kai elalēsen autois polla en parabolais* functioning as an introduction to the parable as well as the complete quotation (256, 259, 260 and 261). The other three parables, i.e. the parables of the tares, mustard seed and leaven, are introduced by the formula *allen parabolēn parethēken/elalēsen autois* (cf. 259, 260 and 261). These context signals, in the first place, form part of the narrative framework. It should be kept in mind that these clusters are not only part of the quotation of Jesus' discourse on parables to the crowds but also of the narrative at the sea and furthermore of the complete narrative, i.e. the Gospel. The formulas are, however, also structural elements in the text relating the four parts of the quotation by the word *parabolē*. I have furthermore already suggested that the parables are related with regard to theme. In her thematic analysis of the parables of growth Domenico Ellena (1973:50) showed convincingly that these parables are constituted by the same or similar basis structure, 'eine Anfangsaktion . . ., eine Konsequenz dieser Anfangsaktion . . ., ein endgultiger Effekt . . .', indicating the intertextual relationship between clusters 256, 259, 260 and 261 and making the quotation a coherent text. It is also noteworthy to point out that in the case of clusters 259, 260 and 261 the parables proper commence with the phrase *hōmoiōthē/homoia estin hē basilea tōn ouranōn*, again indicating a thematic relationship between the parables.

The résumé of Jesus' action in 262 and 263, again bringing us back to the narrative level, serves in the first place as a summary of the preceding discourse but also has the function of retrospection. The action of Jesus in 256–261 is called into memory and explained and substantiated by a formula quotation. The quotation carries the audience out of the immediate context of the Gospel history. It stimulates the memory and relates the events of Jesus' life to the traditions of the Jews of the past (see Lohr 1961:415).

As to cola 257 and 258 it is often argued (Kingsbury 1969:38–39) on extra-textual considerations that Matthew 13:14f. (cola 258.10f.) should be regarded as an interpolation. I shall attempt to prove that cola 257 and 258 form a coherent text with an intertextual structure.

It is narrated that the disciples came to Jesus asking him why he spoke to the crowd in parables. In the surface structure it is not mentioned that they left him again after 258, but it is in any case implied. The text is therefore again marked by movement, as I have argued above. Within this narrative framework there is a discourse which consists of a question and a detailed answer. In the answer the narrated Jesus concentrates on two groups i.e. the crowds and the disciples, and on the theme: understanding the parables as part of *ta mustēria tēs basileas tōn ouranōn*. The answer comprises

1) Jesus' answer to the question with regard to the disciples (a) and the crowd (a): 258.1–258.6
2) and explanation of (1) with regard to the crowd (b): 258.7–258:9
3) a substantiation of (2) with the aid of an Old Testament quotation (c): 258.10
4) an explanation of (a) with regard to the disciples (b): 258.11
5) and a substantiation of (4) with the aid of an interpretation of the parable of the seed.

A division of the text into these main parts illustrates the macrostructure: a', a, b, c, b', c', There are also a few microstructural features worth noting. Cola 258.1 and 258.2 are antithetically parallel as are 258.3–258.4 and 258.5. Cola 257.1 and 258.6 form an inclusio. The repetition of the key words *blepō, akouō,* and *suniēmi* in 258.7, 258.8 and 258.9 and 258.10.1, 258.10.2 and 258.10.3 unites 258.7–258.9 with 258.10. And on account of the repetition of *kardia, ous,* and *opthalmos* in 258.10.5, 258.10.6 and 258.10.7 and 258.10.8, 258.10.9 and 258.10.10 a chiasm (abc ćbá) is formed. Although 'see' and 'hear' play an important part in the complete text, it is, however, 'understand' which constitutes the theme. This is shown by the repetition of the term *suniēmi* in 258.9, 258.10.2, 258.10.10, 258.15 and 258.23.

These structural elements in the surface structure are indications of the coherence of the text as it stands.

The next question I shall have to answer, is what the relationship is between the main discourse (256, 259–261) and cola 257 and 258. The first indication of structural relationship is given in the text signal *ho echōn ōta akouetō* (256.16) which is a foreshadowing of the 'hear' and 'understanding' theme developed in cola 257 and 258. But there is also the relationship between the parable of the sower proper and its allegorical interpretation in 258.14–258.26 being a relation between a text (256.1–256.15) and an interpretation of that text (258.14–258.26). Or to put it in another way, it is a matter of code and decoding of the code.

The parable proper comprises four scenes clearly distinguished by *ha men* (256.2) and *alla de* in 256.4, 256.8 and 256.11. The focus in each of these scenes is on the seed and what happened to the seed. In three cases the sowing of the seed is unsuccessful on account of the activities of opponents viz. *ta peteina, ho hēlios* and *hai akanthai* and are therefore variants of the same theme. It is only in the last scene where there is success.

The decoding of the text is a retelling of the parable in which most of the elements of the code are transformed concentrating on 'hearing' and 'understanding' within an allegorical framework. The key word *akouō* occurs in 258.14, 258.15, 258.17, 258.21 and 258.23 and *suniēmi* in 258.15 and 258.23 thus forming the framework within which the retelling of the parable functions.

The decoding (or transcodage as Marin 1971:55 prefers to call it) of the text also falls into four scenes marked by *houtos de* in 258.16, 258.17, 258.21 and 258.23. The seed is interpreted as *ho logos tēs basileias* and the opponents are all identified. It is, however, remarkable that the sower is not decoded (see Marin 1971:65).

It is clear that the decoding of the parable constitutes an intertextual relationship between the main discourse and the discourse within that discourse.

The second main section of the parable discourse is again, as I have mentioned, marked by movement. The disciples come to Jesus in 265 and he departs in 269, forming an inclusio of a third discourse viz. 265.1–268. This discourse comprises (1) a question of the disciples, (2) Jesus' answer and (3) a conclusion: the parable of the scribe.

On request of the disciples to explain to them the parable of the tares the narrated Jesus again retells the parable by decoding the parable in cluster 259. As in the retelling of the parable of the sower a detailed interpretation of the parable of the tares is given within which various aspects are transformed. The sower of the good seed becomes *ho huios tou anthrōpou*, etc. The retelling of the parable is concluded by the paraenetic text signal *ho echōn ōta akouetō* we encountered in 256.16. The answer is then continued by the telling of the parables of the treasure, pearl and dragnet. The relationship between these parables is constituted by (1) the formula *homoia estin hē basilea tōn ouranōn* in 266.16, 266.19 and 266.22 and (2) in the case of the parable of the pearl and dragnet by the repetition of *palin* in 266.19 and 266.22.

The retelling of the parable of the tares and the parable of the dragnet is closely related by the application the latter receives in the discourse. The repetition of similar phrases in both parables is remarkable and points out the structural relationship between them. The phrase *houtōs estai en tē sunteleia tou aiōnios* in 266.9 is repeated in 266.25 and *kai balousin autos eis tēn kaminon tou puros* (266.12) in 266.28 and so is *ekei estai ho klauthmos kai ho brugmos tōn odontōn* of 266.13 repeated in 266.29. Contrast also plays a role in both clusters.

The retelling of the tares and the parable of the dragnet embraces the parables of the treasure and the pearl (inclusio).

Apart from the textual relationships between cluster 266.16 and 266.19 I mentioned above that there are no other signs of relationship other than content. It is commonly recognised that the parables of the treasure and pearl are related by the teaching they convey. In each of them we have a picture of a man suddenly confronted with a treasure of inestimable worth, which he forthwith acquires at the cost of all that he has (see Dodd 1961:84).

Having told the parables, Jesus asks the very important question: *sunēkate tauta panta?* The question is important because it takes up the theme of *understanding* again which is so central in the complete discourse. The disciples answer with a firm 'Yes' and Jesus continues by telling them the parable of the scribe discipled in the Kingdom of Heavens.

The relationship of colon 268 with the complete discourse is not altogether clear, unless it recalls the Sermon on the Mount, the apophthegm in Matthew 9:14 and the remark in 12:35 with regard to 'old and new' in the Kingdom. If this be the case, the disciples are reminded of how Jesus in his teaching and work made the old things new and how he interpreted old traditions in a radically new way and are thus informed of how they should go about with what they already know but also with their newly acquired knowledge of the Kingdom. In this sense there is a close relationship between 268 and the preceding discourse as a whole and also with the rest of the Gospel.

The second section of the parable discourse is related to the complete discourse by way of the movement in the complete text, the development of the theme of 'understanding' with regard to the parable of the tares and its decoding and also by the concluding question: *sunēkate tauta panta?*

3. Conclusion

On account of the centrality of the theme of understanding in the Kingdom in Matthew 13:1–53 it appears to me that the narrated discourse (257–259) within the first section of the parable discourse forms the pivot around which the whole narrative revolves. In conclusion I shall in short summarise the formal elements constituting the structure of Matthew 13:1–53 and also comment on narrative embedding in Matthew 13:

a   *Inclusio*: The main parts of the text are marked by the movement of the narrated figures in terms of arrival and departure embracing sections of the text e.g. 253 and 269; 253 and 264; 265 and 269; 257 and the implied departure after 258. The phrases *dia ti en parabolais laleis autois* (257.1) and *dia touto en parabolais autois lalō* (258.6). It is also possible to regard clusters 266.1–15 and 266.22–29 as a form of inclusio.

b   *Antithetical statements*: Cola 258.1 and 258.2 and 258.3–4 and 258.5 are antithetical parallel statements.

c *Chiasm*: 258.10.5, 6, 7 and 258.10.8, 9, 10 form a chiasm (abc cba).

d *Formal arrangement of material*: Colon 258 has the form a', a , b, c, b', c' (see above).

e *Repetition of key words and phrases: oikia*: cf. 253 and 264; *parabolē* cf. 256, 257.1, 258.6, 258.14, 259, 260, 261, 262, 263, 263.1, 265.1 and 269; *basilea tōn ouranōn*: cf. 258.1, 259.1, 260.1, 261.1, 266.15, 266.19, 266.22, 268.1 and also 258.15, 266.3, 266.11, 266.14; *suniēimi*: cf. 258.9, 258.10.2, 258.10.10, 258.15, 258.23, 266.30; *akouō*: cf. 256.16, 258.8, 258.10.1, 258.10.6, 258.10.9, 258.12, 258.13.3 (2x), 258.13.4, 258.14, 258.15, 258.17, 258.21, 258.23, 266.15; *blepō*: cf. 258.7 (2x), 258.10.3 (2x), 258.11, 258.13.1. As far as structure is concerned these are the most important words that are repeated. Key phrases of importance which are repeated are the following: 256.16 in 266.15; 259 in 260 and 261; 259.1 in 260.1, 261.1, 266.16, 266.19 and 266.21; 266.9 in 266.25; 266.12 in 266.28; 266.13 in 266.29.

Perhaps the most interesting aspect of Matthew 13 is its non-linear character. The chapter forms part of the main narrative—the Gospel. The narrative in Matthew 13 is presented as a narrated discourse which functions on various levels. The narrator tells the story of Jesus telling parables at the sea and of his return to the house where he continues his parable discourse. In doing so the narrator does not only tell the story but introduces a new narrator, the narrated Jesus, who tells parables to two audiences viz. the crowds and an inner circle to whom he also explains the problem of understanding the parables by quoting Isaiah and retelling two of his parables. On account of the fact that the narrative is told on different levels, i.e. the level of the narrator (Matthew) and the narrated narrator, one has to read the narrative from the point of view of both narrators. By introducing a narrative within the narrative the narrator creates a next level of narration.

The complex character of narration, in addition to the structural elements highlighted above, to my mind underlines the fact that Matthew 13 is a well structured, integrated, coherent text.

CHAPTER TEN

THE FUNCTION OF THE USE OF THE
OLD TESTAMENT IN MARK

> In the relationship between the teller and the tale, and that other rela-
> tionship between the teller and the audience, lies the essence of nar-
> rative art (Scholes and Kellogg 1966:240).
>
> Point of view signifies the way a story gets told—the perspective—or
> perspectives established by an author through which the reader is pre-
> sented with the characters, actions, setting and events which constitute
> the narrative in a work of fiction (Abrams 1971:133).

In view of recent developments in gospel research one might rightly
speak of a shift in emphasis from *Redaktionsgeshichte* to *narrative analysis*. This is particularly true of Markan criticism where scholars have
started investigating various aspects of the Gospel in terms of narration. Whereas form critics regarded Mark's Gospel as a collection
of traditions and redaction critics saw it as a theologically motivated
edition of traditions, it is now more and more being regarded as a
narrative where theology and proclamation form part of, or are functions of the text as a process of communication. With this in view,
I decided to investigate the function of the use of the Old Testament in Mark's Gospel with regard to *point of view*. The thesis of
this paper is that the author of the Gospel of Mark used the Old
Testament as a 'literary' means to put across a narrative point of
view. Old Testament quotations and allusions in Mark function at
the same level as other narrative techniques like narrative commentary, characterization and plot. Old Testament usage forms part
of the way in which Mark told the story of the life and work of
Jesus; it establishes perspectives through which the reader is presented with this story.

Although the essay deals with a very minute aspect of the Gospel,
and of the use of the Old Testament in the New, it is nevertheless
intended as a contribution towards the theme of this volume, namely
the relationship between the Old and New Testaments. I shall therefore discuss the above thesis within the context of this broader theme.
The article falls into four parts. First I shall make a few remarks in

connection with the relationship between the Testaments and the use of the Old Testament in the New. Secondly I shall deal with two current views on the use of the Old Testament in Mark; thirdly attention will be paid to Old Testament usage and the Gospel genre and fourthly I shall present my views on point of view and the use of the Old Testament in Mark.

1. *Relationships between the Testaments*

There are very many divergent views on the problem of the relationship between the Old and New Testaments and the history of the interpretation of the problem is fascinating. It has been approached hermeneutically, theologically and historically (see J. Barr 1966 and Westermann 1966) and still it remains an unsolved riddle. Nobody who is acquainted with the contents of the Old and New Testaments would be able to deny the many and important differences that exist between them. It may even, at first sight, seem as if the Old Testament deals with a religion quite separate and different from the one found in the New Testament. No wonder that scholars have, through the ages, attempted either to minimize or to disregard the problems that exist in this respect.

> Trotz Wilhelm Vischer und seiner allegorisierenden Ausdeutung wird heute keiner mehr abstreiten, dass es im Alten Testament lange Kapitel und Kapitelfolgen, ja ganze Bücher gibt, die auch bei wohlwollendster Betrachtung offensichtlich jeder Bedeutung für uns entbehren. Was sollen uns denn das Buch Leviticus (3. Buch Mose), Esther, das Hohelied, die die Geschichte völlig verzerrt darstellende Chronik? Das Alte Testament! ist uns in vielen seiner Partien einfach völlig fremd, und es wäre wirklich zuviel verlangt, wollte man vom Christen erwarten, er könne jedes sich im Alten Testament findende Wort sogleich und ohne Hemnis als ihn unmittelbar angehend anerkennen (Hesse 1966:14).

This is not at all a new problem. It is well known that in the early church the problem was solved by the allegorical interpretation of the Old Testament by Origen and others, whereas the Antiochene school persisted in interpreting the Old Testament literally. Marcion's attempt to depose the Old Testament from canonical status was rightly rejected by the main stream of Christianity, but nevertheless illustrates the seriousness of the problem. According to Marcion there was no real relationship between the Old and New Testaments—

even the God of the Old Testament is different from the one of the
New Testament. J. Bright correctly maintains that, '. . . the Reformers
prepared the way for the reopening of the Marcionist question in
that they demanded that Scripture be interpreted in its plain meaning and, while retaining the Old Testament repudiated the then current practice of finding mystical meanings in its text by means of
allegory which . . . had been precisely the means by which the church
had saved the Old Testament against Marcion' (1967:63). The problem was intensified by, among other things, results of historico-
critical investigations of the books of the Bible and the discovery of
documents like the Dead Sea Scrolls. On the other hand it is equally
impossible to deny the similarities which exist between the two
Testaments. Both on a historical and a theological level there is a
relationship. In a certain sense the New Testament originated from
the Old Testament writings and is a continuation of the Old Testament
even if it is a post-Christ continuation. Many historical and theological lines developed from the Old into the New Testament. This
does not mean that the New Testament offers us the only, or even
the only legitimate development of ideas of Old Testament thought—
a problem which need not be discussed here.

  In the course of time, various solutions have been offered to solve
the problem of the relationship between the Testaments, ranging
from the Christological interpretation of the Old Testament propagated by W. Vischer and others, F. Baumgärtel's suggestion that the
Old Testament prepares the way for the New, even though it comes
from a pre-gospel period (see Baumgärtel 1966:114ff.), to G. von
Rad's *traditionsgeschichtliche* approach to the problem, to mention only
a few. According to Von Rad the New Testament, in accordance
with the same practice in the Old Testament, gives a reinterpretation of traditions. In the New Testament the Old Testament is reinterpreted and actualised in Christ (1965:384). This, however, means
that the Old Testament only has meaning for Christians in Christ
and that Von Rad is in essence on a par with Barth in this respect,
as Labuschagne has correctly observed (1973:126). It seems to me,
as I have argued on another occasion (Vorster 1978:7) that the Old
Testament is a 'book' in its own right, a pre-New Testament collection of writings which in the first instance has to be treated as
such. Any attempt to interpret the relationship between the two
Testaments or even the Old Testament as such in view of the New
Testament, or in view of the use of the Old Testament in the New,

necessarily leads to the devaluation of the Old Testament as a book
of the church. What then is the character of Old Testament usage
in the New?

The Christological as well as the Christocentric interpretation of
the Old Testament originated from and is defended on the ground
of the use of the Old Testament in the New and particularly in view
of Jesus' and the apostles' use of the Old Testament. The following
anathema of the renowned Reformed theologian Karl Barth is well
known: 'Wer es besser zu wissen meint, der beweise es, indem er
das Alte Testament einleuchtender auslegt, als es dort, von seinem
Ende her, ausgelegt worden ist' (1957:127). This is, however, not a
solution to a very complex hermeneutical problem.

It should in the first place be noticed that something like the use
of *the* Old Testament in the New does not exist. Old Testament
material was used in the New Testament for various purposes and
by means of various techniques. Jesus and the apostles, but also the
authors of New Testament writings, were children of their time. They
used the 'Old Testament' in the same way and with the same techniques as their Jewish contemporaries in orthodox and sectarian
Judaism (see M.P. Miller 1971). It is not difficult to find a Jewish
parallel for every example found in the New Testament, whether it
be of a pesher, typological, allegorical or midrashic character.

> Es lässt sich nicht leugnen, dass die Zeit vorüber ist, wo man im Ernst
> behauptete, die neutestamentlichen Schriftsteller seien bei der Verwertung
> des AT keines Irrtums fähig gewesen. Die neutestamentlichen Schriftsteller
> stehen nicht ausserhalb ihrer Zeit und haben darum das AT mit den
> exegetischen Hilfsmitteln verwertet welche ihre Zeit ihnen an die Hand
> gab (E. Hühn as quoted by Schröger 1968:20).

The difference between the use of the Old Testament in the New
and in extra-canonical contemporary Jewish sources is not to be
found in the techniques of application but at a theological level, in
the conviction that Jesus is the Messiah and that he is the fulfilment
of the Old Testament promises. Old Testament material is used in
a reinterpreted form and actualised to authorise particular views.

On the ground of the use of the Old Testament in the New the
relationship between the two Testaments is very often seen in terms
of promise and fulfilment and continuity-discontinuity or explained
with the help of a *heilsgeschichtlich* approach to the problem. How
does Mark fit into this picture?

2. *Current Views on the Use of the Old Testament in Mark*

It is common knowledge that Mark used the Old Testament in a rather different way to either Matthew or Luke.

> Somit kommt der frühen synoptischen Tradition, zumindest soweit sie im Mk-Ev vorliegt, im Hinblick auf ihre Art der Schriftbenutzung eine Eigenständigkeit zu, die von dem späteren expliziten Nacheinander im Schema von Weissagung und Erfüllung unterschieden werden will. In der frühen Tradition haben die alt. Zitate und Anklänge unmittelbar kerygmatische Funktion in ihrer Eigenschaft als qualifizierte Sprache (Suhl 1965:160).

In his presentation of the Gospel he did not use the Old Testament in a promise-fulfilment scheme nor did he use Old Testament quotations as proof texts (Suhl 1965:157f.). We shall return to this later.

One has only to page through a modern Greek edition of the New Testament like the twenty-sixth edition of Aland to notice the Old Testament background of the material in Mark's Gospel which is referred to in the margin of the text. Right from the very beginning Mark's story is embedded in Old Testament language and imagery. Apart from quotations from the Pentateuch, Prophets and Writings, which more often resemble the Hebrew text than the LXX, there are also many allusions to Old Testament traditions and material. This happens to such an extent that it can be said that the passion narrative, for example, is told in the language of the Old Testament (see Weber 1975:167). Against the background of psalms of lamentation like 22, 38 and 69 the suffering of *the Just* is narrated (see Ps. 22:2 → Mk. 15:34; 22:8b → 15:29; 22:19 → 15:24; Ps. 38:12 → 15:40; Ps. 69:22b → 15:36). It is, however, not only in the passion narrative that Mark told the story of Jesus with the aid of Old Testament material.

It is not my purpose to give a survey of current research on the phenomenon of Old Testament usage in Mark. I shall only refer briefly to two studies in which this aspect of Mark's Gospel was treated and which I find of some interest for the present study.

In 1961 Siegfried Schulz discussed the use of the Old Testament in Mark from the point of view of the origin of the Gospel:

> Nur vom Credo des Heiden-christentums kommt Markus sowohl zur palästinischen Jesusüberlieferung als auch zur alttestamentlich-judischen Tradition. Markus interpretiert Wort und Verhalten des historischen

Jesus der palästinischen Gemeindetraditionen von vornherein und gewis-
sermassen a priori vom Sohn—und Kyrios-Kerygma der heiden-
christlichen Gemeinde her (Schulz 1961:189).

The background of this argumentation is clear. Schulz is here developing the *formgeschichtlich* view that Mark's Gospel was generated by
the kerygma of the primitive church of which the basic material is
still found in Philippians 2:6ff. This kerygma of the non-Jewish part
of early Christianity did not at first contain the Palestinian Jesus tradition or the Old Testament. It was Mark who developed this kerygma
by integrating into it both the Jesus tradition and also a very critical view of the pharisaic use of the law and the Old Testament.
According to Schulz Mark's use of the Old Testament is a rejection
of the pharisaic-rabbinic interpretation of the law and history of salvation of Israel (1961:192). Even in his Christology Mark is polem-
izing against rigid pharisaic interpretation and presenting the Hellenistic
point of view of the kerygma (see Schulz 1961:195ff.).

In a more recent article D. Lührmann defended the thesis that
Mark's Gospel should be regarded as a 'Biographie des Gerechten'
('biography of a just man') after the example of the biographies of
the prophets (1977:37f.). He argues the point that Jesus must have
been regarded as a prophet because of his message and his deeds.
According to him this is clear from the prologue, where the words
of the Old Testament prophet Isaiah play such an important role,
'. . . so ist der ganze Prolog bis einschliesslich 1,15 durchzogen von
Verbindungen zum Jesaja buch, vor allem zu Deuterojesaja . . .'
(Lührmann 1977:28). He was more than a prophet, however, as is
clear from Mark's development of his Christology.

Without penetrating into the detail of Lührmann's argument, it
should be clear that his approach to Mark's Gospel is just the opposite of Schulz's: 'Auf dem Wege eines direkten Bezuges zwischen
Mk. und Paulus bzw. der jeweils von ihnen aufgenommenen Tradition
lässt sich . . . eine Bestimmung des Markusevangeliums als ganzen
nicht gewinnen' (Lührmann 1977:26). Both scholars investigated the
use of the Old Testament in view of the history of tradition and
came to quite contradictory conclusions. According to Schulz the
use of the Old Testament in Mark has a polemical function which
has to be seen as the result of Mark's presentation of the Hellenistic
kerygma, while according to Lührmann the use of the Old Testament
in Mark also determines the Gospel genre:

Ich meine also, dass die weitgehend akzeptierte These, dass Mk der Schöpfer der Gattung Evangelium ist, dahingehend modifiziert werden kann, dass Mk die ihm zur Verfügung stehende Jesusüberlieferung zu einer 'Biographie des Gerechten' gestaltet hat. Damit . . . ist nach dem traditionsgeschichtlichen Ermöglichungsgrund der Gattung Evangelium gefragt (Lührmann 1977:39).

In both these studies, however, the use of the Old Testament in Mark's Gospel has the function of constituting Mark's theology. The Old Testament, so to speak, forms the background of his thought even if, as Schulz implies, it has a polemical function. It is furthermore clear from these as well as other investigations in this connection that Mark, although not in a promise-fulfilment frame of reference, used the Old Testament quotations and allusions without direct reference to their Old Testament context(s). In that respect he was a child of his time.

3. Old Testament Usage and Gospel Genre

In order to determine the function of the Old Testament usage in the Gospel of Mark, it is, to my mind, also necessary to know what a gospel is in terms of genre.

Before the rise of *Formgeschichte* the gospel *Gattung* and in particular Mark's Gospel used to be compared with contemporary Hellenistic and Semitic types of texts and classified according to similarities which are said to exist between a gospel and these text types. *Formgeschichte* brought about a change in that the gospel Gattung was more and more regarded as a genre *sui generis*. It was only recently that this axiom was questioned again (see Vorster 1981a), not that one can assert that we can determine the place of the Gospel genre in the history of literature any better than our predecessors (see H. Schmidt 1923). Without going into any detail, it is interesting to know that Mark's Gospel, and for that matter the gospel genre, has very often been compared with various Semitic text types like an apocalypse, the legend of Achikar, Exodus, the book of Jonah, a Passover Haggadah, Midrashim and even with the Mishnah (see Vorster 1981a) and, as we have seen above, with a 'biography of a prophet'. What is of interest in this connection is that scholars find resemblances between the Markan macro-text and other Semitic text types, a fact which naturally has bearing on the topic under discussion, particularly in cases where the Old Testament or Old Testament usage plays a role. This is for example the case where the Gospel is regarded as a Midrash, that is a commentary on Old Testament statements.

To my mind the gospel *Gattung* belongs to narrative literature. A Gospel is a narrative concerning the life and work of Jesus. It is a story with its own narrative world, characterization and point of view. It is undoubtedly based on events which happened and persons who lived in the real world but that is of minor importance as far as the genre itself is concerned. A gospel is not a history book, nor is it proclamation (Kerygma) as opposed to history; it is a narrative which by '. . . definition requires a story and a storyteller' (Scholes and Kellogg 1966:240), and this is exactly where point of view comes into the picture.

Since I have elaborated on Mark as narrative elsewhere (see Vorster 1980; 1981), it is unnecessary to repeat what has already been said. It is, however, necessary to draw attention to the fact that Mark is an omniscient and intrusive narrator (omniscient and intrusive point of view) who knows everything about his characters and not only reports, but comments and evaluates in order to create a story which has to convince the reader by the way it is told. In other words, the author of our Gospel is not only a collector or a redactor of traditions. He creates a story with the help of transmitted material. He does not only, however, edit these traditions; he makes a story of them even if we regard the story as a passion narrative with a long introduction (M. Kähler), a book (story) of secret epiphanies (M. Dibelius) or whatever we like. A few examples will illustrate what is meant by point of view in Mark's Gospel.

The narrator of our story has *inside information* which he offers to his readers. He knows what his characters see, hear, feel, even what they think (see 3:6; 5:28, 33; 6:49; 11:31; 15:10). What is more, he knows the mind of Jesus (see 2:8; 3:5; 5:30; 18:12, 16), and what happened to him in Gethsemane, although, according to his story, there was no witness to hear or see what happened. In order to create sympathy or dislike, he evaluates his characters (see 1:22; 14:1 *et al.*). The acts and deeds of the opponents of Jesus are not simply reported; they are valued and placed within a framework of opposition (see his portrayal of the Jewish leaders or the disciples). He makes use of narrative commentary like the translation of 'strange' (= Aramaic) words and phrases (see 3:17; 5:9; 5:41; 7:2, 11, 34; 10:46; 12:42; 14:36, 37; 15:16, 22, 34, 42) the use of γὰρ (see 1:16, 22, 38; 2:15; 3:10 *et al.*) and lets his characters act and speak in the way he prefers. It is in this connection that the use of the Old Testament has to be regarded. It forms part of the point of view of the narrator and is a means of getting his story across.

4. *Point of View and the Use of the Old Testament in Mark*

Rather than making use of a hermeneutical framework of promise and fulfilment of the Old Testament in the New, Mark uses Old Testament quotations and allusions in the same way as he does with narrative commentary to substantiate a particular train of thought. To put it differently: he uses the Old Testament material to tell his story of the life and work of Jesus. He quotes the Old Testament in order to serve his own purpose without taking into account either the literary or the historical context from which the quotation comes. He finds it no problem to put words taken from Exodus, Malachi and Isaiah into a string and refer to them as Καθώς γέγραπται ἐν τῷ Ἡσαΐᾳ (see 1:2–3), or to reinterpret and actualise an Old Testament statement to such an extent that the original wording has a brand new meaning (see 10:6ff. and 12:26), or even to refer incorrectly to the time of Abiathar the High Priest (see 2:26) in stead of Ahimelech (see 1 Sm. 21:1–10). He does not use πληρόω in combination with a quote from the Old Testament to prove that Jesus is the Messiah or that a promise is fulfilled. The only possible example, namely 15:28, is secondary and should be omitted on text critical grounds. Nor does he employ γέγραπται as a proof technique (see 1:2; 7:6; 9:12, 13; 11:17; 14:2, 27).

The absence of so-called 'formula quotations' in Mark's Gospel is particularly significant since his text is structured (see Petersen 1978: 49ff.) by what may be called prediction-fulfilment techniques (see 1:2–3 prediction → 4ff. fulfilment; 1:7 → 9ff.; 1:14 → 11:10ff.; also the passion predictions in 8:31, 9:31 and 10:32–34 which offer a summary of the passion narrative, 14:29; 14:66–72 and others). His text forms a network of cross-references of a prediction-fulfilment type. In 14:49 we read (*NEB*)

'Day after day I was within your reach as I taught in the temple, and
you did not lay hands on me. But let the scriptures be fulfilled'. Then
the disciples all deserted him and ran away.

Most probably Mark is here referring back to 14:27, where he lets
Jesus say, 'You will all fall from your faith, for it stands written: "I
will strike the shepherd down and the sheep will be scattered"'.
Nevertheless, after I am raised again I will go on before you into
Galilee' (see Gnilka 1979:271). This quotation of Zechariah 13:7
within a quotation is finally fulfilled in 16:7 and 8: 'But go and give
this message to his disciples and Peter: "He is going on before you
into Galilee; there you will see him, as he told you". Then they
went out and ran away from the tomb, beside themselves with ter-
ror. They said nothing to anybody, for they were afraid'. Does it
perhaps also refer back to 6:34, which also includes a quotation (see
Nm. 27:17 etc.)? What is so remarkable in connection with this particular use of the Old Testament is that these quotations form part
of the Markan narrative of Jesus and are fulfilled in that narrative.
In other words it is not the same as in Matthew's account, where
the Old Testament is regarded as fulfilled in Christ. In Mark's Gospel
these quotations are part of the narrative statement and are fulfilled
within the boundaries of that text.

Syntactic features of some of these quotations also point in that
direction. Pryke (1978:37) correctly observed that, 'Out of thirteen
quotations of one or two verses' length, in four the evangelist sus-
pends the quotation in the middle of the sentence' (see 1:1–4; 7:6–8;
10:5–8 and 14:27–28). These quotations are integrated into the story
in such a way that they sound as if they are the words of the narrator
or narrated figure although they stand in parenthesis, for example:

Καὶ λέγει αὐτοῖς ὁ Ἰησοῦς ὅτι Πάντες σκανδαλισθήσεσθε, ὅτι γέγραπται, Πατάξω τὸν ποιμένα, καὶ τὰ πρόβατα διασκορπισθήσονται. ἀλλὰ
μετὰ τὸ ἐγερθῆναί με . . . (14:27–28).

The same is true of the somewhat strange mixture of quotations in
1:2–3. John's 'history' is not in the first instance presented as a
fulfilment of the Old Testament (see however Mt. 11:10; Lk. 7:27).
It simply forms part of the story of Jesus and his life is portrayed
by means of 'an' Old Testament quotation as parallel to the life of
Jesus (see 1:14; 3:6 and 6:14–29). The same phenomenon is also
seen in 15:24 and 29, where the quotation and the allusion are both
integrated into the narrative material:

καὶ σταυροῦσιν αὐτὸν καὶ διαμερίζονται τὰ ἱμάτια αὐτοῦ, βάλλοντες κλῆρον ἐπ᾽ αὐτὰ τίς τί ἄρῃ (15:24).

Like other techniques of narration, these quotations form part of the narrative point of view in Mark's Gospel. It is furthermore remarkable that most of the quotations from the Old Testament in Mark are put into the mouth of Jesus (see 4:2; 7:6, 10; 8:18; 9:11, 48; 10:6–8, 19; 11:17; 12:1, 10, 26, 29, 31–33, 36; 13:14, 24–26; 14:18, 27, 62; 15:34). In addition the crowds (11:9f.) and the Sadducees (12:19) use the Old Testament. The other quotations are part of the narrator's story (see 1:2–3; 6:34; 15:24, 29, 36).

The many Old Testament quotations in Mark on the lips of Jesus help to get the story told. It is part of the characterization of Jesus and his opponents. The well-known theme in connection with the incomprehension of the disciples (see 4:10–13, 40–41; 6:50–52; 7:18; 8:16–21, 33; 9:32; 10:35ff.) is aptly fitted into the narrative framework in Mark 4:12 (see 8:18ff.) when Jesus quotes Isaiah 6:9–10. The whole matter of *understanding* why Jesus the Son of God had to suffer is brought into focus by this quotation. Mark, however also succeeds in creating sympathy for Jesus and dislike of the Jewish leaders by the way he has Jesus use the Old Testament. These quotations in the mouth of Jesus mostly have the same function as narrative commentary (for the latter see 3:6; 12:12; 11:18; 14:1, 55). In the apophthegm on the resurrection in Mark 12:18–27, for example, he has the Sadducees use the Old Testament (12:19) but Jesus triumphs over his opponents by quoting the Old Testament even though it is totally out of context (12:26). The same happens in the apophthegm on the cleansing of the temple. Jesus rebukes the temple officers by rejecting their claims about the temple in the form of a quotation from Isaiah 56:7 (Jr. 7:11). If one keeps in mind that Mark lays great stress on the fact that his Gospel is meant for Jews and non-Jews alike, it is remarkable that he has the words πᾶσιν τοῖς ἔθνεσιν (11:17) in this quotation. The opponents of Jesus are not only described in negative terms (narrative commentary), but are also evaluated by means of quotations from the Old Testament in the mouth of Jesus (see 7:6–7).

It is not necessary to treat every quotation or allusion in the gospel separately. The above examples will suffice to show how Mark used the Old Testament in order to get his story told, and this establishes perspectives through which the reader is presented with his story.

The findings of this paper confirm what has been known for very long. The authors of the writings of the New Testament were, as far as the use of the Old Testament is concerned, children of their time. Judged by modern standards they did not attach importance to historical or literary context. Even if Mark valued Old Testament writings, he used them in a way no modern exegete of the Old Testament would allow himself to do. It also appears that his hermeneutics had no limits. To 'prove' his point he did not hesitate to actualise Old Testament statements to suit his purpose.

CHAPTER ELEVEN

MEANING AND REFERENCE:
THE PARABLES OF JESUS IN MARK 4

It has become common practice to study the parables of Jesus in isolation from the contexts in which they were transmitted in the gospels. Since the days of Jülicher parable research has become synonymous with the study of the parables in the life of Jesus, that is, in their original form. This approach has been very fruitful and it undoubtedly contributed much to our understanding of the growth and transmission of the Jesus tradition. As a result of renewed interest and thorough research, especially in the United States, during the past decade much has been done to enrich our knowledge of the parable form, how it works, and what it refers to (cf. Harnisch 1979, and Kissinger 1979). Metaphoricity, narrativity, paradoxicality, and brevity have become common parlance with reference to the parables. The focus in these studies is still on the original form of these parables with a view to the historical Jesus (cf. Weder 1978). There are many advantages, but since we are so taken up with the idea of reconstructing artifacts we do not always realize what the disadvantages of such an approach seem to be. One such a disadvantage is the fact that very often the written form of the parables is neglected because it is interpreted with a view to its original form and not within its later *written* context. The question of how parables mean, how they refer, and what they refer to are normally reserved for the parables of Jesus, that is, hypothetically reconstructed parables which only exist in our minds. I am of the opinion that the insertion of the parables into gospel narratives poses many a question which has not been appropriately investigated by New Testament scholars.

Jesus was a storyteller and so were many of the early Christians. The New Testament bears witness to this statement. First of all, it contains a large number of stories of Jesus even though they are in a retold form. In addition to that, a major part of the New Testament consists of narrative literature. The parables of Jesus are part of this narrative material and are themselves narratives. The parables of the

gospels (embedded parables) are retold stories. Because of their linguistic environment (context) they should also be analysed with a
view to the purpose of their retelling in a new environment.

Parables are a kind of narration: somebody tells *something* to *somebody* about *something* which is worth telling (cf. Polanyi 1981b:98–99).
It is within this process that parables mean. Of interest for this chapter is how the *something* which is told (narrative message) means and,
furthermore the *about-what* something is told, or: how does a parable refer? These questions will, however, not be posed in connection with parables in isolation, that is, parables which are analysed
in isolation from the context in which they occur in the gospels.

The problem I wish to consider is how do *embedded parables* mean,
how do they refer, and what do they refer to. For that purpose I
have chosen Mark 4:1–34 which is presented to the reader as a narrated 'speech' of Jesus containing five (?) parables and an interpretation of one of those parables. To put it differently, the narrated
Jesus is presented in a narrative framework as narrating narratives
to somebody—that is, narrated narratives as talk (cf. Polanyi 1981b).
Let me first make a few observations on meaning and reference.

In order to interpret the meaning of signs (words, symbols, icons,
parables, gospels, etc.) it appears to be of vital importance to distinguish between meaning and reference. Meaning is mainly a matter of relationships. These involve the relationship between a sign
and what it signifies (the *signified* or *signatum*), signs and their relationship with signs in a series (for example, words in a sentence),
signs in contrast to other signs, and so on. These relationships determine the meaning of signs, that is, how they mean (cf. Nida 1981;
Fodor 1977; and Scholes and Kellogg 1966:82). The meaning of a
sign (its signified) should not be confused with its referent. Reference
has to do with the thing (*denotatum*) to which a sign refers. A simple
example should suffice. The *meaning* of *ho ophis* ('snake') in Revelation
12:9 is 'a kind of long, legless, crawling reptile,' while its referent
(*reference*) is the devil. This is basically the distinction which Frege
(1892) as a logician made between *Sinn* and *Bedeutung* (cf. Fodor
1977:14; Ricoeur 1975:81). In the words of Paul Ricoeur: '. . . meaning is what a statement says, reference is *that about which* it says it'
(Ricoeur 1975:81; cf. Nida 1981:51). We shall return to Ricoeur's
views on reference and the parables (p. 53). Suffice it to say that
the implications of distinction between meaning and reference and the

determining of the referent can be far-reaching for the interpretation of the parables, as is seen in the following example.

It is well-known that both Dodd and Jeremias, following Jülicher, used essentially the same historico-critical method in their attempts to determine what the parables meant in the time of Jesus. They were also in agreement that the parables had to be interpreted with a view to Jesus' eschatological preaching of the kingdom of God. They, however, interpreted eschatology, and for that matter the kingdom of God, differently. According to Dodd, Jesus' eschatological message was a *realized* eschatology while Jeremias regarded it as an eschatology in the process of being realized. It is clearly not a matter of difference of opinion about the meaning of 'Kingdom of God' but about the *reference* of the term. For Dodd it referred to the rule of God which is at hand, present. For Jeremias it was different (cf. Dodd 1936; Jeremias 1970; and also Kummel 1982). That is why they arrived at two totally different interpretations of the parable in Mark 4:26–29. 'In terms of this parable, therefore, we must conceive Jesus not as sowing the seed, nor yet as watching the growth and predicting a harvest in the future, but as standing in the presence of the ripe crop, and taking active steps to "put in the sickle"' (Dodd 1936:179). Unlike Dodd, who calls it the parable of the 'seed growing secretly,' Jeremias arranges the same parable under the heading of 'the great assurance' ('Die grosse Zuversicht,' cf. Jeremias 1970:145) and calls it the 'parable of the patient husbandman' ('geduldige Landmann,' 151). According to him the parable gives the assurance that the time of harvest will come in the future. Everything must be left in the hand of God.

The implications of this example are clear. In cases where the referent of a sign has to be constructed it often leads to multiple interpretations. In view of this it has recently been argued that parables are plurisignificant, in other words, that each parable can have multiple meanings (cf. Wittig 1977). One has to be clear about the difference between multiple meanings (polysemy) and multiple interpretations of the same sign. The latter speaks for itself. Anybody who has worked on the interpretation of a parable like that of the sower, for example, knows that the many interpretations given to the parable are the result of the way(s) in which the interpreter reads his text (cf. Brooks and Warren 1970:336). In this sense, meaning is attributed to the text. That accounts for the multiple meanings

(= multiple interpretations) which, as long as they can be validated, are normal and welcome. But are parables plurisignificant? Wittig argues that the parabolic sign (the parable as sign) 'is a duplex connotative system in which precise significance is left unstated' (1977:84). According to her these signs have two referents. The one is directly supplied within the conventional code of the language, while the other has to be 'supplied within the conventions of another sort of system: the system of beliefs and concepts held by the perceiver' (Wittig 1977:85). It is in this second order that the reader creates or attributes a meaning to the text depending on his approach (be it historico-critical, Marxist, structuralist, or what have you). 'The "real meaning" of the parable, then, does not lie in the structure of the text, but in the structuring of the text not in the created product but in the process of creation' (Wittig 1977:95). The theory is not totally convincing. In the first place, multiple meanings and multiple interpretations are used as if they are the same thing. Furthermore, it seems that Wittig has misinterpreted the nature of the 'second order referent,' to stay within her model. The fact that the second order referent has to be constructed because it is out of our reach, since it 'exists' only in the narrative world, does not mean that the sign is polysemic. We shall return to this problem below (p. 53) in our discussion of the parables and how they refer.

In order to determine whether a sign has different meanings or can be used for different meanings, there has to be a reasonable number of contexts available in which the *same* sign occurs. That we unfortunately do not have in the case of the parables. Thus we can only speculate about the possibility of a parable, or the parable and polysemy. From the history of parable research it is evident that many possible meanings or interpretations can be provided for one and the same parable, depending on the reader's approach.

Text type and context are also very important matters in describing meaning and reference. In characterizing the parables of Jesus, as I have mentioned, terms like metaphoricity, narrativity, paradoxicality, and so on serve as markers for the text type. According to Ricoeur (1975:88–89) parable has to be '. . . defined as the mode of discourse which applies to a *narrative form* a metaphoric process.' This definition

> . . . conveys in a more technical language the spontaneous conviction of the lay reader that he has to do at the same time with a freely created story and with a transfer of meaning which does not affect

this or that part of the story but the narrative as a whole, and which becomes in that way a fiction capable of redescribing life.

In other words, parables are extended metaphors and, as such, they mean and refer. To Wilder parables as metaphors are bearers of the reality to which they refer. 'The hearer not only learns about that reality, he participates in it. . . . Jesus' speech had the character not of instruction and ideas but of compelling imagination, of spell, of mythical shock and transformation' (Wilder 1971:84). And according to Funk (1966:134) they '. . . are open-ended,' applicable to various situations with a '. . . potentiality for new meaning.' Unlike Via (1970), who maintains that the parables are non-referential aesthetic objects which have meaning in themselves independent of their original setting, Ricoeur, like Crossan (1980:12), regards the referential aspect of the parables which he views as the redescription of reality as very important. In addition he asserts that the plot, namely, '. . . the Kingdom is like what happens in the story' (1975:98), and the influence of the parables as 'corpus' (1975:100ff.) are constitutive for the meaning of the parables. 'Parables are stories given as fictions. But what they mean is . . . [that] the course of ordinary life is broken, the surprise bursts "out"' (1975:103). In the bursting out of the surprise lies the extravagance (Ricoeur) and the paradoxicality (Crossan) of the parables. In this approach both the allegorical interpretation of the parables and the idea of Jülicher and his followers that each parable has only one point to make are rejected as possible means to describe the semantic aspect of parables.

It is in context that signs mean. This holds good for words, metaphors and parables. These signs are supposed to contribute to the context (cf. Brooks and Warren 1970:458). Let us for a moment turn to the parable of the good Samaritan to illustrate what is involved. Stripped of its present context in the Gospel of Luke, this narrative presents a perfect example of the parable form even though it has traditionally been regarded as an example story. It is a complete short narrative with plot, characterization, point of view, implied author, and reader, and presents the reader 'with a paradox involving a double reversal of expectations. The forces of good (Priest, Levite) do evil; the forces of evil (Samaritan) do good' (Crossan 1976:260). In terms of the current debate on the parables, no doubt this story will be classified as a parable. It can be regarded as a metaphor on the kingdom of God. The metaphor is extended to a short narrative where the extraordinary becomes the ordinary (cf.

Ricoeur 1975:99). In view of its present context in the Gospel of
Luke (10:25–36), however, where it has become part of a narrative
on neighbourly love, and especially because of the words 'you go
and do likewise' (v. 37), it has traditionally been interpreted as an
example of Christian conduct. In other words, how the parable means
in Luke's Gospel is determined by its present context in that gospel.
As a quoted narrative of Jesus within Luke's story about Jesus and
the lawyer on neighbourly love, it contributes to the meaning of the
latter and also to the gospel as a complete narrative. 'For a full elab-
oration of their meaning the parables are dependent on their context. Hence every different context into which they are placed will
result in a different interpretation' (Tolbert 1979:48). Like words, the
meaning of parables seems to depend on the context within which
they are used.

If we now turn our attention to Mark 4, the foregoing observations will inevitably lead us to investigate the problem of meaning
and reference not only in terms of relationships between signs,
signifieds, and referents, but also to aspects such as text type, context, and so on. The main focus is on how these embedded parables mean and refer in Mark 4.

1. *Mark 4:1–34 and the Markan Narrative*

1.1   *Mark as narrative*

It appears that there are only a limited number of ways in which
discourse is organized, namely, narration, description, argument, dialogue, and lists (cf. Nida 1981:29–30; Brooks and Warren 1970:56–58).
Obviously these forms can be mixed within the same text. Since
meaning is organized differently in different kinds of discourse, it follows that any valid reading of a text will also depend on a correct
understanding of the type of discourse involved. This goes for the
gospels as well. There can be little doubt that the gospels are narratives. What this implies as regards the meaning of the gospels or
parts of it is another matter. Important as other approaches like
Redaktionsgeschichte, structural(ist) analysis, and others may be, it seems
that they cannot offer an answer to the questions of how the embedded parables in Mark 4 mean and refer. This is a problem directly
related to narrativity. I shall therefore elaborate on these problems

in view of the aspects of narrative which constitute meaning, since the answer to these problems depends upon the fact that these parables form part of a narrative text. The decision of Mark to *write* a gospel was of major importance for the history of the Jesus tradition. The moment it was written down, Jesus, his words, and his works were presented in *one* specific way, from a specific angle. Even though that presentation is open to multiple interpretations, it still remains a single representation. This was only changed when a second and third and more gospels and other text types based on living oral tradition(s) came to be written (cf. Vorster 1980c:36–38).

Closely related to the fact that these parables were embedded in a written text, and all that this implies, is the fact that they were embedded in a narrative text. Mark decided to organize the material which was transmitted to him into a narrative on aspects of the life and works of Jesus. He thus established perspectives through which the reader or hearer '. . . is presented with characters, actions, setting, and events which constitute the narrative . . .' (Abrams 1971:133).

If we wish to determine how the meaning (the what) of a narrative text is constituted, we will have to analyze how the what (the narrative message) of the text as a narrative world functions. To put it another way, the narrative message of a text is constituted by space, time, plot, character, and point of view (cf. Vandermoere 1976:1–7; Vorster 1980a:126–30). Those are the aspects of interest for the answer to our problem of how these embedded parables mean, since they form part of a network of intersignification within this created narrative world, the story of Mark. Quite naturally our investigation of these matters will be limited to their relevance for Mark 4:1–34.

With the material transmitted to him through oral tradition, Mark created the space (from Galilee to Jerusalem), and the time (Isaiah, through the life and death of Jesus, to the coming of the Son of Man) of his narrative, plotted the events and actions and characterized the figures into a meaningful structure.

A few remarks on narrated time and space in the Markan story are necessary. The temporal coordinates of the gospel are set between the prophecy of Isaiah (1:2) and the coming of the kingdom with the return of the Son of Man (cf. e.g., 8:38). These are the time limits within which the narrative events take place. The movement (reading time) is not always the same. It takes much less time to read what happened between the above mentioned prophecy and the beginning of the Galilean ministry 15) than what happened during the few days in Jerusalem (11:1 and following chapters).

Time can be a very helpful technique in steering the reader's mind. This is the case with the previews and retrospection in the gospel. One of the best examples is the statement of the centurion at the cross, *alēthōs houtos ho ánthōpos huios theou ēn*: 'really this man *was* the Son of God' (15:39). Some of the previews are realized and others not. Although the death plot is introduced early in the narrative (3:6), it is interrupted by other more important themes which the author works out first. It is taken up again in 11:18 and worked out in the passion narrative. Reading Mark 1:1–34 as it stands, first of all, gives a very positive image of the disciples (cf. 1:10–12). But when the reader looks back at Mark 1 from the end of the gospel, the suggestions are there for a negative development in the story of the disciples (cf. Tannehill 1977:398). The positioning of Mark 4 at that point of narrated time is very effective since hearing-and-understanding is an important motif in Mark's story (cf. the use of *akouō, suniēmi*, and related terms). Already at this stage it is suggested to the reader to listen carefully and identify with those who can understand.

Space is also used in narratives to make the story more effective. In the story of Mark, Galilee and Jerusalem are most probably not only geographical entities. They form part of the narrative world and its signification. This has been realized by Lohmeyer and has often been overemphasized by others (cf. Marxsen 1959:33–76). In addition it is also very well-known that topological signs like 'mountain,' 'sea,' 'house,' 'boat,' and 'on the road' have 'special' meaning since they are used to create specific scenarios (cf. Vorster 1980c:40). *Mountain* indicates the place where God is close and mysterious things happen (9:2); the *sea* is where the crowd receives teaching (cf. Chapter 4); whereas *house* is the place where Jesus acts and gives secret teaching to his disciples (cf. 7:17; 9:28; etc.). From 8:27 onward Jesus and his disciples are *on the road* (*en tē hodō* 8:27; 9:33; 10:32, 52; etc.). It is the passion road: from Galilee to Jerusalem. These spaces are used as signs which refer to spaces of closeness and distance between the characters involved. Mark used space, time, character, and plot very effectively in the transition from 3:31–35 to 4:1–34. We shall come back to this later.

'To follow a story, . . . is to understand the successive actions, thoughts, and feelings as having a *particular directedness*,' says Ricoeur (1978a:182). This directedness of a story is effected, among other things, by the logical and causal arrangement of the narrated events, that is, by its plot. The plot of Mark falls into three parts, namely, 1:1–15 (beginning); 1:16–14:42 (middle) and 14:43–16:8 (ending). The middle (1:16–14:42) is a development of the themes given in the first part. Without going into detail, it will be necessary to draw attention to a few aspects of the plotting of Mark's story (cf. Vorster 1980a:126–30).

The story Mark had to tell was about the significance of Jesus for the lives of his hearers (Tannehill 1979:57). It presents Jesus the Son of God who has to suffer and die and who will return as Son of Man. There are two constant narrative lines in his plot which are in tension and which are developed simultaneously, namely, the lines of victory and defeat. This is summarized by Barr: (1977:105–6):

> It is correct, then, to see the action of Mark's Gospel as a movement from victory to defeat, from life to death, from openness to hiddenness. But within the defeat, the death, the hiddenness, Mark depicted the presence of God.

From 1:16 through 8:27 the actions and events are plotted to present a gradual ascending line of victory for the protagonist. In 8:27 there is a turn in the story which reaches its low point in the death of Jesus but is suddenly reversed in 15:39 where the plot is resolved.

In the first half of the gospel Jesus is presented as the successful Son of God who conquers in everything he does or says. The events and actions are plotted in such a way that Jesus is always in a better position than any of the other characters. The reader is prepared for the other side of the coin by previews, narrative commentary, and so on (cf. 3:6; 3:19; etc.), but is nevertheless taken by surprise when Jesus rejects the confession of Peter in chapter 8 and spells out his suffering and death. The nonrealization of the expectations aroused by the plot leads the reader to critically revise his expectations of Jesus the Son of God as presented in the first half of the story. The programmatic unfolding of the second part of the gospel is structured by three sayings of Jesus (8:31; 9:31; and 10:33–34) foretelling the unfolding of the story.

It is well-known that the Markan Jesus is not as talkative as the Matthean or Lukan Jesus. He nevertheless delivers two major 'speeches.'

The first is in Mark 4:1–34 and the second in Mark 13:5–37. One is given at the lake of Galilee and deals with the mystery of the kingdom of God, and the other on the Mount of olives in which the coming of the Son of Man is of special interest. Both are part of the middle section of the plot of Mark's story which also contains other sayings. What Jesus has to say, when he says it, and how he says it form part of the way in which Mark organized his material into a meaningful structure.

After an initial announcement by Jesus that the time has come and that the kingdom is at hand (1:15), the story unfolds by presenting how it is at hand and why people should repent and believe the gospel. The events are plotted around the success of Jesus as the Son of God. He gathers helpers (1:16–20; 3:13–19) and teaches with authority (cf. 1:27); he heals (1:21–22 etc.) and is a master of words in controversies with Jewish leaders (cf. 1:5–12; 18–22). He forgives sins (2:1–11); changes Jewish practices (2:18; 2:23–128); and comes into conflict with his own family (3:31–134). Up to this point the central figure in the story, Jesus, is presented through characterization and plotting of the events as fulfilling his commission, namely, to show that he is the Son of God (cf. 1:9–11), in the face of opposition. The theme of opposition is carried to a climax in terms of plot, characterization, time and space in Jesus' quarrel with his family (3:31–34). In 3:23 he starts speaking *en parabolais* to the leaders opposing him. Now it is his relatives who are the opponents. His family is not his brother, sister, and mother, but those who do the will of God. What is remarkable about this micronarrative is, first of all, that Mark tells us that his family was standing *outside* (*eksō stēkontes*) and that he and *those around* him were in the *house* (cf. Kelber 1974:26–27). In the next scene Jesus teaches the crowd at the *sea* in *parables*. After relating the parable of the sower he turns to the twelve and those around him. They are alone and he distinguishes between those *outside* (*tois eksō*), who receive everything in *parables*, and the *insiders*, the twelve and those around him. By putting these traditions into specific space and time settings in his narrative, Mark attempted to get his reader involved in the story of Jesus.

In structuring a narrative, characterization plays a very important role as we have already seen. It is also a vital aspect from the point of view of the reader/hearer. The way in which characters are presented directly influences the reader. No reader will identify with a character who is presented mainly in negative terms, whereas the opposite is true.

In the Gospel of Mark characterization takes place mainly through the narration of action. 'We learn who Jesus is through what he says and does in the context of the action of others' (Tannehill 1979:58). Jewish leaders including the scribes, Pharisees, and Sadducees are characterized negatively throughout the gospel. That is why the reader dislikes these characters and has sympathy with Jesus and what he says and does.

A very important group for our understanding of Mark 4:1–34 are the disciples. Perhaps they are to be regarded as the most complex characters in the gospel, also because they form part of the messianic secret. In the first part of the gospel there are three related scenes in which the disciples are given the function of 'helpers' of Jesus in his own commission. These are the narrative of the call (1:16–20), the choosing (3:13–19), and the mission of the twelve (6:7–13). In these scenes the disciples are evaluated positively. In addition they are positively assessed in our chapter, namely in 4:10–12. Only once in the chapters preceding chapter 4 is there a negative remark about one of them (3:19). 'Thus initial positive evaluation has an important function: it encourages the natural tendency of Christian readers to identify with Jesus' followers in the story' (Tannehill 1979:71). By contrast with this positive presentation, there is a very strong negative characterization of the disciples. It starts with the pericope following our chapter (cf. 4:35–41). In three boat scenes where Jesus is alone with his disciples (4:35–41; 6:45–52; 8:14–21) they are presented as those who fear and do not understand. In 8:34–9:1 they are reestablished and commissioned to follow him even if it is difficult. Throughout the story, despite their close association with Jesus in everything he does and says, they fail to be his true helpers except for the open future and a promised meeting in 16:7. They are even replaced as helpers by other figures like Bartimaeus (10:52); the anointing woman (14:7–8); Simon of Cyrene (15:21); and the centurion at the cross (15:39). Tannehill, who has worked out extensively the characterization of the disciples in Mark, rightly remarks that the reader's initial expectations in connection with the disciples are not fulfilled. This leads to self-criticism and rethinking of what it means to follow Jesus. They nevertheless remain his followers and helpers until the end and this has a critical function for the reader. 'When the disciples are in harmony with Jesus the author intends them to be viewed with approval; when they are not, with disapproval' (Tannehill 1979:69).

'Those around' Jesus are also characterized positively as his followers. We have already referred to the very positive judgement of those around him in 3:31–5. In contrast to his family they are the people who do the will of God. They also appear on the scene in 4:10 where they and the twelve are those to whom the mystery of the kingdom is revealed. They see and understand.

Some of the recurring elements in the characterization of the crowds are: the fact that they are the ones who receive teaching (cf. 2:13; 4:2; 6:34; 8:34); their attraction to Jesus (2:1, 13; 3:22; 5:21, 24); their opposition to the religious leaders (11:18, 32; 12:12, 37); and Jesus' positive attitude towards them (cf. 8:2; 7:14). In chapter 14 there is an unexpected total break between them and Jesus and they join in the demand that Jesus be crucified (cf. 14:43; 15:8). 'Stated in terms of personal relationships, the effect is similar to a close and trusted friend who has an opportunity to save a loved one and instead, for apparently political reasons, is instrumental in causing the loved one's death' (Boomershine 1974:302).

The following characters from the main narrative, from Jesus, are involved in Mark 4:1–34: the crowd, those around him (the disciples), and those outside. How does the characterization of these narrated figures mentioned above affect the interpretation of Mark 4:1–34? As far as the crowd is concerned, one tends to appraise them positively as those who receive the teaching of Jesus and go wherever he goes. Verses 33 and 34, however, raise the question of whether they are not included with the outsiders to whom Jesus speaks in parables. The outsiders are characterized negatively as those who do not receive the mystery of the kingdom. They are continually looking but do not see, they listen but do not hear, and they will not repent and be forgiven (4:12). In view of the fact that the crowd eventually deserts Jesus and participates actively in his trial and death, it could be that they are already regarded as part of the outsiders in chapter 4. If so, the fact that they accompany Jesus from the beginning to the end, see, listen, are taught, and ought to know what he stands for, is all the more remarkable. They are then part of 'those outside' who do not do the 'will of God' those who reject him.

The people around him and the twelve are those who are given the mystery of the kingdom. But they are also those who need special instruction. They ought to understand, but v. 13 gives the impression that they do not seem to understand fully. This is only the start of the disciples' incomprehension, which is fully developed in the remainder of the story (cf. 4:b1; 6:b; 7:18; 8:14–1; 9:10; and 14:40).

Mark 4:1–34 is a crucial point in the narrative as far as characterization is concerned. Up to this stage the reader is encouraged to identify with the disciples and the crowd, associate with them, and dislike the opponents. In a very subtle way the suggestion is made that the reader should think twice. Mark 4:11–12 is turned upside down in 8:17–18. The disciples do not understand! They have eyes but they do not see, have ears but cannot hear, and they do not understand. From now on there is a constant shift in identification between reader and narrated figures, fluctuating between sympathy, dislike, and pity. In 4:1–34 the reader is given a norm to evaluate the characters in the story and himself.

From the perspective of point of view there remain a few observations which will add to our understanding of how Mark 1:1–31 functions as part of the narrative and how the parables in that chapter mean.

We have noted above that Mark created perspectives from which the reader or hearer is presented with the characters and so on. This is what point of view is about. Mark made use of an omniscient and intrusive point of view, as I have suggested elsewhere (cf. Vorster 1980:8–61). The *narrator* of Mark's story knows everything about his characters: what they see, hear, feel, and even what they think (cf. 3:6; 5:28, 33; 6:49; 11:31; 15:10). He knows the mind of Jesus (cf. 2:8; 3:5; 5:30). By arranging his material to suit his purpose, the focus is on the opposition Jesus experienced from the Jewish leaders. They are not only narrated; they are evaluated. For the sake of the reader he comments on strange words and phrases (cf. 3:17; 5:9; 5:41; 7:2, 11, 34; 10:46), uses *gar* in narrative commentary to explain (cf. 1:16, 22, 38), and lets his characters speak in the way he prefers.

What is the function of Jesus' 'speech' in Mark 4:1–34 with reference to point of view? From chapter 1 to the end of chapter 3 Jesus is not very talkative, but what he says is of the utmost importance both for the way in which he is characterized (cf. 1:25, 35;

2:8, 17) and for our understanding of how the narrative means (1:15; 1:44; 2).

From what he says the reader knows his purpose and what he stands for. Like the narrator of the story he is omniscient. He even knows the thoughts of men and tells them that he knows what they think (2:8). From what he says the reader can gather who he is. He is an authoritative leader of people (cf. 1:17; 2:14, 17); he is a miracle worker (1:41; 2:5, 11, 23; 3:3, 5) who commands demons (1:35); he lays down new norms for forgiveness (2:5), fasting (2:18), the Sabbath (2:73), and blasphemy (3:23–29); he is a teacher (cf. 3:23–29). He is the type of character with whom the reader would identify. However, the most important thing is that:

> Jesus's voice provides an evaluative context for understanding the speech and action of the crowds, because Jesus teaches them in a form designed to keep them ignorant of the kingdom, and for understanding the speech and actions of the disciples, because Jesus says that they, like the crowds, are without understanding. And it is Jesus's speech that provides an evaluative context for understanding the words and deeds of the authorities, because it is his speech that corrects and condemns them (Petersen 1978b:109).

From the perspective of point of view it should be noted that three of the public 'speeches' of Jesus in the Gospel of Mark are said to have been *en parabolais*, namely, 3:23–29 on Beelzebul; 4:2–32 (the parable speech); and 12:1 on the parable of the vineyard and the tenants. These must be related to Mark 4:11–12 and 34, where he explicitly states that Jesus made a distinction in his teaching between the twelve and those around him on the one hand, and the outsiders on the other. The distinction between *en parabolais* and the possession of the *mystērion tēs basileias* is very important. The translation 'in parables' fails to render the specific Markan distinction between overt and secret or mystery and riddle. 'Figurative meaning' is perhaps the most distinctive feature of *en parabolais*, although not necessarily in a technical sense. In that sense the sayings regarding the lamp (4:21) and the measure (4:24) are also parabolic, that is, 'parables.' Kelber (1974:32–33) correctly observes:

> ... everything is or occurs in *riddles* to the outsiders (*ta panta ginetai*). This is neither a statement on Jesus' specific use of parables, nor even on the purpose of his teaching in general, but on the nature of his ministry as a whole. The whole ministry is en *parabolais*, i.e. an enigma to outside recognition. This points beyond a specific theory on parables!

'Talking in parables,' in other words, forms part of the way in which the narrated Jesus of Mark speaks to the outsiders, and is directly related to Mark's dialectic of hearing and understanding the message of the kingdom. The purpose is to encourage the reader to get involved in the message of the story of Jesus. Point of view is one of the techniques narrators use to get their story across. It is within this context that the function of the quotation of Isaiah 6:9 in Mark 1:12 has to be viewed.

Mark 1:12 is a well-known *crux interpretum*. It is normally regarded as Mark's view on the purpose of the parables. It has given rise to many theories on the rejection and punishment of Israel. 'Als solche dienen sie (sc. die Gleichnisse) dem Zweck, die Wahrheit zu verhüllen, um über das widerspenstige Volk das Verstockungsgericht zu verhangen' (Gnilka 1979:170).

In view of the function of old Testament quotations in Mark, this seems to me rather doubtful. The quotation should be interpreted as part of the narrative point of view of the gospel and in the light of the motif of *understanding* why Jesus the Son of God had to suffer. Petersen rightly reminds us '. . . that the speech of all characters, including Jesus, is ultimately controlled by the external point of view of the narrator. His plotting of their speeches is an expression of his own ideological standpoint' (Petersen 1978:109), that is, his own conceptual understanding of the world he narrates.

I have elsewhere commented on the function of the use of the old Testament in Mark and need not repeat everything. Most important is the fact that quotations from the old Testament have the same function in Mark as narrative commentary (cf. Vorster 1981a:62-72). It *substantiates* the train of thought. The quotations are often so well integrated into the narrative that they form part of the narrative statement (cf. 1:1-4; 7:6-8; 10:5-8 and 14:27-28). It is often only because of the way it is printed in our modern editions of the New Testament that we read them as quotations. More often they sound like the words of the narrator or narrated figures. It is remarkable that most of the quotations from the old Testament in Mark are in the mouth of Jesus. They form part of the characterization of Jesus and his opponents (cf. 7:6-7). The theme of incomprehension of the disciples, referred to above, is brought into focus in Mark 4:12 (cf. 8:18) when Jesus uses the words of Isaiah 6:9-10, and so also the whole matter of *understanding* why Jesus, the Son of God, had to suffer. Because of the network of signification in a text

it would be wrong simply to read Mark 4:12 as an isolated quotation on the parables and their meaning. Mark is not explaining the
purpose of the parables in the sense of a 'Verstockungstheorie.' Kelber
reminds us that the parable of the sower is not introduced as *a* parable but as teaching *en parabolais* (plural).

> To the outsiders Jesus relates in parabolic riddling fashion, but the
> insiders will be given a chance to learn that he was actually lecturing
> on the present state of the Kingdom. Rather than punish, the par-
> ables will help to reveal what to the outside forms an inaccessible
> riddle, and to the inside takes on the appearance of a mystery. Basi-
> cally, what the Galilean speech advances is a further elaboration of
> the Kingdom theme, but not a thesis on parables (Kelber 1974:33).

Mark 4:10–12 depicts Jesus in relation to his associates and to those
outside. This relationship is a complex one. It has already been
referred to in the preceding part of the narrative (3:31–35) and is
developed at length in the rest of the gospel. In fact, it starts in the
next verse (4:13). The reader is urged to look, listen, and understand, and notice how insider and outsider alike fail to understand
the mystery of the kingdom of God.

Narrative commentary, which is a form of narrative point of view,
also directs the reader. In his attempt to help his reader/hearer Mark
often uses *gar* to indicate how the reader should understand some
point or other (cf. 1:16, 22, 38; 2:15; 3:10). There are two important instances of *gar* in Mark 4:1–34.

It has often been a point of discussion whether or not the Q-logia
in Mark 4:21–25 should also be regarded as 'parabolic' or 'parables.' It seems to me that the use of *gar* in vv. 22 and 25 can help
us. The word indicates how the reader should regard the preceding
sayings. Verses 22 and 25 are to be regarded as commentary on the
logia preceding them, in the same way as 14–20 should be regarded
as commentary on 3–9. Verses 22 and 25 are explanations of vv.
21 and 24.

In Mark 4:1–34, as elsewhere in the gospel when Jesus speaks,
the focus is not on why he says so little but on what he says and
why he says it. As with all the other saying of Jesus in Mark, the
function of the speech is first of all to create an evaluative context
for the reader. Besides the information it offers on how things happen in the kingdom of God, it also provides the reader with norms
to evaluate the actions of other characters in the story. These include
the disciples, those outside, the crowd, and others who participate

in the development of the story of Jesus, the Son of God who has to suffer and die in order to fulfil his commission.

2. How Do the Parables in Mark 4:1–34 Mean?

In order to determine how the parables in Mark 4 mean, it is necessary not only to see chapter 4 of Mark's Gospel as part of the Markan narrative world (as we have done above), but also to examine how the speech is organized internally. Broadly, the speech is structured as follows (cf. also Lambrecht 1969:106ff., especially 109):

Introduction (1–2): Setting (Jesus by the sea of Galilee teaching the *ochlos*)

kai elegen autois . . .
Akouéte (3)
Sower (3–8)
kai elegen, Hos écheiōta akouein akouetō (9)

Once they were alone, those around him and the twelve enquired about the parables.
(Change of setting) (10)

kai elegen autois (11)
  The mystery of the kingdom of God is explained to those inside. To those outside everything comes in parables (+ Isaiah 6:9) (11–12).

kai legei autois (13)
  Because they do not understand he gives an explanation of the parable to those who are supposed to understand (14–20).

kai elegen autois (21)
  'Parable' of lamp (21)
  Explanation of (*gar*) (22)
  ei tis echei ōta akouein akouetō (23)

kai elegen autois, Blepete ti akouete (24)
  'Parable' of measure (24)
  Explanation (*gar*) (25)

kai elegen (26)
  houtōs estin hē basileia tou theou hōs . . .
  Self-Growing Seed (26–29)

kai elegen
  Pōs homoiōsōmen tēn basileian tou theou, ē en tini autēn parabolē thōmen; hōs . . .
  Mustard seed (31–32)

Conclusion (33–34)

> Jesus preached his message to the people (*autois*), using many other
> parables like these; he told them as much as they could understand
> (*kathos edynanto akouein*). He would not speak to them without using para-
> bles, but when he was alone with his disciples, he would explain every-
> thing to them (*TEV*).

The 'speech' forms a self-contained unit with a beginning and an
end, although it has often been pointed out that it must have grown
in the transmission of the tradition (cf. Kuhn 1971:99; Weder 1978:99).
For our purpose we are interested not in the growth of the text but
in its final form. Whether it is a coherent text or not is significant
only inasmuch as this affects our interpretation. Since we have dealt
with the characters of the main narrative involved in the speech we
need not repeat this.

The discourse consists of a narrative framework (1–2 and 33–34)
interspersed with seven quotations. Each quotation has a narrative
introduction (cf. *kai elegen ktl.* in 11, 13, 21, etc.). Because of the
theme of the kingdom of God, which plays a role from vv. 3 to 32,
it is regarded as a discourse and not as separate units of unrelated
speech (cf. Delorme 1979:157–91).

As for the coherence of the discourse, the audience remains a
problem. The narrative starts with Jesus and the *ochlos* (and the twelve
cum suis?). In v. 10 there is a change of setting. The disciples and
those around him are alone with Jesus. There is no indication in
the remainder of the speech that the insiders have returned to join
the crowd. This causes a problem. It is impossible to determine with
certainty whether *autois* in vv. 21 and 24 includes the crowd and the
insiders, or whether the term refers to the insiders only. In 26 and
30 the audience is not mentioned at all, while the crowd (outsiders)
seems to form part of the *autois* of v. 33. That is why scholars have
often drawn attention to the (so-called) tension between vv. 33 and
34. These verses should, however, be regarded as a general summary. The *TEV* translation above renders the Greek well. The tension between 33 and 34 strikes one as more or less serious, depending
on how one interprets the *autois* in vv. 21 and 24 and the intended
audience of vv. 26 and 30.

The expression *kai elegen* in vv. 26 and 30 is striking. It is used
only in this instance and in v. 9 in the speech. Verse 9 seems to
round off the parable of the sower. If the phrase has the same function in vv. 9, 26, and 30, it would imply that from 10 to 33 Jesus
was addressing the insiders only.

One could also argue, however, that except for vv. 10–20 or 10–25 the entire speech is addressed to the crowd.

The complete discourse is built around v. 11, in which the hiddenness and *revelation* of the kingdom of God are the central focus. All five 'parables' to some extent illustrate the hiddenness and revelation of the kingdom of God. First there is the *logos* motif, which occurs nine times in the speech. It has the meaning of 'message' and refers to the preaching of the gospel (of the kingdom of God). The teaching of Jesus (v. 3) is therefore aptly summarized in v. 33 as *elalei autois ton logon*. It is this teaching, his message of the kingdom of God, which is both hidden and revealed.

The recurring motif of *akouō* is also prominent. The word occurs no fewer than thirteen times in the thirty-four verses. Apart from its prominent use in the old Testament quotation in v. 12, it is used in formulas which appeal to the reader, urging him to listen attentively and become one of the insiders (9, 23, 24, cf. 33). In the interpretation of the parable of the sower (14–20), the focus is on *hearing* the word.

It is in this context that we have to pursue the question of how the parables of Mark 4 mean.

Elsewhere (cf. Vorster 1981b) I have drawn attention to the fact that the meaning of the parable of the sower in Mark's gospel is obscured by the modern search for the 'original meaning' of the parables as spoken by Jesus (cf. Crossan 1980:25; Carlston 1975:137). In this search the *relationship* in Mark's narrative between the parable of the sower in 4:3–8 and its interpretation in 4:14–20 is neglected. The two 'texts' are normally analysed in isolation, and each is assigned its own meaning. It is usually argued that Mark 4:3–8 presents us with an earlier form of the parable than the exposition given in 4:14–20. The latter, it is argued, originated from the primitive church and, since it gives an allegorical (metaphorical, according to Weder 1978:112) interpretation of parts of the parable, it should be treated as secondary. Without submitting any reasons Gnilka (1979:161) in his recent commentary on Mark offers an explanation of the meaning of the parable and then asserts that Mark did not care for this particular meaning. According to him, Mark accepted the 'allegorical interpretation' in 4:14–20 as the meaning of the parable. To avoid the problem of whether Jesus could have used allegory or allegorical interpretation, which has been denied since the days of Jülicher, Pesch calls it 'eine allegorisierende Parabel' (1976:

229). Schmithals, on the other hand, maintains that both the text
(4:3–8) and its interpretation (14–20) are the work of the narrator
who was responsible for the *Grundschrift* Mark used in writing his
gospel. Accordingly, the parable has one meaning only, and that is
the 'allegorical interpretation' in Mark 4:14–20. Mark accepted this
meaning (cf. Schmithals 1979:231–33).

This inevitably leads to the conclusion that Mark's text and what
he says are not taken seriously. In answering the question of how
the parables in Mark 4 mean, it is beside the point whether the
parable of the sower as spoken by Jesus originally had another meaning than the one put into his mouth in Mark 4:14–20. Mark edited
and contextualized its interpretation for a specific purpose. By inserting vv. 11–13 between the parable and its interpretation, Mark told
his story from his own perspective. The very fact that he tells the
story of Jesus in this particular way forms part of the composition
of the narrative. It is highly significant that he has Jesus, the teacher,
tell a story and also explain it to the disciples who are presented
as those who, despite their special instruction, often misunderstand
Jesus. The only meaning the parable of the sower has in the Markan
gospel is that given in the explanation of 4:14–20. This has consequences for our question of how these parables mean. We here have
a very rare phenomenon in that the author of the text tells the
reader explicitly how to understand a part of his text. The reader
should note that the meaning of the parable is explained in relation
to the word (*logos*). The sower sows the word. *Logos* as we have noted,
refers to Jesus' message of the kingdom. Each scene of the original
story is interpreted in terms of how, under varying conditions which
influence their reception, people *hear the word* (compare vv. 3 and 14;
4 and 15; 5–6 and 16–17; 7 and 18–19; and 8 and 20). Since the
parable is a short story marked by characterization, plot, and so on,
it is remarkable that both the order of the scenes of the parable and
the plotted line are retained in the exposition. Not every aspect
of the original story is assigned a meaning only those which relate
to 'hear,' 'the seed,' and the conditions which permit or preclude
fruitfulness.

Kelber (1974:27) correctly observes that the *logos* is the main protagonist, who suffers several defeats and gains a resounding victory:
'A threefold failure is set over against a threefold success, but it is
the period of crisis to which special importance is attached.' This is
the mystery of the kingdom revealed: continuous failure, but even-

tual success. In our attempt to answer how the parable means, two things should be kept in mind. Firstly, it is in keeping with the motifs of 'hearing' and the 'word,' and also with hiddenness or the figurative meaning of the parable of the sower, that parts of the story are explained in *context* in a metaphorical (allegorical?) way: the seed is the word, and so on. But secondly, it is important to note that the story character of the original parable is retained. It is plotted in accordance with the plot of the first story. That is why one may well ask whether Mark 4:14–20 is not a *retelling* of the same story as the one in 4:3–8.

From a literary point of view, but also in view of the relationship between the written and oral forms of the stories of Jesus, the question is: should one not consider seriously the problem of whether the same story can be told twice (cf. Polanyi 1981a)? This is a fine example of the problem attending the parables of Jesus. How the story of the parable of the sower means in Mark 4 is directly dependent on the fact that its reinterpretation is a *story that is retold*. The parable of the sower in Mark 4:14–20 is based on the same matrix as Mark 4:4–8 (cf. Polanyi 1981a:332). The same narrative time, space, and plot are found in both stories. The characters the protagonist as well as the opponents are different. By filling out the metaphorical characters, Jesus is presented as having told the same story twice, that is, a new story under new circumstances (contra Huffman 1978:212). It is the same plot which brings about the same paradox. In relating the ordinary, the extraordinary is told by plotting the events into a hyperbole of a threefold 'failure' and a threefold 'success.' Through the unusual 'syntactic' (metaphor) and semiotactic arrangement of the plot the story has its impact.

It is noteworthy that Mark 4:3–8 is written as narrative discourse (*erzählte Welt*), whereas the explanation in 4:14–20 is *direct discourse* (*besprochene Welt*). In other words, the parable itself is recorded in narrated form and its explanation is a discussion of the parable in narrated form. Put another way, the parable of the sower in Mark 4 is presented as narrative within a narrative, whereas its explanation is a narrated discussion within the narrative. Both are, however, *narratives*. In terms of the structure of Mark's narrative, in which narrative discourse and direct discourse are continually alternated, and where the savings of Jesus, as we have seen, often serve the function of presenting the reader with norms, this is not without significance. It gives an indication of how the author wished his readers/hearers to interpret the retold story. It tells us how the parable of the sower *means* in the Markan gospel. What this story means is explained first of all by how it means. In the retelling of the story the metaphorical process is extended in narrative form by filling out the characters by means of motifs, such as 'word,' which are important for the main narrative. The retold story, as well as the original version, refer to the kingdom of God in the Markan narrative that is, as *Mark* presented the kingdom. According to Mark, things happen in the kingdom as they happen in the retold story of the sower. This illustrates some of the consequences of reading the parables in their gospel contexts and also of reading them as (meta-phorical) narratives.

It was said above that the sayings about the lamp and the meas-ure are to be seen as parables or parabolic sayings which, on the strength of the use of *gar* in Mark, should in each case be explained in terms of the meaning supplied in the saying following it. This is how the author leads his hearers to understand Jesus' teaching on the kingdom. Although it is a mystery it will of necessity be revealed like a lamp, which is made to reveal light. But it should also cau-tion the hearer also caution the hearer/reader to be on the alert, because in the measure that he accepts the kingdom he will be meas-ured. The figurative meaning of these sayings is what counts. That is because he who has (insight into the kingdom of God) will be given more, and he who has nothing will forfeit even what he has. This is the way of the kingdom.

How is this message (meaning) created in Mark? Once again the context of the Markan narrative has to be kept in mind, and espe-cially the context of Mark 4:1–34. The parable of the lamp is explained in terms of what is hidden and what is revealed. It is reit-erated in the form of a chiasm:

             a   b
ou gar estin krypton ean mē hina phanerothē

             b'   a'
oude egeneto apokruphon all' hina elthē eis phaneron

The parable of the lamp is a metaphor of the kingdom of God in which the reversal of the order of hidden and revealed is under-lined. It has a strong eschatological tone, strengthened by *hina*. Nothing is hidden unless it is in order that (so that) it will be revealed. The hidden kingdom will be revealed. Again the reader is urged to listen carefully (v. 23). The same basic technique of creating meaning is used in the parable of the measure. An explanation is given in v. 25. 'Those who acknowledge and live according to the conditions set by the invisible Kingdom, will be rewarded, and they will be rewarded beyond all expectations' (Kelber 1974:39).

How these parables mean is not very different from how the parable of the sower means in Mark. The same technique is applied. The metaphorical statements about the lamp and the measure are explained through a reformulation. The point of these reformulations is made in the context. Removed from this context, these sayings would have totally different meanings (cf. Luke 8:16–18). There is little doubt that ultimately the context of these sayings is the only factor determining what they mean. In the case of the parable of the sower, meaning was created by retelling the story in accordance with its new context. The two parabolic sayings about the lamp and the measure were reformulated in the sayings following each one to refer to a certain aspect of the kingdom.

As to the parables about the seed growing secretly and the mustard seed; except for contextual indicators we have no direct clues from the text how the author meant the reader understand them. It is nevertheless clear that these meaning refers to the kingdom, as their introductions indicate.

The parable of the growing seed (4:26–29) is introduced by the formula 'the kingdom of God is like. . . .' In the end it is only a technicality whether one regards it as metaphor or comparison. It is the unusual syntactic and semiotactic arrangement of the 'kingdom,' and the story which affects the meaning. In other words? what matters is the predication of the kingdom of God by an extended narrative. The kingdom 'is similar to that which happens in' the story of the seed growing secretly (cf. Ricoeur 1975:98). The narrative is structured as follows:

$$
\begin{array}{ll}
\quad\quad\quad a & b \\
\left[\begin{array}{l}
\textit{anthrōpos balēton sporon epi tēs gēs} \\
\textit{kai katheudē} \\
\textit{kai egeirētai nykta kai hēmeran,}
\end{array}\right. \\
\\
\quad a' \\
\left[\begin{array}{l}
\textit{kai ho sporos blasta} \\
\textit{kai mēkynētai} \\
\textit{hōs ouk oiden autos.}
\end{array}\right.
\end{array}
$$

b'

> *automatēhe gē karpophorei, prōton chorton, eita*
> *stachyn, eita plērēs sitos en tō starchiu*
> *hotan de paradoi ho karpos, euthys apostellei to*
> *drepanon, hoti parestēken ho therismos.*

The narrative is structured by its plot, characterization, and by narrative commentary. The repetition of seed (a, a') and earth (b, b') draws attention to these components. The seed, the protagonist of the story, yields a harvest, with the aid of the 'earth' which acts as 'helper.' Seed and earth seem to be the characters which are developed in the story, and not the man, since he only features in the opening scene where he introduces the construction of the plot. The story is told in time sequence from sowing to harvest. The whole story is told in direct discourse (*besprochene Welt*) and not in narrative discourse (*erzählte Welt*), which strengthens both its evaluative and its informative function. In the main story we are told that Jesus narrated the story. In his description (direct discourse) he characterizes the narrated figures. The sower sows and then comes and goes only to wait for the harvest. As far as the growing of the seed is concerned he is not active (cf. Carlston 1975:204). The seed grows in a surprising way as the narrative commentary indicates (*hōs ouk oiden autos*). This is highlighted by the automatic (automate) way in which the earth yields fruit; stage after stage follows until the crop is ready to be harvested. This idea is established by an allusion to Joel 3(4):13. It drives home the idea that the harvest is assured. 'From sowing to harvest is a sure and certain step' (Carlston 1975:205). The plot is again worked out in the form of a hyperbole, affecting a contrast between beginning and end. The emphasis is on the surprising automatic movement from the beginning to the final stage.

The Markan context suggests that both 'kingdom of God' and 'word' are important clues to the meaning and reference of the parable. The way in which the *logos* grows is hidden and astonishing. The harvest is guaranteed because the *logos* will bear fruit, thus affirming the mysterious workings of the kingdom. The evaluation of the characters in terms of surprise and certainty has the function of encouraging those who are able to hear.

How the story means is determined by its context and text type. It is a metaphoric narrative within a narrative context. In that context the referents are filled out.

The last in the series, namely the parable of the mustard seed, is

the third seed parable in the speech. It is again introduced by a formula inquiring into the nature of the kingdom: 'With what can we
compare the kingdom of God? or what parable shall we use for it?'
The second part is simply a repetition of the first. The kingdom is
compared to. . . . Things happen in the kingdom as in the story of
the mustard seed. The plot is structured in two scenes:

> *hōs kokkō sinapeōs*
> *hos hotan sparē, epi tēs gēs mikroteron on paatōn tōn*
>   *spermaatōn tōn epi tēs gēs,*
> *kai hotan sparē, anabainei*
> *kai ginetai meidzon pantōn tōn lachanōn*
> *kai poiei kladous megalous, hōste dynasthai hypo tēn*
>   *skian autou ta peteina tou ouranou kataskēnoun.*

The parable of the mustard seed, like that of the seed growing
secretly, is narrated in direct discourse (*besprochene Welt*), reinforcing
the evaluative and informative function in the main discourse. In
Luke 13:18–19 it is rendered in narrated discourse (*erzählte Welt*).
Contrast between small and large is emphasized by the focus on
mikroteron and *meidzon*. There is one character, the mustard seed, and
there are two plotted scenes. The beginning is small, the ending
great. The allusion to Daniel 4 in v. 32 is a qualification of the
greater ending, which probably refers to the fact that the kingdom
'provides protection for all who seek its shelter' (Carlston 1975:159).
The story is plotted hyperbolically.

Meaning is established through contrast and characterization in
a narrative form. In the Markan context, seed most probably refers
to the message of the kingdom. In the kingdom things happen to
that message, just as things happen in the story of the mustard
seed. Carlston (1975:159) correctly remarks: 'Mark's tradition, however, probably did not stress the contrast . . . the parable was probably still understood primarily in terms of the symbol of birds and
branches, as a reference to the inclusion of Gentiles in the growing
church as in Q.'

If we return now to the speech as a whole, and as part of the
Markan narrative, there are quite a number of indications of how
the parables and parabolic logia of Jesus in Mark 4 should be read,
or how they mean. First of all, we have a clue in the way the speech
is structured. It is presented as part of a narrative. What Jesus says
within this narrative is quoted in the form of sayings and narratives.
Unlike the parable of the sower, all the other sayings and parables

are given in direct discourse (*besprochene Welt*), emphasizing their value
as normative statements regarding the kingdom. The reader is involved
in a complex narrative context, characterized by a deepening interest in the distinction between the opponents and helpers of the protagonist. Secondly, the narrative shows the insiders as the only ones
able to understand Jesus' parables, but since they did not understand the parable of the sower, the narrative tells how they are
enabled to understand the parables. How is this done? In the case
of the parable of the sower, meaning is created by retelling the story
in narrative form in a narrative context. The parabolic sayings are
reformulated in accordance with the context. The other two parables, which are not expounded, are to be read as stories quoted in
context. Narrativity remains their basic characteristic. By plotting the
events in the form of hyperboles or paradoxes in all three cases,
the extraordinary quality of the kingdom is rendered in terms of the
ordinary (cf. Ricoeur 1975:99). That is what the reader has to note
and pursue.

3. *Reality Remade, or How Do These Parables Refer?*

In the introduction above I referred to the opinion of Ricoeur who,
in opposition to modern literary criticism, maintains that poetic language such as that of the parables does have a referential function
since 'discourse is open and turned toward a world which it wishes
to express and to convey in language' (Ricoeur 1975:82). He believes
that language is a closed system and that the abovementioned use
of reference is applicable only to signs within a language and not
to signs within a text like a narrative. But in view of the fact that
discourse is based on 'a unit of genre, completely different from the
units of language which are signs' (Ricoeur 1975:81), namely, the *sentence*, its referential aspect is totally different. He argues that the characteristics of a sentence are in no sense a repetition of those of
language. That is why a sentence's characteristics of meaning and
reference are totally different from those of language signs. In view
of this hypothesis, and such theories as Max Black's theory of models, he introduced Mary Hesse's concept of redescription in connection with the referential aspect of the metaphor. In the case of
the metaphor, the first order reference (literal interpretation) is lost
(cf. Wittig 1977:30 above), resulting in a reinterpretation of reality

which brings forth a second order reference, namely, a redescription of reality as a possibility of 'the forming of the world' (cf. Ricoeur 1975:82). Reference as redescription is 'the movement of the internal structure of the work toward its reference, toward the sort of world which the work opens *in front of* the text' (Ricoeur 1975:82). This is very important since, for Ricoeur, reference of a second order is quite unlike reference of the first order. The latter is a movement *backwards* from the sign to what it refers to in the extralinguistic world, whereas second order reference points forward (to an open possibility). 'This hypothesis marks our complete break with structuralism where language functions purely internally or immanently, where an element refers only to another element of the same system' (Ricoeur 1975:81).

Although Ricoeur has been criticized for this view (cf. Crossan 1980:12) it was welcomed by others (cf. the preceding chapter). In an essay on the narrative function he reintroduced this hypothesis in connection with the difference between historiography (writing of history) and fiction, distinguishing between two kinds of reference. As to the first he maintains that historical narratives (historiography) refer to events outside the narrative whereas fictional narratives do not. 'But both historical and fictional narratives have in common an intersecting reference, a reference to historicity, to the fundamental fact that we make our history and are historical beings' (Ricoeur 1978a:177). History gives a description in conventional language whereas fiction gives a redescription, since it suppresses the first order reference and refers in a second order. Both refer to human action: history 'through' relics, documents, and archives, and fiction by redescribing reality. Thus, one cannot say that a literary work (including a parable) is without reference. It is a work with a split reference, that is, a work whose ultimate reference has as its condition a suspension of the referential claim of conventional language (Ricoeur 1978a:194). He feels very strongly about the referential claim of narrative discourse, albeit in the sense that he understands the concept (cf. Ricoeur 1978a:186). It is a very important problem, since it penetrates to the very heart of one of the major unsolved questions of literary criticism in general and New Testament scholarship in particular. It is of importance not only for parable research but also for gospel research as a whole. We shall return to Ricoeur's views, but let us first look at the problem from another angle.

The problem of reference has been described in literary criticism

by likening texts to windows or mirrors (cf. Petersen 1978a:20–21).
Applied to New Testament scholarship Via writes:

> ... one could say that the historical critic looks through the text to
> what it refers or points to [window-WSV] and treats the text as evi-
> dence for something else, while the literary critic looks at the text for
> what it says in itself by means of the patterning or shaping—the inform-
> ing of its content (quoted in Petersen 1978a:5).

To put it differently, what do the gospels or the parables of Jesus
refer to and how? The historical critic will probe the growth phases
of the text to establish 'historical reality,' whereas the literary critic
will look for referential relationships within the text. As to the parables of Jesus, this problem has for a very long time been described
in terms of realism. Writes Dodd:

> In the parables of the Gospels ... all is true to nature and to life.
> Each similitude or story is a perfect picture of something that can be
> observed in he world of our experience. The processes of nature are
> accurately observed and recorded; the actions of persons in the sto-
> ries are in character; ... It (sc. realism) arises from a conviction that
> there is no mere analogy, but an inward affinity, between the natural
> order and the spiritual order, or as we might put it in the language
> of the parables themselves, the Kingdom of God is intrinsically like
> the processes of nature and of the daily life of men (Dodd 1936:20–22).

Remarks such as these can be multiplied. Scholars like Dodd, and
especially Jeremias, did a tremendous job in unearthing a vast amount
of historical knowledge which reveals the background from which
these stories arose. Thus, in their attempt to 'prove' the realism of
the parables of Jesus, they provided us with very useful material for
creating a *frame of reference* without which it would be impossible to
read and validly interpret these stories. Who would have thought
today that in ancient Palestine they used to sow before they ploughed,
as is told in the parable of the sower (cf. Jeremias 1970:7), to name
but one of the realities of the world in which Jesus lived?

At this stage we should remind ourselves of the aforementioned
development in the interpretation of the parables as metaphors. It
was said, amongst other things, that the parables are open-ended
and that a metaphor or parable '... is a bearer of the reality to
which it refers' (Wilder 1971:84); stress was laid on paradoxicality.
Ricoeur (1975:99, 109, 112–18) speaks of the extravagance of the
parables. It was realized in the meantime that 'normalcy' (Crossan)
only holds good for certain aspects of the parables. There are numer-

ous 'atypical features' (Huffman 1978) in the parables which can only be explained as literary devices such as paradox and hyperbole. Let us take the parable of the sower as an example. It occurs in Mark 4:3–8, Matthew 13:3–8, Luke 8:5–8, and the Gospel of Thomas 9. We have seen that in Mark the threefold downward action is 'balanced' by a threefold upward movement. In view of the search for realism the difference between the various versions regarding the *good soil* has given rise to many discussions (cf. Carlston 1975:139; Crossan 1980:40). The various versions read as follows:

> And some of the seed fell into good soil, where it bore fruit, yielding a hundredfold or, it might be sixtyfold or thirtyfold (Matthew 13:8, *NEB*).

> And some of the seed fell into good soil, where it came up and grew, and bore fruit; and the yield was thirtyfold, sixtyfold, even a hundredfold (Mark 4:8, *NEB*).

> And some of the seed fell into good soil, and grew, and yielded a hundredfold (Luke 8:8, *NEB*).

> And others fell on the good earth; and it produced good fruit; it bore sixty per measure and one hundred and twenty per measure (Gospel of Thomas 9 [82, 10], *WSV*).

On the basis of historical investigation it is maintained that a tenfold yield amounts to a good harvest (cf. Crossan 1980:41). Scholars have nevertheless attempted to calculate exactly whether the yield refers to the whole field (Jeremias 1970:149) or to the individual ears (Linnemann 1961:149) and so on. The harvest undoubtedly exceeds actual production, indicating that realism is out of the question. What we have is hyperbole. 'God's harvest at the realization of the kingdom will be a more productive one than a farmer ever reaped. This is revealed by having this sower reap unrealistic amounts' (Huffman 1978:212).

The parable of the mustard seed has also been transmitted in different versions. Unlike in Mark, in Luke 13:19 the mustard seed 'grew to be a tree and the birds came to roost among the Markan version is preferred to its branches.' Traditionally that of Q since it is more mustard plant. However, the question is not whether it is more or less correct. It is a matter of rhetoric. These two examples (of which there are many: cf. Huffman 1978) suggest that trying '. . . to put the "camel through the needle's eye" literally, either by

turning the former into a rope (Mark 10:25 . . .) or the latter into a
pedestrian gate . . .' is rightly rejected as the work of unimaginative
readers (cf. Huffman 1978:220). His view is worth noting:

> I suggest that when Jesus spoke of hiring workmen at the eleventh
> hour, of a mustard seed that grew into a tree, of a farmer reaping
> hundredfold, of a Samaritan offering to reply 'whatever more you
> spend on a Jewish stranger he made use of actor's skills *to convince his
> audiences* (Huffman 1978:220; italics mine).

The foregoing examples indicate a much greater hermeneutical problem, namely, the relationship between a narrative and its reference.
If we say that biblical narratives represent reality, what do we mean?
Is a parable a replica of reality, a representation of reality, an illustration of reality, an icon or symbol of reality? This type of question is important and will be dealt with below. First I shall make a
few observations about the character of the problem in the broader
context of narrativity, namely, the Gospel of Mark. This is the text
into which the parables under discussion are inserted. Besides, I
would postulate that there is not a significant difference between the
ways in which a parable and a gospel refer-both are 'made up' stories, even if not the same genre.

I think it is correct to say that Mark made use of 'real' world
people to fill the narrative roles he created in his story of Jesus. The
pharisees are people who lived in Palestine during the life of Jesus.
Jesus once lived in Galilee and so on; the places, customs and cultural setting are equally realistic. The whole text is embedded in
first-century Palestine. And that is why one has to know the language and the 'real' world of the text This does not, however, help
us to answer the question of a text and its reference. What do the
disciples in Mark, for example, represent? Ernest Best (1977:379)
defined their 'possible roles' in the following way:

(1) They could signify themselves, the original disciples, no more and
no less; this could be a purely historical position. Mark might
approve of them or disapprove.

(2) They could signify a group claiming to continue the position of
the original disciples, and Mark might either favour or oppose the
group.

(3) They could signify some or other contemporary group: (a) the
church as a whole, or (b) a part of the church, e.g. its officials, or
a group of heretics.

(4) They could occupy a purely informatory role, i.e., Mark might believe that past history should determine the present and we should learn from the past.

This example presents the problem of New Testament research on the text and reference *in nuce*. The same phenomenon occurs in Matthean research (cf. Luz 1971) and throughout the narrative material of the New Testament. The most extreme form of the problem is when the disciples in Mark are identified with the so-called heretics in Mark's community; according to this view Mark had to combat a heretical Christology (cf. Weeden 1971; Kingsbury 1981). The following remark by Bultmann is only partly true: '... a literary work or a fragment of tradition is a primary source for the historical details concerning which it gives information' (as quoted by Marxsen 1959:13). Naturally the gospels tell us a lot about the world of their authors (cf. Polanyi 1981b), but that does not mean that the text of a gospel is somehow a reproduction of what actually happened. The text of a gospel does not present a copy of reality. Mark's gospel is not a replica of Mark's supposed community; it is a narrative about the life of Jesus within some or other historical setting. It is reality remade (cf. Goodman 1968; 1978; 1981).

The objection may be raised that, since a gospel narrative and a parable are two different text types, it is incorrect to talk about their referential function as if they belonged to the same type. Naturally one will have to keep in mind the metaphoric nature of the parables. But parables are (metaphorical) *narratives*, and their narrative character is merely an example of extended predication. Predication is given in narrative form. Parables are by nature narratives, some of which occur in a metaphorical context.

Despite the fact that parables are normally regarded as fictional stories or free creations (*'freie erfundene Geschichten'*), there has been a consistent search for 'realism' in the parables or, to put it more positively, for making the horizons of reader and parabolist meet. These things told in the parables are undoubtedly related to first-century Palestine, but this does not imply that parables should be regarded as a report of 'how things really happened.' Anybody would concede that. In other words, although it is absolutely necessary for the interpreter of parables of Jesus to know exactly what 'Samaritan' stands for, why the word refers to more than its meaning in a story by a Jew for Jews, it is just as important for him to know that a

parable is a story. Narrative is the context of meaning of the parables. As fiction, that is as 'made up' stories, they are stories worth
telling (cf. Polanyi 1981b). Are they then so different from gospels
which are also stories? Parables are stories in which reality is remade,
even if in a metaphorical or some other-say, paradoxical manner.
Gospels are also stories in which reality is remade. Let us leave this
problem for a moment and return to the problem of the referential
aspect of parables.

To my mind the so-called open-endedness of metaphors has largely
contributed to the definition of referential function of parables as
redescription. In the sense in which the term is used by Ricoeur it
is nothing other than the open-endedness of metaphor, or the so-called
priority of possibility as opposed to reality (cf. Jüngel 1969). Redescription has to do with the world which is opened in front of the
text (Ricoeur 1975:82) and not with that to which the text refers
('denotation'). To my mind Ricoeur and his followers, in their use
of redescription, are not concerned with the same problem as the
followers of Jakobson, with whom it is natural to speak of the referential function of the text as something purely internal or immanent. This one has to realize. Ricoeur's handling of the narrative
function is too limited and his distinction between historiography and
other kinds of narrative not convincing. Unlike Ricoeur I would say
that even history (writing) is a 'made up' story. Accordingly it would
be simplistic to say '. . . only history may claim to address itself to
events which actually happened, to actual deeds in the past' (Ricoeur
1978:187). History is by its nature plotted; it is poiesis in the Aristotelian
sense of the word (cf. Ricoeur 1978a:192); it is reality remade. Cannot
a historical novel also '. . . claim to address itself to events which
actually happened . . .,' although on a different level? No doubt
Ricoeur would agree to this. Should we not perhaps rephrase the
problem as follows: how can history (writing) and novels, for example, be used to reconstruct 'what happened?' The distinction made
by Scholes and Kellogg between empirical and fictional narrative as
used by Ricoeur is too broad to handle the problem of the referential aspect of both parables and gospels as stories. Are the characters, events, situations, and plots of gospels not 'imaginary' in the
sense that they are the way the gospel writers presented them, that
is, interpretations? Is a gospel 'empirical' in the sense that it 'may
claim to address itself to events which actually happened, to actual
deeds in the past'? It is, in fact, empirical in the sense that it remakes

the deeds, among other things that actually happened, but it is not because it does not reproduce the actual deeds of the past. The characters, events situations, and plots of gospel narratives are not fictional in the sense that they are '*frei erfunden*,' one may say, but they also are not 'empirical' in the above sense. Although historians or biographers, for instance, work with facts, the facts have to be evaluated and interpreted. Facts do not automatically make the narrative, or render the meaning of the narrative (Brooks and Warren 1970:337). We should remind ourselves that we are dealing with narrative discourse and avoid the so-called 'referential fallacy' of '. . . construing the signifier alone as the sign and as referring directly to the real world object without regard for the signified' (Petersen 1978a:39). Umberto Eco (1972:71) correctly says (a) '*Man macht damit den semiotischen Wert des Signifikans (sc. word, text) von seinem Wahrheitswert abhängig;*' and (b) '*Man ist gezwungen, den Gegenstand zu identifizieren, auf den sich das Signifikans bezieht, und dieses Problem führt zu einer unauflösbaren Aporie.*' There is a difference between a gospel and a parable in that the gospel characters refer to characters who lived in Palestine during the first century, whereas those of parable stories need never have existed at all. There might have been such a person as the good Samaritan, but there is no reason why he must have existed. This distinction is made not because of its usefulness for describing the referential aspect of narrative but only to draw attention to a difference between the two types of texts, with due regard for the dangers involved in such a distinction between characters of a narrative

The crux of the problem lies in the nature of narrative itself. Narrative is the remaking of reality (= creating a *narrative world*) through characterization, plot, and other narrative devices. The storyteller creates a world of his own making with its own time, space, characters, and plot, one which is called a 'narrative world.' Even if one were to be as true to the 'real world' as possible in presenting part of it in narrative discourse, one will still be creating a 'narrative world.' And the resemblance between narrative world and real world cannot be seen as a one to one relationship, but as a remaking of the real world. In a sense this is what has been called *mimesis*: their significance is not the actuality of the events, but their logical structure (cf. Ricoeur 1978a:192). Reference is to be analysed not only with regard to the 'real world' but, in the case of narratives, also with regard to the 'narrative world.' Narratives are not merely windows, nor are they purely mirrors: they are both. One could say that 'disciples' in Mark refers to the original followers of Jesus, but one would immediately have to add how they refer and to what they refer in the gospel narrative. Mark's presentation of the disciples has to do with the narrative world he created. The answer as to how they refer is to be found in the way Mark created his narrative world. The same applies to parables.

Perhaps the distinction between representation as *mimesis* and illustration as *symbolic* (cf. Scholes and Kellogg 1966:84) should not be applied to the parable story quite so readily either (cf. Tolbert 1979:90). Even an exaggerated or a paradoxical story like the parable of the lost sheep can be 'an attempt to create a replica of actuality' (= *mimesis*; cf. Scholes and Kellogg 1968:84) in the sense of remaking reality. Parables are not patently symbolic or purely illustrative. They are stories of a specific kind. In parables reality is remade, often in an extreme form. If one is to ask how these stories refer, the answer would be: in the same way as other stories, that is, within their own narrative worlds. The following discussion by Nida of metaphors as icons (for example, speaking of a person as being a 'pig,' 'wolf,' or 'rat') can help us a little further. 'In reality,' he says, 'such metaphors are not necessarily based upon the true behaviour of the objects which form the basis for the figurative meaning, but the figurative extension of meaning is based upon the way in which people regard such animals, irrespective of the actual truth of a situation' (Nida 1981:20). The referents of signs with figurative meaning are *conceptual*. In this sense Ricoeur is correct in asserting that the first order referent (literal thing) is suspended and replaced by a second order referent (cf. Wittig 1977). The redescription he is talking about is in fact the 'narrative world' of literary criticism in the sense of reality remade, and not what he thinks it to be. Even a photograph cannot provide a copy of reality; it is a remaking thereof (cf. Goodman 1978).

Because we do not have the objects, events, abstracts and so on of a 'narrative world' at our disposal in the same way as we 'have' those of the real world, it follows that opinions will differ greatly about what they really are. In view of what narrative discourse is, namely reality remade, it is clear that the signs in a narrative refer internally within this remade reality. The referents of these signs are to be sought within the 'narrative world' of the text, be it a gospel or a parable. The first order reference is suspended, in the words of Ricoeur, to make room for a second order—that of the narrative world. The implication is not that parables as 'fictions redescribe what conventional language has already *described*' (cf. Ricoeur 1978a: 193) but that they describe in conventional language a remade reality.

It therefore becomes clear that the answer to the question of how narratives (including parables as extended metaphors) refer lies primarily in the nature of narrative. Reference is bound to the expression in which it occurs. To put it differently, the nature of reference depends upon the type of content, be it single words, sentences, or discourse. Parables as parables refer, within their own narrative world, and so do gospels. But parables, like gospels, originate from and exist within the real world. That is why there are relationships between the narrative world of a narrative discourse and the real world of which it is part.

Are parables as metaphors open-ended? From the perspective of the reception of a narrative text, it may be said that the text invites the reader to participate in the narrative world of that text. Since reality is remade, it offers new perspectives to the reader. The participation of the reader in the text is stimulated by the way in which the message is structured. It creates a new world of reference, namely, a narrative world. This is the redescription of which Ricoeur speaks.

How does the metaphorical character of parables influence their reference? The 'kingdom of God' is the referent of the narrative message of parables in general. Like all other signs, the reference of parables depends on the environment of the parable. The direct environment of the predicate of parables is normally the kingdom of God. It is to that sign, which as a sign also refers to some referent, that parables refer. If we know what the sign 'kingdom of God' stands for, we would know what is being said about what. This was shown above in the short discussion of Dodd's and Jeremias's interpretation of the parable of the seed growing secretly. It is not all that difficult to determine the meaning of 'kingdom of God,' but what it refers to is often an open question. The story part of a parable, like that of any other narrative, has a referent (or referents) in its own narrative world. The narrative message of this narrative, however, has as referent the kingdom of God. To put it more specifically, if the narrative message of the parable of the sower is that, despite the small beginning, there will be an abundant harvest, then this message would refer to the kingdom of God where '. . . the kingdom is like what *happens* in the story' (Ricoeur 1975:98). Parables refer as stories. In their metaphoric context the message of the story refers to the kingdom of God.

How do embedded parables refer? In our discussion of the parables in Mark 4 in the first part of this chapter, it was shown how the parables and parabolic sayings are not only inserted into the narrative but how they are actually integrated into the network of intersignification of a narrative text. An attempt was made to give a brief survey of the place of Mark 4 in the narrative world of the gospel. It has become clear that these parables became an integral part of the complete narrative and its narrative world. Within the context of the characterization of the disciples as insiders as opposed to outsiders, these parables have to show, so to speak, how the kingdom is a mystery to the insiders and hidden from the outsiders. Because they are used in a context, they refer within that context. The narrative world of the gospel is the world within which parts of these stories in turn refer. In my view this clarifies the importance of *logos* and kingdom of God. These metaphorical stories and statements contribute to the meaning of Mark in a distinctive way. They are stories as communication and contribute to the meaning of the macronarrative.

Embedded parables and parts of such parables have referents in the narrative world of the text into which they are inserted.

5. *Conclusion*

In conclusion, then, let us consider a few things which have emerged from current research on parables. First, parable research in New Testament scholarship is normally conducted with a view to the parables of Jesus, that is, the historical Jesus. The importance is easily understood. In addition it is normally argued that parables should be interpreted according to their referent—the kingdom of God which in turn interpreted in terms of the eschatological preaching of Jesus. This too follows naturally. In the third place, much is made of the fact that the parables of Jesus can be studied in groups, for example, tragic and comic parables; parables of advent, reversal, action; parables of growth, servants and so on, emphasizing that various parables have a 'common' theme. The usefulness of this approach is also self-evident. Furthermore, it has often been argued that context is a very important aspect of the parables of Jesus. Recently New Testament scholars have reached consensus about the form of the parables. As we have said repeatedly, Jesus' parables are spoken of in terms of metaphoricity, narrativity, and paradoxicality (and brevity). All these aspects, however, are emphasized with regard to the parables of Jesus in their original form and meaning.

This approach poses at least two problems. First, there is the fact that little or no attention is paid to the problem of the continuity or discontinuity between the oral and literary phases of the tradition of Jesus. In the above study some of the implications of the recording of Jesus' parables in a macro-text were pointed out. This is another facet of parable research, not the only but nevertheless an important one, which should receive much more attention than has hitherto been the case. Secondly, there is the problem of historical reconstruction. It is well known that we can reconstruct the *Sitz im Leben* of the parables with some certainty, but that from the sources at our disposal it is impossible to reconstruct the historical situation in which Jesus uttered a specific parable. This is a major problem which we will have to face sooner or later. The original parables may be considered stories as communication (cf. Polanyi 1981b). Jesus most probably told these stories not for their intrinsic worth but because he wanted to say something to his followers *about* some point raised in his conversations with them. It is commonly held that this something *about* which he told his parables was the kingdom of God. That is probably correct. But in his talks with his followers, various reasons could have given rise to such stories, not only as illustrations but as a means of communicating something about a topic that cropped up in their conversations. These reasons, these contextual settings in the life of Jesus, have been lost and cannot be reconstructed. Tolbert (1979:49) correctly maintains: 'Unless historical criticism can supply a much more *specific* picture of the historical Jesus or the particular situation in which the parables were first told, historical interpretations of the parables will diverge as widely as modern philosophical or psychological interpretations. . . .' That is why it is so difficult to make comparative studies of the parables in their gospel contexts and in their context in the life of Jesus.

Even more important than the problems of what parables mean and to what they refer is how they mean and how they refer. If we can answer this question we will know the solutions to the other as well.

CHAPTER TWELVE

THE GROWTH AND MAKING OF JOHN 21

The choice of the topic of this contribution has been partly influenced by the presidential address of Professor F. Neirynck at the 44th General meeting of the *Studiorum Novi Testamenti Societas* in Dublin, Ireland, on July 25, 1989. The address, which was later published, gives a clear indication of the many difficulties involved in John 21 (see Neirynck 1990). Neirynck approaches this chapter of John's Gospel from the perspective of the *Vorlage* of parts of John 21 and elaborates on his earlier thesis that John used Luke and not a common source or a pre-Johannine tradition. The second part of his essay deals with the Beloved Disciple, whom he believes the author introduced 'in the story of the Gospel at the dark moments of discipleship' (Neirynck 1990:336). Close to the end of his essay he makes the important observation that 'in recent studies the two positions, the evangelist's addendum or the appendix of a post-Johannine redactor, come closer to one another: the redactor sometimes takes the shape of an evangelist, and chapter 21 is studied as part of the Fourth Gospel' (Neirynck 1990). The importance of this remark should not be underestimated in current research on the Gospel of John, and I would like to pursue the matter further by paying attention to both the growth and the making of John 21.

The purpose of this essay is to draw attention to the far-reaching effects of focusing either on the evolution (growth) of a text or on its production (making), with regard to how a text is perceived, and what problems are discovered and the solutions offered. In the first part of the essay John 21 will be discussed from the perspective of the growth of the text, that is what lies behind the text. The second part of the essay will deal with the same text from the perspective of the making or production of the text.

1. *On the Growth of John 21*

For more than a century interpreters of New Testament documents have been concentrating on the origin of texts, that is on questions relating to the source material in texts. One of the main interests was the sources and or traditions behind final texts. This explains the lack of interest, even in redaction critical studies, in the process of production, and the focus on the growth and influence of precursor texts on the final product. This approach gave rise to certain data beliefs and assumptions about the origin and growth of New Testament writings such as the Gospel of John. Matters of literary dependence, literary integrity, the history and growth of traditions and the influence of precursor texts on the final versions of particular texts were addressed in order to explain how material, which has now been incorporated into edited versions of traditions, was transformed into new texts. Very often these investigations were done with more than one question in mind. Detailed examination of parts of texts was, for example, undertaken primarily to explain the origin and growth of these particular texts, but also with (a) the Synoptic problem, or (b) the relationship between the Gospel of John and the Synoptics, or (c) the historical Jesus in mind. The result is a very complicated concept of what a text is and also how New Testament texts came about. This also applies to John 21. John 21 is normally regarded as a second ending to the Gospel of John, which was added to the first version by a redactor shortly after the Gospel was written. Since there is no manuscript evidence that the Gospel was ever circulated without chapter 21, there is no reason to believe that it is a late addition to the Gospel.

The chapter can be divided into three parts, namely verses 1–14, 15–23 and 24–25. The first part is a story about a miraculous catch of fish (1–8), a meal on the shore (9–13) and a parenthetical observation of the writer: this was the third time that Jesus revealed himself to the disciples. The second section consists entirely of sayings of the risen Jesus. In verses 15–17 Jesus rehabilitates Peter by asking him about his love for Jesus and commissions him to be the shepherd of his sheep. Verses 18–23 consist of remarks by Jesus about the fates of Peter and the Beloved Disciple. Verse 23 is a comment by the writer on the real meaning of Jesus' remark about the fate of the Beloved Disciple. The conclusion of the chapter consists of remarks about the true witness of the Beloved Disciple and the many other deeds of Jesus.

Interpreters of the Gospel have discovered a variety of problems in the chapter, and numerous solutions, hypotheses and assumptions have been offered in the history of interpretation of these few verses from John. John 21 is generally perceived as a complicated text with a complex history of growth and production. It is regarded as an addition to the original Gospel, as I have said, and furthermore as a text which underwent different transformations in its history of development. Let us first turn to the status of John 21 as part of the whole Gospel.

Most scholars seem to think that chapter 21 did not originally form an integral part of the Gospel. It is assumed that the original Gospel ended with John 20:30–31. The categorical statement of Kümmel that chapter 21 is an appendix ('Nachtrag') which cannot be denied because 20:30–31 is undoubtedly the end of a book, indicates the unanimity on the issue (see Kümmel 1965:141 and for a discussion of the unanimity Reim 1976:330). Although there is difference of opinion on the exact nature of the addition, it is often taken for granted that chapter 21 was added to the rest of the Gospel either by the evangelist or by another hand (a redactor). It is regarded either as an appendix, a supplement or an epilogue, depending on the function which is ascribed to John 21, or to views held about the origin and growth of the Gospel. Lindars (1972:618), for example, argues that the chapter cannot be viewed as part of the formal structure of the book and regards it as an appendix—'It has been added soon after the rest was written, possibly at the time of publication to a wider audience than the immediate circle for whom the Gospel was written'—, while Brown and others regard it as the epilogue of the Gospel. He maintains that it was added to the rest of the Gospel by a redactor who was a Johannine disciple 'who shared the same general world of thought as the evangelist and who desired more to complete the Gospel than to change its impact', and that it therefore forms part of the Gospel in its final redaction (see Brown 1972:1081). He correctly observes that there is a vast difference between regarding John 21 as an appendix which is not related to the complete work or an epilogue which is integrated into the complete Gospel: 'Certainly this chapter is more closely integrated into Johannine thought than the "Marcan Appendix" is integrated into Marcan thought' (Brown 1972:1078).

There are different reasons for this state of affairs. I have already mentioned that 20:30–31 is universally taken to be the end of a book and, as Brown maintains, the termination 'seems to preclude any further narrative'. He also mentions other principal reasons— for example that after the blessing in 20:29 on those who have not seen but nevertheless believe, other appearances are unlikely to be related; also that the story in John 21 is awkwardly placed after that of chapter 20. Why would the disciples return to Galilee and fail to recognize Jesus after they had seen him twice after his death in Jerusalem? (Brown 1972:1078). It is bluntly denied that the original Gospel anticipates a need for the continuation of the story by different scholars on these and other grounds (see furthermore Braun 1990:68–69 for a summary of reasons by Mahoney and others). However, it is also widely accepted that, as I have mentioned, there is no manuscript evidence that the Gospel was ever circulated without chapter 21. In view of the agreements and differences between the vocabulary and style of John and the rest of the Gospel, Minear correctly asserts that 'attribution of chapter 21 to a separate redactor must rest on other conclusions than manuscripts, vocabulary or literary style' (Minear 1983:87). For the purpose of this essay it is unnecessary to go into more detail, since arguments for and against are readily available in surveys and works on John 21 (see Thyen 1977:211–270).

In spite of the consensus amongst scholars that the original Gospel ended with John 20:30–31, it appears that the evidence for or against chapter 21 as an addition is inconclusive. This being the case, it becomes all the more important to take seriously the implications of regarding John 21 either as a separate appendix or as an epilogue— albeit an epilogue added to the original Gospel by a redactor—as we shall do in the second part of the essay.

In addition to the status of John 21 with regard to the complete Gospel, the contents of the chapter have been subjected to serious scrutiny in the course of history, especially as far as the origin of the material is concerned. Different parts of the chapter are related to traditions or other texts in the New Testament. The main problem is: Where did the author of John 21 get his material?

First, there is the story of the miraculous catch of fish and a meal in John 21:1–14, which presumably is related either to a hypothetical pre-Johannine signs-source or to Luke 5:1–11, but which has led scholars to opposing conclusions. There are at least three motifs which have to be taken into account in John 21:1–14, namely the fishing motif, the recognition motif and the meal motif. As it stands, the story has at least these three motifs combined in the same story which, according to verse 14—a parenthetical remark for the sake of the readers—was about the appearance of the risen Jesus. The

combination of these motifs and the aside by John leaves the interpreter with a number of problems which have to be addressed in
connection with the origin of the material.

   Different solutions to explain the origin of the material have been
offered which need not be dealt with in detail, but should nevertheless be mentioned for the sake of the argument. The prevailing
hypothesis is that a story of a miraculous catch of fish is the basic
source on which the author of John 21:1–14 based his story. Some
scholars arc of the opinion that the material goes back to the hypothetical σεμεῖα-source as the third σεμεῖον in a pre-Johannine collection of signs (for full details see Neirynck 1990:322). Others consider
the fishing motif as reminiscent of a traditional appearance story.
This, however, implies that Luke 5:1–11, which is now a calling
story, was originally a post-resurrection appearance story which had
been retrojected into the ministry of Jesus (see the proponents of this
view in Neirynck 1990:322, notes 8 and 9). That is why it is often
argued that the transition from miracle story to appearance story is
the result of a fusion or a combination of two or more traditions (see
further Pesch 1969:131–133; Lindars 1972:619 and Schnackenburg
1975:411, who also gives a summary of the findings of Fortna and
Pesch). One may moreover ask what the relationship is between John
1–14 and the logion of Jesus about the 'fishers of men' (Mk. 1:17)—
a tradition which is related to Jesus' ministry in Galilee.

   A detailed comparison between John 21:1–14 and Luke 5:1–11
indicates that there are several agreements between the two stories.
Brown (1972:1090) has a useful summary of similarities. He, however, remarks: 'The similarities . . . make it reasonable to conclude that Luke and John have preserved variant forms of the same
miracle story—we may say independently because there are many
differences of vocabulary and detail' (Brown 1972:1090). However,
the differences also underscore the fact that John's story is a totally
different story from that of Luke. This does not only apply to the
difference between an appearance story and a calling story, but also
to much of the detail. Fortna (1972:67 note 148) goes so far as to
say that the 'two stories stem distantly from the same tradition and
have no more than that in common', while Neirynck (1990:336)
maintains that the author of John used Luke's Gospel as the *Vorlage*
for John 20 and 21. For our purpose it is unnecessary to pursue the
matter further.

   In the case of the hypothetical signs-source it is even more difficult to determine the exact extent of traditional material in John 14:1–11. Various attempts have been made to distinguish between tradition and redaction in John 21,1–14 with varying results (see Schnackenburg 1975:410–411) for the different verses or parts of verses which are regarded as tradition. In this hypothesis the main emphasis is on the use of a pre-Johannine signs-source.

The matter is complicated even more by the postulation of yet another source underlying John 21:1–14 regarding the meal motif in John 21:9–13—especially when verse 7, the recognition of Jesus by the Beloved Disciple, is taken into account. The meal in John 21 is often compared with that of the Emmaus story in Lk. 24:13–35 (see for example Eckhart in Thyen 1977:238 and Brown 1972:1094). In addition, Brown's remark about the statement in the *Gospel to the Hebrews* is noteworthy where we are told that Jesus appeared to James at a meal: 'He took the bread, blessed it, and gave it to James the Just, and said to him, 'My brother, eat your bread, for the Son of Man is risen from among those who sleep' (Brown 1972:1094). There are obviously great differences between John 21:9–13 and the Emmaus story in Luke 24, but the agreements cannot be denied. (Neirynck 1990:324–325 has given a full treatment of the possible relationships and concludes that the traditional theme of the recognition at the meal, as well as the eating scene, 'underwent transformation').

The locality of the appearance story in John 21:1–14, namely Galilee, is also remarkable and has been linked to Mark 16:7 where the disciples, and Peter in particular, are directed to go to Galilee. It is furthermore remarkable that the *Gospel of Peter* 58–60 breaks off with the tradition that the first appearance of the risen Jesus to his disciples took place near the Lake of Galilee after Easter. It is possible that John 21 is based on material from a Galilean tradition of post-resurrection appearances (see Brown 1972:1094).

The foregoing discussion gives an indication of the sources and traditions which presumably underlie the story of the miraculous catch of fish in John 21:1–14. It also gives an indication of the complex nature of the concept 'text' which underlies studies of the New Testament which take the origin and growth as point of departure. This will be discussed in greater detail below. Let us now turn to the rest of the chapter.

The second part of John 21 can also be related to traditions which are found elsewhere in the New Testament, even if similarity is restricted to thought patterns.

The commissioning of Peter in John 21:15–17 has often been compared to Peter's leadership of the church according to Matthew 16:17–19. The latter text is obviously a Matthean interpretation of the original scene during the ministry of Jesus where Simon Peter confesses Jesus as Messiah (Mk. 8:27–29 *par*). According to Matthew, Jesus praises Simon for possessing an insight which the Father must have revealed to him, changes his name to Peter, the rock on which the church has to be built, and gives him the keys of the kingdom. Some scholars think that the post-resurrection period was the original setting for this Matthean interpretation (for further detail see Brown 1972:1088). Although the metaphor is totally different from the metaphor of tending the sheep in John 21:15–17, the idea of Petrine leadership of the church undoubtedly underlie both traditions. Brown proposes that although the sayings cannot be regarded as doublets they may both represent fragments of a longer original post-resurrection appearance narrative, in which Peter is given authority over the church (Brown 1972:1089, see also Bultmann 1968:551–552, who regards Peter's commission to lead the church as an older tradition than the mission commission in Mt. 28:19 and elsewhere). The idea of Peter's leadership is firmly based in tradition.

Neirynck has furthermore drawn attention to the fact that both Peter's commission and the theme of 'following' occur in John 21:19.21 and Luke 5:1–11. He maintains that the interpretation of John 21 in the light of Lk. 5:1–11 has the advantage that it places the story of the catch of fish in the larger context of John 21. In both stories Peter is commissioned to a task expressed in two different metaphors, both of which imply following Jesus (see Neirynck 1990:328–329). He says: 'In John 21, Peter's commission to his pastoral task is the real "parallel" to the fishers-of-men saying' (see Neirynck 1990:329).

It is improbable that the question: 'Do you love me?' which is repeated three times in John 21:16–17 is an allusion to the three times Peter denies Jesus during the trial (see Lindars 1972:619). On the other hand there are intertextual relationships between different details in John 21 and the rest of the Gospel to which we shall return in the second part of the essay.

While Bultmann, for example, maintains that the material in verses 18–23 were composed by the redactor (see Bultmann 1968:554), Brown contends that the redactor may only have joined existing sayings (see Brown 1972:1118). According to Brown, the sayings are very old. The statement in verse 19 is reminiscent of terminology

relating to martyrdom or death for the sake of Christ (see 1 Pt.
4:16). The saying about the Beloved Disciple, on the other hand,
reminds one of the expectation reflected by sayings such as Mark
9:1 predicting that the Son of man would return before the generation of Jesus had died out (see also Mk. 13:30; 1 Thess. 4:15).

The foregoing discussion gives a general picture of the complexities regarding the material from which this chapter originated. There
is yet one other problem which has to be mentioned concerning the
origin of John 21, namely: Who was responsible for compiling the
chapter?

Different people could have been responsible for composing chapter 21. First, there is the author of the rest of the Gospel, the evangelist, as he is generally called. There are, however, also those who
are of the opinion that an editor or editors could have compiled
John 21. It is furthermore possible that most of the material goes
back to the evangelist, even though an editor reworked it. In short,
scholars are of different opinions as to the source of the material;
whether it was handed down orally or in written form, or in both
media, and whether some editor(s) composed the chapter independently of the evangelist, or whether most or some of the material goes
back to the evangelist remains an open question (see Schnackenburg 1975:416–417 for various points of view).

In the preceding treatment of findings, hypotheses and well-informed
speculations about the origin and growth of John 21 there is one
thing missing. There is no clarity on how the end product came
about. What do the following phrases mean: 'was used by the redactor/
evangelist', 'underwent transformation', 'traditions were fused', 'was
handed down orally', 'is based upon', 'stem distantly from', 'was
edited by' and so on? How should one imagine this process? What
did the redactor of John 21 do? If he received the information from
the evangelist orally, did he creatively 'rework' the material, or was
he simply a 'conduit' through which the process of transformation
of tradition flowed?

At this point in time these questions are very important. We as
New Testament scholars do not have answers about the process
of making texts. We have been so involved in the origin of New
Testament material and the transmission of tradition that other important questions have slipped our minds. This can be explained by the
fact that we have mainly concentrated on the origin of material without reflecting on the actual process of making a text. Can we really

answer to an uninformed person simply: Did the compiler/composer/redactor/evangelist of John 21 actually have a copy of Luke 21 as *Vorlage* in front of him when he composed his text? How should we conceive the process of growth of a text? In the next section of the essay the issue of the making of John 21 will be addressed.

2. *On the Making of John 21*

The discussion of the growth of John 21 in the previous section has made it clear that the focus was on the origin of the material in that chapter. It has also become apparent that the phenomenon 'text' has been conceived in causal terms. The purpose of source-influenced studies is to prove the use of sources and to demonstrate the indebtedness of authors of these texts to other texts and their authors, whether actual or proposed texts.

It is, however, possible to study textual relationships from a totally different perspective. This involves a radically different perception of the phenomenon 'text' and also of the role of the interpreter. It also implies a different set of questions.

Literary references to earlier texts, allusions to other texts, and literal or 'free' citations are known to us not only from the New Testament but also from other ancient writings such as Homer. The historico-critical study of the New Testament has opened our eyes to the many intertextual relationships in these writings. What is important, however, is the way in which we regard these relationships.

All texts can be regarded as the rewriting of previous texts. Every text is a reaction to other texts, and textual discourses, whether contemporary or earlier, written or cultural. In the words of Kristeva: 'tout texte se construit comme mosaïque de citations, tout texte est absorption et transformation d'un autre texte' (Kristeva 1969:146). According to this view, the phenomenon 'text' becomes a network of traces, no longer a unitary object which can be known by the interpreter. Each sentence of the network creates intertextual relationships which point to intertextual analogies and connections. 'The intertextual relationships of any work of literature are theoretically infinite, since potentially any sentence of a text (or fragment thereof) may engender a series of presuppositional statements', says Miller 1985:24–25). The theory which lies behind this concept is 'intertextuality'.

There are many and important differences between source-influenced studies and studies based on the theory of intertextuality. The main difference with regard to New Testament study of intertextual relationships concerns the focus of and assumptions regarding these relationships. In source-influenced studies the focus is on the growth of the text and on the intention of the authors/redactors of these texts. The presupposed texts are more or less regarded as citations, embedded into or assimilated by the new text with the focus on the cited text, and the intention of the author/redactor of the final text with his reworking of the cited text. These studies are based on comparisons of two texts, the presupposed cited text and the edited text, with regard to the influence of the source on the final text. This final text is seen from below, that is diachronically. The cited text determines the final text. In intertextuality the focus is on the top— to continue the metaphor. The final text adapts and assimilates the cited text. In fact, the cited text is reworked in such a manner that the former texts are often hardly recognisable. The selection and form of the reworked text now determines the cited text and prompts the reader to read this text intertextually in the broadest sense of the word. An apocalyptic text, for example, would be read in the context of apocalypticism and with reference to other apocalyptic texts and fragments of such texts.

New Testament scholars should have a good understanding of this concept of text. The same story of Jesus, whether a parable, a miracle story, or a chreia, is never the same story in the Jesus tradition when it appears in retold form. The versions not only differ in wording and order, they also differ because they are told in different contexts and communication situations. New selections have been made and the stories in retold form have new functions and are told from new perspectives for new purposes. That is the reason why the reworked versions refer to totally different intertextual texts and discourses.

The matter may be further illustrated by the findings of narratologists and ethno-methodologists who point out that when a story is retold orally the exact words are almost never used and that each time the story is repeated, it 'will be tuned to circumstances in which it is told, delicately reflecting the concerns of the participants and their relationships to each other, to events and circumstances in the story and to the fact that the story is being told at a particular point in a particular conversation to make a point relevant to the topics under discussion at that time' (Polanyi 1981:319). *Retelling* should therefore be regarded as a means of text production, and authors or editors of New Testament writers as readers of texts to which they react. This has far-reaching implications for the study of New Testament documents, including the synoptic problem and the relationship between the Gospel of John and the Synoptic Gospels (see Van Wolde 1989:43–49, especially page 46; and also my contribution in the same book, Vorster 1989c:15–26, where I have pointed out the vast differences between these two strategies of reading texts with regard to New Testament texts).

Van Wolde maintains: 'a writer should neither be regarded as a completely autonomous and conscious authority, nor as a reproducer of previous texts, but as a reader, in continuous interaction with other texts which, for him, function as synchronic texts' (Van Wolde 1989:46). In the reworking of texts and fragments of texts, and in the interaction with other texts it is the author who as a reader of intertextual discourses produces a completely new text. This is best seen when the Gospels are compared as whole texts. Although they tell the 'same' story, each author tells another story which is different from the others. Because of the network of codes and discourses within which an author finds him/herself, a different text comes about with traces of many texts.

John 21 is an excellent example of a text in which the author/redactor has succeeded in making a completely new text. This is not only seen when we compare the traces of other texts which are presumably present, but also when we assign meaning to this text as the product of reworked texts.

We have seen above that different scholars postulate different possible sources underlying John 21. We have also noticed that there is no unanimity about which sources were used by the person who wrote this nor anybody else has drawn up a list of the sources and has given an indication of whether they were written or oral, it is futile to attempt to find out which sources have been used. The author of John 21 obviously made up a new story with the material he had at his disposal. It is improbable that his story is totally 'fictitious', but it nevertheless remains his story, a story which has been written creatively. He obviously combined 'sources' and fragments of sources and made new stories out of his material. From the point of view of the present text, not a single trace of any source mentioned in the first part of the essay was used verbatim by our author.

That, amongst other things, explains why scholars who approach the text from the perspective of source-influenced theories have so many difficulties in ascertaining what is redaction and what is tradition, and in determining whether traditions have been fused or combined or whether they stem distantly from the same tradition. If it were not for the references to traditions and other texts in the margins or footnotes of Greek New Testament editions, and our knowledge of comparable and parallel thought patterns in our documents, probably less time would have been spent on determining the sources, traditions, quotations and allusions in the New Testament.

It should be clear by this time that I have a lot of appreciation for what has been achieved in the past with regard to the use of sources and traditions in New Testament writings, but also that I have a large number of problems in this regard because this approach retards progress in the understanding and interpretation of documents such as John 21.

Let us now turn again to some of the problems which have been treated in the first part of the essay, but now from another perspective.

If we assume that the author of John 21 used traditions of different natures and backgrounds, and that he reworked them into a new text, can we make sense out of what he has done? The idea is not to give a detailed treatment of the complete text, but to comment on aspects which throw light on the implications of concentrating on the making of John 21.

The first thing that needs to be said is the fact that the present (critical) text of the Gospel of John includes chapter 21 as part of it. Whether it was originally written without the chapter is difficult, if not impossible, to determine. For the sake of the argument, and on text-critical grounds, we have to assume that it formed part of the Gospel. Whether it was added shortly after the Gospel was written cannot be determined with any certainty. I therefore proceed from the assumption that as it now stands it forms part of the complete text of John's Gospel.

There are at least two different ways in which it could be treated now. First, as an addition or, secondly, as an integral part of the Gospel. If it is treated as an addition, the question is: what did the person who added it want to achieve? A very interesting proposal has recently been forwarded by Braun who uses the concept of the resisting reader (see Braun 1990). Braun accepts the interpretation that the original Gospel ended with chapter 20 and that John 21 was added. The original Gospel did not need anything beyond John 20. The necessity to write anything beyond n. This narrative situation differed from the original situation from which John 1–20 originally came. John 21 is evidence in itself of a new narrative situation, according to Braun. 'Chapter 21 imposes on the original gospel a configuration of meaning it did not have before' (Braun 1990:70). The old ending was originally satisfying to the reader. Now it is exposed as premature and becomes a premature ending. The redactor respects the received Gospel although he also transgresses it and 'so contests its sufficiency . . . By reopening a closed text the Johannine redactor refuses to absolutize the claims of his precursor' (Braun 1990:70–71). According to Braun there is now an ambivalence between the original Gospel and the new ending, which causes the reader to receive the text with critical ambivalence (Braun 1990:71).

This solution is obviously based on the idea that John 20:30–31 is the original ending of the book and also that a new situation is responsible for the addition of chapter 21. In essence it is a corroboration of the earlier hypothesis that John 21 is an appendix or supplement. It nevertheless gives an interesting interpretation of the chapter as an addition to the original Gospel.

If one accepts the fact that there is no textual evidence that the Gospel was ever circulated without John 21, and tries to understand John 21 as the ending of the story, as readers have done for many ages, it should be seriously considered whether the Gospel with its twenty-one chapters cannot make sense as a whole. It would imply that the last chapter should be considered an integral part of the story line and story world. That this is not an artificial undertaking has been shown by Culpepper, amongst others, who has made a narrative analysis of the literary design of the Gospel (see Culpepper 1983).

Culpepper believes that John 21 is an epilogue, which was added shortly after the completion of the Gospel, but he nevertheless regards the chapter as a necessary ending to the Gospel. According to him the ending is necessary because some unresolved minor conflicts in chapters 1–20 are resolved in 21, notably the conflict between Peter and the Beloved Disciple and Peter and Jesus, and it is also necessary to bring some of the symbols of the Gospel to a climax (Culpepper 1983:96). Culpepper still works with the idea of two separate endings. But is that really necessary?

Let us approach the question from the perspective of the reader and not from the traditional arguments mentioned above. Although John 20:30–31 is normally interpreted as the ending of the original Gospel, it need not be the case. First of all one can regard the 'ending' as a conclusion to the material which has been dealt with in chapter 20, as has been done before (see Minear 1983:87). There is in fact nothing in the wording of John 20,30–31 which compels the reader to regard these statements as the end of a book, despite the consensus of opinion to the contrary. It is not only what is said that matters, but also why it is said. What is done with these words? People do things with words, and readers react to words because communication concerns a process of interaction between sender and hearer or reader (see e.g. Bach and Harnisch 1979). To my mind the author of these words directed these words to the hearers/readers of the Gospel not for the sake of giving information, but in order to prompt them to believe, and as a result share in eternal life.

Too often interpreters of the New Testament are misled by the questions they ask. John 20:30–31 is a typical example. To my knowledge these statements have never been studied from the perspective of what these words *do*. The focus has always been on what they *say*. As soon as one realizes that these words do not only want to inform, but also want to convince the reader that the signs in John's Gospel are related to enhance and generate belief and faith in the Son of God, the picture changes as far as the ending of the Gospel is concerned. (Traditionally the statements in John 20:30–31 have been read as information about the end of the book, but notice the stress on the directive: ταῦτα δὲ γέγραπται ἵνα πιστεύσητε κτλ.) John 20:30–31 is not the ending of a Gospel. It is a summary and conclusion to the chapter.

An additional argument should be discussed briefly. Let us for a moment assume that the original Gospel ended with chapter 21 and not with 20. How should one then explain John 20:30–31? Readers normally read texts from the beginning to the end, even if they are interrupted or if they stop at certain points. What would the effect have been on a reader who would have read John 21 after John 20:30–31 if he/she had understood these words as an ending? Obviously defamiliarisation would have taken place. Having read chapter 21, the attentive reader would have revised his/her understanding of the ending of John 20 and would have realized that it had been misinterpreted, and would have understood that John 20:30-31 was not the end of the Gospel.

It is true that at face value, the link between chapters 20 and 21 seems to be a bit awkward. What is meant by μετὰ ταῦτα in 21:1? Is it simply a conjunction between the two chapters or should one read it consecutively or diachronically? In all probability it has the function of linking two narrative sections. Nothing more and nothing less. Within the story line of John's Gospel the next episode is a presentation of new material by the omniscient narrator who continues his story in the third person. (I am not trying to defend the unity of the Gospel or to refute the idea of a redactor who has edited the original Gospel at this point. All I am trying to do is to show that our data assumptions are determined by our methods and by convention. We are not working with hard facts and that is the reason why experimental work on the New Testament is necessary.) And this part of the story can be read as an integral part of the Gospel as a whole, who wrote the Gospel or edited it in its final form.

If one carefully compares John 21:1-14 with texts such as Luke 5:1-11, it soon becomes clear that it is a totally different story from that in Luke. The author of John 21:1-14 has made up his own story about an appearance of Jesus to the disciples at the Sea of Tiberias. Not only the content but the whole structure of the story has its own Johannine colour. What is reminiscent of other New Testament material is used in such a manner that it forms part of a new story. The author has made a new text for the sake of his readers, to communicate a message which is in no single way comparable to the messages of any of the texts we have mentioned in the first part of this essay. In fact, those texts were reworked to such an extent that John 21:1-14 is a new story and different from any story which we have. The author retold the story and if we compare it with the intertexts mentioned above, the Johannine meaning comes out very sharply. It is not only different from intertexts such as miracle stories in the Jesus tradition, but also from other appearance stories.

There are obviously many traces of other texts in the story, including the ones mentioned above. There are also traces of texts within the Gospel, such as the Beloved Disciple material. In fact, by including the Beloved Disciple in verse 7, the story links up with

the characterization of the disciple in previous sections of the narrative. The same applies to Peter. Both these characters are in focus
in the story which certainly has to be taken into account by the
reader. By concentrating on the text of John and reading it together
with other intertexts it becomes clear how our author selected,
arranged and structured his own text.

The things to which interpreters have drawn attention in the past,
such as symbolism in verses 11 and 13, are characteristic of the
ambiguity of the Gospel and give the story its own Johannine character. The same applies to the rest of the ion to tend the flock, and
where the deaths of Peter and the Beloved Disciple are focused upon.

Let us now turn to the end of chapter 21. If John 20:30–31 is
viewed as the ending of chapter 20, and not necessarily as the ending of the original Gospel, as I have argued above, then John 21:24–25
serves as the ending of the Gospel as a whole.

The use of the plural 'we' in οἴδαμεν in verse 24 has given rise
to much speculation (see Brown 1972:1124 for a thorough treatment
of different standpoints). Since whoever wrote the ending tried to
give the impression that the material in the Gospel originated from
the Beloved Disciple—in fact, that it was written by him—it is also
possible to interpret the 'we' as referring to the Beloved Disciple.
The implication is that the 'we' was used to incorporate the Beloved
Disciple and the support of the Johannine circle by association. As
a speech act, this is a forceful way of drawing the reader to the text
and its truthfulness.

There is good reason to interpret John 21 as an integral part of
the Gospel of John and not simply as an appendix or even as an
epilogue which was added. It is impossible and also unnecessary to
repeat the arguments of Minear in connection with the original functions of John 21. He has convincingly shown how many intratextual relationships there are between this chapter and the rest of the
Gospel. In addition, the many studies on the Beloved Disciple material in John's Gospel indicate that this material is well integrated
into the whole of the Gospel. Thyen (1977:229) is correct in saying:
'Doch nicht allein das 21. Kapitel erreicht so in Vers 24 seine Klimax.
Dies gilt vielmehr zugleich für die gesamte Folge der planvoll, Schritt
für Schritt farbiger werdenden Lieblingsjüngertexte, das als Einheit
begriffen sein wollen'.

The time has come to study John 21 from perspectives other than
its origin. This chapter can be read as a very important part of the

story of the author of the Gospel, his story about Jesus which he himself made out of many different materials at his disposal. The observation was made by Professor Neirynck that this is already taking place. It is an honour to dedicate my contribution to this great scholar of the sources of New Testament texts, and to help open the way for renewed study of what happened when the author created his own text for his own purposes.

Section B.3

Apocalypse

CHAPTER THIRTEEN

'GENRE' AND THE REVELATION OF JOHN:
A STUDY IN TEXT, CONTEXT AND INTERTEXT

> Every genre . . . has multiple distinguishing traits, which however are
> not all shared by each exemplar. If literature is a genre, the idea of
> defining it is misconceived. For . . . the character of genres is that they
> change. Only variations or modifications of convention have literary
> significance (Fowler 1982:18).

Recent analysis of discourse has been dominated on the one hand
by formalism which treats the text as an extension of the syntactic
and logical 4 structuring of the sentence, on the other hand by an
embarrassed empiricism which, in attempting to take into account
the role of context and enunciation in the shaping of text, finds itself
unable to formalise the infinity of possible speech-situations (Frow
1980:73).

1. *Introduction*

Recent discussions of matters concerning the 'genre' of the Revelation
of John have largely been dominated by the results of the *Society of
Biblical Scholarship*-group directed by Professor J.J. Collins (cf. Collins
1979, 1984; Aune 1986 and Hellholm 1986). The group has developed a typology of the apocalypse genre, based on a thorough investigation of a large corpus of ancient writings in order to establish
'. . . distinctive recurring characteristics which constitute a recognizable and coherent type of writing. The initial undertaking, which
focused mainly on aspects of form and content, has been comple-
mented by recent investigations into the 'function' of the genre (cf.
Hartman 1983, Collins 1984, Aune 1986 and Hellholm 1986). I
have discussed some of the merits and the demerits of this approach
in another connection where I contended that it is difficult to speak
of a 'genre apocalypse' and that more attention should be paid to
the mode of writing or the way in which material is organised in a
discourse. I maintained that so-called apocalypses are, first of all,

narratives; if these texts were to be understood, their narrative aspects should be taken seriously. I furthermore maintained that the Revelation of John is a circular letter in narrative form (cf. Vorster 1983). In view of new insights into the problems of genre and the role of the interpretive community in defining the data and the beliefs of researchers, I should like to address the problem of the genre of the Revelation of John anew.

2. *From Architext to Intertext*

2.1   *Three approaches*

The reasons for and the relevance of the study of genre are directly related to views on what texts are and how they function. Generally speaking, there are at least three current approaches to the study of genre in literary theory which have to be taken seriously. These are based on different epistemologies and views of the phenomenon 'text', which obviously have implications for the study of the kinds of texts we find in the New Testament. The three approaches range from the traditional analysis of genre, in terms of the classification of texts based on universal characteristics and the literary history of a particular genre, through the emphasis on the texts as signs of communication in different types of situations and their social settings, to the viewpoint that the classification of texts in genres is subverted by the very nature of text. In view of this it seems necessary to establish a frame of reference for the topic of my essay, in order to determine the relevance of the study of genre in New Testament research. It is necessary both on the grounds of the present state of research into types of texts in the New Testament, including the genre of the Revelation of John, and in view of the fact that there have recently been a few shifts in New Testament studies—from the author to the text to the reader—shifts which have implications for the study of genre and the New Testament.

The main differences between the three approaches mentioned above can be viewed in terms of the role of universals and convention in the definition of genre (cf. Bal 1981:7ff.) and convictions about the nature of texts. While some scholars see genre as something which is based on ontologically determined universal characteristics, others regard it as being fundamentally and historically variable, and conventionally determined.

At the same time, the matter is complicated by the fact that the phenomenon of 'text' (and not only literary text) has become a contentious great emphasis has been placed on texts as signs within the context of communication and the associated interaction between sign and receiver has brought about a number of shifts which have to be taken seriously.

2.2 *Aristotle: universals and convention*

It has become conventional in many circles to analyse genre—with reference to the taxonomy of literary texts in particular—on the grounds of universal characteristics. Texts with presumably similar characteristics are classified in genres, subgenres and even subsubgenres, and the history of the different sets is described on the grounds of a comparison of recurring characteristics. This approach is based on the idea of a set of universal transhistoric characteristics, according to which the whole of literature can be classified. Other so-called non-literary texts are, however, treated in a similar manner, as is the case with the classification of New Testament writings. The purpose is mainly to classify objects, namely texts belonging to the same group (cf. Hempfer 1973 and A. Fowler 1982a+b).

The idea that every kind of literature (literary text) can be classified into one of three fundamental types or genres is traditionally traced back to Aristotle (and Plato). Their ideas, and specifically the few opening sentences of Aristotle's Περὶ Ποιητικῆς, form the architext or source of a very long tradition in the study of genre within the framework of three basic genres, namely epic or prose, drama and lyric, or poetry. This tradition is, however, basically a misconception of what Aristotle and also Plato maintained about mode of presentation and genre, as Genette (1981:61ff.) has shown in a convincing manner. What Plato and Aristotle had in mind was something other than universals, with regard to the classification of texts in the traditional study of genre—especially since the eighteenth century. That does not deny Aristotle's distinction between universal modes of presentation in poetics. In research we should perhaps remind ourselves of what Plato and Aristotle had to say, to see for ourselves the origins of a very influential theory of genre.

In his Πολιτεία Plato uses two kinds of arguments as to why poets should not be allowed in his state (cf. Pl. *Resp.* 3.392). On the one hand there are the arguments of content or λόγος, what is to be said ὡς δεῖ λέγεσθαι and on the other, arguments of form or λέξις, how it is to be said (ὡς λέκτεον). It is the latter kind of argument which is very often, in addition to the introductory remarks of Aristotle in his Περὶ Ποιητικῆς mistakenly used to substantiate systems of genre based on three fundamental types. Both Plato and Aristotle, each in their own manner, spoke about mode of presentation, not about literary genre in the sense of three fundamental literary types. Because of his views on poets, whom he would not allow in his ideal state, lyric is excluded from Plato's limiting discussion of how things are to be said.

Plato maintains that every literary work (everything said by fabulists or muthologists) is a narration (διήγησις) about past, present or future things. This narration can, however, have three different forms. It can be pure narration (ἁπλῆ διήγησις), narration effected through imitation (διὰ μιμήσεως) as in drama where characters narrate by dialogue, or mixed when narrative and dialogue are alternated. These modes of presentation (λέξις) in narration roughly correspond with three literary genres: 'pure narration' corresponds with the dithyramb, 'mixed' with epic, and 'mimetic' with tragedy and comedy. The correspondence does not, however, account for the classification of genre in the traditional sense. In fact, the three modes of presentation have to do with the status of the spokesman. In 'pure narration' the narrator is the speaker, in drama the characters are the spokesmen on behalf of the author and, in mixed forms, the speaker alternates between the narrator and the narrated spokesmen (cf. also Genette 1981:185). Let us now turn to Aristotle.

Aristotle maintains that all kinds (εἴδη) of poetry (ποιητική scil. ποιητικὴ τέχνη)—that is, the making (ποιητική) of epic and tragic poetry, comedy, and dithyrambic poetry—and most music composed for the flute and the lyre can be described as forms of imitation or representation (μίμησίς, μιμέομαι). In other words literature, that is poetics, is seen in the context of the art of representation or imitation and in contrast to science (cf. Empedocles). Aristotle asserts that these forms of imitation can be distinguished because the medium of representation varies, or they represent different things, or the mode of presentation is different (cf. Aristot. *Poet* 1). The distinction between medium (e.g. language, dance, singing), object, and mode of presentation forms the backbone of Aristotle's discussion on the art of imitation. Again, it is striking that lyric is totally absent from his discussion of the art of imitation. The criteria he uses (medium, object and mode) in his description of the art of presentation are directly related to the theme of presentation or imitation. Medium has to do with the question 'in what?' (e.g. in Greek, in prose, in hexameters, in gestures); object with 'what?', and mode with 'how?' (e.g. narrating or showing).

Within the Aristotelian concept of genre the first two criteria are conventional, not universal. The use of one or another language, style, and so on, is conventional. The same holds true for the object or actors. They are presented in conventional terms: as superior (βελτίονες), mediocre (καθ᾽ ἡμᾶς) or inferior (χείρονες). They are distinguished in terms of virtue and vice (ἀρετὴ, κακία). These characteristics have a social dimension. In tragedy and epic drama, the players are of the 'higher' social class, while those of comedy come from the common people.

With regard to the mode of presentation, Aristotle has one category less than Plato. By distinguishing between 'narrating' and 'showing', to use terminology anachronistically, Aristotle did not make provision for the so-called mixed form of Plato. 'Epic' corresponds with 'narrating' and 'dramatic' with 'showing' in the Aristotelian presentation. In his view tragedy and comedy are 'dramatic' because the players (πράπτοντες) are the spokesmen, while epic and parody are in the narrative mode of presentation since they are told by a narrator. The distinctive criterion between possible genres in the Aristotelian concept is that of the situation of the speaker, the mode of presentation. The material is either presented by a spokesman who tells or by persons who show, and these modes can be mixed. Genette (1981:70) has presented these views very clearly in the following graphic form (my translation):

mode object	dramatic	narrative
superior	tragedy	epic
inferior	comedy	parody

Bal (1981:18) correctly observes that Aristotle, and for that matter one can include Plato, does not distinguish between three different genres, but he does distinguish three differences between possible genres! Genres can differ in medium, object and mode of presentation. It is noteworthy that these differences are worked out in the semiotic framework of the art of presentation which includes music, painting and poetic texts. His theory of genre is thus multidimensional, a flexible system which leads to a dynamic and very relative limitation of a corpus (Bal 1981:21), and to something very different from a rigid and magical division of literature into three fundamental categories of universal types of texts namely lyric, epic and drama. Mode of presentation is the only universal aspect in Aristotle's theory of genre. It is a very helpful criterion in distinguishing conventional, that is historically and culturally determined, genres (cf. Bal 1981:21).

Incidentally it is also a matter of convention to approach the problem of genre with a discussion of the architext on the theory of genre, as Bal (1981:9) has convincingly argued. Even Aristotle's Poetics is but one fallible source on the theory of genre! Nevertheless, from the perspective of the analysis of genre with reference to the New Testament, Aristotle's views are important. In the first place, it seems clear that criteria for establishing genre are of the utmost importance. Aristotle's mode of interpretation is of great significance in the study of the types of texts we find in the New Testament, as we shall see below. Secondly, it appears that the study of genre entails more than taxonomy. The mere classification of texts according to shared characteristics can be interesting, but classification for the sake of classification is of little use. It also follows from Aristotle's theory of genre that there are different ways of mapping genre, depending on the criteria used in the process of classification (cf. Bal 1981; A. Fowler 1982a). That there is the possibility of overlapping in the classification of the texts is also clear. In the third place, there is a need to take seriously the problem of the art of presentation in sacred texts, in the light of Aristotle's views on imitation. Lastly, the misconception about the origin of the classification of genre into three fundamental groups, with its long tradition, is an interesting example of the influence of the interpretive community on the course of scientific investigation. These matters are of direct importance to the study of the genre of the Revelation of John.

2.3 *Society, text types and the study of genre*

The relationship between universal (that is, transhistoric) and conventional aspects associated with the origin of genres is complex. What is clear, however, is that new genres originate within society as a reflection of the social situation, and older ones disappear as a result of social changes. Genre therefore seems to be cultural convention in a certain sense. In this respect the questions of the relationship between society and genre—that is, convention and text—and the function of texts become very important. Sociology (cf. E. Köhler 1977), text linguistics (Van Dijk 1977) and sociolinguistics (Halliday 1978) have played major roles in recent years to broaden the study of genre to embrace more than the mere classification of types of texts. Let us start with a few remarks about 'text'.

It is probably true to say that very few terms have become so ambiguous and problematic in literary study as the word 'text'. In text linguistics and deconstruction, specifically, there have been developments with far-reaching implications for our understanding of the connotations of the word 'text'.

In text linguistics, it is the regarding of text as a unitary object, a sign in the process of communication or even a communicative activity, or a network of signifiers (cf. Harty 1985:2ff.), which has given rise to new possibilities in the investigation of genre (cf. Guelich & Raie inclusion of more than literary texts in the concept of 'text', and the emphasis on textness, or well-formedness (cohesion), and texts as signs of communication, the scope of the study of genre has widened and the technical term 'genre' has been replaced by 'text type'. In order to limit my survey to matters relevant to my discussion, I will outline a proposal for the study of discourse genres which reflects current views of a text-linguistic and sociolinguistic nature, without the unnecessary load of formalism which is found in some text-linguistic studies.

Frow (1980:73) regards genre as '. . . a conventional institution: a normative codification of different levels of meaning appropriate to a type of situation'. In this manner the study of genre is related to the semantic, syntactic and pragmatic aspects of texts within a situation of communication. Both text and context are sharply defined in terms of linguistic insights and the primary purpose of texts, namely communication. It is noteworthy that convention, and not 'universal characteristics', 'text type' and 'type of situation', are the catchwords in this approach. Genre is a code like other codes which senders may use in the communication process in a given social context. Following Halliday, Frow (1980:73) regards genre as '. . . the configuration of semantic resources that the member of a culture typically associates with a situation type . . . the meaning potential that is accessible in a given social context . . .': both with regard to what is said and how it is said.

It is proposed that the system of genres should be described by specifying the semantic function with reference to the dominance of field (that is, the type of activity in which the text has significant function), tenor (the status and role relationships involved, interpersonal functions) or mode (the symbolic mode and rhetorical channels or textual function) (Frow 1980:74ff.). Function thus becomes a very significant aspect of text and also of the study al classification of genre in terms of dominance of field, tenor or mode, or the feasibility of such a classification (cf. Fowler 1982:238), is the introduction of the criterion of function as a sociolinguistic category to describe genre. This is an aspect to which I will return.

The advantage of a sociosemiotic approach to genre which is based on text-linguistic insights, is the integration of textual and social aspects as linguistic phenomena. Thus cognisance is taken of both the text and the context of communication as a type of communication situation. A further advantage of the particular approach to genre is the fact that it is not restricted to literary texts alone (cf. also Bal 1981:29ff.).

One of the major objections to the approach is the epistemological premise of textual autonomy and determinacy. The text is regarded as an object that is knowable,

> . . . or the conviction that a text has a centre and an edge, and which is recoverable, whole and unblemished, by the skilled reader (Ryan 1985:8).

With the introduction of the role of the reader in the process of interpretation and the idea of interaction between reader and text, and the reader's contribution to the meaning of the text, which is different from a recovery of the codified meaning of the text, this situation has changed. As Kuenzli (quoted by Ryan 1985:20) maintains:

> Paying attention to the reader is therefore often regarded as a subversive activity which reopens Pandora's box and undermines our hard-earned 'certainties' concerning literary texts. Indeed, a reader-oriented theory exposes our 'objective' analyses as sophisticated 'subjective' readings.

The relationship between text and reader as a process of actualising the meaning of a sign, which can no longer be regarded as a knowable object that has to be decoded, changes the concept 'text' radically, and obviously the epistemology as well (cf. Ryan 1985:20ff.). The real break with past epistemology came with the birth of deconstruction.

4. *The Death of Genre and Literary History*

Deconstruction presents a total break with past epistemologies in literary studies and has convincingly been compared to the Newtonian revolution of quantum theory in the natural sciences (cf. Brink 1985: 10ff.). Two categories which are basic to deconstruction as a literary strategy, and which are of direct interest for this essay on the study of genre, are 'text' and intertext'.

Contrary to views held in text linguistics, text is no longer regarded as an object. It is a process, which exists only in the activity of production. It is

> ... no longer a finished corpus of writing, some content enclosed in a book or is margins, but a differential network, a fabric of traces referring endlessly to something other than itself, to other differential traces. Thus the text overruns all the limits assigned to it so far ... all the limits, everything that was to be set up in opposition to writing (speech, life, the world the real, history, and what not, every field of reference—to body or mind, conscious or unconscious, politics, economics, and so forth) Derrida 1979:84.

Since texts are texts about texts, within a total network, the idea of the origin and the centre of texts, which are so important in pre-deconstructionalist thought, is totally undermined.

Texts do not have meaning because they are structured, but because they are related to other texts and their meanings, in a network of intertextuality. The meaning of a text is the result of the similarities and differences between other texts. Intertextuality refers to the fact that one text is irrevocably influenced by other texts, and that its meaning is determined by its similarities with and differences from other texts. The source of the meaning of a text is therefore not the mind of the author, the reality outside the text; texts are their own source of meaning. Ryan (1985:16) summarises the implications of deconstruction as follows:

> The author does not create meaning because meaning is never present and has to be sought, without success, beyond the text. As a result, the idea of 'book' becomes hopelessly unstable, because no text

is ever singular or unified. Next, the idea of 'interpretation' must be discarded, because under Derridean scrutiny the term erroneously assumes the explication of a concealed but nonetheless present meaning. The two grouping concepts, 'genre' and 'literary history' cease to have validity, because all texts are for Derrida a single expression and not a controlled sequence (the literary historical premise), or capable of being divided into a number of subsets distinguishable by type (the generic premise).

This represents a totally new paradigm and a totally new epistemology. It is not simply a shift from the old to the new.

2.5   *Genre and the study of the New Testament*

For more than half a century New Testament scholars have been occupied with the study of genre in different forms, based on different epistemologies with the assumption that the analysis of genre is in some or other manner relevant. The theory of *Gattungen* (forms) and their *Sitze im Leben*, together with the idea that most of the writings of the New Testament are *Kleiniteratur* (cf. Schmidt 1923), dominated the study of the New Testament for the greater part of the century. A new interest in the study of genre has emerged during the past few decades, very much under the influence of the older theory, but taking into account developments in literary theory and linguistics.

In view of the above, it seems to me that any attempt to write on any aspect of genre in the New Testament—no matter whether one holds the view that genres are based on universals, are conventional, or should be described in terms of function—will have to be defined in terms of some theory of genre. The relevance of the study of genre to the writings of the New Testament is directly related to the theory adopted. Since New Testament scholars are normally interested in deciphering the meaning of these ancient texts of religion, the Derridean position on genre can hardly be taken. On the other hand the idea of intertextuality may help us to explain the compositeness of most of the writings, in terms of rewriting.

In the next section I shall pay attention to current views on the genre of the Revelation of John. My own position will be given in terms of critical observations.

3. The Analysis of Genre in Use: the Revelation of John

3.1 Current views

If anything is clear about the study of the 'genre' of the Revelation of John, it is that it is determined by the data beliefs of New Testament critics as an interpretive community, and based reflectively or un-reflectively on a variety of assumptions and theories. It has, for ex-ample, been described as an apocalypse in the form of a letter (cf. Collins 1977; Hellholm 1986), an apocalypse as an autobiographi-cal prose narrative (cf. Aune 1986), a circular letter in narrative form (Vorster 1983), a drama (cf. Palmer 1943; Bowman 1955; Blevins 1980), liturgy (Shepherd 1960), myth (cf. Halver 1964; Gager 1975), and prophecy (cf. Kallas 1967; Schüssler Fiorenza 1977). It is unnec-essary to explore in detail all the different views. What I have in mind is to discuss the most influential views critically in the light of the information in section one of my essay. Since criteria of form, content and function are mentioned in discussions I will pay atten-tion to these from the perspective of mode of writing, content, and function. I obviously do not contend that how a text is written can be isolated from what is written or why it is written. For the pur-pose of the discussion each aspect will be discussed separately.

3.2 Mode of writing and the genre of Revelation

The Revelation of John starts with the remark that it is a Revelation (ἀποκάλυψις) of Jesus Christ concerning the things that will happen soon, which God gave to John that he might show it to his serv-ants. . . . This is the first time in the history of literature, as far as we are aware, that a revelatory message came to be known as ἀποκάλυψις (cf. Smith 1983:14). Although the phenomena of tran-scendental and metaphysical spaces, events and existents were dis-cussed in the Mediterranean world and Near East prior to the Revelation of John (cf. Hellholm 1983), it is remarkable that no writ-ing prior to the Revelation of John was called an apocalypse. This remark is not insignificant since it is commonly accepted that the term ἀποκάλυψις in John refers to a genre which had already been in existence prior to this book. It is remarkable that no ancient source dealing with the question of literary types and genre ever referred to such a genre—not even in the sense of some kind of literature dealing with transcendental phenomena (cf., however, Betz 1983). Whether it is a designation of a separate genre with its own literary characteristics is another matter. Furthermore, it is not without importance that the ἀποκάλυψις which John received is referred to as words of prophecy (Rv. 1:3; 22:7,10,18,19).

One can easily argue, 'what is in a name?' This would be inappropriate in view of a very long and intensive debate and history of research. As a matter of fact, it would be difficult simply to ignore the serious attempt of the SBL group, as well as that of the International Colloquium on Apocalypticism in Uppsala during 1979, to argue the existence of a separate literary genre, the apocalypse, of which Revelation of John is presumably an example. Let us instead select another starting point.

One of my conclusions in discussing the views of Aristotle above, was the need for criteria *with which to* determine literary genres. Despite the controversy between universalists and conventionalists, 'mode of writing' seems to be the most important distinctive criterion in the study and classification of genre (cf. Bal 1981:21; Van Luxemburg, Bal & Weststein 1981:121). It is in other words possible to classify texts according to the type of speaker involved, and the function of the speaker in a particular text. Where there is one speaker, as in poetry, the text is a monologue. When one speaker allows other speakers in a text to speak as well, the text is organised in the narrative mode. Thirdly, there are texts in which a set of actors are the speakers. These are called dramatic texts. There are obviously also other criteria, such abstract content, theme and physical form (length etc). These can be used to distinguish texts from one another. Events are normally not organised in a logical and chronological way (abstract content) in poems. In addition to the manner of writing this criterion could help distinguish a poem from a narrative or drama (cf. Van Luxemburg, Bal & Weststeijn 1981:120ff.). The relative importance of each criterion for the analysis of genre is self-evident. Physical form can help us distinguish between a novel and a short novel as two different text types in terms of levels of classification—for example, type and subtype. The fact that both are written in the narrative mode, however, immediately calls attention to the narrative code as a code of communication.

The distinction between the modes of writing has significant implications, because every mode has its own way of communicating a message. Similar to the dramatic code, the narrative code has distinctive features. It seems a misconception (cf. Hellholm 1986; also Hartman 1983) to minimise, or perhaps not realise the importance of the narrative code to the so-called apocalypse genre, by dealing with it in a hierarchy of so-called abstractness and concreteness.

Hellholm (1980 & 1986) uses Hempfer's (1973) systematic hierarchisation of genres (*Gattungen*) to classify texts written from an apocalyptic perspective within a linguistic text theory. In addition to the criteria suggested by Collins's group, Hellholm also emphasises the role of function in determining genre. We will return to this later.

Hempfer's classification of literary texts in a hierarchy should be interpreted very carefully when applied to the hierarchisation of ancient texts within the framework of a classification which pretends to be of value for the interpretation as well as for the classification of the texts. Hempfer distinguishes between the transhistoric features (e.g. mode and type of writing) and historic realisations of these features (genres and subgenres) in a hierarchy. are specifications of each other. Starting at the top with narrative as a mode of writing, the next level has a first-person or third-person narrative on the level of a type of writing. 'Novel' as genre would be a specification of a type of writing on a lower level, and 'picaresque novel' as subgenre a specification on an even lower level (cf. also Genette 1981:112ff.). Hempfer's hierarchy is in other words an attempt to arrive at a systematic classification of literary texts, taking into account the transhistoric and historic features of texts. Following this systematic classification, Hellholm maintains that apocalyptic texts can be classified in the following manner:

> Mode of writing—*the Narrative, the Dramatic, the Epic* ... Type of writing—*Revelatory writing* ... Genre—*Apocalypses, Prophetic texts, Discourses* ... Subgenre—Apc. *with o.-w. journey* Apc. *Without o.-w. journey*, Singletexts-. ...

I would like to draw attention to the second level in the hierarchy. In Hempfer's system one would have expected a specification of the mode of writing, such as first-person or third-person narrative. In the case of the Revelation of John, for example, one would expect first-person narrative and not 'Revelatory writing'. On the level of genre the question then arises as to whether one should think in terms of a genre 'revelatory texts', of which I apocalypses and prophetic texts would be subgenres. This is just to show how relative taxonomy is. In addition, it is clear that Hempfer's classification is not without its shortcomings (cf. Bal 1981:25 and Genette 1981: 112ff.). The relationship between the different levels, in terms of that between transhistoric and historic, is not clear at all because it is based on a single principle of inclusion as Genette (1981:112) has shown. Works fall under kinds, kinds fall under genre, and genre falls under modes and types of writing. Aristotle on the other hand had two principles, namely mode and object, which made it possible to classify each genre in terms of mode and object (theme) at the same time, on the same level of a hierarchy. The relationship between transhistoric and historic is much closer than Hellholm's hierarchy allows for.

From the point of view of the genre code there seems little doubt that the mode of writing of the so-called apocalyptic texts is narrative. In the case of the Revelation of John the text is organised in the form of an autobiographic narrative concerning the visions of a certain John. These he received from God (cf. Rv. 1:1) on the island of Patmos. He was ordered to write down his vision and send it to the seven communities of Asia Minor (1:11). The command to write down the revelation, and send it to a specific group of readers, is important for two reasons.

The publication of revelatory material in written form for a specific public is a common feature of Jewish texts written from an apocalyptic perspective (cf. Dn. 12:4; 4 Ezr. 14:24ff.; 45f.). Because of the importance of the contents of the revelation it should be preserved and nobody may alter or add to it in any way (Rv. 22:18f.). This written document should be distributed to a group of people to whom the revelation should be read (Rv. 1:3). It should be written down because the content of the vision is so important to the recipients (cf. also Güttgemanns 1983:12). It deals with things that will happen very soon (Rv. 1:1,3), of which the recipients should be aware. As to the genre code of the document, it is the vision and the mode of writing which the reader should note—its inscripturation. Do the so-called letter formulas (cf. Rv. 1:4ff.; 22:21) and the fact that the text includes seven letters to the communities in Asia Minor not change the genre code of Revelation? Is it not a letter? This leads us to the second reason why the command to write down the vision and distribute it is important.

The long tradition of the presumed genre relationship between the Revelation of John and the letters of Paul (cf. Berger 1974:204f.) is based on a misconception of genre codes and the way in which the material is presented in Revelation. Letters of the kind we find in the New Testament are argumentative texts, not narrative texts. The mode of writing a letter is thus different from that of a narrative.

The structure of the Revelation (cf. Hahn 1979:145–154) is determined by the command related in 1:11. The main segment (Rv. 1:9–22:20) is an account of the vision, its content, how, when, and where it was received and what should be done with it. The authority of the message imparted as secret information in a vision is also given here. Revelation 1:1–8 and 22:6–18 form a frame around the main text (cf. Müller 1983:600ff.). This frame was made necessary by the command in 1:11. Revelation 1:1–3 is a prologue in narrated form serving as a theme and an introduction to the text which has to be read to the seven communities. Since the author is ordered to distribute his revelation to those mentioned, he uses the introductory formulas and ending for a letter (1:4–8 and 2:21) to present his revelation to his recipients. This letter frame does not, however, change the genre code of the text at all. In fact, the beginning and the end of Revelation are, taken together, the story of the fulfilment of the order given in 1:11. The only correlation in respect of genre, between the so-called apostolic letter and Revelation, is in the letter formula, together with the embedded narrated letters used in Revelation. The mode of writing of Revelation is narrative. It starts with a third person narrative; then the main narrative, which is in the first-person mode, is framed with a letter beginning and end.

What about the fact that it was intended to be read (1:3)? Does this not influence the genre code? I mention this for two reasons. Aune (1986:77ff.). has introduced the topic of orality and textuality into the discussion of the genre, and has concluded that the oral reading of texts such as Revelation and the Shepherd of Hermas '. . . constitutes a unique feature of these two apocalypses and argues that '. . . it appears to be an innovative factor in the function of early Christian apocalypses' (1986:78). Firstly, it seems to me that Aune is addressing a problem which is important, but has nothing to do with the genre code. Secondly, Aune's use of function in connection with genre is disputable.

Too little attention is indeed paid by New Testament critics to the fact that the writings of the New Testament were intended to be read aloud to their audience, and to the implications of the construction of meaning. From a reader's perspective this is undoubtedly important. From the perspective of what a text is, and whether one can speak of 'a' message in a text, these matters are important. The question of concern should, however, be whether orality or textuality can influence the genre—for example, change the mode of writing from, say dramatic to narrative. This can clearly not be done. Since there are a number of proponents of the idea that Revelation is a drama, let us take up this approach because it has to do with the performance of the text as a drama.

In 1980 Blevins wrote a very interesting article about the genre of Revelation. Basing his argument on previous research, the uniqueness of the theatre at Ephesus, the nature of Greek tragedy and the resemblances between many details of Revelation and Greek tragedy, Blevins claims that Revelation was conceived as a one-actor play (with chorus), with the theatre of Ephesus in mind.

> We conclude that the writer of Revelation adapted the genre of Greek tragedy because it was a vessel through which his community could interpret its experiences in a troubled time (Blevins 1980:405).

However attractive this proposal may seem, it is clear that one has to force Revelation into the dramatic genre. This is best seen in the many hymnic elements (cf. Nestle-Aland 26; Vielhauer 1975:47; Schüssler Fiorenza 1977:351) that are integrated into the Revelation narrative. These utterances by a variety of speakers can hardly be explained as the lyric role of a chorus in a tragedy, as Blevins argues. They form part of the story of John's transcendental experience and are the words of different speakers in the narrative, not of the chorus acting in a tragedy. In addition, Revelation is clearly not written in dialogue form. On the grounds of mode of writing alone one can make out a convincing case that Revelation is not '. . . an innovative adaptation of Greek tragic drama' (Blevins 1980:405). This is not to say that Revelation was not conceptualised in its mode of presentation, and its use of rhetoric, to be read orally. On the contrary!

Various 'recurring features' of form have been identified by scholars who argue the existence of a separate 'genre apocalypse' (cf. Vielhauer 1964:408ff.; Collins 1979b:28; Hellholm 1986:23). The problem is that, except for the narrative framework which seems to be the distinctive feature, hardly any of these features can be used as criteria for the distinction of genre. The recurring features on the so-called text-syntactic level (form and style, cf. Hellholm 1986:23) which are really text-syntactic, can be found in many macro-texts of a narrative nature. That is why Hellholm's (1986:43ff.) discovery of levels of embedment of communication as '. . . the most striking macro-syntagmatic feature of the generic concept "Apocalypse"' is totally unconvincing. Narrative embedment depends on the number of speakers within a particular narrative, and what they have to say to whom. Matthew 13, for example, is a good illustration that pragmatic embedment of communication levels has nothing to do with a distinctive feature of 'the generic concept "Apocalypse"'. From the perspective of embedment in narrative texts it is not even striking. Obviously the remark about embedment is interesting from the perspective of the making and structure of the Revelation of John. It is, however, not a feature peculiar to texts written from an apocalyptic perspective.

The Revelation of John does not seem to have any peculiar or distinctive feature as regards its mode of writing, to enable one to classify it in a separate class of texts. It is for the greater part a first-person narrative.

3.3 Content as criterion for the genre of Revelation

Perhaps the most important recurring features of the presumed genre of 'apocalypse' are those which can be related to content. Those features are to my mind the dominant characteristics of texts written from an apocalyptic perspective. This is also applicable to Revelation.

It is first of all clear that most of the texts which are classified as apocalypses have to do with some aspect of transcendental reality relating to this world. In other words, texts written from an apocalyptic perspective normally deal with future matters in relation to the present, and with the revelation of events significantly important to the present and (immediate) future of the world, and to the people in the world. Thematically the texts we are referring to normally deal with transcendental realities, events and existents. This is true of texts from all over the Mediterranean world and the Near East prior to, contemporary with and later than Revelation. How can one speak about these matters other than in terms of visions or dreams, or some form of fantasy. This explains the imaginary presentation of the subject matter. In connection with the problem of apocalyptic genre in Greek and Hellenistic literature, Betz (1983:588) regards μῦθος as the apocalyptic literary genre and maintains that

'. . . mythos can speak in human words about things that go beyond the human world and language'. These texts form part of a larger body of fantasy literature (cf. Olsen 1986, Güttgemanns 1983). Muthos, apocalypse and so on are names for texts that speak about the transcendental world from an apocalyptic perspective (cf. Vorster 1983 & 1986). These terms are nothing but classificatory tags for a submode of a broader mode of writing. In this sense it seems to be possible to speak of a subgenre, 'apocalyptic texts' or 'apocalypses', in the way one would speak of picaresque novel as a subgenre of novel. The distinctive characteristic of so-called apocalypses can be described in the light of the apocalyptic perspective of reality.

It is of little use to catalogue characters such as intermediaries or those found in Revelation, or events such as journeys in another world, or narrative techniques such as dreams, visions, and epiphanies, in order to define the genre of 'apocalypses' (contra the tendency in the SBL-group, cf. Olsen 1986:279). What happens is that the genre code of fantastic literature is described superficially, in terms of a large number of events and existents that occur in many texts of fantasy of this kind. The fact that texts such as Revelation normally communicate '. . . a transcendent perspective on human experience' (Aune 1986:88), and the promise of restoration and reversal (cf. Sanders 1983:458) is a dominant distinctive feature, on the grounds of which scholars can agree to view such texts as a distinctive subgenre in the narrative mode.

'What', as described in the Revelation of John, is to be related to 'how' it is described, with regard to the genre of the text. In addition to the narrative code of the genre, the code of imagination or fantasy—which in the case of the Revelation of John has received abundant attention in studies on symbolism, colour, gems, and imagery in the history of research (cf. Böcher 1980:26ff.; Güttgemanns 1983)—is obviously important concerning 'what' is communicated.

3.4   *Function and the genre of Revelation*

The importance of the pragmatic function of language in sociolinguistics cannot be overrated. In a certain sense New Testament scholars realised this very long ago. The original use of *Sitz im Leben* as a sociological category (cf. Bultmann 1970:4) points in this direction. Unfortunately, 'Sitz im Leben' lost its original purpose, and became a means of speculation about a concrete historical situation or context within which a text could have functioned.

I have already pointed out that 'function' has become an important criterion in the description of the apocalypse genre. The problem is that function is used in very broad terms—for example, as social function, that is, literature of the oppressed (cf. Sanders 1983: 456ff.); for the purpose of writing, '. . . intended for a group in crisis with the purpose of exhortation and/or consolation by means of divine authority' (Hellholm 1986:27), for authorization of the message (Hellholm 1986:45, cf. also Aune 1986:89ff.), or as a literary function, namely '. . . to shape one imaginative perception of a situation and so to lay the basis for whatever course of action it exhorts' (Collins 1984:32).

Most of these scholars are working within a text-linguistic framework and that is why it is important to scrutinise their use of function in the light of the sociolinguistic theory about function.

Although there is a difference of opinion about the importance of 'function' in the study of genre (cf. Fowler 1982a:238), it can be very helpful in forming a conceptual framework of the social context '. . . as the semiotic environment in which people exchange meanings' (Halliday 1978:111). In this sense function is not an empirical category but a theoretical device. It is, furthermore, necessary to emphasise that social context and communication context do not refer to a particular historical context. However important the original historical situation out of which the text arose and within which it functioned may be for us, this is not what we have in the case of ancient texts. We have before us the contextless text of the Revelation of John and that is why

> . . . the structure of John's literary world is to be found in the interconnectedness of his language, not in correspondence to some external order of reality (Thompson 1986:147).

The intentions of a speaker (that is, the functions for which a speaker uses language—and for that matter the author of a written text such as Revelation used language) are of an ideational, interpersonal and textual nature. Webb (1986:51f.) following Halliday, gives a valuable summary of the various functions. *Ideational* refers to relating experiences, providing information (experimental), indicating the relationship

between the events described in texts (logical), and using language
to order thoughts (cognitive). *Interpersonal* refers to expressing feelings
(expressive), changing the emotional state of the hearer (emotive),
changing the behaviour of the hearer (imperative, persuasive), establishing the speaker's status (egocentric), changing the status of the
hearer ('Your sins are forgiven'—performative) and establishing and
maintaining contact (phatic). *Textual* function refers to the use of
language to give a particular form to the message, for example, to
signal topic (cf. Rv. 1:1). These are the pragmatic functions of utterances and texts which have to be related to the genre code. This
approach to the pragmatic function is obviously quite different from
the one we have described above, in reference to the views of the
New Testament scholars who are interested in defining function in
pragmatic terms.

It is furthermore clear that social factors determine the construction of a message, and also that the function of the use of language
relates to these factors. Communication between members of a subculture or some sociopolitical, or socioreligious group is determined
by the symbols they share socially which are reflected in their use
of language (cf. Webb 1986:53ff.). In order to be meaningful a text
such as Revelation presupposes a group of people who share a common system of meaning, thus a closely-knit unit with a strong concern for the beliefs of the group (cf. Malina 1986:13ff.). It is within
this framework that one should regard function in the above sense
of the word and relate it to genre.

In our discussion of Frow's conception of genre we referred to his
views on dominance of field, tenor or mode, and the classification
of discourse genres. We have already said that in texts written from
an apocalyptic perspective there seems to be a dominance of content, that is semantic domain (field of discourse). With regard to the
semantic process or function of Revelation it seems as though there
is also emphasis on the instrumental process, that is persuasion and
instruction, as well as on the experiential process of reinforcing
(beliefs). This is, however, a tentative observation only.

If any progress is to be made in connection with the definition of
the genre of texts written from an apocalyptic perspective in terms
of function, these texts need to be studied from a sociolinguistic point
of view within the framework of a theory of genre such as, for example, Frow's, which gives attention to these aspects. It seems to
be clear that the genre theory of Professor Collins's group is not

well enough integrated to take care of the various aspects involved in studying the genre code of texts written from an apocalyptic perspective. Perhaps it is due to the fact that the group has been interested both in establishing and classifying a genre and in demonstrating the relevance of the study of genre for the interpretation of these texts.

4. *What About the Future?*

The two main options for New Testament scholars regarding the study of the genre of Revelation are either to continue the search for a theory of genre which can accommodate the problems involved in studying genre from the point of view of the interpretation of texts, or to accept the challenge of deconstruction and face the death of genre and the birth of intertextuality. Both options are viable on different epistemological grounds.

It is my conviction that the study of genre should be more than the classification of texts. In order to achieve such a goal a theory of genre which integrates classification and interpretation is needed. This has not yet been achieved. In this regard it is important that different genre theories should be tested in order to assess the advantages and disadvantages of every theory. Perhaps it would be a good thing to undermine the present dominance of certain views in the interpretive community by testing other possibilities.

The study of the so-called composite character of the text of Revelation in terms of proposed sources, quotations and redaction urgently needs to be studied from a totally new perspective. The idea of intertextuality as the basis for and explanation of the differential network of meaning components in Revelation seems to be challenging. Taken as a text about other texts in a network, a number of intriguing questions posed by past researchers might be handled in quite another way. In addition, Revelation should be studied as a narrative of fantasy, a submode or subgenre of the revelatory writings. Until recently very little attention has been paid to the narrative character of Revelation. Questions about plot, narrative point(s) of view, characterisation and so on, can help to explore the genre code productively.

I started my essay with two quotations from the writings of Fowler and Frow which have direct bearing on current study of the genre of Revelation. Present investigation of the apocalypse genre has become unnecessarily complicated under the influence of text-linguistic formalism. Authors of other early Christian apocalyptic writings (cf. Weinel 1923; Vielhauer 1964) ventured to make use of the narrative genre code to communicate a message in terms of other-world realities, and similarly the author of Revelation wrote a story on the same lines.

Section B.4

Extra-Canonical Material

CHAPTER FOURTEEN

THE ANNUNCIATION OF THE BIRTH OF JESUS IN THE PROTEVANGELIUM OF JAMES

The purpose of this essay is to study the annunciation of the birth of Jesus in the Protevangeluim of James from the perspective of production and reception of texts in the early church. Both aspects, text production and text reception, throw light on how early Christians contextualized their beliefs, transmitted tradition and retold stories. These insights are necessary for explaining and understanding the development of ideas in early Christianity.

> The literary phenomenon is not only the text, but also its reader and all of the reader's possible reactions to the text—both enonce and enonciation (Michael Riffaterre 1983:3).

1. *Introduction*

In chapter 11 of the so-called *Protevangelium Jacobi* (hence *PJ*), an 'infancy gospel' from the second century, the following narrative is related:

> And she took the pitcher and went outside to fill it with water, when a voice said to her, Greetings, most favoured one. The Lord is with you. He has greatly blessed you among the women. Mary looked around to the right and to the left where the voice came from. Trembling she went into her house and put down the pitcher. She took the purple, sat down on her seat and drew out the purple (threads). Suddenly an angel stood before (her) and said, Don't be afraid Mary. The Lord of all things has been gracious to you. You will conceive of his Word. When Mary heard this she thought by herself and said, You mean, I shall conceive of the Lord, the living God as every woman bears? And the angel went to her and said, No, Mary, not so; for the power of God will overshadow you. That is why the holy child will be called son of the High (= God WSV). You will name him Jesus because he will save his people from their sins. Then Mary said, I am a servant of the Lord before him. May it happen to me as you have said.

In spite of obvious differences between the annunciation of the birth of Jesus in the canonical gospels and this version, there can be little doubt that PJ 11:2–3 is a retelling of the annunciation of the birth of Jesus in Luke and Matthew. From this perspective, namely the retelling of stories in early Christianity, this particular text is of great interest for the study of text production and text reception in the early church. In this article I shall pay attention to aspects of retelling stories, the production of texts and also the reception of texts in the early church by studying PJ 11:2–3. Attention will be paid to the following aspects: Retelling as a means of text production and reception, PJ an infancy gospel? and 'Canonical' and 'apocryphal': the New Testament and PJ 11:2–3.

2. *Retelling as a Means of Text Production and Reception*

Storytelling is one of the characteristic features of early Christianity. Jesus was a storyteller and much of his life and preaching was transmitted in narrative form by his followers. The New Testament as well as great parts of other early Christian literature bear witness to this statement. It is therefore not surprising to find many traces in the canonical gospels of what happened when the Jesus story or parts of it were retold by his followers.

Historico-critical investigation of the formation and growth of the gospel tradition has afforded us with a considerable amount of information about the processes at work in the transmission of the Jesus tradition. By decomposing the written texts of the gospels and constructing possible situations of communication, growth of individual forms and so on, we have a relatively good idea of how the written texts about the life and teaching of Jesus developed through oral stages into written texts. We have, however, also learnt how difficult it is to reconstruct the original words of Jesus, let alone the original contexts of communication, persons, events and processes involved and many other important aspects which are clouded by our ignorance and lack of information. It has furthermore become clear that sayings of Jesus, events in his earthly life and persons with whom he had contact during and before his ministry were transmitted in different ways for different purposes before they were written down. In short, what lies behind the gospel texts is not necessarily reflected by what is related in these texts. To put it differently, the gospels are not verbatim reports of 'what happened'.

The gospels are products of retelling the story and stories of Jesus. His sayings and deeds were put into narrative frameworks, new sayings and stories were created after the models of earlier ones and put onto the lips of Jesus, series of sayings were collected and arranged into narrated discourses and so on. How the written texts of the canonical gospels came about, what lies behind them in the history of their growth and what happened to these texts after they were written down, has been the object of study for very long.

It is, however, not only that which lies behind these texts or the texts themselves that has been studied. Attention has also been paid to the way in which these texts were used and interpreted in and by the early church, that is their *Wirkungsgeschiche*. There nevertheless remains a lot to be done since much of what has been done was done in terms of evaluation and not in terms of explanation. Notwithstanding the results of previous and very useful investigations there is much yet to be learnt about the transmission of tradition in the early church, that is transmission of tradition before and after these texts became inscripturated.

New insights into aspects of the gospel tradition are often gained only by posing 'new' and other questions to the texts involved. Although the narrative character, for example, of many parts of the New Testament and other early Christian literature has been recognized very long ago, the serious study of these texts as *narratives* started only recently. Many of the implications of this approach still await serious investigation. This includes the implications of the phenomenon of *retelling* as a means of text production and reception. New Testament scholars have been aware of the fact that retelling played an enormous role in the transmission of tradition. But have all the problems and possibilities of retelling stories been fully explored? I have elsewhere indicated how this phenomenon of retelling affects our understanding and interpretation of the parables and in particular the reconstruction of the 'original' meaning of the parables (cf. Vorster 1985a). What are the implications of retelling the Jesus tradition? Let us consider the phenomenon of retelling.

The question to be addressed here is whether the *same* story, a parable for example, can be told more than once and what happens when the same story is retold. Or to put it into New Testament

terms, is it possible that Mark, for example, could have retold a
parable in exactly the same way that Jesus had done? Narratologists
and ethnomethodologists disagree about the matter (cf. Polanyi 1981).
The answer to the problem obviously depends on one's definition
of 'story' and 'the same'. It has on the one hand been pointed out
that, when a story is retold orally the exact words are almost never
used in telling the same story and that '. . . each telling will be tuned
to the circumstances in which it is told, delicately reflecting the concerns of the participants and their relationships to each other, to the
events and circumstances in the story and to the fact that the story
is being told at a particular point in a particular conversation *to make
a point* (my italics) relevant to the topics under discussion at that
time' (Polanyi 1981:319). The same also holds true of stories not
embedded into conversations, for example texts embedded into written narratives (cf. the speeches of Jesus in the Gospel of Matthew).
The main point of the argument is that a story is told with a *purpose* in mind and that the 'same' story can be told for different purposes and therefore become a different story (stories)—not only a
different version of the same story. The parables of Jesus are a good
illustration of this.

Context determines the meaning of parables—be it literary context or the context of communication. The meaning of the parable
of the good Samaritan, for example, is evidently influenced directly
by the immediate context into which Luke put the narrative. As it
now stands, it has become part of a narrative on neighbourly love,
especially in view of the words, 'you go and do likewise' (Lk. 10:37).
Luke tells the story with the purpose of illustrating neighbourly love.
Stripped of its Lucan context, it can, however, easily be told for
many other purposes too to make different points depending on the
context into which it is fitted. Each retelling of the story of the good
Samaritan would thus become a 'new' story, although superficially
it seems to be the 'same' story. What is observed here of the parable of the good Samaritan holds true of other stories in the gospel
tradition. Each time a story of Jesus is retold, it becomes in principle another story or a new story according to this view.

One of the implications of this particular approach to the problem is that any attempt to reconstruct the 'original' meaning of a
particular narrative is doomed to fail unless the 'original' story and
its communication context can be reconstructed. Another is that the
retelling of stories is in fact a means of text production. New texts

are created by retelling the 'same' story for a different purpose. We will return to this aspect below.

Polanyi (1981:315) has on the other hand correctly pointed out that on a more abstract level it can be argued that '... multiple tellings may reduce to the same underlying semantic structure in which the same events, set in a similarly constructed storyworld communicate the same global point'. Seen from this perspective it seems possible to retell the 'same' story and even 'other' stories more than once (for the same purpose). The tellings will be the same if they comply with the conditions given in the quote. In other words, if the semantic structure, the storyworld and global point of a story are the same as another telling of that story or any other story, they are the 'same'. It therefore seems possible that two different stories can be told to say the same thing. Is that perhaps illustrated by the seed parables in Mark 4:26–33 for example?

What one should, in view of the aforesaid, keep in mind is that different versions of the same story or even different stories in retold form may or may not be the 'same'. Secondly, that retelling is a kind of text production because retelling can be a way of creating new texts.

Let us pursue the matter a little further and make a few remarks about text reception. During the past decades there has been a shift in the interpretation of texts from the author, via the text to the recipient. Reception criticism (cf. Holub 1984) has become the object of interest in many fields of the study of texts, including New Testament studies. The focus in reception criticism is on two aspects namely the constraints in a text which direct the reader in his reading or reception of that text and secondly on empirical research of how different readers read (receive) a particular text (cf. Segers 1980:9ff.). These reactions of readers of a text are not unimportant to the explanation and understanding of texts. Texts prompt readers in different ways to assign a particular meaning to a given text. That is why Riffaterre (1983:3) can say, 'The explanation of an utterance should not, therefore, be a description of its forms, or a grammar, but rather a description of those of its components that prompt rationalizations. The explanation of a rationalization should not consist in confirming or disproving it in terms of the external standards or yardsticks to which critics have traditionally turned.... A relevant explanation of a rationalization will consist first in accepting the rationalization as a way of perceiving the text...'.

In studying the Jesus tradition in its various receptions in the early church the specific role played by reader's reception deserves special attention. Why did a specific reader in the early church read a text as he did? Did the text prompt that rationalization or were there other factors responsible for a particular reading? Obviously this approach is not the same as seeking the *Sitz im Leben* of a text although results may sometimes concur. In comparing later receptions of a text with the 'original', the focus should in the first place be on the explanation of the rationalization of a particular reading. In this way it seems possible to detect and explain trajectories which were later accepted or rejected by the early church.

Given the fact that storytelling was a common practice in the early church and that stories are told for a specific purpose (e.g. to entertain, inform, persuade, confirm, etc.), retelling of stories found in the canonical gospels seems to contribute considerably to our knowledge about attempts to contextualize the story of Jesus. The early church did not simply transmit tradition. Tradition was used creatively. It is even possible to speak of transmission of tradition as imagination. Let us now turn to PJ.

3. *PJ an Infancy Gospel?*

It is well known that the childhood of Jesus is dealt with in the New Testament only by Matthew and Luke. Mark and John don't include any narratives about the birth and childhood of Jesus. They concentrate on other aspects of his life and teaching. In the period after the New Testament, however, a great variety of writings, the so-called apocryphal gospels, came into existence. These texts are modelled on and focus or elaborate on aspects of the Jesus tradition found in the canonical gospels. They even contain information not found in the canonical gospels—one of the reasons why they are often regarded as 'apocryphal'. These texts do not form a body of similar texts, not with regard to form nor with regard to contents. Schneemelcher (1968:48–51) divides them into three groups:

1. Texts which are clearly related to the canonical gospels, specifically the synoptic gospels, possibly because of common traditions;
2. So-called gnostic gospels in which revelation of the resurrected Lord plays a significant role. Their contents tie in with information found in the canonical gospels but in a 'developed' form and content;

3. Texts which are (legendary) elaborations of aspects of the life of Jesus. The infancy gospels fall into this category because they supplement or expand the infancy stories of Jesus found in Matthew and Luke. PJ is normally regarded as an infancy gospel.

Why were these infancy gospels written? In his treatment of the question, Cullmann (1968:272–274) correctly observes that various reasons can explain the origin of these texts. In the first place we are all aware of how little information is given in the New Testament about the early years of Jesus on earth. Lack of information gives rise to inquisitiveness, a natural eagerness to be informed. One could therefore expect that a considerable amount of information (factive or fictive) could have originated in the early church on this score. Secondly, and I shall return to this below, the need to develop Christology also explains some of this information in these texts. Christological thought originated with the resurrection and developed backwards to pre-existence Christology (cf. Brown 1977:311ff.). The need to relate the moment of the birth of Christ to Christology, forms part of this process. And in the third place early Christian apologetic (in view of Jewish polemic) also explains the origin of some of the material. How Jesus of *Nazareth* could be the promised Messiah who was to come from Bethlehem, demanded explanation. One already notices how Matthew and Luke solve the problem. According to Matthew Jesus and his parents had to leave his birthplace, Bethlehem, for Egypt because of the massacre of the children. On their return they went to Nazareth. Luke on the other hand tells us that Jesus was born in Bethlehem because of a census which caused his parents to go there from Nazareth, their home town. In view of this, obviously a variety of themes found in the Jesus tradition could have been developed for various purposes and because of various needs. Where does PJ fit into the picture?

The title of the book *Protevangelium Jacobi*, which goes back to G. Postel (1510–1581), has become the accepted one. It indicates that the book contains material about the infancy of Jesus which is older than the information contained in the canonical gospels. In the oldest existing manuscript of the book, *Papyrus Bodmer V* (3rd to early 4th century AD), the title is: *The birth of Mary. Revelation of James*. Origen in his commentary on Matthew (10:17) refers to it as *biblos Iakóbou* cf. Delius 1973:17), according to which the brothers of Jesus were born from an earlier marriage of Joseph. In 25:1–2 we read:

I, James, who wrote this (hi)story when a tumult arose in Jerusalem on the death of Herod, withdrew into the wilderness until it was over. I will praise the Lord, God, who gave me the gift of wisdom to write this story.

Grace will be with all those who fear our Lord. Amen.

Birth of Mary.

Revelation.

James.

Peace to the author and the reader.

The James referred to here is presumably James, the brother of Jesus who recounts the life story (*historia*) of Mary, the mother of Jesus. Except for this pseudonymous reference, the author is completely unknown to us and so is also the place of writing. Because of ignorance of the author concerning the geography of Palestine and religious practices there, this country is normally dismissed as a possible place of origin (cf. Smid 1965:20). Other places which are mentioned as places of origin are Syria and Egypt. Although there seems to be no definite reason why Egypt should be preferred to Syria or vice versa, it might be of interest to remind ourselves that most of the virgin birth material probably originated in Syria (cf. Von Campenhausen 1963:13ff. and Hamman 1966:62–69). The book is furthermore normally dated on eternal grounds in the second century (cf. R.M. Wilson 1978, Smid 1965 *et al.*) because it was already known to Clement of Alexandria and Origen. Justin has similar views on related matters (cf. *Apol* I.23, 33) which makes it possible that he also knew the book. But that is disputable. It has been transmitted in various translations contributing to the popularity of the book in the East.

Despite rejection in the West by the Gelasian Decree (ca. 500 AD), where it is listed as an apocryphon not received by 'the catholic and apostolic Roman Church' (cf. Brown *et al.* 1978:248), its influence on the development of mariological tradition and dogma cannot be underestimated. This is confirmed by catholic piety, in art and also in dogma-historical developments within Roman Catholicism (cf. Brown *et al.* 1978:248 and Cullmann 196:279). The infancy gospels, and in particular PJ had a tremendous impact in the early church, the Middle Ages and the Renaissance—even greater than the Bible—on literature and art (cf. Quasten 1950:106). Although Luther rejected the infancy gospels at a later stage in his life, Anne, the mother of Mary, whose name is known to us through PJ, was (cf. Cullmann 1968:275). Needless to say that its reception and influence on Mariology have greatly influenced interpreters of the text. This is obvious from the anti-Roman Catholic as well as Roman Catholic readings and evaluation thereof.

It has been mentioned above that the infancy stories developed certain themes of the childhood of Jesus. In PJ the theme is the birth of Christ from the perspective of the virgin Mary. It relates the life story of Mary, the daughter of a *rich* man Joachim and Anne (Anna); her birth based on the Old Testament story of Hannah (1 Sm. 1–2, cf. PJ 1–5; childhood in the temple (6–8); 'marriage' (cf. 19) to a widower, Joseph, who already had children (9–10); annunciation of the birth of Jesus in Jerusalem (11); visit to Elizabeth (12); Joseph's doubt and comfort by an angel (13–14); vindication of Mary before the High Priest (15–16); birth of Jesus in a cave outside Bethlehem (17–18); vision of Joseph (18); Salome's unbelief about a miraculous virgin birth (19–20); and adoration of the Magi (21). The story ends with Herod's infanticide and the murder of Zechariah, the father of John the Baptist, in the temple (22–24) and the postscript (25) referred to above. In short, the book develops the birth story of Jesus by retelling the annunciation and birth of Jesus within a narrative about his mother.

PJ is a *narrative* consisting of various episodes. Except for chapter 18:2 which contains a vision of Joseph and the postscript in 25, narrated in the first person, the narrative is narrated from a third person omniscient narrative point of view (cf. Chatman 1978:151ff.). The *narrated time* covers the period of the parents of Mary through her birth and childhood, the birth of Jesus to the massacre of the children by Herod and the death of Zechariah. The *narrated space* is mainly Palestine and in particular Jerusalem. The temple, house of the parents, house of Joseph and Mary, the road to Bethlehem and the cave also play a role. The *characters* and the way in which they are presented are determined by the scenarios in which they act. I will mention only the more important ones: *Joachim* and *Anne*: two pious, godfearing, rich, but childless parents who are presented in their emotions from despair to happiness; *Mary*: the protagonist of the story—a long expected child whose childhood is based on the example of Old Testament characters. Her name is hailed by the whole nation because it will be an eternal name remembered by all generations (cf. 6:2, 7:2, 12:2). She is raised for the service of the Lord; kept safely (holy) for the Lord (6:3); beloved of the whole of Israel (7:3). She is fed like a dove by an angel, a *Davidid*, undefiled,

pure virgin (10:1). She is put into the care of a widower—at the age
of 12 (9:1); a willing servant of the Lord 3), working for him in the
temple. She is visited by the angels (cf. 11 *et al.*), bearer of a child
not conceived in a normal way (11); mother of the Lord (12:2, chaste
and complying to the morality of Israel (12:3). She is accused of
unchastity like her predecessor Eve (13:1), but vindicated (16:3). She
is a virgin who abstained from intercourse with Joseph (her husband,
betrothed 13:3, 15:3, 19), betrothed to Joseph (19:1), a mother who
cares for her child (cf. 17:2, 19:2, 22:2); *Joseph*: a widower with children, elected to take care of Mary (9:1), a builder (9:3), a man of
emotion: fear (9:3, 14:1, 17:3), reproach, doubt, suspicion (9:3, 13:1–2)
and joy (13:2). He is a 'father' who cares for the girl (his wife) and
her child (17:3, 22:2); *Jesus*: the child conceived in an abnormal
manner (9:2), whose name shall be Jesus because he will save his
people from their sins (11:3, 14:2, 19:2). He is conceived of the
Holy Spirit (14:2, 19:1), he is the Christ (21:2, 4) and the Christ of
the Lord (21:4), the king to be born for Israel (20:2, 21:2). Soon
after his birth he is capable of taking his mother's breast and being
a great salvation to Salome (20:3). He is a king to be worshipped
(21:2, 3) and is taken care of as are presented in a positive manner
unlike the way they are characterized in the canonical gospels. They
perform religious rites (cf. 6:2, 8:2, 3, 24:1 *et al.*), bless (17:3 *et al.*),
pray (8:3 *et al.*), take care of the temple and determine the norms
(cf. 10:1, 15:3 *et al.*). They seek the will of God in prayer and reveal
it (8:3ff.). They are helpers and not opponents of the protagonist.
This is in agreement with the very positive picture painted of Israel
(people of Israel, the whole nation of Israel, sons of Israel) in PJ
(cf. 1:2, 7:2 *et al.*). Their characterization is such that one gets the
impression that the story is told on their behalf. Since the child is
born *from* Israel *for* Israel they are presented as cooperators in his
coming. From a narrative point of view this is very interesting because
there is reason to believe that the story polemises against views held
by Jews who were contemporaries of the author. In order to convince his readers he presents the Jews who were 'involved' in the
coming of the child positively.

Other helpers in the story are characters like Elizabeth, Zechariah,
the midwives, Simeon, the Magi and angels. Euthine, Herod and
the Romans act as opponents in the development of the story.

The story is built up of short episodes which relate to each other
by various narrative techniques like pro- and retrospection. Previews

are given, for example, in terms of lack which is then later liquidated (cf. 1–8). In 8:2 it is related that Mary became twelve and that the priests held a meeting about her presence in the temple. This information is not, in the first instance, given to inform the reader about the 'Mary of history' or her biography. It serves a purpose in the development of the plot, because the age of Mary is the reason why she has to leave the temple.

This theme is worked out in 8:3ff. and leads to Joseph being chosen to take care of the virgin girl from the temple. These and other narrative techniques such as repetition of formulas (cf. 6:1, 13:3, 15:3, 4, 19:3) and narrative commentary are used in plotting the episodes. One can agree with Cullmann (1968:279) when he says:

> Die ganze Darstellung ist eindrucksvoll und höchst anschaulich und zeugt von Diskretion, Innerlichkeit und Poesie. Wenn der Verfasser auch Quellen aus mündlicher und schriftlicher christlicher Tradition benutzt hat, besonders aber auch viel Stoff aus dem AT, vor allem die Samuelgeschichte, so hat er es doch verstanden, sie zu einem kunstvollen Ganzen zu verbinden. Nur wo die Apologetik es erfordert, scheut er sich nicht, auch größere, ja geschmacklose Züge beizubehalten.

The contents of the book are couched in Old and New Testament imagery and thought and the author was evidently influenced by conventions of the Old and New Testament. Even in language usage and narrative structures similarities between PJ, the Septuagint and the New Testament abound.

Scholars normally agree that PJ does not supply us with new information about the 'Mary of history'. On the contrary, it is mostly regarded as fiction written with an apologetic interest (cf. Brown *et al.* 1978:258). The story is based upon the canonical gospels, but is also the result of the author's vivid imagination (cf. the Salome-episode). This, however, does not imply that the story is completely worthless for historical construction or that it can be dismissed as invented and therefore not true or genuine (cf. Koester 1980:105ff.). This attitude leads to oversimplified statements like the following:

> As it can be shown in several instances that the author arranges his narrative after OT examples, it is certain that he is relating a fictitious historia. As he lived in the second half of the second century no authentic data were available to him. 'Amore Mariae' he writes his tale . . . (Smid 1965:11).

Without arguing the point, I would rather subscribe to the following statement, 'The author of the Protevanglium betrays no use of significant, independent sources for the life of Mary; seemingly, his principal source was the canonical Gospels' (Brown *et al.* 1978:260). It is a retelling of the virgin birth story.

4. 'Canonical' and 'Apocryphal': the New Testament and PJ xi:2–3

New Testament scholars are in agreement that Matthew and Luke offer two *different* accounts of the infancy of Jesus. The stories are narrated from two different points of view with different purposes in mind. They agree only on a very few points. Brown (1977:34–35, cf. Fitzmyer 1973:564) notes the following aspects which they share: Mary and Joseph are the parents legally engaged or married but not living together yet; Joseph is of Davidic descent; an angelic announcement of the birth of Jesus; conception of the child not through intercourse with her husband; conception is through the Holy Spirit; angelic directive about the name Jesus; the angel states that he is to be Saviour; birth takes place after the parents have come to live together; the birthplace is Bethlehem; the child is born during the reign of Herod the Great and the child is reared at Nazareth. Although commentators have often harmonized the two versions into one consecutive narrative the differences and contradictions (cf. Brown 1977:35–36) cannot be wished away or explained in such a manner. In addition to the differences in the genealogies and the lack of parallels in Luke for Matthew 2:2–22 and in Matthew for Luke 1–2 (with the exception of Lk. 1:26–35) there remains a considerable amount of detail in Matthew that can be explained only in view of each evangelist's telling of the story for his own purpose and from his own perspective.

If we compare PJ to the Matthean and Lucan versions with a view to the agreements between Matthew and Luke, there are remarkable agreements and differences. With regard to the agreements the following should be mentioned: an angelic announcement of the birth of Jesus; conception of the child, not through intercourse with her husband; conception through the 'Holy Spirit'; angelic directive about the name of Jesus; the angel states that he is to be Saviour; birth takes place after the parents have come to live together; the child is born during the reign of Herod. On the other hand there are also important differences in this respect: Joseph is an old widower with children to whom the virgin is allotted as wife (cf. 8:3) and whom he takes into his care (ραραλάβαι εἰς πήρησιν cf. 9:1,3); *Mary* is a Davidid (10:1); the birth takes place near Bethlehem in a *cave* (18:1, 19:1–3, 20:3, 21:3) and Nazareth does not play any role in PJ. The author of PJ made use of the New Testament but retold the story just as Matthew and Luke had done with the traditions they used in their narratives.

Let us now consider PJ's retelling of the annunciation of the birth of Jesus which is narrated in Luke 1:26–38 in an angelic appearance to Mary in Nazareth and incorporated into Matthew's version of the birth of Jesus (Mt. 1:18–25) in an angelic appearance to *Joseph* in Bethlehem.

From a form-critical perspective it is interesting to note that the form of biblical annunciations of birth normally has the following pattern: 1. *Appearance* of an angel of the Lord (or the Lord); 2. *Fear* or prostration of the visionary; 3. *Divine* message; 4. An *objection* by the visionary (as to how it can be, or request for a sign); 5. Giving of a *sign* of reassurance (cf. Brown 1977:156). This pattern is found in the birth stories of Ishmael (Gn. 16:7ff.), Isaac (Gn. 17:1ff.), Samson Jd. 13:3ff.), John the Baptist (Lk. 1:11ff.) and Jesus (Lk. 1:26ff., cf. Mt. 1:20–21). 'Such an annunciation was a standard biblical way of preparing the reader for the career of a person who was destined to play a significant role in salvation history, a role already known to the author' (Brown *et al.* 1978:114). Luke has followed this pattern in the annunciation stories of both John the Baptist and Jesus while Matthew, since he inserted this story into another narrative, only partly used the form. A close comparison of Luke 1:26–38 with Matthew 1:20–21 reveals that the authors used the same tradition (not necessarily the same version of the pre-gospel story) to tell *different* stories about the birth of Jesus. Brown 1979:162) summarizes the probable history of the formation of the gospel stories as follows, 'This pre-Gospel annunciation pattern developed in each evangelist's tradition in a different way. As part of an elaborate parallelism between the infant JBap and the infant Jesus, Luke rewrote it and used it to fashion a companion annunciation of the birth of JBap. Since he directed the JBap annunciation to Zechariah, he directed the Jesus annunciation to Mary . . . Matthew (or his tradition) combined the pre-Gospel angelic annunciation of the birth of the Davidic Messiah (with its christological message of begetting through the Holy Spirit) with a popular narrative in which a story of Joseph and the infant Jesus had been modeled upon the adventures of the

patriarch Joseph and the infant Moses, a narrative structured on a
series of angelic dream appearances'. This explains why Luke has
the annunciation made to Mary and Matthew to Joseph.

In PJ's retelling of the New Testament material, the author used
both Luke's (cf. PJ 11:2–3) and Matthew's version (cf. PJ 14:1–2) of
the annunciation. This gave him the opportunity to make two separate episodes of the story to develop his plot. In fact, in his infancy
stories of Luke and Matthew the two versions offered him material
for retelling the birth story more extensively. Instead of harmonizing,
he relates 'Luke's' version to narrate the annunciation of the birth
to Mary, and Matthew's version to elaborate on Joseph's dilemma
and fill out the 'open spaces' in the gospel stories. The differences
between Matthew and Luke thus gave him the opportunity to retell
the story in the way he did. Let us now consider the three versions
in more detail. The double underlining refers to agreements between
Matthew and PJ only.

I shall not discuss minor differences and agreements like the narrative framework of each version as well as the locality of the appearances in Bethlehem (Mt.), Nazareth (Lk.) and Jerusalem (PJ)
which can be explained in view of each author's own presentation
of his story.

The form in which the author of PJ presented his announcement
story closely relates to the 'biblical' form of annunciation stories. It
has the following motifs in common with Luke's version. 1. Appearance of an angel; 2. Fear of the visionary; 3. The divine message
including a. a qualifying description of the visionary, b. the visionary
is addressed by name and urged not to fear because God has inter-
fered in her life, c. a woman is to conceive and bear a child, d. the
name by which the child should be called, e. future accomplishments
of the child; 4. Objection of the visionary as to how this can be
done; 5. Answer to objection. Although the order and contents of
these motifs are not exactly the same there is a number of obvious
agreements between the stories. These agreements are also not
superficial and one might even ask whether the semantic structure
and 'global point' of the stories are the same in view of this. Even
on the surface it is clear from the underlined words that the author
of PJ was influenced by Luke in his choice of wording, but also by
Matthew. The doubly underlined words indicate agreements between
Matthew and PJ.

Are the three 'versions' of the annunciation in view of the apparent

Matthew 1:18

1.18 Τοῦ δὲ Ἰησοῦ Χριστοῦ ἡ γένεσις οὕτως ἦν. μνηστευθείσης τῆς μητρὸς αὐτοῦ Μαρίας τῷ Ἰωσήφ, πρὶν ἢ συνελθεῖν αὐτοὺς εὑρέθη ἐν γαστρὶ ἔχουσα ἐκ πνεύματος ἁγίου. 1.19 Ἰωσὴφ δὲ ὁ ἀνὴρ αὐτῆς, δίκαιος ὢν καὶ μὴ θέλων αὐτὴν δειγματίσαι, ἐβουλήθη λάθρᾳ ἀπολῦσαι αὐτήν. 1.20 ταῦτα δὲ αὐτοῦ ἐνθυμηθέντος ἰδοὺ ἄγγελος κυρίου κατ᾽ ὄναρ ἐφάνη αὐτῷ λέγων, Ἰωσὴφ υἱὸς Δαυίδ, μὴ φοβηθῇς παραλαβεῖν Μαριὰμ τὴν γυναῖκά σου· τὸ γὰρ ἐν αὐτῇ γεννηθὲν ἐκ πνεύματός ἐστιν ἁγίου. 1.21 τέξεται δὲ υἱόν, καὶ καλέσεις τὸ ὄνομα αὐτοῦ Ἰησοῦν· αὐτὸς γὰρ σώσει τὸν λαὸν αὐτοῦ ἀπὸ τῶν ἁμαρτιῶν αὐτῶν. 1.22 Τοῦτο δὲ ὅλον γέγονεν ἵνα πληρωθῇ τὸ ῥηθὲν ὑπὸ κυρίου διὰ τοῦ προφήτου λέγοντος, 1.23 Ἰδοὺ ἡ παρθένος ἐν γαστρὶ ἕξει καὶ τέξεται υἱόν, καὶ καλέσουσιν τὸ ὄνομα αὐτοῦ Ἐμμανουήλ, ὅ ἐστιν μεθερμηνευόμενον Μεθ᾽ ἡμῶν ὁ θεός. 1.24 ἐγερθεὶς δὲ ὁ Ἰωσὴφ ἀπό τοῦ ὕπνου ἐποίησεν ὡς προσέταξεν αὐτῷ ὁ ἄγγελος κυρίου καὶ παρέλαβεν τὴν γυναῖκα αὐτοῦ. 1.25 καὶ οὐκ ἐγίνωσκεν αὐτὴν ἕως οὗ ἔτεκεν υἱόν· καὶ ἐκάλεσεν τὸ ὄνομα αὐτοῦ Ἰησοῦν.

Luke 1:26-38

1.26 Ἐν δὲ τῷ μηνὶ τῷ ἕκτῳ ἀπεστάλη ὁ ἄγγελος Γαβριὴλ ἀπὸ τοῦ θεοῦ εἰς πόλιν τῆς Γαλιλαίας ᾗ ὄνομα Ναζαρὲθ 1.27 πρὸς παρθένον ἐμνηστευμένην ἀνδρὶ ᾧ ὄνομα Ἰωσὴφ ἐξ οἴκου δαυίδ, καὶ τὸ ὄνομα τῆς παρθένου Μαριάμ. 1.28 καὶ εἰσελθὼν πρὸς αὐτὴν εἶπεν, Χαῖρε, κεχαριτωμένη, ὁ κύριος μετὰ σοῦ. 1.29 ἡ δὲ ἐπὶ τῷ λόγῳ διεταράχθη καὶ διελογίζετο ποταπὸς εἴη ὁ ἀσπασμὸς οὗτος. 1.30 καὶ εἶπεν ὁ ἄγγελος αὐτῇ, Μὴ φοβοῦ, Μαριάμ, εὗρες γὰρ χάριν παρὰ τῷ θεῷ. 1.31 καὶ ἰδοὺ συλλήμψῃ ἐν γαστρὶ καὶ τέξῃ υἱὸν καὶ καλέσεις τὸ ὄνομα αὐτοῦ Ἰησοῦν. 1.32 οὗτος ἔσται μέγας καὶ υἱὸς ὑψίστου κληθήσεται καὶ δώσει αὐτῷ κύριος ὁ θεὸς τὸν θρόνον Δαυὶδ τοῦ πατρὸς αὐτοῦ, 1.33 καὶ βασιλεύσει ἐπὶ τὸν οἶκον Ἰακὼβ εἰν τοὺς αἰῶνας καὶ τῆς βασιλείας αὐτοῦ οὐκ ἔσται τέλος. 1.34 εἶπεν δὲ Μαριὰμ πρὸς τὸν ἄγγελον, Πῶς ἔσται τοῦτο, ἐπεὶ ἄνδρα οὐ γινώσκς; 1.35 καὶ ἀποκριθεὶς ὁ ἄγγελος εἶπεν αὐτῇ, Πνεῦμα ἅγιον ἐπελεύσεται ἐπὶ σὲ καὶ δύναμις ὑψίστου ἐπισκιάσει σοι· διὸ καὶ τὸ γεννώμενον ἅγιον κληθήσεται υἱὸς θεοῦ. 1.36 καὶ ἰδοὺ Ἐλισάβετ ἡ συγγενίς σου καὶ αὐτὴ συνείληφεν υἱὸν ἐν γήρει αὐτῆς καὶ οὗτος μὴν ἕκτος ἐστὶν αὐτῇ καλουμένῃ στείρα· 1.37 ὅτι οὐκ ἀδυνατήσει παρὰ τοῦ θεοῦ πᾶν ῥῆμα. 1.38 εἶπεν δὲ Μαριάμ, Ἰδοὺ ἡ δούλη κυρίου· γένοιτό μοι κατὰ τὸ ῥῆμά σου. καὶ ἀπῆλθεν ἀπ᾽ αὐτῆς ὁ ἄγγελος

Protev. Jacobi 11,1-3
(sec. Pap. Bodmer V et ed de Strycker):

1. Καὶ ἔλαβεν τὴν κάλπιν καὶ ἐξῆλθεν γεμίσαι ὕδωρ. Καὶ ἰδοὺ [αὐτῇ] φωνὴ λέγουσα <αὐτῇ>· Χαῖρε, κεχαριτω <μένη· ὁ Κύριος μετὰ σοῦ· εὐλογη> μένη σὺ ἐν γυναιξίν. Καὶ περιέβλεπεν τὰ δεξιὰ καὶ τὰ ἀριστερὰ Μαρία πόθεν αὕτη εἴη ἡ φωνή. Καὶ ἔντρομος γενομένη εἴσῃει εἰς τὸν οἶκον αὐτῆς καὶ ἀναπαύσασα τὴν κάλπιν ἔλαβεν τὴν πορφύραν καὶ ἐκαθάθισεν ἐπὶ τοῦ θρονου καὶ ἕλκεν τὴν πορφύραν. 2. Καὶ ἰδοὺ ἔστη ἄγγελος ἐνώπιον <αὐτῆς> λέγων· Μὴ φοβοῦ Μαρία· εὗρες γὰρ χάριν ἐνώπιον τοῦ πάντων Δεσπότου. Συλλήμψῃ ἐκ Λόγου αὐτοῦ. Ἡ δὲ ἀκούσασα Μαρία διεκρίθη ἐν ἑαυτῇ λέγουσα· Ἐγὼ συλλήμψομαι ἀπὸ Κυρίου Θεοῦ ζῶντος ὡς πᾶσα γυνὴ γεννᾷ; 3. Καὶ ἰδοὺ ἄγγελος ἔστη [αὐτῇ] λέγων αὐτῇ· Οὐχ οὕτς, Μαρία. Δύναμις γὰρ Θεοῦ ἐπισκιάσει σοι· διὸ καὶ τὸ γεννώμενον ἅγιον κληθήσεται υἱὸς Ὑψίστου. Καὶ καλέσεις τὸ ὄνομα αὐτοῦ Ἰησοῦν· αὐτὸς γὰρ σώσει <τὸν> λαὸν αὐτοῦ ἐκ τῶν ἁμαρτιῶν αὐτῶν. Καὶ εἶπε Μαρία· Ἰδοὺ ἡ δούλη Κυρίου κατενώπιον αὐτοῦ. Γένοιτό μοι κατὰ τὸ ῥῆμά σου.

agreements perhaps then after all not different but the same? To answer the question we will first have to discover the 'global point' of each. It will take us too far to discuss all the detail problems involved that have been addressed from various perspectives during the history of research (cf. Von Campenhausen 1962, Dibelius 1932, and Brown 1977).

Matthew and Luke told the infancy stories and parts of it with specific purposes in mind. These relate to curiosity, apologetics and christology (cf. Brown 1977:28ff.). In view of all the differences and contradictions between the versions of Matthew and Luke in their presentations of the infancy stories, it has become evident that both took a greater interest in the theological (= christological) aspects of their stories rather than in the historical or biographical ones. Jesus' origins were made intelligible to their readers against the background of the fulfilment of Old Testament expectations as they understood it (cf. fulfilment quotations in Matthew) or with a view to the history of salvation, that is as *theologoumena*.

There is general agreement that the infancy stories represent the latest phase in the development of the gospel tradition and that Matthew and Luke differ from the rest of the New Testament in this respect. In contrast to Mark they relate christology not only to the resurrection and ministry of Jesus (two-stage christology), but also to his birth and infancy (three-stage christology). It is a very particular kind of three-stage christology which is also different from that of Paul and John who both have a pre-existence christology. 'Their major affirmations in these Gospel introductions bear then on His Christological identification: He is born of God, son of Abraham, son of David, Messiah, Saviour, Lord, and Son of God. To fail to perceive this is to miss the thrust of the infancy narratives' (Fitzmyer 1973:564). It is furthermore argued that christology developed from the resurrection backwards through Jesus' ministry and baptism to his birth and pre-existence. In the pre-gospel traditions found in Paul (compare the sermons in Acts) the identity of Jesus is associated with his being raised from the dead by God (cf. Rm. 1:3–4, Ac. 2:32 *et al.*). In Mark (1:11) he is proclaimed Son of God at his baptism and transfiguration (9:7) while in Luke he is born Son of God (cf. also Matthew).

> The same combined ideas that early Christian preaching had once applied to the resurrection (i.e., a divine proclamation, the begetting of God's Son, the agency of the Holy Spirit), and which Mark had

applied to the baptism, are now applied to the conception of Jesus in the words of an angel's message to Joseph and to Mary... (Brown 1977:31).

In view of this the infancy of Jesus is narrated in Matthew and Luke from the perspective of the identity of Jesus—*who* he is and *how* it happened that he is who he is. His being Son of God and being Son of David are related to each other by associating his sonship with the moment of his conception. Matthew and Luke made their own stories of it by presenting the material each in his own way. With this in mind, let us now consider the 'virginal conception' which is the focal point in PJ.

One of the differences between Matthew and Luke with regard to the conception of Jesus is the fact that Matthew leaves no doubt that the conception of Jesus has already taken place when the angel appears to Joseph. Joseph was not involved in it in any way. (In Luke's version it is a future conception.) Exactly how the conception happens is not told by Matthew. His story, which is unmistakably a story about virginal conception, has definite apologetic nuances. In 1:18 he tells the reader that Mary conceived *before* she and Joseph started living together (got married) but also that he did not have intercourse with her until she bore Jesus (1:25). Added to the angel's announcement, is a *formula citation* (1:22–23) to prove that the conception is a fulfilment of Isaiah's prophecy of a young girl conceiving and bearing a son. In this way Matthew undoubtedly stresses the virginal conception through the Holy Spirit. The child is a Davidid through naming. His father is an ancestor of David (1:19). Through conception, however, he is Emmanuel. Unlike in Luke where Mary plays a more important role in the infancy story, Mary is an instrument of God's action in Matthew. 'Once she has given birth to Jesus, she and the child become the object of Joseph's care (2:13–14, 20–21); and it is Joseph who is given the centre stage of drama' (Brown *et al.* 1978:86). The primary emphasis of the story is the virginal conception by the Holy Spirit.

In Luke it is different. His is not in the first instance a story about virginal conception. In his version the focus is on the future greatness of Jesus, on christology and exceptional conception. 'We should not forget this christology even though there has been more Marian reflection (and literature) based on this scene than on any other in the NT' (Brown *et al.* 1978:112). Having given a rather extensive divine message, Luke tells the reader that Mary is confused about the fact that she will become the mother of the Davidic Messiah, eternal king of the house of Jacob, about *this future* conception. Mary objects by saying that she does not have intercourse with a man (1:34). This objection and the reference to her being a betrothed virgin are the only indications of her virginity. Fitzmyer (1973:567) therefore correctly maintains that, 'When this account is read in and of itself . . . every detail in it could be understood of a child to be born of Mary in the usual human way, a child endowed with God's special favour, born at the intervention of the Spirit of God, and destined to be acknowledged as the heir of David's throne as God's Messiah and Son. Chap. 2 in the Lucan Gospel supports this under-standing even further with its references to Mary and Joseph as Jesus' "parents" (2:41) or as "your father and I" (2:48)'.

The global point of the annunciation story in Luke reminds one of Paul's statement in Romans 1:3–4: 'It is about his Son, our Lord Jesus Christ: as to his humanity, he was born a descendant of David; as to his divine holiness, he was shown with great power to be the Son of God by being raised from death' (GNB). Luke's story is a story about an extraordinary child and its conception. That Luke's annunciation story has been read as a story about virginal concep-tion since the early days of church history cannot be denied. It is well known that Mary's objection, and in particular her question, 'how can this be?', gave rise to much speculation about Mary's igno-rance of how children are conceived, perpetual virginity and a hypo-thetical vow to remain a virgin for the rest of her life (cf. Brown *et al.* 1978:114). Luke 1:34 has ever since been a bone of contention and debate. If one realizes, however, that an objection or request for a sign very often occurs in annunciation stories, in other words, that it need not be a biographical statement, and notice how it con-tributes towards the development of the plot, it becomes another matter. In the case of Luke it offers the opportunity to inform the reader that the conception will be through the Holy Spirit, and to refer to the fact that Elizabeth, who used to be barren, is pregnant *because there is nothing God cannot do* (1:37). After this Mary is satisfied and the angel leaves. It is the Matthean version with its nuances which influenced readers of Luke to interpret Luke's story in view of Matthew's. On the other hand, it is also clear that the lack of clarity in Luke's version (cf. also Matthew) of how the Holy Spirit will be involved in the conception of Jesus; the accusations of Jesus being an illegitimate child (cf. e.g. Celcus, *Logos, Alethēs* 1:32); attempts to explain how Jesus could have been Son of God from his child-hood, and many more aspects of which we find vestiges in the New Testament, could have given rise to readings of Luke with the focus on virginal conception.

The author of PJ used the material of the annunciation stories of the New Testament to propagate the virginal conception, most prob-ably in an attempt to convince his readers of the extraordinary birth of Jesus. The global point of his version ties in with the rest of his narrative. It is an annunciation narrative about a virginal concep-tion which is elaborated upon in various episodes which follow. It serves the purpose of a preview of what is to follow in the rest of the narrative. In telling the story of the virginal conception, PJ is closer to Matthew than to Luke even though he uses Luke's version as his main 'Vorlage', and despite the christological information Luke's version contains. This is mainly due to the fact that the author of PJ embedded this narrative into a virginal conception context. What PJ 11 amounts to, or why it was told, is determined by its lit-erary environment. In spite of its christological content (Son of the Highest, Saviour of his people from their sins), its meaning and ref-erence is determined by the fact that it forms part of the story of *Mary*'s virginal conception. This is made clear by the narrative frame-work of the annunciation story in PJ, the contents thereof and the integration of the material into the complete story.

One of the remarkable differences between PJ and Luke is in the wording of the promise of future conception. According to Luke the angel says καὶ ἰδοὺ συλλήμψῃ ἐν γαστρὶ while PJ has καὶ συλλήμψῃ ἐκ λόγου αὐτου. What does the expression in PJ mean? Unfortunately the question is not completely answered by the text. Mary finds the remark puzzling and deliberates whether she will conceive of the Lord, the living God and give birth like every other woman does. That will not be the case. The power of God will overshadow her. Is συλλήμψῃ ἐκ λόγου αὐτου the same as, or paraphrased by δύναμις γὰρ θεοῦ ἐπισκιάσει σοι? This is of course a possibility because αὐτου refers to δεσπότου in the preceding phrase and δεσπότης is a sub-stitute for θεός in PJ (cf. 2:4, 7:1 *et al.*). Λόγος would thus refer to or be the same as δύναμις γὰρ θεοῦ a term used for the Holy Spirit (cf. Luke 1:35). In 19:1 it is overtly stated that, '. . . ἀλλὰ συλλήμψιν ἔχει ἐκ πνεύματος ἁγίου (cf. The Gospel of the Hebrews in Delius 1973:8). Nevertheless, it is clear that the author did not fill out the 'open space' in the New Testament versions by telling the reader in detail how the conception through the Holy Spirit took place or through which medium the conception happened. Later readings of the phrase gave rise to speculation and even explanation of how conception took place ἐκ λόγου for example, the idea of conception through the ear (cf. Smid 1965:84). In addition it may rightfully be asked whether this formulation shows traces of the *logos* Christology of the second century (cf. Justin, *Apol* 1:33 and Bauer 1967:48ff.).

The omission of the extensive identification of the child by Luke in PJ and the reformulation of Mary's question, Πῶς ἔσται τοῦτο, ἐπεὶ ἄνδρα οὐ γινώσκω; into ἐγὼ συνλήμψομαι ἀπὸ κυρίου τοῦ θεοῦ ζωντος ὡς πᾶσα γυνὴ γεννᾷ; the answer of the angel, οὐχ οὕτως Μαριάμ and what follows, is a deliberate attempt by the author to prompt his reader to understand that the birth is an exceptional one. It is also a preview of an episode which is later taken up and developed in the gynaecological test case story in chapter 19ff. In chapters 17–19 a new episode in the story of Jesus' birth is invented in which the occasion is taken to elaborate upon Mary's remark ἔπει ἄνδρα οὐ γινώσκω (cf. 17:1 and 19:1). Most probably it also already points to what is being stated in 20:1 as οὐ γὰρμικρὸς ἀγὼν περίκειταί μοι. Interestingly enough, the author of PJ did not elaborate on the *how* of the conception through the Holy Spirit. Similar to Luke, the answer to Mary's question concerns the who that will be conceived rather than the how.

Did Matthew, Luke and the author of PJ tell the same story? Superficially one would have to say yes. It seems like yet another story of the annunciation of the birth of Jesus. However, does this reply in the affirmative comply with the conditions discussed above, according to which various versions of the 'same' story can be the 'same'? Matthew and Luke did not in fact tell the same story. Their purposes were different and so were the 'points' of their stories. The author of PJ retold Matthew's and Luke's versions and in his retelling he came closer to telling the same story that Matthew did, where the emphasis is on the virginal conception, even though he relied more on Luke's version of the material. But again he did not tell the same story as Matthew because Matthew used the virginal conception in telling the story of Emmanuel and how he is 'God with us' through conception to resurrection. In PJ the virginal conception is not told—not even in the annunciation story—to explain Christology, but to explain the extraordinary birth of the Messiah.

There should be no doubt that the author of PJ was prompted by the New Testament texts to retell the annunciation story, and

for that matter his whole story in the way he did. By emphasizing
certain motifs found in the New Testament, he retold the virginal
conception story for a purpose which most probably can be linked
to the difficulties which arose when Christology was associated with
the moment of conception. When theologoumena became part of
the life story of Jesus (cf. Dibelius 1932:38ff.) a whole set of problems was generated (cf. Von Campenhausen 1962). The following
remark of Brown about Luke's version (1977:312) is helpful in this
connection, 'The action of the Holy Spirit and the power of the
Most High came not upon the Davidic king but upon his mother.
We are not dealing with the adoption of a Davidid by coronation
as God's son or representative; we are dealing with begetting of
God's son in the womb of Mary through God's creative Spirit'. PJ
lays stress on this mariological directive of the Lucan text and follows Matthew in his identification of Jesus. PJ is a retelling of a the-
ologoumenon which had already been told for various purposes (cf.
Matthew and Luke). It originates from a period when speculation
about the origins of Jesus was in the air (cf. Bauer 1967:29ff.), and
unity and diversity in teaching became a problem of orthodoxy and
heterodoxy (cf. Bauer 1964). With PJ we have, however, not reached
a stage where full-fledged doctrines about the humanity and divinity of Christ have been worked out. PJ reveals a stage of imitative
and imaginative retelling of New Testament material, in many respects
similar to retellings found in the New Testament.

The author of PJ knew the New Testament versions of the conception of Jesus. These versions prompted him in his own situation
to retell the story of Jesus' conception with his own purpose in mind.
In order to smooth out some of the difficulties of the New Testament
versions, he produced a new text, but a text which can be explained
as a rationalization of what is given in the New Testament. He
undoubtedly invented some of the material he offered his reader and
most probably does not supply the person in search for 'how things
really happened' with any 'new' information. The points in which
it deviates from the 'canonical' conversions of the infancy story of
Jesus, with which I have dealt above, can be accounted for either
in terms of the 'integrity' of his story or perhaps as rival traditions.

The purpose of PJ is often said to be the *glorification of Mary*
(cf. Smid 1965:14). It is stated as follows by Cullmann (1968:279),
'Das Ganze ist zur Verherrlichung der Maria geschrieben. Nicht nur
werden implizit die jüdischen Verleumdungen ... besonders kräftig
abgelehnt, sondern alle künftigen mariologischen Themen kündigen

sich schon an . . .'. I am afraid that Cullmann and others who share this view are led by the fact that PJ was used and received by many of its readers as aglorification of Mary and a clear plea for asceticism. But is that the purpose of the story? Is that why it was written or what the text tells? Granted the fact that the virginal conception, virgin birth and enduring virginity (cf. 20:1), is narrated by PJ, one should nevertheless be careful to conclude that its purpose is to glorify Mary. The purpose of the story should rather be looked for in PJ as a retelling of the birth story of Jesus from the perspective of his mother. The author's object was probably not 'to write a (pretty elaborate) mariology in the form of a novel', as Smid (1965:19) contends. Intertextual relationships with texts of the same period (cf. Delius 1973:5ff.) prove that discussions about the origin of Jesus, his birth, and for that matter the virgin birth and Mary's role in the birth of Jesus, was in vogue, so to speak, when our author retold the story of the birth of Jesus. PJ was told primarily with a view to the birth of Jesus, and from the perspective of his mother. That is why it is rightfully called an infancy gospel.

Because retellings of stories are in principle more often not the same as the 'original' it is a pity that extracanonical narratives have been called 'apocryphal'. 'Canonical' and 'apocryphal' reflect, as Koester (1980:105ff.) correctly observes, deep-seated prejudices that have far-reaching consequences. Especially in (fundamentalist) Protestant-dominated areas or countries where the 'sola scriptura' doctrine has unintentionally given rise to ignorance about developments in the early church and neglect of the study of early Christian documents, these terms are naively equated to 'authentic' versus 'inauthentic', 'factive' versus 'fictive', 'historical' versus 'unhistorical', 'true' versus 'false' and so on. The following remark by Brown (1977:33 n. 21) is useful in this connection:

> The relative sobriety of the canonical infancy narratives when compared to the non-canonical ones has been used as an argument for their historicity. But is this a difference of kind (history vs. fiction) or a difference of degree? One might argue that both canonical and non-canonical narratives result from the attempts of Christian imagination to fill in the Messiah's origins, and that in the case of the apocryphal narratives the imagination had a freer and further exercise.

CHAPTER FIFTEEN

1 ENOCH AND THE JEWISH LITERARY SETTING OF THE NEW TESTAMENT: A STUDY IN TEXT TYPES

The writings of the New Testament did not originate in a vacuum. They are in form and content deeply rooted in a Jewish/Hellenistic historical, sociological and literary setting. The term 'setting' is preferred to 'background' because overtones of 'influence' are very often connected to the latter. Keeping in mind the limitations of studying extra-biblical literature from the perspective of the New Testament, the study of literature between the Old Testament and the Mishnah from that perspective proves to be invaluable in creating a frame of reference for a valid reading of the New Testament. What matters most is not the literary influence, but the community of thought between these writings and the mutual ways of expression.

There can be difference of opinion about the correctness of Käsemann's provocative statement that apocalyptic is the mother of Christian theology (see Käsemann 1964a:100; Bultmann 1967b:476–82). There is, however, no doubt that much of what we find in the New Testament is written from an apocalyptic eschatological perspective. It is also at this point that the importance of 1 Enoch as part of the Jewish literary setting of the New Testament becomes clear. Both 1 Enoch and the writings of the New Testament display common features with regard to apocalyptic eschatology. Quite a number of sayings of Jesus in the gospel tradition are 'apocalyptic'. The Olivet discourse in Mark 13 *par* is an apocalyptic speech and the Revelation of John is normally regarded as an apocalypse. Mark's gospel has been called an 'apocalyptic drama' (see Perrin 1974:143ff.) and Q 'the first literary evidence in the New Testament for the existence of Christian apocalyptic . . .' (see Perrin 1974:74), while Beker recently argued a strong case '. . . that the character of Paul's contingent hermeneutic is shaped by his apocalyptic core in that in nearly all cases the contingent interpretation of the gospel points—whether implicitly or explicitly—to the imminent cosmic triumph of God' (1980:19). However difficult it may be to determine the exact character of eschatology in the different layers and writings of the New Testament (see Kümmel 1982) it is obvious that, for various reasons, apocalyptic was formative.

The literature attributed to Enoch was in high regard with early Christianity as can be gathered from references and allusions to Enoch in writings of early Christianity and community of thought in these writings (see Adler 1978:271–278; Charles 1913:180f.). In certain Jewish circles the books of Enoch were regarded as inspired (see the Testaments of the Twelve Patriarchs and Jubilees). They were cherished by the community of Qumran (see Milik & Black 1976). They were quoted in the New Testament and even referred to as ἡ γραφὴ in the Epistle of Barnabas 16:5. If it were not for Augustine and others these books would most probably not have fallen into discredit after the third century.

Paging through Nestle-Aland's list of *loci citati vel allegati* the number of possible references and allusions to Enochic literature catches the eye. Even if one were to exclude those which come from the Book of Parables *BP* on grounds of dating, the number is still substantial. Perhaps more important, however, are those instances where there are common thought patterns between passages from the New Testament and Enochic literature such as transcendence of death, imminent judgement and so on (see Collins 1974; Nickelsburg 1979 *et al.*). It is a pity that knowledge of New Testament scholars about Enochic literature is often limited to the possible influence *BP* could have had on the Son of man Christology. Important as this may be, it is debatable whether this is the most important, let alone only reason, why the study of 1 Enoch can be rewarding for a better understanding of the New Testament.

I have undertaken to prepare an introductory paper to the theme of this volume, that is on '1 Enoch and the New Testament'. Needless to say that such an undertaking proved to be almost impossible within the limits of one single paper. I have therefore decided to limit my article to the so-called 'apocalyptic' or 'apocalypse' genre, an aspect of 1 Enoch and the New Testament which seems very important and necessary. By doing this I hope to offer some introductory information on the nature of the books of Enoch called 1 Enoch, and secondly, perhaps even more important, I hope to further the discussion on the text type 'apocalypse'. The thesis of my paper is that, from a literary and communication point of view, it is wrong to classify the so-called 'apocalyptic' literature as a separate 'genre'. In the next part of my paper a survey will be given of the current debate on the apocalypse as genre. The text types involved in 1 Enoch and the New Testament will then be discussed and conclusions will be drawn.

Despite the progress in the restudy of apocalyptic (see Hanson 1976a:389–413) one may perhaps still say with Betz (1966:392), 'Was Apokalyptik ist, ist umstritten'. And perhaps one should add that the existence and character of the genre 'apocalypse' is debatable.

It has become customary (see Collins 1979a; Hanson 1976a; Stone 1976) to distinguish between 'apocalypse' as a literary genre, 'apocalyptic eschatology' as a religious perspective and structure of thought, and 'apocalypticism' as a sociological ideology. Since these terms may refer to three different things it is argued that '. . . much of the confusion which currently reigns results from a failure to observe these distinctions' (Collins 1979a:3). It is my contention that this distinction is confusing in that it is artificial and responsible for the creation of a separate genre which in fact does not exist. For an understanding of these texts it is the ideology and theological perspective that are important. These texts are the result of an ideology and they are written from the perspective of apocalyptic eschatology.

Apocalyptic eschatology is a perspective '. . . a way of viewing divine plans in relation to mundane realities' (Hanson 1976b:29). It is a continuation of prophetic eschatology which yielded to that of apocalyptic eschatology. 'Gradually God's final saving acts came to be conceived of not as the fulfilment of promises within political structures and historical events, but as deliverance out of the present order into a new transformed order . . .' (Hanson 1976b:30).

Apocalyptic eschatology and apocalypticism should furthermore be seen in connection with the development of ideas and contingency in theological processes and thought of Israel. When prophecy failed, and theology of the law, wisdom theology and so on could not give an answer to existential problems, new theological answers had to be found to old problems. Although it is difficult to determine the exact beginnings of apocalyptic eschatology it seems that the Hellenistic setting of the third century played a substantial role in giving rise to apocalyptic thought patterns (cf. Muller 1973:31–42; Rudolph 1980:221–237). A large number of writings of different kind were written from an apocalyptic eschatological perspective and came to be known as 'apocalypses'.

Both 'apocalyptic' and 'apocalypse' are derived from the title of
the 'Apocalypse of John'. Used with reference to certain writings, it
is argued that apocalypse '. . . designates a literary genre which is
one of the favoured media used by apocalyptic writers to communicate their messages'. It is, however, common knowledge that, 'It
is by no means the exclusive, or even the dominant, *genre* in most
apocalyptic writings but is found alongside many others, including
the testament, the salvation-judgment oracle, and the parable' (Hanson 1976b:29; see Collins 1979a:3). Some of the writings in question
are: Daniel 7–12; 1 Enoch 1–36; 1 Enoch 37–71; 1 Enoch 72–82;
1 Enoch 83–90; 1 Enoch 91–108; 4 Ezra; 2 Baruch and others. It
is noteworthy that all the literature attributed to Enoch is generally
regarded to be of the apocalypse genre (see Fitzmyer 1977; Collins
1979b *et al.*).

The text type or genre 'apocalypse' is normally defined in terms
of formal characteristics and characteristics of content. Matters such
as pseudonymity, revelatory discourses or visions, symbolic language,
unveiling of the meaning of obscurities, systematization and ordering of phenomena, combination of smaller forms like *ex eventu* surveys of history, throne visions, descriptions of the metaphysical world,
paraenesis and prayer are mentioned as distinctive features of the
genre (see Vielhauer 1978:488–90).

In contrast to this view which has been established for quite a
while in the scholarly world Von Rad argued:

> Entgegen immer wieder auftauchenden Behauptungen muss betont wer-
> den, dass die Apokalyptik in literarischer Hinsicht keine besondere
> 'Gattung' repräsentiert. Sie ist im Gegenteil in formgeschichtlicher
> Hinsicht ein mixtum compositum, das uberlieferungsgeschichtlich auf
> eine sehr komplizierte Vorgeschichte schliessen lässt (Von Rad 1965:330
> note 28).

His viewpoint is, however, normally rejected (see Collins 1979a:3f.).
Recent attempts to define the genre of apocalypses have concentrated mainly on the refinement and precision of the characteristics
mentioned above although some very important textlinguistic and
literary factors have also been taken into account. The most important of these are to my knowledge the studies done by the Apocalypse
Group of the Society of Biblical Literature Genres Project (Collins
1979a; 1979b) and that of Hartman (1983).

According to the definition of the *SBL* group a literary genre is
'. . . a group of written texts marked by distinctive recurring char-

acteristics which constitute a recognizable and coherent type of writing' (Collins 1979a:1). These characteristics are based on phenomenological similarity, are independent of historical, functional and social considerations and are established by listing the prominent recurring features in a set of similar texts (see Collins 1979a:2–5). As a result of a survey of 'revelatory literature' limited to approximately 250 BCE to 250 CE, Collins establishes a master-paradigm which is divided into two sections: the *framework* of the revelation and its *content*.

The framework concerns the *manner of revelation* (*medium*: visual, auditory or otherworldly journey; *otherworldly mediator*: angel, Christ and *human recipient*: pseudonymity, disposition and reaction), and *concluding elements* such as paraenesis to the recipient (however rare), instructions to the recipient and a narrative conclusion.

The contents are characterized by a *temporal axis* embracing historical and eschatological events like protology, history, salvation, eschatological crisis, judgement, and salvation, and a spatial axis embracing otherworldly beings and places. Collins (1979a:8–9 reminds us '. . . that no one apocalypse contains all the elements noted in the paradigm . . .' and that '. . . all apocalypses seek to influence the lives of their readers and many imply exhortation to a specific course of action'. There are a few elements pertaining to both framework and contents which are constant: a *narrative* framework in which the manner of revelation is described and a presentation of eschatological salvation and otherworldly realities (see Collins 1979a:9). With this in mind a comprehensive definition of the genre is given, '"*Apocalypse*" is a genre of revelatory literature with a narrative framework, in which a revelation is mediated by an otherworldly being to a human recipient, disclosing a transcendent reality which is both temporal, insofar as it envisages eschatological salvation, and spatial insofar as it involves another, supernatural world' (Collins 1979a:9).

One has to note that the so-called distinctive characteristics the *SBL* group has listed concern the sign system or code of the writings under discussion and not the text type. Since these characteristics occur in different text types such as narratives, expository and argumentative discourses (see below) they can hardly be described as distinctive features of a specific genre. If they are, one would like to know what their functions are with regard to a particular text type. Is the 'narrative framework' mentioned in the definition perhaps the distinctive characteristic or constitutive element of the text type called 'apocalypse'? These are open questions as far as the results of the *SBL* group are concerned. That is not to deny the use and value of listing the typical events, characters, settings and other elements which are found in these texts. Remaining within the limits of their own definition of genre given above one should ask whether the distinctive recurring characteristics the group listed are constitutive of the text type or typical of the perspective or thought system which is presented in these texts.

Hartman's views on what he calls the 'apocalyptic genre' are by and large in agreement with those of the *SBL* group insofar as he also distinguishes between characteristics relating to form and content. One should, however, not be misled since Hartman's definition of constituents of genre regarding contents are dependent on literary and linguistic characteristics. He furthermore maintains that in addition to constituents related to form and content, semantic function of the message of the text and the socio-linguistic function of the genre are also constituents of genre (see Hartman 1983:334). Collins (1979a:1) on the other hand specifically says that '. . . while a complete study of a genre must consider function and social setting, neither of these factors can determine the definition'.

Hartman deals with genre from the perspective of communication, including both the process of text-making and that of text-understanding. He draws on linguistic, literary and sociological insights and sees the purpose of the study of genre not simply to classify but to serve the process of understanding. Author, text and reader are taken into account. Genre therefore has to do with text—and cultural conventions. It creates a certain 'reader's expectation' on the ground of which there is a connection between genre and socio-linguistic situation and function (see Hartman 1983:331f.). He understands the '. . . apocalyptic genre as being something narrower than, say, narrative as genre . . .' corresponding '. . . with a narrower scope in terms of a historically given, cultural context, which contains the conventions that include the genre, its use and understanding' (Hartman 1983:340).

According to Hartman there are two groups of constituents of the apocalyptic genre. The first concerns the 'linguistic characteristics' of a text and includes aspects like style, vocabulary and phraseology, while the second deals with the content of the text on the propositional level. His treatment of constituents are noteworthy. These characteristics are seen with reference to the work as a whole, its parts and the addressees.

With regard to the macro-structure he draws attention to the importance of the structure of presentation, the plot, the main themes, the topic. In the case of apocalypses: the introduction of a divine revelation, the revelation itself in the form of visions, travels or dialogues and a conclusion. This is in some respect related to Collins' framework. In the second place, he argues that the different sections of an apocalypse also have their own characteristics related to the structure and ways of presenting the material in smaller forms. This includes for example the appearance of a heavenly messenger, an *angelus interpres*, who interprets a vision. The relationship between the sections and the whole is seen with reference to their 'function', for example, a heavenly journey is a means of joining heaven and earth and has the function to anchor the authority of the message of revelation to the divine being.

The constituents of genre related to the addressee are treated with reference to semantic and sociolinguistic functions of texts and their parts. Bearing in mind that clauses may have informative, prescriptive, expressive or performative functions, in other words semantic functions, Hartman relates this to the semantic function of the message of a text. He maintains that a typical message of apocalypses is one of comfort and exhortation to steadfastness. In the last instance the constituents of genre should be related to their socio-linguistic function which normally is a cultural convention shared by sender and receptor of the text. He does not, however, attempt to mention a specific socio-linguistic function of the apocalyptic genre except for the remark that the Apocalypse of John was written to be read at the divine service (see Hartman 1983:335). He is of course aware of the fact that there is not necessarily a one-to-one relationship between genre and sociolinguistic function, '... one must be aware of the possibility that apocalyptic, or perhaps eschatological motifs and themes are dealt with in other literary genres' (Hartman 1983:341).

Although there is merit in Hartman's discussion there also are a number of problems. Apparently he regards the apocalyptic genre as a subtype of *narrative* although he does not, as far as I can see, explicitly say so (see Hartman 1983:340). Does he, for instance, regard 'the manner of writing apocalypses' as narrative art? If so, one would have expected him to have made some mention of narrative characteristics of the apocalyptic genre. What are the genre characteristics of the smaller units of apocalypses; are they constitutive of the text type 'apocalyptic genre'? Are the functional relations between units and macrotext to be defined in terms of, for example, joining heaven and earth, or in terms of the 'plot' of the narrative? Are *semantic* and *socio-linguistic* functions also distinctive characteristics of *genre*? Or to put it in another way, is there a one-to-one relationship between apocalyptic genre and semantic function or apocalyptic genre and socio-linguistic function? The answer is undoubtedly 'no'. And for this reason it cannot be regarded as part of a genre constituent, however important it may be in analysing the meaning of the texts.

The main problem with both these models seems to be the question of what genre is and what the distinctive characteristics of specific text types are. Before we turn to 1 Enoch and text types in the New Testament a few remarks should be made about typical features of text types.

It has become clear that many of the traditional approaches to the study of text types (see Hempfer 1973) are not very useful in classifying texts with the view of understanding them. It is furthermore obvious that '. . . to carry out the various functions of communication in language, information must be organized, for discourse does not consist of a random accumulation of words and phrases' (Nida 1981:29).

The ways in which information can be organized are limited. There are basically five ways: narration, exposition, argument, description and listing (see Brooks and Warren 1970:56f.; Nida 1981:29f.). From this point of view there are only a limited number of text types: narratives, expositions, argumentative texts, descriptions and lists. The study of text types therefore concerns the study of characteristics typical of a particular text type. In the case of narratives, for example, narrative features like plot, characterization, setting and so on (see Chatman 1978) are characteristics of this genre, and in the case of the others, features typical to the rhetoric of those genres are characteristic. These 'distinctive recurring features' are not the same as those mentioned by the *SBL* group and Hartman systems or codes like symbolic language. Needless to say that there is more involved in understanding a text than clarifying its genre. On the other hand, it is obvious that it is of the utmost importance to know the working of a particular text type in order to understand it. We can now proceed to restudy the so-called apocalyptic genre with reference to 1 Enoch and text types in the New Testament.

The importance of studying the so-called 'apocalyptic genre' with reference to individual texts in addition to the study of the group of texts which presumably share the same characteristics of genre, is obvious and at this stage of the restudy of these texts also necessary (see Collins 1979a:12; Hartman 1983:339). Among the many issues repeatedly raised in the recent past by scholars in their study of 1 Enoch, there is the question of the text type of 1 Enoch as a collection and of the individual parts. What is the genre of 1 Enoch? The answer to this question is not an easy one and depends on many debatable issues. Let us, therefore, start with a few general remarks about 1 Enoch.

It is generally recognized that 1 Enoch is the result of a very long process of translation, compilation and redaction. The discovery of fragments of leather scrolls belonging to the books of Enoch during 1952 at Qumran caves 1, 2, 4 and 6, made it clear that the process started with Aramaic originals probably composed toward the end of the third century BCE and later, and that they were used by Palestinian Jews during that period. It also became obvious that these manuscripts differed considerably in form and extent from the literature attributed to Enoch known from the Ethiopic version, that is from 1 Enoch (see Milik & Black 1976).

The name 1 Enoch is used to distinguish it from the Slavonic (2 Enoch) and Hebrew Book of Enoch (3 Enoch). It is a collection of traditions dating from various times during the last three centuries BCE and the first century CE. Written mostly in Aramaic, these traditions were collected into the so-called books of Enoch (= 1 Enoch), translated into Greek and from Greek into Ge'ez. These collections of Enochic material were held in high esteem by Jews and Christians (see Milik 1976).

1 Enoch is a composite work consisting of five main parts or books and two appendices. The reason why these parts have been collected and transmitted as 'one' book remains unclear. This was even more so when it became known that the so-called *BP*, cherished by New Testament scholars because of the light it throws on the Son of man tradition, was absent from the Qumran discoveries and most probably did not exist in any form during the period before Christ (see Suter 1981). Since the attempt by Dix (1926) to explain the collection as an Enochic pentateuch compiled as a counterpart to the pentateuch of Moses, several other explanations have been offered to explain the form and literary structure of 1 Enoch. The existence of an Enochic pentateuch at Qumran, with the Book of the Giants taking the place of *BP* in Dix's Ethiopic pentateuch, was propagated

by Milik but has convincingly been refuted (see Dimant 1983:14ff.).
It is nevertheless clear that the hypothesis of an Enochic pentateuch
does not solve the problem of the text type of 1 Enoch. What genre
is 'a' pentateuch in any case?

In analysing the text type of 1 Enoch one has, in view of its history of growth, to distinguish between the text types of the individual books or parts of 1 Enoch and the genre of the complete collection.
Let us therefore briefly review the individual books with a view to
content and way of presentation of content, that is text type. (All
English translations of 1 Enoch are those of Knibb 1978.)

1 Enoch consists of the following parts: 1. The Book of the watchers (*BW*)—chapters 1–36; 2. The Book of parables (*BP*)—chapters
37–71; 3. The Astronomical Book (*AB*)—chapters 72–82; 4. The
Book of dreams (*BD*)—chapters 83–90; 5. The Epistle of Enoch
(*EE*)—chapters 91–105; and 6. Two *appendices*—the Birth of Noah
in chapters 106–107 and the Last book of Enoch to Methuselah—
chapter 108.

The Book of the watchers

> *BW* is embraced by a narrative introduction (1–5:9) and a blessing in
> narrative form (36:4). The introduction (1–5) relates Enoch's vision of
> the day of judgement: vindication of the righteous and admonition to
> the sinners. In its present form chapters 1–5 serve as an introduction
> to the complete text of 1 Enoch. Whether it originally formed part of
> *BW* is another problem (see Hartman 1979:384; Dimant 1983:24).
> Except for 1:1–1:2a which is narrated in the third person style, the
> introduction is presented as a vision in the first person and the con-
> tents about future judgement in the third person narrative style.
>
> In 6:1 the style changes to the past tense when the myth (Nickelsburg
> 1977a) of the fallen angels (see Gn. 6) is presented in retold form and
> punishment is announced (6–11). It forms '... the nucleus and foun-
> tainhead of the traditions in chaps. 1–36' (Nickelsburg 1981b:49).
> Chapters 12–16 proceed from the previous section. Enoch's attempt
> to intercede on behalf of the fallen angels and God's judgement of
> them is then told. It is presented in narrative style. In 17–36 Enoch
> is taken on two cosmic tours guided by angels to places of judgement
> and the ends of the earth. The material is again arranged in first per-
> son narrative style. The journey narrative in chapters 21–7 is told, as
> Nickelsburg (1981b:55) has pointed out, in a stereotyped pattern which
> is repeated in other parts of 1 Enoch (see 17–32; 46–54; 56–58; 61–64
> *et al.*), that is, '... arrival, vision, question, angelic interpretation, bless-
> ing (I came to ... I saw ... I asked the angel ... he said ... Then I
> blessed the Lord)'. In 33:2–4 a preview of chapters 72–82 (AB) is given
> and 34–36 gives a summary of the vision in chapter 76.

The Book of parables

   BP is the most disputed (Knibb 1979; Suter 1981 *et al.*), and because of the occurrence of the heavenly Son of man (see 46:3ff.; 48:2; 62:7, 9) the best known part of the corpus. The book starts with a statement by the third person narrator who announces the '. . . second vision which he saw the vision of wisdom . . .' (37:1) and ends with the remarks in 70:2 by the same narrator that '. . . his name was lifted from those who dwell upon the dry ground to the presence of that Son of man . . .' and two visions of Enoch.

   BP consists of three main prophetic discourses; visions of divine mysteries mostly in the form of first person narratives in 38–44; 45–57 and 58–69. These visions are presented as narratives about Enoch's journeys to the heavenly throne (39:2–41:2), visits to astronomical and other celestial phenomena (41–44; 59–60), and places of punishment (52–56:4). The idea of Noah's flood as a type of final judgement which occurs in 6–11 is repeated here as elsewhere in 1 Enoch (see 54–5, 65, 83 and 106–107).

   The parables announce judgement for the wicked and reward for the just. The narrated setting (space and time) is related to this theme. In addition to Enoch the *dramatis personae* are God and his helpers in the judgement: the elect one, the angels of God and the elect, the righteous and the holy. Also involved as narrated opponents are Azazel, the chief demon, his angels, the kings and the mighty. As a matter of interest it should be noted that Enoch is identified as Son of man in 71:14.

The Astronomical Book

   AB is a treatise on cosmic and astronomical phenomena explaining the laws of operation of the celestial bodies like the sun and moon and a defence of the solar calendar of 364 days (see 75:2). The material is presented in the form of *narrative* (vision) and detailed *description* (see 75:4).

Enoch is taken on a guided tour in the company of the archangel Uriel to secret places like the end of the earth. He is shown the gates through which the sun and moon appear and disappear and much more. An account of what he saw is given to his son Methuselah (79:1). In chapters 80–81 Uriel informs Enoch about the changes that will take place in nature as a consequence of the deeds of the sinners and the coming punishment, and how Enoch blessed the Lord (81:3ff.). Methuselah is instructed to pass the information on to '. . . the generations of eternity' and admonition is given (82).

The Book of dreams

   BD is again addressed to Methuselah (83:1; 85:2) and relates in first person narrative style two of Enoch's visions. The first, concerning the flood and judgement, Enoch saw when he was learning to write, and the second, concerning the history of the world from creation to the messianic kingdom, he saw before he took a wife. The interpretation of the flood as judgement of the Lord in chapter 83 parallels the retelling of this story in chapters 65 and 106–107, as I have mentioned. The prayer in 83:10 is dependent on the angelic prayer in 1 Enoch 9.

The second vision relates in symbolic language the story of the world, that is of Israel, from the appearance (85:3) of the first white bull (Adam) through the coming of the white bull with large horns (the messiah) in chapter 90:37. Animal symbolism dominates the whole narrative. It contains various interesting Jewish traditions about persons and events in the history of Israel (see Klijn 1978; Nickelsburg 1981b:90–94) in which human beings are depicted as animals, the fallen angels as stars, and the seven archangels as human beings. Reality is described as elsewhere in Enoch (see Dn. 7–12) on two levels, '... the earthly realm of history and the heavenly sphere of angelic activity' (Nickelsburg 1981b:93). The book is ended by a description of the emotional state of Enoch (90:41).

The Epistle of Enoch

EE is introduced (91) by a narrative relating how Enoch summoned Methuselah to gather Enoch's wife and children and how he spoke to them about righteousness. In 91:12–17 (see 93) there are reminiscences of the Apocalypse of the weeks in which history is related in 10 weeks of which 7 have already passed. The seventh, the author's own time, is the climax of history and wickedness. 'The plant of righteousness has been pruned to an elect remnant' (Nickelsburg 1981b:146). The eighth is characterized by righteousness, the ninth by judgement, after which the final judgement follows in the tenth week. The Apocalypse of the weeks is *related* in full in chapter 93:1–10.

Chapters 92–105 are composed in the form of a letter ('wisdom teaching') addressed to Enoch's children: '... for all my sons who dwell upon the earth and for the last generations who will practise uprightness and peace' (92:1). As such it is directed to the author's own contemporaries. After a final revelation and instruction from the Lord the readers receive a positive admonition as conclusion to the letter: 'Rejoice, you sons of uprightness! Amen' (105:2).

The body of the letter is carefully structured. It conveys a message of comfort to the readers. They are encouraged not to be in distress about the present situation in which they suffer at the hands of sinners. In the judgement the sinners will be judged by God and the righteous will assist him and be rewarded. The theme of judgement is worked out in the form of the Apocalypse of the weeks (93:1–10), wisdom sayings (93:11–14), woes, exhortations and descriptions of the future.

The rhetoric of the letter is noteworthy. It is a document of persuasion. The reader is appealed to by stereotyped formulae like 'know', 'I say to you', 'I show you', 'I swear to you', 'fear not' (see Nickelsburg 1977b:315f.), and by the presentation of information about the necessity of endurance in present circumstances. Most of the material is organized by way of argument and description which is typical of the letter as argumentative text. In this respect *EE* is different from the other major sections of 1 Enoch. Although the contents are presented from the same perspective, that is apocalyptic eschatology, the material is organized in a different way. This simply illustrates that it is possible to organize apocalyptic material in different text types including narratives and argumentative texts.

Two appendices

1 Enoch is concluded by two narratives. The first concerns the miraculous birth of Noah. The story is told by Enoch about Lamech's amazement concerning the child and Methuselah's voyage to the ends of the earth to consult his father Enoch about the birth. Noah's role in the coming judgement is explained in narrative style by Enoch. It is concluded (107:3) by the return of Methuselah and an explanation of the name of the child, '. . . for he will comfort the earth after all the destruction'.

Chapter 108 tells about another book Enoch wrote for Methuselah '. . . and those who should come after him and keep the law in the last days' (108:1). The book deals with the judgement of the evildoers and vindication of the righteous. It is presented in narrative form with the familiar vision, question and explanation by an angel.

There is little doubt that most of the material in 1 Enoch is organized in narrative style and that except for *EE* each of the major parts function as narrative and should be read as narrative. The only really unique feature of these narratives is the *perspective* from which they are told: the perspective of apocalyptic eschatology. It is furthermore obvious that apocalyptic material can be organized in almost every text type. In 1 Enoch there are examples of narratives, argumentative texts, descriptions, expositions (see the interpretations of angels) and lists (see Stone 1976). All of these are written from an apocalyptic eschatological perspective, which clearly shows that 'apocalyptic' is not a characteristic of genre. The following remark by Collins is not without implication with regard to the so-called apocalyptic genre: 'Enoch 91–104 is . . . an important document for Jewish apocalypticism and apocalyptic eschatology, but it is not in the literary form of an apocalypse' (Collins 1979b:45). It is therefore impossible to regard 1 Enoch 91–104 with Collins (1977:329) as an example of '. . . a group of Jewish writings which are usually recognized as apocalypses'. What is typical about this group of texts is not the *genre* but the code or the sign system of that code. It is in this respect that the results of the *SBL* project can be very helpful.

Texts in which apocalyptic eschatology plays a role characteristically have to do with otherworldly spaces and characters. Events are presented as extraordinary, exotic and miraculous, and use is made of sign systems like numerals, animals, plants, colours, metals, precious stones and so on. Many of these signs are cultural conventions. These codes or signs are used for particular meanings and very often have specific referents outside the narrative world. Unless they can be decoded it is impossible to understand the texts in which they occur. This is clear from the animal apocalypse in 1 Enoch (85ff.). The same is true of Revelation 12.

If one considers the main parts of 1 Enoch individually with a view to genre, the narrative characteristics strike the eye. There are only two text types involved in the main sections of 1 Enoch: narration and argumentation. All but one of the major parts of Enoch are written in narrative style as we have seen. Even *AB* which certainly has a large amount of description is written in the form of narrative and needs to be analyzed as such. With regard to *genre* the following narrative features should be taken into account as characteristics of genre. On the story level: characters, setting, events and plot and on the discourse level, how the story is told, including all aspects of narrative style like narrator, and point of view (see Chatman 1978). Both aspects are important for an understanding of these texts.

It has been mentioned that the greater part of the material in 1 Enoch is presented in the first person. Seen from a literary point of view this is one of various possibilities of presenting narrative material. In the case of autobiographical writings first person narration is common. In our texts, Enoch is presented as a first person narrator who observes events and existents, that is characters, places and time and narrates what he observes from a particular point of view. This is not the place to elaborate on all these aspects except for drawing attention to the fact that these books of Enoch display typical features of narrative texts on the story and discourse level.

The narrative paradigm also offers, to my mind, insight into the problematic distinction between apocalyptic eschatology and the so-called apocalyptic genre. In 'apocalyptic' texts of a narrative, argumentative or of any other character, it is the perspective of apocalyptic eschatology which determines the point of view. Be it judgement, poverty, or whatever theme under discussion, in these texts they are narrated or argued or described or explained or listed from this perspective.

However different the date of writing, place of origin, social and historical setting of the individual books of Enoch, they display the same theological perspective: apocalyptic eschatology. This is important both with regard to the problem under discussion, that is the text type, and the distinction normally made between perspective and text type in the study of these texts. The nucleus narrated in Genesis 5:21–4, amongst others offered the matrix for a series of narrative theologies of crisis. How it started is not the prime interest of this article, but it seems clear that the theology of transcendence (see Collins 1974) arose when theologies of law, wisdom, 'Heilsgeschichte' and so on failed to answer existential problems.

What are the implications of the collection of the individual books into a 'single' work with reference to text type? What is the genre of 1 Enoch?

It is more than clear that the literature attributed to Enoch, as we know these writings from 1 Enoch and Qumran, had undergone a history of growth, transmission and redaction before they were collected into a corpus. Why were they put together and what are the consequences for the genre of 1 Enoch?

In answering the question why the separate books of Enoch were put together, Dimant (1983:29) argues that the biography of Enoch known from Genesis and Jubilees offers the solution: 'Each composition appears to have a distinct biographical reference which decides its place in the corpus. Together the works review the main events in Enoch's life, following the biblical chronology as elaborated by aggadic amplifications'. This would only explain a pre-stage of 1 Enoch since Dimant omits *BP* from the collection on grounds of dating. Such a 'biography' would be classified as 'narrative'. The point is, however, that this hypothesis, like the Pentateuchal theory of Dix and Milik referred to above, does not exactly explain problems of genre. Let us rather return to 1 Enoch.

It is difficult to determine whether chapters 1–5 originally formed part of *BW* or whether they were added at a later stage as an intro-

duction to the complete corpus. In its present form these chapters
serve as an introduction to the complete book and together with the
ending of the book form a narrative framework. Although it would
be difficult to argue that 1 Enoch is a coherent integrated narrative,
there are indications of macro-narrative topics. One should note that
the story of the coming judgement (1 Enoch) is introduced by a
third person narrator who disappears and gives way to the first person narrator Enoch. He sporadically returns to remind the reader
that he is telling the story and also to link parts together. In addition, phenomena like the previews in chapter 33:2–4 (see 72–82),
repetition of themes like judgement and Noah's flood or the recurring of references to the fallen angels, which might be the work of
a redactor, seem to point to attempts at combining the separate parts
into one story. If one would regard the corpus as a macro-text, one
will have to see the individual books of Enoch as sections of a book
which are embedded into a narrative framework. In such a case the
individual books, including *EE*, would be narrated texts in the same
way as descriptions of other smaller units like visions, dialogues and
others which are embedded into a narrative framework, are *narrated*
descriptions, visions and dialogues. The embedding of text types other
than narratives into a narrative framework is a common phenomenon. Seen from this point of view one could regard 1 Enoch as a
narrative.

One can, however, argue that the collection of the major sections
of 1 Enoch into a macrotext is a matter of coincidence. One could
then compare the corpus of Enoch to the New Testament as a collection of books. Despite the relationships between the parts, it is
not possible to see the New Testament as a macro-text in terms of
a single text type. The individual writings belong to different text
types and this will also be the case with 1 Enoch. In this case one
would not speak of the complete text but rather of its parts.

The study of 1 Enoch as part of the Jewish literary setting of the
New Testament also throws light on the text types of New Testament
writings. Does the New Testament offer us an example of the 'apocalyptic' of 'apocalypse' genre?

The common argument, with which I don't agree, is that there
are at least four types of texts or 'Gattungen' in the New Testament:
gospels, a historical monograph, letters and an apocalypse (see
Conzelmann and Lindemann 1975:30ff.). Many smaller forms like
apophthegms, miracle stories and parables are embedded into these

larger 'Gattungen'. Even 'apocalyptic' texts are embedded into larger forms in the New Testament as we have seen above.

Although there are differences of opinion about the genre of the Apocalypse or Revelation of John (see Collins 1977:329), it is normally regarded as an apocalypse on the ground of the features it has in common with 'Jewish apocalypses' (see Collins 1977:330ff.). As a result of his analysis of these features, Collins maintains that '. . . the lack of pseudonymity, *ex eventu* prophecies and the epistolary framework are superficial differences which do not reflect a significant change of perspective'. There is no reason to deny '. . . that the Apocalypse is an apocalypse' (Collins 1977:342). Does this, however, imply that it is an example of a separate text type as far as the New Testament is concerned?

To my mind Revelation is a narrative. Or to be more precise: a narrative presented as a circular letter. Except for the epistolary framework (1:1–8; 22:21) material is organized in narrative style and presented from an apocalyptic eschatological perspective. It is again not the genre as such which is so different from other texts, it is the code, sign system and perspective. Most of the material is presented from the point of view of a first person narrator who observes and relates what he sees. Events and existents are presented from a narrative point of view and the story is made up of mandates (letters) and visions of this and otherworldly places, beings and events. Smaller forms like letters and visions are embedded into the main narrative, which again is embedded into an epistolary framework.

As far as I am concerned then which the material is organized in the form of narratives and those in which argument is the organizing pattern. The gospels, Acts of the apostles and Revelation are narratives, while the letters, including Hebrews, are argumentative texts.

In view of *the way material is organized* in both the books of Enoch and the New Testament especially in the Revelation of John, it seems that 'apocalyptic features' are not constituents or characteristics of genre. They refer to a theological perspective which can be presented in almost any literary form ranging from narrative to lists. This makes it difficult even to classify 'apocalyptic' texts as a sub-genre since the material in a so called 'apocalyptic text' can be arranged in one of the five possible genres mentioned above. When a text is written from an apocalyptic eschatological perspective it will of necessity display certain features, many of which have been listed by the *SBL* group.

Texts which are written from an apocalyptic perspective do not constitute a or text type. Depending on the way the material is organized they belong to different genres (see *BW* in contrast to *EE*). Because of the material they contain, most 'apocalyptic' texts are narratives.

SECTION C
HISTORICAL JESUS

CHAPTER SIXTEEN

JESUS THE GALILEAN

The Gospel of Mark relates us this challenging little episode of Jesus and his disciples who were on their way to the villages of Caesarea Philippi when Jesus asked them (Mk. 8:27–30, *TEV*)

> 'Tell me, who do the people say I am?' 'Some say that you are John the Baptist', they answered; 'others say that you are Elijah, while others say that you are one of the prophets.' 'What about you?' he asked them. 'Who do you say I am?'

> Peter answered, 'You are the Messiah.' Then Jesus ordered them, 'Do not tell anyone about me.'

What followed is known. Even Peter, the closest friend and follower of Jesus apparently had mistaken expectations about Jesus, and according to Mark, did not grasp the significance of what he had just said about the messiaship of Jesus.

After almost twenty centuries of worship, historical study and admiration of Jesus of Nazareth, Christian believers and New Testament scholars alike still grapple with the question: Who was Jesus? This is also the issue I would like to address in this essay. Because of the lack of communication between scholars and the believing community, the diverse points of view which are often taken by scholars on different theological issues, the different theologies which presuppose theological answers given to contemporary social and political problems, and the lack of interaction between lay people and the academic community, there seems to be a yawning gulf between scientific research and the beliefs of the man in the street. I do not pretend that a series of two essays can narrow or even get rid of the schism. But I am convinced that, by taking current research and current beliefs seriously, one can contribute to an understanding of the difficulties and challenges involved in the questions of who Jesus was, what his significance was and, most importantly, what his significance *is* for us today.

I distinguish between 'who Jesus was', and 'what his significance was/is' for the simple reason that who a person is, and what people say or think that person is, are often two totally different things. In the case of Jesus it is even more so.

The first essay deals with two issues. It firstly concerns the question of why there seemingly is confusion, if not total chaos, in the answers given to the question of who Jesus was. I shall secondly give attention to the phrase *Jesus the Galilean* by attempting to situate him in a first-century Galilean historical context. This will on the one hand illustrate the importance of understanding Jesus of Nazareth within the geographical area in which he mostly operated and the historical circumstances under which he lived, and on the other prepare the way for the next essay.

In the second essay I shall develop two possible answers to the question of who Jesus was and also focus on the implications of the points of view that Jesus was either an eschatological prophet or a first-century sage, that is wisdom teacher, or perhaps both. Let me start with the first part of this essay.

1. *Why so Many Answers?*

If I were to ask any lay person, or for that matter any theologian: 'Who was Jesus?' the question would undoubtedly give occasion to a number of different important answers, depending on many things. Some of these answers might even be similar to those reportedly given by the disciples on their way to Caesarea Phillippi. One might say he was the Messiah, while another would argue that he was the Son of God, incarnate. Yet another might maintain that he was the Son of man, and that he will return to judge the sinners and unbelievers at judgement day. It might also be argued that he was the saviour of the world or, in another idiom which is perhaps more familiar today, the liberator of the oppressed. Thus we can continue giving possible answers to the question. A number of these possible answers presuppose church dogma and are formulated from the perspective of the time after the resurrection, while others tend to focus on the time before his death. Or to put it differently: some of these answers relate to his significance for certain people while others focus on who he was when he was on earth.

Some two hundred years ago, in 1778 to be precise, seven fragments of a manuscript in which a scholar of that time had gathered the courage to strip the dogmatic overlayers of the pictures of Jesus painted by the church through the centuries—were published posthumously. I am referring to Reimarus' manuscript 'Concerning the aims of Jesus and his disciples', published by G.E. Lessing. This document, however we might judge it, was the birth of the modern quest for the historical Jesus. Being influenced by the Enlightenment, that is, the eighteenth-century philosophical movement stressing the importance of reason, Reimarus subjected dogmatic beliefs about Jesus, and also the sources from which we know Jesus, to rigorous historical criticism. It soon gave rise to a flood of publications on the question of who Jesus *really* was. Noticing the diffcrences between the Gospels in terms of what Jesus had said and done, scholars came to realise that the Gospels were not history books in the strict modern sense of the word. The differences and agreements were the result of the way in which the Jesus tradition had been transmitted, and the purposes for which the different Gospels had been written. I shall return to this.

For our purpose we will have to take a short cut through two centuries of historical research. During this time critical attempts were made to save the Jesus who once lived in Palestine from the dogmatic, that is, christological, images which the church painted of him, that is, about his humanity and divinity. The phrase 'historical Jesus' was coined to distinguish 'Jesus of Nazareth', the man of flesh and blood, from the 'Christ of faith' of whom we learn in the New Testament, and whose significance was elaborated upon by the church through the ages. What came about is tremendously interesting and fascinating. Researchers' attempts to save the Jesus of history from the dogmas of the church concerning him, resulted in a variety of contemporaneous (that is, eighteenth- and nineteenth-century pictures) of Jesus. For the rationalists he became a preacher of morals, the *idealists* regarded him as the prime example of humanity, the *aesthetes* portrayed him as a genius in the art of rhetoric, while the *socialists* maintained that he was the friend of the poor and a social reformer (see Jeremias 1961:14).

By the end of the nineteenth (Kähler) and beginning of the twentieth (Schweitzer) centuries, at least some scholars argued that, in spite of the admirable motives of their predecessors and fellow New Testament scholars to search for the historical Jesus, one was confronted by the fact that our extant documents were written from the perspective of faith in Jesus, that is, the Christ of faith, and not from the perspective of the historical Jesus. These documents were written long after the events about which they report, and therefore they did not concern the question of who Jesus was, but what his significance was for those who believed in him. It was furthermore asserted that the biblical Christ of faith was what was important for our faith in Jesus, not who he was and what he did. In fact, in certain circles it was even maintained that since it was impossible to go back to the original historical Jesus we would have to satisfy ourselves with the faith of the early Christians about him. As a result for almost half a century there was virtually no quest for the historical Jesus.

Since 1953 there has been renewed interest in the question of who Jesus was, but also into his significance for the early church and for us today. The so-called New Quest has been an attempt to avoid the impression that his humanity was unimportant for faith or that his earthly life was not as important as the fact that he was resurrected. The term 'historical Jesus' also underwent a redefinition and came to be distinguished from the term 'earthly Jesus'. While the former is being used for the historian's answer to the question of who Jesus was, the latter is used with reference to the flesh and blood Jesus who lived in Palestine at the beginning of the first century CE. The main issue was to determine the exact relationship in terms of continuity between the man Jesus who lived on earth, and beliefs about him as the resurrected Christ. What are the historical links between the man of Nazareth and the Christ of faith?

Of particular interest for the purpose of this essay is the renewed interest of scholars in Jesus the Jew. What do we mean when we say that Jesus was a Jew? If we follow the Gospel tradition and say that he was a Jewish teacher, what do we mean by the term 'teacher'? Or a Jewish prophet? Do our sources afford us sufficient material to say what we mean when we call Jesus a Jewish prophet or rabbi? In view of the complex nature of first-century Jewish Palestine, the groups who lived there, the relationships between them, their relationship with the authorities, that is with the Roman rulers, the interaction between Jews and other inhabitants of the country, and so on, these questions are not of academic interest only. In fact, they concern our concept of the past and of Jesus of Nazareth.

In scholarly circles one finds a great variety of images of Jesus the Jew, relating to the different Jewish backgrounds against which the images are located. The following have been proposed by Christian scholars: an eschatological prophet, a political revolutionary, a magician, a Hillelite or proto-Pharisee, an Essene, a Galilean charismatic or a Galilean rabbi. In addition, there are the different Jewish views of Jesus, which add to or complement the variety of views held about his Jewishness. One of the reasons for the many answers to the question of who Jesus was, lies in the lack of sources which would enable us to give a precise description of all the relevant detail. Let us for a moment look at our sources.

I have already referred to the agreements and disagreements between the different Gospels and other documents which report the sayings of Jesus and what he did during his life. This is not the place to deal in detail with the matter, but let us for the sake of illustration return to the Caesarea Philippi incident for a moment. What did Jesus say to his disciples at Caesarea Philippi about carrying their crosses?

> 'If anyone wants to come with me', he told them, 'he must forget self, carry his cross, and follow me' (Mk. 8:35, TEV).

or

> If anyone wants to come with me, he must forget self, take up his cross *everyday* (my italics), and follow me (Lk. 9:23, TEV).

Mark is clearly emphasising that Jesus wanted his followers to be prepared to die for his sake and for the sake of his message. Luke, on the other hand, obviously 'spiritualises' the matter by adding 'every day'. This is just one of the minor, but nevertheless important, differences in wording of the sayings of Jesus, illustrating the fact that the Gospels do not necessarily report the sayings of Jesus *verbatim*. Did he ever have contact with the Samaritans, since only Luke and John report on his visit to Samaria? Why do the travels of Jesus in the Gospel of John differ from those in the other Gospels? How long was his ministry? When was he crucified (see Lk. 24:44 and Jn. 19:31)? Why was Jesus crucified? And, who was finally responsible for his death?

These and many other questions arise when one compares the detail of the different Gospels. They also illustrate one of the problems we have in answering who Jesus was. Our sources, both canonical and extra-canonical, do not answer the question in a clear-cut manner. We may call the Gospels ancient biographies, but like other contemporary ancient biographies, none of the Gospels can be regarded as a life of Jesus where a detailed description is given of his person, life, works and words (see Vorster 1981b). And the same holds good for the extra-canonical material.

In addition to the lack of sources and the difficulties involved in interpreting ancient documents, our knowledge about the past and the culture in which we live also plays a tremendously important part in the formation of our views about Jesus and his significance. I have already referred to the results of the Old Quest. In addition there is the influence of our theological traditions. It has correctly been observed that six so-called salvation events determine theological predispositions, namely the incarnation of Christ, his death and cross, his resurrection on the third day, his ascension, the outpouring of his Spirit at Pentecost, and his second coming or *parousia* (see Bosch 1986:2). Depending on where one puts the emphasis one would have a different theology and a different image of Jesus. Liberation theologians seem to be interested in a Christ who suffers with the oppressed and knows about their agonies and fears, not in a Christ who only offers eternal salvation. They emphasise the incarnation of Jesus. In the reformed tradition (in South Africa at least), the emphasis is strongly on Christ's act of atonement on the cross and eternal salvation. In the place of a suffering Christology one finds a Christology of atonement and eternal salvation. And in many instances even a Christology of victory. And so we can continue (see Bosch 1986:2–6). The influence of all these different views on the question of who Jesus was, and his significance, is obvious. Unless there is tolerance for other views and a willingness to be corrected, Christians will continue to misunderstand each other. The problems are simply implied by the New Testament and its interpretation, and that is why the question of Jesus' identity is so important for us. We tend to misjudge the role that tradition, culture and circumstance plays in our views.

The quest for the historical Jesus concerns our interest in the past and the attempt to understand those who lived in remote times. It also concerns what we think and believe and one should not too easily say that historical problems such as Jesus' identity do not concern us. On the contrary, we are wittingly and unwittingly informed about the past by all sorts of sources that we simply presuppose. That partly explains our current confusion regarding Jesus and his teaching, and our wish to legitimatise a point of view. Let me shortly elaborate on this. I shall illustrate the problem of interpreting who Jesus was by taking two very simple examples from the Gospels as an aid to understanding why different points of view are taken by different theologians who try to argue on the basis of what is found in the New Testament.

My first example is a very simple one, but it nevertheless illustrates a typical problem we are confronted with in our attempts to
say who Jesus was and what he taught. According to Mark 1:17
Jesus called Peter and Andrew and said to them: 'Come with me,
and I will teach you to catch men' (*TEV*). How should we interpret this short metaphorical saying? Did Jesus mean that Peter
and Andrew would become missionaries who would go out and call
people to follow Jesus? Or did he have in mind that they would
become 'fishers of souls', that is, that they would become people
who would gather souls for heaven? It is also possible to argue that
Jesus expected the eschatological judgement of God to come soon
and that he called Peter and Andrew to help him bring home the
people of God without delay (Jeremias 1961:132–133). In what sense
can this saying of Jesus be used in a missionary or evangelism context? The particular interpretation chosen would obviously make a
difference to one's case and how one argues it.

Let us take another example. According to the Gospels Jesus
'cleansed' the temple. But, why would he have done that (Mark
11:15–19 and parallels)? Some interpreters think that the 'cleansing'
refers to prior profanation and that Jesus wanted to purify the temple to fulfil its intended purpose. Others argue that it refers to the
rejection of the Jewish cult by the early church, or that it shows the
power of the resurrected Christ. It is also maintained that the 'cleansing' was a symbolic or prophetic sign which was intended to cause
the repentance of Israel (see Sanders 1985:61–62). Be it as it may,
one thing becomes clear—and that is that our views about who Jesus
was play a significant role in our interpretation of the deeds and
words of Jesus. If we regard Jesus as a religious reformer, we will
argue that the first interpretation (purification) is correct. If we think
that he was an eschatological prophet we might go for the symbolic
interpretation. Let us get a little closer to the problems caused by
present-day views in South Africa about Jesus.

For a variety of good reasons many recent public debates in South
Africa—in which Christian religion and, in particular, Jesus' views
played a role—concentrated on political matters such as violence.
How should we regard the following saying of Jesus with regard to
violence and oppression?

> You have heard that it was said, 'An eye for an eye, and a tooth for
> a tooth.' But now I tell you: do not take revenge on someone who
> wrongs you. If anyone slaps you on the right cheek, let him slap your

left cheek too. And if someone takes you to court to sue you for your
shirt, let him have your coat as well. And if one of the occupation
troops forces you to carry his pack one kilometre, carry it two kilometres . . . (Mt. 5:38–41, TEV).

Is this a plea from the side of Jesus for total submission, passivity
or passive resistance? (See Wink 1987.) Obviously one cannot make
out a case for any of these answers without taking a large amount
of other material into account. But it also underscores the great danger of taking these first-century words out of their context and of
simply applying them to our own complicated situation. Unfortunately
this is what so often happens, at the risk of making illegitimate cultural and religious transfers in order to have Jesus on one's side, so
to speak.

The problem of the historical Jesus teaches us one thing in particular, and that is that Jesus lived in a far distant time in a situation totally different from ours. In spite of all the positive things we
can say about the history of Christian doctrine on Jesus, we also
immediately have to recognise that our views are contaminated by
the distance in time and the minds of men. All theologians and lay
Christian believers can learn one thing from the historical Jesus problem, which is that their views on who Jesus is or was are their own.
Unless these views are scrutinised by rigorous historical criticism they
are nothing more than modern men's images of Jesus. It is only in
a context of interaction and negotiation that we can work out probable answers to who Jesus was and what his views were on particular issues of his time.

Let me summarise. Because of the nature of our sources about
Jesus—the fact that they are limited, that they lived in a totally
different time and culture from our—own and the fact that we stand
in a particular tradition, there is a great need for us to get to know
the past better and to be moderate and tolerant in our views about
Jesus and his significance for today. This is one of a number of reasons why there is such a lively interest in who Jesus was in New
Testament scholarship today. Having clarified the problem, in the
next part of the essay I will concentrate on the phrase *Jesus the
Galilean*, in order to place Jesus in a possible historical context.

2. *Jesus the Galilean*

New Testament scholars agree about a relatively small number of so-called 'facts' in the life of Jesus. The following are taken as indisputable: (1) Jesus was baptised by John the Baptist. (2) He was a Galilean who preached and healed. (3) He called disciples and spoke of there being twelve. (4) He confined his activity to Israel. (5) He engaged in a controversy about the temple. (6) He was crucified outside Jerusalem by Jewish authorities. (7) After his death his followers continued as an identifiable movement. (8) At least some Jews persecuted parts of the new movement, and it appears that this persecution endured at least to a time near the end of Jesus' career (see Sanders 1985:11).

We have already noted that there is no such thing as a bare fact in the history of Jesus research. Even the indisputable facts have to be interpreted. So, if we say that Jesus was a Galilean who preached and healed, we at least have to say what we mean by 'Galilean', 'preaching' and 'healing' in first-century Palestine. We shall, however, for the purpose of this essay concentrate on 'Jesus the Galilean'. Time and space do not allow us to go into detail, but a few remarks are necessary. I shall concentrate on the territory, its inhabitants, the relationship between urban and rural Galilee, and the social situation of Galilee in the time of Jesus.

The general picture of Jesus and his first followers is one of a group of rural, illiterate people who travelled around in Galilee while Jesus preached and healed people. Since the geographical environment of people helps to shape their identity, it is necessary to know what Galilee refers to and who inhabited the area, to test the validity of such a supposition.

The term 'Galilee' means 'circle', which refers to the geographical shape of the area it covers. In the time of Jesus it consisted of Upper and Lower Galilee in the north and south respectively, and the Valley running along the Jordan. As in the rest of Palestine, there is a coastal strip between the Mediterranean Sea and the central hilly area, with a valley on the Eastern side along the Jordan River, north and south of the Sea of Galilee. Galilee is characterised by its mountain ranges and fertile valleys. Unlike other parts of the country, Galilee had a substantial rainfall, making it an important agricultural area, the most productive region of the country. It produced most of the produce used in the ancient world. In addition

to wheat and grain, the vine and the olive grew in abundance. From
ancient export catalogues we know of items such as grain, oil, wine,
different kinds of vegetables and herbs that were exported from
Galilee and Syria to Egypt (see Freyne 1980:172). Because of its
location, the network of roads, and the closeness to the ports of
Sidon, Tyre and Ptolemais, Galilee was one of the most important
importers and exporters in the Near East.

The fishing and glass industry were the two most developed in-
dustries in Galilee. Fishing rights on the shores of the Sea of Galilee
were farmed out at a high price, and methods of preservation and
marketing were developed to improve export (Freyne 1980:174). The
glass-making industry was developed in Hellenistic times (first century BCE). The plain of Acco on the border of Galilee provided the
raw material for the glass (Freyne 1980:175).

It is remarkable that the ministry of Jesus is related to villages
such as Nazareth, Capernaum and others, while large cities such as
Sepphoris and Scythopolis are not mentioned. One should not infer
from the absence of any mention of these cities in the New Testament
that there were no large cities at that time, or that Jesus and his
followers were unacquainted with urban life and practices. Sepphoris,
Tiberias and Scythopolis were within walking distance of Nazareth
and Capernaum. In fact, Sepphoris was less than five kilometres from
Nazareth, where Jesus spent his youth and learnt to be a carpenter.
Before we come to urbanisation and the social status of people in
the region, let us pay attention to the people who lived in Galilee.

Galilee was known as 'Galilee of the Gentiles' (see 1 Macc. 5:15)
in the second century BCE, thus expressing the feelings of the Jews
who lived there. This remained the situation for many centuries.
When Alexander the Great, a Greek from Macedonia, defeated
Darius, king of the Persians, and his armies at Issus in 333, Galilee
was still part of the Orient. The situation was soon changed when
a successor of Alexander, namely Ptolemy I of Egypt, conquered
Palestine and the country became part and parcel of the Hellenistic
world. Occupation forces settled in the country, including in Galilee,
land ownership changed and the people of Israel were subjected to
the influences of the Greek way of life. Many of the Jews, especially
members of the urban upper class—including members of the priest-
hood of the temple—supported Hellenisation. There was, however,
a large number who rejected, and even fought against any form of
Hellenisation. From then on until the middle of the first century

BCE, when the Romans conquered Palestine in 63, the region was unstable and there were constant uprising and unrest. The influential Jewish Maccabean family (the Hasmoneans) led the revolt against the oppressors when Antiochus Epiphanes IV, the Seleucid King of Syria tyrannically suppressed Judaism and profaned the temple in Jerusalem. During the period 167–63 BCE the country was ruled by the Maccabees. They repossessed a great part of the country, including the greater part of Jerusalem. During that period Sepphoris was the administrative centre in Galilee. In 63 BCE Pompey's legions captured Jerusalem and Palestine became part of the Roman empire (see Freyne 1980:22ff.).

Jewish settlement in Galilee followed the Maccabean revolt in 164. Pompey, however, recaptured many of the cities and incorporated them into the Roman administration. Herod the Great made Galilee and Perea part of the Roman province of Judea but, after his death, Galilee and Perea became part of the tetrarchy of Herod Antipas.

By this time Galilee was greatly Hellenised, both politically and socially. The region was ruled and administered in a Roman manner, including trade, tax and infrastructure. Although Aramaic, the lingua franca of the Persian Empire, was still spoken by most Jews, and Hebrew was probably still in use, Greek was the language used in the market-place. It can be assumed that most Jews, including Jesus and his followers, were to a greater or lesser extent bilingual, and could also speak Greek. Latin was the language of the rulers and the military but in most cases these people could also speak Greek and knew the Greek way of life. Galilee was correctly referred to as Galilee of the Gentiles. The region was inhabited by others beside the Jews and these Jews were no longer free from the influences of a cosmopolitan society even though some of them rejected the Hellenistic way of life. Obviously it was socially, economically and politically that the Jews of Galilee were most influenced in the Hellenistic period. They were allowed to practice their religion and worship their God.

One of the aspects which greatly influences one's image of Jesus and his first followers is the relationship between the cities and the smaller villages and towns. Although it is almost impossible to say what the exact relationship would have been between Sepphoris and Nazareth, for instance, one can get a rough picture of the influences that cities in the days of Jesus had on the general population of Galilee.

According to the Jewish contemporary historian, Josephus (*Vit.* 45:235), who also was a leader of a revolt in Galilee against Rome in 66 CE, there were no less than two hundred and four villages in the whole of Galilee. This is quite a number for a region as small in size as Galilee. Capernaum apparently was a large village with a population of ten to twelve thousand (see Overman 1988:162). It was a fishing village similar to other villages on the shore of the Sea of Galilee. The towns and villages which Jesus visited according to the New Testament are all within walking distance, and in the proximity of large cities. This was made possible by the network of roads and routes which were necessary for trade.

One of the most important cities was the capital of Galilee, namely Sepphoris. According to Josephus (*Vita* 45:231, 239 who is one of our main informants in this regard, it was the largest city in Galilee, and the seat of the royal bank and archives. Archaeological evidence furthermore shows that 'there were courts, a fortress, a theatre seating three to four thousand people, a palace, a colonnaded street on top of the acropolis, two city walls, two markets (upper and lower) . . . and the arsenal' (see Overman 1988:164). In addition there were cities such as Scythopolis and Tiberias with similar building constructions and features of ancient cities, such as water systems and aqueducts. In Magdala (Tariceae), a city with a population of forty thousand (Josephus, *BJ* 2:608), there was even a hippodrome, or an arena.

When and how often Jesus and his followers visited these cities is not known. What is, however, clear from the urban imagery of the Gospels and specifically the teaching of Jesus, is that they were acquainted with city life. Overman is correct in saying that: 'One could not live in any village in lower Galilee and escape the effects and the ramifications of urbanization. . . . These lower Galilean cities functioned as regional centers of Roman power and culture and would have been unavoidable in this small area in terms of their influence and impact' (Overman 1988:165).

Although the Gospels depict the activities of Jesus in the region of Sepphoris, that is, the villages of Nazareth, Cana and Nain, and the area of the western shore of the Sea of Galilee, these activities presuppose a setting which includes urban centres as an integral part. In his teaching Jesus refers to courts, the market-place, financial investment which earns interest, the absence of a landlord, images which indicate that he was familiar with city life. One also has to

remember that agriculture 'in the Roman empire was intimately connected with urban environments' (D.R. Edwards 1988:170) and that
commerce made the movements of Jesus to the coastal area of Sidon
and Tyre, the villages of Caesarea Philippi and the cities of the
Decapolis, possible. It was in an environment of cities that Jesus
operated because of the market and commercial networks. Import
and export networks also played a role.

> The broad sweep of Galilee's import network is indicated by a host
> of items including Babylonian beer, medium beer, Egyptian barley
> beer, smoked fish/lentils from Egypt, cheese from Bythinia, mackerel
> from Spain, wines, asses from Lydia, purple dye from Tyre, jewelry
> from Egypt (as well as parchment and papyrus) (Edwards 1988:175).

It is within this context that we have to imagine the activities of
Jesus. The specific rural and agricultural aspects of his activities and
teaching are embedded into the highly urbanised and commercial
setting of Galilee in the first century CE. Jesus was not unaware of
the people who lived in the cities and who administered the country.
Other important matters are how society was structured and who
played which roles.

In the Gospel tradition the peasants made up the bulk of the population. They were obviously of the lower class. Like the peasants,
the artisan class (of which Jesus, Paul, and the fishermen were members) was also part of the lower class who lacked power. They were
not indigent, but as a class in society they did not have power and
influence except in their own circles (see Saldarini 1988:201). The
poor, and the bandits (some of whom lived in caves in the moun-
tainous areas of Galilee), also belonged to this group of society.

The governing class was very small. According to Saldarini (1988:
200) perhaps one to two percent of the population formed part of
this upper class. It was made up of both hereditary aristocrats and
appointed bureaucrats (Saldarini 1988:200). They owned the land
and controlled the political power and wealth in the region. Through
taxation, confiscation, and the selling of offices they acquired wealth
and influence. Another important group in the society was the so-called
retainer class:

> The *retainer class*, perhaps 5% of the population, served the needs of
> the ruler and the governing class. To some extent they shared in the
> life of the elite, but not in its direct power. Soldiers, bureaucratic
> government officials, various kinds of servants, religious leaders, and

educators were all necessary for the functioning of society, and as a group they had a great impact on society and culture (Saldarini 1988:201).

The most important people in this group for our purpose are the Pharisees and the scribes. We get to know them as religious opponents of Jesus in the Gospels and tend to forget that we do not know exactly how the Pharisees earned their daily bread. That is why we think of them only in their roles as religious leaders. But how did Jesus and his followers experience them as members of the retainer group in society, serving the interests of the upper class? The scribes were obviously people of learning who could read and write and would have been archivists, secretaries, and so on in the administration of the Roman Empire.

This is not the place to go into a detailed analysis of possible conflict concerning power between the upper and the lower classes. It is difficult to say exactly how revolutionary Galilee was at the time of Jesus because of the lack of evidence, and because any information about the revolutionary situation before the Jewish/Roman War is read into the period (e.g. for that concerning the Zealots, see Horsley 1988:184). Obviously there would have been tension (see Freyne 1980:208ff.). Perhaps economic pressure and the problem of foreign rulers could have given rise to messianic and apocalyptic hopes among the lower class. Evidence, however, is lacking. It is nevertheless possible that Jesus of Nazareth could have been *understood* as an opponent of the *status quo*, not to speak of as a rebel. Whatever the historical value of the Caesarea Philippi event, it is possible that some of his followers would have seen him as a messianic figure. The fact that he specifically mixed with the lower class and preached his message to them, makes it possible that, even though it was not necessarily his intention, some would have regarded him as a leader of the have-nots.

The peasants and the fishermen alike were heavily taxed. In addition to the secular tax they had to pay to the state they were also obliged to pay a religious tax since tithing was regarded as compulsory. One can even talk of a 'rural proletariat'. This is clear from the Gospels where we read of day labourers (Mt. 20:1–16), hired servants (Mk. 1:20), vineyard workers (Mk. 12:1–10), beggars (Lk. 16:6), and fishermen who worked all night without success (Lk. 5:11).

The foregoing gives us a rough picture of the situation in which Jesus operated. It is too early to answer the question of who Jesus

was. However, we can already place him within a concrete historical situation, namely that of Galilee of the early first century. Being
a member of the lower class of a society who had to labour for their
daily bread in the most beautiful part of Palestine, somebody who
had an openness towards the sufferings of the majority of the people, and a religious Jew with a message, he could have been interpreted from many different perspectives by his followers and his
contemporaries, as well as by the members of the upper class and
the retainer class when they became aware of his activities and what
he had to say. He also must have been well informed as far as other
persons with 'a message' in Galilee were concerned. As in other
places in the Hellenistic world there were many different people,
each with their own philosophy of life. Whether he had heard popular philosophers and itinerant teachers is not known, but it is possible. In any case the picture of Jesus and his early followers as a
group of rural, and perhaps even uninformed people, seems to me
improbable. It has become clear that they must have been subjected
to and informed by the situation in which they lived—that is, a small
region, fifty by twenty four kilometres in size, with a highly developed system of trade and commerce.

In the next essay I shall continue my construction of Jesus the
Galilean and concentrate on the two possible images: Jesus the eschatological prophet and Jesus the Jewish sage.

CHAPTER SEVENTEEN

JESUS: ESCHATOLOGICAL PROPHET
AND/OR WISDOM TEACHER?

In a previous essay on the question of Jesus' identity (*Jesus the Galilean*, Chapter Seventeen in this volume), I concentrated on the reasons for the apparent confusion in the answers to the question, and also paid attention to the phrase *Jesus the Galilean*. It was an attempt to draw attention to the difficulties involved in trying to answer the question of who Jesus was, and indicate the importance of finding an answer to the question within a first-century Palestinian context. I underscored the need for rigorous historical investigation and an awareness that historical criticism always involves construction of images. In fact, I asserted that the historical Jesus problem teaches us that our views on who Jesus was or, for that matter, who he is, are based on different assumptions and convictions.

This essay deals with three possible answers to the question of who Jesus was. I will discuss the question of whether Jesus was an eschatological prophet, a wisdom teacher, or perhaps both. It is an attempt to get to grips with the different images of Jesus which currently dominate New Testament scholarship. These images are forced upon us by the New Testament as well as by the results of New Testament scholarship. I would furthermore like to emphasise the fact that there are currently other images defended by scholars, such as the liberator of the oppressed, a revolutionary and so on. To my mind, however, both the state of scholarship and the images of Jesus in the ancient sources at our disposal make it necessary for us to take seriously the images of prophet and teacher. The implications of viewing Jesus as eschatological prophet and/or wisdom teacher will become clear by the end of this essay.

I will first, at some length, discuss some of the reasons why there are currently two opposing images of Jesus among New Testament scholars, namely the images of Jesus as an eschatological prophet or a wisdom teacher. These two images will then be discussed separately in the next two sections of my essay. In the end an answer will have to be given to the question of whether it is necessary to

put the images in opposition. An attempt will be made to deal with
these matters within the context of first-century Palestine and not
simply within the framework of twentieth-century thought.

1. *Why Two Opposing Images?*

One of the main reasons for the opposing views on Jesus' identity,
is that the *nature of our sources* on Jesus makes it possible to have
different views. The Gospels are our main sources. These documents
were written forty or more years after the death and resurrection of
Jesus, and they are in no way to be viewed as history books in the
modern sense of the word. No single Gospel gives us a historical
account of the life and works of Jesus in an exact, chronological and
word-for-word manner.

Until the beginning of this century it was thought that Mark's
Gospel was the oldest of the four, and that it gave us a reliable picture of who Jesus was. It became clear, however, that the Gospel
of Mark, like the other Gospels, had given us an image of Jesus constructed by its author for a specific audience in a specific situation
and for a specific purpose, even though he made use of traditional
material. Mark did not invent all the material he used in writing his
Gospel. On the contrary, he made use of sayings of Jesus, stories
about him and the things he did, but he cast this material into *his*
story of Jesus in order to communicate something about Jesus to his
audience. He also invented some of the material he wrote about
Jesus and ascribed it to Jesus. In this manner he created an image
of Jesus to fit his own purpose and needs. The same holds true for
the authors of the other Gospels who, like Mark, told their stories
about Jesus from a post-resurrection perspective for their own purposes.

The Gospels presuppose a history of growth and a process of
transmission of material about Jesus, his life, the things he did and
said. How the making of the Gospels exactly took place is not altogether clear. Whether Mark, for example, had all sorts of written
material at his disposal and whether he compiled his story from this
by including some and omitting other material is not known. It is
normally thought that he relied greatly on oral tradition about Jesus,
and that his Gospel grew out of this source. Be that as it may, for
our purpose it is necessary to keep in mind that the image of Jesus
of the Gospel in Mark is Mark's image, and that he used the works

and sayings of Jesus to create that image. Some of the sayings and deeds which we find in the Gospels are not authentic. They were ascribed to Jesus by early Christians who did not entertain the fears we do concerning historical 'correctness'. These people used the material about Jesus to inform others about his significance and not about the historical question of his exact identity. This explains why they changed some of his sayings and used others in totally different contexts.

In addition, one also has to keep in mind the relationship between the Gospels of Matthew, Mark and Luke, often referred to as the synoptic problem. These Gospels are called synoptic, that is, 'seeing together', because they are so similar. They tell the story of Jesus to a large extent in the same sequence, and with a great similarity in wording. These similarities are normally explained by literary dependence. One author copied from another, and used the material for his own story. There is, nevertheless, a substantial amount of material which cannot be explained in this way. Matthew and Luke have a lot of material in common, which does not appear in Mark. If Mark's Gospel is the oldest of the three, and if Matthew and Luke used Mark, as is often argued, they must have made use of a common source consisting mainly of the sayings of Jesus, as well as of other sources at their disposal. This is called the two-source hypothesis. It may be schematised as follows:

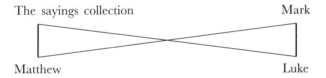

This process of the formation of the Gospels is important for historical construction of who Jesus was. If we take into account the hypothetical 'Sayings collection', normally called Q—from the German word 'Quelle', the equivalent for 'source'—we have at least four broad images of Jesus. Q leaves the impression that Jesus was a teacher, a speaker of aphorisms—that is, pithy sayings expressing general truths—while Mark, for example, who also lays emphasis on Jesus as a teacher, portrays Jesus as the suffering Son of God. So, who was Jesus?

The question becomes far more challenging when we notice that

the certain sayings of Jesus are given in different contexts and that
the same material is used for different purposes by the authors of
our sources. Even the Lord's Prayer is given in two versions in
Matthew and Luke. This means that the Jesus tradition was used
and interpreted after his death in different contexts for different purposes, and also that the present-day historian has to interpret this
material very carefully to construct an image of Jesus. It implies that
the images we get of him from the tradition as we find it in the
Gospels, can be different from the Jesus who once walked the earth.
Jesus the Galilean need not necessarily have been the apocalyptic figure that Mark portrays (see Mack 1987).

In addition to the difficulties caused by the nature of our sources,
there also is the history of interpretation of these sources which has
its own implications for answering who Jesus was. For almost a century Jesus has been interpreted within the framework of Jewish eschatology and apocalyptic (see Perrin 1963). Both his teaching and who
he was came to be seen within the framework of the expectation of
the end of the world, the last judgement, the resurrection and his
second coming or parousia.

In many circles, if not in most, the eschatological interpretation
of the teaching of Jesus and of Jesus as an eschatological prophet
became dominant. During recent times a growing number of scholars, especially in the United States, however, have started questioning the eschatological framework in which Jesus and his teaching
have been placed during the twentieth century (see Borg 1986 and
Mack 1987). It has been argued that the idea of apocalyptic eschatology in the teaching of Jesus was a later development in the Jesus
tradition, and that Jesus himself was probably more of a sage than
an eschatological prophet. A new frame of understanding is developing, making it clear that it is possible to conceive of Jesus as a
wisdom teacher in non-eschatological terms. The Jesus tradition lends
itself to both interpretations and it remains to be argued which is
the more authentic in terms of the earthly Jesus. Let us briefly pay
attention to a few of Jesus' sayings in this regard, to illustrate how
his teaching can be interpreted within an eschatological or a wisdom framework.

The so-called Beatitudes of Jesus are well attested (see Mt. 5:3–11
and Lk. 6:20–23) and are normally regarded as part of the authentic sayings of Jesus—not necessarily in their present number and
form, but in general. Matthew's version reads as follows (*TEV*):

Happy are those who know they are spiritually poor;
The Kingdom of heaven belongs to them!

Happy are those who mourn;
God will comfort them!

Happy are those who are humble;
they will receive what God has promised!

Happy are those whose greatest desire is to do what God requires;
God will satisfy them fully!

Happy are those who are merciful to others;
God will be merciful to them!

Happy are the pure in heart;
they will see God!

Happy are those who work for peace;
God will call them his children!

Happy are those who are persecuted
because they do what God requires;
the Kingdom of heaven belongs to them!

Happy are you when people insult you and persecute you and tell all kinds of evil lies against you because you are my followers. Be happy and glad, for a great reward is kept for you in heaven. This is how the prophets who lived before you were persecuted.

How should we interpret these sayings? Are they apocalyptic blessings or conditions for entering the kingdom (see Guelich 1976)? If we take the term 'kingdom of heaven', which is the Matthean expression for 'kingdom of God', to refer to the apocalyptic reign of God and the coming of a new world, these sayings should be regarded as *apocalyptic blessings*. The poor, the humble and those of similar status will be blessed by God when the new world starts. The roles will be overturned as Luke says. Those who are happy will be those who are sad! But is it necessary to interpret these sayings from an apocalyptic perspective? Should they not rather be interpreted as *general truths* in kingdom terminology? Think of the Old Testament Proverbs where we have the proverbs and maxims of a sage comparable to the Beatitudes. Did Jesus not attempt to bring about a revolution in values among people who were distressed and oppressed? Will the peacemakers not be those who take upon themselves the task of the ruling class who normally bring about peace? Did he not try to create a new frame of reference, a new value system, by expressing his views in terms of practical skills to cope with life? If so, these sayings of Jesus could be interpreted as the sayings of a sage and not necessarily as apocalyptic blessings.

The Beatitudes are but one of many examples of how it is possible to interpret the sayings tradition of Jesus within a wisdom framework and not an apocalyptic, eschatological one. This simply implies that it is possible to interpret the Jesus tradition in ways that differ from the current dominating prophetic eschatological manner. But we are not ready to argue a case for or against an eschatological or a wisdom image of Jesus. Let us now consider the two images separately.

2. Jesus the Eschatological Prophet

According to the New Testament, Jesus was viewed by some as a prophet (Mt. 21:11; Jn. 4:19; 9:17; see Mk. 8:28). With reference to himself Jesus said: 'A prophet is respected everywhere except in his home town and by his own family' (Mt. 13:57 TEV).

He started his career by being baptised by, and becoming a follower of John the Baptist, who was an apocalyptic prophet. According to Mark (1:14–15), he then set off to *preach* the gospel in Galilee. His teaching contains sayings which are comparable to the sayings of prophets. Like the prophets of old he made statements about current situations, he preached and made known the will of God. According to the synoptics he predicted future events (see Mk. 13 par) and behaved like a prophet. This and many other reasons explain why scholars often argue that Jesus was probably an eschatological prophet, who proclaimed the imminent coming of the kingdom (see Hengel 1981; Sanders 1985).

Since there is general agreement about the central place of the kingdom of God in the teaching of Jesus, and also that eschatology and apocalyptic were dominant features of Jewish thought in the time of Jesus, New Testament scholars have accepted the eschatological nature of the teaching of Jesus as an axiom, and Jesus has been conceptualised in terms of a Jewish eschatological or apocalyptic prophet for the past hundred years. It simply means that Jesus was seen as somebody who understood his ministry in terms of Jewish eschatological expectations, in fact as *the* eschatological prophet.

Eschatology has to do with the last things, that is, the end of the world, death, afterlife, a new world and so on. Although the term is not used consistently by biblical scholars, and in the case of Jesus is often used synonymously with apocalyptic, one should not get the impression that there was only one eschatological or apocalyptic view in the time of Jesus. For our purpose we will use the term eschatology in this essay to refer to the Jewish expectation that the world will come to an end, including the last judgement, resurrection, and dawn of a new age (see Borg 1986:81).

'Prophet' is used in the sense of somebody who is regarded or who sees him/herself as a person who serves as a means of communication between the divine and the human worlds (Wilson 1985: 826). Prophetism concerns the past, present and the future, and prophets express themselves about all three these aspects of time. Being an eschatological prophet therefore means being informed about the past, present and future with relation to the will and plans of God. In order to understand the image of Jesus as an eschatological prophet, it is necessary to rehearse briefly the history of interpretation of Jesus within an eschatological, apocalyptic framework.

Before the publication of the epoch-making book of Johann Weiss on the preaching of Jesus on the kingdom of God, the kingdom was explained solely on ethical grounds. According to Ritschl, Jesus 'saw in the Kingdom of God the moral task to be carried out by the human race' (see Perrin 1963:16). Weiss severely criticised these views and argued that Jesus was convinced that he was standing at the end of the world and the end of history, and that the judgement was at hand. The kingdom of God was an apocalyptic concept, according to him; it was a future event which was on the verge of coming.

It was, however, the renowned Albert Schweitzer who interpreted and propagated some of these ideas of Weiss, and who challenged nineteenth-century research into the historical Jesus by focusing on the imminence of the kingdom of God.

Schweitzer believed that the whole life, work and teaching of Jesus was dominated by his expectation of the end of the world as we find it in Jewish apocalyptic. This expectation influenced Jesus' ethical teaching, which Schweitzer called 'interim-ethics'. It means that the ethics of Jesus were valid only for the period before the coming of the final end, a sign of real repentance. Building his arguments on the mission of the disciples in Matthew 10 and sayings such as: 'I tell you there are some here who will not die until they have seen the Kingdom of God come with power' (*TEV*) Schweitzer came to the conclusion that the failure of the kingdom to arrive caused a turning point in the life of Jesus. He did not expect his disciples back before the coming of the kingdom, but when this did not happen, he changed his mind. Jesus decided to hasten the sufferings of which we read in Matthew 10, and deliberately went to Jerusalem to provoke the authorities to kill him so that he could be transformed into the eschatological Son of man by the intervention of God (see Perrin 1963:31).

Subsequent research rejected many of Schweitzer's arguments, especially Jesus' change of mind, but retained the conceptual model of eschatology or apocalyptic. Because of the ambiguity in the Jesus tradition concerning the present and the future aspects of the kingdom, different explanations were devised of which the so-called 'realised eschatology' model of the British scholar C.H. Dodd is the most influential.

Dodd accepted the general consensus that the 'kingdom of God' was an apocalyptic concept. He, however, asserted that for Jesus the kingdom was present in his own ministry, thus realised. He also argued that those sayings which refer to the future coming of the kingdom do not refer to a future coming in this world, since it has already fully arrived in the ministry of Jesus; they refer to something beyond time and space as an ultimate fulfilment in a world beyond this one (see Perrin 1963:58).

Many scholars after Dodd paid attention to the present and future aspects of the kingdom of God and consensus started growing concerning the arrival of the kingdom in the ministry of Jesus. In this way a hermeneutical framework—that is, a framework of understanding—came into being both by interpreting the Jesus tradition in terms of Jewish expectations of the end of the world, and by consensus among scholars. Jesus and the early Christians were seen as people who expected the end of the world soon.

The important point I would like to emphasise for our purpose is the fact that scholars reached agreement on the *frame of reference* within which the Jesus tradition had and has to be interpreted. Almost everything that he said and did has to be interpreted within this frame of reference. Let us, however, take the matter a little further.

One of the most thorough interpretations of Jesus as an eschatological prophet in recent times is that of Sanders, to whom I referred in my previous essay (see Sanders 1985). He argues that Jesus (and his disciples) expected the coming of the kingdom in the near future and also that they would play an important role in the kingdom (Sanders 1985:118). He built his case on a thorough interpretation of aspects of the expectation of the restoration of Israel in the ministry of Jesus.

He starts his argument with an analysis of Jesus and the temple. According to him the cleansing of the temple should be interpreted as a symbolic act signifying the destruction of the temple. But destruction obviously points to restoration, which is confirmed by the sayings of Jesus on the destruction of the temple. 'He [Jesus] intended . . . to indicate that the end was at hand and that the temple would be destroyed, so that the new and perfect temple might arise' (Sanders 1985:75). In other words, Jesus proclaimed the restoration of the temple and of Israel. Like the prophets of old he proclaimed the plan of God, destruction and restoration. It is this thesis that forms the backbone of Sanders's study.

Turning to other indications of restoration eschatology Sanders argues that Jesus first became a follower of John the Baptist who was an eschatological prophet. He, however, saw his own ministry as being the proclamation of the kingdom 'which, it would appear, he regarded as the next final step in God's plan of redemption', and saw himself as engaged in the final act of history (Sanders 1985:93). The Twelve also point to Jesus' understanding of his task as including the restoration of Israel. Although national repentance and judgement do not play such a significant role in his teaching, there is some indication that Jesus fits well in the role of a prophet with the eschatological expectation of the restoration of Israel.

Sanders (1985:124) is convinced that the distinctiveness of the first-century world-view is that it was eschatological, in the apocalyptic sense of the word, and that Jesus shared this view. He accordingly interprets the theme of the kingdom of God in the teaching of Jesus with respect to this world-view. The term refers to the ruling power of God (Sanders 1985:126), and is used in the teaching of Jesus referring both to the present and to the future. This major problem of New Testament interpretation is solved differently by scholars. For Sanders the emphasis is in the end on the future coming of the kingdom. Jesus expected the kingdom in the immediate future (Sanders 1985:152).

In short, most of what we know about Jesus makes one think that he fits well into the role of a prophet of restoration according to Sanders (1985:222). John the Baptist called on the whole of Israel

to repent before the coming judgement and Jesus started his career
as a follower of John. Jesus called twelve disciples which points to
the restoration of Israel. In accordance with the Jewish expectation
of restoration Jesus expected the temple to be destroyed and restored.
And after his death and resurrection the disciples worked within such
a framework.

It is undoubtedly possible that Jesus was an eschatological prophet,
in first-century Galilee. The Jewish historian, Josephus, witnesses to
this fact (see Feldman 1988 and also Hengel 1981). Whether he was
in fact such a prophet is another matter. Sanders's study is obviously directly influenced by the Jewish eschatological framework into
which he fits Jesus. His arguments are directed by this model of
interpretation. And within this framework his image of Jesus as an
eschatological prophet makes sense. The question therefore remains:
How valid is this framework?

3. *Jesus the Wisdom Teacher*

I have noted above that the eschatological framework into which
Jesus and his teaching have been fitted during the past century has
been called into question in the recent past on several grounds. In
this section I shall pay attention to the possibility of viewing Jesus
as a sage or a teacher of wisdom in first-century Palestine.

There are many indications in the synoptics that Jesus was regarded
as a teacher. According to Mark (4:38 *et al.*), one of his main activities was to teach the disciples and other people. Mark says that people regarded his teaching as 'new' and that it amazed them (Mk.
1:27; see Mt. 7:28; 22:33 *et al.*). His disciples called him 'teacher'
(Mt. 8:19 *et al.*) and his teaching was put into long speeches by the
authors of the Gospels (see Mt. 5ff.). Our sources tell us that he
taught in synagogues (Mt. 4:23 *et al.*), at the sea shore (Mk. 4:1) and
in many other places, giving the impression that he was an itinerant
teacher. He was, however, also called 'rabbi' (Mk. 9:5 *et al.*) and the
question immediately arises as to what kind of teacher he was. This
is not a simple question and we will have to consider it thoroughly.

The synoptic tradition does not tell us that Jesus taught in a school
or that he had a regular group, except for the disciples, whom he
educated. Therefore we have to go to the form and content of his
teaching to see whether we can in any way discern what kind of
teacher he was.

The teaching of Jesus, as we have it in the Gospels, consists of his sayings, which are given on their own sometimes in groups, embedded in short stories, dialogues and longer speeches. An important part of the sayings material consists of parables, proverbs, metaphors and so on. In short, a great deal of Jesus' teaching was done in aphoristic form—short pithy sayings—expressing a general truth, as I have said above, and embedded in different contexts. Consider the following (Mt. 6:19–34, *TEV*):

> Do not store up riches for yourselves here on earth, where moths and rust destroy, and robbers break in and steal. Instead, store up riches for yourselves in heaven, where moths and rust cannot break in and steal. For your heart will always be where your riches are.

> The eyes are a lamp for the body. If your eyes are sound, your whole body will be full of light; but if your eyes are no good, your body will be in darkness. So if the light in you is darkness, how terribly dark it will be!

> No one can be a slave of two masters; he will hate one and love the other; he will be loyal to one and despise the other. You cannot serve both God and money. This is why I tell you not to be worried about the food and drink you need in order to stay alive, or about clothes for your body. After all, isn't life worth more than food? And isn't the body worth more than clothes? Look at the birds flying around: they do not sow seeds, gather a harvest and put it in barns; yet your father in heaven takes care of them! Aren't you worth much more than birds? Can any of you live a bit longer by worrying about it? And why worry about clothes? Look how the wild flowers grow: they do not work or make clothes for themselves. But I tell you that not even King Solomon with all his wealth had clothes as beautiful as one of these flowers. It is God who clothes the wild grass—grass that is here today and gone tomorrow, burnt up in the oven. Won't he be all the more sure to clothe you? How little faith you have! So do not start worrying: 'Where will my food come from? or my drink? or my clothes?' (These are the things the pagans are always concerned about.) Your Father in heaven knows that you need all these things. Instead, be concerned above everything else with the Kingdom of God and what he requires of you, and he will provide you with all these other things. So do not worry about tomorrow; it will have enough worries of its own. There is no need to add to the troubles each day brings.

Examples of this type of aphoristic teaching of Jesus can be multiplied. They give the impression that they were given by somebody who was able to offer instruction about practical skills to cope with different situations in life. The sayings of Jesus often contain values for ethical conduct and the pursuit of a lifestyle which is worth following. That is why it is necessary to determine what kind of teacher would have given such instruction.

The aphoristic nature of the teaching of Jesus reminds one of the Proverbs of the Old Testament and other wisdom texts. Wisdom, however, refers to many things and before we draw any conclusions it is necessary to pay attention to what we mean by wisdom and whether it is possible to call Jesus a teacher of wisdom.

Wisdom ranges from practical skills such as those of the crafts- man, the art of government, cleverness, the skill to cope with life, and the pursuit of ethical conduct. It belongs to God and is associ- ated with creation and the Law in the Old Testament (see Murphy 1985:1135). It is a term which is applied to a variety of things: 'an insight into the world, a spirituality . . ., a literature' (Humphrey 1989:50). Like other theologies, wisdom theology is a perspective on God and the world. Unlike eschatological and apocalyptic theology it does not focus on the end of the world. It focuses on this world and its orderliness. God is the giver of wisdom and the wise one is the person who finds wisdom and lives according to it.

Although the New Testament does not have an example of wis- dom literature the phenomenon is definitely not absent. This is espe- cially true of the teaching of Jesus. He was regarded as a sage who was even wiser than Solomon (Lk. 11:31), and as we have seen, much of his teaching was given in aphoristic form, which is typical of wisdom teaching. Both the form and the content of the teaching of Jesus make it possible to view him as a wisdom teacher. The teaching is presented in the synoptics as that of a sage who instructs and exhorts people on many topics including happiness, love of one's enemies, doing good, blessing, praying, turning the other cheek, offering one's cloak, generous lending, applying the golden rule, mercy and many other things.

We have noted above that it is not possible to answer the ques- tion of who Jesus was by taking the Gospels at face value. It is there- fore necessary to pursue the image of Jesus as a wisdom teacher a little further.

I have referred above to the growth of the Gospel tradition and have made mention of the hypothetical source Q. Q mainly con- sists of the teaching of Jesus in the form of sayings. It probably did not contain much narrative material and was therefore totally different from the synoptics and John, which present the Jesus material in narrative form. Like the Gospel of Thomas, Q presents Jesus as teacher. Q is therefore currently regarded as part of the sapiential literature like Proverbs and other texts. In its oldest form Q probably only contained wisdom material. It implies that one of the oldest ways of viewing Jesus was to see him as a wisdom teacher who gave instructions and admonitions (see Kloppenborg 1987). Did the compiler of Q preserve an authentic image of Jesus, perhaps *the* authentic picture of Jesus?

From the viewpoint of first-century Jewish theology it is undoubtedly possible that Jesus could have been a wisdom teacher who was interested in instructing people on how to cope with life and pursue ethical conduct. Wisdom was a traditional perspective in Jewish theology and wisdom thinking was 'in the air', so to speak, in the first century. This can be seen from the works of the Greek popular philosophers, but also from the Jewish-Hellenistic authors of the period (see Kloppenborg 1987 and Mack 1987). Wisdom forms part of the culture of the period and it is not impossible to see Jesus in the religious role of a wisdom teacher travelling around in Galilee instructing people on how to live a meaningful life by changing their value systems (see Theissen 1989). Galilee was a place where people of different walks of life, in different life situations, and of different cultures were gathered during the time of Jesus. That is why one has to see the earthly Jesus first of all in that context and not in the context of the Jerusalem cult. Mack (1988b:608) maintains that: 'A Cynic Jesus does appear to fit the Hellenistic cast to Galilean culture much better than the apocalyptic Jesus'.

The question might immediately arise: what about the term 'kingdom of God' in the teaching of Jesus? Is it not an eschatological term? And does it not mean that the wisdom teaching of Jesus should be seen within that framework?

'Kingdom of God' is a very complex term and scholars do not agree on its meaning and reference. Generally speaking there is consensus that it simply means the rule of God. But what it refers to in the teaching of Jesus is quite another matter. This is not the place to go into detail. Mack has made it clear that it is not necessary to understand the term exclusively in eschatological terms and that the eschatological interpretation is dependent upon Mark's apocalyptic presentation of Jesus. Building on the work of Perrin he reminds us that Perrin has shown that 'kingdom of God' is not a concept that occurs very often in apocalyptic texts and that only four of the kingdom of God sayings which are ascribed to Jesus could have any claim to authenticity, namely Mark 1:15a; Luke 11:20; Luke 17:20–21 and Matthew 11:12 (Mack 1987:10). Mack puts the term into a larger cultural context and shows that 'kingdom' is what rulers had, that is 'sovereignty, majesty, dominion, power, domain' (Mack 1987: 11). He argues that 'kingdom' became a metaphor for sovereignty, freedom, and confidence, which were typical characteristics of the sage in popular Stoic and Cynic philosophy. The sage is the only ruler as Philo says. 'Kingdom of God' would not have called up apocalyptic images in this type of context. It would have been interpreted rather within the framework of wisdom. Mack (1988b) has convincingly shown that it is unnecessary to interpret the term 'kingdom of God' eschatologically in the oldest layer of Q. It has to be interpreted as part of the wisdom teaching of Jesus.

Noteworthy is the fact that the three instances in which the term occurs outside early Christian texts are found in Hellenistic-Jewish texts. The following example from the *Sentences of Sextus* 307–11, as quoted by Mack (1987:15), is worth mentioning, even though the document is not from the same period as the synoptics:

> A wise man presents god to humanity.
> Of all his works, god is most proud of a sage.
> Next to god, nothing is as free as a wise man.
> A wise man shares . . . in the *baislea tou theou*.

If Jesus was a sage he could have used the term 'kingdom of God' to underscore the sovereignty and rule of God in wisdom terms. The idea that God was ruling was common to traditional Jewish thought although it was not often expressed in terms of the 'kingdom of God'. The term 'kingdom of God' is unusual in Aramaic and as Perrin (1967:38) maintains, it 'would never be found in Aramaic'.

The many occurrences of the term 'kingdom of God' in the teaching of Jesus probably point to the fact that he used the term. To my mind it stands for the rule of God and it was used by Jesus as one of the leading symbols in his instruction. One should see it as part of the conviction of Jesus that one should acquire the skill of becoming wise.

Taking into account the evidence of the synoptics, it seems possible to see Jesus as a wisdom teacher. Does that, then mean that he was not a prophet?

4. Jesus: Eschatological Prophet and/or Wisdom Teacher?

Answers to the question of who Jesus was differ greatly in terms of eschatological/apocalyptic or wisdom theology. It is obvious from our sources that Jesus was a charismatic leader who succeeded in making followers and changing ideas. He performed miracles and taught people how to live a happy life in accordance with the will of God. But who was he? Did he fit the roles of both a preacher and a wisdom teacher, or was he one and not the other? If we consider the different frameworks within which he should have fitted if he were both, they involve the following: preaching and teaching, prophetic proclamation and rhetorical persuasion, eschatology or apocalyptic and wisdom (see Mack 1988b).

It is possible that prophetic proclamation could include the genre of wisdom. One should therefore not make it an either/or situation from the outset. On the other hand, one should also ask whether eschatology/apocalyptic and wisdom are not two totally different perspectives on life. While the prophet is a channel through which the divine communicates and proclaims what is right and wrong in the current situation and what will happen in the future, the wisdom teacher is somebody who instructs people how to live a meaningful life. With regard to Jesus one should therefore start at another point. Perhaps the most appropriate point is the fact that our sources do not give us a historical picture of who he was. They tell us about his significance, about his reputation, but not of who he was. Let us therefore consider the question from another angle.

The cornerstone of the conviction that Jesus and his ministry should be interpreted eschatologically comprises the 'coming Son of man' sayings. They also form the basis for the eschatological interpretation of the concept 'kingdom of God'.

A number of the sayings of Jesus speak of the future coming of the 'Son of man'. This figure is portrayed as someone who will play an important role in the final judgement (Mk. 8:38, *TEV*):

> If a person is ashamed of me and of my teaching in this godless and wicked day, then the Son of Man will be ashamed of him when he comes in the glory of his Father with the holy angels.

These and similar sayings convinced scholars that Jesus thought the final judgement and the end of the world to be imminent. The point, however, is whether these sayings are authentic Jesus sayings or whether they are based on an apocalyptic interpretation of Jesus, and therefore put on his lips. There is growing consensus that Jesus referred to himself as the 'son of man', that is, 'I' or 'man', but that the future 'Son of man sayings' are not authentic (see Borg 1986:87ff.). If this is the case, the main cornerstone of the eschatological Jesus becomes problematic.

The term 'kingdom of God' is also not essentially an eschatological term. It simply refers to the reign of God, his sovereignty. Because it is normally conceived of in terms of an eschatological framework in the teaching of Jesus, it is interpreted eschatologically and apocalyptically as we have seen above. There seems to be little, if anything, compelling in the conviction that the term should be interpreted eschatologically. Without the coming Son of man sayings its eschatological interpretation is without foundation. The implication is that eschatological interpretation of Jesus and the kingdom of God in the light of the coming 'Son of man' sayings becomes questionable. It also means that the image of Jesus as an eschatological prophet becomes problematic. However, much research has to be done before we can reach a totally convincing conclusion about Jesus having been an eschatological prophet. As I have said, for a century scholars have been convinced that the teaching of Jesus was couched in Jewish eschatological hopes. It is too early to make final judgements as to whether Jesus was an eschatological prophet or a wisdom teacher. There are many other things involved which also have to be accounted for. Let us consider the following.

One of the most important facts in the life of Jesus was that he was baptised by John and that he then became a follower of John. John was an eschatological prophet who proclaimed repentance and judgement. The question therefore arises as to what the relationship was between John and Jesus. Was John the final eschatological figure or was he the forerunner of the final figure, as the followers of Jesus took him to be after the death of Jesus?

According to our sources there are obvious differences between John and Jesus. While John was an ascetic, living and preaching in the desert, Jesus mixed with sinners and was regarded as a wine drinker and a glutton. John's mission was to separate the wheat from the chaff, and his disciples fasted, while Jesus and his disciples apparently did not. Jesus' mission was to include sinners, while John called for the repentance of the nation. It is thus possible that Jesus embarked on a mission quite different from that of John when he started 'preaching' the gospel in Galilee. To me it seems possible, as Boers (1989) has indicated, that the followers of Jesus, unlike Jesus himself, regarded John as the final eschatological figure after his death. 'Jesus understood the kingdom of God to have been inaugurated by John the Baptist, which meant that it had already arrived, whereas his followers expected its coming with the return of Jesus as the Son of Man, which placed it in future' (Boers 1989:45). This implies that Jesus embarked on a mission of making the 'kingdom of God' known to the people. Unlike John he did not preach as an eschatological preacher. He instructed people about the skills of life in the kingdom. Whoever was willing to listen to him could acquire a new value system. He created a symbolic reality for people who were distressed and lost and oppressed, and gave them reason to find life meaningful.

The time is ripe to reconsider fundamentally the question of who Jesus was. It is too early to say whether we are misled by the eschatological lens through which early Christians like the first followers and Mark saw him after his death. Much more has to be done on the wisdom trajectory before we can say with any certainty that Jesus was not an eschatological prophet, and that he was a wisdom teacher.

The teaching of Jesus was radical. It was not revolutionary in the modern sense of the word. He was mistaken by the Romans as a messianic pretender and a danger to the Empire, and was killed on the cross. After his death he was put into many religious roles because of his significance for his followers. Before his death he enabled people, by his teaching, to cope with life and to pursue a lifestyle in accordance with his perception of the will of God.

CHAPTER EIGHTEEN

THE RELEVANCE OF JESUS RESEARCH
FOR THE 'NEW' SOUTH AFRICA

In a recent publication on Jesus and postmodernism James Breech correctly observes that the evangelical slogan, 'Jesus is the answer', expresses a conviction held by all Christians 'for they believe that the tradition within which they live originated with Jesus of Nazareth' (Breech 1989:13). He convincingly shows that most of the patterns of life and social and religious structures adopted by Christians as part of the new reality that Jesus inaugurated, were, however, not invented by Jesus. It is probably also true that many of the theologies which are allegedly based on him and his teaching are in no way related to Jesus of Nazareth. Breech discusses the question: 'If Jesus is the answer, what is the question?' I would like to link up with this and ask: If Jesus is the answer, who is this Jesus?

This essay deals with the problem of the historical Jesus from the perspective of doing theology in the 'new' South Africa. My conviction is that theologians in South Africa are obliged, for the sake of the church, Christian faith, and the morality of science, to come to grips with the current polarisation between traditional and contextual theology. I am furthermore convinced that Christology will have to be one of the priorities on the theological agenda. It is also clear to me that the only way this can be done meaningfully would be to overcome the current impasse between traditional and contextual (in the sense of Third World) theologians, concerning Jesus of Nazareth. Unlike in the past, where christological differences were discussed from the perspective of 'Christology from above', future discussion will have to start with the problem of the historical Jesus and Christology 'from below', the nature of historical construction and the metaphorical character of theological language. I will come back to this.

The essay deals with the problem of the identity and significance of Jesus, current issues in historical Jesus research, current images of Jesus in South African christologies and possible ways out of the dilemma of opposing views on Jesus.

1. *The Identity and Significance of Jesus*

The New Testament documents make it more than clear that there was difference of opinion about the identity of Jesus, even when he was still on earth. Some regarded him as John the Baptist, others as Elijah, others as one of the prophets and also as a messiah (Mk. 8:27–30). When the stories about him were written down from a post-resurrection perspective these images multiplied. This process did not stop. In the end different significances were ascribed to Jesus and he received many names, including Lord, the Word, Son of God, and so on. The early church continued this process and by the time of Chalcedon doctrines were developed concerning his humanity and divinity. What his understanding of himself was is difficult, if not impossible, to determine. However, it was only after the New Testament documents were written that 'christologies' really started competing. New Testament authors, and the early church, do not seem to be too concerned about the different names Jesus was given. This was a problem that only arose later.

New Testament writings do not differentiate between who Jesus was and who people said he was. In fact, the authors of the New Testament concern themselves with the significance of Jesus and not primarily with his identity. I distinguish between 'who Jesus was' (his identity) and 'what his significance was/is' for the simple reason that who a person is, and what people say or think that person is, are often two totally different things. Both aspects are nevertheless important to the question of who a person was/is. In the case of Jesus it is even more so.

One of the major problems of Christology is the status of 'is' sentences used with reference to Jesus. In the sentence: 'Jesus is the Son of God', 'is' is often understood in an ontological, and not a metaphorical sense. That is why Christology has been such a bone of contention through the ages of church history. There is, however, no clear-cut answer to the question of the status of 'is' sentences about Jesus, unless one believes that informed speculative Christology has ontological status, which is debatable. It is, however, apparent that any 'is' sentence about Jesus has to be interpreted and that these sentences can be interpreted differently. It also follows that sentences about the identity of Jesus and his significance are not the same and that both kinds of sentences are expressions of language. To put it differently: both kinds of sentences, historical and christological, can be regarded as hypothetical. To my mind christological sentences can best be explained as metaphorical expressions of theological reflection and of faith.

The search for the historical Jesus has to do with 'is' sentences of a *historical* nature, while many of the christological statements have bearing on the significance of Jesus for believers. The Old Quest bears witness to the fact that scholars of the eighteenth and nineteenth centuries were interested in the question of who Jesus *really* was in an attempt to save the Jesus of history from the dogmas of the church concerning him.

Another important issue which has been in vogue since the beginning of the twentieth century, and is of significance for our discussion, is the well-known difference between the historical Jesus and the Christ of faith. The man of flesh and blood, Jesus of Nazareth, is not the person portrayed in the New Testament. Jesus of the New Testament is the Christ of faith. 'Jesus of Nazareth' refers to his identity, while 'Christ of faith' is used in connection with his significance. Needless to say, it is exactly the relationship between the two concepts 'historical Jesus' and 'Christ of faith', and the problem of the continuity between the historical Jesus and the Christ of faith, that gave rise to the so-called New Quest for the historical Jesus in 1953 (see Käsemann 1954).

For many the term 'historical Jesus' refers to the man of flesh and blood, the earthly Jesus, as used in the Old Quest. 'Historical Jesus' has, however, undergone redefinition in the New Quest and is since being used by New Testament scholars as the historian's answer to who Jesus was (see Robinson 1983:26ff.). This is also the way in which I shall use the term in this essay. The search for the historical Jesus is a historical issue, it concerns historical construction and should be understood in this way. It concerns the identity of the man of flesh and blood, Jesus the Galilean.

2. *Current Issues in Historical Jesus Research*

There is currently a lively interest in historical Jesus studies, not only as an academic enterprise, but also 'because we are committed to public accountability' (Funk 1985:7). In the United States of America,

scholars attached to both the Westar Institute and the Society of
Biblical Literature are intensively involved in Jesus research, while
the Claremont School of Divinity has a special project on Q. The
international *Societas Novi Testamenti Studiorum* also started a seminar
on the historical Jesus in 1990 and a large number of individuals
are involved in some or other aspect related to Jesus research (see
e.g. Hollenbach 1989). Because of the lack of space, I will concentrate on a few issues which are important for the theme of this essay,
not because they are the only ones being researched, but because
they indicate the kind of current interest in the historical Jesus. I
shall deal with the following: the world in which Jesus lived in
first-century Palestine, the Jewishness of Jesus, and the works and
words of Jesus. In the end I shall give attention to two religious roles
into which he is currently fitted.

2.1   *First-century Palestine*

The world of Jesus is currently studied from archaeological, socio-
historical, and sociological (including economic, political and cultural)
perspectives. Major publications have already seen the light of day
with far-reaching implications for our understanding of the context
within which Jesus and his first followers lived and worked (see e.g.
Hollenbach 1989).

Jesus started his public career in Galilee and ended it in Jerusalem
where he was crucified. That is why it is rather important to see
Jesus first of all within the context of Galilee, and not in the context of the Jerusalem cult (see also Vorster 1990a).

Galilee was greatly Hellenised, both politically and socially, at
the time when Jesus started his public career (see Freyne 1980).
The region including its trade, tax and infrastructure, was ruled and
administered in a Roman manner. Although Aramaic, the *lingua
franca* of the Persian Empire was, still spoken by most Jews, and
Hebrew was probably still in use, Greek was the language used in
the marketplace. It can be assumed that most Jews, including Jesus
and his followers, were to a greater or a lesser extent bilingual.
Urbanisation was no strange phenomenon in Galilee and the region
was inhabited by others beside the Jews. These Jews were no longer
free from the influences of a cosmopolitan society even though some
of them rejected the Hellenistic way of life. 'One could not live in
any village in lower Galilee and escape the effects and ramifications

of urbanization . . .' (Overman 1988:165). Obviously the Jews in Galilee were influenced socially, politically and economically in the Hellenistic period.

The bulk of the population was made up of the lower class, comprising the peasants and artisans, the poor and the bandits. They did not have power and influence—except in their own circles. Jesus and his followers also belonged to this class of society. The governing and the retainer classes were relatively small. According to Saldarini (1988:200) the governing class who, with all the power and influence, formed one or two per cent of the population, while the retainer class (the soldiers, bureaucratic government officials, religious leaders and others) formed perhaps five per cent. Through taxation, confiscation, and the selling of offices the ruling class acquired wealth and influence.

It makes quite a difference whether one views Jesus in such a context or simply fits him into a context where the Jerusalem cult is the dominating factor. The specific rural and agricultural aspects of his activities and teaching are embedded into the highly urbanised and commercial setting of Galilee in the first century CE Jesus was not unaware of the people who lived in the cities and who administered the country. Being a member of the lower class of a society who had to labour for their daily bread in the most beautiful part of Palestine, somebody who had an openness towards the sufferings of the majority of the people, and a religious Jew with a message, he could have been interpreted from many different perspectives by his followers and his contemporaries, as well as by the members of the upper class and the retainer class when they became aware of his activities and what he had to say. He also must have been well informed as far as other persons with 'a message' in Galilee were concerned. As in other places in the Hellenistic world there were many different people, each with a different philosophy of life. Whether he had heard popular philosophers and itinerant teachers is not known, but it is possible. In any case the picture of Jesus and his early followers as a group of rural, and perhaps even uninformed, people seems to me improbable. It has become clear that they must have been subjected to and informed by the situation in which they lived.

Because of sociological studies we have also come to a better understanding of the relationship between religion, education and economics, which were all embedded into the family of politics in first-century Palestine (see Malina 1987). Too often the world of Jesus is seen in compartments and he is viewed only in a religious or a political role. That is a mistake.

2.2   *The Jewishness of Jesus*

It is sometimes forgotten that Jesus was a Jew and not a Christian— or even the first Christian. This makes quite a difference to our image of who Jesus was. In order to understand Jesus in his own context it is important first of all to ascertain what kind of Jew he was. What do we mean when we say that Jesus was a Jew? If we follow the Gospel tradition and say that he was a Jewish teacher, what do we mean by the term 'teacher'? Or a Jewish prophet? Do our sources afford us sufficient material to say what we mean when we call Jesus a Jewish prophet or a rabbi? In view of the complex nature of first-century Jewish Palestine, the groups who lived there, the relationships between them, their relationship with the authori- ties—that is, with the Roman rulers—the interaction between Jews and other inhabitants of the country, and so on, these questions are not of academic interest only. In fact, they concern our entire con- cept of the past and of Jesus of Nazareth.

   In scholarly circles one finds a great variety of images of Jesus the Jew, relating to the different Jewish backgrounds against which the images are located. The following have been proposed by Christian scholars: an eschatological prophet, a political revolutionary, a magi- cian, a Hillelite or proto-Pharisee, an Essene, a Galilean charismatic or a Galilean rabbi (see Harrington 1987). In addition, there are the different Jewish views of Jesus, which add to or complement the vari- ety of views held about his Jewishness. One of the reasons for the many answers to the question of who Jesus was lies in the lack of sources which would enable us to give a precise description of all the relevant detail. It nevertheless becomes clear how important it has become to answer the question about the identity of Jesus (see also Vorster 1990a).

2.3   *The works and words of Jesus*

New Testament scholars have good reason to suspect that not all the works and words which are ascribed to Jesus in the Gospel tra- dition are authentic. They agree about a relatively small number of

so-called 'facts' in the life of Jesus. The following are taken as indisputable: (1) Jesus was baptised by John the Baptist. (2) He was a
Galilean who preached and healed (performed miracles). (3) He called
disciples and spoke of there being twelve. (4) He confined his activity to Israel. (5) He engaged in a controversy about the temple. (6)
He was crucified outside Jerusalem by Jewish authorities. (7) After
his death his followers continued as an identifiable movement. (8) At
least some Jews persecuted parts of the new movement, and it appears
that this persecution endured to a time near the end of Jesus' career
(see Sanders 1985:11).

There is obviously no such thing as a bare fact. And, even if we
agree on the authenticity of the mentioned facts in the life of Jesus,
we still have to interpret them. Why did Jesus, for example, 'cleanse'
the temple? Some interpreters think that the 'cleansing' refers to prior
profanation and that Jesus wanted to purify the temple to fulfil its
intended purpose. Others argue that it refers to the rejection of the
Jewish cult by the early church, or that it shows the power of the
resurrected Christ. It is also maintained that the 'cleansing' was a
symbolic or prophetic sign, which was intended to cause the repentance of Israel (see Sanders 1985:61–62). The point I wish to make
is clear. 'Facts' do not make sense on their own. They have to be
interpreted.

In the case of the words of Jesus it is even more difficult to determine their authenticity. Scholars are continuously trying to find ways
of determining what is authentic and what is not (see Boring 1988).
There is general agreement that Jesus spoke about the 'kingdom of
God'. But what did the term refer to? Was it an eschatological/apoc-
alyptic term, or was it used in a totally different sense by Jesus (see
Mack 1987). It is furthermore apparent that Jesus taught in parables. How should parables, however, be read? They are nowadays
generally viewed as metaphorical, open-ended narratives. But should
they be interpreted in the eschatological framework within which
they have been understood for the better part of this century (see
Dodd 1961 and Jeremias 1970)?

To my mind Jesus created a framework of understanding by the
use of metaphorical stories regarding the kingdom of God. By using
open-ended stories he created a reality which enabled his hearers to
see the world in which they lived as a place where God ruled and
where life was worthwhile. He put across a value system which
enabled people to cope with their daily lives (see also Breech 1989).

2.4 *Jesus and religious roles*

Jesus has been fitted into different religious roles during the past. A
lively debate is presently being conducted as to whether he should
be seen as an eschatological, apocalyptic prophet or as a wisdom
teacher (see Vorster 1990a). The view that eschatology is the dominating theme in the teaching of Jesus is presently being questioned
and subjected to serious scrutiny (see Borg 1986 and Mack 1988b).
For a century scholars have promoted the idea that the only appropriate way to understand the message of Jesus is to take its apocalyptic dimensions into account. There are, however, scholars who
argue that *Mark* was responsible for the apocalyptic framework into
which the early church put Jesus. It is maintained that apocalyptic
eschatology is a later development in the Jesus tradition. These scholars argue that Jesus should rather be viewed as a wisdom teacher—
that is—as somebody who promoted insight into the issues of living,
and how to cope with life. By doing this he caused a revolution in
the value system of his contemporaries. It is furthermore argued that
it is not necessary to understand him as a wisdom teacher in eschatological terms.

This is not the place to pursue the matter further. What is clear
is that there is a need for further study on the identity of Jesus, and
that it is irresponsible to put him into religious or other roles which
do not fit the context of first-century Palestine. This is only possible through rigorous historical study of the sources at our disposal
and by applying our knowledge of the first century in historical
construction.

The present state of New Testament research urges one to be
careful to avoid making claims about Jesus too easily, and attempting to put him into modern roles. This also holds for our claims
about his significance and the early church's understanding of
Christology.

3. *Current Images of Jesus in South African Christologies*

Historical Jesus research has played no significant role in South
African theology. In fact, it is in most cases rejected as irrelevant
for the faith of the believer or for serious theology—that is—for
Christology. Even in New Testament scholarship there has been virtually no serious study of the matter. Only in the last decade or so

has a limited amount of interest developed in the subject. His identity and significance were simply divorced and all the emphasis was put on the his significance.

Although Professor A.B. Du Toit of the Faculty of Theology at the University of Pretoria was the first New Testament scholar to devote a chapter of the South African series *Guide To The New Testament* (vol. IV, 257–281) to the topic, he was recently reported as having said that scientific discussions and theories about Jesus could enrich one's insights, but they could also be false tracks. That is why they should not be taken too seriously (Van der Linde 1990:13). Our fundamentalistic background explains why the historical Jesus is not seriously studied by South Africans, according to Du Toit. Such study is seen as a threat. Our theories will come and go, but Jesus will stay, according to him (Van der Linde 1990:12–13); the study of the historical Jesus is thereby dismissed.

Du Toit is probably correct in ascribing the lack of serious study of the historical Jesus in South Africa to Fundamentalism. Historical criticism has never been one of the characteristics of South African theology. I would go as far as asserting that one of the major problems with South African theology is that it has escaped, to its own disadvantage, the sobering effects of the Enlightenment. Historical criticism never became part of South African theological thought structures. Because of the negative attitude toward biblical criticism, theologians and church people have never been seriously confronted by historical problems in the interpretation of the Bible in South Africa.

Even prominent theologians like Jonker (1977:68) and Bosch (1979:45) reject the study of the historical Jesus outright because of its inconclusiveness. Referring to nineteenth-century historical Jesus studies, Bosch (1979:45) maintains that the historical Jesus always remains the Jesus of the historian! One can, ironically enough, ask: Is any historical construction anything other than the making of a historian? Does that not also apply to Christology? What is the ontological status of expressions of faith? We will have to return to this problem.

It is, on the other hand, strange how much is made of the life of Jesus in traditional theology when it comes to Christology. Like other Christian theologians, South African theologians also relate their christologies to one of six so-called salvation events in the 'life' of Jesus. These events are: the incarnation of Christ, his death and crucifixion, his resurrection, his ascension, the outpouring of his spirit at Pentecost, and his second coming or *parousia*. Liberation theologians emphasise the incarnation. They seem to be interested in a Christ who suffers with the oppressed and knows about their agonies. In the reformed tradition (in South Africa at least), the emphasis is on Christ's act of atonement on the cross and on eternal salvation. Others focus on the ascension and prefer a Christology of victory (see further Bosch 1986:2). The influence of all these christological positions on the identity and significance of Jesus is obvious. In all these christological views there is a striking absence of historical study of the events on which they are based.

For traditional theologians, Jesus of the New Testament is the 'historical' Jesus, or rather the 'earthly Jesus' as he is presented in the New Testament. This is, for instance, confirmed by the extensive study by König on Jesus as the last one (see König 1980). König interprets the whole life of Jesus in the light of eschatological salvation history. He refers to critical scholars but never takes seriously the tremendous historical problems involved in describing the life of Jesus, or even any of the events in the life of Jesus as they are presented almost at face value in the New Testament. There seems to be no understanding of the history of traditions concerning Jesus, and all the material is harmonised into an eschatology of the salvation acts of Jesus. It would seem an understatement to assert that traditional theologians in South Africa are unaware of the historical Jesus problem. If that is not the case, they prefer to ignore it and reject it.

Despite their emphasis on Christology 'from below' and on the importance of context and praxis, the case for the historical Jesus does not seem any better when it comes to Third World christologies. One should be very careful not to misunderstand the term 'historical Jesus' in Third World Christology, including Black Christology (see e.g. Chikane 1985). Although the emphasis is on Jesus in his historical context as the Jesus who liberated the poor, Third World theologians are normally not concerned with the historical Jesus problem. An exception is perhaps Segundo (1985). This is, however, debatable. Smit (1987:6–9), in his very useful survey of Third World christologies, indicates that the term 'historical Jesus' is used with four different meanings by Third World theologians. It is, first of all, used in the sense of Jesus as he is described in the Gospels. Related to this usage is the second—sense the reference of the term to the humanity of Jesus. In the third place it refers to 'Jesus in history' as he appears in his actions towards the poor and oppressed. And, fourthly, the term historical Jesus refers to the suffering people of God in the present, in the spirit of Matthew 25. The Gospels' handling of Jesus' concern for the poor forms the cornerstone of liberation Christology. It is argued that Jesus sided with the poor as one of them, and that his human response to the poor and the oppressed implies that he also sides with the poor and the oppressed of today (see also McGovern 1989:62–82 and Nicolson 1990).

The case of Black Theology is not any different as far as the study of the historical Jesus is concerned. Black theology also prefers a Christology from below. Like other Third World theologies, Black theology is approached from the concrete situation within which Christians find themselves, normally seen in the context of poverty and oppression. In the light of this situation it is asked what the New Testament texts have to say to Blacks. In other words, who is Jesus in this situation? Jesus is viewed in political terms as the one who identifies with the poor and the oppressed, and who is committed to their liberation (applicable literature in Nicolson 1990).

> Incarnation means identifying with humanity. It means identifying with humanity's weakness, suffering and pain. It means identifying with the struggles of the people (Chikane 1985:46).

This is not the place to elaborate on the role of Jesus in Black Christology. He clearly plays a dominant role as a political saviour in liberating terms. In spite of enquiries I made, I could not find any Black theologian who reflected on the historical Jesus problem except in Jesus' role as political liberator. Like in liberation Christology and also in traditional (White) South African theology, Jesus is taken at face value from the New Testament. The difference with traditional theology is that he is clearly put into another role. The 'white' role of Jesus is deliberately rejected: 'South African Black Theologians are convinced that the truth about Jesus has been obscured by Western theology' (Chikane 1985:41). Salvation has a different meaning (see Nicolson 1990).

Despite the apparent differences between traditional and Black Christology they do not differ as far as the role of the study of the historical Jesus problem is concerned. Jesus is obviously seen from a totally different perspective and salvation is differently interpreted in Black Christology. The two christologies agree in that the historical

Jesus problem is not taken seriously at all. Jesus of the New Testament is the historical Jesus no matter how differently he is seen in the different christologies!

These differences have become a polarising factor in doing theology in South Africa! Traditional and Black Christology cannot be reconciled if theologians of both convictions are not willing to look at their christological dispositions afresh and in consultation. Is there a way out of the christological dilemma in South Africa?

5. *Is there a Solution for the Christological Dilemma in the New South Africa?*

The inhabitants of South Africa are currently confronted with one of the most interesting and challenging periods in its history. The term 'new South Africa', however ambiguous and often undefined, is intended here as a description for the process of transition which is taking place in all possible areas of society in present-day South Africa. Although the term is very vague, I use it here with reference to the socio-political changes which are taking place in the country, as well as with reference to the post-apartheid, hopefully democratised society, which will come about as a consequence of these changes.

This 'new' South Africa will probably also be new as far as theology is concerned. It is possible that both traditional and Black Christology will collapse. What might happen is that for certain people in South Africa the apocalyptic view of Jesus as the coming one would be intensified, especially for those who interpret their situation as marginal. Others might experience disappointment that the liberating Jesus, in spite of political changes, has not taken away poverty and suffering, because 'If we hold out hopes of imminent divine intervention in our own lives, we are flying in the face of history' (Nicolson 1990:221). If this happens, theologians will have a duty to re-address Christology.

It seems to me the duty of Christian theologians, if they hold onto the importance of the Bible and the New Testament as the source of theology, to sit down (together) and take the New Testament seriously and ask: Who is the Jesus we are reading about in the New Testament, and what role did he play when he was on earth? The next thing will be to re-address the slogan 'Jesus is the answer' in order to get to know the question for which he is an answer. In this regard the study of the historical Jesus can help us to discard our notions of the many roles into which he has been cast in the course of the history of the church. If we furthermore realise that there is a yawning abyss between the first and the twentieth centuries, and that God is not immediately available to intervene and solve our problems, we might also learn how to address some of the problems with the abilities and insights he has given us, that is without making the first-century Jesus a twentieth-century problem solver.

The study of the historical Jesus will not solve all our christological problems. On the contrary! Nonetheless, it is inappropriate to make claims about and on behalf of Jesus without trying to find out who he was. The arguments of Bosch and Du Toit, mentioned above, have clearly nothing to do with historical argumentation, that is why they do not hold true. If we wish to say anything about the past, whatever it might be, we are by definition obliged to make historical constructions. Historical constructions are constructions and not reconstructions—that is why they are not always the same, and why they always have to be put to the test. People who reject the search for the historical Jesus nevertheless have their own views on his identity. They are just not willing to put their views on the table for discussion. Unless, of course, they silently maintain that the Jesus of the New Testament is the earthly Jesus.

The fact that there are so many views on the historical Jesus need not disturb us. What should disturb us is the unwillingness of people to put their beliefs to the test. We, perhaps more than anyone else, will have to analyse our views of Jesus critically. This might help us to discuss the polarising views on Christology because these christologies are based on views about Jesus.

With regard to the historical study of Jesus, Batdorf (1984:212) makes the following important remarks:

> [W]e need as participants in the quest (1) to abandon the myth of objectivity, (2) to formulate for public inspection what our personal hermeneutic prejudices are, (3) to formulate for public inspection the total image of Jesus on the basis of which our investigations proceed, and (4) to make explicit how personal bias and total Jesus image are related to each other and to the canon's insistence on reading the story in its totality.

These words also apply to our formulation of Christology. Polarisation makes people intolerant. The New Testament and church history teach us that there is a need to be tolerant about Christology. 'Either/or' christologies lead to rejection. This also means that in the new South Africa we will have to be willing to tolerate differences of opinion and even different christological views, but with the willingness to subject our beliefs to scrutiny. Again the study of the historical Jesus might help us gain insight into the origin of our own christological convictions if we compare them with the outcome of historical Jesus research.

The image of Jesus as a wisdom teacher helps one to realise that one of the functions of his teaching was to help people to cope with life. Wisdom is insight, wisdom is craft, wisdom comes from God. The values which Jesus stood for, the fact that he told open-ended stories to develop insight, and the fact that his own story was open-ended help one to realise that there is hope for anybody who takes his/her cue from Jesus.

It is hermeneutically impossible to transfer Jesus and his message from the first to the twentieth century; it is also impossible to make universals out of possible principles in the life and teaching of the historical Jesus. But it is possible to start with him and move on through the centuries if we allow ourselves to be informed about values for life, even if we have formulated some ourselves.

There is a need for the historical study of Jesus in South Africa because such study is relevant for informing Christians about the origin of their tradition. It is also necessary because it might help us to form and to rectify our faith in him and our beliefs about him. Contextual theologians, including Black theologians, should be credited for their awareness of the contextual nature of theological reflection since all theology is contextual. In the case of the historical Jesus it is important that we remind ourselves of the two contexts which we are involved in with regard to such a study. The first is the first-century context. The second is the context of the historian/theologian. Both contexts are equally important for appropriate understanding. The mistake of traditional theology is being unaware of the importance and influence of the modern theologian's context in theological reflection. The mistake of Black theology is that the importance of the historical context of Jesus and the distance between then and now are disregarded. Let us take up the challenge of theology in the new South Africa and work on what we have in common. The one thing contextual and traditional theologians have in common is Jesus. Our answers to who he is we do not have in common. That is why the historical study of Jesus is relevant for the new South Africa.

I do not think that the study of the historical Jesus will afford us answers to all our daily problems in the new South Africa. The one thing it will, however, do is to make us a little more humble in our claims of having answers to difficult questions.

With Kuitert I believe that everything is politics, but politics is not everything (see Vorster 1988c), and that relevance should therefore not be restricted to the political arena. Religion should not be a dividing factor in a community, it should be the very factor which makes life meaningful. If Jesus is the answer, we are obliged to say who he was. To do that in an informed manner makes it necessary to do historical inquiry into the origins of faith as well as the 'facts' on which these origins were based. Historical study does not provide the basis for faith, but it does give answers to the origins of faith (see Boers 1989:xvi). It does not give an answer to the meaning of Jesus, either, but it does explain what significance Christians attach to the 'facts'.

CHAPTER NINETEEN

REDACTION, CONTEXTUALIZATION
AND THE SAYINGS OF JESUS

As a result of the cul-de-sac in gospel research in the late sixties
various attempts have been made during the past decade to dis-
mantle and reassemble the categories of this aspect of New Testament
scholarship (the terms 'dismantling' and 'reassembling' were introduced into New Testament scholarship by J.M. Robinson 1971). It
has been suggested that more attention should be paid to the final
text of the gospels as the compositions of 'authors' who made extensive use of traditional material and the implications thereof (see
Güttgemanns 1970; Perrin 1972; Vorster 1980b). Several attempts,
relating to the literary activity of the evangelists, the relationship
between the oral and literary phases of the gospels, the gospels as
autosemantic texts, aspects of the study of the gospels as narratives,
to mention only a few, followed as a response to this challenge (see
amongst others Kelber 1979; Petersen 1978; Tannehill 1977; Vorster
1980b). The sayings of Jesus form a very substantial part of the
gospel tradition. In view of the aforesaid it follows that also the sayings of Jesus can be studied from perspectives other than the traditional. One of these perspectives, namely that the sayings are part
of a particular text-type, deserves our attention.

Every context, however, has its context (on the importance of context in the study of meaning see Vorster 1979a:13 and Sawyer 1972:
4–26; also J.E. Barnhart 1980:501–513 for other aspects of context).
The fact that *Redaktionsgeschichte* is still in vogue in many circles cannot be ignored. The reason for this is that Redaction critical study
of the gospels has proved to be fruitful in many ways. There are,
however, limits to every method. This is very well illustrated in the
review of three recent commentaries on Mark (see Luz 1980).

The same holds true of new approaches to the study of the gospels
as narratives. Both have their own context. The following short study
is an attempt to analyze some of the implications of the *redaction* (in
the redaction critical sense of the word) and *contextualization* of the
sayings of Jesus in the gospels. Contextualization refers to the situational

context within a text and the world of reference of a literary unit
(word, sentence, term). In a written text it involves more than the
immediate linguistic context. Every component of a text is contextualized within the complete text. The type of contextualization
depends on the type of text involved. (For further usages see Vorster
1979a:13 and Sawyer 1972:6–10.)

I shall limit myself to a discussion of the phenomena in the Gospel
of Mark. The thesis of this study is that the author of the Gospel
of Mark used the sayings of Jesus as a literary means to put across
a narrative point of view and as a form of characterization. In this
paper *Point of view* and *characterization* are used in the technical sense
of the word. The latter is evident and the former '. . . signifies the
way a story gets told—the perspectives established by an author
through which the reader is presented with the characters, actions,
setting and events which constitute the narrative . . .'. (Abrams 1971:
144–148); for further detail on point of view in Mark (see Vorster
1980a:8ff. and Petersen 1978b:97–121). This study falls into two
parts: in the *first* problems in connection with redaction and contextualization are discussed and in the *second* Mark 14:61–62 is treated
in detail.

1. *Redaction and Contextualization: Some Problems*

The sayings of Jesus in the gospels have for the greater part of this
century been studied as individual sayings in isolation, that is in view
of their formation, growth and transmission and not in the first place
as part of the context within which they were finally written down.
This has enormously enriched our knowledge about the things Jesus
said, could have said and did not say. With the rise of *Redaktionsgeschichte*
it became clear that the sayings of Jesus have an additional (third)
Sitz im Leben namely their *redaction* by the individual evangelists. (The
use of the term *Sitz im Leben* has become very misleading and problematic, see Güttgemanns 1970:82ff.) It resulted in study of the share
of the evangelists in the final redaction of these sayings. The purpose was to establish the theology of the individual evangelists and
it was evident that these sayings could be of great importance. The
implications of the *redaction* of the sayings of Jesus have to my mind
not been taken seriously because of the presuppositions of redaction
critics and also because '. . . the importance of studying the composition of each Gospel' (see Tannehill 1977:386) has not fully been

recognized in Redaction criticism. Redaction criticism is based amongst others on the disputable assumption that there is a direct continuity between the oral and literary phases of the gospel tradition (see Kelber 1979 for a discussion of the problems involved). Accordingly the literary phase is studied in view of its origin and growth and not as a written text. Or to put it another way, the redactional phase of the gospels is studied in view of the tradition from which it evolved (see Strecker 1979c). In order to illustrate the implications of such an approach I shall briefly discuss three different examples.

The logion of Jesus in Mark 8,38 forms part of a cluster of sayings (8,34–9,1) on the importance of his suffering and death for his followers. The importance of the structure and composition of the pericope is evident (cf. La Fontaine & Beernaert 1969; and Vorster 1979a:175ff.). It forms a very important part of Mark's narrative and especially of his presentation of Jesus as teacher (see Reploh 1969).

The signs of Mark's redactional activity are evident and need not be elaborated upon (see Pryke 1978:17,163). In its present form the logion fits well into the immediate context and also into the story of Mark and his presentation of Jesus. It is, however, evident from a casual reading of commentaries or relevant material on the logion that ἐπαισχύνομαι amongst others causes great difficulties. To my knowledge O. Michel was the first to establish the semantic aspect of ἐπαισχύνομαι by referring to the synoptic parallel of the logion in Luke 12,8ff./Matthew 10,32ff. and its history of tradition and transmission (see Michel 1940 and Vorster 1979a:141f. for a comprehensive treatment of the logion in this respect). As a result it has been asserted that ἐπαισχύνομαι is a synonym of ἀπαρνέομαι that it is Pauline, or has a Pauline colour, or that it is '... eine gräzisierte und vielleicht nachpaulinische Modifikation des semitischen ὁμολογεῖν und ἀρνεῖσθαι (see Käsemann 1954–55:257; also Vorster 1979a:144f.), or that it originated from the missionary vocabulary of the Hellenistic Church. Of late Schmithals contended: 'Statt (bekennen und) "verleugnen" wählt er den "christlichen" bzw. "paulinischen" Begriff "schämen", der wie ein Vergleich mit anderen Stellen zeigt (Roum. 1,16; 2 Tim. 1,8.16; IgnSm. 10,2; Herrn Sim. VIII 6,4), die Scheu vor dem gefährlichen öffentlichen Bekenntnis ausdrückt. Damit aktualisiert Mk. den Spruch' (see Schmithals 1979:394). There is no reason to accept that Mark is referring to public confession. This idea is based on an incorrect reconstruction of the history of the meaning of ἐπαισχύνομαι. (On the oldest form of the logion, see Vorster 1979a:169ff.)

Interesting as this summary of the results of the initial impulse of Michel's hypothesis may be, it appears that this semantic constellation cannot stand the test of a semantic analysis. There is no reason to accept that ἐπαισχύνομαι has the meaning of ἀπαρνέομαι. Knowledge of semantic domains of New Testament vocabulary helps us realize that the two words belong to two totally different semantic fields, the one to *interpersonal relations* and the other to *emotional events* and also that they are not synonyms (see Vorster 1979a:193). Variance in the transmission of the logion with regard to ἐπαισχύνομαι and ἀπαρνέομαι can be explained without having to accept the semantically impossible, let alone the assumption that the logion in Mark refers to public confession (Vorster 1979a:171f.; also Zimmermann 1979:26f.). Mark has one form of the logion which Luke also retained in 9,26 and this logion makes sense as it stands within the Markan contextualization. (The fact that Luke retained the ἐπαισχύνομαι-form of the logion is not without significance. Why did he not change the verb in accordance with the form in 12,8ff.) Having edited the material he placed the saying in a particular setting in order to further his presentation of Jesus, the suffering Son of Man who is also the Son of God. Central to his narrative is the motif of incomprehension which is part of Mark's attempt to convince his readers/hearers of *his* Jesus (Mk. 4:10–13, 40–41; 6:50–52; 7:18; 8:16–21, 33; 9:32; 10:35ff; see Vorster 1980b:43ff.). If somebody feels ashamed about this Jesus, let him know that the Son of Man will also feel the same about him. It is within this context, that is, within Mark's narrative world. Within his arrangement of transmitted material and his redaction thereof that ἐπαισχύνομαι has meaning and not in view of the history of the transmission of the logion. To put it another way, the meaning of a Jesus-logion or parts thereof is in the first place determined by its immediate environment. Redaction and contextualization are determining factors in this respect.

My second example is of a rather different nature. The fact that both conservative and critical scholars ignore the relationship in Mark's narrative between the parable of the Sower in Mark 4:3ff. and its interpretation in 4:13ff. has often struck me (see Vorster 1975 for a treatment of the problem and relevant literature). The two texts are normally analyzed in isolation and each allotted its own meaning. Whether it is argued, as normally happens, that Mark 4:3ff. presents us with a form of the parable which is much closer to the original words of Jesus than the exposition given in 4:13ff., an exposition which originated from the primitive church, or not, does not matter. The two pericopes are normally treated separately and in isolation from each other. They are in other words not regarded as a text and an explanation of that text as Mark tells us but as two separate texts. It is interesting in view of this remark to note that Gnilka in his recent commentary on Mark first of all affords us with an explanation of the meaning of the parable and then asserts that Mark, however, did not care for this particular meaning of the parable. According to him Mark accepted the 'allegorical interpretation' in 4:13ff. as the meaning of the parable (see Gnilka 1978:161). It is impossible in this type of approach not to remember the words of Wellek and Warren (1973:164):

> ... the mixture of textual criticism, literary history in the special form of source study, linguistic and historical explanation, and aesthetic commentary in many editions seems a dubious fashion of literary scholarship justified only by the convenience of having all kinds of information between two covers.

In accordance with his views on the origin of Mark's Gospel Schmithals on the other hand rejects the form-critical explanation of this parable and also the idea that its exposition in 4:13ff. presupposes a secondary development. According to him both text (4:3ff.) and interpretation of that text (4:13ff.) are the work of the narrator who was responsible for the 'Grundschrift' Mark used in writing his gospel: 'Da aber Bild und Deutung harmonisch zusammenpassen und ausserdem das Bild selbst keine Spannungen oder Erweiterungen zeigt, muss man die Suche nach postulierten Vorformen des Gleichnisses und deren Bedeutung überhaupt aufgeben und sich an den vorliegenden literarischen Bestand halten der keinerlei Anlass gibt hinter ihn zuruckzufragen. Gleichnis und Deutung durften Werk des Erzahlers sein' (see Schmithals 1979:231f.). Accordingly the parable has one meaning only and that is the 'allegorical interpretation' we know from Mark 4:13ff. Mark accepted this. He, however, divided the text and its interpretation by inserting between them the so-called parable theory, Schmithals (1979:234) maintains.

As far as the Markan narrative is concerned Schmithals is correct. His view on the 'Grundschrift'-hypothesis, however, is another matter (see Luz 1980:649ff.). What the original meaning of the parable was, is beside the question now. What matters is that Mark edited and contextualized the parable and its interpretation for a specific purpose. By inserting the parable theory and having Jesus explain the parable Mark has his story told from a perspective of his choice. (The problem of why Jesus the Son of God had to suffer, is brought into focus by the quote from Isaiah 6:9–10 in Mark 4:12, see Vorster 1981b:62–72.) The very fact that he tells the story of Jesus in this particular way, namely to have Jesus the teacher say something and explain it to the disciples who are presented as those who often misunderstand, although they receive special instruction, forms part of the composition of the narrative and has to be taken seriously (see Reploh 1969).

Let us now turn in the third place to yet another type of problem. A very interesting aspect in connection with the study of the sayings of Jesus in Mark is that he included considerably less sayings of Jesus in his narrative than either Luke or Matthew. This has given rise to various questions. It is evident that the answers you get, depend on the questions you ask. 'Die Wahl der Fragenstellung bestimmt das Vorgehen' (see Richter 1971:189). A large variety of solutions have been suggested to the problem of the paucity of sayings in Mark (see Boring 1977). The problem is often related to the question whether Mark knew Q (see Dibelius 1971:262f.). In his attempt to explain the phenomenon in form-critical categories Martin Dibelius for example argued that the narrative tradition and the sayings tradition initially were two separate traditions. Since Mark attempted to describe only the narrative tradition the paucity is not strange. From a redaction-critical point of view a large number of answers has been devised. Boring gives the following review of four of these, 1. Mark *presupposes* the existence of Q or a similar collection. 2. Mark *historicizes* his material, relating them to the story of the pre-Easter Jesus. 3. Mark *selects* his material to correspond to his emphasis on the cross-resurrection kerygma. 4. Mark *opposes* some kind or kinds of Christianity represented to some extent by the speech materials (see Boring 1977:4). What is remarkable about this display of 'Hypothesens freudigkeit' (see Luz 1980:653), is that in most cases it is not the text of the Gospel of Mark or the redaction and contextualization of the 'few' sayings in that text which is taken into account in answering the question. It is that which lies behind the text or in the mind of the author. Amazing as it is, even in Redaction criticism the question remained, 'Why so few sayings?'. Interesting as this may be it is not all that important when the focus is upon the redaction and contextualization of the sayings. More important than, 'Why so few?' is 'Why did Mark include the sayings of Jesus in his narrative?' or perhaps more correctly, 'What is the function of the sayings material in the Gospel of Mark?'.

To review the fore-going problems: The fact that Mark has edited and contextualized the sayings of Jesus in his composition has implications which redaction critics have not realized because of their focus on the relationship between redaction and tradition. This applies to various levels of meaning starting with the semantics of single words and ending with the meaning of the composition as a whole. Approaching the problem from the perspective of the genre of Mark the study of text type problems, especially as far as the gospels are concerned, cannot be overestimated, see Vorster 1981a—and the function of these sayings within that text type, throws new light on the sayings in Mark's Gospel.

2. Mark 14:61–62

The decision to *write* a gospel was a major one in the history of the transmission of the Jesus tradition. The moment it was written Jesus was presented to the receivers of that text in one particular way (see Vorster 1980b). This presentation was only changed when a next gospel and other text types presenting Jesus in other ways came to be written. Whether Mark was a conservative redactor (see Pesch 1976:22) or a creative author (see Vorster 1980b) makes no difference to the importance of the fact that the tradition was written down. Mark decided to compose a narrative on aspects of the life and works of Jesus with the help of material transmitted by way of narration. To get his story across he established certain perspectives through which the reader or hearer '. . . is presented with the characters, actions, setting and events which constitute the narrative . . .' (see Abrams 1971:133). The essence of his narrative lies in the relationship between the teller (Mark) and those who hear or read his narrative (see Scholes and Kellogg 1966:240). Consequently it is possible to approach the sayings of Jesus from the perspective of what Mark achieved or attempted to achieve with their redaction and contextualization in his Gospel. Their relationship with tradition does not play any role in this approach.

Although Jesus is not as talkative in Mark as he is in the other gospels, what Mark has him say, the way in which he has him say it, and the occasions on which he has him say something in his narrative world, form a very important aspect of his characterization of Jesus and the way he gets his story told. (This is not to say that Mark invented all the material in his narrative. The arrangement, the redaction and the way he tells the narrative is his own work, see Vorster 1980b:39ff.) It is well known that Jesus is presented in Mark's Gospel as the Son of God who had to suffer. To achieve this Mark made use of various narrative techniques. In his plotting of the story of Jesus he is presented in the first half of the Gospel as the successful Son of God who conquers in everything he does or says (for a more comprehensive treatment of the structuring of the narrative events, that is the 'plot' of Mark's Gospel and characterization elsewhere, see Vorster 1980a:126–130).

While he is presented in a sympathetic way his opponents, including his disciples create a feeling of dislike and aversion because of what they say and do. Although the reader is prepared for the other side of the success story he is in any case taken by surprise when Jesus rejects the confession of Peter and spells out his suffering and death (see 8:27ff.). The programmatic unfolding of the second part of the Gospel is structured by the three sayings of Jesus (8:31; 9:31; 10:33f.) fore-telling the unfolding of the story. The importance of these three sayings for the structure of the Gospel of Mark has been noticed by many, see Strecker 1968:121–142; also Güttgemanns 1970:221ff. In short, what Jesus does or says contributes to the way in which the story gets told. I shall briefly discuss one saying namely Mark 14:62 as a constitutive element in the composition of Mark's narrative.

It cannot be denied that the trial of Jesus before the Sanhedrin (Mk. 14:53–65) presents serious problems of a historical nature (see Gnilka 1978:284ff.). As a result much of what is told in this pericope is attributed to the redactional activity of Mark (see Pryke 1978:22, 173; also Kaziersci 1979:167ff. especially 185–189; and Steichele 1980:284–286). These questions aside, from the point of view of the narrative composition the main question is what did Mark achieve with the question of the high priest and Jesus' response? Mark tells us, 'Again the High Priest questioned him: "Are you the Messiah, the Son of the Blessed One?" Jesus said, "I am; and you will see the Son of Man seated at the right hand of God and coming with the clouds of heaven"' (NEB). The response of Jesus to the question whether he is the Christ (Messiah) and the Son of God is straightforward. I am the Christ, I am the Son of God; I, the Son of Man, shall sit at the right hand of God and I shall return with the clouds! Both what Jesus says and the form in which he says it— the answer of Jesus is composed of the phrase ἐγώ εἰμι followed by a free quotation from Ps. 110,1 and Dan. 7,13 with reference to the Son of Man—are important. 'Like the questions and answers in 4:10–12 (see 4:13ff.), 8:27–31, and 13:3–37, Jesus' response goes beyond the question, showing that for Jesus (and the narrator) the answer is the important thing, not the question', Petersen (1978:75) correctly argues. In view of Mark's presentation of Jesus and the Jewish leaders in the previous parts of his narrative the reader is able to understand both the question of the high priest and the response of Jesus—be it on two levels though! In Mark's Gospel there is a tension between who Jesus is according to the narrator and who his opponents deem him to be (see Mk. 8:27–31; 10:47; 12:35 *et al.*) which is reflected in the question and answer of Mark 14:61–62.

It has furthermore to be kept in mind that the narrative is structured by what may be called prediction-fulfillment techniques (Petersen 1978:49ff.). A statement or prediction is made and later on in the narrative it is put into practice or fulfilled. A few examples will suffice: 1:2–3 prediction → 1:4ff. fulfilment; 1:7 → 1:9ff.; 1:14 → 11:10ff.; the passion predictions in 8:31, 9:31 and 10:32–34 referred to above, which offer a summary of the passion narrative, and 14:29, 14:66–72. At this stage of the passion narrative the reader is already aware of the fact that Jesus is Son of God, the Son of Man the conqueror who has to suffer, die and return, but is again surprised in view of 8:27ff. by the fact that he is made known as *the Christ* who as Son of Man will *be seated at the right hand of God.* Jesus' response to the high priest identifies three periods in Jesus' career as the Son of man: (1) his time as a character whose actions are plotted in the narrative, namely, the time of the passion of the Son of man; (2) the time after it when he will be seated at the right hand of Power until (3) the time of his parousia at the end, when the kingdom, properly understood in relation to the Son of Man, will come (cf. Petersen 1978:75). By having Jesus answer the high priest with a composite quotation from the Old Testament Mark created the possibility of referring back to what has already been told about Jesus as well as to the post-resurrection time in his narrative when the Son of Man will sit next to God.

The fact that the answer is given in the form of an Old Testament quotation is in view of Mark's use of the Old Testament not without significance. Although Mark's narrative is couched in the thought and imagery of the Old Testament his use of the Old Testament, especially the quotation thereof is remarkable and different from especially Matthew's usage. The use of the Old Testament in Mark's Gospel has the same function as narrative commentary (see Vorster 1981a:69ff.), namely to substantiate the train of thought. The quotations are often so well integrated that they form part of the narrative statement (see 1:1–4; 7:6–8; 10:5–8 and 14:27–28), and sound like the words of the narrator or narrated figures. Most of the quotations from the Old Testament in Mark are put into the mouth of Jesus (see 4:2; 7:6, 10; 8:18; 9:11, 48; 10:6–8, 19; 11:17; 12:1, 10, 26, 29, 31–33, 36; 13:14, 24–26; 14:18, 27, 62; 15:34). These sayings are part of the characterization of Jesus and his opponents. It helps the reader understand Jesus and reject his opponents (see 7:6–7). It creates sympathy for Jesus and dislike in the Jewish leaders. Quotations from the Old Testament have thus the same function in Mark (see 7:6–7; 12:26) as narrative commentary (see 3:6; 11:18; 12:12; 14:1, 55). By quoting the Old Testament, even though it is totally out of context, Jesus triumphs over his opponents (see 12:26). In Matthew's account the Old Testament quotations are often used to show that they were fulfilled in Christ while Mark used them as part of the narrative statement which is fulfilled within his narrative (see for example 1:2–3 → 1:4ff. in its relation to 16:7–8). This is also the function of Mark 14:62 which refers both to the past and to the future within the story time (see Petersen 1978:49–80 for a more comprehensive treatment of *story time* and *plotted time* in Mark's narrative). The redaction of the saying and its contextualization in this particular narrative scene was done on purpose.

Redaction and contextualization form part of the composition of a text. The fact that attention has been focused for so long on the relationship between redaction and tradition has meant that the real issues of the text, its nature and meaning have been overlooked. Texts are written to be read or heard. In the case of narratives like the gospels it proves fruitful to investigate the text from the point of view of the reader and not only from the viewpoint of its growth and origin. The authors of narratives edit and contextualize material with a specific purpose in mind. From the few examples treated above it is evident that the most important implication is the fact that the meaning of a narrative text is first of all to be looked for in the text itself and not in its growth and/or origin. This is the case on the level of the word, sentence and larger semantic units. Since the gospels are narratives there are factors other than the relationship between redaction and tradition which are constitutive as far as meaning is concerned in a text. As a result of the redaction and contextualization of the sayings of Jesus it is essential to study them as part of the text and not in isolation.

SECTION D

LITERARY ANALYSIS

CHAPTER TWENTY

A READER-RESPONSE APPROACH
TO MATTHEW 24:3–28

By this time it is common knowledge among New Testament scholars that the reader plays an active role in assigning meaning to a
text. The reception of Matthew 24 makes it clear that this text has
prompted readers to assign different, even contradictory, interpretations to the text or to parts of it. It is interesting to page through commentaries, articles and translations to see what scholars say the text
is about. Captions such as 'Discourse on the last things' (McNeile
1957:343), 'Endzeitrede: Das Kommen des Weltrichters' (Schweizer
1973:293), 'Prophecies and warnings' (*NEB*), 'The Testament of
Jesus-Sophia' (Burnett 1981) and 'The Matthean apocalypse' (Brown
1979), reveal how different readers describe the 'substantive content'
(Lafargue 1988) of Matthew 24 (see also Kloppenborg 1979 and
Köhler 1987 for early receptions of the text). Since reading is more
than the discovery of the meaning which is seemingly inscribed into
a text, it is not strange that different readers, who are themselves
semiotic topics (see Vorster 1989a:60–61), interact with the text and
actualise its meaning potential differently.

This essay is based on the assumption that reading is an interactive process between a text and a reader. It is furthermore assumed
that texts do not have meaning. Meaning is arrived at by the dialec-
tical process between a text, which evokes a response from the reader,
and the reader who assigns meaning to the text, or responds to the
text. It is also assumed that the (implied) reader is inscribed into the
text and that a real reader has a role in creating meaning by responding to codes inscribed into the text (see Vorster 1989b; also Anderson
1983; Burnett 1990; Phillips 1990). The essay therefore deals with
what the text does to the reader, and how the reader responds to
the text. Attention will be paid to how Matthew 24:3–28 evokes a
reader's response and what strategies the readers apply as they read
the text. Since I was invited to approach the text from a have chosen the title accordingly. I have, however, taken the liberty not to
restrict myself to a specific form of reader-response criticism. The

essay is based on reception theory in general (see Lategan 1984:10ff.; also Porter 1990). Special attention will be paid to the question of whether the speech deals with the fall of Jerusalem or with the return of the Son of man. With this in mind, matters such as the function of the use of the *futurum*, the conjunction γάρ, the motif of alertness, and defamiliarisation are treated.

1. *On Reading Matthew 24:3–28*

Matthew 24:3–28 forms a very small fragment of the Gospel as a whole, and also only a fragment of the speech of Jesus in Matthew 24–25. From the perspective of this essay it is, however, impossible to read these few verses without being informed by the preceding material, and also by what follows (see Howell 1990). A few preliminary remarks are therefore in order.

The material preceding Matthew 24 is important because it 'constitutes the reader's "education"' (Burnett 1985:92). By a variety of codes and strategies the reader is equipped to read later parts of the text.

Reading concerns the process of interaction with the text. Each word, sentence, event or character creates certain expectations which are either fulfilled or disappointed in the reading process. The reader therefore engages in forming expectations and revising these expectations by reading the text sequentially and by processing the information. By the time the reader of Matthew's Gospel reaches chapter 24, he/she is well informed about the characters, events and standards of judgement.

Matthew 24:3–28 forms part of Matthew 24:4–25:46, one of five major narrated (see Vorster 1987a) speeches of Jesus in the Gospel (chapters 5–7; 10; 13; 18; 24–25). At this stage the reader not only knows that Jesus is the most important character in the story but also that, unlike the Pharisees or even the disciples, he is a reliable character. Like the narrator of the story, he is omniscient. He knows what other characters feel, think and plan. It is also known that whenever he speaks important information is given to the reader, and that he presents the 'viewpoint of God' (Mt. 16:23; see also Kingsbury 1986:32ff.).

Burnett (1985; see also Van Aarde 1982) has convincingly shown that when the reader reaches chapter 24, he/she knows that when-

ever Jesus appears, he is 'God with us', and that he is revealing the
'plan of God'. The reader also knows that he will most probably be
revealing an important message to the disciples, and therefore to the
readers of the Gospel in 24:3–28. On different occasions in the preceding material he instructs his disciples and reveals to them his
point of view (5:1; 13:10, 36; 15:12 and 18:1). Simply from the
redundant information that is given by the text, the reader knows
certain things which might be expected. The phrase Καθημένου δὲ
αὐτοῦ ἐπὶ τοῦ Ὄρους τῶν Ἐλαιῶν (24:3), for example, initiates the
expectation that Jesus will authoritatively reveal something, because
the reader is educated that whenever Jesus sits, he teaches with
authority (see 5:1–2; 13:1–3 and 15:29). It is also known that the
'mountain' (see Donaldson 1985) is a place of revelation in the Gospel
(see 5:1; 28:16; also 8:1; 14:23; 15:29; 17:1, 9; 26:30).

The fact that the disciples approach Jesus is also not without
significance. They are his immediate followers, to whom he reveals
the plan of God. The reader is expected to identify with his message to them.

It is, however, not only the information that precedes chapter
24:3–28 that is important to the reader. What follows similarly determines the response of the reader to the text. In fact, in the process
of reading the reader has to revise, for instance, the idea that the
proclamation of the message is restricted to the Jews only as it is
said in chapter 10. In different ways, as we shall see, the reader is
re-educated by the story. In short, the text does something to the
reader. It directs the reader and initiates certain responses.

2. On Prompting the Reader in Matthew 24:3–28

If one wants to know how Matthew 24:3–28 evokes a response from
the reader, one has to address the following question rigorously: what
do the words, the sentences, the sections of the text, and the speeches
of Jesus do? Not simply what the text means, or what it refers to.
The focus is thus not only on what is said, but also why it is said.
In this way one is able to determine the purpose of what is narrated in Matthew 24.

One should keep in mind that people do things with words. When
asked a question, for instance, the hearer or reader is prompted to
formulate an answer or to perform a deed. A prohibition urges the

hearer not to do a certain thing, and a warning advises a person to take care. Forms of speech like sentences, questions and so on are therefore not only concerned with what they say, but also with their purpose or with what they do. By saying something, the speaker performs an act (see e.g. Bach & Harnish 1979). This also holds true for the words and sentences in the story of Matthew.

The narrated speech of Jesus in Matthew 24 is introduced by a description of a new setting and a request by the disciples (24:3). There is a change of scene, but is there a change of topic? And what did the narrator of the story do with these words?

The preceding section (23:34–24:2) deals with the rejection and judgement of Jerusalem and her leaders and the prediction of the destruction of the temple. It has been argued on many and different grounds by scholars that the speech of Jesus in chapters 24–25 is a continuation of the theme of the destruction of the temple. The repetition of ταῦτα in verses 2 and 3 has led many interpreters to conclude that the question of the disciples, 'when will these things be?' refers to the destruction of the temple, and that Matthew 24:4–50 gives an answer to the question. Does it? It will only be possible to answer this question after we have dealt with the content of the speech.

Once the reader has learn no problem with Jesus being able to speak about future things and make predictions. In fact, this has often occurred in the preceding parts of the story. In terms of narrated and discourse time ('erzählte und besprochene Welt'), it immediately becomes evident that there is a change in the use of tenses in Jesus' speech. Most of the verbs are put in the future and present tenses, which are typical of the tenses used for discussing matters. It is also characteristic of the future tense, especially in predictions and assertions, that they express the belief of the speaker and his or her desire that 'the hearer have or form a like belief' (see Bach and Harnish 1979:41). It is therefore possible to infer from the use of tenses in Matthew 24:3–28 that the Matthean Jesus wishes his disciples to share his beliefs about the future. He performs a speech act by what he communicates. To put it differently: the text (of the Matthean Jesus) prompts a response from the disciples.

On the level of the reader of the Gospel of Matthew the same thing happens. Having presented Jesus as the reliable character who now speaks about future things, the narrator also expects the reader to share Jesus' beliefs about the future.

It is, however, important to pursue this matter further. The speech starts with the words: βλέπετε μή τις ὑμᾶς πλανήσῃ. The phrase is formulated in the form of a prohibition. Prohibitions, like all other linguistic directives such as questions, requirements and so on, 'express the speaker's attitude toward some prospective action by the hearer' (Bach & Harnisch 1979:41). The force (purpose) of the phrase is to warn the reader not to be led astray. In other words, what the phrase does is to direct the reader to take a certain action, that is, to be on the alert. It does not so much inform the reader as it instigates an action. The same happens in verses 6, 14, 15, 16, 17, 18, 20, 23 and 26, where prohibitions and requirements are mentioned. The disciples are warned to be on the alert, not to be troubled or disturbed, to witness, to be conscious of the times in which they live, to take preventive action, to pray and not to be misled.

If one carefully investigates the different directives referred to in the speech, it becomes clear that they structure the speech. This happens to such an extent that the main thrust of the speech comprises an appeal to the reader to maintain a state of alertness, and to await the return of the Son of man faithfully. From the perspective of what the text does it can be argued that it directs the reader to adopt a particular attitude, that is, to be on the alert, take heed and be warned. This view is undergirded by the way in which the prohibitions and commands are substantiated.

The use of the conjunction γάρ in the Gospel of Matthew reveals many interesting features with regard to its narrative function (see Edwards 1990). It is evident that the reliability of references to the future in any discourse mainly depends on the authority and reliability of the speaker. Jesus is the appropriate character in Matthew's Gospel to make statements about the future, since he is presented as a wholly reliable character. His reliability is already established in the so-called framework of the Gospel (1–4:22) by different γάρ-clauses used by different characters (see Edwards 1990:642–646, 652). The effect of these statements is to show the reader that the events referred to are part of the divine plan of God, and that 'the reader should expect God's control over events whether it is explicitly stated or not' (Edwards 1990:642).

It is furthermore remarkable that this conjunction γάρ often occurs in the sayings of Jesus which reveal his assumptions. They form part of his narrative point of view, which is presented as the viewpoint of God.

In Matthew 24:3–28 γάρ is used no less than six times as part of Jesus' directives to the disciples (5, 6, 7, 21, 24, 27). These φάρ-clauses predict the appearance of false messiahs, the delay of the final consummation, the advent of wars, famines and earthquakes, and the sudden return of the Son of man. All of these clauses, which are in the form of predictions, substantiate preceding commands. Their effect is that the reader has to be on the alert because the return of the Son of man will be preceded by horrifying events. In one case (v6), the theme of God's plan, which plays an important role in the narrative from the start, is called to mind and used as the reason why the disciples should not be troubled (δεῖ γὰρ γενέσθαι).

The effect of the directives that Jesus gives to the disciples is moreover strengthened by the technique of repetition of words such as πολλοὶ and τέλος, of negative events, and of themes such as false messiahs.

It is evident from the speech acts performed in this speech that Jesus wished his disciples to believe that they could expect a turbulent future. Although he phrased his statements in general (apocalyptic) form, they nevertheless convey the idea of difficult times awaiting the hearer before the return of the Son of man. Even the reference to τὸ βδέλυγμα τῆς ἐρημώσεως from the Book of Daniel (Mt. 24:15), and the references to the flight to the mountains of Judea (Mt. 24:16) should not be interpreted primarily in terms of historical references in the time of the disciples or the author of the Gospel. These signs form part of the narrated world which portrays difficult times of persecution and misery. They all help to impress the disciples/readers with the difficulties which will precede the return of the Son of man. What is, however, important to realise is the observation that the effect of the directives in the speech is to keep the listeners on their toes. They have to be on the alert and live with a view to the return of the Son of man. There is an urgent appeal for them to take care. As a narrated speech the material also has to be read on the level of the reader, and not only on the level of the disciples as hearers. The speech acts serve the same purpose on this level that they do on the level of the disciples. The reader receives the same instructions since he/she is inscribed in the text. This is clear from the command in verse 15: ὁ ἀναγινώσκων νοείτω. This statement is very important with regard to the response of the reader, since it determines the location of the reader of the Gospel of Matthew (see also Mt. 27:8; 28:15).

The reader of the Gospel finds him/herself in the period after the

resurrection and before the return of the Son of man. This is evident from the fact that the text refers to a reader outside the text
of the Gospel in which the resurrection is narrated. 'He who reads'
the speech, refers to the reader of the Gospel. This also helps the
reader to decide whether this speech of Jesus is about the destruction of Jerusalem or about the return of the Son of man.

The first part of the question in Matthew 24:3, namely πότε ταῦτα
ἔσται; might have led the reader to wonder whether the speech
would deal with both the destruction of Jerusalem and the return
of the Son of man. The interpretation of this part of the question
has been a bone of contention among interpreters of the Gospel for
many years. Different solutions have been offered to explain the
apparently ambiguous question (see Burnett 1981:8ff. and especially
198ff.). Let us first turn to the 'substantive content' of the speech
again. A few remarks on the 'return of the Son of man' are necessary.

Although παρουσία can obviously be used for the meaning 'to be
present', it is improbable that this is the case in Matthew 24:3. The
disciples clearly want to be informed about the return of the Son of
man and the end of the age. The tern παρονοία occurs five times in
the Gospel, and only in chapter 24 (vv. 3, 27, 30, 37, 39). Considering the specificity of the question τί τὸ σημεῖον τῆς σῆς παρουσίας;
and the fact that the Matthean Jesus refers to the return of the Son
of man three times in the speech, there seems to be little reason to
doubt that Jesus' speech gives an answer to the question. Although
verse 30 refers only to the sign of the Son of man, and not to his
return, the reader would undoubtedly understand this sign in conjunction with verse 27. The 'return' is, in other words, implied in
verse 30. The return of the Son of man is a formative principle in
the speech.

It is furthermore evident that 'Son of man' refers to Jesus. Because
the reader has been educated by the preceding material in the Gospel
that 'Son of man' is another name for Jesus (see 8:20; 9:6 etc.), and
even that he will return some time in the future as the Son of man
(10:23) and as judge (13:41), the reader knows that the Son of man
in chapter 24 is Jesus. The reader also knows that the speech is
first of all an answer to the question about the return of Jesus. The
third part of the question of the disciples concerning the end of
the age is answered indirectly in Matthew 24:3–28, and more fully
in chapter 25. But what about the first part, 'When will these things
happen?'

Burnett (1981:206) and others have argued that there is a caesura

between 24:2 and 3 and, following Walker, that the καί between the
first and second parts of the question should be read epexegetically:
'Tell us, when will this happen, that is (καί), what will be the sign
of your Parousia and the consummation of the Age?' (Walker as
quoted by Burnett 1981:207). This is a possible solution to the problem, and the conjecture of a caesura explains the break between
24:2 and 3. However, from a reader-response perspective, it seems
to me that the speaker (Jesus) flouts the question of t he does not
want to pursue the topic of the destruction of Jerusalem and the
temple any further. He breaks the maxim of relevance in the disciples' question and pursues the matters posed in the second and third
parts of the question (see Botha 1989:158 for a discussion of the
principle). The disciples are furthermore defamiliarised—that is, put
into a different perspective from the one the reader is used to—a
strategy which is common in the synoptic gospels (see Resseguie
1984) and which also plays a role in Matthew 24.

Chapter 23 has educated the reader that Jesus has rejected Israel,
in particular Jerusalem, and that he has predicted the destruction of
the temple. The latter is dealt with briefly in verse 2. Because of
the repetition of the pronoun ταῦτα in verses 2 and 3, it is quite
natural that the reader would expect Jesus to continue with the
theme in his answer to the disciples. By the end of the speech the
attentive reader would realise that Jesus has defamiliarised the familiar by speaking about his return and the end of the age and not
about the destruction of the temple. He/she will then revise the
question and realise that Jesus does not fulfil the expectation by
ignoring the question. For the (implied) reader of the Gospel, who
probably lived in a period after the destruction of the temple, and
who might have been familiar with the destruction of the temple
and Jerusalem, this defamiliarisation creates the opportunity of seeing the novelty in the story of Jesus.

There are other examples of defamiliarisation in Matthew 24 which
are equally important. It is often argued that there is a contradiction between Matthew 10:5 and 23 on the one hand and 24:15 on
the other (see also 28:19). It is thought that in Matthew 10 the focus
is still on the exclusivity of the mission of the disciples to Israel, and
that this presents a different view from later material, where the
good news of the man of Nazareth is understood in universal terms.
From the perspective of the reader of the Gospel, he/she is educated by the story that, in chapter 10, the disciples were ordered to
go and proclaim the message to Israel only. But, as the story devel-

ops, it is also learnt that Israel is rejected. When the reader reaches 24:15, the familiar is completely defamiliarised. A new message is given by rephrasing familiar material. Since Israel has rejected the proclamation of the message (see Mt. 23), the proclamation would be directed to all the nations.

Another example of defamiliarisation is the fact that no definite answer is given of exactly when the return will be. Since the reader knows that Jesus is a reliable character, it would seem obvious that he/she would also know when the return of the Son of man will be, and when the age will end. However, the disciples (and therefore the readers as well) are told that they should faithfully await the coming of the Son of man. Not even the Son knows the exact time (24:36). The expectation of the disciples/readers is disappointed, and instead they receive a very definite injunction: be on the alert!

3. *Conclusion*

Reader-response criticism does not offer answers to all the questions that are raised by ancient texts such as the Gospel of Matthew, not to mention the difficulties involved in such a complicated text as Matthew 24. Since the emphasis is on the reader, and how a text elicits a response from the reader, aspects of the communication between texts and readers/hearers are highlighted. With its focus on what texts do, and not only on what they mean, a neglected aspect of textual interpretation in New Testament scholarship receives attention. It has been illustrated that Matthew 24 directs the reader to read this part of the Gospel in the light of earlier parts, and that the speech acts used in the text help the reader to build an image of what the text does. It is in this way that a contribution is made to the interpretation of this very difficult early Christian text. Since the essay offers a discussion of a fragment of a fragment of a text, it is obviously incomplete. The aim, however, has been to illustrate how focusing on what the text does to evoke the response of the reader, and how the reader responds to the text, helps one to understand Matthew 24:3–28. Because of a lack of space, no attention has been paid to the detailed interpretation of every word or sentence, or to genre and other difficulties. The use of technical jargon has been limited to a few expressions. The informed reader will nevertheless recognise that the essay has been based, among other things, on insights from narrative, reception and speech act theories.

CHAPTER TWENTY ONE

THE READER IN THE TEXT: NARRATIVE MATERIAL

The notion 'reader in the text,' however ambiguous and paradoxical, has become part of the jargon of New Testament scholars. Because of the many ways in which the concept is used by literary theorists and the variety of applications in literary and New Testament studies, it is necessary to review the theoretical background of the notion as well as its potential for analyzing and interpreting narratives in the New Testament.

The purpose of this essay is to address the following problem areas concerning narratives in general and narratives in the New Testament in particular: Is there a reader 'in' the text? Who or what is the reader in the text? And, how is the reader in the text? Since every text is constructed with specific readers in mind, the question arises whether heuristic devices like the 'implied,' 'encoded,' or 'model reader' can help the flesh-and-blood reader to follow the contours of the text presentation and to actualize the text? I will confront these problems theoretically and methodologically with a view to the interpretation of narratives in the New Testament. In order to achieve this, I will first pay attention to the problem of the reader in the text in literary theory. Against this background, the second major part of the essay will address the phenomenon of the reader in the text in New Testament narratives.

The theme of the essay will be treated in terms of structural semiotic literary theory, keeping in mind the rhetorical and phenomenological background out of which the notion of 'reader in the text' developed. It is assumed that in the context of reception theory, the phenomenon 'text' is not simply an object which has an immanent meaning, but that it is part of a communication transaction in which both the generation of meaning by the author of the text and the attribution of meaning by the consumer of the text (the reader) are significant.

1. *A Reader in the Text?*

1.1   *The reader*

The reader is said to be 'in the text' because of his/her/its presence as an image, created by the author, and because of his/her/its encoding in linguistic signs and textual strategies. This image has to be constructed by the real reader. What does this mean?

The idea of a reader in the text originated with Wayne Booth's concept of an implied author in 1961 and its counterpart, the so-called implied reader, which he and others later developed. According to Booth (1983:138): 'The author creates ... an image of himself and another image of his reader; he makes his reader, as he makes his second self, and the most successful reading is one in which the created selves, author and reader, can find complete agreement.' This view is seminal to numerous developments by Iser (1974) and others (cf. Chatman 1978 and Suleiman & Crosman 1980). In order to come to grips with the theoretical implications of the reader in the text, it is necessary first to look at its counterpart, the implied author.

The first thing to notice is that the implied author is not identical with the real author, even if there may be an occasional overlap (Rimmon-Kenan 1983:87). According to this view (cf. Booth 1983:420–31) the implied author is the governing and organizing principle in, or implied by, the narrative text, the source of the judgments and values embodied in the text. It chooses what we read and how we read, and exerts power over our reading process. It is the implied author that chooses the detail and quality that is found in the work or implied by the work. Its function is to instruct the implied reader how to read by the signs of its presence in the text. It knows what is invented and that all the work's norms may not hold in 'real life.' An implied author may embody totally different views and values in a narrative than the author who created the implied author. That is why implied authors in different works of the same author need not be and often are not the same. The implied author is created by the real author, but as the term says, it is implied in the text. How? According to Booth (1983:70–71) as an image:

> As he writes, he creates not simply an ideal, impersonal 'man in general' but an implied version of 'himself' that is different from the implied authors we meet in other men's works.... Whether we call

this implied author an 'official scribe,' . . . it is clear that the picture the reader gets of this presence is one of the author's most important effects.

Although impersonal, the implied author's presence in the text is implied in terms of personal traits. It is an author with beliefs and values and interests. It is inscribed in the text in linguistic, literary, rhetorical, and other signs and traces from which the real reader has to infer its profile. But it is not simply a 'set of implicit norms' or a mere literary construct as Rimmon-Kenan (1983:88) would maintain. According to him it is not possible to 'cast it in the role of the addresser in a communication situation.' The detection of the implied author, and thus also the implied reader in the text, is directly influenced by the view of its role in communication. Because of the importance of a proper understanding of the function of the implied author, I will discuss the relation between the implied author and the narrator before we proceed to the implied reader.

It is common knowledge that every story has a storyteller (narrator) and somebody to whom the story is told (narratee), no matter whether it is an oral or a written story. But the real author is not identical with the narrator. Even in the case where the author tells the story (author = narrator) it is necessary to pay attention to the voice of the narrator as a narrative instance. Distinct from the real author, the narrator also differs from the implied author. Chatman (1978:148) makes the following observation about the implied author which can help us determine the relation between the two:

> He is 'implied,' that is, reconstructed by the reader from the narrative. He is not the narrator, but rather the principle that invented the narrator, along with everything else in the narrative, that stacked the cards in this particular way, had these things happen to these characters, in these words or images. Unlike the narrator, the implied author can tell us nothing. He, or better, it has no voice, no direct means of communicating. It instructs us silently, through the design of the whole, with all the voices, by all the means it has chosen to let us learn.

Chatman is correct in distinguishing between implied author and narrator, but he fails to see the place of the implied author in the communication process. His observation about the 'instruction' the implied author gives has to be taken a little further.

Although the implied author does not tell, at least it instructs the reader how to read. When the reader is misled by an unreliable narrator, it is the implied author who enables the correction of false views. This is done, for instance, by way of the order of material, opposing perspectives, and other correctives which are encoded in the text. In the case of irony, for example, the reader is activated by the difference in 'world view' between the implied author and the narrator, as Brink (1987:148) correctly observes. The implied reader is the organizing principle, even the interpreting principle, behind the narrator, and as such serves as an important participant in the narrative communication situation (cf. Brink 1987:149). The implied author is obviously a literary construct, as Rimmon-Kenan (1983:88) maintains, but this does not mean that it is a contradiction in terms to cast it in the role of a participant in narrative communication. It is implicitly in the text as the one who instructs the reader how to read.

1.2   *The implied reader*

The implied author, as we have seen, has a counterpart in the implied reader. Similar to the implied author, this is also a literary construct, the profile and image of which has to be constructed by the real reader. Its presence in the text is similar to that of the implied author. It is not identical with the real reader of the text. Not even the original, first flesh-and-blood readers are to be thought of as identical with the implied readers.

Implied readers can be envisaged as the readers intended by the authors as readers or hearers of their narratives. Even though they 'can never know their actual readers,' authors cannot make artistic decisions without prior assumptions (conscious or unconscious) about their audience's beliefs, knowledge, and familiarity with conventions' (Rabinowitz 1980:234). The 'authorial audience,' as Rabinowitz calls the intended actual readers, is of great importance for the reader since the text of any work is designed with this audience in mind and, as he argues (1980:244), 'we must—as we read—come to share its characteristics if we are to understand the text.' This is in agreement with the view of Booth (1983:138–39) that the implied reader is the reader we have to be willing to become in order to bring the reading experience to its full measure.

In Booth's opinion (1983:428–29), the implied reader is the kind of reader selected or implied by a given narrative whose values and beliefs must, at least temporarily, accord with the values and beliefs of that narrative. The implied reader must be a relatively credulous listener within the narrative, who accepts the narrative as it is told without questioning its values or events and existents. And furthermore he/she/it has to be capable of refusing to become the implied reader of an unreliable narrator. In this way the implied reader is enabled to interpret complex ironic structures in a narrative.

1.3 *The reading process*

These ideas about the presence of the reader in the text were developed by Iser (1974) with regard to a textual condition and the production of meaning in the reading process and by Eco with regard to the role of the reader in narrative fiction. Both views are important for our development of the idea of the reader in New Testament narratives.

Iser, who approached the notion of an implied reader from a phenomenological perspective, was mainly interested in the actions involved in responding to a text in order to produce meaning. He maintains (1978:34) that the implied reader:

> embodies all those predispositions necessary for a literary work to exercise its effect—predispositions laid down, not only by an empirical outside reality, but by the text itself. Consequently, the implied reader as a concept has his roots firmly planted in the structure of the text; he is a construct and in no way to be identified with any real reader.

Criticism has been made of Iser for defining the implied reader in purely literary terms as almost synonymous with the structure of appeal of a literary work, thus making the 'reader' a term which is 'senseless, if not downright misleading' (Holub 1984:85). If not seen in terms of its paradoxical nature as a reader who is present in the text both as an image, as Booth argues, and in terms of the directives in the reading process, the term obviously becomes misleading. The point is however, that one should take the notion of implied reader as a literary construct seriously with regard to its presence in the text—in other words, the way it is present in the text. I would agree that too much focus on the encoding could easily distract critics from the idea that they are still busy with inferring an image of the reader from all the components of the text.

Using the ideas of Roman Ingarden, Iser argues that in the absence of the sender of the text and with the inability of the text to react as a participant in the communication transaction, there are directives in the text which guide the reader in the reading process. These directives are defined with regard to the so-called 'Leerstellen,' that is 'gaps' or 'open places,' 'negation,' and 'negativity,' three modalities of indeterminacy or 'Unbestimmtheit' present in the text. These modalities operate on both the syntactic and paradigmatic levels. On the syntactic level, for instance, the breaks in a narrative between episodes or in the plot line, changes in perspective, and the clashes in presentation, offer the real reader the opportunity to fill in the gaps thus created and to return to previous interpretations in attributing meaning to the presented material. On the paradigmatic level, negation takes place when the ideas with which the real reader comes to the text are shattered, and the repertoire is changed. Negativity is involved when something in a text entices the reader to replace its direct meaning with a deeper meaning (cf. Iser 1978:228 and Koopman-Thurlings 1986).

It is not only what is in the text, but also what is not in the text, which directs the reader to make an appropriate reading of the text, according to Iser. Silence can be very effectively used by authors to direct readers in attributing meaning to a narrative, as Booth (1983: 271–301) has also convincingly shown. The ending of the Gospel of Mark is a very good example of what the author says by not saying anything.

1.4   *Codes in the text*

With respect to the presence of the reader in the text, Eco (1979) has made valuable observations about the production of meaning by reading the codes in the text. According to him, these syntactic, semantic, and pragmatic codes define the reader in the text, which he calls the 'model reader.' He maintains (1979:7) that:

> The author has ... to foresee a model of the possible reader (hereafter Model Reader) supposedly able to deal interpretatively with the expressions in the same way as the author deals generatively with them.

He furthermore contends that the text selects its appropriate reader (1979:7), and also that it projects an image of such a possible model reader through the choice of: '*a specific linguistic code*,' '*a certain literary style*,' and '*specific specialization-indices*.' Some texts even presuppose a specific encyclopedic competence (think of the model reader of an apocalyptic text!). These codes are often not only implicit, but also explicit, as in the case of children's literature where typographical signals and direct appeals play such an important role. In a philosophical treatise, on the other hand, the reader's intellectual profile is determined bythe sort of interpretive operations he is supposed to perform' (Eco 1979:11). In this sense the 'author' and 'reader' become textual strategies according to Eco.

The model reader is also encoded in the structure and rhetoric of the text. In the case of narratives, this means being encoded in the plot and all the other aspects which form part of the narrative mode, such as point of view, characterization, time, and order.

Eco developed the notion of the reader in the text much further than Booth or Iser and made it an encompassing concept of what is encoded in a text with regard to and for the sake of the reader. To say it in the words of Rimmon-Kenan (1983:119):

> ... the 'reader' is ... a construct, a 'metonymic characterization of the text' ..., an 'it' rather than a personified 'he' or 'she'.... Such a reader is 'implied' or 'encoded' in the text 'in the very rhetoric through which he is required to 'make sense of the content' or reconstruct it 'as a world.'

1.5 *Summary*

This is not the place to criticize the foregoing models of the reader in the text. I shall rather give a summary of what I regard as the essence of the notion of the reader in the text and the purpose for which it can be used. The summary must also serve as my opinion of what the reader in the text is.

The reader in the text is a literary construct, an image of a reader which is selected by the text. It is implied by the text, and in this sense it is encoded in the text by way of linguistic, literary, cultural, and other codes. It is not identical to any outside flesh-and-blood reader. It is an image that is created by the author which has to be constructed by thereal reader through the reading process in order to attribute meaning to the text, that is to actualize the text. The construction of the reader in thetext is central to the establishment of the meaning of a narrative according to this view (cf. Ruthrof 1981:122).

The purpose of constructing the reader in the text is not to move from the text to the context of communication outside the text, that

is, to the actual reader or even the actual author, but to establish
a meaning of a narrative.

2. *The Reader in New Testament Narratives*

Modern narratology is not necessarily directly applicable to ancient
narrative material, for there have been many and different developments in the art of storytelling of which the ancients had no idea,
and modern narratology must deal with these developments and with
theoretical matters concerning modern narratives. On the other hand,
ancient theorists like Aristotle laid the basis for modern thought about
many aspects of modern literary theory. Narration is, moreover, one
of the very few ways of organizing material in a discourse. It is basic
to human communication. One can, therefore, expect similarities
between modern and ancient narratives. Developments during the
last decade in narrative approaches to New Testament material have
indicated the advantages in analysing the narratives in the New
Testament with the help of modern narratological tools. The present question is whether theory about the reader in the text reviewed
above is applicable to New Testament narratives. If so, in what manner and for what purpose? Before answers are ventured, let us first
make a few general statements about New Testament narratives and
present some features peculiar to them.

2.1 *Narrative in the New Testament*

A very substantial part of the New Testament is presented in the
narrative mode. In addition to the Four Gospels of Matthew, Mark,
Luke, and John, the Acts of the Apostles and the Revelation of John
are narratives. Furthermore, a large number of smaller narrative
units are embedded in the Gospels and Acts of the Apostles. But
we also find material which is organized in narrative style in argumentative texts of the New Testament. The parables of Jesus, miracle stories, and Paul's presentation of the difference of opinion
between himself and Peter in Galatians are good examples of short
stories in the New Testament. These texts display characteristics
which are different from those normally dealt with in narratology.
Most of them are religious and were told for religious purposes, that
is, for communication about religious matters. They were intended

to be read aloud to audiences of hearers and not to be read silently by individual readers as we now read them (cf. among others Aune 1979). The first to hear the stories after they had been written down consisted of both newcomers and committed followers of a new religion. Many of these narratives contain materials which were transmitted orally. This makes the phenomenon of intertextuality and the reader in the text all the more important. Their significance for the subcultures for whom they were intended also makes them different from ordinary stories, even though they still remain stories. We also have to keep in mind the fact that in the end they became part of a set of canonized books, the Christian Bible, which, as a collection, is made up of two testaments.

As Christian scriptures, they are read and used for devotional purposes, in search for meaning in life, as sources for the making of sermons, as historical sources, etc. Undoubtedly these overcodings will play a role in the reading process. But for the purpose of this essay it will not be possible to pay attention to all the implications of these sorts of overcoding in the course of history. I shall limit my discussion by bracketing out the implications of canonization.

The above mentioned texts are said to be narratives because they have the characteristics of narratives. One of the distinctive criteria for classifying texts and determining genre, is the type of speaker involved in a text and his/her function (cf. Bal 1979:21; Van Luxemburg, Bal, & Weststeijn 1982:121). In the case of one speaker, as in poetry, the text is a monologue. When one speaker allows other speakers in a text also to speak, the text is organized in the narrative mode. New Testament narratives are characterized as narratives by this feature among others.

Most New Testament narratives are told by omniscient narrators who allow other speakers like Jesus also to tell stories or simply to speak. That is why these texts also have various narratees. The narrator in the Gospel of Mark tells the story of Jesus to an unidentified narratee. But Jesus also speaks. Jesus tells stories to the crowd and informs his disciples secretly. He even has an inside hearer group among his disciples when, in Mark 13, he informs the four disciples about the future and about their conduct in the light of the coming future (cf. Vorster 1987b). Thus, within the narrative world of Mark, there are different narratees as there are different narrators. The main narrator, whom we may call Mark, is not a separate voice as we often find in modern novels. He narrates the story on behalf

of the author, and that is why we may call him an authorial narrator. This does not imply that he is identical with the blood-and-
flesh author. The narrator is an intratextual communicant. The same
can be said of narrators and narratees in the other Gospels and in
Acts. The we-passages in Acts, of course, pose their own problems
in terms of narrators and readers in the text (cf. Kurz 1987:208–219);
the narratee is identified as Theophilus. In the Revelation of John,
the text is organized in the form of an autobiographic narrative concerning the visions of a certain John (cf. Vorster 1988b). In all these
narratives, authors and readers are implied in the text. They have
to be distinguished not only from the actual authors and readers,
but also from the narrators and narratees. These authors and readers
have to be constructed by the actual reader from the many codes
which I mentioned above. The following diagram illustrates the different communicants involved in New Testament narratives.

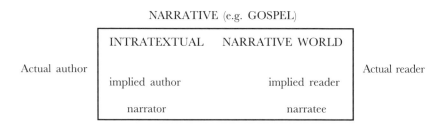

2.2 *Transactions in the text*

The implied author and implied reader as well as the narrator and
narratees are intratextual communicants, while the actual author and
the actual readers/hearers are outside the text. Similar to communication in other stories, in New Testament narratives communication is a transaction between the text and its intratextual communicants
and the actual reader. The actual author disappears behind the narrative presented. It is in this respect that the reader in the text, the
author in the text, the narrator and the narratee, the presentation
of the story, the emplotment, order, time, events, and other existents in the narrative world become important. Also important for
the establishment of the profile of the reader in the New Testament
narratives is the relationship between the presentational process, the
presented world, and the implied reader or reader in the text.

2.3 *Narrative world*

Ruthrof has convincingly argued that the way in which a story is presented, the world presented in a narrative, and the reader in the text are functions of one another. There is a direct relationship between the implied author of any particular text and the implied reader in that text. The implied reader forms a complement of the implied author. Let us give a few examples taken from his book (1981:138): In myth, where the narrator functions as an authority, the narrative world is presented as a dictate and the implied reader as a minor. In a parable, where the narrator is a preacher, the world is presented as analogue and teaching and the implied reader functions as a believer, normally with limited faculties. In prophecy, the narrator is a prophet who presents the world as divine vision and future truth to rebellious believers as implied readers. And in a narrative of ideas, the narrator is presented as an ideological visionary who presents the world as ideology to disciples. Omniscient narration normally involves a narrator who is clairvoyant. He presents the narrative world in unrestricted terms, especially as mental processes, to initiates.

If we now turn to New Testament narratives, it seems to me clear that Ruthrof's insights can help us further in establishing profiles of readers in the text. Let us look at a few examples in which the profile of the reader in the text is in direct relation to the presented world and to the image of the implied author.

The parables of Jesus are presented in the New Testament as narratives told by an authority on the Kingdom of God in which the world is disclosed in the form of 'ideology' about another way of looking at reality. The parables are addressed to minors with limited intellectual faculties due to the fact that they do not have the same insight as the narrator. These 'minors' are often presented as believers, or, in the case of Mark, initiates who find it difficult to grasp the riddle, but who are nevertheless informed as to how to listen and understand. Mark 4:11–12 is very interesting in this respect: 'To you has been given the secret of the kingdom of God, but for those outside everything is in parables; so that they may indeed see but not perceive, and may indeed hear, but not understand; lest they should turn again, and be forgiven.' To the initiates the mystery is given; they have the ability to understand. The outsiders however receive everything in parables, that is, riddles which remain riddles.

The implied reader is obviously one who has to become a hearer who is able to hear (cf. however Sternberg 1986:49). The movement from hiddenness to revelation in Mark's Gospel is one of the ways in which the implied reader is structured. It is common knowledge that the Gospel of Mark is structured by the so-called messianic secret. With a large number of subtleties the narrator encodes the riddle of how the Son of God, although a miracle worker, could die on a cross. The reader in the text is | obviously a decoder of the riddle, somebody who can follow the movement from hiddenness to revelation.

The image of the apocalyptic visionary of the Revelation of John, presenting visions of otherworldly realities to a subculture whose members have to overcome the pressures of their society, undoubtedly implies a reader in the text who has to accept the authority of these visions. He/she has to be an insider in apocalyptic imagery and symbolism, a believer in the triumph of God in the second coming of Christ. The story of Jesus according to Matthew, on the other hand, obviously implies a totally different reader. The story is told from the perspective of how Jesus, 'God with us,' is present in the community of followers. The narrator is an observer in the life and works of Jesus, the Jew. The reader in the text is a follower who has to take the evidence seriously and live as a witness of the will of Jesus.

The implications of the relation between the presentational process, the presented world, and the reader in the text, are obvious. This relationship helps to create an image of the reader in the text which directs the actual reader. It is in this connection that peculiarities of New Testament narratives come into play. Most narratives are religious. The presentation is, therefore, also about religious communication which determines the image of the reader in the text. Beliefs and values obviously form part of the image one constructs of readers in texts. The worldview presented in the miracle stories of Jesus, for instance, influences the image of the readers. The readers in the text of the miracles of Jesus are readers who believe not only in healing practices but also in nature miracles. Actual readers are invited to accept this worldview and to share the characteristics of the stories if they are to understand the texts.

2.4 Coding in New Testament texts

Every aspect of encoding is relevant and needs to be taken into account when the profile of the reader in any New Testament narrative is established. Although it will not be possible to go into all the detail, a few matters need our attention.

Since the structure of any text is designed with the reader in mind, traces of the reader in the text are to be looked for on all the levels of the structure and functions of narratives. Pro- and retrospection, gaps and indeterminacy, selection and organization, are signs of the reader, as Iser and Eco have indicated. All the narrative features such as plot, characterization, point of view, narrative commentary, order of narration, and time and space give clues to the actual reader in his or her construction of an image of the implied reader. Granted that the reader in the text is the total equipment an actual reader needs to actualize an appropriate reading of a text, every word, every group of words, every sentence or cluster of sentences become important. Every aspect of the text matters because the reader in the text is the ideal decoder of the complete text and not only of an aspect of it. As Kingsbury says, 'the important thing to keep in mind is that it is the implied reader who is silently and invisibly present throughout Matthew's story to attend to every word' (1986:37). Knowledge of the basic dictionary of the text, as well as knowledge of the rhetoric of narratives, are important aids in establishing the reader in New Testament narratives, as R.M. Fowler's investigation of irony and narrative commentary in Mark clearly shows (1981:155, 157). I shall limit my discussion of these matters to two further examples to indicate the presence of the reader in New Testament narratives. The first concerns the ending of Mark.

The shorter ending of Mark's Gospel leaves the story open-ended. Many actual readers and critics find Mark 16:8 so abrupt that a variety of suggestions have been offered to explain or complete the ending. From a literary point of view it can, however, be argued that the refusal of our narrator to say more and to leave the response of the women unnarrated stimulates the imagination (Moule 1965: 132–33; cf. Petersen 1980; Magness 1986). This explanation fits well the very structure of the Gospel of Mark. I have already mentioned that the presentation of the story of Jesus in the Gospel of Mark as a riddle which was deliberately encoded as such by the narrator invites the reader to become an insider who is able to decode the mystery of the death of Jesus. The lack of understanding by the disciples, prospection of what is to come (cf. Mark 8:31, 9:31 and 10:33), and reliability of the narrator, to mention only a few things, help us build an image of the reader in the text who has to react to the unnarrated response of the women to the report of the news of the resurrection. The suspension of the end of the story is a very suggestive and powerful way to stimulate the reader. Taking into account the fact that the reader in Mark's text is somebody who has to decode the riddle, one immediately senses that he or she is a reader who is able to respond to the silence in the text by becoming, unlike the disciples who lack understanding in the greater part of the Gospel of Mark, an understanding follower of Jesus.

Characterization in narratives also gives valuable indications of the reader in the text, because the reader either has to identify with or reject characters. The traits given to characters are, therefore, indicative of the image of the reader in the text who is intended to reject certain characters and to identify with others. Characterization of Jesus in the Gospel of Mark, for example, in comparison with opponents of Jesus or with Peter, clearly illustrates the point. The image of Jesus as reliable in every aspect, over against the disciples, including Peter (cf. Vorster 1987a), indicates that the image of Jesus and his point of view is to be accepted; the reader in the text is expected to reject the image of those who oppose and do not understand Jesus. Incomprehension is a trait of the disciples, but not of the reader in the text. The reader in the text is someone who understands and is willing to become a follower of Jesus the Crucified. Both structure and characterization give insight into the image of the reader in the text, an image which the actual reader constructs from the codes in the text. In addition to the syntactic and semantic aspects, the pragmatic aspect of New Testament narratives has to be considered to help establish the image of readers in New Testament narratives.

2.5 *Pragmatic functions*

The study of the reader in the text from the perspective of pragmatic function is especially appropriate since New Testament narratives were doubtless written to convince and persuade hearers and readers. In this respect special attention should be given to the sociolinguistic aspect of language and in particular of religious language. Language is a social interaction. That is why statements, sentences, paragraphs, etc. can have different functions in accordance with the context and participants of communication (cf. Chatman 1978:162ff.; and Halliday 1978:19f.). These include expressive, exhortative, informative, social, and persuasive pragmatic functions. Narrative commentary in the Gospel of Mark introduced by γὰρ (cf. 1:16, 22; 2:15; 3:10, 21 and others) is normally informative, but one can make out a good case that the commands to be silent (cf. 1:44) or the lack of understanding of the disciples (cf. 4:13), on the other hand, have the function to persuade. These pragmatic functions obviously help determine our image of the reader in the text. Let us now turn to the reader in the text and intertextuality and then to a few remarks about the fact that New Testament narratives were intended to be read aloud to an audience of listeners.

2.6   *Intertexts*

The use of the Old Testament in narrative material, such as the Gospel of Matthew, points to the importance of intertextual competence of the reader in the text. In the Gospel of Matthew, the knowledge of the reader in the text concerning the Old Testament is used to bring about a new understanding of the story of Jesus and also to reinterpret the Old Testament. In this manner, an interaction takes place between the texts that are quoted and Matthew's text. The reader in the text is presented as a reader who knows about other texts and who can use his intertextual competence to interpret the story of Jesus in the light of a reinterpretation of other texts which are quoted (cf. Rabinowitz 1980). The same happens in the other Gospels, in Acts, and also in the Revelation of John.

2.7   *Auditory structuring*

That New Testament narratives were not intended to be read silently but to be heard also influences the image of the reader in the text. The very structure of New Testament narratives is often determined by the fact that these narratives were intended to be read to audiences. Studies on redundancy in Matthew, like those of Burnett and Anderson, demonstrate one way that the intended reader/hearer pre-structured the text of Matthew.

2.8 *Summary*

Rather than attempt a comprehensive treatment of readers in the
text of New Testament narratives, this essay seeks to answer the
question of whether and how the reader is present in these narratives and for what purpose one constructs the image of the reader
in the text. It has become clear that there are many different clues
in New Testament narratives from which the actual reader is able
to construct an image of the reader in the text. I have indicated a
few of these, but others are to be found. Culpepper, for example,
has made valuable observations about the implied reader in the
Gospel of John by asking what the narratee, whom he presents as
the implied reader, knows and when he or she knows it. The same
can obviously be done with the other narratives of the New Testament
in order to establish images of readers in the text. As to the purpose of establishing the profile of the reader in the text, it has also
become clear that this is related to the meaning the actual reader
attributes to the text. It helps in the actualization of a specific interpretation or reading of a particular narrative.

3. *Conclusion*

In conclusion I would like to make a few remarks about the possibilities
and the limitations of the theory concerning the reader in the text
with regard to the interpretation of New Testament narratives.
3.1—The shift in emphasis from author to text to reader in the
process of interpretation of the New Testament was a necessary and
meaningful shift. It was necessary as the documents came to be interpreted as ancient documents within a theoretical framework of communication and not merely as artefacts to be interpreted in view of
the intention of the author, their origin, or as texts without authors
or readers. This has given rise to reflection about the nature of New
Testament documents as textual messages between senders and
receivers. Because of the focus on the text, much more attention had
to be paid to the nature of texts and how they function. The rediscovery of the narrative character of a large number of New Testament
writings and the application of insights of narratology, ancient and
modern, and what that implies with regard to the reading of these

texts, opened the possibility of rephrasing old questions and offering new answers within new theoretical frameworks. The outcome of the application of this interest in texts and readers is in many ways still open since much work still has to be done. By interpreting the New Testament from the perspective of the reader in the text, as has for instance been done in volume 31 of Semeia, additional possibilities and limitations will be discovered.

3.2—One of the most important limitations is the fact that there is, to my mind, no possibility of using the reader in the text to go directly through the text to the flesh-and-blood original readers. The fact that the New Testament consists of texts without their original contexts of communication need not be a problem in connection with New Testament narratives and communication or in connection with the phenomenon of the reader in the text. It is, however, remarkable how scholars attempt to use the notion of the reader in New Testament texts to move from this reader to the actual first-century readers. Petersen (1984:39–40), among others, to my mind, overstresses the potential of the reader in the text by relating the implied reader to 'extratextual communicants, to people who belong to the text's historical, interpretive context.' In spite of Culpepper's awareness that a characterization of the narratee (as implied reader) can only be used in a debate over the actual, historical audience on the assumption that the narratee is identical to the actual reader, he (1983:206–37) nevertheless establishes a profile of the narratee within the framework of this debate. To my mind one should avoid the temptation to infer historical information about the actual readers from the reader in the text unless it can be confirmed by other extratextual data. It is theoretically impossible to make inferences from the reader in the text about the actual readers of first-century Christian narratives except in terms of broad generalities. This is not to deny the important principle of historical criticism that a text is evidence for the time in which it was written. I only wish to stress the fact that the profile of a reader in the text is constructed in the first place to enable the reader to attribute meaning to a text, and that it is an intratextual construct. In this respect New Testament narratives are similar to other narratives.

3.3—Another limitation is the fact that the reader in the text is something which has to be constructed, an image of an imaginary reader. It is here that the interpreter comes into the picture and the role of the reader becomes a matter of either the reader controlling the text or the reader being controlled by the text. It is furthermore true that it is impossible to escape the hermeneutic circle. 'I construct the images of the implied reader gradually as I read a work, and then use the images I have constructed to validate my reading' (Suleiman 1980:11).

CHAPTER TWENTY TWO

READER-RESPONSE, REDESCRIPTION, AND
REFERENCE: 'YOU ARE THE MAN' (2 SAM. 12:7)

> ... reading a text narratively (reading it 'for the story') means asking above all questions that have narrative relevance—questions generally referring back to the proairetic dimension and the story line—and finding answers to them. If attempting to read a narrative maximally involves questions and answers about any and all of its meaningful aspects, reading it minimally involves questions and answers about what happens (Price 1982:110).

Notwithstanding the following remarks in connection with reception, redescription, and reference of the parables of Jesus, Lategan (1985:67) finds my views on reference too restrictive and limiting. I wrote:

> From the perspective of the reception of a narrative text, it may be said that the text invites the reader to participate in the narrative world of that text. Since reality is remade, it offers new perspectives to the reader. The participation of the reader in the text is stimulated by the way in which the message is structured. It creates a new world of reference, namely, a narrative world (cf. p. 138 above, also Lategan & Vorster 1985a:62).

In his reaction to that essay, Lategan maintains that reference should be related to all aspects of the communication act, including sender, text, and receptor. In this way, he says, the context in which reference functions is appropriately widened. 'This wider context has an important role to play when determining the more immediate reference of a story or statement' (Lategan 1985:67). He argues that the referential status of a text is not restricted to 'what it refers to' immanently, or outside the text (backwards), but also in front of the text.

To avoid unnecessary misunderstanding, and also to further our discussion, I have decided to analyze the story of Nathan and David in Samuel 12 with a view to reader-response, redescription, and reference. Lategan refers to this story twice in his two chapters in Lategan & Vorster (1985:3–25; 67–93) as a case in point. In the latter he offers us his reception of the parable and its application.

The thesis I wish to propound in this essay is the following: *The referential status of a sentence, or for that matter of a cluster of sentences like a story, is directly related to its semantic function.* An adequate response to what a text (a sentence, for example) refers to depends on its semantic function. It makes quite a difference whether a language unit is descriptive or nondescriptive (social, expressive, or instrumental; cf. Lyons 1977:50). The thesis will be argued by (1) discussing different (modern) receptions of Nathan's parable and its application in 2 Samuel, and (2) by analyzing reception, redescription, and reference with regard to the story as embedded in 2 Samuel. In addition, the thesis will be worked out by discussing some theoretical aspects of the problem and applying them to the text under discussion.

1. *Modern Receptions of Nathan's Parable*

The story of David's affair with Bathsheba and the consequent rebuke by Nathan has captured the imagination of many a student of the Old Testament. The parable of Nathan and its application in the David, Uriah, and Bathsheba episode is most revealing when it is studied from the perspective of reception, redescription, and reference. It reads as follows (*NEB* translation):

> The Lord sent Nathan the prophet to David, and when he entered his presence, he said to him, 'There were once two men in the same city, one rich and the other poor. The rich man had large flocks and herds, but the poor man had nothing of his own except one little ewe lamb. He reared it himself, and it grew up in his home with his own sons. It ate from his dish, drank from his cup and nestled in his arms; it was like a daughter to him. One day a traveller came to the rich man's house, and he, too mean to take something from his own flocks and herds to serve to his guest, took the poor man's lamb and served up that.' David was very angry, and burst out, 'As the *Lord* lives, the man who did this deserves to die! He shall pay for the lamb four times over, because he has done this and shown no pity.' Then Nathan said to David, 'You are the man. This is the word of the *Lord* the God of Israel to you: "I anointed you king over Israel, I rescued you from the power of Saul, I gave you your master's daughter and his wives to be your own, I gave you the daughters of Israel and Judah; and, had this not been enough, I would have added other favours as great. Why then have you flouted the word of the *Lord* by doing what is wrong in my eyes? You have struck down Uriah the Hittite with the sword; the man himself you murdered by the sword of the Ammonites,

and you have stolen his wife. Now, therefore, since you have despised me and taken the wife of Uriah the Hittite to be your own wife, your family shall never again have rest from the sword." This is the word of the *Lord*: "I will bring trouble upon you from within your own family; I will take your wives and give them to another man before your eyes, and he will lie with them in broad daylight. What you did was done in secret; but I will do this in the light of day for all Israel to see."' David said to Nathan, 'I have sinned against the *Lord*.' Nathan answered him, 'The *Lord* has laid on another the consequences of your sin: you shall not die, but, because in this you have shown your contempt for the *Lord*, the boy that will be born to you shall die.'

Even a cursory reading of 2 Samuel 12 makes it clear that Nathan's parable and its application is a textbook example for illustrating problems of the interpretation of ancient texts. A number of very important questions arise in connection with communication: Why did the communication between Nathan and David first fail and eventually succeed? Is it because Nathan's story is ambiguous, or is it because of David's expectation as a hearer that he heard the story incorrectly? Why are both David's and Nathan's hearings 'possible'? Is it because stories are by nature plurisignificant and for that reason open to multiple interpretations? Is it possible in principle that the story refers both immanently and to the extra-linguistic world, or, as Lategan would have it, in front of the text, opening up a new possibility for David? All these and many other questions arise when the text is read with a view to reference and reader-response. We are in the fortunate position of having two (narrated) hearings of the same story, the one by a receptor (David) and the other by the sender of the story (Nathan as interpreter, in his remark to David about the 'correct' hearing of the story). The fact that the parable and its application are embedded in a larger text adds to the interest and complexity of its interpretation.

Nathan's parable and its application form part of the so-called 'Succession Narrative' (*Thronfolgegeschichte*), generally taken to consist of 2 Samuel 9–20 plus 1 Kings 1–2. Hardly any other text in the Bible could better illustrate the influence which views on text type have on reader-response and reference. Although it is almost universally agreed that the *Succession Narrative* is a well-told story, it is certainly not its narrative characteristics which received the most attention or had the greatest influence on its interpretation. It was only recently that scholars started paying attention to the text as *narrative*. This is of direct relevance for our purpose, since classificatory tags like history, poetry, legend, parable, and so on tend to lead or mislead the reader.

In recent years (cf. Gunn 1978:20) the *Succession Narrative* has been characterized as 'history,' 'political propaganda,' 'wisdom' and/or 'didactic literature,' and also as 'story, told in a traditional vein, as a work of art and entertainment' (Gunn 1978:38). Some regard it as the beginning of historiography (cf. von Rad). 'This document is Israelite history writing at its very best. As a result of this writers historical scholarship, the last part of the reign of David is one of the best documented periods in the history of Israel' (Tucker 1971:36). Although this view has not gone without challenge (cf. Whybray 1968), it has influenced generations of scholars for whom the story as such refers backwards to events and persons outside the text. According to this view the semantic function of the story is descriptive. It describes persons in the real world, how they lived and what they did, and real events.

According to Rost (1926), however, the real concern of the story is with dynastic politics. It was written during the early years of Solomon's reign to propagate his glory. The theme is his succession. The Solomonic date obviously facilitated this reading. The purpose is to justify Solomon's succession. Together dating and purpose influence the meaning and reference of the story since it is related to a particular situation in the real world.

Taking his cue from the story of David and Bathsheba, Delekat (1967) argues for the anti-Davidic and anti-Solomonic polemic of the narrative as a whole. Both anti- and pro- propaganda trends discovered during the history of research allegedly originate from different stages in the growth of the story (cf. Veijola 1975). This makes the problem of meaning and reference a very complicated matter, because it becomes almost impossible to know to which layer of tradition any part of the final story refers, let alone the problems of semantic function and cohesion.

Whybray (1968:47) regards the *Succession Narrative* as a political document, a novel '. . . albeit a historical one—rather than a work of history properly speaking. No doubt purely literary and artistic aims and the desire to entertain the reader occupied an important place in the author's mind.' Moreover the work was designed as teaching material, that is, didactic literature, written from the same perspective as Wisdom literature (Whybray 1968:13). The problems with such an approach, where historicity, perspective (wisdom), narrativity (novel), and semantic function (teaching) are mixed, are clear. How could any reader possibly know exactly what the story means or what it refers to? At the other end of the spectrum are the views of Gunn. He acknowledges the historicity of persons and events, but nevertheless regards the story of king David as '. . . entertainment which demands the active engagement of those entertained, which challenges their intellect, their emotions, their understanding of people, of society and of themselves' (Gunn 1978:61). According to him (1978:61) the narrative is not fiction in the sense of 'frei erfunden,' although it is possible—as in the case of Icelandic stories—'. . . to detect demonstrably fictitious or highly conventional elements in the stories.' From this perspective the *Succession Narrative* is to be read as a story, for example, a historical novel, as remade reality. The semantic function of the text is nondescriptive, that is, social, expressive, and instrumental.

It is already becoming clear that an adequate reading of our embedded parable of Nathan and its application would very much depend on one's views about the macrotext into which it is embedded. If it is regarded as history writing, meaning and reference would be construed in terms of description. Other views on the text type will equally influence one's reception of the text. It needs to be said further, however, that the shift from considering it history writing to political propaganda and beyond is an indication that scholars are taking increasingly seriously the narrative character of the story of king David.

The history of the reception of Nathan's parable and its application is equally interesting. The relationship between the parable and its literary context in 2 Samuel has given rise to many different readings of the text. Since the days of Schwally and Gunkel, serious objections have been raised (among others) about the authenticity of this David story in view of the so-called incompatibility between the parable of Nathan and its application in 2 Samuel 12. According to Schwally, it is hardly possible to reconcile David's struggle for the life of the son of Bathsheba with his sentence on the man who stole the lamb from the poor man in the story of Nathan. Moreover, he also finds it difficult to accept both the image of Nathan as the prophet who rebukes the king for his affair with Uriah's wife and the later picture of him (1 Kgs. 1) in his involvement to secure the succession of Bathsheba's second son to the throne of David as images of the same man (cf. Simon 1967:208). These two observations, as well as attempts to reconstruct 'what actually happened,' ruled the scene of interpretation of the story of Nathan and David for a very long time.

Various solutions to the problem of the relationship between Nathan's parable and its application have been offered, ranging from hypothetical interpolations to detailed discussions of the possible juridical background of the story told. In all these readings the reconstruction of the events which are not told ('What actually happened') plays a very important role.

> Our chapter contains no answer to the questions that deeply interest us. Had anyone of the court divulged to Uriah what had transpired between his wife and the king? Can we possibly attribute to him any deliberate intention to fail the king's designs and interpret his words as a daring protest against the injustice perpetrated against him? (Simon 1967:21).

According to Garsiel (1976:24): '. . . the Bible has apparently failed to elucidate . . .' problems such as: 'To what extent was Bathsheba herself responsible for David's affair with her? Did Uriah know about her adultery? Exactly how was the murder of Uriah accomplished?' These matters undoubtedly play a role in how the reference of the text is construed.

Two recent attempts to explain the relationship between the parable and its context focused on the juridical character of the parable. According to Simon there are five examples of juridical parables in the Old Testament (2 Sam. 12:1–14, 14:1–20; 1 Kgs. 20:35–43; Isa. 5:1–7; and Jer. 3:1–5). His definition of a juridical parable is most revealing:

> The juridical parable constitutes a *realistic* story about a violation of the law, related to someone who had committed a similar offence with the purpose of leading the unsuspecting hearer to pass judgement on himself. The offender will only be caught in the trap set for him if he truly believes that the story told him *actually happened* and only if he does not detect prematurely the similarity between the offence in the story and the one he himself has committed. . . . The realistic dress of the juridical parable, on the other hand, is intended to conceal the very fact that it is a parable (Simon 1967:220–21; italics mine).

The description is influenced by Simon's interpretation of the application of the parable. It does not offer us a description of what a 'juridical' parable is, but tells us for what purposes such a story may be used. As a consequence he presumes that the story (juridi-

cal parable) describes a 'real legal problem,' and that it should be
read in view of *that* problem. The metaphorical nature of the text
type parable is replaced by a so-called 'realistic story' character of
the juridical parable, in order to mislead the person who is guilty
of the transgression to which the parable refers. This conclusion is
doubtful. These parables are not ambiguous in the sense that they
can be read both as stories and as reports of what had actually happened. Because the reader is, on the one hand, unaware of the reason why the parable is being told, and, on the other, being presented
as a reader (hearer) who reads stories as reports (description), communication fails. Simon's definition of a juridical parable invites the
reader to look for certain information in the text which in the end
he will also find. This is seen best in the analyses of both Simon
and Seebass (1974): '. . . Nathan's story should be examined for traces
of a real legal problem justifying its being brought by a third party
(the prophet) to the notice of the king' (Simon 1967:226). In this
way juridical problems are imposed in the story. According to Seebass (1974:203) there are two irritating juridical problems involved
in 2 Samuel 12:1–15: Does the transgression which is narrated in
the parable (theft) justify the death sentence (cf. v. 5)? How can
David be forgiven (juridically) for what he had done by simply plead-
ing guilty (cf. v. 13: 'I have sinned against the *Lord*')? By reading
these two questions into the text he concludes that the parable told
by Nathan only corresponds to David's transgression if the case
intended is not one of theft but of the exploitation of superior force
against the poor. 'On this basis v. 11f. are original, v. 13 a frank
acceptance of the verdict, and v. 14 the preservation of the legal
rights of Uriah' (Seebasss 1974:211). Admittedly this reading of the
parable and its application offers solutions to the *supposed* incompatibility between the parable and its context in 2 Samuel. But does it
really take the story in 2 Samuel seriously? The narrator of the
Nathan and David story in 2 Samuel had no interest, as far as I
can see, in the two problems posed by Seebass. Neither did he want
to inform the reader about all the missing data which scholars like
Garsiel and others find so important. By imposing these problems
on the text, the text is read through a filter which makes it refer to
and mean accordingly—be it a filter of Solomonic dating, deuteron-
omistic morality, or whatever the case may be. It should also be
noted that in these attempts to construct the meaning of the text by
filling in 'missing' data or making it refer to a 'real legal problem,'

a reader-expectation is created which need not necessarily be that
of the text but rather that of an enriched text.

Let us now turn to Lategan's reception of the parable and its
application (1985:81). According to him it is the story character of
Nathan's parable that puts David at ease. It causes him to identify
with a fictive character, however incorrectly, because he sees this
poor man as a man of flesh and blood. He is taken by surprise
when he is told that he is the man who took the poor man's lamb.

> It is important to notice that the embedded story of the rich man and
> the poor man, which forms a perfectly self-contained unit on its own,
> only functions in this context because of the tacit identification of David
> with the rich man. Without this 'outside' reference, the tension cre-
> ated by the parable would not exist and the point missed (Lategan
> 1985:81).

He denies the fact that parables as stories refer immanently. He
insists that they refer to the outside world by virtue of the fact that
this particular parable refers to David: '. . . because they presuppose
a wider referential context, parables become one of the most effective
vehicles of redescription.'

Apparently Lategan did not notice that we here have an ideal
model of reader-response and expectation related to text type.
According to our narrator, David did not hear the parable as parable at all. It is therefore not correct to think that the story character of Nathan's parable put David at ease and that as story (second
order reference) it opened the possibility for David to step outside
his first order context, that is, his literal real world situation.
Incidently, David heard the parable as a *description* of what actually
happened (first order reference). He identified with the poor man
because he regarded him as the victim of exploitation. Is the so-called
'identification' of David as 'the man' an indication of how parables
refer to the outside world? Certainly not. Because the parable is used
to say something about somebody, its meaning is referred to by a
comparable meaning in the events of the narrated world of king
David. What he has done according to our narration is compared
to what somebody has done in the fictitious world of the parable.
The parable is applied and, because of the application, there is a
relationship of reference between text and application. One should
furthermore also note that it is not the historical David who is said
to be 'the man' of the parable but the narrated David. This observation is not without importance, as I will argue below. In its appli-

cation, the parable indeed has an outside reference. It is used to say something about somebody (the narrated David) in the narrative world of the text into which it is embedded. It is only in this sense that it is used as a redescription of reality—to use Ricoeur's term—to help redescribe the reality of the narrated David.

In his attempt to apply and defend Ricoeur's theory of redescription as reference in front of the text, Lategan misread the story of Nathan and its application. The semantic function of the parable of Nathan is directly related to its application in the story of David not because parables '. . . presuppose a wider referential context,' but because they can be used to say something about somebody or something.

This short survey of a few readings of our text as embedded into the *Succession Narrative* clearly indicates that, despite universal agreement on the narrative character of 2 Samuel, the story is not read as story. It is also clear that historical interests dominate most readings of the text, not, in the sense of seeing the text as part of a specific historical period but rather as referring to historical events and persons. As we have seen, it is argued that even the parable of Nathan refers to some real legal problem or to the historical David.

In the next section reader-response, redescription, and reference will be discussed in view of this thesis and with regard to 2 Samuel 12:1–15.

2. *Reception, Redescription, and Reference*

It is unfortunate that reference is too often used in theological literature in connection with the historicity of events and persons mentioned in biblical texts. In this way a semantic problem (reference) is changed into a historical one (historicity) and the problems of text semantics are neglected.

In view of the difference of opinion among scholars about the exact nature of *reference* and Ricoeur's views on *redescription* as a particular kind of reference to reality, which play such an important role in Lategan's discussions above, it seems necessary to return to the problem again.

The difference between *endophoric* and *exophoric* use of reference items in language communication appears to be basic to the interpretation of texts. In any discourse, reference to something which has already been mentioned or will be mentioned is necessary (cf. Halliday and Hasan 1976:305). Consider the sentence: 'The following morning David wrote a letter to Joab and sent Uriah with it' (2 Sam. 12:14). The endophoric use of the items 'following morning' and 'it' is clear. 'Following morning' should be interpreted with reference to the previous evening mentioned in 2 Samuel 12:13 and 'it' with reference to 'letter' in the same sentence. The co-text (context), that is, the preceding statements as well as what follows, are instructive for construing the meanings of these items. Do these items, however, also refer to extralinguistic referents in the world outside the text? Does the situation in which the communication took place also constitute the meaning of items in the sentence? Are they, in other words, also exophoric? A clear-cut answer is not easy, since the existents and events in this sentence are first of all *narrated* existents and events. Even David and Uriah are in the first instance the narrated David and the narrated Uriah. Some would undoubtedly argue that David, and perhaps also Uriah, refer to the David and Uriah who happened to live in Israel long ago. But are these extralinguistic referents constitutive in constructing the meaning of this language communication? I will come back to this below.

Let us now look at another example. In 1 Corinthians 3:1–2 Paul says: For my part, my brothers, I could not speak to you as I should speak to people who have the Spirit. I had to deal with you on the merely natural plane, as infants in Christ. The use of reference in these sentences is clearly exophoric. 'I' refers to 'Paul' of flesh and blood and 'you' to 'those out there in Corinth.' Both persons and events point to extralinguistic referents in the first place. Not that the endophoric use of reference items in this kind of statement is denied. However, it is the *situational context* that is constitutive for constructing the meaning in these utterances. In fact, the interpretation of reference items in statements like these depends on situational information, while the interpretation of those mentioned in the previous example depends on the information of the co-text. Text type seems to have a great influence on the referential status of utterances. These two very simple examples, one of which comes from a narrative text and the other forming part of an argumentation, sufficiently illustrate the complicated nature of reference. Not only are there different kinds of reference, but reference also depends on the *nature* of the communication act (narration, exposition, argument, description, listing: cf. Brooks and Warren 1970:56–57; Nida

1981:29–30), its context, and the situation in which it happens. 'Reference . . . is a context-dependent aspect of utterance meaning' (Lyons 1981:220).

The relational aspect of reference is made clear by the following remarks by Lyons. He asserts that reference is: '. . . the relation that holds between *linguistic expressions* and what they stand for in the world, or universe of discourse . . .' and that '. . . it is a relation that holds between speakers (more generally, locutionary agents) and what they are talking about on particular occasions' (Lyons 1981:220). The first of these remarks could be interpreted in terms of Halliday and Hasan's application of exophoric and endophoric use of reference, the importance of which we have already noted. In the second remark we are closer to the problems involved in Lategan's relating of reference to reception. In this case reference is defined within the framework of a language communication act, where speaker and receptor are involved in construing 'what they are talking about.' Both parties play an active role in the construction of reference; the speaker by using 'some appropriate expression' (Lyons 1977:177) and the receptor by actively decoding what the speaker attempts to communicate. Obviously communication will fail or be distorted when the coding or decoding is done inadequately. For instance, when a speaker's narrative is read as description there would be a disagreement between 'what they (= speaker and receptor) are talking about.' This has been illustrated above with a survey of receptions of the *Succession Narrative*. Two things should be noted. In order to communicate properly both speaker and receptor should be in agreement in their construing of 'what they are talking about.' Secondly, 'what they are talking about' is a semantic phenomenon. In view of this, let us return to my thesis about semantic function and reference.

The distinction between the different semantic functions of the same or different units of language, like phrases or sentences, has far-reaching implications for our present discussion and also for the interpretation of texts. In the words of Lyons (1977:50):

> Many semanticists have talked as if language was used solely, or primarily, for the communication of factual information. Others have maintained that making statements descriptive of states-of-affairs is but one of the functions of language; that it also serves, as do our other customs and patterns of behaviour, for the establishment and maintenance of social relationships and for the expression of our personality.

Undoubtedly not all statements in biblical texts have the semantic function of communicating 'factual information,' that is, of being descriptive. Think of admonitions, miracle stories, parables, and other kinds of statements which function semantically in a non-descriptive way. In Mark's Gospel, for example, the miracle stories are used (semantically) to characterize Jesus and his opponents.

Seen from the perspective of the so-called speech-act theory (cf. Chatman 1978:161–66), the same sentence may be used for different meanings in accordance with the speech act which is performed. The same sentence may be uttered as an assertion, a warning, a prediction, a promise, a threat, or whatever illocutionary act involved. This would obviously influence both the meaning and the reference of such an utterance.

Because the semantic function of sentences may be descriptive or non-descriptive, and because different speech acts may be involved in performing the same sentence, it is absolutely necessary that speaker and receptor have to know exactly 'what they are talking about.' This also holds for written communication. The fact that different text types (narration, exposition, argument, description, and listing) do not necessarily refer in the same way as far as exophoric reference is concerned also has important implications for our discussion. This is where Ricoeur's theory of *redescription* comes into the picture in connection with non-descriptive texts like narratives.

In my essay on the parables of Jesus (chapter 11 in this volume, also Lategan & Vorster 1985:27–65), I have argued that Ricoeur is not addressing the problem of *what the speaker and receptor are talking about (reference)* in the case of metaphors and parables, but about what they *are*, that is, a remaking of the world (cf. above). In his attempt to break with the idea that narratives refer immanently to the reality of a narrative world, Ricoeur concerns himself with what a narrative achieves. According to him, narratives reshape reality; they refer in front of the text (cf. Ricoeur 1979:124). His distinction between *productive* and *reproductive* reference in connection with fiction is useful insofar as it clearly distinguishes descriptive from nondescriptive language usage. In fiction, reality is present not in a reproduced sense of a given original (the existing thing) outside the text to which it could be referred. Fiction produces reality, and therefore *absence* (of an original) and *unreality* should not be confused. Unlike a photograph, where the original is absent, fiction produces reality by combining components '. . . derived from previous experience'

(Ricoeur 1979:125). The original is not reproduced. Writing a poem, telling a story, construing an hypothesis, a plan, or a strategy: these are kinds of contexts of work which provide a perspective to imagination and allow it to be productive (Ricoeur 1979:125). This also holds for metaphors, which are very good examples of redescription of reality because they are semantic innovations. His remarks about fifteenth-century Flemish painters illuminate his understanding of redescription.

> Painting, with them, remains mimetic in the sense that aspects of the reality are restored, but painting only reaches its goal under the condition of inventing the medium of that mimesis. Ever since, imitation is no longer a reduplication of reality but a creative rendering of it (Ricoeur 1979:138).

The same holds for poetry, which is also a redescription of reality. Up to this point Ricoeur is clear, but to my mind a shift then takes place between what a fiction (painting, metaphor etc.) *is*, and what a fiction *does* (can do). This difference is best illustrated by the following remark about models and fiction:

> Models in turn provide us with the more accurate account of what we have attempted to describe as productive reference. To the extent that models are not models *of* . . . i.e., still pictures of a previously given reality, *but models for*, i.e., heuristic fictions for redescribing reality, the work of the model becomes in turn a model for construing in a meaningful way the concept of the productive reference of all fictions, including the so-called poetic fictions (Ricoeur 1979:140–41; italics mine).

He simply asserts, without substantiation, that a fiction *is* a redescription as well as a redescription *for*. With this in mind, it is difficult to relate productive reference—which is the name for the creative and non-descriptive semantic function of 'fictions'—to reference *in front of the text*. By remaking reality, be it in a narrative, metaphor, painting, or whatever other 'fiction,' a text is created of which the meaning has to be decoded. Peak communication will only be possible if the receptor is able to construe the meaning of what the sender is talking about in his redescription of reality. In the end productive reference appears to be the network of reference (for example, the narrative world of a story) which is created by writers of poems, story-tellers, et cetera when they redescribe reality by means of new combinations (of existing and non-existing things).

The problem with Ricoeur's view on redescription is that they are too inclusive. He wants both to explain and also to create reality, and uses the term 'productive reference' for both activities. That is one of the reasons why Lategan's application of the concept of redescription to the growth and communication of biblical texts is problematic. The possibilities which texts create do not depend on reference in front of but on the making of new texts.

With this in mind, let us now consider again the parable of Nathan and its application in 2 Samuel. It has, to my mind, been adequately indicated that the *Succession Narrative* is a *story* (cf. Gunn 1978, and Bar-Efrat 1978). This I will not—except for a few necessary remarks below—argue any further. It follows, however, that if 2 Samuel 12:1–14 is embedded into a narrative, it should also be read as part of that narrative.

The story of David, Uriah, and Bathsheba is told at a crucial point in the development of the plot of the story of king David. In 2 Samuel vv. 11–12, a complication takes place in the plot when David ironically attempts to *take* the wife of Uriah by force. Unlike the previous section, where David is presented as a king content to be *given* a kingdom by Yahweh (cf. 2 Sam. vv. 2–5), he is now presented as a keen schemer who does everything possible to seize a wife for himself (cf. Gunn 1978:97). The episode gives the pattern of intrigue, sex, and violence in a nutshell which '... is played out at length in the subsequent story within David's own family' (Gunn 1978:98). This violent seizure of Uriah's wife is not accepted by Yahweh without serious consequences for his kingdom (2 Sam. 12:8–11). Gunn (1978:98) is correct when he says: 'However precisely one interprets Nathan's parable in relation to its setting ... it is absolutely plain that it encapsulates the essence of David's dealing with Bathsheba, the episode is the story of the rich man who *took* the poor man's lamb.' The story and its application is used to characterize David by the application of various narrative techniques including irony. Irony is a very effective device for steering the reception of the text. It is often used to develop characterization and to set norms of judgement for the reader. I have already referred to the ironic contrast between David being given a kingdom and his attempt to seize a wife. The tension between retribution and forgiveness, which is not absolutely solved in the story, is heightened by the ironic treatment of David in connection with the death of Uriah. Even Yahweh's role in the story '... retains a measure of ambivalence if not an undercurrent of irony' (Gunn 1978:98). Because of his faithfulness to his principles and his king, Uriah ironically brings about his own death. He even unwittingly carries out his own death sentence. David ironically passes judgement upon himself after hearing the parable of Nathan. Bar-Efrat (1978:22) remarks correctly: 'Often the irony serves to express criticism of the characters concerned in an implicit and indirect way.' This is exactly the purpose of irony in the David, Uriah, and Bathsheba story, which is told primarily to characterize David the king.

Speeches and actions are also very important aspects of characterization. They provide the reader with information about narrated figures and how the sender wants the receptor to see them. This is particularly true of the story of David and Bathsheba. Notice how the characters are presented to the reader through the eyes of the narrated David and *not* through the eyes of Bathsheba. How he sees and meets the characters is narrated. This is part of the way in which David is shaped for the audience (receptors). In the end the reader either identifies or rejects the character because of his characterization. In an almost matter-of-fact manner David is presented as a deviser of plans in order to take the wife of Uriah. If the plan does not work out, the next is implemented. In the end, he succeeds at the cost of the life of Uriah. But this success is a failure, however, since he pronounces himself guilty by misinterpreting the parable of Nathan. The flow and development of the story (*Succession Narrative*) is made possible by this reaction to Nathan's story. In short, a reading of the story of David which does not take seriously the narrative character of 2 Samuel is bound to distort the communication between text and reader. 2 Samuel clearly is a redescription of reality. It is not a reproduction or a replica. It invites the reader to participate in a network of significances created by a combination of events and people. The function of the story is *non-descriptive in* the above sense of the term.

3. *Semantic Function and Reference*

Let us now consider again Nathan's parable and its application with a view to reception, redescription, and reference in the light of the thesis of this essay.

The semantic function of the statement 'You are the man' should be read with reference to its context. It forms part of a narrative and has the function of pointing back to the *narrative world* of an embedded narrative. This embedded narrative (Nathan's parable) is used in 2 Samuel to characterize David negatively. His character is shaped by the story of Nathan as well as by his reception thereof. To the reader, however, he is presented as acceptable again by his confession of guilt. It is not possible to read the sentence 'You are the man' as an ontological statement about the 'real' David who used to be king of Israel; neither does it refer outside the main narrative world of 2 Samuel to the real world; David is also not identified as *the man*. The narrated David is told that, by taking Uriah's wife, he acted the role of the character who took the poor man's lamb in Nathan's parable. Ricoeur's distinction (1978b:248) between two functions of 'to be' is helpful in this respect. On some occasions 'is' is used to denote equivalence, but 'is' can also be used as a simile, 'to be like.' The actions of David are to be compared to those of the man in Nathan's story: David is like . . . or acted like. . . . The following remarks of Halliday and Hasan are equally illuminating:

> Either the reference item is interpreted through being IDENTIFIED with the referent in question; or it is interpreted through being COMPARED with the referent . . . (1976:309).

> Comparison differs from the other forms of reference in that it is based not on identity of reference but on nonidentity: the reference item is interpreted, not by being identified with what it presupposes, but by being compared with it (1976:313).

Notice that in our sentence the reference item *you* (David), is *compared* to a character in Nathan's story and not vice versa. It is not the story of Nathan as such that refers to an outside referent in 2 Samuel 12. In its application a character outside the story is compared with a character in the story. Because of its application to a particular situation in the narrative world of 2 Samuel, the story of Nathan, like that of the Good Samaritan in Luke, has a performative semantic function. It denounces the action of a narrated figure and characterizes him negatively. It also is an anticipation of David's confession of guilt and makes clear what this confession refers to.

Nathan's story is, like any other parable, a self-contained unit. It can stand on its own and has a meaning of its own. It is a complete story with plot, characters, and point of view. Like the parables of Jesus, it can, however, be used in different contexts with different meanings and for different purposes.

In our context it is used for a very specific purpose which also determines its semantic function. The fact that David read the story as a report, while Nathan intended it as a story about David's handling of his affair with Uriah's wife, explains the lack of communication between David and Nathan and also tells the reader how to read it. The modern reader might miss quite a bit of the subtle information embedded into the context of Nathan's story which the ancient reader would have enjoyed. In his recent article Peter Coxon (1981), for example, draws attention to the fact that in chapter 11, David is the agent on four occasions of *šlh* in his manipulation of the situation. In chapter 12 it is Yahweh, however, who sends Nathan to David to rebuke him. The terminology used by Uriah to reject David's encouragement to enjoy conjugal rights with his wife also appears in Nathan's story (cf. 'eat,' 'drink,' and 'to lie with'). 'Ancient audiences would have relished the thick irony which laces the narrator's account of the ewe lamb in the next chapter when the same terminology reappears' (Coxon 1981:249). Suffice it to say that the repetition of terminology, with its ironic effect, adds to the fact that 2 Samuel is a network of internal reference.

The relationship between the parable of Nathan and its application can only be properly understood if the context within which it occurs is taken seriously. This context is a narrative. If it is taken into account that the parable is used to say something about the narrated David of 2 Samuel, and how crucial the episode of David, Uriah, and Bathsheba is for the development of the plot, the comparison of the narrated David to the rich man will be the focal point in a search for what it refers to. The semantic function of the story—that is, characterization—determines its reference and referential status. The story of Nathan in 2 Samuel does not refer to some 'real legal problem,' as Seebass and others would think, but is used like the story of the Tekoite woman to characterize David as a man who was too clever by half. The norms of judgment of his action are given in the text. 'Nathan the prophet denounces David's behaviour concerning Bathsheba and Uriah, and David himself confesses his guilt. . . . His confession demonstrates, for all his misdemeanor, his moral greatness' (Bar-Efrat 1978:24). The reception of the text is determined by its text type and so is the semantic function and reference.

CHAPTER TWENTY THREE

LITERARY REFLECTIONS ON MARK 13:5–37:
A NARRATED SPEECH OF JESUS

1. *Introduction*

From the point of view of interpretation, there seems to be hardly any other chapter in the New Testament which offers as many challenges to the interpreter as does Mark 13. On the semantic level there are a few intriguing problems which have puzzled scholars through the ages. Although the meaning of the *bdélugma tes eremóseos* of verse 14, for instance, is clear, there still remains uncertainty about the reference of the term. Whether the chapter was written from an apocalyptic perspective is a bone of contention between scholars, and about the origin and the literary history of the chapter there will always be difference of opinion. On the Christological level the problem of the imminent parousia has given rise to many and divergent 'solutions' for the difficulties of verse 30 and so there are many other detail problems which scholars attempt to solve in view of their understanding of the chapter and its relation to the rest of the Gospel of Mark.

The purpose of this essay is not to give answers to the many 'unsolved' problems of Mark 13 (cf. Beasley-Murray 1983; Brandenburger 1984; Wenham 1975). What I have in mind is to approach this chapter from a different perspective than is usually done by New Testament scholars in order to throw light on aspects of Mark 13 which are normally neglected. It has been the custom to study this chapter from the perspective of its origin and growth. With the exception of a few articles (cf. Hallbäck 1981; Petersen 1980, 1984), even in the latest extensive studies on Mark 13 the focus is on the literary history and the origin of this chapter (cf. Brandenburger 1984) and not on the text as a text or a communication. Important and interesting as this might be, there is no reason why the interpretation of this chapter should be restricted to this very limited perspective (cf. Lambrecht 1967; Pesch 1968). I will approach the chapter from a literary point of view with the focus on Mark 13:5–37 as a narrated speech and not on the literary history or the extratextual context to which it could possibly refer. It is impossible to give an exhaustive interpretation of the speech in a single essay. Therefore I shall concentrate on a few aspects only. In the first part of the essay attention will be paid to the fact that Mark 13 is presented to the reader as a narrated speech and what this implies for the interpretation of this chapter. The second section deals with the place of Mark 13 in the Gospel of Mark. The problem of time is of special interest here. In the third place narrative point of view and the function of apocalyptic and paraenesis in Mark 13 will be discussed. The essay will be concluded by a few summary remarks.

2. A Narrated Speech

After more than a century of critical scholarship following the hypothesis of T. Colani that Mark supposedly used and expanded an existing apocalypse in compiling Mark 13, it is almost impossible to escape the haunting questions concerning the origin and growth of this chapter. This is what scholars have been studying and not the text in its final redaction as part of the Gospel of Mark. In spite of the paradigm switch which is taking place in New Testament studies—where the emphasis is on the texts of the New Testament as communications and not on their origin and growth—it still very often is the literary history of texts and not what they are and how they communicate, which intrigue the minds of New Testament scholars. This should not prevents scholars from testing new hypotheses and applying new methods of interpretation. On the contrary, it should rather invite us to test and revise basic presuppositions and to develop new answers to old questions.

To say that Mark 13:5–37 is a narrated speech may not seem very important. The term, however, is not as innocent as it may seem. The basic presupposition behind the term is that the Gospel of Mark is a narrative and that the speech in Mark 13 is part of that particular narrative and should be read in the light of these presuppositions. This too may not seem to be of particular interest to those who are used to referring to the gospels or parts of them as narratives. But, as we shall see below, the approach followed in this essay implies a different perspective of Mark 13 than the usual 'historical' one. The application of a set of different questions to the text is also implied, since the approach is that of structural semiotics (cf. Genette 1980). There are not many ways in which material can be organized in a discourse (cf. Brooks & Warren 1970:56f.). Narration is one. The way in which material is organized is important both with regard to the production and the reception of texts. It is important regarding the production of texts because of the conventions which are followed. When a person, for example, produces a narrative, he almost involuntarily uses the codes of the narrative genre. And the same happens to the receiver in the decoding process. He also has to read the text in accordance with its codes in order to produce an adequate reading. Asserting that a particular text is a narrative would, therefore, mean that the text reveals certain characteristics.

In order to tell a story one needs a storyteller, a story and an audience (cf. Scholes & Kellogg 1966:240). A narrative consists of a series of events forming a story which is told by a narrator to a narratee. The events are arranged in terms of space and time, performed by a limited set of 'actors' and told from a specific perspective. In this way a narrative world is created. This in short is what a narrative is and how it works. To avoid any misunderstanding a few extra remarks will have to be made.

It is important to note that when an author of flesh and blood writes or tells a narrative he creates (cf. Chatman 1978:19) a narrative message (the contents or 'what' of the narrative) by using certain narrative techniques (the 'how' of the narrative). He selects and arranges the events and existents (e.g. space, time and actors) and uses a narrator and a narrative point of view inside the text as the means by which he tells the narrative. The important thing to notice here is that by telling or writing a story the author creates an image of events and personages in order to communicate something to his audience. This image is his image. The following diagram visually explains some of the aspects involved in the communication of a narrative.

With this in mind let us now turn to the Gospel of Mark. That Mark's Gospel is a narrative, cannot be doubted. The discourse is organized in narrative style and the story is communicated by means of a narrator. In writing a story Mark created an image of events and personages in the life of Jesus in order to communicate something to his readers. The story he created is Mark's image and the narrative world is his narrative world. He selected and arranged his

NARRATIVE (e.g. GOSPEL)

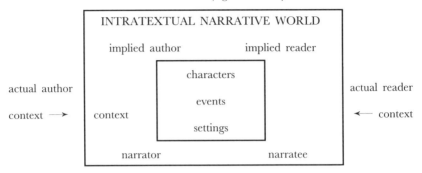

context of communication

material in terms of order and space and it is he who decided on what each character will do or say and when. Even if Mark closely followed tradition and 'historical events', it was still he who created the image of a not too loquacious Jesus or disciples who lack understanding. When we read Mark's gospel we are guided by his text through pro- and retrospection, gaps and indeterminacy, selection and organization, and the modification of expectations (cf. Iser 1974, 1978) to assign meaning to the image he created. This is how we create our own image of Mark's image. What is done or said in a gospel should therefore be interpreted in view of the fact that it is narrated. This is of particular interest with regard to Mark 13.

In view of the fact that the sayings material in the gospels have been studied in terms of historical reliability, authenticity and the reconstruction of the teaching of Jesus, it is not surprising that Mark 13:5–37 causes so many problems in this connection. Amongst other things, it was the idea of the imminent parousia in Mark 13 and the resulting problem of the possibility that Jesus might have been mistaken (cf. Hooker 1982:79), which have given rise to the conclusion that Mark 13:5–37 is in its present form a secondary speech based on a Jewish or Christian fly leaf. As Brandenburger (1984:21) remarks: 'Als inzwischen fast einhellig vertretenes Ergebnis der kritischen Forschung kann festgehalten werden dass in Markus 13 keine historische Rede Jesu vorliegt'.

From a literary point of view the words '. . . that in Mark 13 we do not find an historical speech of Jesus', are of particular interest. On what grounds can we expect a narrated speech like Mark 13:5–37

to be 'an historical speech of Jesus'? Even if we take into account
the fact that in an oral culture people were able to recall the exact
words of a speaker far better than those who are exposed to writing and reading, there seems no reason why ancient speeches in
narrative form should be historical or even verbatim reports, as
some seemingly expect them to be. This does not apply only to the
speeches in the New Testament as is clear from the following remarks
by the ancient Greek historian Thucydides (Thuc. Hist. I.22, Loeb
translation):

> As to the speeches that were made by different men. either when they
> were about to begin the war or when they were already engaged
> therein, it has been difficult to recall with strict accuracy the words
> actually spoken both for me as regards that which I myself heard and
> for those who from various other sources have brought me reports.
> Therefore the speeches are given in the language in which as it seemed
> to me, the several speakers would express on subjects under consid-
> eration the sentiments most benefitting the occasion, though at the
> same time I have adhered as closely as possible to the general sense
> of what was actually said.

These words clearly indicate the problems involved in narrating direct
speech in ancient times. But it also points to the role and purpose
of speeches in narrative texts like the history of the Peloponnesian
war. This is, however, not the main point I wish to make. Narrated
speeches have to do with the presentation of material in a discourse—
a problem which has puzzled man for many centuries. The perspective from which something is narrated and the way in which it is
presented clearly influence the information given.

In his *Republic* (*392–395*) Plato contrasts two ways of presentation
by distinguishing between simple narration (*diegesis*) and imitation
(*mimesis*). In connection with the Iliad he writes:

> . . . the poet himself is the speaker and does not even attempt to sug-
> gest to us that anyone but himself is speaking. But what follows he
> delivers as if he were himself Chryses and tries as far as may be to
> make us feel that not Homer is the speaker, but the priest, an old
> man. . . . 'But when he delivers a speech as if he were someone else,
> shall we not say that he then assimilates thereby his own diction as
> far as possible to that of the person whom he announces as about to
> speak?'. . . . 'And is it not likening one's self to another in speech or
> bodily bearing an imitation of him to whom one likens one's self?'
> 'Surely'. 'In such case then, it appears he and the other poets effect
> their narration through imitation' (Pl. Resp. 393, Loeb translation).

In order to explain the difference between what he calls *diegesis* and *mimesis* Plato rewrites the end of the scene between Chryses and the Achaeans as *diegesis*. He indicates the difference in directness between the two modes of presentation. Imitation is much more direct and gives the impression of less distance between the reader and what is told. It is in this connection that Genette (1980:162) correctly observes that, '... the narrative can furnish the reader with more or fewer details ... and in a more or less direct way and can thus seem ... to keep at a greater or lesser distance from what it tells'.

The use of the word 'seem' is very important since in the end any narrative is a presentation of reality and creates the illusion of *mimesis*. For our purpose two things are very important. Firstly, it is clear that speeches have narrative functions. They create the illusion of directness. Secondly, they are invented as an aid to other narrative means of conveying a narrative message. Both these aspects have to do with the nature of narrative and how they work. Narratives are not descriptions of reality. In a certain sense they are the remaking of reality. And this holds good even for narratives which pretend to make use of historical persons and events.

Mark 13:5–37 is a speech which should not in the first place be analysed outside its narrative context. As a narrated speech it has a narrative function within the story of Jesus according to Mark. One can compare it to the parables of Jesus which receive their messages in the gospels from their narrated contexts of communication. Mark 13 has meaning within the narrative context of this gospel. In fact, it can be argued that the reader of the Gospel of Mark is educated through the reading of the preceding twelve chapters on how to read the speech (cf. Burnett 1985), as we shall see below. It has to do with the image Mark created of Jesus. This makes it in principle impossible to start any discussion about what Jesus had said, could have said and would have said in connection with either the future of Jerusalem or the return of the Son of man on the grounds of Mark 13:5–37 as it stands. The narrative character of the speech makes it necessary to reconstruct Jesus' words, if one is interested in what the earthly Jesus had to say. That is, however, something different from reading or interpreting the meaning or message of the narrated speech as a narrated speech of a narrated figure. To enjoy and understand a narrative the reader has to suspend his own feelings and beliefs and accept those of the text, argues Booth (1983:137).

This is a very important guideline for us, New Testament critics, who were educated to read the gospels not as narratives but as layers of tradition.

If we accept the fact that the author of the gospel presented Mark 13:5–37 as a narrated speech in order to convey a part of his message about Jesus, it will be necessary to consider some of the implications with regard to its place in the Gospel of Mark.

3. Narrative Time and Context

Both the length of the speech and the place in the gospel narrative have been noticed as remarkable by scholars in the past. It is well known that the Jesus of Mark's gospel is not very talkative. Barring the speech on the parables in chapter 4, Mark 13 is the only long speech in Mark. What, if anything, is the significance of this in terms of the narrative? And secondly, is there any significance in the fact that Mark 13 is placed before chapters 14–16 (cf. Grayston 1973–1974)?

The importance of temporal aspects of the Gospel of Mark has in the past been related mostly to the question of the dating of the gospel and the temporal stance of the readers with regard to the narrated material. Interesting as this may be, there are other aspects of time in the gospel which, from a literary point of view, need our attention first.

Time like space, plays an important role in the communication of a narrative message. In fact, it is part of the narrative message. When studying time in a narrative it is necessary to distinguish between various elements. It is particularly helpful to make a distinction between the *story* (*fabula*) that is the basic story material or signifiers; the *narrative text* or *narrative discourse* that is the *fabula* transformed into an artistic structure of chronology and logic (*sjuzet* the signified); and the *act of narration* or *narration*. These are also referred to as *histoire, recit and narration* (cf. Genette 1980). There is an interdependence between these narrative elements, and authors make use of different devices to manipulate material in terms of these elements, as we shall see below. These distinctions make it possible to differentiate between story time and narrative time and to study the significance of the time aspect of a narrative by comparing story time and narrative

time and the effect of arrangement (order), duration and frequency
(cf. Genette 1980:33–160; Petersen 1978a:49–80). Let us consider
the order of Mark's narrative first with reference to Mark 13.

The order in which Mark emplotted his material becomes remarkable when the chronological sequence of the story is compared to
that of the narrative. The events in the narrative leading to chapter 13 have to do with things which occurred in and around Jerusalem
(A). Then in chapter 13, when they leave the temple the remark (B)
by one of the disciples about the wonderful buildings gives rise to
the Olivet speech (C). In narrative time most of the preceding events
have to do with the past, the Olivet discourse, however, concerns
the future. There is a switch both in narrative content (fall of Jerusalem
and parousia (D) which is predicted) and in narrative tense. Until
chapter 13 the narrative was, with the exception of predictions and
narrative commentary, told in the past tense (imperfect, aorist and
historic present) and in the narrative mode (*erzählte Welt*). In chapter 13:5–37, on the other hand, there is a change in narrative tense
(mostly future tenses) and mode (*besprochene Welt*). The narrator returns
to past events in chapters 14–16 when he relates the events (E) preceding the trial of Jesus, his trial (F), crucifixion (G), death (H), burial
(I) and resurrection (J). The chronological order of these events in
the story time is: 1,2,10,3,4,5,6,7,8,9. In other words, the chronological order of the basic material (story) out of which Mark made
his narrative text is different from that of the order in the narrative. In Mark 13 the author introduces another narrator Jesus who
looks forward and narrates events which are still to come. That is
what changes the chronological order in the narrative. Whereas the
narrator of Mark's story usually looks backward in time and narrates past events, in the Olivet discourse Jesus looks forward.

If we compare narrative time with story time, the order of Mark's
emplotted narrative is most remarkable and thus also the place of
Mark 13 in his narrative. The result of our comparison can be
expressed as follows: A(1) B(2) C(3) D(10) E(5) F(6) G(7) H(8) I(9).
Is there anything significant in Mark's ordering of the material in
this manner? Is this perhaps a means of foregrounding and accen-
tuating the contents of the speech for the sake of the readers?

The rearrangement of story time in narratives is not unusual. It
is in fact quite customary to find all sorts of rearrangements of time,
like pro- and retrospection, in narratives. This is the way in which
the reader is directed through the narrative. This is how the reader

is invited to take part in the narrative, to form expectations and to modify his expectations. And it is also true of Mark's gospel. It has, for example, been noticed by Petersen (1978a & b, 1980, 1984) that one of the important plot devices of this gospel is prediction and fulfilment, which is a form of rearrangement of story material. The reader is directed through the narrative by this device because predictions as well as their fulfilments are emplotted within the narrative (8:31; 9:31; 10:33ff. and the passion narrative). In the case of Mark 13 it is different. These predictions are not fulfilled (emplotted) inside the narrative. Contrary to the reader's expectation which is grounded on the way in which he is educated by the text, Mark does not tell what happened with the predictions Jesus makes in Mark 13. Literarily, Petersen (1980, 1984) finds this aspect of Mark 13 very significant and offers an interesting interpretation of the chapter on the basis of the 'unfulfilled' predictions. I shall return to this below. Fact is that the fulfilment of the predictions of Mark 13 are not emplotted in Mark's narrative, which underscores the question whether the placing of Mark 13 in the order of the narrative has any significance.

Another aspect of narrative time which might help us answer the question is that of *duration*. Duration has to do with the amount of time it takes to narrate an event (or events) in the story. It often happens that a narrator mentions a period (e.g. youth) in the life of a person but spends pages on one single event in the person's life. The amount of time devoted to the passion narrative in Mark, for example, is relatively extensive in comparison with other events. The only way of measuring the time spent in a narrative on an event or events, is to measure the amount of space taken to tell the event. The relative importance of an event is often determined by the space given to it in narrative time. The comparison between story time and text time is therefore based on the basis of space. If an author devotes twenty pages to one day in the life of the protagonist and one line to his birth, he clearly regards the former as more important for his purpose. The events which receive more attention are those which take most narrative space. The effect of longer or shorter narrative space is that of acceleration and deceleration, accentuation or generalization. Let us now turn to Mark 13.

I have already observed that Mark 13:5–37 takes relatively much space in comparison with what Jesus has to say in the rest of the Gospel of Mark. If we compare the length of Mark 13:5–37 to that

of the summaries given, for instance, of the miracles which Jesus
performed (cf. 1:32–34), or the resurrection narrative (16:18), it becomes clear that the speech in Mark 13 is undoubtedly accentuated
and focused upon. There is a deceleration in narrative speed. In the
material preceding the Olivet discourse the tension builds up through
the amount of events that are told. But all of a sudden the narrative speed is decelerated by the introduction of a long speech. There
is a pause in the narrative. In view of the fact that it is Jesus that
speaks, the narrative becomes more dramatic and a scenic impression is made on the reader. Taken together, there seems to be little reason to doubt the importance of and the accent on the contents
of the speech given by the narrative devices of order and duration.
This explains the significance of the order in which Mark narrated
Jesus' speech. Before the trial, death, and resurrection the reader is
called to a halt. The material is foregrounded for the sake of the
reader to reflect upon in order to 'understand' what 'followed' (in
the narrative of Mark!), and to instruct the reader about his own
conduct. The question now arises as to what the author wanted to
achieve with the speech since he obviously placed a lot of weight
on the contents thereof.

4. *Narrative Point of View, Apocalyptic and Paraenesis*

In Mark's gospel, like in any other narrative, the story of Jesus is
presented by the narrator from a certain perspective or viewpoint.
Narrative point of view signifies the perceptual, conceptual, and ideological way in which the story gets told (cf. Abrams 1971:133
Chatman 1978:151ff.). It is the means by which the reader is directed
to identify with the message of the narrative and to accept the norms
of judgement presented in the text. Petersen (1978b) has correctly
observed that until chapter 13 the reader is educated to accept the
view presented by Jesus and the unclean spirits and to view Jesus
in terms of the things of God (cf. 8:33) and not in terms of man,
as the other characters in the narrative, including the disciples, do.
The other characters wrongly view Jesus as the worldly messiah and
do not understand his mission. The disciples' lack of understanding
is woven like a golden thread through the fabric of the text. The
reader knows, because he is given the information by the narrator,
that Jesus is the Son of God and what his fate as Son of man is

(cf. 4–10); that death, resurrection and parousia await Him. The disciples, however, are presented as characters who are unable to comprehend.

> ... they do not comprehend what the reader is given to comprehend, namely that messiah and kingdom are to be understood in terms of death. resurrection, and parousia of Jesus. the Son of man who is the Son of God (Petersen 1984:47).

In literary terms, it means that Jesus is a reliable character because his perspective is presented by the narrator as trustworthy, while the disciples are unreliable (cf. Petersen 1980:161). With regard to Mark 13 this is rather important. Is Jesus presented as reliable? And what about the disciples? We will return to this.

It is not only through the eyes of the narrator that the events in the text are perceived. It is also possible to present the story from the perspective of a character in the story, in which case such a character is referred to as a 'focaliser' (cf. Genette 1980:189ff.). It is the narrator of the Gospel of Mark that presents Jesus in Mark 13 as a narrator. Embedded into Mark's narrative, which is told from a particular perspective, is the speech (the story about the future) of Jesus being told from the perspective of Jesus who is the focaliser in Mark 13:5–37. In the chapters preceding Mark 13 the narrator presented the viewpoint of Jesus as being trustworthy and established the norms of judgement through that point of view. What is the message and the perspective of Mark 13? Let us start with a few remarks about the closure of Mark's story with regard to Mark 13 in order to explain the difficulties of interpretation that are involved.

In two thought provoking articles Petersen (1980, 1984) argued that Mark 13 should be seen as the key to the plot of Mark's story. In view of the fact that Petersen gives a literary interpretation of Mark's gospel, and also because of the importance of his findings, I will rehearse in some detail parts of his argument. He maintains:

> Unlike the understanding of all other characters in the story, the twelve disciples' understanding is contrary to the intent and expectations of the reliable character, Jesus. For the plot to be resolved and this theme to be closed, something closural must either happen or be firmly implied (Petersen 1980:161).

He then goes on to show that Mark 13 is Jesus' story about a conflict of eschatological interpretations. On the one hand there is the eschatology of the false messiahs and prophets who proclaim that the messiah has come. They pretend that with his coming the end, that is the kingdom of God, has also set in and as a token they perform signs and wonders. On the other hand, there is the viewpoint of the disciples, who in chapter 13 '. . . have reversed the position they held before Jesus' death and resurrection' (Petersen 1984:47). When did this reversal take place? Petersen (1984:49) maintains that although the reversal is not described in the text of Mark, and although the predictions of Mark 13 are not fulfilled in the text of Mark, the reversal is addressed in the meeting of Jesus with his disciples in Galilee, which is predicted (but not described) in the section after Mark 13 (cf. 14:28; 16:7).

> Because he insists that the disciples, or at least four of them, remained in their false messianist position until the meeting in Galilee, Mark is saying of the later false messianists that their credentials are false because they have not been processed through Galilee (Petersen 1984:49).

According to Petersen the closure of the story is thus, firmly implied, namely in the meeting of the disciples with Jesus in Galilee. The closure of Jesus' story in Mark 13 is implied in the return of the Son of man. Both events take place in the continuum of Mark's narrative world. The intended reader, however, is aware of the change the disciples had undergone through their meeting with Jesus in Galilee because in the continuum of Mark's story the Galilee encounter did happen. The return of the Son of man still has to happen. The Galilee meeting supplies the basis for the reader to believe that the Son of man will return. Jesus thus remains a reliable character throughout the whole narrative and the reader can be convinced that the things of God dominate.

> The message of Mark's narrative is therefore not that the disciples were indeed a dull lot, or that they were such until Galilee, but that those proclaiming that Messiah and Kingdom have come are not to be believed because Jesus already disclosed the error of their views to four of his disciples and because these disciples themselves experienced a dramatic realization of that error which had once been their own (Petersen 1984:166).

For Petersen Mark 13 tells the story of Jesus about the reversal the disciples will undergo with respect to their views about Jesus. He has indeed made a number of very important observations about the Gospel of Mark and his views are especially challenging with respect to the interpretation of Mark 13. There are, however, a few things in his interpretation, which, from a literary point of view, are problematic. I fully agree that the closure of Mark's gospel is strongly implied in the Galilee episode and that the reader is invited to read Mark 13 in view of the reliability of the narrator, Jesus. However, it seems to me that Petersen wrongly interprets the story of Mark 13:5–37 as a story which relates the reversal of the viewpoint of the disciples because the reader knows that it had taken place in the Galilee episode. Let us therefore return to the text of Mark 13:5–37.

Unlike most of the information in Mark's narrative, Mark 13:5–37 is a speech about the future. It is a 'narrative' about future conflict written from an apocalyptic point of view in paraenetic style. The cast of characters includes, on the one side, the false messiahs and prophets (cf. 13:5,22), the unidentified 'they' of 13:9 and 11, and persecutors and helpers of the false messiahs and prophets. Opposed to these characters are the disciples to whom the story is told. Included in this narrative role are the 'elect' (13:20,22,27) referred to as the 'many' (13:5) and those who are persecuted (13:9–13). The helpers in this role are the Holy Spirit (13:11), the Lord (13:20), the angels (13:27) and the fig tree (13:28–29). It is a story about conflict and torment in which persecution and deception will play an enormous role. In addition to persecution the false messiahs and prophets will pretend that they are Jesus, the Messiah (13:5). They will even perform signs and miracles (13:22) to lead astray the elect. The time co-ordinates of the narrative are indicated by phrases introduced by *hotan* and *tote* and references to events which will come about (beginning), and (end) by the return of the Son of man (13:26). The latter (end) is imminent, it will occur in the time of the contemporaries of Jesus: 'I tell you this: the present generation will live to see it all' (13:30 NEB). The former (beginning) lies in the near future although not even the Son knows the exact time of 'that day' (13:32). There is a necessity for the conflict to take place—it must happen (13:7). The gentile mission also first has to take place (13:10). The narrative space includes earthly and heavenly scenes. In terms of the plot of the 'narrative' the task set for the false messiahs and prophets is to lead astray the elect (disciples), which will only be accomplished if the opponents of the false messiahs (the elect) are unable to read the signs, and do not endure and keep in mind the paraenesis they receive.

In addition to the fact that the speech of Jesus is told in the future tense while most of Mark's text is told in the past tense, there is a shift in, what may be called the 'conceptual perspective'. I am here referring to the way of representing things, the symbolic universe of Mark 13:5–37. Jesus is still presented as the One who sees things in God's terms. There is a change in the conceptual perspective by the introduction of a new way of presenting material. What I mean is the theological perspective from which the material is presented— the way in which Jesus sees the world and its future in the narrative of Mark. This is not the place to enter into the scholarly debate about whether Mark 13 is apocalyptic or not (cf. Brandenburger 1984), but a few remarks seem to be necessary.

The main difficulty concerning the theological perspective of Mark 13:5–37 is that of definition. Apocalyptic is used in many confusing ways and that explains the difference of opinion with regard to the supposedly apocalyptic nature of Mark 13. Following the research of Hanson (1976) and others, apocalyptic to my mind (cf. Vorster 1986) refers to a crisis phenomenon and apocalyptic eschatology to a meaning system, a theological perspective. Apocalyptic usually arises when the values and structures of a society lose all meaning for some minority group within a particular society and are replaced by a new symbolic meaning system. It is therefore at once a crisis phenomenon and an all-embracing approach to life in which the future determines the present. It is not concerned with the future only. Adherents of apocalyptic are not merely interested in the future. The contents of their visions and revelations also affect their views on the present and the past. Because life is seen in relation to the future there is great emphasis on correct conduct and ethics. Eschatology is of paramount importance. The past, present and future are interpreted in terms of the expectation of a new future or age and a new world in which supernatural space (heaven) and figures play an important role. Against this background one may ask how apocalyptic is Mark 13?

It is difficult not to read Mark 13 in its intertextual relationships and to overlook the traces of apocalyptic imagery in the chapter (cf. Brandenburger 1984). The eschatological conflict and the promise of the return of the Son of man are obviously two of the master symbols of a new symbolic universe which the text offers, making it different from the previous sections. Mark 13:5–37 presupposes a new context of communication. The material given in Mark 13:5–37 refers to a narrative world which is different from that in the previous chapters and the reader is expected to have a different frame of reference from the previous sections in Mark's story in order to understand the codes of the text. Chapters 1–12 undoubtedly generate certain expectations about the future by previews and hints through which the reader is educated on how to read Mark 13. He is aware of the return of the Son of man (cf. 8:38), of future suffering for the sake of Jesus (8:27–9:1) and of the imminent coming of the kingdom (9:1). Most of this information is, however, related to the death and resurrection of Jesus which the reader is expected to see as something which has to happen to the Son of God. In Mark 13 conduct is determined by the coming of the end which will be sudden, and not by the death and resurrection of Jesus. End-time events are given in images which are familiar to those who are acquainted with apocalyptic imagination and theology. That determines the new context of communication. On the ground of the reliability of Jesus as character the reader is entrusted through the eyes of Jesus with a view of what will happen in the immediate future. The future and future events are presented to the four and thus to the reader as new knowledge. Things that will happen, of which they did not have to the faintest clue, are now made known to the four. They are in addition told how to react to the new situation which will arise.

One of the recurring problems in the interpretation of Mark 13:5–37 is that of reference. This does not only apply to verse 14 which remains a *crux interpretum* with regard to the speech as can be seen in the history of interpretation (cf. Brandenburger 1984:49ff.). It also applies to the speech as a whole and to texts written from an apocalyptic perspective in particular. It is obvious that these texts, like any other text, refer in some way or another and that extratextual realities play a role in this regard. It should, however, not be forgotten that the primary function of texts written from an apocalyptic perspective is not to refer to extratextual realities. In the case of Mark 13:5–37 it is clear that the speech has a function with regard to the complete narrative and that it creates a narrative world of its own within the narrative world of Mark's gospel. It is the image of a future of conflict, persecution, tribulation, cosmic changes and the unexpected coming of the Son of man which is used to persuade the four to be on the alert, and not the events in the extratextual world to which each narrated event could possibly refer. That is why one should determine the semantic function of the text rather than its possible reference to extratextual realities. In the history of the interpretation of Mark 13 it appears to have been the other way

round. Far more importance was attached to the possible historical
inferences that could be made, than to the semantic function of these
intertextual realities. I am not saying that texts written from an apocalyptic perspective do not reflect the real world out of which they
arose, only that their primary function should not be looked for in
terms of extratextual reference. I will return to this problem below.
First, there is a need to reflect on the semantic function of Mark
13:5–37. Our text is an interesting mixture of apocalyptic imagery
and paraenesis. It is remarkable that almost everything which is said
to, and thus about the four to whom the speech is directed, is done
by way of imperatives (cf. *blepete* in 13:5,9,23,33; *me throeisthe* in 13:7;
me promerimnate in 13:11; *proseúchesthe* in 13:18; *me pisteúete* in 13:21;
máthete in 13:28; *ginoskete* in 13:28,29; *blépete agrupneîte* in 13:33; *gre-
goreîte* in 13:35,37 and the singular subjunctives in 14–16). It is
expected from the four disciples to act in a certain way during the
end time. This is of particular interest with regard to the interpretation of the text, since language is used to some end. To use language is to do things; it is to make language perform one or more
functions (cf. Chatman 1978:162ff.; Halliday 1978:19f.). The question may rightly be asked what the function of language is in Mark
13:5–37. Is it to inform the reader about all the events which are
referred to in the chapter, or is it to persuade the reader? To me
there seems to be little doubt about the answer. The use of imperatives is self-explanatory. Mark 13:5–37 was not in the first instance
written to inform the four about the future, but rather how to expect
the future—that is, to be prepared for the future by being alert and
aware of what to expect. It is the paraenetic mode of expression
which dominates the text, not in the sense of 'ethical' admonitions,
but of the stringing together of imperatives of conduct. The imperatives in Mark 13:5–37 have the same characteristics as paraenetic
admonitions which are devised as ethical precepts (cf. Perdue 1981:
242–246). On the basis of the authority and trustworthiness of Jesus
these imperatives are given to '. . . define the ideal behaviour for
those entering into a new social position or group' (Perdue 1981:
249). Perhaps the most important remark made by Perdue (1981:249)
for our purpose is that these admonitions call the recipient to serious reflection about his initial entrance into his present position,
which is a matter of resocialization. Does the language of Mark
13:5–37 lead the reader to such reflection before he reads the closure of Mark's story? The language used in Mark 13 is used to do

something and that is to convince the reader about the perspective of Jesus, that is the life and works of the Son of God seen in terms of the things of God—the suffering and return of the Son of man. To accept the story the reader has to take a different stance than the one taken by the disciples.

One has to keep in mind the development of the plot of Mark's narrative in an attempt to understand Mark 13. The reader has of God, namely the idea of a kingdom and messiahship which is not of man. Until Mark 13 he is prepared to accept the predictions of the suffering, death and resurrection on the ground of the reliability of Jesus. In terms of redundancy the reader is in fact well prepared for the death and resurrection of Jesus. Mark 13 is however, of vital importance for the time after the resurrection and for the implications of his being Son of God, who will return as Son of man. It substantially undergirds the total resocialization of the reader who has to accept the view that the Son of God had to suffer and that the end is not yet, neither with the death and resurrection of Jesus nor with rumours about end time signs like wars (cf. 13:7). It implies a closure of the plot in the future.

It seems to me that Petersen's interpretation about the disciples and their reversal in Mark 13 cannot be accepted. He infers too much from Mark 13 and in the end ignores the text and its directives for the reader. He regards the disciples as the protagonists of the story—not a set of orders of conduct to disciples who lack understanding (cf. Petersen 1980:165). This is best seen in the following remark:

> Some who were declared false by Jesus, proclaim that the messiah has come, and with him the end, that is, the Kingdom of God, while prophets attest to the eschatological presence by performing signs and wonders (13:6.21–23). Opposed to the messiahs and prophets are the four disciples who, in this story. say that the end is not yet but that it will come next when, with cosmic signs, the Son of man will come in clouds with great power and glory (13:24–27,29) (Petersen 1980: 165–166).

This is the hub of Petersen's interpretation. It stands and falls with the question whether 'in this story' the four disciples say that the end is not yet—as he maintains—or whether they are expected to say so—as I have argued above. I do not doubt that the disciples, according to the text, are expected to say that the end is not yet and so on, and that their role is that of opposing the protagonist, that is the false messiahs and the false prophets. They are not the protagonists in the story of Jesus in Mark 13:5–37. They are once again given the instruction to comprehend the implications of story of Mark. They are undoubtedly not presented in their after-Galilee meeting (in the real world or continuum of Mark's narrative world), but in their state of incomprehension. They are again, as in chapters 1–12, put in the privileged position of receiving inside information on the after-resurrection period and are expected in the continuum of Mark's story to make the viewpoint of the things of God their own.

Much of what Petersen has to say in connection with Mark 13 is useful. He seems, however, in his literary interpretation of the text to have been led by historical inferences about the first flesh and blood readers and the problem of the 'historical' as well as the literary closure of Mark's gospel. In the long run Mark's disciples are not personages in a narrative world but real persons. The task of the interpreter becomes one of establishing what the real readers knew and what their positions were. Once this is established the text is interpreted in the light thereof. The reason for this is found, amongst others, in Petersen's use of the term 'implied reader'. For him the implied reader is not a textual construct (cf. Booth 1983:137; Iser 1978:34), a reader encoded in the text, but a real flesh and blood reader implied by the text. This is misleading and nothing less than the construction of a possible reader. His results are not literary but rather historical, based on inferences made from the text. There is a very sophisticated mixture of literary and historical information in these studies as is seen in the following remark:

> From a literary perspective, therefore, Jesus' predictions are the implied author's fictions, based on his knowledge of events that are either past or present (Petersen 1984:45).

Is fiction now becoming factual and is that the reason for the historical inferences? One should remember that all we have is the text, a contextless text and that in the first place the Gospel of Mark is a narrative, rather than a history of Jesus and his disciples.

There is enough literary grounds to argue the importance of the fact that Mark 13:5–37 is a narrated speech and that its position in the order of the narrative is significant. The narrative message of the text ties in with the theme of the incomprehension of the disciples. From an apocalyptic perspective they are admonished to reconsider their position as followers of Jesus and encouraged to resist the persecution, tribulation and false messages of the false messiahs and prophets who will try to lead them astray. Similar to the closure of the Gospel of Mark in 16:8, Mark 13 is an openended story. The reader is left with the gap of the fulfilment of the Galilee episode, but also with the gap of the fulfilment of the predictions in Mark 13. This is one of the significant ways in which the reader is guided to read the text constructively. It leaves the reader with the strong expectation of an imminent parousia. It is very difficult for a modern reader, who is accustomed to the delay of the parousia, not to realise that Mark wrote a story for people who lived a long time ago.

5. *Conclusion*

A literary interpretation of Mark 13 can never pretend to solve all the problems in the text. It can only offer a particular reading of the text based on certain presuppositions as we have seen above. What is more, there is more than one literary reading possible in accordance with literary vantage points. I have not tried to give an exhaustive treatment of the narrated speech. I have simply dealt with a few, to my mind important, problems. In the first place it seems clear that much more attention should be spent on the narrative character of Mark 13, also on the fact that the speech in Mark 13 is told from the perspective of a reliable character who is trusted to talk about the future, even though he himself confesses that he does not know everything (13:32). The point of view from which he offers his information will also have to be studied in greater detail, but from a literary and not a literary comparative viewpoint. In the third place much more attention should be paid to semantic function in New Testament studies.

CHAPTER TWENTY FOUR

CHARACTERIZATION OF PETER
IN THE GOSPEL OF MARK

The role of Peter in the Gospel of Mark has been studied from various perspectives during the past. These include attempts to 'reconstruct' the 'real' Peter from Petrine, or as others argued, anti-Petrine strands in Mark's material, as well as descriptions of Mark's presentation of the person and position of Peter. In recent years the gospels have been subjected to various forms of narrative analyses and the narrated figures have been studied with respect to their narrative roles. This study explores the possibility of studying the shaping and function of Peter as a character in Mark's story of Jesus. In order to avoid misunderstanding the first part of the paper deals with theoretical aspects of roles, characters and narrated figures. In the second part a construction made of what Mark's Peter is like.

1. *Theoretical Reflections*

Gospel criticism has been enriched in recent years by increased attention to the gospels as *narratives*. Contrary to the past where the focus was mainly on the origin, growth and making of the gospel material, recent studies concentrated on narrative aspects of the gospels. This involved a paradigm switch both in terms of research methods and results. A new set of questions was introduced and new answers were developed to old problems. This also applies to the study of figures or persons narrated in the gospels. Whereas past studies concentrated mainly on historical problems in connection with narrated persons in the gospels, for example Jesus, recent investigators started to pay attention to literary aspects of the gospels and for that reason to narrated figures as characters in the storyworld of these texts (cf. e.g. Culpepper 1983:101ff.; Malbon 1983:29ff.; Rhoads & Michie 1982:101ff.; Tannehill 1977:386ff.).

Peter has been the object of investigation in many studies during the past, including some on Peter in the Gospel of Mark (cf. Brown,

Donfried & Reumann 1973; Best 1978:547ff.). These range from
studies with a dogmatic interest in the primacy of Peter and apostolic succession (cf. Pesch 1980) to historical studies on the person
of Peter (cf. Cullmann 1960) and Mark's presentation of him in his
gospel. In addition to the traditional view of Papias (cf. Eus. HE
111:39) that Mark was Peter's interpreter and the influence of this
view on investigators about Peter and Mark's gospel, quite a number of attempts has been made to infer biographical data about him
from the gospel by filling in the 'open spaces' in Mark's story and/or
doubting the historicity of different aspects of his presentation (cf.
Klein 1961). Mark's presentation of Peter has been judged differently
by different scholars. Bultmann (1970:275) argues that there is an
anti-Petrine trend in Mark's gospel and according to Weeden (1971:56)
Peter is the spokesman of an erroneous Christology. The following
remark of Achtemeier (1973:62) is not altogether inconceivable in
view of this type of approach to the gospels, 'The way one answers
the question of Mark's attitude toward Peter will depend in part on
one's analysis of Mark's theological outlook and his purpose in writing the Gospel.' The fundamental insight here is the fact that texts,
like the gospels, reflect the interests of the redactors of the material
they contain, and that these redactors were exponents of the communities they represent. That explains Achtemeier's remarks about
'Mark's attitude' and 'theological outlook'. The question, however,
is whether it is possible at all to infer Mark's attitude toward Peter
from the text and whether Mark's picture of Peter is determined in
the first instance by his so-called theological outlook and purpose of
writing. In other words, is the shaping of Peter and his function in
the narrative dependent upon matters such as Mark's attitude towards
Peter or upon Mark's theological outlook? In what follows I will
argue that Peter is a *character* in Mark's *narrative* and not in the first
place, a historical person. Mark shaped the character Peter in view
of the narrative function(s) he attributed to the character. Whether
this shaping and function(s) coincide with the Peter who lived on
earth during the ministry of Jesus, what Mark's attitude was towards
him, and whether there is a (historical) pro- or anti-Petrine trend in
Mark's gospel, are matters of historical concern which can hardly
be determined by any study which has the presentation of Peter in
Mark's gospel as its aim. This is not to deny the importance of historical studies, or the possibility of inferring historical data from texts
like gospels, but simply to state the importance of studying the gospels

for what they are: narratives. In this article the characterization of Peter in Mark will be examined in view of the way in which the character is shaped and also in the light of its narrative function. A few remarks on what I mean by characterization are necessary. I will first deal with this and then analyse the characterization of Peter in the gospel.

2. *Narratives, Persons, Roles and Characters*

There is only a limited number of ways in which material is organized in a discourse. Communication of material takes place by *narration, exposition, argument, description* and *listing* (cf. Brooks & Warren 1970:56f.). These ways of communicating also represent different text types. There can be no doubt that gospels are narratives, and that smaller units like dialogues which are embedded into these narratives, are presented as narrated texts, for example narrated dialogues. Once this is recognized the question arises how narratives work. What are the characteristics of narratives? And how should they be read? Are gospels narratives of a special kind? Is it possible to apply modern theories of narratology to texts which are commonly regarded as the end product of processes of transmission of oral tradition? These and many other questions have been of interest to investigators of the gospels and their narrative character during the past decade. There are obviously many divergent views on detail aspects of the matter, but the narrative character of gospels seems to be something which cannot be denied and which has to be taken into account in any study of the gospels and their way of communication.

One of the fundamental insights gained from the narrative analysis of the gospels is that these texts do not give us descriptive accounts of 'what really happened'. They are constructs which reflect an author's attempt to relate the story of Jesus for a specific purpose to an audience who most probably heard the narrative but did not read it individually. From the perspective of text production this observation means that the author produced a narration of events and persons in which he organized the material according to his purpose. Mark deliberately constructed a story of Jesus with a beginning, a complication and a resolution, and shaped the material in the way he preferred in spite of the fact that he was using traditional material. It is within this world, Mark's storyworld, that things

happen, and people act. This might not seem important. But the
implications are far-reaching. Mark's story is a story and not a *verbatim*
account of what happened. Whoever wishes to answer the question,
'Who is Peter according to Mark?', will either have to construct 'the'
Peter of history by way of historical construction or will have to
rephrase the question to, 'What is the character Peter like in Mark's
story?' These two questions represent two basically different approaches
to the gospel material. The first deals with the problem of text and
'reality', that is with the person of the Peter who lived on earth;
while the latter is concerned with Peter 'on paper', that is a personage in a text (cf. Bal 1979). These questions also call for concern about the function of texts in the process of communication.

Every communication is not necessarily a communication of information, and texts, be they sentences or larger units or even gospels
for that matter, may have a variety of functions. The primary function of certain texts are indeed *informative*. Texts give information or
describe matters mentioned in them. Others, however, are expressive. They express ideas, feelings, convictions, and so on, in aesthetic
language. Yet others are formulated in such a manner as to *persuade*
the reader, or simply to serve a *social* purpose (cf. Chatman 1978:162ff.;
Halliday 1978:19f.). These semantic functions are of paramount importance for the process of communication, as well as for the understanding of texts such as gospels. In short, both the shaping of a
text and the function of a text are important aspects in reading or
understanding a text.

Mark's gospel is a narrative, and narratives are shaped by the way
in which the material is arranged, personages presented, the points
of view from which material is narrated, the narrative space and
time, and other narrative characteristics. In his shaping of his narrative, Mark constructed a world of ideas, a symbolic universe, within
which events and existents like characters, space and time interact
(cf. Chatman 1978). Let us for a moment return to the 'storyworld'
of Mark.

Mark wrote a story and thereby created an *image* of events and
personages in the life of Jesus in order to communicate something
to his reader(s) through this image. There can be difference of opinion about the original semantic function and what it was that he
intended to communicate, but this is not the place to argue that
point. What is of importance is to notice the implications of the fact
that Mark created a 'world', a storyworld. A story, like the Gospel

of Mark, is an author's image, his construction of the information he presents to his readers. In addition, one should not forget that, because a story is a communication, there are readers involved as well. Reading is also an act of construction. Like text production, reading is a process of production. The literary phenomenon is not only the text, but also its reader and all of the reader's possible reactions to the text—both *énoncé* and *énonciation* (Riffaterre 1983:3). From the perspective of the reader an image of an image is constructed and this construction is the reader's reaction to the text (cf. also Petersen 1984). Reading is a mental process and therefore one could say that the reader's image of the events and existents in a text is the way in which the reader sees them. The image of the text generates an image within the mind of the reader. What happens then when the characters in a story are studied, is that a particular kind of reader analyses the way in which the character is presented in the text by reflecting on his image of the character ('What is the character like?' (cf. Chatman 1978:19ff.)). Are these 'characters' in Mark's story then different from persons, and is it correct to speak about characterization in the Gospel of Mark?

It is true that it is impossible to apply all insights of modern research on narratology to ancient literature like the gospels. For that reason one should be careful not to read too much into a text. But given this condition, one should also take seriously the fact that the gospels are narratives and that one could therefore expect narrative characteristics, like characterization, in these texts. It is perhaps not correct to expect the same forms and degree of characterization in a gospel as one would expect in modern short stories. But there is also no reason to no doubt the presence of characters in gospel stories. Nor is there any reason to take Cullmann (1959:101) seriously when he says that there is no difference in treatment of the person of Peter among the synoptic gospels (cf. also Gewalt 1975:21). The actors are not simply persons as we will see later on. They are personages in the story worlds of narratives.

Literary theorists differ considerably about the exact nature of characterization (cf. Chatman 1978; Bal 1979). In accordance with different literary theories the 'persons' who act in narratives are analysed mainly in terms of characters and/or role functions. What is a character and what is a role? Let us start by saying that the characters in a story are not persons. The main difference between a person and a personage or character is that persons are of blood and flesh while characters are of paper (Bal 1979:2). This brings us back to the remarks about a story as being images of the events and existents which are related. Characters greatly determine the nature of any kind of narrative. They act, speak, and experience things in narratives. What they say and do determine the reaction of the reader to them. The way in which their actions and their words are involved in the development of the story also determine their characterization, that is, what they are like. Characterization is thus a very complex matter. Of importance is not only what an author directly says about a character, but also what he does not say and what is told or shown directly and indirectly about matters which concern the development of the story and as such the character. Words and images determine characters since that is the way in which they are shaped.

The only source of information about characters is the text. Sometimes a character is explicitly described, but implicit information is no less important. If Peter is said to have been called as a follower, does he also act as a follower? The whole story, all the events and characters are the source from which a reader might derive his image of a character. Direct and indirect information about a character influence the image a reader may have about a particular character, but this image is also influenced by the way in which the narrative is structured logically and chronologically. The relationship between these two aspects of characterization has given rise to various theories about characterization. Since the days of Aristotle who deals with characterization in his *Poetics*, there has been difference of opinion about the relationship between plot and characterization. Some regard characterization as an aspect or function of plot (the chronological and logical structure), while others put sharp focus on the way in which a character is 'described' or named independent of its relationship with the plot (cf. Chatman 1978:110ff.). When the emphasis is mainly on the likeness of a character, traits of characters are investigated. Aristotle speaks of four character traits in drama (*Poet* 15.1–6) and argues that a character should be *good, appropriate or natural, like a person,* and *consistent* (cf. Lausberg 1960:594ff.). And in similar fashion Foster introduced the idea of so- I called *round* and *flat* characters, where round characters are lifelike, complex and surprising and flat ones not (cf. Bal 1979:2). Useful as these categorizations may seem, they do not really help us in describing the

characterization of characters. Chatman (1978:125), who builds on
the idea of Barthes that reading is a process of naming, and that
one element to be named is the traits of a character, speaks of a
trait as, '. . . a narrative adjective out of the vernacular labelling a
personal, quality of a character, as it persists over a part or whole
of the story . . .' 'Incomprehension' would be one of the traits of the
disciples in Mark and 'fallible' would be another. These names or
traits, which are obviously culturally coded (Peter is a Galilean), and
which are explicit as well as implicit, are very useful in any attempt
to envisage what a character is like in a story. It also gives a much
more open possibility of describing characters.

In structuralist circles 'characterization' has been studied in close
relationship with plot and semantic function. One has to keep in
mind that, according to structuralists, there is a difference between
a character and a narrative function or role (cf. Propp), or actant
(cf. Greimas). In Mark the Jewish leaders, the disciples, and the
crowd function as *Opponents* of Jesus who is the *Subject* in the story.
Since the same 'character' can perform different functions in a story,
the disciples, however, also function, with the demons and others,
as *Helpers*. The actions and actants in the story are related to the
plot, which can be schematized as follows (cf. Vorster 1982a:144ff.):

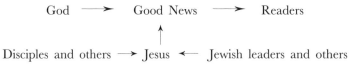

Donor ⟶ Object ⟶ Beneficiary

Helper ⟶ Subject ⟶ Opponent

A Subject is helped by a Helper and opposed by an Opponent in
his attempt to acquire an Object or to give it to a Beneficiary. The
process is started by a Donor who wants the Beneficiary to get the
Object. In the case of Mark:

God ⟶ Good News ⟶ Readers

Disciples and others ⟶ Jesus ⟵ Jewish leaders and others

The advantage of this approach is the formal way in which narrative roles are related to plot, which is not complex if understood
within the framework of this approach. The disadvantage thereof is
the impossibility to build a mental image of a particular character
with the help of such an analysis. In view of this Chatman (1978:119)

correctly observes that characters should be autonomous beings and not mere plot functions. On the other hand it is also true that there is a direct relationship between characterization and plot in a story.

In the following section the insights above will be used in a description of the character Peter in the Gospel of Mark. Special attention will be given to the way in which the character is shaped and to certain traits which are highlighted.

3. *Peter in Mark*

It is clear from the beginning that Peter is not a mere 'walk-on' in Mark's narrative. He is one of the characters who receives a relatively large amount of attention in the story and is also one of the characters who, through his shaping, greatly influences the reader's identification with Jesus. Peter's characterization as well as his narrative role(s) is closely linked to Jesus, the protagonist or Subject of the story, and to other characters like the disciples, the crowd and others. It has often been said that Peter is portrayed both positively and negatively in Mark's-gospel (cf. Achtemeier 1973:61ff.) and reasons have been sought to explain this state of affairs. In addition it has been argued that the role of the followers of Jesus is composite and complex (cf. Breytenbach 1984; Malbon 1983; Tannehill 1977; Vorster 1980c:43–4). I am convinced that this observation is true of characterization in general in the Gospel of Mark and in particular of the characterization of Peter.

In researching the character of Peter in the Gospel of Mark, I paid special attention to direct as well as indirect definition of the character. It soon became clear that, although it is a very useful distinction, the character Peter is almost exclusively shaped indirectly. Peter is one of the *Helpers* of Jesus in the plot of the story, perhaps the most important one. And for that reason his characterization is part of the characterization of the Helpers, that is the followers of Jesus. On the other hand, Peter is also at times presented as an Opponent of Jesus, in fact as *the* Opponent of Jesus who reveals a total lack of understanding (cf. Mk. 8:27ff.) In the following I will very briefly indicate the instances where the character is defined *directly* before I turn to the *indirect* definition.

3.1 *Direct characterization*

There are a few interesting remarks in Mark's gospel which directly pertains to the character Peter. Close to the beginning of the narrative the reader is told that Jesus saw *Simon* and his brother Andrew casting a net in the Sea of Galilee. They are invited to join Jesus on the promise that he would make them 'fishers of men'. The reader is told that they followed him (1:16–18). In verse 16 the narrator remarks, '. . . for they were fishermen' (1:16). In Mark narrative commentary, uttered for the sake of the reader, is often, like here, introduced by a γάρ-statement (cf. 1:22, 38; 2:15; 3:10 *et al.*). In view of this, it can be argued that the remark is not simply made in passing. This social setting of the first 'helpers' of Jesus is not unimportant. Immediately after the incident another two fishermen, John and James, are also called and they too decide to follow him. 'Fishermen' and 'followers' introduce two important aspects of the narrative world of Mark's gospel. In fact, Galilean fishermen are called as his first followers and they obey him. Galilee forms an important part of the narrative space and so do the inhabitants of Galilee. In contrast to the religious leaders, who are the opponents of Jesus in this gospel, the Galileans are his followers and the main audience of his message. The play on 'fisher'—'fishers of men' both characterizes Peter (and Andrew) and also functions as a preview to a task they are given in the plot which they can either accomplish or cannot: They have to be fishers of men. They immediately accept the task and follow Jesus. The theme of following, which is perhaps the most important aspect of Peter's characterization, as well as one of the most complex aspects of characterization in Mark, will be discussed below. Indirectly the impression is created that Peter (and Andrew) reacted on the spur of the moment—a motif which is repeated in connection with Peter (cf. Mk. 8:32; 14:28). A few traits of the narrated figure are thus introduced: a fisher from Galilee who might become a fisher of men, a follower of Jesus, an impulsive person, but also a person who is willing to obey at first sight.

Other instances where Peter is defined directly are in fact very few. The reader learns that Peter and Andrew had a house in Capernaum and that he had a mother-in-law (1:29–30); that he was one of an inner group of the helpers of Jesus consisting of four (Peter, Andrew, John, James: cf. Mk. 1:29; 13:3; cf. also beginning of the list of Twelve in 3:16ff.) or three (without Andrew 5:37; 9:2;

14:33); that he had companions (1:36); that his name used to be Simon (cf. 1:16, 29, 30, 36; 14:37) but that it was changed when Jesus gave him the name Peter on the occasion of the appointing of the Twelve, after which he is called Peter eighteen times in the story; that he was called Satan (cf. Osborne 1973:187ff.) by Jesus and told that he was thinking as man and not as God (8:33); that he (one of the Three) was afraid at the transfiguration (9:6); that despite his conviction that he would not fail Jesus (14:29–31, he followed Jesus at a distance (14:54) when he was arrested and denied him three times (14:66–72); but when he remembered his promise he broke down and wept (14:72). His Galilean pronunciation betrayed him (15:70). These references clearly indicate the complexity of the character Peter. In terms of the norms of the narrative, there is a guile positive as well as a negative side to this character. From the narrator's point of view Peter is the first and the most important follower of Jesus, but he is also the one who fails Jesus in the most critical situations. From the point of view of Jesus, on the other hand, the same complex figure is portrayed. There is a very close relationship between Jesus and Peter, although Peter is also rejected with very harsh words. The point of view of the narrator as well as that of Jesus directly influences the reader and because of the complex nature thereof the , reader is invited both to identify with and to reject Peter. This will become even clearer when the indirect definition is discussed below.

3.2 *Indirect characterization*

It will be impossible to treat separately each case where Peter is mentioned in the Gospel of Mark or where indirect definition of the character Peter plays a role. The reason for this is not only a matter of space but rather a matter of the interwovenness of the text. I have therefore decided to discuss the indirect definition of the character in terms of themes such as association, following, fear, incomprehension and so on.

Personages in narratives are often characterized by association or environment. I have already indicated that Galilee, fishermen, discipleship, the Twelve, are important indicators of the narrative existents which determine the image of characters in the Gospel of Mark. In the case of Peter it is his association with Jesus but also with the followers of Jesus that is important. It is his being a follower of Jesus both in terms of success and failure, that invokes an image of what sort of character Peter was like.

The next two examples are both illustrative of how association or environment plays a role in the characterization of Peter. In 1:29 he is in the company of members of the 'Big Three/Four', that is Peter, Andrew, John and James, who are the privileged and direct associates of Jesus on special occasions in the narrative (cf. 5:37; 9:2; 13:3; 14:33). They get to the house of Simon and Andrew where Simon's mother-in-law was ill in bed with fever. The four men privately observe the power of Jesus to heal, and are 'served' by Peter's mother-in-law (cf. 1:31). The fact that Peter was married is underplayed by the focus on his association with Andrew, John and James and the healing of his mother-in-law. As a follower of Jesus he is directly involved in the story of Jesus, his deeds and his words, both as an observer and as a helper. The success of Jesus is his success and the opponents of Jesus his opponents. Being in the company of Andrew, John and James furthermore signals his membership of an inner group of the followers who are privileged to accompany Jesus on very private occasions (cf. 5:37; 14:33) and to observe and hear things from which other characters are excluded (cf. 9:2; 13:3ff.). The episode gives a preview of the intimate relationship between Peter and Jesus which is developed in the remainder of the story. A similar thing happens in 1:35–8, but here a negative aspect of the character is signalled. The narrator tells that 'Simon and his companions' went out to search for Jesus and to inform him that everybody was looking for him. The answer of Jesus, however, is a suggestion that 'Simon and his companions' do not understand the mission of Jesus (1:38–39). It is thus the first indication of the theme of the incomprehension of Peter and the disciples in Mark's gospel. This trait of Peter will be discussed below.

The two episodes just mentioned are indicative of aspects of the characterization of Peter which are developed in Mark's story. I Although they are only suggested here, two important traits are introduced, namely the important place Peter has in the world of Mark, but also that Peter did not fully understand the mission of Jesus. Both need to be treated in more detail.

In the narrative about the appointment of the Twelve (3:13–19) Simon is mentioned as the first of the Twelve and given the name Peter. Earlier on he was called Simon. At first sight this might seem very innocent. However, both the order of the names and the change of names are important for the portrayal of Peter in Mark's gospel. It is remarkable that Peter is mentioned as the first of the Twelve and that only Peter, John and James, members of the inner group of Three/Four receive other names. John and James are called *Boanerges*, that is, for the sake of the reader: *Sons of Thunder*. Let us first consider the order of the names.

Simon and Andrew were the first followers according to 1:16–20 and Simon was mentioned first. In 1:36 it is *Simon* and his companions that are referred to. Already at this stage of the story it seems that it is not without reason that Peter is mentioned first. What becomes clear at a later stage in the story, namely that Peter is a kind of spokesman for others and that there is special focus on him (cf. 5:37; 8:27–33; 9:2–13; 10:28–30; 1:12–22; 13:3ff.; 14:29–31, 32–42, 54, 66–72; 16:7), is already suggested by the placing of his name in the calling of the fishers and the Twelve. Even within the inner group Peter is singled out for special attention on two occasions (cf. 9:2–13; 14:32–42).

It should be noticed that the focus Peter receives in the instances mentioned above, evoke a very complex image of him and his privileged position. He is not only singled out to be first in terms of importance and success (cf. 1:16; 3:16; 5:37; 10:28–30; 13:3ff.; 16:7, and in a restricted sense 8:29), but also in terms of impulsiveness and failure (cf. 8:33; 9:6; 14:29–32, 32–42, 54, 66–72). One of the introductory remarks in the narrative about the appointment of the Twelve is about the task they had to accomplish: 'He appointed twelve as his companions, whom he would send out to proclaim the gospel, with a commission to drive out devils' (3:14, *NEB*). According to the narrator they only partly accomplish the task (cf. 6:13 and 9:18; 28, 33; 14:32–72). This ties in with the ambivalence of the characterization of the disciples (the Twelve) [and other followers of Jesus (cf. Malbon 1983)] in general and Peter in particular. Peter and the disciples are called to be the special agents of Jesus and receive special information (cf. 3:13–19; 4:10ff.; 6:7ff.; 9:30–1 etc.), but do not understand. They fear and reject him (cf. 4:13; 6:51–2; 8:14–21; 14:10, 50, 66–71). By placing him in the important position of being the first follower, the first of the Twelve, and the one who is singled out for special attention, Peter is portrayed with the others as the disciple of success and failure.

The change of the names in the list of the Twelve is important for two reasons. In the first place it is remarkable that Peter, John and James are mentioned in this order with Andrew being the following name on the list. Only the first three received new names and they are important members of the inner group. Does that tell the reader anything special about the character Peter? Secondly the change of the name of Simon to Peter deserves attention because with one exception he is called Peter throughout the narrative after the change (14:37). It is difficult to determine why the inner group sometimes consists of four members and sometimes of three. Except for the apocalyptic discourse given to the four in chapter 13, it is only in the calling narrative (1:16ff.) [and the appointment of the Twelve (3:13ff.)] that the four are referred to as a group. On three very important occasions in the narrative, the inner group has only three members (5:37ff.; 9:2ff.; 14:33ff.). The stories of the transfiguration and Gethsemane are of special interest for our purpose. In 9:5 it is Peter who takes the word almost impulsively without really knowing what to say, 'Rabbi . . . how good it is that we are here! Shall we make three shelters, one for you, one for Moses, and one for Elijah?' (*NEB*). The narrative commentary, 'For he did not know what to say; they were so terrified' (9:6), is illuminating as far as the shaping of Peter's character is concerned. Out of fear and ignorance he reacts impulsively. The story of Gethsemane where he is portrayed as failing completely in the hour of Jesus' distress, also throws special light on Peter's character. The inner group is told about Jesus' distress and is instructed to remain awake while he goes to pray. They fall asleep, however, and on his return Jesus addressed *Peter*, 'Simon, are you asleep? Were you not able to stay awake for one hour?' (14:37). In addition to Peter's failure to stay awake, Jesus' question is important. First of all we should remind ourselves about the close relationship existing between chapters 13 and 14 (cf. Tannehill 1977:402–3). The disciples are warned that they will have to face situations of persecution and that they should watch and not fall asleep (13:9–13, 33–37). This heightens the attention paid to the disciples' and to Peter's failure in chapter 14. From the point of view of Jesus, and not only from that of the narrator, Peter fails Jesus in his hour of distress. It is furthermore remarkable that Peter is called Simon. Why? He is called Simon prior to his renaming in the narrative of the appointment of the Twelve, and here. The narrator creates the impression that the change of name had to do with the appointment of Peter as one of the Twelve. Being the first of the apostles, he is Peter. But in the hour of total distress, when he fails

Jesus, the name Simon recalls the time before the appointment. Perhaps one should, however, not read too much into the name Simon in 14:37.

One of the prominent threads in the texture of Mark's text is *following* or *discipleship*. This is perhaps the most complex and composite theme as Malbon (1983) and others have argued. Although the disciples are not the only followers of Jesus (cf. crowd, women and individuals) in the gospel narrative they are the most prominent. In his thought-provoking thesis Weeden (1971) maintains that Mark's presentation of the disciples reflects his polemic against the historically false Christology which he wished to oppose and correct. According to him there are three stages in Mark's presentation: *unperceptiveness* (1:16–8:26), *misconception* which starts with Peter's confession, and *rejection* when Judas's plans to betray Jesus 'erupts into an outright rejection of Jesus and his messiahship' (cf. Weeden 1971:32ff., especially 38). This is a very negative view of Mark's portrayal of the disciples and has been rejected on both historical and literary grounds. I would rather agree with Tannehill (1977), Malbon (1983) and others that Mark's representation of the disciples is a literary attempt to prompt the reader to prepare for discipleship and to make it clear that discipleship is no easy task. Discipleship is portrayed in this gospel in a positive as well as a negative way. Jesus's companions both follow him and betrayed him, and the same group and the same individual obey as well as misunderstand him. In this manner they are both helpers and opponents in the plot. What is Peter's position?

Peter is the first follower of Jesus. Without objection he leaves his boats and follows Jesus in order to become a fisher of men (1:16–20, cf. also 10:28–30). He and others accompany Jesus on his journey through Galilee to Jerusalem, observing his deeds and listening to his teaching. In the company of the other disciples Peter receives special instruction (cf. ch. 4, 8, 13). He is allowed to accompany Jesus on special occasions (5:37ff.; 8:27ff.; 9:2ff.; 13:3ff.) and as one of the Twelve partly accomplishes the task they receive at their appointment. On the other hand, however, it is also clear that Peter is a fallible follower of Jesus. Like the other disciples he does not understand precisely what it means to follow Jesus because he does not understand what Jesus stands for, as we shall see below. Peter is in fact the one who is rebuked in strong terms because he thinks like men and not like God (8:33) about the mission of Jesus. It is because of him and for his sake, as I will argue, that the exact meaning of following is proclaimed in overt terms in 8:34–9:1. He promises to follow Jesus even if everybody else falls away, and insists that he will not deny Jesus (14:28ff.). In the end he follows Jesus unobtrusively (ὁ Πέτρος ἀπὸ μακρόθεν ἠκολούθησεν αὐτῷ 14:54) and denies Jesus three times (14:66ff.). When he realizes that he failed, he bursts into tears (14:72). There is no sign of Peter being a non-follower of Jesus in Mark's gospel, not even in the passion narrative. His presence at the trial, be it il at a distance, should be interpreted positively (cf. however Klein 1961). 'To be present at all is a mark of followership, but remaining "at a distance" is a mark of fallibility for Peter and for the women' (Malbon 1983:43). At the end of the story there is a remark which signals the invitation to the disciples and to Peter to a continual following of Jesus in Galilee (16:7). Peter's characterization, and also the disciples' characterization as followers of Jesus, do not end on a negative note. Instead, the relationship between Jesus and his followers is re-established (cf. Boomershine 1977:309).

Two other aspects which deserve attention in connection with the characterization in the Gospel of Mark of the disciples in general and Peter in particular, are fear and incomprehension. Both the fear and the incomprehension of the disciples form part of the so-called messianic secret. It is remarkable that, despite special instruction, the disciples do not understand (cf. 4:10–13, 40–1; 6:50–2; 7:18; 8:16–21, 33; 9:32; 10:35ff.) and that they are often afraid because they lack insight (cf. 4:41; 6:50; 9:32; 10:32). These two aspects occur in many parts of the gospel but are particularly relevant in the first section which is structured for the greater part by the theme of seeing, hearing and not understanding (especially 4:1–8:26, cf. Petersen 1980). On the one hand the disciples are special agents appointed to help Jesus in the accomplishment of his task (1:16ff.; 3:13ff.; 6:7ff.), men who receive special instruction, as I have indicated. On the other hand they fail, however, to be his helpers, through lack of understanding. In a certain sense Peter's confession forms the climax of the theme of misunderstanding, but it is also the starting-point in the unfolding of the theme in 8:27–16:8. Petersen (1980:217) correctly maintains, 'The composition of Mark 4:1–8:26 depicts the unfolding of the disciples' incomprehension despite Jesus' expectations of them and despite his attempts to explain things to them. They, who were the recipients of the mystery of the kingdom of God that was concealed from others, proved to understand no more than the others. Thus the narrator leads us to expect that 8:27–10:45/52 will disclose both Jesus' response to this state of affairs and the disciples' reaction to his response.'

Peter's confession is preceded by the narratives of the leaven of the Pharisees and of Herod (8:14–21), and the healing of a blind man at Bethsaida (8:22–6). In the first Jesus queries the comprehension of the disciples twice by asking them. 'Have you no inkling yet? Do you still not understand? (οὔπω νοεῖτε οὐδὲ συνίετε). Are your minds closed? You have eyes: can you not see? You have ears: can you not hear? Have you forgotten?' (8:17). And in verse 21, 'Do you still not understand?' (*NEB*). These questions are a continuation of the theme of the misconception of the disciples which runs like a golden thread through the story. Despite their special instruction the disciples do not really know who Jesus is and what his mission is about. They are presented as his closest followers and friends who see and hear what he teaches, yet they do not comprehend who he is. There is good reason to think that the healing of the blind man at Bethsaida is a metaphorical narrative about the same theme. Initially the man can ill see only vaguely (8:24) and Jesus has to lay his hands on his eyes again before he can see properly. The two narratives are a closing of a cycle suggesting, as Petersen has indicated, that the reader will be informed I about the reaction of Jesus. This reaction to the state of affairs in the development of the relationship between Jesus and the disciples is started with the narrative about Peter's declaration at Caesarea Philippi.

Mark 8:27–9:1 has a very complicated history of tradition and making which reveals that Mark has used traditional material to form a very important episode in the shaping of the story of Jesus and in the portrayal of Peter (cf. Vorster 1979a:141ff.; Achtemeier 1973:64ff.). This is not the place to elaborate on this aspect of the pericope, neither is it the place to discuss the problems in connection with the historicity of the material. What is important here is to notice how Mark shaped the character of Peter taking into account the fact that Mark deliberately arranged and presented the material in order to develop his narrative. This is made clear by the differences and agreements between the various versions of the whole section (8:27–9:1) in Matthew and Luke.

The reader is introduced to a discussion between Jesus and the disciples on a journey to the villages of Caesarea-Philippi about the question as to who men say that Jesus is. Some say John the Baptist, others Elijah while yet others think that he is one of the prophets. The question put to the disciples is, 'Who do you say I am?' (v. 29a). Peter, as happens elsewhere in the story, takes the word and answers, 'You are the Messiah', after which Jesus orders them to remain silent. This charge of Jesus is one of a set of similar charges which belong to the so-called messianic secret of Mark. Those characters in the story who glimpse his identity or experience his power are ordered to remain silent (cf. 1:25, 34, 44; 3:11–12; 5:43, 7:26; 8:26; 9:9). Jesus then continues to foretell his passion, death and resurrection (8:31). This passion prediction is repeated twice in the remainder of the story (9:31; 10:33–4). These predictions contribute greatly to the development of the story, both with respect to the incomprehension of the disciples and the way in which the reader is guided to a correct understanding of who Jesus is. Peter's immediate reaction to the passion prediction is a refusal to accept the suffering of the Son of man. Peter rebukes Jesus, indicating his incomprehension of Jesus and his mission. From the readers's point of view, the scene is very important. At first glance Peter's confession that Jesus is the Messiah is a very 'positive' declaration. But this impression is corrected very strongly since what the narrator wants the reader to realize is that the disciples and Peter as their spokesman misconceive of who Jesus is. The evaluation of the character Peter by the norms of the protagonist is very important here. The reader is forced to dissociate himself from Peter because his ideas are like those of men, he does not know and also does not want to know about the suffering of Jesus. His image of Jesus the Messiah is not the image Jesus wanted him to have and unless this is corrected Peter would remain thinking of Jesus in terms which are not God-like (8:33). There is a total reorientation of the reader's image of Jesus, Peter, and the Jesus-Peter relationship in this pericope. The reader is prompted to rethink the success of Jesus in the previous part of the story and to recap the theme of misconception which is suggested from time to time. Peter's declaration is put into very sharp focus when for his sake, that is in order to correct his image of Jesus the Messiah, the theme of following is overtly developed in 8:34–9:1.

Although Peter is not directly addressed in Mark 8:34, he undoubtedly still remains the focus for the reader. Peter's confession is highlighted by the set of sayings about following. For his sake and on the ground of his declaration Jesus in no uncertain terms teaches what following is all about. If Jesus then is the Messiah, but not in the sense of the Messiah Peter had in mind in Mark's story, what does it then mean to follow Jesus, the Son of man who will suffer? In contrast to Peter's conception of the Messiah who will not have to suffer and die, Jesus tells the crowd and the disciples that following entails a total rethinking of one's own position, hardships and persecution. There is a direct relationship between what his followers do and what will happen when the Son of man returns, which will be soon (cf. 8:38; 9:1). Following Jesus is no easy task. One has to know who he is and what it means to follow him. The contrast between the misconception of Peter about Jesus and the following of Jesus, has direct influence on the portrayal of Peter. Peter is characterized as the spokesman of the disciples, the first disciple to declare him as the Messiah, a disciple with a total misconception of who Jesus is, and somebody who has to be instructed again about the implications of following Jesus. In fact, he is given a new task. In the following section of the story Peter has to show whether he accepts the challenge of following Jesus. On this aspect we have already elaborated above and have seen how Peter is portrayed as the fallible, unobtrusive follower of Jesus to the end. There is no reason to think that Peter is portrayed as a follower who rejected Jesus as the suffering Son of man. His image is that of a follower who persisted in following Jesus even though he failed him to the extent of denial. Another striking aspect of Peter's portrayal, as we have already seen, is that Peter remains the fearful disciple (cf. 9:6, 32; 10:32; 14:54).

Mark 8:27–9:1 is in a certain sense a turning point in the story of Mark. From this point onwards there can be no doubt either about Jesus and his mission, or about the task of the helpers of Jesus. They have a well-defined task and misconception would be no excuse.

4. Conclusion

We have concentrated mainly on the depiction of Peter by focusing on what the narrator directly or indirectly tells the reader about him. All the cases where Peter acts have been referred to and have been taken into account. A few words need to be said about those instances where Peter speaks. Characters act and speak and it is through their acting and speaking that they are revealed to the reader. In the case of Peter in the Gospel of Mark it is clear that he is not allowed to speak too much. What he has to say is, however, very interesting regarding his portrayal (cf. 8:29; 9:6; 10:28; 11:21; 14:28). By what he says he reveals his incomprehension (8:29; 11:21; 14:28), his embarrassment and his perplexity (9:6; 14:68, 71). What he says, turns out to be 'wrong' (8:29) and words that are not confirmed by deeds or do not come true in the story (14:28).

In Mark's gospel, Peter is both a Helper and also an Opponent in the development of the plot. Contrary, however, to those characters, who are Opponents from the beginning to the end of the story (e.g. the religious leaders), Peter does not become a final obstacle in the way of the protagonist to achieve his goal. Because of misconceptions about his mission and his identity Peter opposes Jesus instead of helping Him. This ambiguity in his role is basic to his characterization. The traits which are characteristic of Peter in the gospel are developed in terms of this ambiguity. This is best seen in Peter as the fallible follower of Jesus. At the beginning of the story he accepts the task of follower and he is appointed as the first of the Twelve who are given a special task. The task is fulfilled but not completely. Because of their lack of comprehension they do not understand and Peter does not accept his mission.

He is rebuked and hesitatingly fulfils the task of a follower in terms of 8:34–9:1. In the end he turns out to be an unobtrusive follower who becomes aware of his lack of insight. Only after this happens, he realises that he was told that he would deny Jesus. With regret he falls into tears. This is part of the schema of prediction-fulfilment in the story of Peter. He is told that he would deny Jesus, he refuses to accept that and only later on realizes with regret that he was wrong. The same happens with the passion predictions. Only later on Peter sees the fulfilment of the words of Jesus. Peter is shown to the reader much more than he is told. Indirect definition plays a bigger role than direct definition. His character is shaped mainly by indirect definition and this is in accordance with his role function in the plot of the story.

The semantic function of the characterization of Peter should be seen in terms of the theme of following. The reader is invited to identify with the fallible follower Peter whose story is left open-ended (cf. Mk. 16:7). As a communication the portrayal of Peter both repels and attracts the reader. How much of what is told about Peter in the Gospel of Mark is historical and how much goes back to the creative mind of Mark, remains an enigma. Being a character in a story, the Peter of Mark is a personage.

CHAPTER TWENTY FIVE

THE NEW TESTAMENT AND NARRATOLOGY

> The right to tell one's own story is a weapon of the marginalized in
> the struggle against identity in a world of uniformity (Fackre 1983:347).

What role does narratology have to play in the interpretation of the
New Testament? A prominent one, I would argue. Was Jesus not a
storyteller, and were the early Christians not committed to promote
their beliefs by telling all sorts of stories? Are there not many narrative texts in the New Testament? And is narratology not the study
of narrative? Let me begin my discussion of the topic with a few
general remarks about New Testament studies and literary theory.

New Testament scholars are by definition literary as well as historical critics. Their field of study includes ancient documents and
the world out of which these documents arose. In view of this, it
could be expected that New Testament scholars would form part of
the scientific circle of literary and historical critics. Furthermore, it
could be expected that scholars with a mutual interest, for example
literary critics who are all interested in 'texts', would in some way or
another influence one another with regard to their reflection and
their practice. This is obviously a positive and perhaps even an ide-
alist view of a scientific circle. Theory is not always in accordance
with practice and this, in addition to other reasons, will explain why
some literary critics, including New Testament critics, are presently
reflecting on the possibilities of narratology and reception theory
while others are involved in the study of deconstruction, and yet
others are totally unaware of theories literature on which they base
their interpretation of texts.

In this regard the history of New Testament research reveals an
interesting insight into the history and *Wirkungsgeschichte* of the science of literature. Wittingly and unwittingly New Testament scholars
have been influenced by current ideas in literary circles. It is not
difficult to show how the interest of New Testament scholars, mov-
ing from *author* to *text* to *reader*, has directly been influenced by exactly
the same theories of literature which influenced literary critics in
other fields of literary study. Positivism, Structuralism, Phenomenology,

Marxism, Feminism, Reception Aesthetics and other perspectives formed and form the basis of the symbolic universes of scholars of the New Testament in the same way as those of their colleagues in other literary disciplines. The only reason why I mention this all too obvious fact, is because it is not always taken into account by practitioners of New Testament criticism and also not by those literary critics who are unaware of the work which is being done by New Testament scholars. It is often the case that scholars are unaware of the philosophical basis of their respective disciplines or of the reasons why they practice their discipline in a particular way. This holds true for many biblical scholars also in connection with those theories, which influence their approach to ancient texts.

These few preliminary remarks set the parameters of my understanding of the theme of my article. I am aware of the fact that my view of what the New Testament is, what the science of literature is, what interpretation is and so on, determine my understanding of the topic. In view of this and other limitations such as the fact that it is not common practice in our country that New Testament and other literary critics share and exchange ideas, in other words that one cannot necessarily suppose mutual knowledge about the subject matter, I will attempt to deal with this topic in the first place as a New Testament critic who also realises that his task is a literary one. In addition to the introduction the article comprises two sections. Firstly I shall develop the theme from a literary-historical perspective by taking into account aspects of the history of New Testament research, and in the second section aspects of the New Testament as part of the narrative legacy of ancient times will be treated with a view to the implications of insights of narratology for the study of New Testament texts.

1. *Nature of the New Testament Texts and the History of Research*

For many the New Testament is a book, a holy document written shortly after the founding of the church in the first century of the Christian era. This is partly due to the way in which the New Testament is presented to the modern reader, a single book comprising a number of documents divided into chapters and verses, or as the second section of a book, the Bible. It would be agreed that the understanding and interpretation of any form of communication,

including a written document, is to a great extent determined by
the way in which it is presented. While gestures, tone of voice and
other factors, in addition to the way in which the material as such
is organised, play a role in communicating a message, cover, title,
subtitle and many other aspects of presentation, among other things,
determine the way in which a written document is read and understood. Perhaps this is the one, most important fact to remember
when the New Testament is approached rom a literary perspective.
The New Testament is a collection of ancient writings written by
different authors from different perspectives for different reasons and
probably for different purposes. It is not one book, it is a collection
of books. The titles, presentations of modern editions and versions
of New Testament writings, divisions into chapters, paragraphs and
verses are all but original. These aspects reveal the purpose for which
these documents came to be used, namely as lectionary units and
preaching material of a religious community.

However, although all these reading indicators may be necessary
and helpful, they certainly distract the attention of readers from the
character and purpose of these writings. Before they became the
canonised documents of a new religion, that is a sect of Judaism,
they existed individually as texts written for specific purposes by
people who were members of a minority group, in many ways a
marginalised group, who had to promote their own convictions and
beliefs. In short, early Christians produced writings to further their
convictions, and current presentations of these documents in modern versions with titles, divisions of chapters, verses and so on are
fictions, however well-intended and helpful they might be for the use
of the New Testament in the church. But what are these writings?
From a literary-historical point of view, depending of course on what
is meant by the term, this is an intriguing question, which, for the
purpose of the discussion of the topic, needs to be illuminated.

The history of research in connection with early Christian documents
is revealing. Perhaps the most influential period in the scientific
research of these texts is the nineteenth and twentieth centuries. Since
the Reformation the so-called grammatical-historical, or literal meaning of Scripture had been promoted in contrast to the deeper and
spiritual meaning of earlier ages. It was, however, in the previous
century, and especially in the early part of the twentieth century that
biblical writings came to be viewed in terms of current convictions
about literature. Under the influence of a variety of historistic and

positivistic assumptions, biblical writings came to be studied in view of their origin and evolution and as part of the current convictions of their time of origin. The history of literature, especially the history of early Christian literature, became the history of the growth and evolution of early Christian writings, that is the study of the sources upon which the final texts were presumably based. In accordance with current scholarship, it was asserted that early Christian writings were of secondary value, *Urliteratur*, in fact that they were not literary at all (see Overbeck 1954). In his epoch-making essay on the place of the gospels in the history of literature, K.L. Schmidt (1923), for instance, maintained that the gospels were cult legends, *Kleinliteratur*, and comparable to folk stories, not to the so-called *Hochliteratur* of Greek and Hellenistic authors. Under the influence of these and other views on the origin of cultic texts, the gospels and other New Testament writings came to be regarded as second-rate productions of cultic communities the end products of a process of transmission of oral traditions which were collected and written down. A very sophisticated methodology, called *Formgeschiche* (form criticism), was developed to study the history of the origin and growth of the oral (and written) sources which lay behind the written texts. On the assumption that it was possible to study the origin and growth of inscripturated texts in their original oral forms, the history of early Christian literature became the hypothetical literary-historical study of forms behind the written texts (see Bultmann 1970 and Dibelius 1971). The written texts were broken down into smaller units (*Gattungen*) such as parables, controversy stories, miracle stories, and so on, separated from the contexts within which they were transmitted in written form and studied like archaeological artefacts by tracing their development through the presumed layers of transmission which are hidden behind the written text. In terms of biblical criticism, study of the literary history of biblical writings became the study of the growth and origin of texts.

This is not the place to evaluate the so-called historico-critical reconstruction of early Christian writings. I simply wish to highlight the very influential hypothesis that early Christian writings like the gospels, were the products of cultic communities and not of individual authors, and that the study of the history of these texts should be a study of their growth and origin, rather than of their resemblance to other texts. Although much attention was paid to the study of form, the main emphasis was on the history and transmission of

smaller literary units, that is on forms within a form, and not on
the textual characteristics of the forms such as gospels, acts or apocalypses into which these smaller units were embedded. In view of
this the so-called literary character of the New Testament was denied
and it was concluded that Christian literature started to be written
in the second century when authors adopted Graeco-Roman standards (see Norden 1958:451ff.; Overbeck 1954). With the emphasis
mainly on the so-called non-literary character of New Testament
writings, it is clear why and how it happened that early Christian
writings such as the gospels came to be regarded as *sui generis*. What
happened was that scholars first of all based their views about the
form or genre of the writings of the New Testament on the aforementioned presumed literary history of these texts and furthermore
valued the form of these writings in the light of so-called criteria of
literary characteristics of contemporary and earlier Graeco-Roman
writings. The problem of genre is, however, much more complicated,
as we all know. A few remarks in this connection will help to explain
the importance of the narrative paradigm in any discussion of the
literary history of these writings.

There seems to be little agreement between literary theorists about
the nature and characteristics of genre (see Hempfer 1973). Generally
speaking, genre refers to a group of literary texts which are related
to one another by shared resemblances. That explains why genre
is very often described by comparison of generic features of types
and sub-types, for example drama, epic, lyric, novel, biography,
sonnet and so on. It is, however, also possible to describe 'genre' in
terms of text types, that is, in accordance with the organisation of
the material in a given text, for example narrative, argument, exposition, description and listing. The latter approach to the problem
of classification of text types seems to be useful, since it is possible
to apply significant textual criteria to describe a particular text.

If one considers the writings of the New Testament from the
perspective of text type, that is in view of the way in which the
material is organised in a particular discourse, the matter becomes
interesting, and the history of early Christian literature a totally
different case. Irrespective of the subclasses into which the different
New Testament writings can be divided, it seems to be clear that
there are mainly two types of texts presented in the New Testament
and that they are of a narrative and non-narrative character. The
material in the letters of the New Testament is organised in the form

of argumentation or exposition while the gospels, *Acts of the Apostles* and the so-called *Revelation of John* are narratives.

The following New Testament writings can be regarded as narratives: The *Gospels of Matthew, Mark, Luke* and *John, Acts of the apostles*, and *Revelation of John*. Roughly speaking, there seems to be enough reason to subdivide these texts into three subclasses, although it should be remembered that these subdivisions do not imply that the texts are not narratives. Gospels form a separate subclass. In addition, the *Acts of the apostles* and the *Revelation of John* can be classified separately. In spite of the objections raised by proponents of the evolutionary view of early Christian literature mentioned above, there seems to be no serious reason why cognisance should not be taken of the textual resemblances between these texts and other Graeco-Roman and Semitic texts of a narrative nature. The writings of the New Testament fit well into a very long tradition of Greek and Semitic narrative literature, even though they cannot be compared on literary artistic levels.

2. *The New Testament and the Narrative Legacy of the Past*

Although it would be impossible to maintain that the gospels were written under the influence or even on the model of ancient biographies like the lives of philosophers or emperors of Greek and Roman authors (see Vorster 1984b), the biographical aspects of these narratives should nevertheless be considered (see Dihle 1983). Luke-Acts, that is the *Gospel of Luke* and the *Acts of the apostles* as a cycle, has on the other hand, on the ground of narrative criteria successfully been compared with ancient novels written during the first three centuries after Christ. These include The *Acts of Thomas, The Alexander romance, Chaereas and Callirhoe, Clitophon and Leucippe, Daphnis and Chloe, The Ephesian story, Theagenes and Chariclea, Joseph and Asenath, The life of Aesop, The golden ass, The pseudo-Clementines* and the *Satyricon* (see Praeder 1981). There are, however, those who regard the *Acts of the apostles* as Hellenistic history (see Plümacher 1972) which, of course, is also a form of narrative. Texts written from an apocalyptic perspective can also be classified as a subclass of narrative. These texts became popular during the period between the Old and New Testaments. Because they are concerned with supernatural realities, symbolic language and concealing codes play a prominent part. The content of these texts is determined by the idea that this world is passing away and that a new world is coming. The past and present are read through the lens of a coming future, which is revealed by means of visions, dreams and messages transmitted from the supernatural realm (see Vorster 1985b).

These few remarks illustrate how deeply embedded a major part of the texts of the New Testament is in the narrative tradition of ancient Greek and Semitic literature. Let us now, in view of some insights of narratology, turn to a few implications of the fact that the gospels. the *Acts of the apostles* and the *Revelation of John* are narratives.

There can be little doubt that Jesus was a story-teller and that early Christians transmitted and established their newly found convictions by retelling the story and stories of Jesus. This was a very powerful, but also natural way of promoting the ideas of a new religion. The gospels contain a great variety of short narratives ranging from parables, controversy stories, and legends, to miracle and biographical stories. While the *Acts of the apostles* relate the narratives in the lives of the apostles in their attempt to propagate their beliefs from Jerusalem to Rome. The *Revelation of John* on the other hand, presents us with the creative imagination of an early Christian who tried to persuade his readers to persist under difficult circumstances by telling them about things revealed to him from an apocalyptic perspective.

From a narratological point of view, these stories offer a variety of insights into the art of storytelling in ancient times. The narrative paradigm furthermore presents the reader of New Testament narrative texts with challenging problems and possibilities in the interpretation of these narrative texts.

Since the days of Aristotle (see his *Poetics*) it has been realised that both the *narrative message* (narrative world of events, existents, sequence, structure, time and space) and *narrative means* (narrator, point of view, style, language, commentary and so on) are the building blocks of any story (see Chatman 1978, also Genette 1980). It has been argued that the essence of narrative art lies in '. . . the relationship between the teller and the tale, and the other relationship between the teller and the audience' (Scholes and Kellogg 1966:240).

In spite of the fact that the authors of gospels have in view of the results of gospel criticism been regarded as collectors and redactors of tradition, it has been realised during the last decade that they have in a very significant way contributed to the presentation and structuring of their material (Vorster 1980b). It has in fact become clear that gospels are narratives, that the material they contain is presented through narrative means and also that their messages are narrative messages (see e.g. Culpepper 1983; Edwards 1985; Kingsbury 1986; Malbon 1983; Rhoads and Michie 1982 and Tannehill 1977). While these texts have been the object of historical reconstruction for many years and in many ways have been regarded as windows through which the real world behind the texts can be seen, the narrative paradigm has brought new challenges for those who have come to realise that, despite the fact likeness-character (see T.R. Wright 1984:396) of early Christian narratives like the gospels and Acts of the apostles, they still remain man-made representations of narrative worlds and works (see Petersen 1984). Let us consider a few matters in this regard.

With the exception of the *Revelation of John* all other narrative texts in the New Testament are presented by third person narrators from an omniscient narrative point of view. In the Gospel of Mark, for example, the narrator knows everything that needs to be known about the characters and events in his story, even the thoughts, feelings and emotions of the characters (see Vorster 1980b:58ff.). He knows that Jesus silenced demons because they knew him (1:33–34); that the disciples thought he was a ghost and were afraid because they did not understand (6:49–52); that the Pharisees thought to test Jesus (8:11); that Peter did not know what to say (9:6); that Jesus knew about the conversation of his disciples (9:33–35) and so on. He even knows what happened to Jesus in Gethsemane although, according to his story, there was no witness to hear what was happening. He reports what Jesus prayed (14:35) when Jesus was alone, simply because he knows everything. He knows the minds of his characters (3:6) but withholds the information from Jesus. He knows their emotions (1:27, 41; 4:41; 14:4, 11, 19) what they see and hear (14:67; 15:35) and even what they think (2:6, 8). For the sake of the reader the narrator comments on the thoughts (see 2:6, 8) and actions of characters (1:22b; 2:18; 3:6; 5:30). He explains strange terminology (e.g. Aramaic in 5:41) and narrates the actions of the characters in an evaluative manner and in this way affords the norms of judgement for his reader.

The same holds true of the narrators of the other gospels and the Acts of the apostles who are also third person narrators who relate their stories from an omniscient point of view. In the case of the Revelation of John it is different. In accordance with other apocalyptic texts, and the content of the message, the story of John is told from a first person perspective. Because of the type of information with which the reader is presented, that is imaginative presentations of other-worldly realms and events. this observation is not without significance. In contrast to the gospels and acts the author of the *Revelation of John* is supposedly telling his readers about the world and time to come and accordingly, because the otherworldly is unknown to mankind, he makes use of a first person narrator to whom the mysteries have been revealed. In accordance with conventions of his time he uses symbolic language and concealing codes.

Another aspect which is of paramount importance for the interpretation of New Testament narratives, is the phenomenon of story-world. It is not so much the fact that the events and existents of these stories are foreign to a modern reader, as the idea that these worlds are narrated worlds that often cause problems. Indeed, the world view or symbolic universes of these texts are very unfamiliar to people who live in a modern society. That one can, however, attempt to understand. In addition to knowledge of Greek, social and cultural conditions and customs of those times and information about the geography and history of the peoples involved, one needs to understand that these texts are narratives and that the world they present is a narrative construction. This is a very important discovery for historically-minded people who tend to focus on the fact-likeness of much of the information in these texts. Is Peter of the Gospel of Matthew not the Peter who lived in Galilee during the life of Jesus, and are the cities and towns not the ones we know from history and archaeology? Yes indeed, but one also has to say no immediately. They are the characters and existents in the story-world of the New Testament narratives. For literary critics it might be obvious that the worlds of stories are narrated worlds and not descriptions of how things 'really were and how they really happened'. For many New Testament critics on the other hand, this is a frightening idea on many scores, despite the fact that it is common knowledge that the gospels and acts are not so-called historical accounts. Some would accept the narrativity of certain characters and events, of certain stories, for example the parables, but it would be difficult to convince them of the narrative implications of the gospels and acts as such. This is so in spite of their rejection of the nineteenth century idea that Mark wrote a history of the life of Jesus. Let us develop the problem a little further.

What if one were to argue that the gospels and acts are historical

narratives, as some do? From a narrative point of view this is a very
interesting problem. I have elsewhere argued (Vorster 1984a:115ff.)
that even in the writing of history there is no one-to-one correspondence between object and description because neither linguistic
signs nor historiography functions in that way. In short, historical
description is nothing more than narrative, that is remaking of reality. It is in this remaking of reality that the challenge of the narrative paradigm lies for readers of the New Testament and especially
for critics who make the narrative character of the writings under
discussion seriously. Are these narratives thus fiction? Obviously they
are, but this is an unfruitful way to look at these writings because
of the superficial way in which fiction is very often handled. Fiction
is used here in the sense of man-made, that is remaking of reality.
In the same way as it is impossible to repeat any historical fact, it
is impossible to narrate 'facts' without remaking them. And in this
way New Testament narratives are undoubtedly fictions which invite
the reader to enter into their story worlds.

Because of the importance of the historical basis of Christian faith,
among other things, a lot of effort has been put into the discovery
of the original form of the utterances and narratives of Jesus. A case
in point is the historico-critical research of the parables during this
century (see Jeremias 1970).

Parables are metaphorical narratives, short stories of which Jesus
apparently told quite a number in his attempt to resocialise his hearers in terms of their religious thinking. If one compares the different
versions of the same parable in the different gospels, it becomes clear
that these stories had undergone various changes according to the
context of communication (see Mk. 4 against Mt. 13). Closer investigation also reveals that the authors of the different gospels used
these parables, which are mostly selfcontaining stories, in contexts
which often not only vary in the different gospels (see Mt. 13:31–32;
Mk. 4:30–32 and Lk. 13:18–19), but also used them in contexts
which they apparently created for the purpose of conveying a particular meaning by imposing the context onto the parable. This is
clearly the case with the parable of the good Samaritan which Luke
used to answer the question of who is one's neighbour (see Lk. 10:29,
31–35 and 36–37)

> 'And who is my neighbour?' Jesus replied, 'A man was on his way
> from Jerusalem down to Jericho when he fell in with robbers, who
> stripped him, beat him, and went off leaving him half dead. It so hap-

pened that a priest was going down by the same road; but when he saw him. he went past on the other side. So too a Levite came to the place, and when he saw him went past on the other side. But a Samaritan who was making the journey came upon him, and when he saw him was moved to pity. He went up and bandaged his wounds, bathing them with oil and wine. Then he lifted him on to his own beast, brought him to an inn, and looked after him there. Next day he produced two silver pieces and gave them to the innkeeper, and said, 'Look after him; and if you spend any more, I will repay you on my way back'. 'Which of these three do you think was neighbour to the man who fell into the hands of the robbers?' He answered, 'The one who showed him kindness.' Jesus said, 'Go and do as he did' (NEB).

Luke inserted the story of the Samaritan into this particular context to illustrate the point of neighbourliness in a divided society. Obviously this story can be used on its own, that is without the context into which Luke put it, and within other contexts to convey other messages such as fellowship and sympathy. From a narrative point of view two very important questions arise. The first is related to the fact that it was fashionable in New Testament studies to reconstruct the 'original' form and meaning of the parables in the mouth of Jesus (see Jeremias 1970). The second has to do with the retelling of stories. Is it possible to tell the same story twice?

Unless we assume that Jesus told parables for the sake of parables, that is for the purpose of religious entertainment and not to make a point or to convey a particular message, it seems to be futile to search for the original form and meaning of these metaphorical stories (see Frye 1979). Even if it were possible to reconstruct the original form, it is in no way possible to recover the contexts of communication in the life of the earthly Jesus (see Vorster 1985b).

The second question is perhaps even more interesting. Since much of the debate about the gospels concern the relationship between them and how the agreements and disagreements can be explained this is not an unimportant matter. In fact, it is a very fundamental question. Literary scholars do not seem to agree about the possibility of telling the same story twice (Polanyi 1981). One thing, however, is clear. As soon as the 'same' story is told in another context of communication the narrative message is viable to change. This is not only true of parables, but also of other narratives (see A. Fowler 1982b), even for the story of Jesus as we can gather from the four narratives, that is the four gospels, we have in the New Testament.

3. *Conclusion*

To conclude: it seems to me that not only is it possible for New Testament scholars to learn a lot from insights of narratology offered by modern theorists, it is also possible to gain insights into the nature of New Testament narratives. There is undoubtedly a need to rethink the history of early Christian literature from a perspective where much less emphasis is put on the growth and the origin of texts and more on the written texts and the way in which the material they contain is organised. Despite the important contributions of scholars who studied the New Testament documents with view to their pre-literary stages, one has to remember that it was the written documents which became the literary legacy of early Christianity and not their origins. Once it is realised that narrative is one of the few ways in which material can be organised into a discourse. both the literary history of some of the documents and their narrative nature become important, more important even than the so-called literary or non-literary character of New Testament writings. With regard to the interpretation of the New Testament, the narrative nature of the gospels, acts and the apocalypse has far-reaching implications. For people who are historically-minded and who care for so-called 'facts', the discovery of the narrative nature of New Testament writings often poses major problems. On the other hand, when it is accepted that much of the material is narrated, it is also possible to view the documents from a totally different perspective and to discover the possibilities of narration. As a form of text production, early Christian narratives furthermore provide the student of ancient texts with invaluable insights into the creative imagination of ancient men who were committed to the story of Jesus. Narrative research conducted during the last decade has fruitfully contributed towards a better understanding of these texts (see Hahn 1985).

SECTION E

INTERTEXTUALITY

CHAPTER TWENTY SIX

THE PROTEVANGELIUM OF JAMES
AND INTERTEXTUALITY

'. . . tout texte se construit comme mosaïque de citations, tout texte est
absorption et transformation d'un autre texte' (Kristeva 1969:146, 255).

The relationship between early Christian writings, precursor and
contemporary ancient writings has been a topic of great interest in
biblical and patristic studies. The abundance of material on the
use of sources, the use of the Old Testament, quotations from and
references to other documents, influences, and parallel statements,
illustrate the value scholars attach to the phenomenon of textual relationships.

Most of these studies focus on sources and the search for influences, and not, for example, on the *function* of traces of anterior texts
in later texts. Little attention, if any, is paid to the function of these
traces either with regard to the production or with regard to the
readers of these texts. Despite the renewed interest in rewriting the
literary history of the gospels, for example, considering more than
the intracanonical material, the phenomenon of intertextual relationships seems to be blurred by the emphasis on source and tradition
criticism as the only way in which these relationships are normally
studied. It might be a good thing to investigate other possibilities of
explaining the relationships between early Christian texts in order
to come to a better understanding of the literary history of early
Christian literature. (see also Koester 1984:1463–1542 and Crossan
1985 in this regard.) The problem is that most of the studies on the
literary history of the gospels are fixated on the canonical gospels
and on the origin and growth of the material. Perhaps the concept
of *intertextuality*, that is *the theory of the relationship between texts* which
will form the basis of this essay, can throw some light on aspects of
the problem. It will obviously take much more than a single essay
to investigate the possibilities of intertextuality as a heuristic device
in the study of early Christian literature.

To say that *intertextuality* is *the theory of the relationship between texts*, is a minimum definition of the concept as Pfister (1985:11) correctly remarks: 'Dies ist unumstritten; umstritten jedoch ist, welche Arten von Beziehungen darunter subsumiert werden sollen'. Stierle (1983:7) furthermore correctly remarks: 'Jeder Text situiert sich in einem vor-handerlen Universum der Texte, ob er dies beabsichtigt oder nicht'. Let us make the problem more concrete.

Suppose an uninformed, but interested reader finds any commentary or translation with notes on the *Protevangelium of James* in a bookshop, reads the book, and approaches you with the following questions: 'I notice that mention is made of sources, and references to Old and New Testament texts. Can you explain to me how the *author* went about in writing this story? Since I do not know much about biblical writings, can you tell me whether all the references I found in that book on the Protogospel are citations? Did the author of the text have a copy of all the manuscripts which are referred to? Were the intended *readers* so informed that they would have noticed all the sources and supposed quotations referred to in this book on the Protogospel? Were the intended readers expected to have so much information available that they would have been able to use the biblical texts from which these references supposedly came as a foil against which the story should be read?' It would not be an easy task to explain to a novice in the field of critical biblical scholarship how we conceive of the production and reading of ancient documents. On the other hand, have we really given enough thought to the use of sources, citations, references and influences in early Christian literature, or are we satisfied with identifying possible sources and influences? Perhaps one can rephrase these questions of an hypothetical reader and ask ourselves what the implications are of all the references about sources and influences in our commentaries and translation notes on ancient texts both in view of the making of texts and their reception.

What are the relationships between texts and their precursors and why and how did ancient authors use other texts in writing their own texts? This is what this essay is about. It is an exercise in the problem of intertextuality. It is an attempt to explain the use of and references to other texts in view of how discourses are written and how they are read. It is not a study about the sources and the influences behind the *Protevangelium of James* (hence PJ), in terms of origin. The essay is based on the hypothesis that a text should not be regarded as a unitary object which is knowable. A text is not a completed work with a centre and an edge which is recoverable by the skilled reader (Ryan 1985:8). It should rather be regarded as '. . . a differential network, a fabric of traces referring endlessly to something other than itself, to other differential traces' (Derrida 1979:84).

Although 'intertextuality' is a modern concept which is used to explain intertextual relationships, the phenomenon is known from ancient times (see Pfister 1985:1–30 for an excellent survey of the use of the concept in recent research). Literary references to precursor texts are known from Homer, Ovid and Virgil, to mention only a few authors. They used anterior texts and imitated others when they produced their own texts in ancient times. This, as such is not all that important. What is important is how the relationship between texts is viewed. Since all texts can be regarded as the rewriting of previous texts, pretexts, and are reactions on other texts, it is far more important to pay attention to the relationship between texts than to identify the precursor texts and references and then to leave it open to the reader to guess how these references came about and what they imply to the reading of the text. It is the relationship with other texts or parts of texts which make the reading of texts possible.

The rest of the essay falls into two parts. The first deals with PJ and intertextuality from the perspective of text production. In the second, attention is paid to PJ and intertextuality from the perspective of text reception. Both parts focus on the function of intertextual relationships in PJ.

1. *Imagination as Plagiarism*

This heading is taken from Federman's unfinished 1976 paper, '*Imagination as Plagiarism*'. One sometimes gets the impression that early Christian and pagan writers had no scruples about the use of material from other writings in their own without acknowledgement, because of the lack of a system of reference to sources. There are obviously those like Matthew, who uses citations with reference to his sources. This is for a specific reason as is clear from the so-called 'fulfilment quotations'. But very often, as in the case of Mark, the Old Testament is frequently quoted or alluded to without mention of the source. In such cases the 'quotations' are so integrated into the text that they form part of the narrative material and simply

serve the flow of the narrative. If it were not for our knowledge and
the bold print in modern Greek editions, one would not even have
thought about quotations or how these traces of texts refer to anterior texts. What are the implications of this imaginative use of precursor texts?

One way of looking at the phenomenon is to regard it as plagiarism. Another would be to look into the whole problem of the
relationship between texts. PJ is a very good example of the imaginative use of precursor texts. From the perspective of both the production and the reading of a story like PJ the relationship between
texts is revealing.

Very little is known about the childhood of Jesus from the New
Testament. Except for Matthew and Luke the rest of the New
Testament does not deal with that part of the life of Jesus. In the
period after the New Testament many open spaces in the life of
Jesus were filled in by authors of the so-called apocryphal gospels.
They did that for different reasons. Some of the material, fictive or
factive, obviously came into existence on the ground of inquisitiveness, and a natural eagerness to be informed, as Cullmann (1968:
272–274) has correctly observed. He also points out that there was
a need to develop Christology, and that Christian apologetic in view
of Jewish polemic can explain the origin of some of the material.
For these purposes new narratives were created by retelling older
ones and filling in open spaces with unknown material. PJ, a second century 'infancy gospel', is such a writing in which the birth
story of Jesus was retold from the perspective of his mother's birth
and marriage and open spaces in his life story were thus filled in
for apologetic and christological reasons.

PJ is a retelling of the annunciation and birth of Jesus within a
narrative about his mother. It consists of various episodes, all of
which, except for chapter 18,2 and the postscript in 25, are told
from the third person omniscient' narrative point of view. It relates
the life story of Mary up to the birth of Jesus (1–16), the annunciation and birth of Jesus (17–21), the infanticide, death of Zechariah
and postscript (22–25). Mary is presented as the daughter of a *rich*
man Joachim and Anne, her birth is based on the Old Testament
story of Hannah (1 Sam. 1–2, cf. PJ 1–5). Chapters 6–8 deal with
her childhood in the temple, after which her 'marriage' (cf. 19) to
a widower, Joseph who already had children (9–10), is recounted.

This is followed by the annunciation of the birth of Jesus in Jerusalem (11); visit to Elizabeth (12); Joseph's doubt and comfort by an angel (13–14); vindication of Mary before the High Priest (15–16); birth of Jesus in a cave outside Bethlehem (17–18); vision of Joseph (18); Salome's unbelief about a miraculous virgin birth (19–20) and the adoration of the Magi (21). The story ends with Herod's infanticide and the murder of Zechariah, the father of John the Baptist, in the temple (22–24), and a postscript. From a thematic point of view, PJ obviously has a lot in common with New as well as Old Testament stories. The problem we are discussing, however, is how one should regard the intertextual relationships and references of which there are many, and also different kinds?

It is commonly accepted that the author of PJ based his narrative mainly on 'biblical' material. In the high days of source criticism it was argued that the infancy stories of Matthew and Luke as well as PJ could be derived from a common Hebrew source (Resch), or that PJ should be viewed as the source of the canonical stories in Matthew and Luke as Conrady suggested (see Smid 1965:193). These views have been replaced by the idea that the author of PJ made up a story to glorify Mary by using Old and New Testament material as sources. In one of the most recent commentaries on PJ, there is an abundance of references to Old and New Testament material and especially to words and phrases from the so-called Septuagint. The commentary of Smid (1965), mainly consists of references to possible sources. Although he emphasises the experimental character of his work with regard to LXX, he nevertheless refers to LXX words, phrases and sentences wherever possible. In accordance with Laurentin, Smid regards the contents of PJ '. . . as "exégèse midrashique" of the birth-stories on the first two chapters of both St. Matthew and St. Luke' (Smid 1965:8), and agrees with a number of scholars that the LXX is another source of PJ both with regard to language usage and motives:

> The matriarchs of the O.T. provided the model for Mary, together with the heroines of younger tales such as Judith and Tobit. In this matter again, it is difficult to decide what is intentional and what is involuntary (Smid 1965:11).

Van Stempvoort (1964:410–426) has made a thorough study of PJ and the Books of Susanna and Tobit and has drawn attention to similarities. He has also pointed out that there is a relationship between the interpretation of some of the material common to PJ and writings of the early church.

How one should account for the presence of sources, quotations, references, motifs, and language usage which is in agreement with that of LXX, is not directly explained by Smid and those who are mainly interested in identifying these matters. Except for the odd remark, such as the next quote, one finds it difficult to imagine how an author, like the one who wrote PJ would have gone about in writing his story. Referring to Radermacher, Smid (1965:11) asserts:

> The author was a child of his time. Quotation was an engrained habit and undoubtedly a general characteristic of the atticising period. 'Christians or pagans,' these writers have a passion for quoting, for seeking support in the work of their predecessors.

In addition he also contends that the story is a mere fiction of the author's imagination. Although he used biblical sources, he did not have additional sources at his disposal which made his version possible (Smid 1965:43). In other words, he used biblical sources to create a fiction.

It is not difficult to spot that our author used a variety of themes, expressions and words similar to those found in the Old and New Testament. The following examples prove the point:

PJ 2,3 cf. 1 Sam. 1,5;
PJ 4,1 cf. Luke 1,13 and 1 Sam. 1,11;
PJ 4,2 cf. Luke 1,13;
PJ 5,1 cf. Luke 18,14;
PJ 6,3 cf. Luke 1,25 and Gen. 30,23 *et al.* also Prov. 11,30; 13,2 and Phill. 11; Jas. 3,18;
PJ 7,1 cf. 1 Regn. 1,21–23;
PJ 7,2 cf. Luke 1,48;
PJ 9,2 cf. Num. 16,32;
PJ 11 cf. Matt. 1,20.21 and Luke 1,26.28.30.31.35.38;
PJ 12,1 cf. Luke 1,42.48;
PJ 12,2 cf. Luke 1,42–43.48;
PJ 12,3 cf. Luke 1,56;
PJ 13,1 cf. Gen. 3,13; 2 Cor. 11,3; 1 Tim. 2,14;
PJ 13,3 cf. Luke 1,34;
PJ 14,1 cf. Matt. 1,19;
PJ 14,2 cf. Matt. 1,20.21.24;
PJ 15,4 cf. I Pet. 5,6;
PJ 16,1 cf. Num. 5,11–31;
PJ 17,1 cf. Luke 2,1;

PJ 18,2 cf. Josh. 10,12; Hab. 3,11; Ezek. 31,15; Matt. 8,26; Ps. 75,9;
  Isa. 14,7 and Hab. 2,20;
PJ 19,2 cf. Luke 2,30–32;
PJ 19,3 cf. John 20,25;
PJ 21,1 cf. Matt. 2,2.4.S.7.9–11.12.16;
PJ 22,1 cf. Matt. 2,16;
PJ 22,2 cf. Luke 2,7;
PJ 23,3 cf. Matt. 23,35;
PJ 24,4 cf. Luke 2,25–27

The question is, however, what do we then mean when we use terms like 'source' and 'quotation' in this connection? Despite the fact that one should say that PJ is couched in 'biblical' thought and language, verbal agreement in terms of longer sentences or passages is rather limited. Even in passages where there is a very close relationship with the pretext, verbal agreement in longer sentences is rare, as is clear from chapter 11 as I have indicated elsewhere (see Vorster 1986 and also chapter 14 in this volume). There seems to be much more involved in the use of 'biblical' material in PJ than the mere seeking of support in the work of predecessors because of time conventions. The question is whether 'source' should be conceived of in a neutral sense as the body of knowledge available to the author, or should we think of 'source' in a more dynamic way. Are 'sources' the pretexts to which the story refers which our author used, rejected, absorbed and transformed, which the reader should keep in mind? If the first option is chosen, one would regard the quotations and allusions to 'biblical' and other material as part of the 'vocabulary' of the author. In the second view, more emphasis is put on the way in which the sources were transformed into a new story.

In the earlier essay (chapter 14 in this volume) on the annunciation of the birth of Jesus in PJ, I maintained that the canonical infancy stories prompted the author of PJ to retell the story. In doing so, he produced a new text by using tradition creatively. As a reader our author was not only a receptor of tradition, he also produced meaning by reading and retelling creatively. This would mean that he rewrote anterior texts and in this manner created a text which refers to other texts. On the ground of his acquaintance with Old Testament stories, most probably in their Greek versions, the New Testament infancy stories and so on, an interesting interplay between texts came into being when he created his text. I am, however, of opinion that not all traces of anterior texts are equally important with regard to intertextuality.

In his commentary on PJ, Smid has paid special attention to 'the' LXX as a 'source' of PJ. It is difficult to know exactly how he envisages LXX as a 'source' in the production of PJ. The many references to words common to PJ and LXX in his commentary create the impression that our author deliberately used 'Septuagintal' words and expressions. If that had been the case, one would obviously expect these traces also to refer to the pretexts. This can hardly be the case with all the words and expressions referred to by Smid. One will have to take into account that the similarity in language usage between LXX and PJ should in the first place be ascribed to convention. Since the things which are spoken about in LXX, the New Testament and early Christian writings are very similar, a certain degree of similarity can be expected. There is undoubtedly a preference for particular words and expressions in 'religious talk' of the nature we find in PJ and LXX. LXX and the New Testament form part of the competence of our author. Because he used pretexts from the Old and New Testament like the stories of Hannah and the infancy story of Jesus, his language resembles biblical expressions and thoughts. That appears to me the only reasonable way to account for the similarity of words and expressions apart from free quotations in PJ, LXX and the New Testament. Motifs derived from pretexts such as the story of Hannah cause intertextual relationships between PJ and LXX, not words and expressions which occur in different contexts. An example will help to illustrate the point.

There seems to be a resemblance between the two texts, rather on the ground of the similarity in story stuff and not because our author 'quoted' words from 1 Sam. 1,5 in PJ 2,3. If that is not the case one would have to argue that PJ 2,3 refers back to 1 Samuel and that our author 'changed' 'the Lord' of 1 Samuel to 'the Lord God'. It would also be expected from the 'informed' reader to notice the subtle change and to assign meaning to the change. This seems to me farfetched (cf. also PJ 4,1 to Luke 1,13; PJ 4,1 to 1 Sam. 1,11.28; PJ 5,1 to Luke 18,14 etc.). By saying this I am not denying the similarities in diction between PJ, LXX and the New Testament. I am allowing for possibility of religious language as a social convention.

Even where there is a very close relationship between PJ and pretexts, as in the case with PJ and the infancy stories of the canonical gospels, there is a significant lack of direct quotation. In passages like PJ 11 (the annunciation of the birth of Jesus), where the narrative comes very close to the gospel stories, our author retold the story in such a manner that the pretext material became integrated into his text. That also holds for the free quotations. 'Quotations' therefore become very subtle allusions to pretexts in terms of motifs and not in terms of exact wording.

From the perspective of production PJ is a very good example of the implications of retelling stories. Because the author of PJ made use of 'biblical' language, themes and topics, there is no doubt that he created a text which presents itself as an absorption and transformation of other texts. The author made his own narrative by retelling a number of pretexts.

The episodic nature of PJ accounts for the various pretexts which were used in writing the story. But on the whole it is the Lucan version of the infancy story of Jesus which served as basis for PJ as is clear from the presence of Lucan material. The following episodes are retellings of pretexts. In PJ 1–7 aspects of 1 Samuel 1 and were used. The episode about the assigning of Mary to Joseph by a sign in PJ 9 probably refers to the scene at the baptism of Jesus in Mark 1,9. The annunciation of the birth of Jesus in PJ 11 (cf. also 12) is undoubtedly a retelling cf. the annunciation in the synoptic tradition as I have argued elsewhere (Vorster 1986 & chapter 14 in this volume). There is a close relationship between PJ 16 where Mary is given the bitter water to drink to prove her innocence and Num. 5,1–11. In PJ 17 there are traces of Matt. 1 and Luke 2. The birth in Bethlehem in a cave relates this episode to the synoptic tradition but also to cave traditions as Smid (1965:125–127) has indicated. Traces of the motif of the standstill of nature are found in both the Old and New Testaments and elsewhere (e.g. Josh. 10,12; Hab. 3,11; Ezek. 31,15; Matt. 8,26 and especially Ps. 75,9; Isa. 14,7; Hab. 2,20). The 'gynaecological test' as a proof for faith has reminiscences of John 20,25. The story of the Magi in PJ 21 is an obvious reworking of Matt. 2,2 and probably similar stories about the birth of a claimant to the throne and the reaction of the older ruler. Smid (1965:151), draws attention to the fact that PJ 21 and 22 contain the 'stock formula' which occurs in literature about the struggle between the old and the new leader as Erdmann has pointed out, namely the ruler becomes aware of the birth of a claimant to the throne; the old ruler is alarmed; the persecuted child escapes from danger; innocents are killed or persecuted in his stead. The infanticide in PJ 22 again refers to Matt. 2 and PJ 23 and 24 has references to Luke 1.

The remarkable thing about PJ is not that the author used pretexts, free quotations, allusions and bits and pieces of precursor texts. However, he integrated these 'rests' into a new story which refers back to other texts, and this makes these references significant. The precursor texts and traces thereof, prompted our author to tell his own story about the birth of Jesus, which is different from the stories of the pretexts. In spite of all the resemblances between 1 Sam. 1 and 2 and PJ 1–7 (see Smid 1965:62), the story of Mary's birth and youth is not exactly the story of the birth and youth of Samuel. But Samuel's story clearly is the intertext of Mary's, and by referring to that story, Mary's story becomes all the more meaningful since it also refers to other intertexts like the infancy story of Jesus in Luke. It is this network of references which is of importance to the reader.

2. *Reading as Intertextual Assignment of Meaning*

If it is true that PJ is a transformation of a variety of pretexts which places the story into a network of intertexts, the relationship between these texts will be a matter of concern for the reader. Reading is not a neutral process. Like text production it is a dynamic process in which intertextual references play a significant role. It is important also to keep in mind that PJ as a whole forms part of a set of texts which deals with the birth story of Jesus, and in addition with stories of important religious leaders as we shall see below. Let us illustrate this point by looking at the title of PJ first and then at a few examples from the text.

The title *Protevangelium of James*, commonly used in the West since the sixteenth century, indicates that the book contains material about the childhood of Jesus which precedes the information given in the canonical gospels (see De Strycker 1968:5). It is, however, also possible that the title implies that the book contains material which precedes the material in Matthew and Luke chronologically (cf. De Goeij 1984:37). Van Stempvoort (1964:410) also contends that 'The most correct title is, properly speaking, that used by Origen: *The Book of James...*'. After a trip to the East where he discovered a

Greek manuscript of the book, the French humanist Guillaume Postel published his Latin version of this book in 1552 under the title *Proteuangelion, on siue de Natalibus Iesu Christi et ipsius matris Virginis Mariae sermo historicus diui Iacobi minoris consobrini et fratris Domini Iesu, Apostoli primarii et episcopi christianorum primi Hierosolymis.* Since then the text has become known in the West as the *Protevangelium Jacobi,* or Protevangelium of James, while in the East it remained to be called *The Birth of Mary* (De Strycker 1968:5), to which was sometimes added *Revelation of James* (cf. Papyrus Bodmer V) in accordance with the postscript in chapter 25,1–2:

> I, James, who wrote this (hi)story when a tumult arose in Jerusalem on the death of Herod, withdrew into the wilderness until it was over. I will praise the Lord, God, who gave me the gift of wisdom to write this story.
> Grace will be with all those who fear our Lord. Amen.
> Birth of Mary.
Revelation.
James.

Peace to the author and the reader.

In his commentary on Matthew (10,17), Origen refers to it as 'The Book of James' (see Delius 1973:17). The James referred to here is presumably James, the brother of Jesus who recounts the life story of Mary, the mother of Jesus, and his birth.

The different titles tell us about the contents as well as the history of reception of the text. The reference to James in the postscript and doxology, whatever its origin, as well as the addition 'revelation' which is not original, obviously served to authenticate the contents of the story. It was intended for the reader who, as Postel did many centuries later, had to relate it to James, the brother of Jesus. The title, *Birth of Mary*, preferred and used in the East, on the other hand gave rise to a long '*Wirkungsgeschichte*' in private reading and liturgy as is clear from the history of the transmission of the text (De Strycker 1968). In spite of its rejection by the Gelasian Decree (ca. 500 AD) as an apocryphon not received by 'the catholic and apostolic Roman Church' (see Brown *et al.* 1978:248), the influence on the evolution of mariological tradition and dogma is obvious from literature and art in the early church, Middle Ages and the renaissance (cf. Quasten 1950:121–122 and Cullmann 1968:279). In Protestant circles where extracanonical texts are often treated with suspicion, PJ is regarded as 'glorification of Mary'. Title and contents clearly prompted readers to read the story differently.

Concerning the problem of reference and the relationship between texts a very interesting observation can be made from the different titles. Both titles 'Protevangelium Jacobi' and 'Birth of Mary' undoubtedly refer back to the text. 'Protevangelium' obviously stresses the fact that the story contains material prior to the birth of Jesus, while 'Birth of Mary' focuses on Mary's birth. 'Das Ganze ist zur Verherrlichung der Maria geschrieben. Nicht nur werden implizit die judischen Verleumdungen . . . abgelehnt, sondern alle kunftigen mariologischen Themen kundigen sich schon an' (Cullmann 1968:279); see also Smid 1965:14. By the different emphases the story either becomes part of texts that deal with the *childhood of Jesus* or of *the story about Mary*. To put it differently, these titles either relate PJ to the intertext 'infancy story' of Jesus, or to the intertext 'religious story of Mary'. Whenever PJ is seen as a story about the birth of Jesus and what has happened before, it is normally grouped with other stories about his childhood like the ones found in Matthew and Luke, and other extracanonical stories such as the 'Childhood of Jesus according to Thomas'. It furthermore becomes part of an intertext which might be termed 'childhood stories of religious leaders', as has been correctly observed by the *Religionsgeschichtliche Schule*. Dibelius (1932) gives a useful survey of the relevant material.

On the other hand the '*Wirkungsgeschichte*' of PJ also indicates that in certain circles it became part of texts concerning the glorification of Mary, be it in a positive or a negative sense.

These few remarks about the different titles of PJ help us to realise how the story became part of two different sets of intertexts, and in fact two meaning systems because of its absorption into intertexts. Once the text came to be read, readers were prompted to bring the text into relation with other texts. What is true of the reading of a text, is also true of the making of a text, since writing can be regarded as rewriting of other texts.

Metatexts like titles often tell us a lot about the reception of ancient texts and their reading in relation to other texts. This is illustrated by the letters of Paul and especially by the deutero-Pauline letters. The importance of intertextuality and the reading of texts is, however, not restricted to metatexts only. It is actually the way in which texts and parts of texts refer to intertexts and pretexts that is so important for the reading of a particular text. Various aspects of texts like names of persons, characters, motifs, episodes and complete texts allude to other texts and cause intertextual relationships. Let us therefore look at a few aspects of the phenomenon in PJ.

Characters play a very important role in narratives. Those characters which are known from pretexts are therefore important points of contact between texts. When a reader encounters a character in a particular text which he already knows from another text, two texts are activated, the text he is reading *and* the pretext. The reader who is acquainted with Luke will undoubtedly recall Mary's presentation in Luke when he reads PJ. The Mary of PJ will be read against the background of previous knowledge. Any divergence from the pretext will be significant and will help the reader to understand the character in the text he is reading at the time. Let us look at Mary, Joseph and the Jewish religious leaders in PJ from this perspective.

In PJ Mary is the protagonist. She is presented as the long expected child of Joachim and Anne, two pious, godfearing, *rich*, but childless parents. Her childhood is based on the example of Samuel. Her name is hailed by the whole nation because it will be remembered by all generations (cf. 6,2; 7,2; 12,2). Her mother raises her for the service of the Lord and keeps her safely (holy) for the Lord (6,3). She is the beloved of the whole of Israel (7,3). She is fed like a dove by an angel, a *davidid*, undefiled, pure virgin (10,1). She is put into the care of a widower at the age of twelve (9,1). She is a willing servant of the Lord (11,3), working for him in his temple. She is visited by the angels (11), bearer of a child not conceived in an normal way (11). She is the mother of the Lord (12,2), chaste and complying to the morality of Israel (12,3). Like Eve she is accused of unchastity (13,1), but vindicated (16,3). She is a virgin who abstained from intercourse with Joseph (her husband, bethrothed 13,3; 15,3.19), bethrothed to Joseph (19,1), a mother who cares for her child (17,2; 19,2; 22,2).

If we compare the characterization of Mary in PJ and Luke, there is undoubtedly a very close relationship between the two portrayals. In spite of the fact that PJ elaborates on aspects which are not narrated in the pretext like the birth and childhood of Mary, the Mary in PJ refers to Mary in Luke. With regard to the intertext 'childhood of Jesus' there are, however, very significant differences between PJ and Luke which immediately draw attention. Unlike Luke where she is presented as a poor woman, our author makes her the child of rich parents. The reader who is familiar with Luke's theme of

poverty and Mary's portrayal as a poor servant of the Lord (cf. Luke
1,48), would find the difference significant. In his assigning of meaning
to the character, this change in character traits will play a role. The
same is true of Mary being a Davidid. It does not only tie in with
the presentation of Joseph in PJ as a widower, but also undoubtedly
on Mary as the Davidic descendant of Jesus and not on Joseph who
had to take care of this very special virgin.

In his presentation of the birth story of Jesus narrated from the
perspective of his mother, it is not only the additional material that
prompts the reader to build his own image of the character of Mary,
but also her transformation into a new character. Readers who notice
the difference between PJ and Luke would react differently and
attempt to explain the divergence of PJ in different ways, as the history of the reception of PJ clearly indicates.

The presentation of Joseph is also something which immediately
strikes the reader who knows him from the infancy stories of the
canonical gospels. Unlike the Joseph of Luke and Matthew, PJ's
Joseph is a widower with children (9,2) and a builder (9,3). He is
also presented as a man of doubt and *suspicion* (cf. 13,1–2). This is
somewhat different from the character known from Luke and Matthew.
With regard to the story of our author, however, and his emphasis
on the virginity of Mary, the Davidic descendance of Jesus, and the
role of Joseph in the life of Mary, his presentation of the characters
is coherent.

In the third place there is a noticeable difference between the
Jewish religious leaders of PJ and those of the canonical gospels. In
the canonical gospels the Jewish religious leaders are characterised
negatively. They are the opponents of Jesus. In PJ they are presented positively. They perform religious rites (cf. 6,2; 8,2.3; 24,1).
They bless (17,3), pray (8,3), take care of the temple and determine
the norms (cf. 10,1; 15,3). They are the helpers and not the opponents in the plot of the narrative. This rearrangement of the material of the intertext enables the author to tell his story from his own
point of view, and to make his own point. It also prompts the reader
to comprehend the text as something which is different from the
pretext and as an independent realisation of the intertext 'childhood
of Jesus'.

PJ's allusion to familiar characters activates different texts to which
the reader reacts. On the ground of his knowledge of the pretext,
the reader expects certain things to happen and to be told when he
encounters an allusion. The allusion to and the intertextual rela-

tionship between the different texts thus enable the reader to assign meaning to the text he is reading. This is the function of traces of precursor texts in later texts. They draw the reader into the dialogue which exists between texts. This function of traces is conformed by the function of pretexts in PJ.

I have already referred to the fact that there is a resemblance between the first few chapters of PJ and 1 Sam. 1 and 2. Smid (1965:62) among others, draws attention to the following: Joachim like Hannah is reproached with childlessness. He also refuses to eat. Anne, the mother of Mary, is reproached by a woman, and so is Hannah. Before the birth of the child both Hannah and Anne dedicated their children to the service of God. There is a comparison between the grieving of Hannah and the lament of Anne. Both Mary and Samuel are presented in the temple and spend their lives there.

Immediately when the reader starts reading PJ and notices some of the motifs common to the story of Samuel, the pretext is activated. On the ground of these allusions he expects certain things to happen in accordance with the pretext. In the narration of the story of Mary, however, the author had his own point to make. The reader is prompted to fill in the story of Mary with his knowledge of the story of Samuel, but also to correct his version by taking seriously the point of the new story and the differences with the pretext. While Samuel is prepared for a 'ministry', Mary is prepared to become the virgin mother of Jesus. The allusion to the story of Samuel is simultaneously an allusion to the intertext 'childhood of Jesus', which invites the reader to activate that intertext too.

In each episode of PJ where a relationship with another text can be established, one notices exactly the same thing. The pretext is activated by an allusion and the new context of narration highlights the differences. Subsequently the reader is drawn into the process of assigning meaning to PJ on account of precursor texts. PJ 16,1–3 undoubtedly have traces of Num. 5,11–33 where cases of wives with suspicious husbands are treated (cf. also Josephus *Ant.* 3,27–274; Philo *De spec.leg.* III,62 and *m.Sota* 2 and 9). The reader. who is acquainted with the intertext on the treatment of women who are suspected of adultery, activates the intertext and reads PJ in this context. But our author retold the information with regard to Mary in order to emphasise the miraculous conception and birth of Jesus and her vindication before the High Priest. In similar manner the very interesting chapter 18,2 where the narrator changes from a third to a first person narrator and Joseph's vision of the standstill of nature is recounted, other arrests of nature are called into memory. In the end it is, however, yet another episode in the structuring of the miraculous birth of Jesus as part of the intertext 'childhood of Jesus'.

There are many allusions in PJ to other texts, the most important of which are those which activate the intertext 'childhood of Jesus'. It is in this regard that our author had a point to make. In new circumstances, probably in the second century, he felt the need to retell the story of the virgin birth of Jesus. With the help of different pretexts he created a new story and subsequently produced a new exemplar of the intertext 'childhood of Jesus' stories. There is no reason to deny his inventiveness or his vivid imagination. On the other hand one cannot overlook the imaginative use of pretexts in telling his own story. By referring back to the canonical stories of the miraculous birth of Jesus and by retelling the story for quite another purpose the author invites the reader into the world of intertextual relationships and the experience of the assignment of meaning by selection and correction of first impressions.

A long period of scrutinising early Christian documents in view of historical awareness and the aid of historico-critical methods have enabled us to rid ourselves of many misconceptions and beliefs about the origin of these documents. It has also caused scholars to approach these documents with a limited and restricted viewpoint. This essay has been an experiment, an attempt to look at the allusions in PJ to precursor texts from quite another angle. Instead of looking for sources and influences, I assumed that all texts, including PJ, are writings on writings and that allusions to other texts enable the reader to assign meaning to the being read text. I am of the opinion that there is the possibility of progress in the researching of these ancient documents if we accept the work of our predecessors who emphasised the use of sources, but reformulate the problem in view of production and reading and not in terms of origin and transmission only.

The phenomenon of intertextuality, limited in this essay to written texts, seems to me a challenge to new ways of investigating the relationship between texts and the implications thereof. It is a great honour to dedicate this essay to Professor Klijn. He has influenced me in many ways and has taught me not to restrict my views on early Christianity to those presented by the canonical writings. Early Christian faith was after all a dynamic process, not a closed system. This is one of the fascinating aspects of a short story like PJ.

CHAPTER TWENTY SEVEN

THE PRODUCTION OF THE GOSPEL OF MARK: ESSAY ON INTERTEXTUALITY

1. *Introduction*

Modern informed readers know the Gospel of Mark from critical Greek editions with text-critical and other notes in the margins. These notes inform them not only about the history of the transmission of the final text, but also about allusions and quotations in the text. In addition, it is commonly maintained that the Gospel was originally written in Greek, and that the final text represents a rather lengthy history of growth. For more than a century attempts have been made to explain the origin of the gospel material and to interpret the space between the related events and the final inscripturation of the contents of the Gospel. For that reason the emphasis has been on the growth and not on the making of the Gospel. Very few scholars have taken the production of the written Gospel seriously. Certain data beliefs and assumptions concerning the Gospel have become so dominant that very little progress has been made in the history of interpretation of the Gospel (see e.g. Peabody 1987:3ff.).

In this essay I will discuss the importance of the unsolved problem of the production of the Gospel of Mark. To achieve my goal, I will first pay attention to current views on the origin of the material. The idea is to illustrate the implications of the traditional focus on the origins of the Gospel. In the next part of the essay I will turn to the production of the Gospel from the perspective of intertextuality. In this section I will focus on the implications of a totally different perception of the phenomena of text and textual relationships.

2. *Mark and its Predecessors*

It is no longer possible to determine with any certainty who Mark, as we normally call the author of the Gospel of Mark, really was. Neither is it absolutely certain how he went about writing his Gospel and where he got his material from. A period of three or four decades must have passed after the death of Jesus before Mark decided to write his story. What happened during that period lies in the dark.

It is normally argued that the followers of Jesus transmitted his words and deeds by telling and retelling things he did and said. In view of the folkloric nature of many of the stories of and about Jesus, the aphoristic character of many of his sayings, the many parables he apparently told his followers, and the role of oral communication in that period, it is probable that Mark was informed about the story of Jesus by way of tradition. It is also probable that his audience would have known these traditions and others, such as the institution of the Lord's Supper, and controversy stories. It is therefore possible to argue that Mark based his written story of Jesus on traditional material which he received and decided to put into written form. This is also the way in which the origin of the material was explained in the early church. The earliest witness to the authorship of Mark is the quotation from Papias of Hierapolis (c. 140 CE) in the history of Eusebius (Hist. Eccl. III 39:15), according to which the Gospel was based on memory of the things Peter had told Mark (see also Breytenbach 1992).

What other sources did Mark use? One of the interesting things about early Christian literature is that although there was only one Jesus, we have many Gospels. The Gospels of Matthew, Mark and Luke—the so-called Synoptic Gospels—are closely related and have much material in common. Some form of dependence is therefore presumed (see Sanders & Davies 1989). The dominant assumption is that Matthew and Luke made use of Mark in compiling their Gospels, and that they also had a hypothetical collection of sayings of Jesus normally called Q (that is, 'Quelle' = 'source'), at their disposal when they wrote their Gospels. On the grounds of this hypothesis it is much easier to explain the origin of the Gospels of Matthew and Luke than it is to explain that of Mark. The question therefore arises whether Mark also had other, perhaps written, sources in addition to the 'traditional material' referred to above when he wrote his Gospel.

First of all there is the so-called Old Testament. It is probable that Mark had copies of the Old Testament in either Greek or Hebrew in written form at his disposal. Whether he had these copies on his desk is difficult to determine. This is also not the place to argue the problem. That his Gospel echoes the Old Testament is clear from both the quotations and the many allusions to Old Testament writings. There are, moreover, large chunks of material in the Gospel, such as a collection of miracle stories, parables, an apocalyptic speech and the passion narrative, for example, which have prompted scholars to investigate the possibility of other written sources behind the Gospel of Mark (see Vielhauer 1975:332–336 and Neirynck *et al.*, 1992:646). The passion narrative is presumably related to the Gospel of Peter, which is basically a passion story (see Crossan 1988); Mark 13 is based on an earlier Jewish leaflet (see Brandenburger 1984); Mark 4 on a collection of parables, and the miracle stories in chapters 5 and 7 on catenae of miracle stories (see Kuhn 1971). It has furthermore been proposed that some of the sayings material is also related to the material found in Q (see e.g. Neirynck 1991:421ff.). In addition, it has been argued that Mark's Gospel is based on an original lost *Urmarkus* or *Grundschrift* being either the 'proto-Mark' or 'deutero-Mark', or that it is a revision of the *Secret Gospel* referred to by Clement of Alexandria (see Koester 1990:273ff.). However it may be, there seems to be little evidence that Mark invented the material in his Gospel.

From the perspective of the making of the Gospel, different viewpoints have been advanced in accordance with views on the role attributed to the person who was finally responsible for composing the Gospel. Mark has been regarded as a collector, a composer, a redactor (editor) and an author (see Vorster 1980b). These perceptions are based on data assumptions. Underlying assumptions concerning authorship, the phenomenon text, text types, the history of early Christianity, the origin of early Christian literature and other aspects of the Gospel are responsible for the current state of affairs. Let us briefly discuss this viewpoint since I have treated the problem elsewhere in more detail (see Vorster 1980b).

In the 1920's the idea that Mark was written by an author was replaced by the current view that he was nothing more than a collector of traditions. The Gospels were regarded as Kleinliteratur, the products of the transmission of tradition by illiterate, unknown persons—a collective community (see Schmidt 1923 & Güttgemanns 1970). Mark's task was to collect these traditions and to put them into a narrative framework. His contribution was limited to the collection of material which he knitted into a loose composition of episodes concerning the deeds and works of Jesus. Mark was regarded as a stringer of pearls (see Schmidt 1923:127f.) or a collector of traditions (Dibelius 1971:3). This should be understood against the background of the emphasis on the interest in what lies behind the text and not what is in the text.

The situation changed in the late 1950's with the rise of the so-called redaction-critical approach to the Gospels (see Marxsen 1959 & Peabody 1987). The material in the Gospel was increasingly regarded as edited tradition—an idea which goes far back, but one that had only recently developed. Although the Gospel as a whole came into focus, the interest was in the redaction of tradition. This resulted in detailed investigations concerning tradition and redaction in the Gospels. In the case of Mark it was extremely difficult to determine exactly what could be regarded as tradition and what could not, because of the absence of copies of the presumed sources. On the basis of style, regular occurrence of certain words and phrases, views that were peculiar to the specific Gospel, so-called seams or breaks in the text and other features, scholars reached a certain degree of consensus about redaction and tradition in the Gospel of Mark.

Mark's (theological) emphasis was determined by interpreting his redaction of tradition. At least a certain amount of creativity—however limited—was ascribed to the redactor. Mark's own contribution to the story of Jesus came into focus, despite the fact that he was soon described as a conservative redactor (see Pesch 1976). The emphasis which Wrede (1969) had put on Mark's creativity in 1906 was newly appreciated.

In circles where Mark was regarded as a composer, he received more credit for what he had achieved, and attention was given to the Gospel message as a whole. It was, however, only in the late 1970's that scholars started paying serious attention to Mark's Gospel as a narrative, and to Mark as an author or author/narrator and to the Gospel as an autonomous text.

The renewed interest in Mark as author and his Gospel as a narrative opened new possibilities in the interpretation of different aspects of the Gospel. It was discovered that the story had been told from a certain narrative point of view, why time and space play an important role in the Gospel, and that characters, including Jesus, were presented in conjunction with the story line—in short, that narrative analysis posed new challenges to interpreters of the Gospel (see Vorster 1980b; Hahn 1985 & Moore 1989). Perhaps the most important single contribution of this approach is the fact that interpreters were forced to take the Gospel as a complete text seriously. It also implied that the transmitted text—and not its history or the origin of parts of it—was placed in the centre of interest. This does not imply that the text was interpreted a-historically as is so easily incorrectly assumed by critics who regard narrative analysis of the Gospel as an extension of redaction criticism (see Zwick 1989).

This short survey clearly indicates that the emphasis that was put on the growth of the Gospel also determined the role of the person who was responsible for the final text. One can safely say that there has been little reflection on the role of the person who produced the Gospel, except for the descriptions I have mentioned, namely collector, composer, redactor and author. How one should picture Mark editing tradition in written or oral form by changing a word here and there, adding a sentence or two, rearranging the order of material, putting the traditional material into a narrative frame and joining separate units or episodes—as redaction critics make us believe—is difficult to imagine. There is much more to the production of a text than traditional views would allow. As long as the Gospels are perceived mainly from the perspective of their growth, the process of production is blurred. What is needed is serious reflection on the production of texts from the perspective of what happens when other texts, whether oral or written, are included in or absorbed by a new text. The traditional approach is anti-individualistic because the driving force behind the Gospels is the anonymous community.

In addition to the assumption that the message (meaning) of the Gospels can be studied from the perspective of their origin, and that the authors were redactors and not authors in the proper sense of the word, the idea of influence also plays an important role. The assumption is clearly that Mark was influenced by his sources. One should be very careful with this type of argument. If Mark is simply regarded as an exponent of the community within which he stood, it may be thought that his task was to put into words what the community thought. From the insights of Sociology of Knowledge we are aware that all knowledge is context-bound. But that does not imply that there is no place for creativity. On the contrary, even oral storytellers tell the 'same' story differently in different contexts and under different circumstances, although their knowledge is bound to their contexts.

A further problem with the traditional approach to the Gospel of

Mark is that the final text is not sufficiently distinguished from its history of growth. This is due to the text concept which underlies the approach. As we have seen it is not the text as such that is studied, namely a new edition of a text, but a text which should be divided into segments of redaction and tradition.

In the next section an attempt will be made to take the fact seriously that Mark probably did not invent the material, but that he nevertheless made up his own story of Jesus for his own purposes and in his own circumstances. This will be done from the perspective of the production of the text and not from its growth.

3. *The Production of Mark: Mark and Precursor Texts*

I have already mentioned that there is no certainty about the identity of the author of the Gospel or about his audience. It is probable that he was a bilingual Jew, and it is possible that he wrote his Gospel for an audience in either Galilee or in Rome (see Vorster 1990b & 1991). We do not know what the place where he wrote his Gospel looked like, whether it was a study in a private house, or some other room where he had different manuscripts at his disposal. We assume that much of his material was known to him through the tradition in which he stood. It is also possible, as I have already said, that he had some manuscripts of Old Testament writings available.

The main thing, however, is that we have a text, written in Greek with different allusions to and quotations from precursor texts. This last observation underscores the fact that Mark as a reader/hearer of texts reacted to different intertextual codes, and thus created a new text which refers to different texts and codes intertextually. These include parables, miracle stories, controversy stories, bibliographies, stories of cult heros, speeches about the future, stories of suffering and resurrection stories. In addition Mark apparently knew themes, words, phrases and stories from the Old Testament. He must have had acquaintance with the Elisha cycle and with other performers of miracles. He must also have known the economic, political and other cultural codes of his time. However, we still do not know exactly how he went about creating his story of Jesus—that is, how he made his Gospel.

Two recent attempts at explaining the making of the Gospel are, however, worth mentioning. Mack (1988:322–323) maintains that Mark's Gospel was '. . . not a pious transmission of revered tradition. It was composed at a desk in a scholar's study lined with texts and open to discourse with other intellectuals. In Mark's study were chains of miracle stories, collections of pronouncement stories . . .' Mack assumes that Mark had different Hellenistic Jewish texts, the Scriptures and other Christian texts in his study. One need not agree with Mack, but he has at least given some thought to what might have been possible in the production of a text in the first century.

Botha P.J.J. (1989:76–77), on the other hand, maintains that the Mediterranean world of the first century was predominantly oral. Mark came from an oral community and his Gospel should be seen as oral literature. Mark told his story of Jesus orally and at some stage dictated it to somebody who wrote down his words. It still bears the signs of oral literature. Again, Mark is taken seriously as the producer of a text and not simply as a conduit through which a stream of tradition flowed, or a (passive) exponent of a community out of which his text arose (see also Vorster 1980b).

The next question is whether we can say more about the actual process of the making of the Gospel by using a concept of the phenomenon text which is different from the concept we know (the traditional approach we have dealt with above), and by asking different questions concerning the making of texts. My hypothesis is that a concept of text different from the one we are used to in New Testament scholarship, and a rethinking of the process of production, can help us understand the Gospel of Mark and its relation to precursor and other texts. This would, however, imply a total rethinking of the traditional approach.

The idea that any text is a network or mosaic of different texts referring to other texts is challenging. The concept 'intertextuality' has not been sufficiently explored by New Testament scholars (see however Draisma 1989; Phillips 1991; Vorster 1992).

There is no reason to doubt that the written Gospel of Mark echoes many different precursor texts and intertextual relationships. In this regard the use of the Old Testament in Mark's Gospel is helpful. I have elsewhere argued that Mark's use of the Old Testament is totally different from that of Matthew or Mark who use the Old Testament within a promise-fulfilment scheme (see Vorster 1981). Allusions to and quotations from the Old Testament are usually absorbed into Mark's story in such a manner that, except for a few cases where he specifically mentions the origin of the quotation, the allusions and quotations form part of the story stuff. They are so embedded into the story that, if it were not for the references in the margins and a knowledge of the Old Testament, the reader would not have noticed that Mark uses an allusion or a quotation (see Mk. 15:24). This is best seen in Mark's story of the passion of Jesus.

It has often been noticed that psalms of lamentation such as Psalms 22, 38 and 69 concerning the suffering of the just, are knitted into the passion narrative in such a manner that one can say that the passion narrative of Mark is narrated in the language of the Old Testament. The point is, however, that the allusions and 'quotations' form such an integral part of the passion narrative that it is impossible for the naive reader to realize that the text is enriched by its intertextual relationships concerning the suffering of the Just.

One of the significant things about the use of the Old Testament in Mark is that he had no respect for the original context of the quotations and allusions to Old Testament writings in his text. The story of John the Baptist at the very beginning of the Gospel proves the point. In the first place the very first quotation (Mk. 1:2–3) does not come from Isaiah the prophet, as Mark asserts. It is a composite reference to Exodus 23:20, Malachi 3:1 and Isaiah 40:3 which he connects to Isaiah the prophet. The quotation is taken out of context and worked into his story of John and Jesus in order to show the relationship between the two. The beginning of the Gospel does not prove the fulfilment of the Old Testament, it characterises John as the predecessor of Jesus. Only at a later stage does the reader realize the resemblance between the apocalyptic John and the apocalyptic Jesus.

One of the inferences one should make from the use of the Old Testament in the Gospel of Mark is that the author created a new story with the aid of intertextual codes that helped him to communicate his own point of view. The Old Testament quotations and references formed part of the new story that Mark created in order to convince his readers of his point of view concerning Jesus and the implications of Jesus' life, works and words for the prevailing situation.

Somebody may argue that the Old Testament is a special case and that it does not say much. However, let us argue the use of traditional material in the Gospel of Mark from the perspective of intertextuality.

It is an illusion to think that Mark was a conservative redactor. In fact, Mark not only reshaped his story of Jesus by retelling the story for the sake of a particular situation, he also told it from his own perspective. Whether he transmitted tradition 'conservatively' or 'creatively' is of little significance. Even eyewitnesses shape their messages for their own purposes. Vansina (1985:5) correctly observes:

> ... [M]ediation of perception by memory and emotional state shapes an account. Memory typically selects certain features from the successive perceptions and interprets them according to expectation, previous knowledge or the logic of 'what must have happened', and fills the gaps in perception.

This is all the more true of the Jesus tradition which has been shaped by eyewitnesses as well as those who retold the tradition for their own purposes and in their own circumstances. That is already clear from the different versions of the same stories of and about Jesus in the canonical gospels. First of all we do not have any (un-biased) eyewitness reports; furthermore, the retelling of the Jesus tradition was done in different circumstances for different purposes. This is, for instance, confirmed by the 'same' version of the 'same' parable in different contexts in the different gospels. Retelling of the 'same' event or word of a specific person involves creativity.

What is apparent regarding the use of the Old Testament in Mark seems to be even more applicable to the tradition incorporated in the Gospel of Mark. Let us take individual units such as controversy stories between Jesus and his opponents in the Gospel of Mark as an example.

From a form-critical perspective most of these stories presuppose a sociological situation of conflict in early Christianity. In addition, some of the stories are transmitted in Mark's Gospel in a mixed form—that is, a story which relates conflict between Jesus and opponents within the framework of a miracle story. These stories seem to have been created around a saying of Jesus and reflect situations in early Christianity which the other evangelists used in their own stories about Jesus. In retold form, these stories were used not only for different purposes but also for different messages, depending on new situations.

Retelling involves creativity, whether in oral or in written form. It is impossible to tell the 'same' story twice. Each telling has its own context and its own message. The truth of this statement is confirmed by the retelling of the stories of the Old Testament within the Old Testament, as well as in later Jewish literature. Each time a story or event is retold, it is done for a specific purpose and from a specific point of view. In other words, each account involves creativity. The same applies to oral transmission of history.

Even if Mark's version of narrative units is based on authoritative transmission of tradition, or on written accounts of certain chunks of material in his Gospel, he made up his own story by putting the narrative units into the order he wanted and into the framework he developed. It is important and significant to see that Mark knitted the Jesus tradition into a new narrative web of his own.

Even if he had based his version of Jesus' speech on the Mount of Olives in Mark 13, for instance, on an existing Jewish flyleaf, as is often assumed, this narrated speech of Jesus, which is a network of quotations and allusions to the Old Testament, has its own Marcan message and function (see Vorster 1987b). As it stands, it refers back to precursor texts and to intertextual codes of apocalyptic disruption and disaster, but it also takes up the apocalyptic theme of the imminent coming of the Son of Man, which is a Marcan creation (see Mack 1987). The same applies to other material in the Gospel of Mark which can probably be connected to pre-Marcan collections or pre-Marcan written or oral compositions.

In addition to the many studies on the texts behind and in the Gospel of Mark, two recent attempts have been made at describing the Gospel as the rewriting of Old Testament stories. Although I am not convinced about the total outcome of either (see Roth 1988; Miller & Miller 1990) they have both indicated how important it is to regard Mark's Gospel as a creation of a new text. The Millers correctly observe that New Testament writers created what they call new midrashim on older texts. They argue that Mark did not simply interpret the Old Testament midrashically. Mark created a new midrash—that is, new scripture in typical Jewish fashion. This is another way of seeing the importance of creativity in Mark's Gospel. It also supports my argument.

We have already noticed that Mark did not hesitate to use the Old Testament out of context, and that it is probable that he did the same with the tradition he received. This simply underscores our notion that he retold tradition for his own purposes. By doing this Mark created a new text from other texts, traces of which can be seen in his text.

The relationship between the final text of the Gospel of Mark and precursor and other texts is an intertextual relationship. There is no causal relationship between this new text and the texts out of which Mark made his text. Mark quoted other texts, and his story alludes to other texts and absorbed other texts. This is how his story becomes meaningful and different from other stories with the same theme when the reader interprets Mark's texts in the light of other texts known to him/her.

There is a total difference between an attempt where the Gospel of Mark is understood from the perspective of its production, and an attempt where it is understood from the perspective of its growth. The first approach seriously considers that any allusion or quotation from another text forms an integral part of the new text, even when it seems to be out of context. The latter regards the final text, which has relationships with precursor texts, as the result of a causal process.

CHAPTER TWENTY EIGHT

INTERTEXTUALITY AND *REDAKTIONSGESCHICHTE*

In a recent article on the Gospel of Mark and *Redaktionsgeschichte* (hence RG) it was correctly observed that in spite of new approaches in Marcan research during recent times, RG has dominated this research for the last thirty years and still does so in some circles (cf. Black 1988:19–39). This observation holds true of Gospel research in general in spite of the awareness of manifold uncertainties concerning the theory and practice of RG and the fact that in some circles it is argued that a paradigm shift is taking place in New Testament scholarship calling into question the assumptions on which RG, for example, is based (see Martin 1987:370–385 and also Vorster 1988d: 31–48). In such a situation it seems appropriate to reconsider the basic assumptions of such a method of interpretation and to investigate the appropriateness of current views in the light of other methodologies and theories dealing with the same problems. Since intertextuality is a modern theory about relationships between texts and RG has to do with the relationship between texts, the assumptions of RG should be tested in the light of current views on text relationships. It is the purpose of this article to compare the agreements and differences between RG and intertextuality in order to point out the possibilities which an intertextual approach to the relationship of texts and fragments of texts in the New Testament offers. The term intertextuality will be reserved in this essay for the modern concept of intertextual relationships as it will be developed below.

The relationship between early Christian writings, precursor and contemporary ancient writings has been of great interest in the study of the New Testament. Studies on the use of the Old Testament in the New, the use of sources, and literary dependence between documents of the New Testament abound. This illustrates the great importance scholars attach to the existing or supposed relationships between texts in the writings of the New Testament.

Very few of these studies focus on the *function* of traces of anterior texts in later texts. And normally there is little awareness of the importance of the study of textual relationship with regard to the

production and reception of these writings. Scholars are mostly interested in the study of sources and their influences in the focused texts.
Such studies furthermore tend to focus upon agreements and differences between texts in order to prove that sources were in fact used
and to demonstrate the originality of users of other texts or their
conservativeness in the transmission of tradition. Developments in
this regard which have taken place in literary circles urge us to consider the possibilities which these developments offer the New Testament scholar in the study of intertextual relationships. The shift
in focus from author-oriented to text—and reader-oriented study of
New Testament texts simply compels us to look at matters such as
intertextual relationships afresh. In addition there also seems to be
a great difference between perceptions which focus on the growth
of texts and those which attend to the making and reception of texts.
I will attempt to address some of the implications involved by focusing on RG as a methodological strategy to address the relationship
between texts and on intertextuality as a modern theory concerning
text relationships. In the first part of the essay I will develop the
main assumptions underlying the theory and practice of RG with
regard to text relationships. Then I will pay attention to the phenomenon of intertextuality and lastly I will take Mark 13 as an example of a complicated text in order to demonstrate the differences
and agreements between redaktionsgeschichtlich and intertextual
approaches to this text with regard to production and reception.

The thesis I wish to propose in this essay is that the literary notion
of intertextuality can be fruitfully applied in the study of the production and reception of New Testament writings with regard to the
relationship between these texts and texts or fragments of texts produced prior to or after the New Testament writings were written.

1. *Redaktionsgeschichte*

RG is concerned with the composition of texts. The redactors of the
individual Gospels are regarded as persons concerned '. . . with the
composition of new material and the arrangements of redacted or
freshly created material into new units and patterns, as well as with
the redaction of existing material' (Perrin 1970:1; see also Rohde
1966:1–22). Practitioners of RG are therefore interested in the activities of the redactors of texts, who are moreover regarded as the-

ologians. The theological intentions of the redactors are found in the redaction of their material and that is why tradition should be distinguished from redaction. It is obvious that RG is author—and not text—or reader-oriented. The way the redactor thought theologically, the way in which he compiled the material, the way in which he manipulated tradition to suit his intentions, are of the things which are of importance for the production process.

RG proceeds from the assumption that there is literary dependence between the synoptic Gospels, and also that there is some relationship between the material in John's Gospel and the synoptic Gospels. In most circles the so-called two source hypothesis, according to which Matthew and Luke used Mark and the so-called Q source and other material peculiar to each of them, is still accepted by many scholars as the best explanation for the agreements and differences between the three Gospels. John made use of other sources in compiling his Gospel, but there also seems to be some relationship, although different from the relationship between the material of the Synopics, between some of the material in John and the Synoptics, according to this argument. RG therefore presupposes an intertextual relationship between the Gospel texts and fragments of these texts on the ground of the use of sources, oral or written, in the production of these texts. It is obvious that according to this view on the relationships of texts in the Gospel tradition it would be easier to determine the implications of relation between Matthew and Luke and their precursor texts than between either Mark or John and their precursor texts, since these precursor texts are presupposed. We do not have copies of the supposed sources of Mark and John. The main point is that RG is a form of source-influence study.

The role of the redactors of the Gospel material in the production of the texts is nevertheless not always clear, because it is not often explicitly said how scholars conceive of the process of production.

For some scholars the continuity between tradition and redaction is of great importance, while others come very close to regarding the redactors of Gospel material as creative authors. Obviously this influences the perception of the relationship between redaction and tradition, that is the relationship between texts and fragments of texts. Pesch, for instance, regards Mark as a conservative redactor but according to Mack the situation is totally different (see Pesch 1976:15–23 and Mack 1988:321–324). Pesch (1976:23–24) maintains that: '. . . der Redaktor Markus ist kein Inventor, sondern Bearbeiter von Tradition, er verhält sich kaum literarisch produktiv, sondern "unliterarisch" konservativ'. Mack, who perhaps should not be seen as an proponent of RG in the traditional sense of the word, holds that:

> Mark's Gospel was not the product of divine revelation. It was not a pious transmission of revered tradition. It was composed at a desk in a scholar's study lined with texts and open to discourse with other intellectuals. In Mark's study were chains of miracle stories, collections of pronouncement stories in various states of elaboration, some form of Q, memos on parables and proof texts, the scriptures, including the prophets, written materials from the Christ cult, and other literature representative of Hellenistic Judaism. It would not be unthinkable that Mark had a copy of the Wisdom of Solomon, or some of the Maccabean literature or some Samaritan texts and so on (Mack 1988:322–4).

The differences between the two points of view are far-reaching as far as the relationship between texts, and also the making of the Gospel of Mark are concerned. While Pesch holds the view that there is a direct continuity between tradition and redaction, and thus that Mark was dictated by his sources, Mack maintains that Mark *transformed* tradition. In his view Mark created a new text, and transformed precursor texts into a totally new fabric—'a highly conscious scholarly effort in fabricating a new text . . .' (Mack 1988:322, n. 3). The idea of transformation of texts is something totally different from what Pesch has in mind. For him the relationship between Mark's texts and precursor texts is one of sources and influences. Another group of scholars regard the redactors of the Gospel material as exponents of their communities, thus little more than the conduits through which the stream of tradition originating with Jesus flowed (see Strecker 1971:10). The relationship between the texts (tradition and redaction) is one of continuity and influence between source and receptor. The redactor is little more than a compiler in the making of these texts. This is the direct opposite of somebody who argues that Mark transformed tradition into a new text. Underlying the two viewpoints is a different concept of what a text is. To this problem we will return below.

Another basic assumption of RG is that the final written Gospels are the products of inscripturation of written and oral sources or traditions, and that there is a relationship of continuity between the final texts and their precursors. It is taken for granted that the incorporation of oral material into written texts does not change the precursor text. It is assumed that precursor (oral) texts are changed only by the editing of their content. That is why the pre-written texts can supposedly be reconstructed from the written text and be compared. This is a highly problematic assumption as we shall see below (cf. also Güttgemanns 1970:223–231).

Although proponents of RG advanced the idea that the Gospels should be analysed as wholes and not as fragments, they hardly ever rid themselves of the concept of influence and dependence regarding the production of texts. The final texts are the products of growth and not of creative activity, they often argued.

2. *Intertextuality*

Intertextuality is concerned with the relationship between texts (cf. Pfister 1985:11 for an excellent survey of the concept in current research). This is, however, a minimum definition because of the many ways in which intertextuality is conceived and the many relationships which are involved. It is therefore necessary to comment on this definition in order to get a clearer picture of the phenomenon. Since we are interested in the implications of intertextuality concerning the interpretation of text relationships in the New Testament, the theory will be related to New Testament scholarship and New Testament texts.

It seems imperative, from what I have said above about the presuppositions of RG that the relationship between source-influence studies in the traditional sense of the word and intertextuality has to be clearly defined. Secondly it will also be necessary to ponder on the phenomenon text, since this is basic to current views on intertextuality in literary criticism. Out of this will follow what the implications are for the study of the relationship between texts from an intertextuality point of view.

Traditional source-influence studies need not necessarily be regarded negatively as Miller (1985:19) has correctly observed. The study of sources and influence of texts on other texts is the historical forerunner of intertextuality. The concern of this approach was (and for current practitioners still is) to prove the use of sources in a focused document and to demonstrate the debt of the focused text to a precursor text. New Testament scholars are accustomed to this kind of approach since the early days when the relationships between the

Gospels became a problem which had to be clarified. It was, however, with the rise of the historico-critical methods and especially
with the arrival of *Literarkritik* as a methodological strategy to determine source that special attention was given to the matter. Not only
were actual texts regarded as source for other texts (the synoptic
problem!), but scholars also started working with presupposed texts
in cases where the actual precursor texts were not available. Concepts
like *oral sources* and *tradition* formed part of the total strategy to explain
the origin of written texts and to gain meaning to these texts. No
doubt that this approach found its ebb tide in RG where the sources
did not have to be proved, but were simply taken for granted. In
RG sources are regarded as 'artefacts' which can be compared to
final texts in order to demonstrate the intentions of the redactors,
even though in many cases the interpreter has to work with presupposed and not actual texts.

The presupposed texts are more or less viewed as citations embedded into, or assimilated by the new text. The final text is compared
to its intertext (cited text) in view of the intention of the author of
the text. This is obviously a valid approach if the agreements and
differences between focused text and intertext is the only aspect we
have to take into consideration, and if we only concentrate on the
author and his/her *intentions*. Depending on whether the redactor is
regarded as conservative or innovative, judgements are made about
the meaning of the 'citations' in their new environment.

What I am saying here is not to be taken negatively or as a straw
man which has to be demolished. On the contrary. It is necessary
to know exactly what we have been doing all the way in the application of these methods. The theory of source-influence study is
based on firm convictions and domain assumptions concerning texts
and their origin and growth. These assumptions and convictions have
to be tested from time to time no matter what the results and consequences are. Miller (1985:13) makes the following very valuable
and valid remark about source-influence:

> To refer to text A as being the source of or exercising an influence
> on text B is really to refer to author A's intersubjective relation-
> ship with author B. Our very manner of speaking of source-influence
> studies ... betrays our fundamental ways of thinking about them as
> an author-oriented enterprise the nature of which the critic must un-
> cover.

This is especially true of New Testament scholarship, where until recently, all the focus in studies of interpretation was author-oriented, as I have pointed out above. This has to do with a number of things of which our views on text are not the least important. Recently much more attention has been given to communication of ancient documents. The result was a re-evaluation of what the role of the text and the reader is in the process of interpretation. But before we get to that perhaps we should sum up the purpose and practice of source-influence studies.

Source-influence studies are based on a particular view of what a text is. In New Testament scholarship texts are generally regarded as something which has developed into written documents and that it is possible to determine the presupposed texts on which these documents supposedly were based. The purpose of source-influence studies is to prove the use of sources and to demonstrate the debt of the authors of these texts to the precursor texts, be they actual or presupposed texts.

In order to show the difference between the traditional approach to intertextual relationships and intertextuality, it is now necessary to make a few observations about the phenomenon text within the context of intertextuality.

Intertextuality is based on a new notion of what text is. Baktin, Barthes, Kristeva and many others have developed a radically new concept of what a text is and how it works. It is, however, necessary to point out that the phenomenon of intertextuality is not at all new or modern. What is different is the way in which the phenomenon is perceived. Literary references to precursor texts, allusions to other texts, citations, be they verbatim or 'free' are known to us from Homer and other ancient makers of texts. The ancients, similar to what we do, made use of anterior texts, imitated other texts, and alluded to precursor and contemporary texts in producing their own texts. This is not at all new or important. What is important is the way in which we regard these relationships.

All texts can be regarded as the rewriting of previous texts, and also as reactions to texts. Kristeva coined the following very useful metaphorical sentence which forms the basis of the modern view on intertextuality: '. . . tout texte se construit comme mosaïque de citations, tout texte est absorption et transformation d'un autre texte' (Kristeva 1969:146 and 255). This is also the Barthesian notion of

the mosaic concept of text as a series of quotations. He forcibly
states it as follows:

> L'intertextuel dans lequel est pris tout texte, puisqu'il est lui-même
> l'entre-texte d'un autre texte, ne peut se confondre avec quelque orig-
> ine du texte: rechercher les 'sources', les 'influences' d'un oeuvre, c'est
> satisfaire au mythe de la filiation: les citations dont est fait un texte
> sont anonymes, irrépérables et cependant déjà lues: ce sont des cita-
> tions sans guillemets (Barthes as quoted by Miller 1985:21).

This should make sense to New Testament schcolars who know that
if it were not for the references in the margin of printed editions
and italics or bold print indicating quotations, most of the allusions
and quotations in New Testament texts would be unknown because
they are integrated into the text. Unless an author specifically says
that he is quoting (cf. formula quotations in Matthew), the sources
simply remain anonymous and form part of the code system of the
given text for the reader. What these allusions and quotations can
do is to recall intertexts as codes of reference and meaning (see
Miller 1985:25). This notion of text conceives of text as:

> ... a mosaic composed of many fragments of linguistic matter quoted
> from anonymous sources, a collage of pieces of language brought into
> spatial proximity and inviting the reader to create some sort of pat-
> terning by forcing them to discharge some of their interrelational energy
> (Miller 1985:24).

Text become a network of traces, it is no more a unitary object
which is knowable, or a completed work with a centre and an edge
which is recoverable by the skilled reader (see Ryan 1985:8). Each
sentence of this network creates intertextual patterns and points to
intertextual connections:

> ... the intertextual relationships of any work of literature are theoret-
> ically infinite, since potentially any sentence of a text (or fragment
> thereof) may engender a series of presuppositional statements (Miller
> 1985:24–25).

Three things come very sharply into focus in such an approach. First
of all it is clear that the phenomenon text has been redefined. It
has become a network of references to other texts (intertexts). Secondly
it appears that more attention is to be given to text as a process of
production and not to the sources and their influences. And thirdly
it is apparent that the role of the reader is not to be neglected in
this approach to the phenomenon of text.

In producing sentences the maker of any text creates a fabric which points to many other prior texts. However, the texts that really matter are those intertexts which have been used in comparable contexts. Birth stories, for example, point to other birth stories and so do apocalyptic texts. 'Birth story' is the intertext within which other texts of similar content function and point to. The text type presupposes a particular context of utterance to which the utterance is related (cf. Miller 1985:25 and also Vorster 1988d:262–275). Apocalyptic texts illustrate the point. They are related to contexts in which these type of utterances are 'normal'. Readers read birth stories as birth stories, that is within the range of that intertext.

Whereas RG's interest lies with the intentions of the redactors and the ways in which they edited tradition, proponents of intertextuality focus on texts as networks pointing to other texts, not to the intentions of the author. It moreover becomes clear that readers play an active role in the assigning of meaning to the focused text. In the place of an object which has meaning has come a network calling for reaction by the reader. Depending on his/her repertoire of intertexts the reader (also the critic as reader) will assign meanings to the text or fragments of texts. In this manner intertextual relationships are made meaningful for the reader.

The theory of intertextuality also holds promises for the writing of the literary history of any given corpus such as early Christian literature. Up till now much of the story of early Christian documents has been written from the perspective of the use of sources and influences. It is clear to me that with the focus on early Christian writings as texts that have been produced a fresh look at these documents might throw light on textual relationships which have been blurred by the traditional approach to the literary history of the corpus. Such a history will, however, not have to be restricted to the canonical writings, or if so it will be necessary to include extra-canonical writings in order to make clear the ways in which early Christian authors transformed tradition into new texts. Intertextuality need not be restricted to relationships between a focused text and its precursors. A text can also be seen in relation to later texts. The story of the birth of Jesus in Luke and Matthew can, for example, be seen in relation to what the author of the Protogospel of James made out of it. And the Protogospel of James can be seen in relation to yet other intertexts of birth stories of important people or in relation to the life story of Mary (see Vorster 1988a; chapter 26 in this volume) In the next section the textual relationships in Mark 13 will be briefly considered.

3. *Intertextual Relationships in Mark 13*

Mark 13 offers interesting challenges with regard to the study of intertextual relationships. It is one of the most complicated texts in the New Testament as far as its relationship with pre-texts and co-texts is concerned. It forms a network of signs pointing to other signs outside the text, of allusions and quotations which remind the skilled reader of many other similar signs and sentences. Let us first look at the detail.

Mark 13:5–37 is presented in Mark as a narrated speech of Jesus about the future. It has often been observed that it basically consists of sayings of Jesus, of which most also occur in the apocalyptic discourse of Matt. 24 and Luke 21. There are, however, a number of sayings which also appear in other parts of Matthew and Luke. Mark 13:11 also occurs in Luke 21:14–15, but in addition is also found in Luke 12:11–12, Matt. 10:21–22 and John 14:25–26. Mark 13:12–13 occurs in Matt. 24:9–13 and Luke 21:16–19, but is also found in Matt. 10:21–22 and Did. 16:4–5. And so we can continue pointing out relationships between sayings of Jesus appearing in the apocalyptic discourses of Mark 13, Matt. 24 and Luke 21 and between Mark 13 and other texts in Matthew, Luke, John and the Didache. There also seem to be textual relationships to other writings of the New Testament. Mark 13.7 can be compared to Rev. 1:1; 13:14 to 2 Thess. 2:3–4; 13:22 to Rev. 13:13; 13:24 to Rev. 6:13; 13:29 to Phil. 4.5, Jas. 5.9, Rev. 3:20; 13:37 to Acts 20:31, 1 Cor. 16:13, 1 Thess. 5:6:10 and 1 Pet. 5:8. Taking this into account it can hardly be denied that Mark 13 has all sorts of relationships with texts in the New Testament prior to and after the making of this speech. There are also relationships with Old Testament and other texts. First there are direct quotations. The 'abomination of desolation' of verse 14 has its background in Dan. 12:11; 11:31 and perhaps 9:27. Mark 13:24 is also a quotation taken from the Old Testament (cf. Isa. 13:10; Joel 2:10; 3:4, 15 and Isa. 34:4). Mark 13:26 probably has its background in the wording of Dan. 7:13–14. The following list contains possible allusions to Old Testament texts:

Mark 13	Old Testament
6	Jer. 29:9
7	Dan. 2:28–29, 45
8	Isa. 19:2; 2 Chron. 15:6
12	Micah. 7:6
13	Micah. 7:6, 7; cf. Dan. 12:12
14b	Gen. 19:17
16	Gen. 19:17
18	Dan. 12:1; Joel 2:2; Exod. 9:18; Deut. 4:32
22	Jer. 6:1:3; Dt. 1:3:2
27	Zech. 2:6; Deut. 30:3–4
31	Isa. 51:6

The following remark by Perrin (1963:133) is revealing:

> We have a series of quotations and allusions woven into the text of the chapter and taken *verbatim* from the LXX or Theod., which is often quite different from the Hebrew (or Aramaic) ... All this is absolutely different from the usage elsewhere in the recorded teaching of Jesus in Mark.

In addition to the relationships mentioned above, there also seem to be relationships between Mark 13 and other extracanonical texts of importance. Mark 13.8 can be compared to 4 Ezra 13:30–32; and 13:13 to 4 Ezra 6:25.

From quite another perspective other textual relationships to Mark 13 are also suggested. More than a century ago it was proposed by T. Colani that Mark supposedly used and expanded an existing apocalypse in compiling the speech which he put on the lips of Jesus. The text on which he based the speech presumably consisted of the material now quoted in Mark 13:7–8, 12, 14–20 and 24–27. This Jewish apocalypse originated in Jerusalem in 40 CE during Caligula's reign and was spread as a fly leaf in the days of hardship. The hypothesis was replaced by another, based on the assumption that Mark 13 was based on a Jewish Christian apocalypse consisting of verses 7–8, 9b (10), 11–13, 14–20, 21–22, 24–27 and 28–31. (Brandenburger 1984:21–42 gives a useful survey of the problem of a 'Vorlage'.)

Summarising the above information on possible text relationships between Mark and other texts we note that Mark 13:5–37 has traces of other texts known to us, and that it is furthermore assumed that it is based on a source which is now non-existent. Mark 13 forms a network of relationships with other texts outside the Gospel of Mark. Both with regard to the production and the reception of texts Mark 13 offers a very good example of the complexities of text relationships.

From a *redaktionsgeschichtlich* perspective attention is focused on the relation between redaction and tradition. Most studies done from this perspective deal with the relationship between the final text and the presupposed Jewish or Jewish-Christian texts. (See Breytenbach 1984:280–281 for a survey of *redaktionsgeschichtlich* studies on Mark 13 and also Wenham 1984.) Attempts are made to prove the existence of such a presupposed text or texts and to demonstrate the relationship between the final text and these texts. Mark's indebtedness to and his agreements and differences with the pretext form the focus of these studies. Even in the case of Hartman, who regards the text as a Christian 'midrash' on the Book of Daniel, the main interest falls on the way in which the redactor reinterpreted tradition and Old Testament prophecy (see Hartman 1966). This is not the place to go into the detail of these studies. The results are well known. No real progress in the understanding of the text can be expected from that perspective as is clear from the original study of Pesch on Mark 13 and his later attempts to interpret the same text anew with the help of RG as strategy. One can, however, learn much from the detail of these studies and the mine of information which has been brought together in these studies. The main problem, however, is the fact that all these studies simply focus on text relationships between redaction and tradition, while the text offers a network of other relationships of equal and more importance. Again it is not my intention to belittle these studies done from a *redaktiongeschichtlich* point of view, but simply to draw the attention to the fact that these studies concentrate on a particular point of view, namely the importance of the distinction between redaction and tradition, sources and influence! Let us now turn to a short discussion of an intertextual approach to Mark 13:5–37 in order to show the agreements and differences between the two approaches.

Any attempt to interpret Mark 13 intertextually will have to take a number of things seriously. In the first place it is necessary to bear in mind that the final text of Mark 13:5–37 presents itself as a narrated speech about the *future* of a very particular kind. The intertext 'speeches about the future' forms a very rich corpus of material. In the Gospel tradition we have the Olivet discourses as intertext, but we also have the farewell discourses of John. Mark 13:5–37 is related to prophetic speeches about the future, like the Book of

Daniel. Because of its apocalyptic language and imagery it also calls into mind apocalyptic speeches (see Brandenburger 1984:13). One can also think of the many testaments which contain apocalyptic sections as the intertext of the speech. Similar to most of these Mark 13:5–37 has a paraenctic function. Mark took great trouble in making this speech work. Its placing in the Gospel is significant and so is the fact that the reader is prepared to accept its contents as authoritative since Jesus is a reliable character in the story of Mark. (Cf. also Petersen 1980:151–66 and Vorster 1987a:203–24.)

These intertexts limit possible readings of the text. Because of the similarity of the context in which 'speeches about the future' are uttered the reader is invited to read the text within that kind of context. Anybody who reads Mark's Gospel immediately notices the differences in code when he/she reaches this speech. It would not be possible not to notice the change in story time, narrative perspective and cast of characters. The text's codes point to 'speeches about the future'. In the second place the reader is invited to read Mark 13 in comparison to the intertext 'speeches about the future'. Obviously the speeches of Jesus about the future will take an important place in such a reading. As in RG agreements and differences will play an important role. But these agreements will not be read with a view to influence and sources. When Mark 13 is read within the context of other speeches of Jesus about the future, including all the discourses of revelation in extracanonical Gospels, the peculiarities of Mark 13 are emphasized by the agreements and the differences.

Thirdly it is also important to take into account that Mark has created a network of traces referring almost endlessly to other texts both inside and outside the New Testament. This speech is a product of his own making regardless of where he got the material from. Mark produced a speech similar to the speeches in the history of Thucydides or the Acts of the Apostles. He gathered together possible sayings of Jesus in connection with the future to get his readers to react in a certain manner. He wanted them to believe that the 'gospel of Jesus Christ' (Mark 1:1), which in real terms is a contradiction in terms, has some significance for their present actions because of its future implications. His *making* of a text which alludes to many other texts is to be taken seriously.

An intertextual reading will have to be limited also. It is not necessary to follow up each allusion to every single intertext since all allusions are not of the same importance. Mark created a text which undoubtedly points to many other texts because of the many allusions we have mentioned. On the other hand one should keep in mind that he absorbed many fragments of texts into his own speech by convention and not necessarily to get his reader to react to each little aspect of his text. Some limits have to be put to intertextual reading.

As he does in RG the reader may infer from the text possible presupposed texts on which Mark based his speech. His/her purpose would, however, not be to prove the use of sources or to determine the influence of presupposed texts, but to compare the focused text to texts which could have been uttered in similar contexts as the focused text and how they would have prompted the presupposed readers to react to them.

In conclusion I would like to draw together the agreements and differences between studies based on intertextuality and RG. The main difference seems to be the concept *text*. The two methods of interpretation are incompatible in this respect. Viewing a text as a network of fragments of texts which refer endlessly to other texts because of the absorption of other texts, is something totally different from studying the agreements and differences between a focused text and its sources. Source-influence is not the focus point of intertextuality. As a strategy intertextuality has totally different objectives than RG does. Even though agreements and differences between focused and intertexts are important the emphasis in intertextuality is different. Intertexts form the context of interpretation because they are uttered in contexts similar to the focused text. While RG focuses on the redactor and his activities intertextuality takes the fact that authors produce texts seriously and that readers react to these texts by assigning meaning to them. Again there is a big difference. In intertextuality a text does not have meaning. Meaning is assigned to the text by intertextual reading in accordance with the function of the intertexts of the focused text.

To conclude this essay in this *Festschrift* I would like to say that Professor Van Iersel is one of the critical scholars who allowed himself the pleasure of reading beyond the limits of critical New Testament scholarship. It was a great privilege to know him during all the years in which we developed as critical readers, that is since the days of historico-critical study of the New Testament through structuralism and reception theory. It is an honour to dedicate this essay to Professor Van Iersel. I have learnt many things from him, not the least of which is to be an alert reader.

BIBLIOGRAPHY

Abrams, M.H. 1971. *A Glossary of literary terms*. 3rd ed. New York: Holt.
Abudarham, S. (ed.) 1987a. *Bilingualism and the Bilingual: An Interdisciplinary Approach to Pedagogical and Remedial Issues*. Windsor: Nfer-Nelson.
——— 1987b. Terminology and Typology, in Abudarham (ed.) 1987a, 1–14.
Achtemeier, P.J. (ed.) 1978. *Society of Biblical Literature 1978 Seminar Papers I*. Missoula: Scholars Press.
——— 1973. Peter in the Gospel of Mark, in Brown, Donfried & Reumann 1973, 57–73.
Adler, M.K. 1977. *Collective and Individual Bilingualism: A Sociolinguistic Study*. Hamburg: Buske.
Adler, W. 1978. Enoch in Early Christian Literature, in Achtemeier (ed.) 1978, 271–276.
Aland, K. 1967. *Synopsis Quattuor Euangeliorum*. Stuttgart: Württembergische Bibelanstalt.
Altaner, B. & Stuiber, A. 1966. *Patrologie. Leben Schriften und Lehre der Kirchenväter*. 7. Aufl. Freiburg: Herder.
Anderson, H. 1985. 4 Maccabees (First Century A.D.), in Charlesworth 1985, 531–564.
Anderson, J.A. 1983. Matthew: Gender and Reading. *Semeia* 28, 3–27.
Anderson, J.C. 1985. Double and Triple Stories, The Implied Reader, and Redundancy in Matthew. *Semeia* 37, 71–89.
Attridge, H.W. 1984. Historiography, in Stone 1984, 157–185.
Aune, D.E. 1986. The Apocalypse of John and the problem of genre. *Semeia* 36, 65–96.
——— 1989. *The New Testament in its Literary Environment*. Philadelphia: Westminster.
Baarda, T., Klijn A.F.J. & Van Unnik W.C. (eds.) 1978. *Miscellanea Neotestamentica I*. Leiden: Brill (Supplements to Novum Testamentum 47).
Baarlink, H. 1977. *Anfängliches Evangelium: Ein beitrag zur näheren Bestimmung der theologischen Motive im Markusevangelium*. Kampen: Kok.
Bach, K. & Harnish R.M. 1979. *Linguistic Communication and Speech Acts*. Cambridge: MIT.
Bal, M. (red) 1981. *Literaire genres en hun gebruik*. Muiderberg: Couthino.
——— (red) 1979. *Mensen van papier. Over personages in de literatuur*. Assen: Van Gorcum.
Bar-Efrat, S. 1978. Literary Modes and Methods in the Biblical Narrative in View of 2 Samuel 10–20 and 1 Kings 1–2. *Immanuel* 8, 19–31.
Barnhart, C.L. 1980. What makes a dictionary authoritative, in Zgusta, L. (ed.) 1980, *Theory and methord in lexicography: Western and non-Western perspectives*. Columbia: Hornbeam Press, 33–42.
Barnhart, J.E. 1980. Every Context has a Context, *SJT* 33, 501–513.
Barr, D.L. 1977. *Toward a Definition of the Gospel Genre: A Generic Analysis and Comparison of the Synoptic Gospels and the Socratic Dialogues by Means of Aristotle's Theory of Tragedy*. Ann Arbor: University Microfilms.
Barr, J. 1966. *Old and New in Interpretation: A Study of the Two Testaments*. London: SCM.
——— 1968. Common Sense and Biblical Language. *Bib* 49, 377–387.
——— 1969. *Biblical Words for Time*. London: SCM.
——— 1970. Which Language did Jesus speak? Some Remarks of a Semitist. *BJRL* 50, 9–29.

——— 1985. The question of religious influence. The case of Zoroastrianism, Judaism, and Christianity. *JAAR* 63, 201–235.

Barth, K. 1957. *Die Kirchliche Dogmatik III/l.* 3. Auflage. Zürich: Evangelischer Verlag.

Bartholomaus, W. 1974. *Kleine Predigtlehre.* Koln: Benziger.

Batdorf, I.W. 1984. Interpreting Jesus since Bultmann: Selected Paradigms and their Hermeneutic Matrix, in *Society of Biblical Literature 1984 Seminar Papers.* Chico: Scholars Press, 187–215.

Bauer, W. 1964. Rechtgläubigkeit und Ketzerei im ältesten Christentum. Hrsg. von G. Strecker. Aufl. Tübingen: Mohr (BHT 10).

——— 1967. *Das Leben Jesu im Zeitalter der neutestamentlichen Apokryphen.* Darmstadt: Wissenschaftliche Buchgesellschaft.

Baumgärtel, F. 1966. Das hermeneutische Problem des Alten Testaments, in Westermann 1966. *Probleme alttestamentlicher Hermeneutik. Aufsatze zum Verstehen des Alten Testaments.* München: Kaiser (TB 11).

Beardslee, W.A. 1970. *Literary Criticism of the New Testament.* Philadelphia: Fortress Press.

Beasley-Murray, G.R. 1983. Second thoughts on the composition of Mark 13. *NTS* 29, 414–420.

Beek, M.A. 1968. De opstanding in de apokalyptische literatuur. *Gereformeerd Teologisch Tijdschrift* 68, 15–26.

Beker, J.C. 1980. *Paul the Apostle. The Triumph of God in Life and Thought.* Edinburgh: T. & T. Clark.

Berger, K. & Colpe, C. (Hrsg.) 1987. *Religionsgeschliche Textbuch zum Neuen Testament.* Göttingen: Vandenhoeck & Ruprecht.

Berger, K. 1974. Apostelbrief und apostolische Rede. *ZNW* 65, 190–231.

Bertram, G. 1950. s.v. 'Auferstehung I (des Kultgottes)' in *RAC*.

Best, E. 1977. The Role of the Disciples in Mark. *NTS* 23, 377–401.

——— 1978. Peter in the Gospel according to Mark. *CBQ* 40, S47–58.

Betz, H.D. 1966. Zum Problem des religionsgeschichtlichen Verständnisses der Apokalyptik. *ZThK* 63, 391–409.

——— 1979. *Galatians: A Commentary on Paul's Letters to the Churches in Galatia.* Philadelphia: Fortress Press.

——— 1983. The problem of apocalyptic genre in Greek and Hellenistic literature, in Hellholm 1983, 577–598.

Black, C.C. 1988. 'The Quest of Mark the Rcdactor: Why has it been Pursued, and What has it Taught Us?' *JSNT* 33, 1988, 19–39.

Black, M. 1967. *An Aramaic Approach to the Gospels.* 3rd ed. Oxford: Clarendon.

Blevins, J.L. 1980. The genre of Revelation. *RevExp*, 393–408.

Bloom, H. *et al.* 1979. *Deconstruction and Criticism.* London: Routledge.

Blumenberg, H. 1961. Wirklichkeitsbegriff und Moglichkeit des Romans. in: Jauss H.R. (ed.) 1961. *Nachahmung und Illusion.* Munich: Fink, 9–27.

Böcher, O. 1980. *Die Johannesapokalypse.* Darmstadt: Wissenschaftliche Buchgesellschaft.

Boers, H. 1971. *Theology out of the Ghetto: A New Testament Exegetical Study concerning Religious Exclusivism.* Leiden: Brill.

——— 1989a. *Who was Jesus? The Historical Jesus and the Synoptic Gospels.* San Francisco: Harper & Row.

——— 1989b. Review of *Greek-English lexicon of the New Testament based on semantic domains,* 2 vols. Edited by Johannes P. Louw and Eugene A. Nida. New York: UBS. *JBL* 108, 705–707.

Boomershine, T.E. 1977. *Mark, the storyteller. A rhetorical-critical investigation of Marks passion and resurrection narrative.* Ann Arbor: UMI.

——— 1974. *Mark, the Storyteller: A Rhetorical-Critical Investigation of Mark's Passion and Resurrection Narrative.* New York: Union Theological Seminary.

Booth, W.C. 1961. *The Rhetoric of Fiction.* Chicago: University of Chicago Press.

——— 1983. *The rhetoric of fiction.* 2nd ed. Chicago: University of Chicago Press.

Borg, M.J. 1986. A Temperate Case for a Non-Eschatological Jesus. *Foundations and Facets Forum* 2, 81–102.

Boring, M.E. 1977. *The Paucity of Sayings in Mark: A Hypothesis. Society of Biblical Literature 1977 Seminar Papers*. Missoula: Scholars Press.

———— 1988. The Historical-Critical Method's 'Criteria of Authenticity': The Beatitudes in Q and Thomas as a Test Case. *Semeia* 44, 9–44.

Bosch, D.J. 1979. *Heil vir die Heidene: Die Christelike Sending in Teologiese Perspektief*. Pretoria: N.G. Kerkboekhandel.

———— 1986. Dissension among Christians: How do we handle Contentious Issues? in De Villiers (ed.) 1986, 1–8.

Botha, J. 1989. Die Louw & Nida-woordeboek: 'n Kragtige nuwe hulpmiddel vir die eksegeet, prediker en Bybelvertaler. *In die Skriflig* 23, 1–23.

Botha, J.E. 1989. *A study in Johannine style: History, theory and practice*. D.Th. Thesis, University of South Africa, Pretoria.

Botha, M.E. 1984. *Metaforiese Perspektief en Fokus in die Wetenskap: Die Rol van Geloof, Mite en Taal in Wetenskaplike Teorievorming*. Potchefstroom: Potchefstroom University for Christian Higher Education.

Botha, P.J.J. 1989. Die Dissipels in die Markusevangelie. Unpublished D.D.-thesis. Pretoria: University of Pretoria.

Bowman, J.B. 1955. The Revelation to John: Its dramatic structure and message. *Int* 9, 58–70.

Brandenburger, E. 1984. *Markus 13 und die Apokalyptik*. Göttingen: Vandenhoeck & Ruprecht.

Braun, H. 1969. *Jesus. Der Mann aus Nazareh und seine Zeit*. Berlin: Kreuz.

Braun, W. 1990. Resisting John: Ambivalent Redactor and Defensive Reader of the Fourth Gospel. *SR* 19, 57–91.

Breech, J. 1989. *Jesus and Postmodernism*. Minneapolis: Fortress.

Breytenbach, C. 1984. *Nachfolge und Zukunfterwartung nach Markus. Eine methodenkritische Studie*. Zurich: Theologischer.

———— 1992. *Mnemoneyein*: Das sich-erinnern in der urchristlichen Überlieferung: Die Bethanienepisode (Mk 14:3–9/Jn 12:1–8) als Beispiel, in Denaux, A. (ed.) 1992. *John and the synoptics*. Leuven: Peeters, 548–557.

Bright, J. 1967. *The Authority of the Old Testament*. London: SCM.

Brink, A.P. 1985. Transgressions: A quantum approach to literary deconstruction. *Journal of Literary Studies* 1, 10–26.

———— 1987. *Vertelkunde: 'n Inleiding tot die Lees van Verhalende Tekste*. Pretoria: Academica.

Broich, U. & Pfister M. (eds.) 1985. *Intertextualität: Formen, Funktionen, anglisistische Fallstudien*. Tübingen: Niemeyer.

Brooks, C. & Warren, R.P. 1970. *Modern rhetoric*. 3rd ed. New York: Harcourt.

Brown, R.E. *et al.* (eds.) 1978. *Mary in the New Testament. A collaborative Assessment by Protestant and Roman Catholic Scholars*. Philadelphia: Fortress.

Brown, R.E., Donfried K.P., & Reumann J. (eds.) 1973. *Peter in the New Testament. A collaborative assessment by Protestant and Roman Catholic scholars*. Minneapolis: Augsburg.

———— 1972. *The Gospel according to John (xiii–xxi). Introduction, Translation, and Notes*. London: Chapman (The Anchor Bible).

———— 1977. *The birth of the Messiah. A Commentary on the infancy narratives in Matthew and Luke*. London: Chapman.

Brown, S. 1979. The Matthean apocalypse. *JSNT* 4, 2–27.

———— 1989. Philology, in Epp & MacRae (eds.) 1989, 127–147.

Büchsel, F. 1944. Die Griechische Sprache der Juden in der Zeit der Septuaginta und des Neuen Testaments. *ZAW* 19, 132–149.

Bultmann, R. 1965. *Das Verhältnis der urchristlichen Christusbotschaft zum historischen Jesus*. 4th ed. Heidelberg: Carl Winter.

―――― 1967a. *Exegetica. Aufsatze zur Erforschung des Neuen Testaments.* Ed. by E. Dinkler. Tübingen: Mohr.

―――― 1967b. Ist die Apokalyptik die Mutter der christlichen Theologie? Eine Auseinandersetzung mit Ernst Käsemann, in Bultmann 1967a, 476–82.

―――― 1968. *Das Evangelium des Johannes.* 10th ed. Göttingen: Vandenhoeck & Ruprecht (Meyers Kritisch-Exegetischer Kommentar).

―――― 1970. *Die Geschichte der synoptischen Tradition.* 8. Aufl. Göttingen: Vandenhoeck & Ruprecht.

―――― 1971. *Die synoptischen Tradition. Egänzungsheft.* Bearbeitet von Gerd Theissen und Philip Vielhauer. 4. Aufl. Göttingen: Vandenhoeck & Ruprecht.

Burger, P. 1977. Rezeptionsasthetik Zwischenbalanz (III): Probleme der Rezeptionsforschung. *Poetica* 9, 446–71.

Burnett, F.W. 1981. *The Testament of Jesus-Sophia: A Redaction-Critical Study of the Eschatological Discourse in Matthew.* Lanham: University Press of America.

―――― 1985. Prolegomenon to reading Matthew's eschatological discourse: Redundancy and the education of the reader in Matthew. *Semeia* 31, 91–109.

―――― 1990. Postmodern Biblical Exegesis: The Eve of Historical Criticism. *Semeia* 51, 51–80.

Caird, G.B. 1980. *The Language and Imagery of the Bible.* Philadelphia: Westminster Press.

Cancik, H. (ed.) 1984. *Markus-Philologie: Historische, literargeschichtliche und stilistische Untersuchungen zum zweiten Evangelium.* Tübingen: Mohr.

Carlston, C.E. 1975. *The Parables of the Triple Tradition.* Philadelphia: Fortress Press.

Chatman, S. 1978. *Story and Discourse: Narrative Structure in Fiction and Film.* Ithaca: Cornell University Press.

Cazelles, H. 1970. *TWAT* 1, 481–485.

Charles, R.H. (ed.) 1913. *The Apocrypha and Pseudepigrapha of the Old Testament in English. With Introductions and Critical and Explanatory Notes to the Several Books. II. Pseudepigrapha.* Oxford: Clarendon.

Charlesworth, J.H. (ed.) 1983. *The Old Testament Pseudepigrapha. I. Apocalyptic literaure & testaments.* New York: Doubleday.

―――― 1985. *The Old Testament Pseudepigrapha. II. Expressions of the 'Old Tesament' and legends, Wisdom and philosophical literature, prayers, psalms and odes, fragments of lost Judeo-Hellenistic works.* New York: Doubleday.

Chatman, S. 1978. *Story and discourse. Narrative in fiction and film.* Ithaca: Cornell University Press.

Chikane, F. 1985. The Incarnation in the Life of the People in Southern Africa. *JTSA* 51, 37–50.

Clevenot, M. 1985. *Materialist Approaches to the Bible.* New York: Mary Knoll.

Colish, M.L. 1985. *The Stoic Tradition from Antiquity to the Early Middle Ages.* 2 vols. Leiden: Brill.

Collins paperback English dictionary, The 1986. London: Collins.

Collins, J.J. 1974. Apocalyptic Eschatology as the Transcendence of Death, *CBQ* 36, 21–43.

―――― 1977. Pseudonymity, historical reviews and the genre of John. *CBQ* 39, 329–43.

―――― 1979a. Introduction: Towards the morphology of a genre. *Semeia* 14, 1–20.

―――― 1979b. The Jewish apocalypses. *Semeia* 14, 21–49.

―――― 1984. *The apocalyptic imagination: An introduction to the Jewish matrix of Christianity.* New York: Crossroad.

Conzelmann, H. & Lindemann, A. 1975. *Arbeitsbuch zum Neuen Testament.* Tübingen: Mohr (Uni-Taschenbücher 52).

―――― 1979. χαίρω κτλ., in *TWNT* 9, 50–62.

―――― 1972. Literaturbericht zu den synoptischen Evangelien, *TRu* 37, 220–272.

―――― 1978. *Geschichte des Urchristentums.* Göttingen: Vandenhoeck & Ruprecht.

Coxon, P.W. 1981. A Note on 'Bathsheba' in 2 Samuel 12,1–6. *Bib* 62, 247–50.
Cross, F.M., Lemke W.E. & P.D. Miller (eds.) 1976. *Magnalia Dei: The Mighty Acts of God. Essays on the Bible and Archaeology in Memory of G. Ernest Wright*. Garden City: Doubleday.
Crossan, J.D. 1974. A Basic Bibliography of Parable Research, *Semeia* 1, 236–256.
———— 1976. Parable, Allegory and Paradox. in: Patte, D. (ed.) 1976. *Exploration of the Possibilities Offered by Structuralism for Exegesis*. Pittsburgh: Pickwick, 267–318.
———— 1979. *Finding is the First Act: Trove Folktales and Jesus' Treasure Parable*. Missoula: Scholars Press/Philadelphia: Fortress Press.
———— 1979/80. Paradox Gives Rise to Metaphor: Paul Ricoeur's Hermeneutics and the Parables of Jesus. *BR* 24/25, 20–37.
———— 1980. *Cliffs of Fall: Paradox and Polyvalence in the Parables of Jesus*. New York: Seabury.
———— 1985. *Four other gospels: Shadows on the Contours of Canon*. Minneapolis: Fortress.
———— 1988. *The cross that spoke: The origins of the passion narrative*. San Francisco: Harper & Row.
Cullmann, O. 1959. c.v. 'Petros' in *ThWNT*.
———— 1960. *Petrus. Junger-Apostel-Martyrer. Das historische und das theologische Petrusproblem*. 2. Aufl. Zurich: Zwingli.
———— 1968. Kindheitsevangelien, in: Hennecke, E. 1968. *Neutestamentliche Apokryphen in deutscher Übersetzung*. 4. Aufl. Hrsg. von W. Schneemelcher. Tübingen: Mohr, 272–274.
Culpepper, R.A. 1983. *Anatomy of the Fourth Gospel. A Study in Literary Design*. Philadelphia: Fortress.
Dalman, G. 1965. *Die Worte Jesus: Mit Berücksichtigung des nachkanonischen Jüdischen Schrifttums und der Aramäischen Sprache*. Darmstadt: Wissenschaftliche Buchgesellschaft.
De Beer, C.S. 1985. Representasie en Disseminasie. *Journal of Literary Studies*. 1(3), 1–9.
De Goeij, M. 1984. 'De Geboorte van Maria of Het Protevangelie van Jakobus' in Klijn, A.F.J. (ed.) 1984. *Apokriefen van het Nieuwe Testament. I*. Kok: Kampen, 31–45.
Deissmann, A. 1965. *Light from the Ancient East: The New Testament Illustrated by Recently Discovered Texts of the Graeco-Roman World*. Rev. ed., tr. by R.M. Strachan. Grand Rapids: Baker.
Deist, F.E. & Vorster W.S. (eds.) 1986. *Words from Afar: The Literature of the Old Testament*. Cape Town: Tafelberg.
Delekat, L. 1967. Tendenz und Theologie der David-Salomo-Erzahlung, in: Maas, F. (ed.) 1967. *Das ferne und nahe Wort*. (BZAW 105). Berlin: Topelmann, 26–36.
Delius, W. 1973. *Texte zur Geschichte der Marienverehrung und Marienverkundigung in der Alten Kirche*. 2. Aufl. von H.-U. Rosenbaum. Berlin: De Gruyter.
Delorme, J. (ed.). 1979. *Zeichen und Gleichnisse: Evangelientext und semiotische Forschung*. Dusseldorf: Patmos.
Demandt, A. 1979. Was heisst 'historisch denken'? *GWU* 30, 463–478.
Den Boer, W. 1968. Graeco-Roman Historiography in its Relation to Biblical and Modern Thinking. *HistT* 7, 60–75.
Derrida, J. 1976. *Of grammatology*. Baltimore: John Hopkins University Press.
———— 1979. Living on: Border lines, in: Bloom H. *et al.* 1979. *Deconstruction and criticism*. London: Routledge, 75–176.
De Santos Otero, A. 1975. *Los evangelios apocrifos*. 3. ed. Madrid: Biblioteca de Autores Christianos.
De Strycker, E. 1968. *De Griekse Handschriften van het Protevangelie van Jacobus*. Brussel: Paleis der Academiën.
De Villiers, P.G.R. (ed.) 1986. *Healing in the Name of God*. Pretoria: University of South Africa.

Dibelius, M. 1932, *Jungfrauensohn und Krippenkind. Untersuchungen zur Geburtsgeschichte Jesu im Lukas-Evangelium.* Heidelberg: Carl Winter.
———— 1966. *Die Formgeschichte des Evangeliums.* 5th ed. Tübingen: Mohr.
———— 1971. *Die Formgeschichte des Evangeliums.* 6. Aufl. Tübingen: Mohr.
Dihle, A. 1970. *Studien zur griechischen Biographie.* 2. Aufl. Göttingen: Vandenhoeck & Ruprecht.
———— 1983. Die Evangelien und die biographische Tradition der Antike. *ZThK* 80, 33–49.
Dimant, D. 1983. The Biography of Enoch and the Books of Enoch. *VT* 33, 14–29.
Di Marco, A. 1977. Der Chiasmus in der Bibel, 3. Teil. *LB* 39, 38–57.
Dix, G.H. 1926. The Enochic Pentateuch. *JTS* 27, 29–42.
Dodd, C.H. 1936. *The Parables of the Kingdom.* Welwyn: Nisbet.
———— 1944. *The Apostolic Preaching and its Developments: Three Lectures.* London: Hodder & Stoughton.
———— 1953. *New Testament Studies.* Manchester: The University Press.
———— 1961 [1936, 1955]. *The Parables of the Kingdom.* London: Collins.
Donaldson, T.L. 1985. *Jesus on the mountain: A study in Matthean theology.* Sheffield: University of Sheffield (JSOT Supplement Series).
Dorsch, T.S. 1965. *Classical Literary Criticism.* Harmondsworth: Penguin.
Downing, F.G. 1984. Cynics and Christians *NTS* 30, 584–589.
———— 1988. *Christ and the Cynics: Jesus and Other Radical Preachers in First-Century Tradition.* Sheffield: Sheffield University (JSOT Manuals 4).
Draisma, S. (ed.) 1989. *Intertextuality in biblical writings: Essays in honour of Bas van Iersel.* Kampen: Kok.
Dressler, W. 1973. *Einführung in die Textlinguistik.* 2d ed. Tübingen: Niemeyer.
Du Plessis, I.J. 1980. Realiteit en Interpretasie in die Nuwe Testament. *ThEv* 13, 25–41.
Du Toit, A.B. 1983. s.v. 'Freude' in *TRE* 11, 585–86.
———— (ed.) 1980. *Die Sinoptiese Evangelies en Handelinge: Inleiding en Teologie.* Pretoria, N.G. Kerkboekhandel (Handleiding by die Nuwe Testament 1).
Eagleton, T.T. 1983. *Literary Theory: An Introduction.* Oxford: Basil Blackwell.
Eco, U. 1972. *Einführung in die semiotik.* Uni-Taschenbücher 105. Munich: Fink.
———— 1977. *Zeichen.* Frankfurt: Suhrkamp.
———— 1979. *The Role of the Reader: Explorations in the Semiotics of Texts.* Bloomington: Indiana University Press.
Edwards, D.R. 1988. First Century Urban/Rural Relations in Lower Galilee: Exploring the Archaeological and Literary Evidence, in *Society of Biblical Literature 1988 Seminar Papers.* Atlanta: Scholars Press, 169–182.
Edwards, O.C. 1977. Historical-Critical Method's Failure of Nerve and a Prescription for a Tonic: A Review of Some Recent Literature. *Anglican Theological Review* 59, 115–134.
Edwards, R.A. 1985. *Matthew's Story of Jesus.* Philadelphia: Fortress.
———— 1990. Narrative implications of gar in Matthew. *CBQ* 52, 636–655.
Eliade, M. 1967. *From primitives to Zen. A thematic sourcebook of the histoy of religions.* London: Collins.
———— 1987. *The Encyclopedia of Religion.* 16 vols. New York: Macmillan.
Ellena, D. 1973. Thematische Analyse der Wachstumsgleichnisse, *LB* 23/24, 48–62.
Elliott, J.H. 1988. The fear of the leer: The evil eye from the Bible to Li'I. Abner. *Foundations & Facets Forum* 4, 42–7 1.
Elliott, J.K.E. (ed.) 1976. *Studies in New Testament Language and Text. Essays in Honour of George D. Kilpatick on the Occasion of his sixty-fifth Birthday.* Leiden: Brill (Supplements to Novum Testamentum 44).
———— 1989. Review of Johannes P. Louw and Eugene A. Nida (eds.), *Greek-English lexicon of the New Testament based on semantic domains,* 2 vols. New York: UBS. *NT* 31, 379–380.

Enzenberger, C. 1981. Die Grenze der literarischen Utopie. *Akzente* 1, 44–60.

Epp, E.J. & MacRae G.W. (eds.) 1989. *The New Testament and its Modern Interpreters.* Philadelphia: Fortress.

Fackre, G. 1983. Narrative Theology: An Overview. *Int* 37, 341–364.

Farmer, W.R. 1964. *The Synoptic Problem: A Critical Analysis.* New York: Macmillan.

Federman, R. 1976. 'Imagination as Plagiarism [an unfinished paper . . .]' *NLitHist* 8, 563–578.

Feldman, L.H. 1988. Prophets and Prophecy in Josephus, in *Society of Biblical Literature 1988 seminar papers.* Atlanta: Scholars Press, 425–441.

Fenton, J.C. 1959. Inclusio and Chiasmus in Matthew, in Aland K. and Cross F.J. (eds.) 1959. *Studia Evangelica: Papers presented to the International Congress held at Christ Church, Oxford.* vol 1. Berlin: Akademie-Verlag, 174–179.

Ferguson, E. 1987. *Backgrounds of Early Christianity.* Grand Rapids: Eerdmans.

Finkel, A. 1964. *The Pharisees and the Teacher of Nazareth: A Study on their Background, their Halachic and Midrashic Teachings, the Similarities and Differences.* Leiden: E.J. Brill.

Fitzmyer, J.A. 1970. The Languages of Palestine in the First Century A.D. *CBQ* 32, 501–535.

———— 1973. The Virginal conception of Jesus in the New Testament. *TS* 34, 541–75.

———— 1977. Implications of the New Enoch Literature from Qumran. *TS* 38, 332–45.

Fodor, J.D. 1977. *Semantics: Theories of Meaning in Generative Grammar.* Sussex: Spires.

Fokkema, D.W. & Kunne-Ibsch, E. 1977. *Theories of Literature in the Twentieth Century: Structuralism, Marxism, Aesthetics of Reception, Semiotics.* London: Hurst.

Ford, D. 1979. *The abomination of desolation in Biblical eschatology.* Washington D.C.: University Press of America.

Fortna, R.T. 1972. *The Fourth Gospel and its Predecessor.* Philadelphia, Fortress.

Fowler, A. 1982a. *Kinds of literature: An introduction to the theory of genres and modes.* Oxford: Clarendon Press.

———— 1982b. Using Literary Criticism on the Gospels. *The Christian Century,* May 26, 626–629.

Fowler, R.M. 1981. *Loaves and Fishes: The Function of the Feeding Stories in the Gospel of Mark.* Chico: Scholars Press (SBLDS 54).

———— 1985. Who is 'the Reader' in Reader-Response Criticism? *Semeia* 31:5–23.

Frankemolle, H. 1982. Kommunikatives Handeln in Gleichnissen Jesu: Historisch-kritische und pragmatische Exegese. Eine kritische Sichtung. *NTS* 28, 61–90.

Frazer, J.G. 1963. *The Golden Bough. A Study in Magic and Religion.* London: Macmillan.

Frey, G. 1970. Hermeneutische und hypothetischdeduktive Methode. *Zeitschrift für allgemeine Wissenschaftstheorie* 1, 35–40.

Frey, E. 1974. Rezeption literarischer Stilmittel. *ZLL* 4, 80–94.

Freyne, S. 1980. *Galilee: From Alexander the Great to Hadrian 323 B.C.E. to 135 C.E. A Study of Second Temple Judaism.* Wilmington: Michael Glazier.

Friedrich, G. 1973. Das bisher noch fehlende Begriffslexikon zum Neuen Testament. *NTS* 19, 127–152.

———— 1974. Zur Vorgeschichte des Theologischen Wörterbuchs zum Neuen Testament. *TWNT* 10, 1–52.

Friedrich, J., Pohlmann, W. & Stuhlmacher, P. 1976. Zur historischen Situation und Intention von Röm 13:1–7. *ZTK* 73, 131–166.

Frow, J. 1980. Discourse genres. *Journal of Literary Semantics* 9, 73–81.

Frye, R.M. 1970. Literary Criticism and Gospel Criticism. *Theology Today* 36, 207–219.

Fuchs, W.P. 1979. Was heisst das: 'Bloss zeigen, wie es eigentlich gewesen'? *GWU* 30, 655–667.

Funk, R.W. 1966. *Language, Hermeneutic, and Word of God: The Problem of Language in the New Testament and Contemporary Theology.* New York: Harper & Row.

———— 1985. The Issues of Jesus. *Foundations and Facets* Forum 1, 7–12.

Gadamer, H.-G. 1975. *Wahrheit und Methode.* 4th ed. Tübingen: Mohr.

Gager, J.G. 1975. *Kingdom and community.* Englewood Cliffs: Prentice Hall.

Garland, D.E. 1979. *The Intention of Matthew 23.* Leiden: E.J. Brill. (Supplements to Novum Testamentum 52).

Garsiel, M. 1976. David and Bathsheba. I, II & III. *Dor le Dor* 5, 24–28, 85–90, 134–37.

Geeraerts, D. 1986. *Woordbetekenis: Een overzicht van de lexicale semantiek-* Leuven: Acco.

Genette, G. 1981. Theorieën van literaire genres: Inleiding in de architekst, in Bal 1981, 61–120.

———— 1980. *Narrative Discourse.* Trans. J.E. Lewin. Oxford: Basil Blackwell.

Gerhart, M. 1979. Imagination and history in Ricoeur's interpretation theory. *Philosophy Today* 23, 51–68.

Gewalt, D. 1975. *Das 'Petrusbild' der lukanischen Schriften als Problem einer ganzheitlichen Exegese. LB* 34, 1–22.

Gilbert, M. 1984. Wisdom literature, in Stone 1984, 283–324.

Gilliam, H. 1976. The Dialectics of Realism and Idealism in Modern Historiographic Theory. *HistT* 15, 231–256.

Gnilka, J. 1979. *Das Evangelium nach Markus. (MK 1–8:26).* Zurich: Benziger. (EKKNT II/1)

———— 1979. *Das Evangelium nach Markus. (MK 8:27–16:20).* Zürich: Benzinger. (EKKNT II/2)

Goodman, N. 1965. *Fact, Fiction and Forecast.* 2d ed. Indianapolis: Bobbs-Merrill Co.

———— 1966. *The Structure of Appearance.* 2d ed. Indianapolis: Bobbs-Merrill Co.

———— 1968. *Languages of Art: An Approach to a Theory of Symbols.* Indianapolis: Bobbs-Merrill Co.

———— 1969. *Languages of Art: An Approach to a Theory of Symbols.* London: Oxford University Press.

———— 1978. *Ways of World making.* Sussex: Harvester.

———— 1981. Wege der Referenz. *Zeitschrift für Semiotik* 3, 11–22.

Grayston, K. 1973–1974. The study of Mark xiii. *BJRL* 56 371–387.

Greenspoon, L.J. 1981. The origin of the idea of resurrection, in Halpern, B. & Levenson, J.D. (eds.), 1981. *Traditions in transformation. Turning points in biblical faith.* Winona Lake: Eisenbrauns, 247–321.

Grimm, G. 1975. *Literatur und Lesen.* Stuttgart: Reclam.

———— 1977. Receptionsgeschichte: Pramissen und Moglichkeiten historischer Darstellung, in: Jager, G., Martino A. & Sengle, F. (eds.) 1977. *Internationales Archiv fur Sozialgeschichte der deutschen Literatur,* vol. 2. Tübingen: Niemeyer, 144–186.

Guelich, E. & Raible, W. 1975. Textsorten-Probleme, in Moser, H. (ed.) 1975, *Linguistische Probleme der Textanalyse.* Düsseldorf: Pedagogischer Verlag Schwamm, 144–197.

Guelich, R.A. 1976. The Matthean Beatitudes: 'Entrance-Requirements' or Eschatological Blessings? *JBL* 95, 415–34.

———— 1982. *The Sermon on the Mount: A Foundation for Understanding.* Waco: Word Books.

Guillaumont, A., *et al.* 1959. *The Gospel according to Thomas.* Coptic text established and translated by A. Guillaumont, *et al.* Leiden: E.J. Brill.

Gunkel, H. 1910. *Zum religionsgeschichtlichen Verständnis des Neuen Testaments.* 2. Aufl. Göttingen: Vandenhoeck & Ruprecht.

Gunn, D.M. 1978. *The Story of King David; Genre and Interpretation.* Sheffield: University of Sheffield. (JSOT Supplement Series 6).

Güttgemanns, E. 1970. *Offene Fragen zur Formgeschichte des Evangeliums: Eine methodologische Skizze der Grundlagen-problematik der Form- und Redaktionsgeschichte.* München: Kaiser (*BEvT* 54).

———— 1971a. Die linguistisch-didaktische Methodik der Gleichnisse Jesu, in: E. Güttgemanns (ed.) 1971. *Studia Linguistica Neotestamentica: Gesammelte Aufsatze zur linguistischen Grundlage einer Neutestamentlichen Theologie.* Munich: Kaiser, 99–183. (*BEvT* 60).

———— 1971b. *Offene Fragen zur Formgeschichte des Evangeliums.* 2d ed. Munich: Kaiser (*BEvT* 54).

———— 1978. *Einführung in die Linguistik für Textwissenschaftler.* Bonn: Linguistica Biblica.

———— 1979. Die Funktion der Erzählung im Judentum als Frage an das christliche Verständnis der Evangelien. *LB* 41, 5–61.

———— 1983a. In welchem Sinne ist Lukas 'Historiker'? Die Beziehung von Luk 1,1–4 und Papias zur antiken Rhetorik. *LB* 54, 5–61.

———— 1983b. Die Semiotik des Traums in apokalyptischen Texten am Beispiel von Apokalypse Johannis 1. (Unpublished paper read at the SNTS seminar meeting, Canterbury, 1984).

Haekel, J. 1965. Zur Frage der endzeitlichen 'Auferstehung' in den Religionen der Naturvölker. *Kairos* 7, 237–241.

Haenchen, E. 1951. Matthaus 23. *ZTK* 48, 38–62.

Hahn, F. 1979. Zum Aufbau der Johannesoffenbarung in Böcher, O. *et al.* (eds.) 1979. *Kirche und Bibel: Festgabe für Bischof Eduard Schick.* Paderborn: Schöningh, 145–154.

———— (ed.) 1985. *Zur Formgeshichte des Evangeliums.* Darmstadt: Wissenschaftliche Buchgesellschaft.

———— (ed.) 1985. *Der Erzähler des Evangeliums: Methodische Neuansatze in der Markusforschung.* Stuttgart: Katholisches Bibelwerk.

Hallback, G. 1981. Der anonyme Plan: Analyse von Mk 13:5–27 im Hinblick auf die Relevanz der apokalyptichen Rede fur die Problematik der Ausage. *LB* 49, 38–53.

Halliday, M.A.K., & Hasan, R. 1976. *Cohesion in English.* London: Longman.

Halliday, M.A.K. 1978. *Language as social semiotic: The social interpretation of language and meaning.* London: Arnold.

Halpern, B. & Levenson J.D. (eds.) 1981. *Traditions in Transformation. Turning Points in Biblical Faith.* Winona Lake: Eisenbrauns.

Halver, R. 1964. *Der Mythos im letzten Buch der Bibel: Eine Untersuchung der Bildersprache der Johannes Apokalypse.* Hamburg: Reich.

Hamman, A. 1966. Sitz im Leben des Actes Apocryphes du Nouveau Testament, in: Cross, F.L. (ed.) 1966. *Studia Patristica 8, Part 2: Patres Apostolici; Historica, Liturgica, Ascetica et Monastica.* Berlin: Akademie (TU 93).

Hanson, P.D. 1975. *The Dawn of Apocalyptic.* Philadelphia: Fortress.

———— 1976a. Prolegomena to the Study of Jewish Apocalyptic, in Cross, Lemke & Miller (eds.) 1976, 389–413.

———— 1976b. s.v. 'Apocalypticism' in *IDB* suppl. vol.

Harnisch, W. 1979. Die Metaphor als heuristisches Prinzip. Neuerscheinungen zur Hermeneutik der Gleichnisreden Jesu. *VF* 24, 153–189.

Harrington, D.J. 1987. The Jewishness of Jesus. *BibRev* 3, 32–41.

Hartlich, C. 1978. Historisch-kritische Methode in ihrer Anwendung auf Göttingen Geschehnisaussagen der Hl. Schrift. *ZTK* 75, 467–484.

———— 1980. Is de historisch-kritische methode achterhaald? *Concilium* 16, 7–12.

Hartman, L. 1966. *Prophecy Interpreted, The Formation of some Jewish Apocalyptic Texts and of the Eschatological Discourse Mark 13 par.* Lund: Gleerup.

———— 1979. *Asking for a Meaning. A Study of 1 Enoch 1–5.* Lund: Gleerup (CB. NT 12).

———— 1983. Survey of the Problem of Apocalyptic Genre, in Hellholm (ed.) 1983, 329–343.

Harty, E.R. 1985. Text, context, and intertext. *Journal of Literary Studies* 1, 1–13.

Harvey, V.A. 1967. *The Historian and the Believer: The Morality of Historical Knowledge and Christian Belief*. London: SCM.

Hassan, I. 1987. *The Postmodern Turn: Essays in Postmodern Theory and Culture*. Ohio: Ohio State University Press.

Hauck, F. 1942. μακάριος κτλ. in *TWNT* 4, 365–67.

Hellholm, D. (ed.) 1983. *Apocalypticism in the Mediterranean world and the Near East: Proceedings of the international colloquium on apocalypticism, Uppsala, August 12–17, 1979*. Tübingen: Mohr.

——— 1980. *Das Visionenbuch des Hermas als Apokalypse: Formgeschichtliche und texttheoretische Studien zu einer literarischen Gattung. 1 Methodologische Voruberlegungen und makrostrukturelle Textanalyse*. Lund: Gleerup.

——— 1986. The problem of apocalyptic genre and the Apocalypse of John. *Semeia* 36, 13–64.

Helm, R. 1956. *Der antike Roman*. 2. Aufl. Göttingen: Vandenhoeck & Ruprecht.

Hempfer, K.W. 1973. *Gattungstheorie. Information und Synthese*. München: Fink (UTB 133).

Hengel, M. 1973. Historische Methoden und theologische Auslegung des Neuen Testaments. *Kerygma und Dogma* 19, 85–90.

——— 1979. *Zur urchristlichen Geschichtsschreibung*. Stuttgart: Calwer.

——— 1981. *The Charismatic Leader and his Followers*. Edinburgh: T. & T. Clark.

——— 1984. Entstehungszeit und Situation des Markusevangeliums, in Cancik (ed.) 1984, 1–45.

Hernadi, P. 1976. Literary Theory: A Compass for Critics. *Critical Inquiry* 3, 369–86.

Hesse, F. 1966. *Das Alte Testament als Buch der Kirche*. Gütersloh: Gütersloher Verlagshaus.

Hill, D. 1967. *Greek Words and Hebrew Meanings: Studies in the Semantics of Soteriological Terms*. Cambridge: Cambridge University Press.

Hoffmann, P. (ed.) 1988. *Zur neutestamentlichen Überlieferung von der Auferstehung Jesu*. Darmstadt: Wissenschaftliche Buchgesellschaft.

Hohendahl, P.U. 1974. Einleitung: Zur Lage der Rezeptionsforschung. *ZLL* 4, 7–11.

Hollenbach, P. 1989. The Historical Jesus Question in North America Today. *BTB* 19, 11–22.

Holub, R.C. 1984. *Reception Theory: A Critical Introduction*. London: Methuen.

Hooker, M.D. 1982. Trial and tribulation in Mark xiii. *BJRL* 65, 78–99.

Horbury, W. 1982. The benediction of the minim and early Jewish-Christian controversy. *JTS* 33, 19–61.

Horsley, R. 1988. Bandits, Messiahs, and Longshoremen: Popular Unrest in Galilee around the Time of Jesus, in *Society of Biblical Literature 1988 seminar papers*. Atlanta: Scholars, 182–199.

Howell, D.B. 1990. *Matthew's inclusive story: A study in the narrative rhetoric of the first Gospel*. Sheffield: University of Sheffield (JSOT Supplement Series).

Huffman, N.A. 1978. Atypical Features in the Parables of Jesus. *JBL* 97, 207–20.

Humphrey, H.M. 1989. Jesus as Wisdom in Mark. *BTB* 19, 48–53.

Humphreys, R.S. 1980. The Historian, his Documents, and the Elementary Modes of Historical Thought. *HistT* 19, 1–20.

Iser, W. 1974. *The implied reader. Patterns of communication in prose fiction from Bunyan to Beckett*. Baltimore Johns Hopkins University Press.

——— 1976. *Der Akt des Lesens*. Munich: Fink.

——— 1978. *The act of reading: A theory of aesthetic response*. London: Routledge & Kegan.

——— 1980. Interview with R.E. Keunzli. *Diacritics* (June), 57–74.

Jakobson, R. 1960. Linguistics and Poetics. in: Sebeok T.A. (ed.) 1960. *Style in Language*. Cambridge, MA: M.I.T. 350–377.

Japp, U. 1977. *Hermeneutik: der theoretische Diskurs, die Literatur und die Konstruktion ihres Zusammenhanges in den philologischen Wissenschaften*. Munich: Fink.

Jauss, H.R. 1969. Paradigmawechsel in der Literaturwissenschaft. *Linguistische Berichte* 3, 44–56.

——— 1974a. Literary History as a Challenge to Literary Theory. in: Cohen, R. (ed.) 1974. *New Directions in Literary History*. London: John Hopkins University Press.

——— 1974b. *Literaturgeschichte als Provokation*. 5th ed. Frankfurt: Suhrkamp, 11–41.

——— 1975. Der Leser als Instanz einer neuen Geschichte der Literatur. *Poetica* 7, 325–44.

Jellicoe, S. 1969. Septuagint Studies in the Current Century. *JBL* 88, 191–199.

Jeremias, J. 1961. Der gegenwärtige Stand der Debatte um das Problem des historischen Jesus, in Ristow & Matthiae (eds.) 1961, 12–25.

——— 1970. *Die Gleichnisse Jesu*. 8. Aufl. Göttingen: Vandenhoeck & Ruprecht.

Jonker, W.D. 1977. *Christus, die Middelaar: Wegwysers in die Dogmatiek*. Pretoria: N.G. Kerkboekhandel.

Jülicher, A. 1963. *Die Gleichnisreden Jesu*. Darmstadt: Wisenschaftliche Buchgesellschaft.

Jungel, E. 1962. *Paulus und Jesus*. Tubingen: Mohr.

——— 1969. Die Welt als Moglichkeit und Wirklichkeit: Zum ontologischen Ansatz der Rechtfertigungslehre. *EvT* 29, 417–42.

——— 1978. *Gott als Geheimnis der Welt: Zur Begrundung der Theologie des Gekreuzigten im Streit zwischen Theismus und Atheismus*. 3d ed Tubingen: Mohr.

Junker, D. & Reisinger, P. 1974. Was kann Objektivität in der Geschichtswissenschaft heissen, und wie ist sie möglich? in Schneider T. (ed.) 1974. *Methodenprobleme der Geschichtswissenschaft*. München: Oldenburg, 1–46.

Kähler, C. 1974. Studien zur Fonn- und Traditionsgeschichte der biblischen Makarismen. Diss. Jena: Friedrich-Schiller-Universität.

Kallas, J. 1967. The Apocalypse—an apocalyptic book? *JBL* 86, 69–80.

Käsemann, E. 1954. Das Problem des historischen Jesus. *ZTK* 51, 125–153.

——— 1954–55. Sätze Heiligen Rechtes im Neuen Testament, in *NTS* 1, 248–260.

——— 1964a. *Exegetische Versuche und Besinnungen II*. Göttingen: Vandenhoeck & Ruprecht.

——— 1964b. Die Anfänge christlicher Theologie, in Käsemann 1964a, 82–104.

Kaziersci, C.R. 1979. *Jesus, the Son of God: A Study of the Markan Tradition and its Redaction by the Evangelist*. Würzburg: Echter (Forschung zur Bibel 33).

Kelber, W.H. 1974. *The Kingdom in Mark: A New Place and a New Time*. Philadelphia: Fortress Press.

——— 1979. Markus und die mündliche Tradition, *LB* 4, 5–58.

——— 1983. *The Oral and the Written Gospel. The Hermeneutics of Speaking and Writing in the Synoptic Tradition, Mark, Paul and Q*. Philadelphia: Fortress.

Kempson, R.M. 1977. *Semantic Theory*. Cambridge: Cambridge University Press

Kermode, F. 1979. *The Genesis of Secrecy*. Cambridge, MA: Harvard University Press.

Kingsbury, J.D. 1969. *The Parables of Jesus in Matthew 13. A Study In Redactioncriticism*. Richmond: John Knox.

——— 1972. The Parables of Jesus in Current Research. *Dialog* 11, 101–7.

——— 1976. *Matthew: Structure, Christology, Kingdom*. Philadelphia: Fortress.

——— 1981. The 'Divine Man' as the Key to Mark's Christology: The end of an era? *Int* 35, 243–57.

——— 1986. *Matthew as Story*. Fortress: Philadelphia.

Kissinger, W.S. 1979. *The Parables of Jesus: A History of Intrepretation and Bibliography*. Metuchen: Scarecrow (ATLA Bibliography Series 4).

Kjaurgaard, M.S. 1986. *Metaphor and Parable: A Systematic Analysis of the Specific Structure and Cognitive Function of the Synoptic Similes and Parables Metaphors*. Leiden: Brill.

Klein, G. 1961. Die Verleugnung des Petrus. Eine traditionsgeschichtliche Untersuchung. *ZTK* 58, 285–328.

Klijn, A.F.J. 1978. From Creation to Noah in the Second Dream-Vision of the Ethiopic Henoch, in Baarda, Klijn & Van Unnik (eds.) 1978, 147–59.

——— 1983. 2 (Syriac Apocalypse of) Baruch (Early Second Century A.D.), in Charlesworth 1983, 615–652.

Kloppenborg, J.S. 1979. Didache 16:6–8 and special Matthean tradition. *ZNW* 70, 54–67.

——— 1984. *The Literary Genre of the Synoptic Sayings Source.* (Ph.D. Diss., University of St Michael's College) Ottawa: National Library of Canada.

——— 1986. Blessing and Marginality: the 'Persecution Beatitude' in Q, Thomas and Early Christianity, *Foundations and Facets Forum* 2, 35–56.

——— 1987. *The Formation of Q: Trajectories in Ancient Wisdom Collections.* Philadelphia: Fortress.

Knibb, M.A. 1978. *The Ethiopic Book of Enoch. A New Edition in the Light of the Aramaic Dead Sea Fragments, II: Introduction, Translation and Commentary.* Oxford: Clarendon.

——— 1979. The Date of the Parables of Enoch: A Critical Review. *NTS* 25, 345–359.

Koester, H. & Robinson, J.M. 1971. *Entwicklungslinien durch die Welt des frühen Christentums.* Tübingen: Mohr.

——— 1971a. *Trajectories through early Christianity.* Philadelphia: Fortress.

Koester, H. 1971. Ein Jesus und vier unsprüngliche Evangeliengattungen, in Koester & Robinson 1971, 147–190.

——— 1971a. One Jesus and Four Primitive Gospels, in Koester & Robinson 1971a, 158–204.

——— 1980. Apocryphal and Canonical Gospels. *HTR* 73, 105–30.

——— 1980. *Einführung in das Neue Testament.* Berlin: De Gruyter.

——— 1984. Überlieferung und Geschichte der frühchristlichen Evangelienliteratur', (Principat: Religion vorkonstantinisches Christentum: Leben und Umwelt Jesu; Neues Testament, Forts. [Kanonische Schriften und Apokryphen]) in Haase W. 1984. *Aufstieg und Niedergang der Römischen Welt* 25,2. Berlin: De Gruyter, 1463–1542.

——— 1990. *Ancient Christian Gospels: Their history and development.* London: SCM.

Köhler, E. 1977. Gattungssystem und Gesellschaftssystem. *Romantische Zeitschrift für Literaturgeschichte* 1, 7–22.

Köhler, W.-D. 1987. *Die Rezeption des Matthäusevangeliums in der Zeit vor Irenäus.* Tübingen: Mohr.

König, A. 1980. *Jesus die Laaste.* Pretoria: N.G. Kerkboekhandel.

Koopman-Thurlings, M. 1984/85. Tekstinterpretatie en Open Plek: Over de Bruik-baarheid van Isers 'Leerstellen'. *Spektator: Tijdschrift voor Nederlandsetiek* 14(6):398–411.

Kosseleck, R. & Stempel, W.-D. (eds.) 1973. *Geschichte: Ereignis und Erzählung.* München: Fink.

Kosseleck, R. 1973. Ereignis und Struktur. in: Koselleclc, & Stempel (eds.) 1973, 560–571.

Krentz, E. 1975. *The Historical-Critical Method.* London: SPCK.

Kristeva, J. 1969. Σημειωτικὴ. *Recherches pour une sémanalyse.* Paris: Editions du Seuil.

Kuhn, H.-W. 1971. *Ältere Sammlungen im Markusevangelium.* Gottingen: Vandenhoeck & Ruprecht (SUNT 8.8).

Kümmel, W.G. 1965. *Einleitung in das Neue Testament.* 14th ed. Heidelberg: Quelle und Meyer.

——— 1970. *Das Neue Testament: Geschichte der Erforschung seiner Probleme.* 2. Aufl. Freiburg: Karl Alber.

——— 1982. Ein Jahrhundert Erforschung der Eschatologie des Neuen Testaments. *TLZ* 107, 81–96.

——— 1985. Das Urchristentum. II. Arbeiten su Spezialproblemen. *TRu* 50, 132–164.

Kurz, W.S. 1987. Narrative Approaches to Luke-Acts. *Bib* 68, 195–220.

Labuschagne, C.J. 1973. De Verhouding tussen het Oude en het Nieuwe Testament. *RW* 15, 118–132.

Lafargue, M. 1988. Are texts determinate? Derrida, Barth, and the role of the bib-lical scholar. *HTR* 3, 341–357.

Lambrecht, J. 1967. *Die Redaktion der Markus Apokalypse. Literarische und Strukturuntersuchung.* Rom: Bibelinstitut.

——— 1969. *Marcus Interpretator: Stijl en Boodschap in MC. 3,20–24,34.* Brugge: Desclee de Brouwer.

Lampe, P. 1987. *Die stadrömischen Christen in den ersten beiden Jahrhunderten.* Tübingen: Mohr (WUNT 2,18).

Lapide, P. 1983. *The Resurrection of Jesus. A Jewish Perspective.* Minneapolis: Augsburg.

Lategan, B.C. & W.S. Vorster 1985. *Text and Reality: Aspects of Reference in Biblical Texts.* Philadelphia: Fortress.

Lategan, B.C. 1973. Tradition and Interpretation: Two Methodological Remarks. *Neotestamentica* 7, 95–103.

——— 1977. Structural Interrelations in Matthew 11–12. *Neotestamentica* 11, 115–29.

——— 1978a. Het Motief van de Dienst in Galaten 1 en 2. in: Grosheide, H.H. *et al.* (eds.). 1978. *De Knechtsgestalte van Christus.* Kampen: Kok, 76–84.

——— 1978b. Structural Analysis as Basis for Further Exegetical Procedures in: Achtemeier, P.J. (ed.) 1978. *Society of Biblical Literature 1978 Seminar Papers I.* Missoula: Scholars Press, 341–360.

——— 1979. The Historian and the Believer, in Vorser, W.S. (ed.) 1979. *Scripture and the use of Scripture.* Pretoria: Unisa, 113–134.

——— 1984. Current issues in the hermeneutical debate. *Neotestamentica* 18, 1–17.

——— 1988. Why so Few Converts to New Paradigms in Theology? in Mouton, Van Aarde & Vorster (eds.) 1988, 65–78.

——— 1988b. Louw & Nida: 'n Nuwe begrip in Griekse woordeboeke vir die Nuwe Tetsament. *Scriptura* 25, 48–5 1.

——— 1994. Revisiting *Text and Reality. Neotestamentica* 28 (3), 121–136 (Special Edition).

Lausberg, H. 1960. *Handbuch der literarischen Rhetorik. Grundlegung der Literaturwissenschaft.* München: Max Hueber.

Leipoldt, J. 1923. *Sterbende und auferstehende Götter. Ein Beitrag zum Streite um Arthur Drew's Christusmythe.* Leipzig: Dichtertsche Verlagsbuchhandlung.

——— 1988. Zu den Auferstehungsgeschichten, in Hoffmann 1988, 284–296.

Leitch, V.B. 1983. *Deconstructive Criticism: An Advanced Introduction.* New York: Columbia University Press.

Le Roux, J.H. 1994. A brief description of an intellectual journey: On Willem Vorster's quest for understanding. *Neotestamentica* 28 (3), 1–32 (Special Edition).

Lindars, B. 1972. *The Gospel of John.* London: Oliphants (New Century Bible).

Link, J. 1979. *Literaturwissenschaftliche Grundbegriffe.* 2d ed. Munich: Fink.

Linnemann, E. 1961. *Gleichnisse Jesu: Einfuhrung und Auslegung.* Göttingen: Vandenhoeck & Ruprecht.

Lohr, C.H. 1961. Oral Technigues in the Gospel of Matthew, *CBQ* 23, 403–435.

Louw, J.P. & Nida, E.A. (eds.) 1988. *Greek-English Lexicon of the New Testament Based on Semantic Domains.* 2 vols. New York: United Bible Societies.

Louw, J.P. 1979. The Greek New Testament wordbook. *BiTr* 30, 108–117.

——— (ed.) 1985. *Lexicography and translation: With special reference to Bible translation.* Cape Town: Bible Society of South Africa.

——— 1985a. The present state of New Testament lexicography, in Louw 1985: 97–117.

——— 1985b. What dictionaries are like, in Louw 1985: 53–81.

——— (ed.) 1986. *Sociolinguistics and communication.* London: United Bible Societies.

Lüdemann, G. & Schröder 1987. *Die Religionsgeschichtliche Schule: Eine Dokumentation.* Göttingen: Vandenhoeck & Ruprecht.

Lührmann, D. 1977. Biographie des Gerechten als Evangelium. Vorstellungen zu einem Markus-Kommentar. *WuDNF* 14, 25–50.

——— 1984. *Auslegung des Neuen Testaments.* Zürich: Theologischer Verlag.

Luz, U. 1971. Die Junger im Matthausezangelium. *ZNW* 62, 377–414.

——— 1980. Markusforschung in der Sackgasse? *TLZ* 9, 641–655.

——— 1985. *Das Evangelium nach Matthaus (Mt 1–7)*. Neukirchen: Benzinger Verlag. (EKKNT I/1).

Lyons, J. 1977. *Semantics I*. Cambridge: Cambridge University Press.

——— 1981. *Language, Meaning and Context*. London: Fontana.

Maahs, C.H. 1965. *The Makarisms in the New Testament: A Comparative Religions and Form Critical Investigation*. Diss. Tübingen: Eberhard-Karls-Universität.

Maartens, P.J. 1980. Mark 2: 18–22: An Exercise in Theoretically-Founded Exegesis. *Scriptura* 2, 1–54.

Mack, B.L. 1987. The kingdom sayings in Mark. *Foundations & Facets Forum* 3, 3–47.

——— 1988a. The Kingdom That Didn't Come: A Social History of the Q Tradents, *Society of Biblical Literature 1988 Seminar Papers I*. Atlanta: Scholars.

——— 1988b. *A Myth of Innocence: Mark and Christian Origins*. Philadelphia: Fortress.

Macquarrie, J. 1967. *God-Talk: An Examination of the Language and Logic of Theology*. London: SCM.

Magness, J.L. 1986. *Sense and Absence: Structure and Suspension in the Ending of Mark's Gospel*. Atlanta: Scholars Press.

Malbon, E.S. 1983. Fallible Followers: Women and Men in the Gospel of Mark. *Semeia* 28, 29–48.

Malina, B.J. 1986. *Christian Origins and Cultural Anthropology: Practical Models for Biblical Interpretation*. Atlanta: John Knox.

——— 1987. Wealth and Poverty in the New Testament and its World. *Int* 41, 354–367.

Maloney, E.C. 1981. *Semitic Interference in Marcan Syntax*. Chico: Scholars Press.

Maren-Griesbach, M. 1977. *Methoden der Literaturwissenschaft*. 6. Aufl. München: Francke (Uni-Taschenbücher 121).

Marin, L. 1971. Essai d' ánalyse structurale d'uan reacit-parabole: Matthieu 13,1–23, *Etudes Théologiques et Religieuses*, 35–74.

Marshall, I.H. (ed.) 1977. *New Testament Interpretation: Essays on Principles and Methods*. Exeter: Paternoster.

Martin, J.P. 'Toward a Post-critical Paradigm' *NTS* 33, 370–385.

Martin, R.A. 1987. *Syntax Criticism of the Synoptic Gospels*. Lewiston: Edwin Mellen.

Marxsen, W. 1956. Bemerkungen zur 'Form' der sogenannten synoptischen Evangelien, *TLZ* 81, 345–348.

——— 1959. *Der Evangelist Markus: Studien zur Redaktionsgeschichte des Evangeliums*. Göttingen: Vandenhoeck & Ruprecht.

——— 1964. *Einleitung in das Neue Testament: Eine Einführung in ihre Probleme*. Gerd Mohn: Gütersloher Verlagshaus.

Mayer, R. 1965. Der Aufersehungsglaube in der Iranischen Religion. *Kairos* 1965, 194–207.

McCullagh, C.B. 1984. *Justifying Historical Descriptions*. Cambridge: Cambridge University Press.

McFague, S. 1983. *Metaphorical Theology: Models of God in Religious Language*. London: SCM.

McGovern, A.F. 1989. *Liberation Theology and its Critics: Toward an Assessment*. Maryknoll: Orbis.

McKim, D. (ed.) 1986. *A Guide to Contemporary Hermeneutics: Major Trends in Biblical Interpretation*. Grand Rapids: Eerdmans.

McKnight, E.V. 1978. *Meaning in Texts*. Philadelphia: Fortress Press.

McNeile, A.H. 1957. *The Gospel according to St. Matthew: The Greek text with introduction, notes, and indices*. New York: Macmillan.

Meeks, W.A. 1983. *The First Urban Christians: The Social World of the Apostle Paul*. New Haven: Yale University Press.

Meijer, J.A. 1976. *Oecumenische Taal: Beschouwingen over het Nieuw-Testamentisch Grieks in de Laaste Twee Eeuwen*. Groningen: De Vuurbaak.

Merklein, H. 1984. *Jesu Botschaft von der Gottes Herrschaft: Eine Skize*. 2nd ed. Stuttgart: Verlag Katholisches Bibelwerk.
Metzger, B.M. 1983. The Fourth Book of Ezra (First Century A.D.), in Charlesworth 1983, 517–560.
Michel, O. 1940. Zum Sprachgebrauch von ἐπαισχύνομαι in Röm. 1,16, in Paulus 1940, 36–53.
Milik, J.T. & Black, M. 1976. *Enoch, The Book of Enoch: Aramaic Fragments of Qumran Cave 4*. Oxford: Oxford University Press.
Miller, D. & Miller, P. 1990. *The Gospel of Mark as midrash: On earlier Jewish and New Testament literature*. Lewiston: Mellen.
Miller, M.P. 1971. Targum, Midrash and the Use of the Old Testament in the New Testament. *JSJ* 2, 29–82.
Miller, O. 1985. Intertextual Identity, in Valdcas & Miller (eds.) 1985, 19–40.
Minear, P.S. 1983. The Original Functions of John 21. *JBL* 102, 85–98.
Moore, S.D. 1989. *Literary criticism and the Gospels: The theoretical challenge*. New Haven: Yale University Press.
Moule, Charles F.D.L. 1965. *The Gospel According to Mark*. Cambridge: Cambridge University Press.
Mouton, J., Van Aarde, A.G. & Vorster, W.S. (eds.) 1988. *Paradigms and Progress in Theology*. Pretoria: Human Sciences Research Council.
Mouton, J. & Joubert, D. (eds.) 1990. *Knowledge and Method in the Human Sciences*. Pretoria: Human Sciences Research Council.
Mulder, M.J. (ed.) 1988. *Mikra. Section 2, v. 1: Text, Translation, Reading and Interpretation of the Hebrew Bible in Ancient Judaism and Early Christianity*. Assen: Van Gorcum (CRINT).
Müller, K. 1985. Die Religionsgeschichtliche Methode. Erwägungen zu ihren Verständnis und zur Praxis ihrer Vorzüge an neutestamentlichen Texten. *BZ* 29, 161–192.
Müller, U.B. 1983. Literarische und formgeschichtliche Bestimmung der Apokalypse des Johannes als einem Zeugnis fruhchristlicher Apokalyptik, in Hellholm 1983, 599–620.
Murphy, R.E. 1985. s.v. 'Wisdom' in *HBD*.
Mussies, G. 1971. *The Morphology of Koine Greek as Used in the Apocalypse of St. John: A Study in Bilingualism*. Leiden: Brill (Supplements to Novum Testamentum 27).
——— 1972. *Dio Chrysostom and the New Testament*. Leiden: Brill.
——— 1976. Greek in Palestine and the Diaspora, in Safrai & Stern (eds.) 1976, 1040–1064.
Nations, A.L. 1983. Historical Criticism and the Current Methodological Crisis. *SJT* 36, 59–71.
Naumann, M. (ed.) 1975. *Gesellschaft-Literatur-Lesen*. Berlin: Aufbau-Verlag.
——— 1977. Das Dilemma der 'Rezeptionsasthetik.' *Weimarer Beiträge* 23, 5–21.
Neirynck, F. 1990. John 21. *NTS* 36, 321–336.
——— 1991. Recent developments in the study of Q, in Neirynck, F. (ed.) 1991. *Evangelica II: 1982–1991: Collected essays*. Leuven: Peters, 409–464.
——— et al. 1992 (compls.). *The Gospel of Mark: Accumulative bibliography 1950–1990*. Leuven: Peters.
Nickelsburg, G.W.E. (Jr.) 1972. *Resurrection, immortality, and eternal life in intertestamental Judaism*. Cambridge: Harvard.
——— 1977a. Apocalyptic Message of 1 Enoch 92–105. *CBQ* 39, 309–328.
——— 1977b. Apocalyptic Myth in 1 Enoch 6–11. *JBL* 96, 383–405.
——— 1979. Riches, The Rich and God's Judgement in 1 Enoch 92–105 and the Gospel according to Luke. *NTS* 25, 324–344.
——— 1981a. Enoch, Levi and Peter: Recipients of revelation in upper Galilee. *JBL* 100, 575–600.
——— 1981b. The Books of Enoch in recent research. *RSR* 7, 210–217.
Nicolson, R. 1990. *A Black future? Jesus and Salvation in South Africa*. London: SCM.

Nida, E.A., *et al.* 1983. *Style and Discourse: With Special Reference to the Text of the Greek New Testament.* Cape Town: Bible Society of SA.

Nida, E.A. 1981. *Signs, Sense, Translation.* Pretoria: University of Pretoria.

Nipperdey, T. 1979. Kann Geschichte objektiv sein? *GWU* 30, 329–342.

Norden, E. 1958. *Die Antike Kunstprosa: Vom VI. Jahrhundert v. Chr. bis in der Zeit der Renaissance.* 5th ed. Stuttgart: Teubner.

Oepke, A. 1950. s.v. 'Auferstehung II (des Menschen)' in *RAC*.

Olsen, L. 1986. Zombies and academics: The reader's role in fantasy. *Poetics* 15, 279–285.

Orchard, B. & Riley, H. 1987. *The Order of the Synoptics: Why Three Synoptic Gospels?* Macon: Mercer University Press.

Osborn, E. 1981. *The beginning of Christian philosophy.* Cambridge: The University Press.

Osborne, B.A.E. 1973. Peter. Stumbling-block and Satan. *NT* 15, 187–90.

Ossege, M. 1975. Einige Aspekte zur Gliederung des neutestamentlichen Wortschatzes (am Beispiel von δικαιοσύνη bei Matthaus). *LB* 34, 37–101.

Overbeck, F. 1954 [1882]. *Über die Aufgabe der patristischen Literatur.* Darmstadt: Wissenschaftliche Buchgesellschaft.

Overman, J.A. 1988. Who were the First Urban Christians? Urbanization in the First Century, in *Society of Biblical Literature 1988 seminar papers.* Atlanta: Scholars Press, 160–168.

Palmer, F. 1943. *The drama of the apocalypse.* New York: Macmillan.

Palmer, R.E. 1969. *Hermeneutics.* Evanston: Northwestern University Press.

Patte, D. 1976. *What Is Structural Exegesis?* Philadelphia: Fortress.

Patte, D. (ed.) 1976. *Semiology and Parables: Exploration of the Possibilities Offered by Structuralism for Exegesis.* Pittsburgh: Pickwick.

———— 1980. One Text: Several Structures. *Semeia* 18, 3–22.

Paulsen, H. 1978. Traditionsgeschichtliche Methode und religionsgeschichtliche Schule. *ZThK* 75, 20–55.

Paulus, R. (ed.) 1940. *Glaube und Ethos. Festschrift für G. Wehrung.* Stuttgart: Kohlhammer.

Peabody, D.B. 1987. *Mark as composer.* Macon: Mercer.

Perdue, L.G. 1986. The Wisdom Sayings of Jesus. *Foundation and Facets Forum* 2, 3–35.

Perdue, L.G. 1981. Paraenesis and the Epistle of James. *ZNW* 72, 241–256.

Perrin, N. 1963. *The Kingdom of God in the Teaching of God.* London: SCM.

———— 1967. *Rediscovering the Teaching of Jesus.* London: SCM.

———— 1970. *What is Redaction Criticism?* Philadelphia: Fortress.

———— 1971. The Modern Interpretation of the Parables of Jesus and the Problem of Hermeneutics. *Int* 25, 131–48.

———— 1972. The Evangelist as Author: Reflections on Method in the Study and Interpretation of the Synoptic Gospels and Acts. *BR* 17, 5–13.

———— 1976. *Jesus and the Language of the Kingdom: Symbol and metaphor in New Testament Interpretation.* London: SCM.

Pesch, R. 1976. *Das Markusevangelium.* Freiburg: Herder. (HTKNT II/I).

———— 1968. *Naherwartungen: Tradition und Redaktion in Mk. 13.* Düsseldorf: Patmos.

———— 1969. *Der reiche Fischfang. Lk 5,1–11/Jo 21,1–14.* Düsseldorf: Patmos.

———— 1980. *Simon-Petrus. Geschichtliche Bedeutung des ersten Jungers Jesu Christi.* Stuttgart: Hiersemann.

Peters, C.H. 1977. How Important Are Historical Events for Religion? Reflection on G.E. Lessing's Philosophy of Religion. *CuTM* 4, 229–234.

Petersen, N.R. 1978a. *Literary criticism for New Testament Critics.* Philadelphia: Fortress Press.

———— 1978b. 'Point of View' in Mark's Narrative. *Semeia* 12, pp. 97–121.

—— 1980. The composition of Mark 4:1–8:26. *HTR* 73, 185–217.

—— 1980. When is the End not the End? Literary Reflections on the Ending of Mark's narrative. *Int* 34, 151–166.

—— 1984. The Reader in the Gospel. *Neotestamentica* 18, 38–51.

Pfister, M. 1985. Konzepte der Intertextualiät, in Broich & Pfister (eds.) 1985, 1–30.

Phillips, G.A. 1990. Exegesis as critical praxis: Reclaiming history and text from a postmodern perspective. *Semeia* 51, 7–49.

—— 1991. Sign/text/différence. The contribution of intertextual theory to biblical criticism, in Plett, H.F. (ed.) 1991. *Intertextuality*. Berlin: De Gruyter.

Pike, K.L. 1966. Etic and emic standpoints for the description of behavior, in Smith, A.G. (ed.), *Communication and culture: Readings in the codes of human interaction*. New York: Holt, Rinehart and Winston, 152–163.

Plümacher, E. 1972. *Lukas als hellenistischer Schriftsteller: Studien zur Apostelgeschichte*. Göttingen: Vandenhoeck & Ruprecht.

Polanyi, L. 1981a. Telling the same story twice. *Text* 1, 313–36.

—— 1981b. What stories can tell us about their teller's world. *Poetics Today* 2, 97–112.

Porter, S.E. 1990. Why hasn't Reader-Response Criticism caught on in New Testament Studies? *Journal of Literature and Theology* 4, 278–292.

Pötscher, W. 1965. Die Auferstehung in der klassischen Antike. *Kairos* 7, 208–215.

Praeder, S. 1981. Luke-Acts and the Ancient Novel. Unpublished paper presented at 1981-SBL meeting.

Price, G. 1982. *Narratology: The Form and Function of Narrative*. Berlin: Mouton.

Pryke, E.J. 1978. *Redactional Style in the Markan Gospel*. Cambridge: Cambridge University Press (SNTSMS 33).

Quasten, J. 1950. *Patrology* I. Utrecht: Spectrum.

Rabinowitz, P.J. 1980 What's Hecuba to Us? The Audience's Experience of Literary Borrowing. in: Suleiman & Crosman (eds.) 1980, 241–263.

Reese, J.M. 1988. Review of Johannes P. Louw and Eugene A. Nida (eds.), *Greek-English lexicon of the New Testament based on semantic domains*, 2 vols. New York: UBS. *BTB* 18, 150–151.

Reim, G. 1976. Johannes 21: Ein Anhang? in Elliott (ed.) 1976, 330–337.

Reiser, M. 1984. *Syntax und Stil des Markusevangeliums im Licht der hellenistischen Volksliteratur*. Tübingen: Mohr (WUNT 2/11).

Reploh, K.-G. 1969. *Markus-Lehrer der Gemeinde. Eine redaktionsgeschichtliche Studie zu den Jüngerperikopen des Markus-Evangeliums*. Stuttgart: Katholisches Bibelwerk (SBM 9).

Resseguie, J.L. 1984. Reader-Response Criticism and the Synoptic Gospels. *JAAR* 52, 307–324.

Rhoads, D. & Michie, D. 1982. *Mark as Story: An Introduction to the Narrative of a Gospel*. Philadelphia: Fortress.

Richter, W. 1971. *Exegese als Literaturwissenschaft. Entwurf einer alttestamentlichen Literaturtheorie und Methodologie*. Göttingen: Vandenhoeck & Ruprecht.

Ricoeur, P. 1973. Sprache und Theologie des Wortes in: Léon-Dufour, X. 1973. *Exegese im Methodenkonflikt*. Munich: Kösel-Verlag, 201–221.

—— 1975. Biblical Hermeneutics. *Semeia* 4, 27–148.

—— 1976. *Interpretation Theory: Discourse and the surplus of Meaning*. Fort Worth: Texas Christian University Press.

—— 1978a. The Narrative Function. *Semeia* 13, 177–202.

—— 1978b. *The Rule of Metaphor: Multi-disciplinary Studies of the Creation of Meaning in Language*. London: Routledge & Kegan Paul.

—— 1979. The Function of Fiction in Shaping Reality. *Man and World* 12, 123–141.

Riffaterre, M. 1983. *Text production*. New York: Columbia University Press.

Rimmon-Kenan, S. 1983. *Narrative Fiction: Contemporary Poetics*. London: Methuen.

Ringgren, H. 1987, s.v. 'Resurrection', in Eliade, M. (ed.) 1987.

Ristow, H. & Matthiae K. (eds.) 1961. *Der historische Jesus und der kerygmatische Christus: Beitrage zum Christusverständnis in Forschung und Verkündigung*. Berlin: Evangelische Verlagsanstalt.

Robbins, V.K. 1988. The Chreia, in Aune, D.E. (ed.) 1988. *Greco-Roman Literature and the New Testament*. Atlanta: Scholars Press, 1–24.

Robinson, J.M. 1971. The Dismantling and Reassembling of the Categories of New Testament Scholarship, *Int* 25, 63–77.

――― (ed.) 1977. *The Nag Hammadi Library in English: Translated by the Coptic Gnostic Library Project of the Institute for Antiquity and Christianity*. Leiden: Brill.

――― 1983. *A New Quest of the Historical Jesus*. Philadelphia: Fortress.

Rohde, J. 1966. *Die redaktionsgeschichtliche Methode: Einführung und Sichtung des Forschungsstandes*. Hamburg: Furche Verlag.

Roloff, J. 1973. *Das Kerygma und der irdische Jesus: historische Motive in den Jesus-Erzählungen der Evangelien*. 2nd ed. Göttingen: Vandenhoeck & Ruprecht.

Rossouw, H.W. 1980. *Wetenskap, Interpretasie, Wysheid*. Port Elizabeth: University of Port Elizabeth.

Rost, L. 1926. *Die Überlieferung von der Thronnachfolge Davids*. Stuttgart: Kohlhammer (BWANT III/6).

Roth, W. 1988. *Hebrew Gospel: Cracking the Code of Mark*. Oak Park: Meyer-Stone Books.

Rüger, H.P. 1984. Die lexikalischen Aramaismen im Markusevangelium, in Cancik (ed.) 1984, 73–84.

Rüsen, J. 1980. Zum Problem der historischen Objektivität. *GWU* 31, 188–198.

Rudolph, K. 1980. Sphia und Gnosis, in Tröger, K (ed.) 1980. *Altes Testament, Früjudentum, Gnosis*. Gütersloh: Mohn, 221–237.

Ruthrof, H. 1981. *The Reader's Construction of Narrative*. London: Routledge & Kegan.

Ryan, R. 1985. Pathologies of epistemology in literary studies. *Journal of Literary studies* 1, 3–42.

――― 1988. Introduction: Postmodernism and the Question of Literature. *Journal of Literary Studies* 4, 247–258.

Rydbeck, L. 1967. *Fachprosa, vermeintliche Volkssprache und Neues Testament: Zur Beurteilung der sprachlichen Niveau-unterschiede im nachklassischen Griechisch*. Uppsala: Uppsaliensis Academiae.

Sabourtin, L. 1976. The Parables of the Kingdom, *BTB* 6, 115–160.

Sacks, S. 1975. Reception and Interpretation of Written Texts as Problems of a Rational Theory of Literary Communication. in: Ringbom, H. (ed.) 1975. *Style and Text, studies presented to N.E. Enkvist*. Stockholm: Spraaktoerlaget Skriptor, 339–408.

――― (ed.) 1978. *On metaphor*. Chicago: Chicago University Press.

Safrai, S. & Stern, M. (eds.) 1974. *The Jewish People in the First Century. Section 1, vol. 1: Historical Geography, Political History, Social, Cultural and Religious Life and Institutions*. Assen: Van Gorcum (CRINT).

Saldarini, A.J. 1988. Political and Social Roles of the Pharisees and Scribes in Galilee, in *Society of Biblical Literature 1988 seminar papers*. Atlanta: Scholars Press, 182–199.

Sanders, E.P. & Davies, M. 1989. *Studying the Synoptic Gospels*. London: SCM.

Sanders, E.P. 1983. The genre of Palestinian Jewish apocalypses, in Hellholm 1983, 447–460.

――― 1985. *Jesus and Judaism*. Philadelphia: Fortress.

Sawyer, J.F. 1972. *Semantics in Biblical Research. New Methods of Defining Hebrew Words for Salvation*. London: SCM (SBT 4).

Schmidt, H. (Hrsg.) 1923. *'Eucharisterion': Studien zur Religion und Literatur des Alten und Neuen Testaments:. Festschrift für H. Gunkel*. Vol. 2 Göttingen: Vandenhoeck & Ruprecht.

Schmidt, K.L. 1923. Die Stellung der Evangelien in der allgemeinen Literaturgeschichte, in Schmidt, H. (Hrsg.) 1923, 50–134.

——— 1964. *Der Rahmen der Geschichte Jesu. Literarkritische Untersuchungen zur ältesten Jesusüberlieferung*. Darmstadt: Wissenschaftliche Buchgesellschaft. (First printed in Berlin, 1919).

Schmidt, S.J. 1980. Fictionality in Literary and non-Literary Discourse. *Poetics* 9, 525–46.

Schmidt, W.H. 1982. *Einführung in das Alte Testament*. 2. Aufl. Berlin: De Gruyter.

Schmithals, W. 1979. *Das Evangelium nach Markus 1*. Würzburg: Echter (OTKNT, 1/1–2).

Schnackenburg, R. 1975. Das Johannesevangelium III. Freiburg: Herder (HTKNT 4/3).

Schneemelcher, W. 1968. Typen apokrypher Evangelien, in: Hennecke, E. 1968. *Neutestamentliche Apokryphen in deutscher Übersetzung*. 4. Aufl. (Hrsg. von W. Schneemelcher) Tübingen: Mohr.

Schniewind, J. 1930. Zur Synoptiker-Exegese, *TRu* NF 2, 120–189.

Schoedel, W.R. & Wilken R.L. 1979. *Early Christian Literature and the Classical Intellectual Tradition: In Honorem Robert M. Grant*. Paris: Editions Beauchesne.

Schoedel, W.R. 1984. Theological Method in Irenaeus (*Adversus Haereses* 2. 25–28). *JTS* 35, 31–49.

Scholes, R. & Kellogg, R. 1966. *The Nature of Narrative*. New York: Oxford University Press.

Schröger, F. 1968. *Der Verfasser des Hebrärbriefes als Schriftausleger*. Regensburg: Pustet (BU 4).

Schulz, S. 1961. Markus und das Alte Testament. *ZTK* 58, 184–197.

Schürer, E. 1973–1987. *The History of the Jewish People in the Age of Jesus Christ (175 B.C–A.D. 135)*. 3 vols. A new English version, rev. & ed by G. Vermes, F. Millar & M. Black. Edinburgh: T. & T. Clark (Vol. I: 1973, Vol. II: 1979; Vol. III: 1987).

Schurman, H. 1969. *Das Lukasevangelium*. 1 Teil. Freiburg/Basel/Wien: Herder (HTKNT 3).

Schüssler-Fiorenza, E. 1977. Composition and structure of the book of Revelation. *CBQ* 39, 344–366.

——— 1986. Toward a Feminist Biblical Hermeneutics: Biblical Interpretation and Liberation Theology, in McKim, D. (ed.) 1986. *A guide to contemporary hermeneutics: major trends in biblical interpretation*. Grand Rapids: Eerdmans.

Schweitzer, E. 1973. *Das Evangelium nach Matthäus*. Göttingen: Vandenhoeck & Ruprecht (NTD 2).

Seebass, H. 1974. Nathan und David in II Sam 12. *ZAW* 86, 203–11.

Segers, R.T. 1980. *Het Lezen van Literatuur: Een Inleiding tot een Nieuwe Literatuurbenadering*. Baarn: Ambo.

Segundo, J.L. 1985. *The Historical Jesus of the Synoptics*. Maryknoll: Orbis.

Sevenster, J.N. 1968. *Do you know Greek? How much Greek could the First Jewish Christians have known?* Leiden: Brill (Supplements to Novum Testamentum 19).

Shepherd, M.H. 1960. *The Paschal Liturgy and the Apocalypse*. Richmond: John Knox.

Shipley, J.T. (ed.) 1970. *Dictionary of World Literary Terms*. Boston: The Writer.

Silva, M. 1980. Bilingualism and the Character of Palestinian Greek. *Bib* 61, 198–219.

——— 1983. *Biblical Words and their Meaning: An Introduction to Lexical Semantics*. Grand Rapids: Zondervan.

——— 1989. Review of Johannes P. Louw and Eugene A. Nida (eds.), *Greek-English lexicon of the New Testament based on semantic domains*, 2 vols. New York: UBS. *WTJ* 51, 163–167.

Simon, U. 1967. The Poor Man's Ewe-lamb. An Example of a Juridical Parable. *Bib* 48, 207–42.

Smid, H.R. 1965. *Protevangelium Jacobi. A commentary.* Assen: Van Gorcum.

Smit, D.J. 1987. Christologie uit 'n Derde Wecreldperspektief: 'n Literatürondersoek 1. *Scriptura* 23, 1–49.

Smith, M. 1983. On the history of αροκαλυτω and αροκαλυψις, in Hellholm 1983, 9–20.

Snyman, A.H. 1988. Resensie van Louw, J.P.; Nida, E.A.; Smith, R.B. en Munson, K.A. *Greek-English lexicon of the New Testament based on semantic domains*, 2 vols. New York: UBS. *NGTT* 29, 407–408.

Sone, M.E. (ed.) 1984. *Jewish writings of the Second Temple period. Apocrypha, Pseudepigrapha, Qumran-secretarian writings, Philo, Josephus.* Assen: Van Gorcum.

Soskice, J.M. 1985. *Metaphor and Religious Language.* Oxford: Clarendon.

Steichele, H.-J. 1980. *Der leidende Sohn Gottes.* Regensburg: Pustet (BU 14).

Steinmetz, H. 1975. Rezeption und Interpretation: Versuch einer Abgrenzung. *Amsterdamer Beiträge zur älteren Germanistik* 3, 37–81.

Stemberger, G. 1972a. Das Problem der Auferstehung im Alten Testament. *Kairos* 14, 273–290.

———— 1972b. *Der Leib der Auferstehung. Studien zur Anthropologie und Eschatologie des palastinischen Judentums im neutestamentlichen Zeitalter (ca 170 v.Cr[sic]-lOO n.Chr).* Rome: Biblical Institute.

———— 1973. Zur Auferstehungslehre in der Rabbinischen Literatur. *Kairos* 15, 238–266.

———— 1979. s.v. 'Auferstehung der Toten, I/2. Judentumn' *in TRE.*

Stempel, W.-D. 1973. Erzählung, Beschreibung und der Historische Diskurs. in: Koselleck R. & Stempel W.-D. (eds.) 1973. *Geschichte-Ereignis und Erzählung.* Munich: Fink, 325–346.

Stern, F. (ed.) 1970. *The Varieties of History. From Voltaire to the Present.* 2nd ed. London: Macmillan.

Sternberg, M. 1986. *The Poetics of Biblical Narrative: Ideological Literature and the Drama of Reading.* Bloomington: Indiana University Press.

Stierle, K. 1983. Werk und Intertextualität, in Schmid W. & W.D. Stempel (eds.) 1983. *Dialog der Texte: Hamburger Kolloquium zur Intertextualität* Wien: Wiener Slawistischer Almanach Sonderband 11, 5–26.

Stone, M.E. 1976. Lists of revealed things in the apocalyptic literature, in Cross, F.M., Lemke, W.E. & Miller P.D. (eds.) 1976: 414–452.

Stone, M. (ed.) 1984. *Jewish Writings of the Second Temple Period. Section 2, vol. 2: Apocrypha, Pseudepigrapha, Qumran Sectarian Writings, Philo, Josephus.* Assen: Van Gorcum (CRINT).

Strack, H.L., & Billerbeck, P. 1926, 1928. *Kommentar zum Neuen Testament aus Talmud und Midrasch.* I, IV. Munich: Beck.

———— 1969. *Kommentar zum Neuen Testament. IV.2. Exkurse zu einzelnen Stellen des Neuen Tesaments. Abhandlungen zur neutesamentlichen Theologie und Archäologie.* 5. Aufl. München: Beck.

Strawson, P.F. 1971. *Logico-linguistic Papers.* London: Methuen.

Strecker, G. 1968. The Passion and Resurrection Predictions in Mark's Gospel. *Int* 21, 121–442.

———— 1971. *Der Weg der Gerechtigkeit: Untersuchung zur Theologie des Matthäus.* Göttingen: Vandenhoeck & Ruprecht.

———— 1972. *Handlungsorientierter Glaube. Vorstudien zu einer Ethik des Neuen Testaments.* Berlin: Kreuz.

———— 1979. *Eschaton und Historie: Aufsätze.* Göttingen: Vandenhoeck & Ruprecht.

———— 1983. Neues Testament (NT), in G. Strecker (ed.) 1983. *Theologie im 20. Jahrhundert.* Tübingen: Mohr, 61–145.

———— 1984. *Die Bergpredigt: Ein exegetischer Kommentar.* Göttingen: Vandenhoeck & Ruprecht.

Stuhlmacher, P. 1979. *Vom Verstehen des Neuen Testaments: Eine Hermeneutik*. Göttingen: Vandenhoeck & Ruprecht.

Suhl, A. 1965. *Die Funktion der alttestamentlichen Zitaten und Anspielungen im Markuseangelium*. Gütersloh: Gütersloher Verlagshaus.

Suleiman, S.R. & Crosman, I. (eds.) 1980. *The Reader in the Text: Essays on Audience and Interpretation*. Princeton: Princeton University Press.

Suleiman, S.R. 1980. Introduction: Varieties of Audience-Oriented Criticism. in Suleiman & Crosman, 1980, 35.

Tabachovitz, D. 1956. *Die Septuaginta und das Neue Testament: Stilstudien*. Lund: Gleerup.

Talbert, C.H. 1977. *What is a Gospel? The Genre of the Canonical Gospels*. Philadelphia: Fortress Press.

Tannehill, R.C. 1977. The disciples in Mark. The function of a narrative role. *JR* 57, 386–405.

―――― 1979. The Gospel of Mark as Narrative Christology. *Semeia* 16, 57–95.

Te Selle, S.M. 1974. Parable, Metaphor, and Theology. *JAAR* 42, 630–45.

Teeple, H.M. 1982. *The Historical Approach to the Bible*. Evanston: Religion and Ethics Institute.

Thausing, G. 1965. Betrachtung zur Altägyptischen Auferstehung. *Kairos* 7, 187–194.

Theissen, G. 1977. *Soziologie der Jesusbewegung: Ein Beitrag zur Entstehungsgeschichte des Urchristentums*. München: Kaiser.

―――― 1989. Jesusbewegung als charismatische Weltrevolution. *NTS* 35, 343–360.

Thiselton, A.C. 1980. *The Two Horizons: New Testament Hermeneutics and Philosophical Description with Special Reference to Heidegger, Bultmann, Gadamer, and Wittgenstein*. Exeter: Paternoster Press.

Thom, J.C. 1987. The Journey Up and Down: Pythagoras in Two Greek Apologists. Unpublished paper read at a meeting of the South African Society of Patristic and Byzantine Studies, Johannesburg, October 1987.

Thompson, L. 1986. A sociological analysis of tribulation in the Apocalypse of John. *Semeia* 36, 147–174.

Thyen, H. 1977. Aus der Literatur zum Johannesevangelium. *TR* 42, 211–270.

Tolbert, M.A. 1979. *Perspectives on the Parables: An Approach to Multiple Interpretations*. Philadelphia: Fortress Press.

Traugott, E.C. & Pratt, M.L. 1980. *Linguistics for Students of Literature*. New York: Harcourt and Brace.

Troeltsch, E. 1913. Über historische und dogmatische Methode in der Theologie, in Troeltsch, E. 1913. *Gesammelte Schriften. II. Zur religiösen Lage, Religionsphilosophie und Ethik*. Tübingen: Mohr, 729–753.

Tsekourakis, D. 1974. *Studies in the Terminology of Early Stoic Ethics*. Wiesbaden: Steiner.

Tucker, G.M. 1971. *Form Criticism of the Old Testament*. Philadelphia: Fortress Press.

Tuckett, C. 1983. *Reading the New Testament: Methods of Interpretation*. London: SPCK.

Turner, N. 1963. *A Grammar of New Testament Greek, Vol. 3: Syntax*. Edinburgh: T. & T. Clark.

―――― 1976. *A Grammar of New Testament Greek, Vol. 4: Style*. Edinburgh: T. & T. Clark.

Updike, J. 1972. *Seventy Poems*. Harmondsworth: Penguin Books.

Valdeas, M.J. & Miller, O. (eds.) 1985. *Identity of the Literary Text*. Toronto, University of Toronto Press.

Van Aarde, A.G. 1982. God met Ons: Die Teologiese Perspektief van die Matteusevangelie. Unpublished D.Th. Thesis, University of Pretoria.

―――― 1994. Tracking the pathways opened by Willem Vorster in historical Jesus research. *Neotestamentica* 28 (3), 235–252 (Special Edition).

Van der Horst, P.W. 1974. Musonius Rufus and the New Testament: A Contribution to the Corpus Hellenisticum. *NovT* 16, 306–315.

—— 1975. Hierocles the Stoic and the New Testament: A Contribution to the Corpus Hellenisticum. *NovT* 17, 156–160.

—— 1981. Cornutus and the New Testament: A Contribution to the Corpus Hellenisticum. *NovT* 23, 165–172.

Van der Linde, I. 1990. Charismatiese Moralis, Revolusionecre Soldaat of Apokaliptiese Profeet? *Vrye Weekblad* 31 Augustus 1990, 13–14.

Van der Merwe, P.P. 1962. Vers en Simbool: 'n Ondersoek na die Simbool in sy Betrekking op die Poësie. Unpublished D.Phil. Thesis. Stellenbosch: University of Stellenbosch.

Van Dijk, T.A. 1977. *Text and context: Explorations in the semantics and pragmatics of discourse.* London: Longman.

Van Huyssteen, W. 1987. *The Realism of the Text: A Perspective on Biblical Authority.* Ed. by De Villiers PGR, 55 pp. Pretoria: University of South Africa.

Van Luxemburg, J., Bal, M., & Weststeijn, W.G. 1981. *Inleiding in de literatuurwetenschap.* Muiderberg: Couthino.

—— 1982. *Inleiding in de Literatürwetenschap.* 2nd ed Muiderberg: Coutinho.

Van Peursen, C.A. 1972. *Feiten, Waarden, Gebeurtenissen.* Kampen: Kok.

Van Stempvoort, P.A. 1964. The Protevangelium Jacobi: The sources of its Theme and Style and their bearing on its Date. *SE* 3, 410–426.

Van Unnik, W.C. 1978. *Flavius Josephus als historischer Schriftsteller.* Heidelberg: Schneider.

—— 1979. Luke's Second Book and the Rules of Hellenistic Historiography, in Kremer J. (ed.) 1979. *Les Actes des Apôtres: Traditions, Rédaction, Théologie.* Leuven: Duculot, 37–60 (BETL 48).

—— 1979. Theological Speculation and its Limits, in Schoedel & Wilken (eds.) 1979, 33–43.

Van Wolde, E. 1989. Trendy Intertextuality, in Draisma (ed.) 1989, 43–49.

Vandermoere, H. 1976. *The Study of the Novel: A Structural Approach.* Leuven: Acco.

Vansina, J. 1985. *Oral tradition as history.* London: James Currey.

Veijola, T. 1975. *Die ewige Dynastie: David und die Entstehung seiner Dynastie nach der deuteronomistischen Darstellung.* Helsinki: Suomalainen Tiedeakatemia.

Vergote, J. 1938. s.v. 'Grec biblique' in *DBSup.*

Verryn, T.D. (ed.) 1987. *Reflections on Religion.* Pretoria: University of South Africa.

Via, D.O. 1975. *Kerygma and Comedy in the New Testament: A structuralist Approach to Hermeneutic.* Philadelphia: Fortress Press.

—— 1970. *Die Gleichnisse Jesu: Ihre literarische und existentiale Dimension.* München: Kaiser. (BEvT 57).

Vielhauer, P. 1964. Apokalypsen und Verwandtes: Einleitung, in Schneemelcher, W. (Hrsg.) 1964. *Neutestamentliche Apokryphen: In deutscher Übersetzung II. Apostolisches Apokalypsen und verwandtes.* 3. Aufl. Tübingen: Mohr, 405–427.

—— 1975. *Geschichte der urchrislichen Literatur. Einleitung in das Neue Testament: Apokryphen und die Apostolischen Väter.* 2. durchgesehene Druck. Berlin: De Gruyter.

Visagie, P.J. 1978. Die vraag na die Grondstruktuur. I & II. *Tydskrif vir Christelike Wetenskap* 14, 4–37, 34–59.

Von Campenhausen, H. 1962. *Die Jungfrauengeburt in der Theologie der alten Kirche.* Heidelberg: Carl Winter.

Von Fritz, K. 1970. s.v. 'Epictetus' in *OCD*, 324.

Von Rad, G. 1965. *Theologie des Alten Testaments.* Vol II. München: Kaiser.

Von Tischendorf, K. 1966. *Evangelia Apocrypha.* Hildesheim: Georg Olms.

Vorster, W.S. 1975. Hoe Konsekwent dink Eksegete? *Theologica Evangelica* 8, 126–135.

—— 1977. *'n Ou Boek in 'n Nuwe Wereld Gedagtes Rondom die Interpretasie van die Nuwe Testament.* Pretoria: University of South Africa. (Inaugural lecture).

—— 1978. The Relevance of the New Testament for the Interpretation of the Old Testament. *OTSSA* 20/21, 190–205.

—— 1979a. *Aischunomai en Stamverwante Woorde in die Nuwe Testament.* Pretoria: University of South Africa.

—— 1979b. The Structure of Matthew 13. *Neotestamentica* 11, 130–138 (also Addendum to *Neotestamentica* 11, 34–39).

—— 1980a. 'Die evangelie Volgens Markus: Inleiding en Teologie.' in: Ed. Du Toit, A.B. 1980. *Die Sinoptiese Evangelies en Handelinge: Inleiding en Teologie.* Pretoria: N.G. Kerkboekhandel, 109–155.

—— 1980b. 'Mark: Collector, Redactor, Author, Narrator?' *Journal of Theology for Southern Africa* 31: 46–61.

—— 1980c. 'Die Tekssoort Evangelie en Verwysing.' *Theologia Evangelica* 13:27–48.

—— 1981a. 'The Function of the Use of the Old Testament in Mark.' *Neotestamentica* 14:62–72.

—— 1981b. On the Origins of Christianity: A Religio-Historical Perspective, in W.S. Vorster (ed.). *Christianity among the Religions.* Pretoria: UNISA, 36–56.

—— 1981c. *Wat is 'n Evangelie? Die Plek van die Tekssoort Evangelie in die Literatuur-geskiedenis.* Pretoria: N.G. Kerkboekhandel.

—— 1982a. De structuuranalyse, in A.F.J. Klijn, (ed.) 1982, *Inleiding tot de studie van het Nieuwe Testament.* Kok: Kampen, 127–52.

—— 1982b. 'Redaction, Contextualization and the Sayings of Jesus.' in: Delobel, J. (ed.) 1982. *Logia: Les paroles de Jésus—the Sayings of Jesus. Mémorial Joseph Coppens.* 59. Leeuven: Peters, 491–500 *(BETL).*

—— 1983. 1 Enoch and the Jewish literary setting of the New Testament: A study in text type. *Neotestamentica* 17, 1–14.

—— 1984a. The Historical Paradigm: Its Possibilities and Limitations. *Neotestamentica* 18, 104–123.

—— 1984b. 'Der Ort der Gattung Evangelium in der Literaturgeschichte.' *VuF* 29:2–25.

—— 1985a. Meaning and reference. The parables of Jesus in Mark 4, in: Lategan B.C. & Vorster W.S., *Text and reality. Aspects of reference in Biblical Text.* Philadelphia: Fortress (Semeia Supplements).

—— 1985b. Gelykenisse in Konteks: Matteus 13 en die Gelykenisse van Jesus. *Hervormde Teologiese Studies* 41, 148–165.

—— 1986. Texts with an apocalyptic perspective, in Deist, F.E. & Vorster, W.S. (eds.), *Words from afar: The literature of the Old Testament.* Cape Town: Tafelberg, 166–185.

—— 1987a. 'Characterisation of Peter in the Gospel of Mark.' *Neotestamentica* 21:57–76.

—— 1987b. 'Literary Reflections on Mark 13:37: A Narrated Speech of Jesus.' *Neotestamentica* 21:91–112.

—— 1988a. The protevangelium of James and intertextuality, in Baarda, T., Hilhorst, A., Luttikhuizen, G. & Van Der Woude, A.S. (eds.), *Text and testimony: Essays on New Testament and apocryphal literature in honour of A.F.J. Klijn,* 262–275. Kampen: Kok.

—— 1988b. '"Genre" and the Revelation of John: A Study in Text, Context and Intertext.' *Neotestamentica* 22:103–23.

—— 1988c. 'Alles is Politiek, maar Politiek is nie Alles nie': Het Kuitert gelyk? *Hervormde Teologiese Tydskrif* 44, 917–933.

—— 1988d. 'Towards a Post-critical Paradigm, Progress in New Testament Scholarship? in J.H. Moulon, A.G. van Aarde & W.S. Vorster (eds.), *Paradigms and Progress in Theology,* Pretoria, 31–48.

—— 1989a. The In/Compatibility of Methods and Strategies in Reading or Interpreting the Old Testament. *Old Testament Essays* 2, 53–63.

—— 1989b. The Reader in the Text: Narrative Material. *Semeia* 48, 21–39.

—— 1989c. Intertextuality and Redaktionsgeschichte, in Draisma (ed.) 1989, 15–26.

—— 1990a. On Presuppositions and the Historical Study of the Jewishness of Jesus, in Mouton and Joubert (eds.) 1990, 195–211.

———— 1990b. Bilingualism and the Greek of the New Testament: Semitic interference in the Gospel of Mark. *Neotestamentica* 24, 215–228.
———— 1991. Om te vertel dat Jesus Christus die lydende Seun van God is: Oor
Markus en sy teologie, in Roberts, J.H. *et al.* (reds) 1991. *Teologie in konteks.*
Halfway House: Orion, 32–61.
———— 1992. The growth and making of John 21, in Van Segbroeck, F. *et al.* (eds.)
1992. *The four gospels: Festschrift Frans Neirynck.* Leuven: Peeters, 2207–2221.
Webb, V.N. 1986. Some aspects of the sociolinguistics of Bible translation and exe-
gesis, and of religious language, in Louw, J.P. (ed.) 1986. *Sociolinguistics and com-
munication.* London: United Bible Societies.
Weber, H.-R. 1975. *Überlieferung und Deutung der Kreuzigung Jesu im neutestomentlichen
Kulturraum.* Stuttgart: Kreuz.
Wedderburn, A.J.M. 1987. *Baptism and resurrection. Studies in Pauline theology against its
Graeco-Roman background.* Tübingen: Mohr.
Weder, H. 1978. *Die Gleichnisse Jesu als Metaphern: Traditions- und redaktionsgeschichtliche
Analysen und Interpretationen.* Göttingen: Vandenhoeck & Ruprecht.
———— 1980. Zum Problem einer 'Christlichen Exegese.' *NTS* 27, 64–82.
Weeden, T.J. 1971. *Mark. Traditions in conflict.* Philadelphia: Fortress.
———— 1979. Recovering the Parabolic Intent in the Parable of the Sower. *JAAR*
47, 97–120.
Weinel, H. 1923. Die spätere christliche Apokalyptik, in: Schmidt, H. (Hrsg.) 1923.
*Eucharisterion: Studien zur Religion und Literatur des Alten Testaments. H. Gunkel-Festschrift
11. Zur Religion und Literatur des Neuen Testaments.* Göttingen: Vandenhoeck &
Ruprecht, 141–173.
Weinreich, U. 1963. *Languages in Contact: Findings and Problems.* The Hague: Mouton.
Weinrich, H. 1973. Narrative Theology, in Metz, J.B. & Joshua, J.P. 1973. *The
Crises of Religious Language.* New York: Herder & Herder, 46–56 (*Concilium* 85).
Wellek, R. & Warren, A. 1973. *Theory of literature.* 3rd ed. Harmondsworth: Penguin.
Wendland, P. 1912. *Die urchristlichen Literaturformen.* Tübingen: Mohr.
Wenham, D. 1984. *The Rediscovery of Jesus' Eschatological Discourse.* Sheffield: University
of Sheffield (JSOT Supplement Series).
———— 1975. Recent study of Mark 13, parts 1 & 2, *TSF Bulletin* 71, 1–9 & 72,
6–15.
———— 1977. Source Criticism, in Marshall, I.H. (ed.) 1977. *New Testament Interpretation:
Essays on Principles and Methods.* Exeter: Paternoster, 139–152.
———— 1982. Review Article of Weder, H. 1978. *Die Gleichnisse Jesus als Metaphern.
Traditions- und redaktionsgeschichtliche Analysen und Interpretationen* (Göttingen: Vandenhoeck & Ruprecht) *JSNT* 14, 119–23.
Westermann, C. 1966. *Probleme alttestamentlicher Hermeneutik. Aufsatze zum Verstehen des
Alten Testaments.* München: Kaiser (TB 11).
White, H.V. 1975. Historicism, History, and Figurative Imagination, in Nadel, G.H.
(ed.) 1975. *Essays on Historicism.* Middletown: Wesleyan University Press, 48–67.
———— 1980. The Value of Narrativity in the Representation of Reality. *Critical
Inquiry* 7, 5–27.
Whybray, R.N. 1968. *The Succession Narrative.* London: SCM.
Wilckens, U. 1961. Review of M. Dibelius 1959. *Die Formgeschichte des Evangeliums.*
(3rd ed. Tübingen: Mohr) *TLZ* 86, 274.
Wildekamp, A., Van Montfoort, I. & Van Ruiswijk, W. 1980. Fictionality and con-
vention. *Poetics* 9, 547–567.
Wilder, A.N. 1971. *Early Christian Rhetoric: The Language of the Gospel.* Cambridge,
MA: Harvard University.
Wilmsatt, W.K. 1954. *The Verbal Icon.* Lexington: University of Kentucky.
Wilson, R.R. 1985. s.v. 'Prophet' in *HBD.*
Wilson, R.M. 1978. s.v. 'Apokryphen des Neuen Testaments' in *TRE.*

Wink, W. 1987. *Jesus' Third Way. The Relevance of Non-Violence in South Africa Today*. Johannesburg: South African Council of Churches.

Wissmann, H. 1979. s.v. 'Auferstehung der Toten, I/1. Religionsgeschichtlich' in *TRE*.

Wittig, S. 1977. A Theory of Multiple Meanings. *Semeia* 9, 75–103.

Wrede, W. 1969. *Das Messiasgeheimnis in den Evangelien. Zugleich ein Beitrag zum Verständnis des Markusevangeliums*. 4th ed. [1st ed. 1901] Göttingen: Vandenhoek und Ruprecht.

Wright, R.B. 1985. Psalms of Solomon (first century B.C.), in Charlesworth 1985, 639–670.

Wright, T.R. 1984. Regenerating Narrative: The Gospels as Fiction. *RelS* 29, 389–400.

Wuellner, W. 1981. Narrative Criticism and the Lazarus Story. Paper read at the 1981 meeting of the SNTS, Rome, Italy.

Zimmermann, B. 1974. Der Leser als Produzent: Zur Problematik der rezeptionsästhetischen Methode. *ZLL* 4, 12–26.

Zimmermann, F. 1979. *The Aramaic Origin of the four Gospels*. New York: Ktav.

Zwick, R. 1989. *Montage im Markusevangelium: Studien zur narrativen Organisation der ältesten Jesusüberlieferung*. Stuttgart: Katholisches Bibelwerk.

INDEX OF AUTHORS